Law in Social Theory

The International Library of Essays in Law and Society

General Editor: Austin Sarat

Titles in the Series

Law and Religion
Gad Barzilai

Police and Policing Law
Jeannine Bell

Law and Society Approaches to Cyberspace
Paul Schiff Berman

Law and Families
Susan B. Boyd and Helen Rhoades

Rhetoric of Law
Marianne Constable and Felipe Gutterriez

Law in Social Theory
Roger Cotterrell

Ethnography and Law
Eve Darian-Smith

International Law and Society
Laura Dickinson

Legal Lives of Private Organizations
Lauren Edelman and Mark C. Suchman

Courts and Judges
Lee Epstein

Consciousness and Ideology
Patricia Ewick

Prosecutors and Prosecution
Lisa Frohmann

Intellectual Property
William T. Gallagher

Human Rights, Law and Society
Lisa Hajjar

Race, Law and Society
Ian Haney Lopez

The Jury System
Valerie Hans

Regulation and Regulatory Processes
Robert Kagan and Cary Coglianese

Crime and Criminal Justice
William T. Lyons, Jr.

Law and Social Movements
Michael McCann

Colonial and Post-Colonial Law
Sally Merry

Social Science in Law
Elizabeth Mertz

Sexuality and Identity
Leslie J. Moran

Law and Poverty
Frank Munger

Rights
Laura Beth Nielsen

Governing Risks
Pat O'Malley

Lawyers and the Legal Profession, Volumes I and II
Tanina Rostain

Capital Punishment, Volumes I and II
Austin Sarat

Legality and Democracy
Stuart A. Scheingold

The Law and Society Canon
Carroll Seron

Popular Culture and Law
Richard K. Sherwin

Law and Science
Susan Silbey

Immigration
Susan Sterett

Gender and Feminist Theory in Law and Society
Madhavi Sunder

Procedural Justice, Volumes I and II
Tom R. Tyler

Trials
Martha Merrill Umphrey

Law in Social Theory

Edited by

Roger Cotterrell

Queen Mary and Westfield College, University of London, UK

ASHGATE

Published by
Ashgate Publishing Limited
Gower House
Croft Road
Aldershot
Hants GU11 3HR
England

Ashgate Publishing Company
Suite 420
101 Cherry Street
Burlington, VT 05401-4405
USA

Ashgate website: http://www.ashgate.com

British Library Cataloguing in Publication Data
Law in social theory. – (The international library of
essays in law and society)
1. Social jurisprudence
I. Cotterrell, Roger (Roger B.M.)
340.1'15

Library of Congress Control Number: 2006921292

ISBN 0 7546 2508 7

Printed and bound in Great Britain by TJ International Ltd, Padstow, Cornwall

Contents

PART IV LAW AS DISCOURSE, SYSTEM, FIELD: HABERMAS, LUHMANN, BOURDIEU

PART V FOUCAULT, DISCIPLINE AND REGULATION

PART VI SOVEREIGNTY, GLOBALIZATION AND THE RULE OF LAW

Acknowledgements

The editor and publishers wish to thank the following for permission to use copyright material.

American Sociological Association for the essay: Jack P. Gibbs (2003), 'A Formal Restatement of Durkheim's "Division of Labor" Theory', *Sociological Theory*, **21**, pp. 103–27.

Berghahn Journals for the essay: Roger Cotterrell (2004), 'Constructing the Juristic Durkheim? Paul Huvelin's Adaptation of Durkheimian Sociology', *Durkheimian Studies*, **10**, pp. 56–69.

Blackwell Publishing for the essays: Pablo De Greiff (2002), 'Habermas on Nationalism and Cosmopolitanism', *Ratio Juris*, **15**, pp. 418–38; Michael King and Anton Schütz (1994), 'The Ambitious Modesty of Niklas Luhmann', *Journal of Law and Society*, **21**, pp. 261–87; Nancy Fraser (2003), 'From Discipline to Flexibilization? Rereading Foucault in the Shadow of Globalization', *Constellations*, **10**, pp. 160–71; Martti Koskenniemi (2004), 'International Law as Political Theology: How to Read *Nomos der Erde*?', *Constellations*, **11**, pp. 492–511; William E. Scheuerman (2001), 'Franz Neumann: Legal Theorist of Globalization?', *Constellations*, **8**, pp. 503–20.

Canadian Journal of Law and Society for the essay: Reza Banakar (2001), 'Integrating Reciprocal Perspectives: On Gurvitch's Theory of Immediate Jural Experience', *Canadian Journal of Law and Society*, **16**, pp. 67–91.

Cardozo Law Review for the essays: Michel Rosenfeld (1996), 'Can Rights, Democracy, and Justice be Reconciled through Discourse Theory? Reflections on Habermas's Proceduralist Paradigm of Law', *Cardozo Law Review*, **17**, pp. 791–824. Copyright © 1996 Cardozo Law Review; originally published in 17 Cardozo Law Review 791; Gunther Teubner (1996), '*De Collisione Discursuum*: Communicative Rationalities in Law, Morality, and Politics', *Cardozo Law Review*, **17**, pp. 901–18. Copyright © 1996 Cardozo Law Review; originally published in 17 Cardozo Law Review 901; Jiří Přibán (2003), 'Stealing the Natural Language: The Fiction of the Social Contract and Legality in the Light of Nietzsche's Philosophy', *Cardozo Law Review*, **24**, pp. 663–81. Copyright © 2003 Cardozo Law Review; originally published in 24 Cardozo Law Review 663; David Dyzenhaus (1994), '"Now the Machine Runs Itself": Carl Schmitt on Hobbes and Kelsen', *Cardozo Law Review*, **16**, pp. 1–19. Copyright © 1994 Cardozo Law Review; originally published in 16 Cardozo Law Review 1.

Droit et Société for the essays: Roger Cotterrell (2004), 'Emmanuel Lévy and Legal Studies: A View from Abroad', *Droit et Société* , **56–57**, pp. 131–41; Mauricio García Villegas (2004), 'On Pierre Bourdieu's Legal Thought', *Droit et Société*, **56–57**, pp. 57–71.

Oxford University Press for the essay: Victor Tadros (1998), 'Between Governance and Discipline: The Law and Michel Foucault', *Oxford Journal of Legal Studies*, **18**, pp. 75–103.

Sage Publications for the essays: Wolfgang Schluchter (2002), 'The Sociology of Law as an Empirical Theory of Validity', *Journal of Classical Sociology*, **2**, pp. 257–80; Ronen Shamir (1993), 'Formal and Substantive Rationality in American Law: A Weberian Perspective', *Social and Legal Studies*, **2**, pp. 45–72; Wolf Heydebrand (2003), 'Process Rationality as Legal Governance: A Comparative Perspective', *International Sociology*, **18**, pp. 325–49; Barbara A. Misztal (2003), 'Durkheim on Collective Memory', *Journal of Classical Sociology*, **3**, pp. 123–43; Gunther Teubner (2001), 'Economics of Gift – Positivity of Justice: The Mutual Paranoia of Jacques Derrida and Niklas Luhmann', *Theory, Culture and Society*, **18**, pp. 29–47; Roger Cotterrell (1996), 'The Rule of Law in Transition: Revisiting Franz Neumann's Sociology of Legality', *Social and Legal Studies*, **5**, pp. 451–70.

Washington University Law Quarterly for the essay: Harold J. Berman (1987), 'Some False Premises of Max Weber's Sociology of Law', *Washington University Law Quarterly*, **65**, pp. 758–70.

Every effort has been made to trace all the copyright holders, but if any have been inadvertently overlooked the publishers will be pleased to make the necessary arrangement at the first opportunity.

Series Preface

The International Library of Essays in Law and Society is designed to provide a broad overview of this important field of interdisciplinary inquiry. Titles in the series will provide access to the best existing scholarship on a wide variety of subjects integral to the understanding of how legal institutions work in and through social arrangements. They collect and synthesize research published in the leading journals of the law and society field. Taken together, these volumes show the richness and complexity of inquiry into law's social life.

Each volume is edited by a recognized expert who has selected a range of scholarship designed to illustrate the most important questions, theoretical approaches, and methods in her/his area of expertise. Each has written an introductory essay which both outlines those questions, approaches, and methods and provides a distinctive analysis of the scholarship presented in the book. Each was asked to identify approximately 20 pieces of work for inclusion in their volume. This has necessitated hard choices since law and society inquiry is vibrant and flourishing.

The International Library of Essays in Law and Society brings together scholars representing different disciplinary traditions and working in different cultural contexts. Since law and society is itself an international field of inquiry it is appropriate that the editors of the volumes in this series come from many different nations and academic contexts. The work of the editors both charts a tradition and opens up new questions. It is my hope that this work will provide a valuable resource for longtime practitioners of law and society scholarship and newcomers to the field.

AUSTIN SARAT

William Nelson Cromwell Professor of Jurisprudence and Political Science

Amherst College

Introduction

How can social theory aid legal studies? And why might law be an important focus for contemporary social theory? This collection of essays is intended to suggest answers and show something of the range and richness of interactions between legal studies and the work of social theorists.

But what is social theory? The question is more complex today than it was three or four decades ago. Then, social theory was often regarded as the body of general theory associated with the academic discipline of sociology. Today, however, social theory is the preserve of no particular academic discipline. It cannot usefully be confined by the sometimes arbitrary demarcation lines that define each of the disciplines concerned in one way or another with human relations or social experience. In this book, less than half of the included essays are written by scholars who would be likely to label themselves unambiguously as sociologists. And, similarly, many theorists whose work is discussed here could not be so labelled. Social theory depends on, and feeds into, sociological traditions in a broad sense, but it often combines resources from many knowledge-fields – for example, history, philosophy, anthropology, political theory, legal theory and literary theory – as well as much research that resists any simple categorization.

Social theory can be defined as systematic, historically informed and empirically oriented theory that seeks to explain the nature of the social. And the social can be taken to mean the general range of recurring forms or patterned features of interactions and relationships between people. The social is the ongoing life of human beings lived alongside and in relation to others; the compendium of institutions, patterns of interaction, networks, systems and structures of collective life resulting from human coexistence. So it is the collective life of human groups and populations, but also the life of individuals in so far as this is shaped by their relation to those populations or groups. The social is a realm of solidarity, identity and cooperation, but also of power, conflict, alienation and isolation; of stable expectations, trust and confidence, but also of violence, disruption and discontinuity.

Very often the social has simply been called 'society'. Many social theorists of the nineteenth and twentieth centuries analysed what they considered to be the defining features of 'modern society', contrasted with earlier forms. The idea of modern society indicated the social as a realm that, in the urbanized and industrialized West, had substantially freed itself from earlier (premodern) determinants, especially those of religious and traditional authority. Modern society was seen as organized increasingly not by dictates of religion or by traditional statuses, but through the choices and commitments of individuals as autonomous, rights-bearing citizens. Its typical morality was secular and focused on individual freedom and autonomy. Its guarantee of security lay in the sovereignty of the nation-state. Its political outlook demanded the extension of democracy as the only acceptable legitimation of political power. And its engine of social change seemed to be free economic enterprise and individual opportunity. In such a context, modern law would necessarily shed its remaining religious and traditional overtones.

Law could be portrayed (especially in the work of the German sociologist Max Weber) as expressing a kind of moral and political neutrality, its task being to provide clear, predictable, general rules in terms of which individual projects could be pursued and conflicting interests rationally compromised. Law's destiny, on this view, would be to mix abstract formality with instrumentalism: it would be governed less by moral principle than by social or economic goals.

This was not, however, the only scenario that could be indicated for law in modern society. An alternative view points law not away from morality but *towards* particular moral values that are especially compatible with complex modern society. On this view (developed notably by the French sociologist Emile Durkheim) the law and morality of modern society must (and, on the whole, increasingly do) affirm the human worth of the individual, whatever his or her class, creed or social position. In complex modern society with its highly specialized division of labour, people may have little in common, adopting different occupational roles, lifestyles and outlooks. In these conditions, the legal and moral affirmation of a common humanity is needed to create an interpersonal respect that can bridge the differences between people and facilitate their integration into society. Modern law tends, on this view, to focus increasingly on protecting the human dignity and personal autonomy of every individual. This value system of moral individualism may often be trampled on in practice, but social theory shows it to be appropriate to modern society. Indeed no other value system can adequately underpin the whole of modern law. At least, such is Durkheim's view.

Orientations

Weber's and Durkheim's social theories provide the starting point for this book. Although their characterizations of the social and the place of law in it may, at least in some respects, be outdated, their work still provides much of the vocabulary of social theory, and so they continue to provide a useful starting point for understanding the transformations of law and society today. Wolfgang Schluchter's essay (Chapter 1) provides an excellent guide to what remains important in the views on law of these classic theorists of the early twentieth century.

Unlike many other sociolegal writers on Durkheim, Schluchter focuses not just on the problematic early theses in Durkheim's first book, *The Division of Labour in Society*, but on his work as a whole, which provides rich, though currently neglected, resources for sociological study of the relations of law and morality, and especially for a sociology of human rights (cf. Cotterrell, 1999). As regards Weber, Schluchter devotes attention not just to his famous posthumously published manuscript on sociology of law but also to his lengthy, often neglected, critical essay on the jurist Rudolf Stammler (Weber, 1977), which offered an important opportunity for Weber to distinguish and compare juristic and sociological understandings of law and rules. Most importantly, for our present purposes, Schluchter uses his summation of the essentials of Durkheim's and Weber's ideas on law to emphasize how central these ideas are to their social theory as a whole. These two writers are now considered classic theorists of sociology of law, but Schluchter properly emphasizes that their approaches give little warrant for seeing this field as a mere subdiscipline of sociology. Rather, Weber and Durkheim see legal inquiry as central to social studies. For Durkheim, Schluchter notes, '[s]ociology is first of all a comparative sociology of law' (p. 5), and law is nothing less than '*the* precondition of the constitution of social life' (p. 4). For Weber, too, it is one such precondition.

Thus, in Schluchter's persuasive interpretation, modern social theory's primary founding classics make law *entirely fundamental* to their concerns. Law is at the heart of social theory and the contrasting analyses of it in Durkheim's and Weber's work indicate different directions in which sociolegal inquiries can develop.

Legal Form and Legal Rationality: Max Weber's Legacy

Much has changed since Weber was writing in early twentieth-century Germany. His main legacy for sociolegal studies is his analysis of kinds of legal thought, especially of what he termed formal rational law which, in its most abstract form, depended on the logical interrelating of legal ideas independently of the particular contexts of their application. Law in this form tended towards a pure calculus independent of moral or policy considerations. Weber saw formal legal rationality of this kind as a product of certain Western legal systems, one aspect of a multifaceted rationalization of spheres of social life which had emerged historically only in the West and had come to define the unique character of its civilization. Formal legal rationality, with its calculability and predictability, was important to the development of capitalist economic activity but also, and in more obvious ways, to the establishment of modern forms of government and bureaucratic administration.

Weber's significance for sociolegal inquiry today is very much tied up with the destiny of formal rationality in law. Was this rationalization a phase that is now passing? Are law and governmental regulation ceasing to be characterized by formal rationality and answering to new imperatives? Since Weber always saw rationalization processes as aspects of wider cultural, economic and political developments, these questions have broad implications. Ronen Shamir (Chapter 2) uses a Weberian framework to consider aspects of modern legal thought in the United States. He associates the American legal realist movement in the first half of the twentieth century with a reaction against formal legal rationality and a move towards a more substantive legal focus driven by social reform goals; with the decline of realism, however, a move back towards legal formalism has occurred. Shamir suggests a pendulum swing thesis: movement between formal and substantive legal rationality may correspond to 'the interplay between periods of stability and reform in the political arena' (p. 47). Shamir's essay shows imaginatively how Weber's ideal types of legal thought can inspire reflection on general features of change in legal systems. Yet there are some dangers of abstracting Weberian ideas from their dense cultural matrix. For Shamir, types of legal rationality seem like legal styles, while for Weber they are an aspect of civilization. And although it is justifiable to link legal realism with New Deal politics, it should be recalled that the most influential realist of all, Karl Llewellyn, thought that New Deal politics 'threw the whole emerging [realist] line of inquiry off-centre' and, if anything, hampered its development (Llewellyn, 1960, p. 14).

Wolf Heydebrand (Chapter 3) rightly points out the ambiguities of Weber's pure types of legal rationality (an ambiguity that allows Shamir, controversially, to associate formal rationality with Anglo-American common law). Heydebrand is concerned with currently emerging forms of legal rationality and he identifies a new form: process rationality. He comments usefully on Weber's typology and its problems before elaborating the characteristics of process rationality. A logic of 'informal negotiated processes' (p. 58), it is a byproduct and agent of economic and financial globalization. Globalization promotes and requires pragmatism and open-ended, constantly renegotiated economic relations. Formal rationality seems too rigid. So does substantive rationality if it ties law to fixed aims or values. As regulation increasingly operates through private processes it requires flexibility, diversity and negotiability. One might, indeed, ask how far this is *legal* rationality at all, but this is a matter to return to in Part V.

Harold Berman (Chapter 4) raises a dissenting voice against the widely shared view that Weber's work on law is historically sound and realistic even if changes in law and society may be gradually overtaking it. Berman discusses, interestingly, the reasons for Weber's popularity in sociolegal studies, but he also emphasizes that there are important things that the Weberian method of ideal (pure) types cannot grasp, especially the sense of a historical consciousness or self-awareness that informs social institutions and the idea of tradition as a process rather than an object. Berman emphasizes that, although the interpenetration of fact and value is an important matter for any social theory of law, Weber's sociology, with its positivist rejection of evaluation, provides few resources for addressing this.

Law, Experience and Belief: Durkheim, Durkheimians and Beyond

Given that Emile Durkheim and Max Weber were contemporaries and that both were leaders in the developing field of sociology and deeply interested in law, it is remarkable that their work inhabits entirely separate intellectual universes. Law's dependence on, and contribution to, morality are never far from Durkheim's concerns, while they hardly figure in Weber's. Thus a great deal of Durkheim's writing about law concerns the values it embodies and its contribution to wider currents of thought and belief. Yet Durkheim is best known for the early, limited and crude theses on law contained in his first book and not for the more satisfactory approaches of his later work (Cotterrell, 1999). Jack Gibbs's essay (Chapter 5) is a valuable attempt at reconsidering Durkheim's early arguments in *The Division of Labour* and at presenting them in a form that holds out the prospect of testing their empirical claims. In doing so he devotes much attention to Durkheim's theses about law. Gibbs's approach highlights the problems and inadequacies of Durkheim's theses but also shows how they could be extended. Given that discussions of them have so often quickly concluded that they are either too vague or historically inaccurate, Gibbs' approach seems to be a move forward.

Barbara Misztal (Chapter 6) shows one way in which Durkheim's thought can be productively developed. Being much concerned with the common ways of thinking that unite a population, many of which are expressed in law and morality, Durkheim offers guidance for the study of the collective memory. Collective memory is a society's historical consciousness and sense of continuing shared identity, based partly on myths and always a matter of emotion no less than reason. Collective memory can be powerfully shaped and reinforced by law, Misztal notes, through symbols and rituals (such as constitutional documents, recurring ceremonies and representations of historical events) which law and government rely on and refer to (cf., for example, Osiel, 1995). In the rebuilding of society and law after regime change (as in post-communist Central and Eastern Europe), such matters are especially salient, she suggests. Thus, Durkheim provides resources for the study of law's interactions with culture. While law can impact on collective memory, popular consciousness shapes it too, resisting legal manipulations, because memory exists in individuals' minds, and Misztal suggests (faithful to Durkheim's sense of the irreducibility of social facts) that their memory is of facts which can only be manipulated in interpretation to a limited extent.

Durkheim did not work alone and he attracted legal specialists to his close circle of collaborators. Their writings on law remain much neglected. Very little has been translated into English and, since Durkheimian approaches to sociology became unfashionable in France after the Second World War, Durkheimian legal theory has generally been ignored. Certainly, much of it is dated, limited by crude evolutionary assumptions and excessively speculative. Yet some of it suggests lines of thought that could be productively followed in new ways. The Lyon law professors Paul Huvelin and Emmanuel Lévy were much respected members of Durkheim's circle and tried to develop his ideas to bring them closer to the concerns of lawyers and legal activists. The only essays (as far as I am aware) available in English on these two jurists are included here as Chapters 7 and 8.

Durkheim's view of law is often considered somewhat passive, treating law primarily as a reflection and support of culture, rather than as a powerful, autonomous social agency or directing force which is how many lawyers see it. Huvelin tries to correct any Durkheimian passivity and emphasizes modern law's coercive power. At the same time his speculations on magic and the origins of private rights open our eyes to the diversity of elements that may have created modern ideas of law over long ages of social development.[1] Lévy's work, by contrast, resolutely seeks to politicize Durkheim. Like Misztal, Lévy focuses especially on law's links with collective understandings but, combining Marxist and socialist influences with his Durkheimian point of departure, he sees the realm of collective beliefs as a terrain of conflict in which law is both weapon and prize. Lévy harnesses Durkheimian ideas about law and belief to a radical politics that, for all the datedness of its appeal to class solidarity, entirely dispels any lingering sense of conservatism in the Durkheimian outlook.

Georges Davy's work (Chapter 9) on the evolution of contract is another important contribution to legal sociology from the original Durkheim group. Like Huvelin, Davy was concerned with the question of how certain fundamental ideas of private law evolved, given that law, for the Durkheimians, begins its history as an entirely social and collective matter, intertwined with religion. Perhaps the most significant of these ideas – so familiar to the modern lawyer yet so problematic when seen in a broad context of social development – is the idea of contractual obligation, especially as regards future performance. This is the central focus of Davy's work on contract. Like Marcel Mauss's better-known work on gift relationships (Mauss, 1990), Davy's study illustrates that the Durkheimian emphasis on law's roots in culture provokes a rethinking of contract as something more, at least in its origins and moral structure, than just a device of economic exchange.

Georges Gurvitch, who succeeded to Durkheim's sociology chair at the Sorbonne in Paris, is the 'beyond' in the title of Part III. His work is not Durkheimian, yet as Reza Banakar notes (Chapter 10), it builds on Durkheim in certain respects, especially in its ultimate linking of law with collective values and beliefs. Gurvitch's social theory of law is not much cited today but, where it is, this is almost always for its relevance to the idea of legal pluralism – the idea of many legal orders coexisting in the same social space. Durkheim, like Weber, largely assumes that law is state law and that the social to which law relates is politically organized society, the society whose boundaries are those of the nation state. But Gurvitch thinks differently. He identifies many kinds of law linked with many different levels of social life and types of sociality. If this can be confusing (with no less than 162 different kinds of law being tediously categorized),

Banakar nevertheless thinks that Gurvitch's time may have come. Unusually and usefully, he applies Gurvitch's ideas in specific empirical contexts to highlight a central idea of legal pluralism: that law can be experienced in many different forms, some unconnected with, or unmediated by, the state and some in conflict with state law.

In my view, Gurvitch's theory is too complex, abstract and schematic to be directly useful. However, it does indicate some promising directions, all of which Banakar highlights. First, it links types of law not to specific social groups or institutions but to abstract forms of sociality (we might call them types of community) found in many different combinations, or networks, in reality. In so far as contemporary law increasingly operates beyond state jurisdictional boundaries or in networks within them, this approach that links law to communities, rather than to the state, may be helpful. Second, Gurvitch emphasizes the interdependence of legal philosophy and legal sociology, an interdependence too long denied. Third, he stresses the pervasiveness of law in social life: law need not be seen as an alien force intruding only when things go seriously wrong, but as a welcome routine ordering, fundamental to social existence. As Banakar puts it, 'our everyday life is permeated by forms of jural experience' (p. 194).

Law as Discourse, System, Field: Habermas, Luhmann, Bourdieu

The question of law's legitimacy – its claim to authority over those it purports to regulate – has long been a concern of social theory. Michel Rosenfeld (Chapter 11) points out that modern legitimacy claims tend to move in one of two directions, each of which is problematic. An appeal to democracy (the most common claim) risks the arbitrariness of majority decision (51 per cent is enough even if 49 per cent are opposed; far less than 50 per cent can win the day if the opposition is divided). On the other hand, an appeal to some universal standard of justice runs up against the problem that ideas of justice are always rooted in the experience of particular communities and therefore not truly universal. Jürgen Habermas's proceduralism seeks to escape this dilemma. It relies on consensus reached through free, uninhibited debate in which all voices are heard: law's legitimacy is based in both democracy and the protection of rights founded in a universal moral consensus. Rosenfeld asks whether this proceduralism is sufficient in itself to provide legitimacy, or whether it depends on a prior commitment to particular, contingent substantive norms. He argues the latter, so that a 'pure' proceduralism cannot in fact provide a prescription for justice adequate to deal with all the conflicts of contemporary pluralistic societies. Nevertheless, Habermas shows indirectly the contribution that proceduralism can make towards shaping the values presupposed in a legal system.

Pablo De Greiff notes that Habermas's hugely influential ideas about law have developed in two stages (Chapter 12). His early work subordinated legal legitimacy to the requirement of a universalistic moral principle. Norms could be valid only if they satisfied a principle of universalization realized through rational discourse. Later, in his major book on law, *Between Facts and Norms*, first published in German in 1992, Habermas indicated different principles of validity of laws and moral norms, adding, for law, a separate principle of democratic legitimacy. De Greiff links this development to Habermas's discussions of cosmopolitan justice and especially his advocacy of new European governmental and legal institutions. Habermas's ambiguity between (i) making the universality of morality a part of law and (ii) the apparent rooting of law in a particular community that gives it democratic legitimacy raises many issues for his cosmopolitan prescriptions.

Gunther Teubner's discussion of Habermas (Chapter 13) provides a link to the autopoietic theory of Niklas Luhmann, from which Teubner draws much inspiration. Focusing, like De Greiff, on the change in Habermas's view of law, Teubner emphasizes his 'decisive move' towards recognizing 'a plurality of discourses – and their concomitant rationalities' (p. 270). Alongside law are morality, ethics, pragmatics and negotiation. Habermas's hope is still that these discourses can be integrated, but he does little to examine how and in what form. Teubner notes that law itself shows some ways in which 'collisions' between discourses are managed. Like Habermas, he assumes (problematically, in my view) that law is best seen as a single discourse, but his essay eventually moves on to different ground from that of Habermas. Unconcerned here with law's moral or democratic bases of legitimacy, Teubner implies instead that law might be a freestanding discourse, holding itself up by its sheer discursive self-awareness and functional utility.

This is, indeed, Niklas Luhmann's position. While Michael King and Anton Schütz elaborate Luhmann's view of law (Chapter 14), Teubner (Chapter 15) explores its strengths and weaknesses in a brilliant comparison of Luhmann's work on law and economy with that of Jacques Derrida. In Chapter 14 King and Schütz show how Luhmann has tried to bypass many issues that troubled earlier social theory. Tradition and substantive values, for Luhmann, no longer securely underpin legal rationality. Law has become a self-reproducing discourse, taking information from an environment which it understands entirely in its own terms and processing this information to make it intelligible and useful in the carrying out of law's discursive function. This function is simply to code as 'legal' or 'illegal' the situations or actions brought to law's attention. And, like Derrida's deconstruction, Luhmann's sociology emphasizes the paradox of self-observation that characterizes law: law can indicate its identity, separate from its environment, only by using the criteria (legal/not legal) that it *already presumes* as the basis of its discursive identity.

Teubner admits what has long been seen as the central weakness of Luhmann's theory: its inability to analyse the relations between discourses or systems in a satisfactory manner. But, against Derrida, he notes that the problem of paradox, which Derrida sees as a scandal for knowledge-systems such as law, appears, in Luhmann's perspective, as no problem at all. For Luhmann, legal discourse, like other discourses, progresses through its continual displacement of founding paradoxes (hiding them in doctrinal complexity). Indeed, this phenomenon is familiar to most theoretically minded lawyers. Curiously, as Teubner explains, Luhmann and Derrida complement each other's theoretical blind spots. While Luhmann dispels the practical problem of legal paradox (showing that, in practice, it is normally not really a problem at all), Derrida provides the vital idea of an unreachable but indispensable justice – a justice that represents the search for satisfactory relations between law and the discourses alongside which it must exist. While Luhmann leaves the relations between discourses as a mystery, Derrida presents it as a vital quest.

Pierre Bourdieu is also concerned with legal discourse, but in a different way. Mauricio García Villegas (Chapter 16) sees him as much influenced by his French sociological heritage and there are surely Durkheimian elements in his cultural understanding of legal discourse. Bourdieu's thinking may appeal particularly to those who find recent social theory's concerns with legal discourse too abstract and juristic in orientation. His sociological focus is on practice and its cultural milieux. Like, for example, Emmanuel Lévy, Bourdieu sees law as a major form of symbolic power for which different social groups compete; law intervenes where habitus provides insufficient social regulation. But, Villegas notes, Bourdieu's view may be too limited by certain French legal and sociological traditions. It may underemphasize the diversity and plurality of law as a social field.

Foucault, Discipline and Regulation

The work of another, vastly influential French scholar, Michel Foucault, has had an ambiguous and controversial relation to law. Foucault's significance in this context is in his famous discussions of the normalizing disciplines that have developed to dominate modern life. Initially these emerged in particular institutional settings such as the factory, the school, the clinic, the prison and the asylum, but they extended to become more generalized patterned routines and professionalized practices that shape individuals, their identity, expectations and responsibilities. For some sociolegal writers the problem in interpreting Foucault has been not only to decide the relation between these disciplinary forms and law. More specifically, it has been to explain his apparent dismissal of law as something which discipline has largely replaced as the dominant normative structure of social life. Legal scholars and sociolegal researchers have been bewildered by Foucault's apparent ignorance of the vast range of regulatory forms and strategies that contemporary law uses, and its interplay with disciplinary practices such as those of psychiatry, medicine, social work and education.

Victor Tadros shows, in a richly illustrated discussion of the interplay of law and discipline (Chapter 17), that law, for Foucault, is not what his critics have often taken it to be: coercive sovereign power exercised through enacted rules. Foucault may have had only himself to blame for the misunderstanding since he uses the term 'juridical' to mean precisely this exercise of coercive power – the sovereign's right of force – and argues that it has been marginalized in favour of the disciplines and flexible strategies of governmental provision and direction (governmentality). Tadros argues that Foucault distinguishes the juridical from law (see also Ewald, 1990). While the juridical represents a concentration of coercive force in legal form, law embraces a vast range of regulatory strategies and devices. Hence, Foucault's critics misunderstand his claims. Discipline works in alliance with and sometimes through law (as in treatments applied to convicted offenders). Tadros shows how fundamental Foucault's challenge is to simplistic invocations of 'freedom' in much liberal thought. The regimes of discipline define freedom not as a space outside regulation but as the *experience* of that regulation (including self-regulation). It is the realm of security, peace and order that innumerable disciplines create and define.

Whether Foucault provides adequate resources for understanding contemporary regulation is, however, an open question. While Tadros's essay traces in detail the past trajectories of discipline and governmentality, Nancy Fraser and Nikolas Rose (Chapters 18 and 19) discuss, in different ways, the range of governance strategies and practices that are becoming familiar in societies such as those of Britain and the United States. Rose looks at strategies that appeal to ideas of community not only to harness local support for regulation, but also to free it from the need to address society as a whole. In modern nations the social first registered as 'civil society', the sphere of social interaction between autonomous individual citizens. Later, as

Rose describes, it became an arena for governmental intervention associated with the welfare state. While the social is not 'dead', the era of this generalized welfare-oriented governmental intervention is passing. Much more varied strategies enlisting private interests and initiatives, and using contracting as a device of government, are becoming established. Fraser takes matters further. In her view, globalization has begun to displace the disciplinary and governmental strategies described by Foucault. The scenario she paints has much in common with Heydebrand's process rationality (Chapter 3).

The sociolegal message of Tadros, Rose and Fraser is that law's place in a continuum of social regulation is rapidly changing. The issue is not the jurists' old chestnut, 'What is law?', but rather, 'How can we usefully conceptualise the tasks and forms of regulation today?'

Sovereignty, Globalization and the Rule of Law

The changing forms of regulation, the bases of law's ultimate claims to legitimacy, its relations with morality and governmental power: all these matters are brought into sharper relief as law takes on an increasingly transnational character or develops new international forms. If a new world order is gradually forming, what legal shape will it take? Can there be an effective transnational rule of law?

These questions may be the most fundamental ones for social theory of law to address today. But, as has been noted, the classic theorists of modern society usually assumed that 'society' was the politically organized society of the nation-state, firmly bounded by state borders. Similarly, modern legal theory has generally viewed 'law' as the law of the nation state, international law being considered an extension of this, developed to govern relations between states. Legal and social theory still lack adequate accounts of the emerging forms of transnational law.

One approach might be to develop traditional approaches to international law. On that basis, this law primarily concerns relations between states as legal actors, but is overlaid by law created transnationally by non-state agencies and law applicable transnationally to non-state subjects. Ultimately, then, all such law is seen as derived from agreement between states or from their shared custom. A different approach would be to see law as gradually freeing itself from its ties to the sovereign authority of states. As such, its institutional forms are taking on a life of their own, so that, for example, municipal courts become a model for courts of transnational jurisdiction (such as the International Criminal Court, the European Court of Human Rights or the European Court of Justice). These seek independent legitimacy using strategies much like those that municipal legal institutions follow in this quest (appeals to shared cultural values, historical tradition, procedural efficiency, compatibility with democracy and so on). Legal practice, too, becomes transnational without changing its professional character, transnational rule-setting agencies arise and the idea of transnational enforcement of law becomes increasingly familiar.

Theorizing law beyond state boundaries entails re-examining law's relation to state sovereignty, and social theories of sovereignty explore the social conditions that make sovereignty a practical possibility or necessity. As Jiří Přibáň (Chapter 20) points out, Nietzsche saw the political philosopher Thomas Hobbes as a 'bold spirit' (p. 425) because he was unafraid to identify war and social chaos as the conditions that give rise to sovereign power and law.

Behind legal order are the demons that gave birth to it and that it keeps out of sight. Přibán rejects romantic appeals to 'authenticity' as a basis of political legitimacy, authenticity meaning here an ideal of the social as some kind of pure, natural world: a brotherly community, a realm of natural law, a paradise of noble savages, or a condition of total individual fulfilment or freedom. Totalitarianism, relentlessly trying to create such mythical conditions, leads to state terror. Even in less dangerous forms, the politics of authenticity is misguided, in Přibán's view. Authenticity 'never enters the field of law and politics uncorrupted' (p. 432). Fictions like Hobbes's social contract are needed to transform natural conditions into law. Přibán warns us to see law as it is, as rules and power, and not to confuse politics with ethics.

Where, then, does sovereignty stand today? Does it even exist in contemporary pluralistic societies? Contemporary legal theory often suggests not, playing down the concept of sovereignty or excluding it. Law is portrayed as a system of rules (Hart, 1994) or norms (Kelsen, 1967), needing no concept of sovereignty to animate it. Yet such theories are haunted by the deeply disturbing ideas of the German jurist Carl Schmitt who wrote during the first half of the twentieth century and in the context of the disasters of European history in that period. Schmitt argues that it is a liberal delusion that sovereign power can be displaced in favour of a 'neutral' legal order operating like the rules of a game. Liberalism sees government as existing to protect the private sphere, setting rules that mark out areas of freedom. Parliament, Schmitt notes, is supposed to represent the range of private interests publicly but, crucially, it thereby not only makes the public sphere prey to private interest groups, but also disguises the need for fundamental decisions; it favours unending compromise, or decisions driven by dominant interests rather than a sense of national good.

For Schmitt, sovereignty is indispensable, as Hobbes showed, but even Hobbes did not take matters far enough. In trying to rationalize sovereignty in terms of a social contract he allowed the possibility of its being rationally challenged. For Schmitt, a constitutional order requires an ultimate, absolute power of decision immune to rational challenge or debate because such a power is needed to protect this order during crises when legal rules no longer provide answers and political compromises are not possible.

Schmitt strips from the concept of sovereignty the abstraction that legal philosophy often attaches to it: for him, it is simply a capacity for certain people to do particular things without challenge. He points to its ultimate location in myth and sentiment, and its necessary potential for raw violence unconstrained by law, morals or public opinion. As David Dyzenhaus (Chapter 21) suggests, Schmitt challenges liberal theorists to defend the adequacy of their view of authority against his powerful critique – a critique that is all the more deeply disquieting because it founds his dangerous authoritarian alternative, now indissolubly linked with the moral disasters of fascism.

That the social conditions of sovereignty are an important topic for contemporary social theory is made clear by recent debates about an emerging new legal world order. In this context, Martti Koskenniemi (Chapter 22) discusses Schmitt's 1950 book on international law. 'Whatever Schmitt's political choices,' Koskenniemi notes, 'readers have been struck by the expressive force of his critiques when applied to contempory events' such as the war on terrorism (p. 466). Schmitt contrasts what he calls 'the new nomos of the Earth' (p. 466) with the previous European international order, the *ius publicum europaeum* (IPE), existing for a century until the First World War. The IPE ended the era of unlimited religious wars and assumed a formal legal equality between sovereign states. Wars became secular military duels between states rather than efforts to destroy populations, lay waste to territory, criminalize the enemy, or conduct moral or religious crusades. The interest of Schmitt's book is less in his romanticized view of the IPE than in his analysis of what is succeeding it. In this 'new nomos', war becomes moralized again, whole enemy populations are criminalized, police actions against states are undertaken in the name of an international regime of law and order pitted against delinquent violators of peace. Most importantly, all of this is used cynically to justify the unfettered coercion of weaker nations by technologically and economically dominant ones. Sovereignty no longer provides a defence of national integrity.

Koskenniemi points out the plausibility of Schmitt's description of the new nomos of the world (delayed in its full emergence by the uneasy power balances of the Cold War). But coupling this with nostalgia for the old rivalries of sovereign states seems bizarre. The logic of Schmitt's thinking on sovereignty is surely towards a single international sovereign (not a multitude of independent states or even, as he thought, of homogeneous regions). It is towards a sovereign that can decide on the exception, the case that escapes all rules: thus, towards a superpower unilateralism. But, for Schmitt, this sovereignty could be founded only on myth, and there seems to be no available 'world myth' to correspond to national myths or to collective memories (cf. Chapter 6). On a Hobbesian view, a world sovereign would have to be seen to have the power to protect all the world and promote the welfare of everyone in it. Conditions for a fictional world social contract simply do not exist. Perhaps, then, there is no alternative but to turn back to the slow, laborious, frustrating task of building a transnational legal order that can exist apart from *all* claims of national sovereignty and can develop forms of democracy to give it some protection against colonisation by the powerful.

So democracy and the rule of law return as pressing themes. In this context, the final two chapters of this book consider Franz Neumann's sociology of the rule of law. Neumann's work brings us full circle, in that it can be seen as a response to both Weber and Schmitt. While Weber ambiguously associates capitalist economic activity with formal legal rationality, Neumann emphasizes the way in which corporate capitalism potentially undermines formal rationality in law and makes it harder to maintain and justify the guarantees of legal equality and certainty associated with the rule of law. Neumann points to a need to rethink the rule of law today, setting it its in social contexts and considering (as he tried to do in his mid-twentieth century era) the historical conditions that give it meaning and significance (see Cotterrell, Chapter 23).

William Scheuermann (Chapter 24) takes matters further. Neumann's still valuable attempt to rethink relations between legal formality and developing capitalism can, Scheuermann thinks, be extended to take account of changes in capitalism that are associated with globalization. Neumann accepts Schmitt's view of the declining significance of the nation-state and of the inadequacy of liberal legal thought when seen in social theoretical perspective. Against Schmitt, however, Neumann emphasizes the overriding value of the rule of law and rejects Schmitt's retreat to a cynical *realpolitik*. Neumann remains a thought-provoking theorist for our times, if only because he keeps an unswerving commitment to values of legality and democracy while stressing the importance of examining the meaning of these values in the particular historical and social contexts in which they are pursued.

ROGER COTTERRELL

Note

1 Huvelin's work on magic and ancient Roman law is still cited with respect a century after he wrote: see Rives (2002). His suggestion of abandoning the concept of organic solidarity is not only echoed in some Durkheimian literature (see Pope and Johnson, 1983) but may represent Durkheim's own later position: see Cotterrell (1999, p. 109).

References

Cotterrell, R. (1999), *Emile Durkheim: Law in a Moral Domain*, Stanford, CT: Stanford University Press/ Edinburgh: Edinburgh University Press.
Ewald, F. (1990), 'Norms, Discipline, and the Law', *Representations*, **30**, pp. 138–61.
Hart, H.L.A. (1994), *The Concept of Law* (2nd edn), Oxford: Clarendon Press.
Kelsen, H. (1967), *The Pure Theory of Law*, trans. M. Knight, Gloucester, MA: Peter Smith. Reprint, 1989.
Llewellyn, K.N. (1960), *The Common Law Tradition: Deciding Appeals*, Boston, MA: Little, Brown.
Mauss, M. (1990), *The Gift: The Form and Reason for Exchange in Archaic Societies*, trans. W.D. Halls, London: Routledge.
Osiel, M.J. (1995), 'Ever Again: Legal Remembrance of Administrative Massacre', *University of Pennsylvania Law Review*, **144**, pp. 463–704.
Pope, W. and Johnson, B.D. (1983), 'Inside Organic Solidarity', *American Sociological Review*, **48**, pp. 681–92.
Rives, J.B. (2002), 'Magic in the XII Tables Revisited', *Classical Quarterly*, **52**, pp. 270–90.
Weber, M. (1977), *Critique of Stammler*, trans. G. Oakes, New York: Free Press.

Part I
Orientations

[1]

The Sociology of Law as an Empirical Theory of Validity

WOLFGANG SCHLUCHTER Rupprecht-Karls-University Heidelberg

ABSTRACT Contrary to current tendencies, the founders of sociology as a discipline regarded the sociology of law as an integral part of social theory. Law and its historical variations were treated by them as a constitutive component of social life. This can be demonstrated especially with regard to Émile Durkheim and Max Weber. It also provides an opportunity to highlight the differences between these authors, not only in methodological but also in substantive terms. In the essay it is shown how both authors treated law in comparative and developmental perspectives and varied in assessing the role of penal law and human rights in the course of history. Connections to the current theoretical debate in Germany are also drawn.

KEYWORDS Durkheim, human rights, penal law, sociology of law, Weber

Introduction: The Sociology of Law between General Social Theory and Application

I would like to begin the following essay with a preliminary remark. I am well aware of the fact that within the title that I have chosen for this essay there lurks the danger of a naturalistic fallacy. However, I am concerned not with the distinction between validity (*Geltung*) and facticity but rather with the distinction between various *sorts of validity* that reciprocally presuppose one another. From my point of view, the sociology of law is concerned not merely with legal effectiveness but rather with legal effectiveness in relation to validity. One can investigate this issue with regard to the 'classical writers' of the 'discipline', who therefore stand at the center of my further reflections.

The fund of 'classical writers' is of course great; too great for my restricted purposes. Émile Durkheim, Max Weber, Eugen Ehrlich and Theodor Geiger are only a few of the names that may come to mind. I shall confine myself to Weber and Durkheim. The reason is simple. For both Weber and Durkheim, the sociology of law is principally an aspect of *general* social theory.

We can distinguish two conceptions in treating law sociologically: one views law either as *a*, or perhaps even *the*, precondition of the constitution of social life; or one views law as a particular institutional realm. In the first case, the sociology of law is part of general social theory; in the second case, it is a field of sociology that specifies and applies general social theory in view of a particular context. Whereas with the 'classical authors' the first conception prevailed, in the course of a century the second conception came to the foreground. This has resulted in the sociology of law becoming one of the numerous 'sociologies of' (*Bindestrichsoziologien*), or, in other words, a subdiscipline of sociology. At present, the first conception of law appears to be gaining ground again. Of course, both conceptions are not mutually exclusive; however, it does make a difference which of them is emphasized.

It is precisely for this reason that a review (*Rückbesinnung*) of the origins of the sociology of law in Durkheim and Weber is useful. I would like to introduce the comparison between these two authors with two theses. First, for both Durkheim and Weber, law is primarily a precondition of the constitution of social life that is to be elucidated within the framework of general social theory, and only secondarily an institutional realm to which this general social theory is bound to be applied. Second, the social theory of Durkheim and Weber, respectively, leads to a very different understanding of law.

I shall begin my comparison with a presentation of Durkheim's general position in four steps: (1) a positive science of the rules of conduct; (2) outline of a science of morals and rights; (3) the two laws concerning the development of penal law; and (4) human rights as penal law.

Émile Durkheim

A Positive Science of the Rules of Conduct

Durkheim developed his sociological program very early and indeed primarily through a highly peculiar combination of two lines of reasoning, namely the French, in which sociology was conceived as a positive science or social physics, and the German, in which, under the influence of the historical schools, a positive science of morals had arisen. The French line was primarily represented by Auguste Comte, who, with the help of his law of the three stages in the development of the human mind and his law of the hierarchy of sciences, wanted to raise sociology as a positive science of social life to become the leading science of the modern stage (see especially Comte, 1956: 5ff. and 205ff.). The German line was primarily represented by Wilhelm Wundt, who in his *Völkerpsychologie* provided an illustration of how this leading science would have to be formed into a science not only of humankind and its morals, as with Comte, but also of various peoples and their morals.[1] It can also be said that, according to Durkheim, French Cartesianism and German Kantianism should be combined within the new science of sociology, understood as a kind of social psychology, while both are decisively modified through an empirical-inductive procedure. An *inductive physics* of morals and rights was to replace the previous *deductive metaphysics* of morals and rights. Thus, certainly from the very beginning for Durkheim, morals (*Sitten*) and rights (*Recht*) were not physical but rather mental, and not individual but rather social facts, arising through an *association* of individuals, possessing thereby a character *sui generis* and great historical variability.

Outline of a Science of Morals and Rights

At the center of this *science of morals and rights*, therefore, stands the comparative analysis of rules of conduct reinforced by sanctions. The comparisons are set up inter-culturally and inter-temporally. Already in Durkheim's opening lecture of his 'Cours de science sociale', which was held in the winter semester 1887–8 at the University of Bordeaux and which is to a certain extent the starting *and* constant reference point of his doctrine,[2] one finds the decisive designations concerning the object and method of this new science. Launched into the world by economists, then constituted by Comte, consolidated by Spencer, determined by Schäffle, and specialized by the economists and jurists (of the historical school), as Durkheim puts it, the object and method of this new science are to be defined along the following lines.

1. Every society possesses a certain number of *common ideas and sentiments* that are passed on from generation to generation. These phenomena are of a mental nature, but they are resistant to any discernment by individual psychology, and can be identified only by social psychology, a *Völkerpsychologie à la* Wundt.
2. Some of these *common ideas and sentiments* refer to the practice of social life and are obligatory. They are formulated as *maxims* that are addressed to the individual and demand respect and compliance.
3. Some of these *maxims* are so important to society that it sets up *organs* in order to guarantee this observance and compliance. As soon as this is the case, moral judgments and condemnations are turned into 'juridical formulas' (Durkheim, 1981: 46). At this point, a sociology of law may stand beside a sociology of morals.
4. Even economic phenomena, which are centered in the first place on self-interest and not on duty, must be placed in this context. Economics, just as the sociology of morals and law, is a *social science*.

The focus of this science of morals and law is accordingly upon the sociological analysis of rules, particularly *rules of law* from a comparative perspective. Sociology is first of all a comparative sociology of law.

As a matter of fact, Durkheim's first substantial studies, in particular his famous investigation into the social (not economic) division of labor, are in essence analyses of a sociology of law. If later he means to say that at the beginning of social development everything was religion (which implies that a turn towards a sociology of religion occurs in his work), then in his early work it is said that at the beginning everything was law, and, more precisely, penal law, even if not yet formalized, codified and organized.[3] Sociology *as* sociology of law proceeds in this connection from the assumption that the development of law accompanies social development (correspondence thesis), and, furthermore, that law is a symbol (representation thesis) and, therefore, suitable to serve as an indicator for social conditions (scientific thesis). In addition it assumes that customs are secondary to law (hierarchy thesis) and it concerns itself, unlike economics, not with self-interested but rather with dutiful action, above all because collective life is an expression of obligations. However, whoever speaks of obligation, according to Durkheim (1988: 97), must at the same time speak of coercion (thesis of coercion). The decisive conclusion that is associated with this position therefore maintains: it is not true that an action offends the common conscience because it is criminal, but rather it is criminal because it offends the common conscience. The core of the common conscience, however, is formed by those ideas and sentiments congealed into maxims that are passed on from generation to generation and that are held as 'sacred'. Sociology therefore ultimately involves not only a sociology of law, but, more precisely, a *sociology of penal law.*

Durkheim's sociology accordingly commences with an analytical dissection of the concept of 'rule' and a classification of rules derived therefrom.[4] Important to him first of all is whether or not a rule of conduct is reinforced by sanctions. If it is reinforced by sanctions, then it becomes important what kind of sanction is applied, whether appellate, for instance through an appeal to conscience, or impairing, which indeed carries a further sense. If it is impairing, it can provide retribution or the restoration of the status quo ante. This is the meaning of Durkheim's well-known distinction between repressive and restitutive law. It is analytical and relatively independent from concrete matters of law, although an affinity exists between it and the latter (penal law versus the rest of law) (see Figure 1).[5]

However, within social life law does more than play this negative role involving retribution or restoration, along with protecting society from deviant behavior. It also plays a positive role through producing solidarity. The rules of law indeed ultimately represent simply those ideas and sentiments that are recognized by members of a society as desirable and considered as obligatory, *because* they are for them exemplary. Like law in its negative role, so too law in its positive role may serve two main goals. It founds either a similarity between the members of a society or a (complementary) dissimilarity. In the first case, the (positive) solidarity is mechanical and in the second organic. Repressive law represents the first, whereas restitutive law represents the second. The typology of

FIGURE 1. DURKHEIM'S TYPOLOGY OF RULES OF CONDUCT

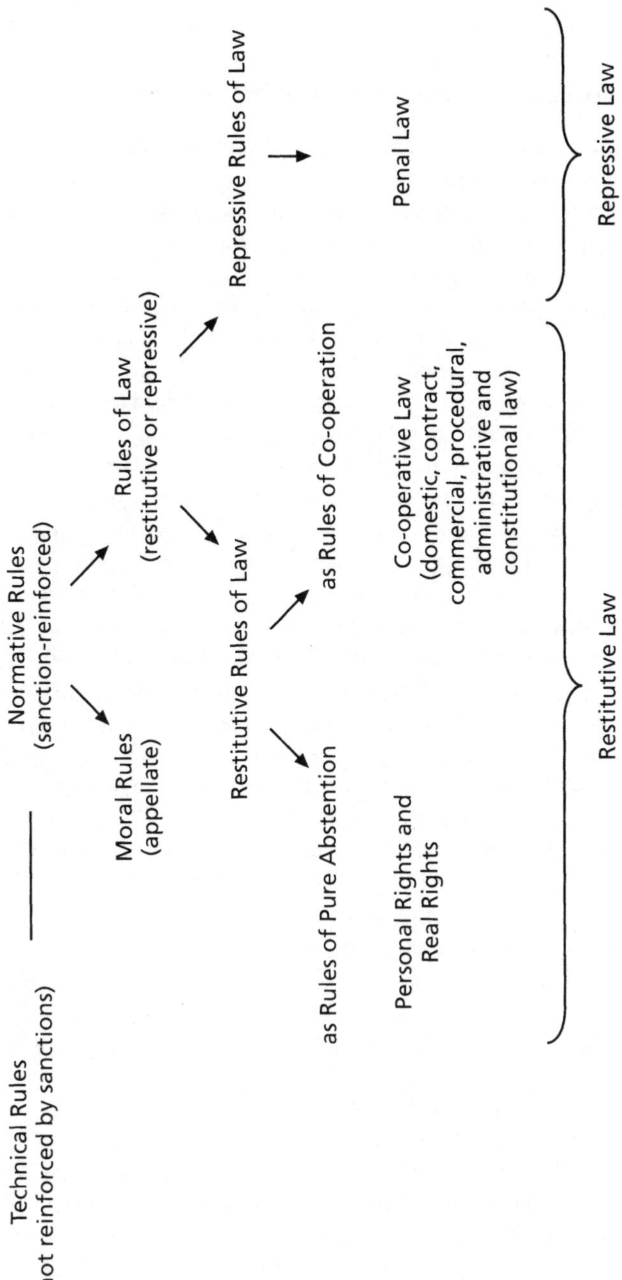

rules of conduct is rendered complete in Durkheim's work through a typology of solidarities (Figure 2).

The Two Laws Concerning the Development of Penal Law

The range, intensity and solidity of the common conscience of a society are, for Durkheim, therefore, closely connected with a consciousness of law that at its core is a consciousness of penal law. Around this core, concentric circles are formed, whereby the distance from the core says something about how intense and firm the shared ideas and sentiments still are (Figure 3). Of course, not only dutiful but also self-interested action is well regulated and can therefore help establish solidarity. This was Durkheim's great discovery in working upon the division of labor, from which he wrested a 'moral' dimension. For he recognized that even the division of labor under certain circumstances can produce solidarity, though a solidarity of a particular kind. He called it, as has already been said, organic, in contradistinction to mechanical. However, from his theoretical perspective, organic solidarity cannot be the result of self-interested action alone. No matter how rational and calculated it may be – and it may also include the insight that under certain conditions it is more advantageous to co-operate voluntarily with others if one wants to increase one's gains – the co-operation based upon self-interest will, according to Durkheim, never yield a stable social order. Towards that end, it requires dutiful action to be joined to self-interested action. That, however, refers to rules of conduct reinforced by sanctions. Hence, organic solidarity is more than contractual solidarity. It is based ultimately upon *repressive* sanctions. If these become weaker, then the intensity and solidity of the common conscience suffers. Every society, even modern society, remains therefore in the final analysis centered on penal law.

Durkheim started with the assumption that the development of law is characterized by the fact that restitutive law *replaces* repressive law. The more a society underwent a division of labor, the less it could be guided with the help of repressive law and the more it became dependent upon restitutive law. Although in the beginning everything in fact had concerned penal law, this could not remain so in a society based upon the division of labor, because its members became increasingly dissimilar to one another. For this reason, the relative range of penal law shrank with social development, while in contrast, especially co-operative law grew. In a society in which the similarity between its members decreased, penal law would lose not only its range, but also its intensity and solidity.[6]

In his later writings, Durkheim would modify these all too simple theses that still informed his studies on the social division of labor by combining the idea of a *substitution* of repressive law by restitutive law with the idea of an *evolution* of repressive law. According to this insight, penal law undergoes a development not only in relationship to restitutive law, but also *in itself*. (The same holds true of course also for restitutive law.) Penal law does actually regress with the increasing

FIGURE 2. DURKHEIM'S TYPOLOGY OF SOLIDARITIES

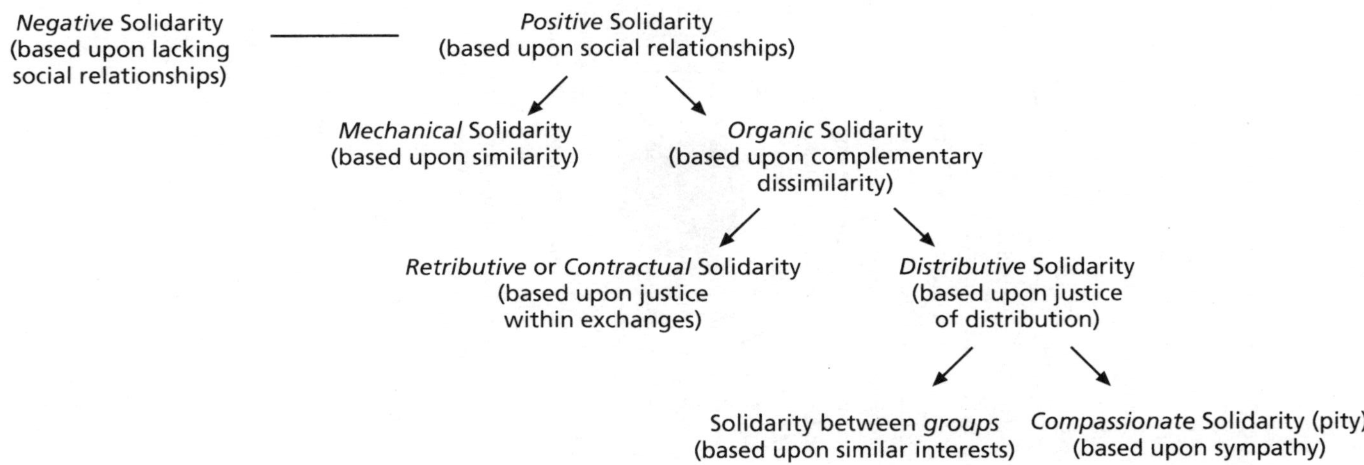

FIGURE 3. RANGE, INTENSITY AND SOLIDITY OF THE COMMON CONSCIENCE ACCORDING TO DURKHEIM

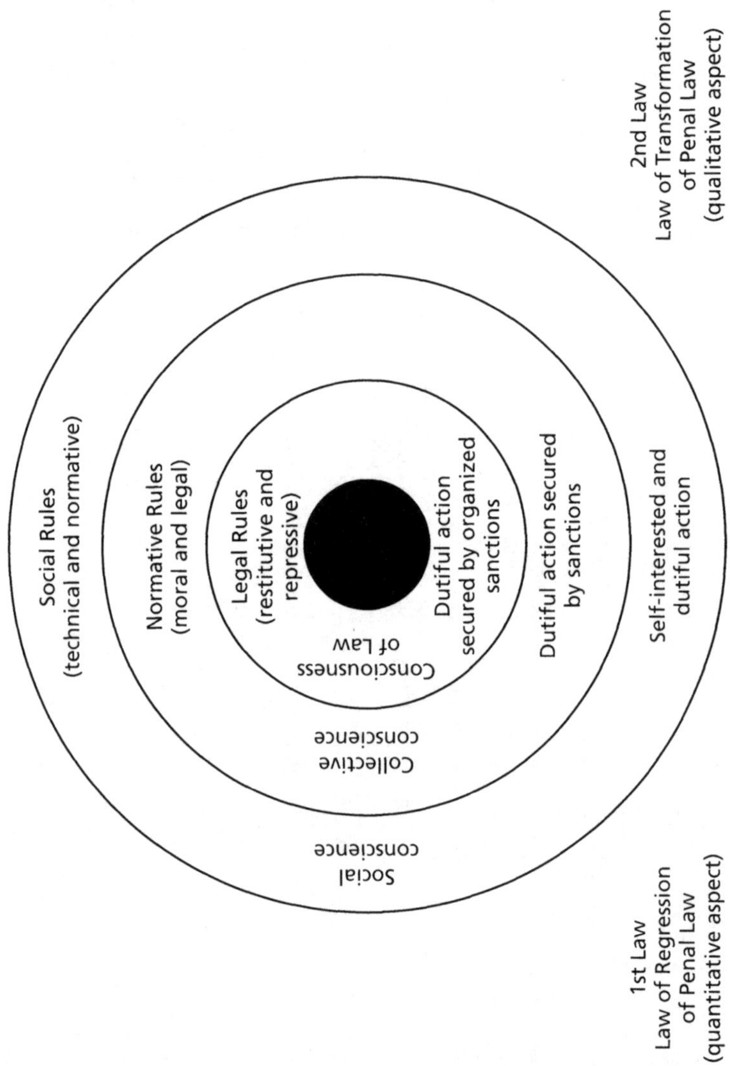

division of labor in society (quantitative aspect); however, at the same time, it fundamentally changes its character (qualitative aspect) and can therefore still form the core of a society based on the division of labor. Reflected in this fundamental change is a radical change in the shared ideas and sentiments. They no longer 'sanctify' the social group, but rather the individual, to the extent that the latter represents humanity. In the place of the cult of the group there arises the cult of the individual.

Durkheim consequently distinguishes between *two* laws in the development of penal law: the law of regression and the law of transformation.[7] The law of *regression* states that the range of the repressive core shrinks with social development; that all social bonds that derive from similarity lose cohesive force; that restitutive law advances at the expense of repressive law; and that all this is a consequence of increasing individualization. The law of *transformation* states that, above all, the intensity and solidity of the repressive core change; that the social bonds that are due to the complementary dissimilarity gain cohesive force in comparison to those from similarity; and that the repressive core is still preserved, though in a new form. All this becomes especially apparent in the changing conception of punishment.

Durkheim's view here is unusually modern. If one translates his analyses into contemporary terms, it could be said that the principle of retribution is sublimated into a principle of guilt, while the principle of prevention is enlarged through special prevention. Individualization here consists in the growing importance of the subjective component with respect to the prohibited action. Hence, modern penal law takes into account mistake of law (*Verbotsirrtum*), necessity as excuse (*entschuldigenden Notstand*), and lack of criminal capacity (*Schuldunfähigkeit*).

However, individualization also consists in the growing significance of the idea of re-socialization. General prevention, deterrence of the general public and the strengthening of a consciousness of law continue to exist, but they are complemented by special prevention, deterrence of the perpetrator from repeating his offense, and, above all, encouragement of his re-socialization. Bound up with individualization – from the cult of the group to the cult of the individual – is, therefore, at the same time a process of subjectivization and psychologization – from physical to psychical punishment. Michel Foucault later analyzed this occurrence in *Discipline and Punish* (1976), essentially as a successor of Durkheim, although with an entirely different objective.[8]

Human Rights as Penal Law

If one pursues this early classification of rules of law throughout Durkheim's work, it becomes clear that it already contains those two kinds of repressive rules of law that later are more emphatically elevated into a perspective of the evolution of humankind, namely those rules that protect the group and those that do the same for the individual. The more the *collective ideal* of individualism gains ground, which therefore, for Durkheim, prescribes not an egotistic but rather a *moralistic* individualism, the more do individual rights take precedence over group rights.[9] The science of morals and rights describes from a comparative perspective how humanity's development of law culminates in human rights and human obligations. While human beings counted for nothing or at least little in simple societies, in complex societies they would count for almost everything, at least since the political revolution of the 18th century.

What Kant had posited a priori, namely that the human being is an end in itself, Durkheim develops historically. The human being as an 'owner with contractual capacity' is not only embedded within the concrete group life of a society based on the division of labor with its intersecting social circles, but is also always above any concrete group life. It is, indeed, not the concrete human being whom modern repressive law ultimately protects, but rather the ideal of the human being, the Individual, *la personne humaine*, that is to say, the humanity in him or her. In 'higher societies', rules that obligate the state to protect this Individual therefore also possess the highest authority. Of course, it should more precisely be said that they *should* possess it. Any statistical investigation in Durkheim's time or even today would show that things are in no way at an optimum in regard to respect and compliance with human rights and obligations.

Let us now summarize Durkheim's perspective concerning the developmental history. In segmentary societies, however extensive and interlocking, particularistic group rights and obligations take precedence over the rights and obligations of the individual, but in societies with division of labor this is otherwise. Here the relationship is reversed. Particularistic group rights and obligations must now attempt to integrate into themselves universalistic human rights and obligations (Figure 4). These, however, are conceived by Durkheim as rules of penal law!

As has been already indicated, Durkheim, beginning in 1895, would increasingly ground the development of law in the development of religion. Within the development of religion arises the distinction between sacred and profane objects, which is also carried out within the development of law, particularly the development of penal law. There is, it is true, a process of secularization, but this is to be sharply distinguished from the process of profanation. Through the process of secularization, religion is not destroyed, but rather recast. Human rights and obligations must, therefore, ultimately be embedded in a *civil religion* by which they are linked together with societal rights and obligations – civic, professional, familial. One can further say that they thereby become contextualized.

Because civil religion, unlike a redemptive religion, is ultimately weak in cohesive force, the law again attains, precisely in modern society and in spite of its partial descent from religion, a central significance, though only that law that is connected to an organized apparatus of sanctions. All this, however, then poses a

FIGURE 4. THE CONSTRUCTION OF THE SCIENCE OF MORALS AND RIGHTS

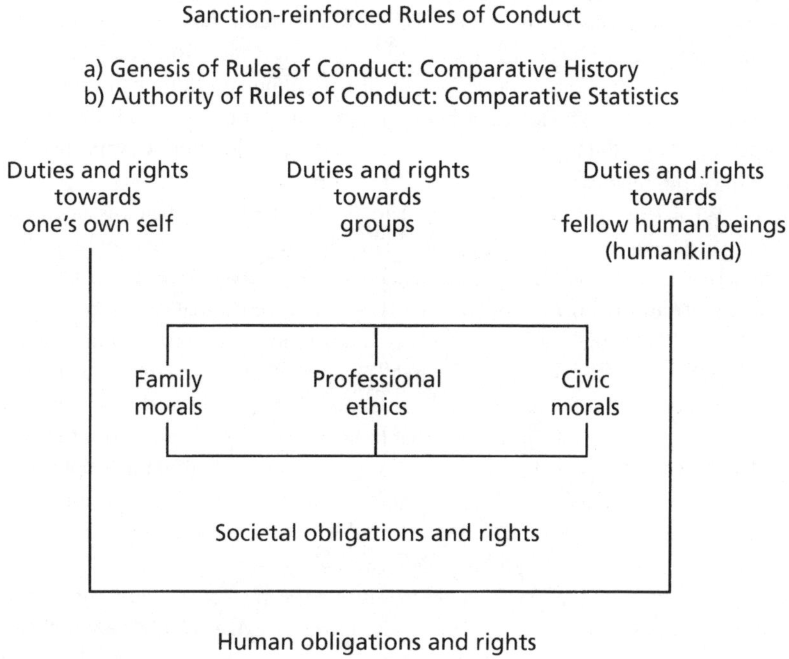

problem for human rights and obligations in Durkheim's time just as today. Therefore, he would have certainly welcomed more recent developments in international law to the effect that the sovereignty of the state and its so-called 'internal affairs' are relativized with respect to human rights and obligations.

In regard to Durkheim's social theory, the sociology of law, therefore, plays a major role. Strictly speaking, society is conceived as a system of law (*Rechtssystem*). Law is not only *one*, but *the* precondition of the constitution of social life.

This is not the case in Max Weber, to whom I shall now turn, again considering his work in four steps: (1) an interpretive science of social action; (2) an outline of a typology of social relationships, orders and organizations; (3) formal and substantive rationalization of law; and (4) human rights as a regulative idea.

Max Weber

An Interpretive Science of Social Action

In his 'Basic Sociological Terms' ('Soziologische Grundbegriffe') written in 1919–1920 as part of his newest formulations for his contribution to the *Outline*

FIGURE 5. ARCHITECTURE OF THE 'BASIC SOCIOLOGICAL TERMS' ACCORDING TO WEBER

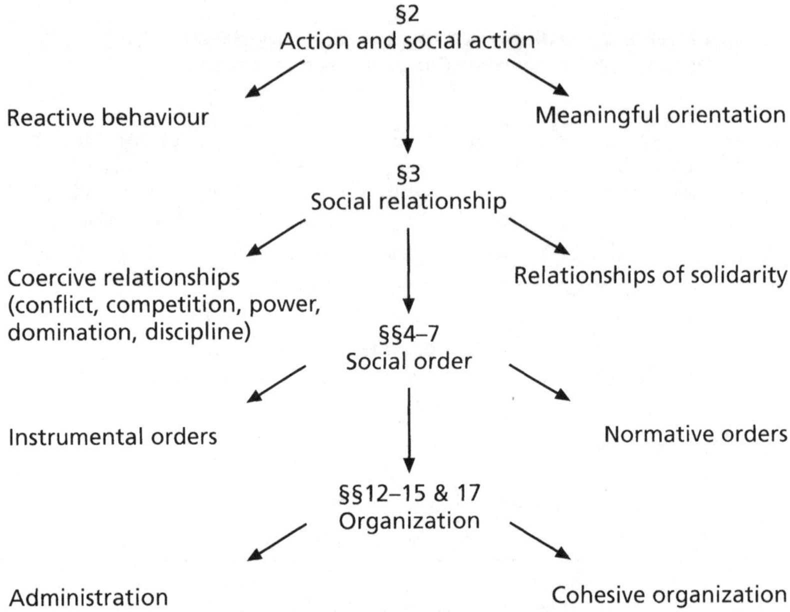

of Social Economics (*Grundriss der Sozialökonomik*), Max Weber defines sociology as a science 'concerning itself with the interpretive understanding of social action and thereby with a causal explanation of its course and consequences' (1978: 4). Three claims stand out in this definition. First, sociology is an empirical science (*Erfahrungswissenschaft*) that, like all empirical sciences, strives for valid explanations. Second, sociology explains its phenomena through 'action types', which are constructed as adequate on the level of meaning, while starting out from the subjectively intended meaning of actors. Third, sociology also explains its data by means of structural principles, that is, it methodically alternates between the micro and macro level without restricting itself to either one. It therefore requires basic concepts that are level-specific. This can be illustrated with regard to the architecture of the 'basic sociological terms' that stretch from action to social action, to social relationships, societal orders, and to organizations, accordingly displaying level-specific concepts that stand not in a genetic but rather in a *logical* sequence (Figure 5).

Since sociology is concerned with action within the context of structures, it can also employ interpretive explanation in addition to mere observational explanation, an idea that was foreign to Durkheim. For Weber, action is related to meaning and meaning is incorporated into structures that restrict and at the same time render possible action, while themselves being produced and reproduced only in action.

Outline of a Typology of Social Relationships, Orders, and Organizations

Weber's reflections on law are a constituent aspect of these basic concepts. In order to understand this correctly, one needs to become aware of two related contexts. The first concerns Weber's dispute with Rudolf Stammler, who in 1906 had come out with, in his own view, an improved second edition of his socio-philosophical investigation into the historical materialist conception of economy and law. Weber's 'basic terms', or categories, were originally developed 'in order to show what Stammler "should have meant" ' (Weber, 1968: 427), particularly in regard to a sociological formulation of the concept of law. The second context concerns Weber's contribution to the *Handbuch der politischen Ökonomie* (*Handbook of Political Economy*), later called *Grundriß der Sozialökonomik* (*Outline of Social Economics*), for which he intended to write under the title of 'Economy and Society' also on 'Economy and Law', first, on their 'relationship in principle' and, second, on the 'epochs up to the present'.[10]

Among the texts that were found after Weber's death in his literary remains, two correspond approximately to this table of contents: (1) 'The Economy and the Orders' ('Die Wirtschaft und die Ordnungen'), of which there are two versions – an early one, presumably from the period before 1910, and a later one not older than 1913; and (2) the text known as his sociology of law, which, however, one should not misunderstand as a mere 'sociology of', that is, as a sociology of a specialized area. On the contrary, it is concerned with the development of law in relationship to the development of the other societal orders and powers (*der gesellschaftlichen Ordnungen und Mächte*), and indeed in a universal historical perspective that considers this development, on the one hand, as a process internal to law and, on the other hand, as external to law.

What may be derived from these texts with regard to our present interests? I shall begin with the text 'The Economy and the Orders'. It deals with the relationship of the legal order to the economic order, but also with the relationship of the legal order to the conventional order and to custom, and, finally, with the significance and limits of legal coercion (*Rechtszwang*) in relationship to the economy. Thus, it is in fact centered upon the *fundamental* relationship between law and economy from a sociological point of view. The text also involves, as has already been implied, an attack upon Stammler. The following remark renders this particularly clear:

> Above all, Stammler confuses the ideal validity of a norm with the assumed validity of a norm in its actual influence on empirical action. The former can be deduced systematically by legal theorists and moral philosophers;

> the latter, instead, ought to be the subject of empirical observation. Furthermore, Stammler confuses the normative regulation of conduct by rules whose 'oughtness' is factually accepted by a sizable number of persons, with the factual regularities of human conduct. These two concepts are to be strictly separated, however.
>
> (Weber, 1978: 326)

How does Weber himself arrive at these conceptual distinctions that he insists upon? To begin with, he strictly distinguishes between two ***points of view***: the legal, and the social economic or sociological. This leads him to the distinction between two ***kinds of validity*** concerning norms that reciprocally presuppose and must be related to one another: the ***normative*** and the ***empirical***. After that, he strictly separates between two ***regularities of conduct***: the mere ***factual*** and that ***directed by rule*** (Figure 6). This leads him to the distinction between convention, law and ethics, on the one hand, and mere custom, on the other. Conduct directed by rules, however, is particularly suited for becoming an order (***ordnungs-tauglich***). Thus, the kind of rule and its guarantee conditions the order that arises from it.

Weber worked this early typology of societal orders into his 'Basic Sociological Terms' from 1920 but in a modified form, insofar as between this early typology and the 'Basic Sociological Terms' lies the unfolding of his sociology of domination (*Herrschaftssoziologie*) in whose center stands the concept of legitimacy. Accordingly, in Section 5 of 'Basic Sociological Terms' he says:

> Action, especially social action which involves a social relationship, may be guided by the belief in the existence of a legitimate order. The probability that action will actually be so governed will be called the 'validity' (*Geltung*) of the order in question.
>
> (1978: 31)

And he continues further below: 'Only then will the content of a social relationship be called an order if the conduct is, approximately or on the average, oriented toward determinable "maxims".' We may add that these maxims can be technical as well as normative. Then follows the qualification: 'Only then will an order be called "valid" if the orientation toward these maxims occurs, among other reasons, also because it is in some appreciable way regarded by the actor as in some way obligatory or exemplary for him' (1978: 31). This, however, is ultimately the case only for normative maxims.

Within these definitions are included: (1) both concepts of validity; (2) both concepts of regularity; (3) the distinction between an instrumental and a normative order; and (4) in regard to the normative order, the distinction between the conventional order and legal order. However, in connection with the

FIGURE 6. WEBER'S (EARLY) TYPOLOGY OF SOCIAL ORDERS

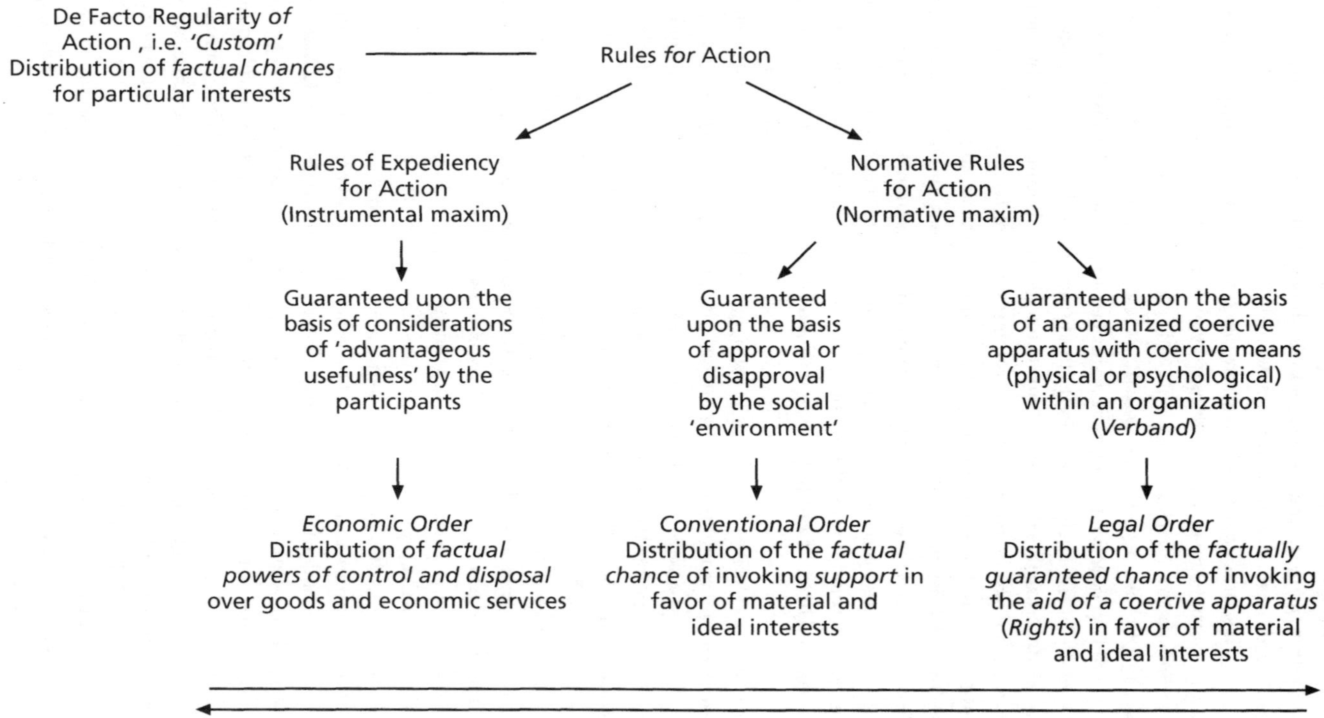

legal order, Weber now emphasizes legitimacy in the sense of an empirically provable belief in legitimacy. This is a consequence of his sociology of domination, which had been developed in the meantime.

The *sociology* of law therefore assumes as its main topic the empirical validity of the legal order consisting of a sum of legal propositions as opposed to legal *dogmatics* (*Rechtsdogmatisk*), which occupies itself with the normative validity of those propositions, whether these be a product of customary law or enacted law. A legal proposition connects a state of affairs with a legal consequence (if *A*, then *B* should follow), and since it is characteristic of this connection that this does not always occur, it must be guaranteed by means of a coercive apparatus. Here arises the greatest proximity to Durkheim, although in this regard Weber simultaneously thinks more in depth about gradations. Thus, law may also be indirectly guaranteed or even unguaranteed without losing its character as *law*, and where it is guaranteed, the guarantee need not be by the state for it may also be extra-state or pre-state. To law, however, correspond rights. Weber defines a right sociologically as the chance factually guaranteed to a person by virtue of the legal order 'of invoking in favor of his ideal or material interests the aid of a "coercive apparatus" which is in special readiness for this purpose' (1978: 315).[11] In turn, this right can be indirect – for example, a by-product of other rights – or direct, and as such either inherent or acquired.

Six points are important in connection with Weber's concept of an empirical legal order. First, every empirical legal order contains gaps. The depiction of the objective meaning of legal propositions as a system in itself logically closed and without contradictions is an ideal of legal dogmatics that is never entirely obtainable. Second, in every empirical legal order, legal propositions are more or less valid. Even this way of looking at things in terms of degrees ultimately contradicts the ideal of legal dogmatics. Third, the degree of empirical validity of a legal order is usually dependent upon the validity of other normative orders, in particular conventional norms, but also norms of ethics. Fourth, legal orders are not only linked 'in a fluid graduation' with ethics, convention and custom. There are usually several legal orders in a society that are in conflict with one another and with other orders so that one may speak of a 'battle of the orders'. Fifth, legal orders regulate only a small portion of action – grasp 'only fragments of the same' (Weber, 1972: 194)[12] – and they can certainly be normatively valid, but empirically completely powerless. Sixth, although legal orders are only capable of becoming more or less rationalized, there are three developments that have become important from the perspective of the history of law and that fall under the heading of the rationalization of law: (a) the standardization of the legal order; (b) its relative autonomization compared to other normative orders; and (c) the monopolization of legal coercion through the state. The latter, however, is, according to Weber, the result of the development of the market.

> The universal predominance of the market consociation requires on the one hand a legal system the functioning of which is *calculable* in accordance with rational rules. On the other hand, the constant expansion of the market, which we shall get to know as an inherent tendency of the market consociation, has favored the monopolization and regulation of all 'legitimate' coercive power by *one* universalist coercive institution through the disintegration of all particularist status-determined and other coercive structures which have been resting mainly on economic monopolies.
>
> (1978: 337)

In contrast to Durkheim, for Weber law is therefore not *the*, but rather only *one* precondition of the constitution of social life. Of course, it gains in importance from his point of view with increasing societal differentiation because that process can also, or even primarily, be described as a legalization (*Verrechtlichung*) of social relationships. In this connection, law undergoes a thorough change. Weber, unlike Durkheim, expressed this process in terms of the formula of a formal and substantive rationalization of law.

Formal and Substantive Rationalization of Law

It is here impossible to provide an account of Weber's encompassing presentation of the various epochs up to the present as found in his manuscript on the sociology of law. However, unlike Durkheim, he does *not* see this development from the point of view of a change in repressive and restitutive law and their interrelationship. Instead, he is interested in demonstrating that contemporary law is primarily the result of a process of *formal* rationalization in adjudication and lawfinding (*Rechtsfindung*) that produces, as a dialectical counter-movement, so to speak, the demand for a substantive rationalization of law on the part of the legally interested parties. The modern legal order not only exists in tension with other societal orders, but is also governed by an idea of law that in itself is tension-ridden. Drawing on Gustav Radbruch, it can be said that it consists of a tension between the idea of justice, on the one hand, and the idea of legal certainty (*Rechtssicherheit*) and expediency, on the other. Wherever law is formally rationalized, legal certainty and expediency inevitably take the lead. This becomes apparent, according to Weber, in the four principles that predominate throughout modern lawfinding. First, it is determined by a principle of subsumption according to which lawfinding is to consist in the application of an abstract legal proposition to a concrete state of affairs. The characteristics of the facts of the case must, in this connection, be general and unambiguous. Second, it is determined by a principle of construction according to which by means of legal logic a subsumption must be able to be obtained for every concrete state of affairs. Such means are at the same time rationally controlled and of an immanent legal nature. Third, it is determined by a principle of coherency according to which valid law is to be represented as a seamless system of legal propositions. This coherency is the result of a logical analysis of meaning and the conceptualization of legally relevant relationships of life. Fourth, it is finally determined by a principle of relevance according to which nothing may be considered as legally relevant that cannot be construed in legal terms. This refers to the difference between the facts of the case and the concrete state of affairs, and the 'irreality' of law (see especially Weber, 1972: 395ff.).

Weber treats in detail the powers that have advanced particularly in the Occident this formal rationalization of law, including the political and hierocratic powers, the exponents of various schools of law, the various groups of legally interested parties, and the organizational composition of the legal order itself. As differentiated as all of this is – and from it one already sees the distance from Durkheim – what about the substantive rationalization of law? What about justice in this context of legal certainty and expediency?

Human Rights as Regulative Idea

Weber, of course, also describes the counter-movements to legal formalism. They are, in the first place, of a thoroughly intrinsic legal nature. He refers, for instance, to the displacement of the formally bound law of evidence by the free evaluation of proof, the displacement of the formally bound characteristics of the facts of the case by taking into account the real intentions of the parties, and the increasing consideration of 'mental attitudes' during the ascertainment of legal consequences. However, he refers above all to the penetration of vague legal concepts into formal law such as good faith and fair dealing, or fair practice (*gute Sitten*). Even more important are the developments extrinsic to law. Particular groups of interested parties, and especially the legal ideologists, according to Weber, wanted to *substitute* substantive justice for formal legality (see Weber, 1972: 507). Weber locates such leading groups supporting an anti-formalism within the monarchical welfare bureaucracy as well as among the social democrats and the ideologists of the status of legal practice. They all held in common the wish to place formal law into the service of a political and ethical postulate external to law, and they thereby also tended to level out the differences between a legally extrinsic and legally intrinsic substantive rationalization.

For Weber, it is one of the distinguishing features of contemporary law that with the decline of natural law the legal system as a whole was transposed from an external to a legally internal postulate of justice. Today modern formal law knows at best only a few transcendental principles of law that, as Hermann Heller once formulated it, can be understood as building principles of legal content with an ethical claim to validity.[13] To such building principles, which in the first place are culturally *bound*, there undoubtedly belong human rights, which Durkheim had shifted into the center of his attention to 'higher societies' and which Weber considered essential to the life of modern citizens. Kant's insight, for

Weber, also holds true that human beings are ends in themselves and should never be degraded to a mere means as they would then forfeit their own dignity. Nevertheless, Weber certainly would never have thought of interpreting human rights as penal law. He was not even certain whether they could be understood as *detached* from a cultural group, and consequently as universalistic in the constitutive sense. Of course, if one does not at the very least *presume* such a universalism, then the formal rationalization of law stands in danger of autonomizing legal certainty and efficiency, while no longer bringing legal formalism into a tension-rich balance with the idea of justice as a constituent part of the idea of law. Just as too great a substantivization can undermine the productive capacity of modern law, so too can the uncoupling of its formal rationalization from any legally extrinsic or intrinsic substantive rationality.

Future Perspectives: A Return to the Sociology of Law as General Social Theory?

Let us begin our concluding remarks with a summary comparison of the two classical authors of the sociology of law whom we have here considered. What do they have in common and what not? Without a doubt they share in common the attempt to elucidate the limits of the economic interpretation of social life, along with the non-economic presuppositions and consequences of economic orders, in particular that of the capitalist market economy. Durkheim pursues this in his study of the social division of labor in direct contrast to utilitarian social theory, while Weber does the same in his investigations of the rise of modern capitalism in direct contrast to, on the one hand, historical materialism and, on the other, the neoclassical school of economics. For both, law plays an eminent role in these confrontations. However, how they define the role of law is what differentiates them.

1. For Durkheim, law is the *core* of social life, while for Weber it is only one important causal component among others. In spite of the increasing tendency towards legalization (*Verrechtlichungstendenz*) to which modern societal orders are subjected, it always grasps only a *fragment* of action and nothing more.
2. For Durkheim, law is a symbol of social life and therefore in the first place part of *culture*, while for Weber law is *order* and therefore in the first place part of the configuration of order within which social life takes place.
3. For Durkheim, there exists, disregarding occasional times of crisis, a *correspondence* between the development of law and social development, while for Weber the development of law proceeds in part *autonomously* and also acquires its *own proper sphere* (*Eigenrecht*) as compared with other developments.

4. For Durkheim, the differentiation of law is part of the functional differentiation of modern societies, while for Weber the differentiating of law means in the first place a differentiation of values with different normative dignity in regard to which an institutional differentiation, a differentiation of orders, can then follow.

In reducing the above to a formula of key words, one may speak of core versus fragment, of culture versus order, correspondence versus autonomy, and of functional differentiation versus differentiation of values. These differences mark out distinct conceptions of law within the framework of very different social theories.

Is this embedding of the sociology of law within general social theory antiquated? I think not. If one considers the contemporary scene in Germany, it may be said that two of its most prominent social theoreticians only quite recently undertook precisely such an integration. First, Niklas Luhmann treated law within the framework of his general theory of social systems as a differentiated, operatively closed and independently structured subsystem that develops through structural coupling with other subsystems.[14] Second, Jürgen Habermas (1992) assigned to law – within the framework of his general theory of communication, which is founded in language philosophy – a bridging function between communicative and administrative power through which it is to cope with the dual task of modern societies, namely to ensure social integration as well as system integration.

Of course, the theoretical foundations of these two approaches are completely different from those of Durkheim and Weber. And the differences between them are at least as marked as those which can be said to exist between these two thinkers. Also, the role that is thereby ascribed to law differs from the judgment of our classical writers. In the view of our classical authors, at any rate, law is neither an autopoietic system (as in Luhmann) nor could it secure the 'double' integration of modern societies, in spite of the fact that at least Durkheim undoubtedly came very close to such notions. At least, Weber did not undertax (like Luhmann) nor overtax (like Habermas) the role of law in social life. Perhaps for this reason one should after almost a century recall more often these classical writers of the sociology of law, before adopting without reservation the autopoietic or linguistic-pragmatic turns in social theory.

Translated by Steven Vaitkus

Notes

1. Durkheim, after his studies at the *École Normale Supérieure* and starting off as a teacher of philosophy at a *Gymnasium* in Saint-Quentin, undertook a study trip to Germany in 1885 that led him to Berlin and to Leipzig, from where there emerged two longer texts that belong to the constitutive components of his sociology: 'Philosophy at German Universities' and 'The Positive

Science of Morals in Germany' (both in German translation in Émile Durkheim, *Uber Deutschland Texte aus den Jahren 1887 bis 1915* [1995]).

2. Durkheim, starting in 1890, regularly held the course 'Leçons de sociologie Physique des moeurs et du droit' at the *Faculté des lettres* of the University of Bordeaux, and later at the Sorbonne The manuscript of this lecture, which has been edited from Durkheim's posthumous works, appeared in German translation under the title *Physik der Sitten und des Rechts Vorlesungen zur Soziologie der Moral* (Durkheim, 1991).

3. In retrospect Durkheim wrote in 1907:

> I read Wundt in 1887, but it was only in 1895 that I obtained a clear sense of the prominent role played by religion in social life In that year I found for the first time the way to tackle sociologically the study of religion. This was a revelation for me The lecture of 1895 marks such a decisive turning point in the development of my thinking that all my previous investigations had to be once more gone over, so as to be brought into harmony with these new ideas. Wundt's *Ethik*, which was read eight years earlier, had nothing at all to do with this change in orientation It rests totally upon the studies into the history of religion undertaken by me and in particular the reading of the works by Robertson Smith and his school.
>
> (Durkheim, 1975· 404; see also Durkheim, 1995: 241)

4. The clearest formulation in this regard occurs of course in a later text, namely in the article 'The Determination of Moral Facts', from 1906, where Durkheim clarifies the difference between technical and moral rules, and more generally between rules of prudence and happiness and those of obligation by means of a *Gedankenexperiment* The question is: how are action and the consequence of action connected, 'naturally' or 'artificially', analytically or synthetically? Where the latter is the case, the connection is established by sanctions (see Durkheim, 1967· 84ff and especially 93f.).

5. Durkheim's classification does not follow the usual distinction between private law and public law The decisive criterion of demarcation in regard to matters of law concerns rather the kind of sanction involved Even this criterion, however, cannot always be maintained Thus, for example, American law recognizes so-called 'punitive' damages, hence a combination of repressive and restitutive law

6. Durkheim's analysis is unsatisfactory because it is not clear what 'member' means Is he talking about individuals or social units; and if about social units, about (occupational) groups or institutional domains as carriers of functions? In addition, he vacillates between an analytical and concrete use of the mechanical–organic distinction. This has engendered considerable confusion in the secondary literature and has led to unusable remedial constructions (e g to the distinction between social integration and system integration). See in this regard above all Lockwood (1992)

7. The relevant text can be found in Durkheim's *Journal sociologique* (1969. 245–73), carrying the title 'Deux lois de l'évolution pénale'

8. For Foucault, it was a matter of rendering visible, behind the apparent humanization of punishment and its execution, the deep dehumanization which arises through the anonymization of punishment and through the reorientation of punishment towards psychical disciplining.

9. For a more extended analysis of this point, see 'Uber Individualismus' in Schluchter (2000)

10. See in this regard the 'table of contents' (*Stoffverteilungsplan*) outlined by Max Weber for this collective from May 1910 printed in *Max Weber-Gesamtausgabe III/6* (1994 766ff , especially 768).

11. Weber, by the way, later replaces the concept of 'coercive apparatus' (*Zwangsapparat*) employed in the older manuscripts with the concept of 'a staff engaged in enforcement' (*Erzwingungsstab*)

12. [The precise German phrase which Schluchter cites from Weber is not explicitly rendered in the English translation and thus the independent translation given here See Weber, 1978 331]

13. See in this regard, also with reference to Hermann Heller and Max Weber, Schluchter (1998. 223ff).

14. See Luhmann's *Das Recht der Gesellschaft* (1993) and also his most recent *Ausdifferenzierung des Rechts Beiträge zur Rechtssoziologie und Rechtstheorie* (1999) Luhmann was already concerned with law before his autopoietic turn See, for instance, his two-volume *Rechtssoziologie* (1972)

References

Comte, Auguste (1956) *Rede über den Geist des Positivismus.* Hamburg: Meiner. [Comte, Auguste (1844) *Discours sur l'esprit positif.* Paris.]

Durkheim, Émile (1967) *Soziologie und Philosophie.* Frankfurt: Suhrkamp. [Durkheim, Émile (1924) *Sociologie et philosophie.* Paris: Félix Alcan. (Durkheim, Émile (1974) *Sociology and Philosophy.* New York: Free Press.)]

Durkheim, Émile (1969) *Journal sociologique.* Paris: Presses Universitaires de France.

Durkheim, Émile (1975) *Textes: 1. Éléments d'une théorie sociale.* Paris: Les Éditions de Minuit.

Durkheim, Émile (1981) *Frühe Schriften zur Begründung der Sozialwissenschaft*, ed. and trans. Lore Heisterberg. Darmstadt and Neuwied: Luchterhand. The particular essay referred to is the German translation of Durkheim, Émile (1888) 'Cours de science sociale: Leçon d'ouverture', *Revue internationale de l'enseignement* 15: 23–48.

Durkheim, Émile (1988) *Über soziale Arbeitsteilung. Studie über die Organisation höherer Gesellschaften*, 2nd edn. Frankfurt: Suhrkamp. [Durkheim, Émile (1994) *De la division du travail social.* Paris: Presses Universitaires de France. (Durkheim, Émile (1964) *The Division of Labor in Society.* New York: Free Press.)]

Durkheim, Émile (1991) *Physik der Sitten und des Rechts. Vorlesungen zur Soziologie der Moral.* Frankfurt: Suhrkamp. [Durkheim, Émile (1969) *Leçons de sociologie. Physique des mœurs et du droit.* Paris: Presses Universitaires de France. (Durkheim, Émile (1983) *Professional Ethics and Civic Morals.* Westport, Connecticut: Greenwood Press.)]

Durkheim, Émile (1995) *Über Deutschland. Texte aus den Jahren 1887 bis 1915*, ed. Franz Schultheis and Andreas Gipper. Konstanz: Univ.-Verl. Konstanz. [The essays referred to in note 1 are the German translations of Durkheim, Émile (1887) 'La philosophie dans les universités allemandes', *Revue internationale de l'enseignement* 13: 313–38; 423–40 and Durkheim, Émile (1887) 'La science positive de la morale en Allemagne', *Revue philosophique* 24: 33–58; 113–42; 275–84.]

Foucault, Michel (1976) *Überwachen und Strafen. Die Geburt des Gefängnisses.* Frankfurt: Suhrkamp. [Foucault, Michel (1975) *Surveiller et punir. La naissance de la prison.* Paris: Éditions Gallimard. (Foucault, Michel (1977) *Discipline and Punish: The Birth of the Prison.* Harmondsworth: Penguin.)]

Habermas, Jürgen (1992) *Faktizität und Geltung: Beiträge zur Diskurstheorie des Rechts und des demokratischen Rechtsstaats.* Frankfurt: Suhrkamp. [Habermas, Jürgen (1996) *Between Facts and Norms: Contributions to a Discourse Theory of Law and Democracy.* Cambridge: Polity.]

Lockwood, David (1992) *Solidarity and Schism: 'The Problem of Disorder' in Durkheimian and Marxist Sociology.* Oxford: Clarendon Press.

Luhmann, Niklas (1972) *Rechtssoziologie*, 2 vols. Hamburg: Rowohlt. [Luhmann, Niklas (1985) *A Sociological Theory of Law.* London: Routledge and Kegan Paul.]

Luhmann, Niklas (1993) *Das Recht der Gesellschaft.* Frankfurt: Suhrkamp.

Luhmann, Niklas (1999) *Ausdifferenzierung des Rechts. Beiträge zur Rechtssoziologie und Rechtstheorie.* Frankfurt: Suhrkamp.

Roth, Guenther (1992) 'Interpreting and Translating Max Weber', *International Sociology* 7: 449–59.

Schluchter, Wolfgang (1998) *Die Entstehung des modernen Rationalismus: Eine Analyse von Max Webers Entwicklungsgeschichte des Okzidents.* Frankfurt: Suhrkamp.

Schluchter, Wolfgang (2000) *Individualismus, Verantwortungsethik und Vielfalt.* Weilerswist: Velbrück Wissenschaft.

Weber, Max (1968) *Gesammelte Aufsätze zur Wissenschaftslehre*, 3rd edn. Tübingen: J.C.B. Mohr (Paul Siebeck).

Weber, Max (1972) *Wirtschaft und Gesellschaft*, 5th, rev. edn. Tübingen: J.C.B. Mohr (Paul Siebeck).

Weber, Max (1978) *Economy and Society*, 2 vols. Berkeley: University of California Press.

Weber, Max (1994) 'Stoffverteilungsplan für das "Handbuch der politischen Ökonomie"', pp. 766–74 in *Max Weber-Gesamtausgabe II/6.* Tübingen: J.C.B. Mohr (Paul Siebeck).

Wolfgang Schluchter is Professor of Sociology at the University of Heidelberg, Germany. Among his publications in English, which he authored or co-authored, are the following: *Max Weber's Vision of History* (1979, together with Guenther Roth); *The Rise of Western Rationalism* (1981), *Rationalism, Religion, and Domination* (1989); *Paradoxes of Modernity* (1996); *Max Weber and Islam* (1999, together with Toby E. Huff), *Public Sphere and Collective Identities* (2001, together with Shmuel N Eisenstadt and Björn Wittrock)

Address: Institut für Soziologie, Universität Heidelberg, Sandgasse 9, 69117 Heidelberg, Germany [email. wolfgang schluchter@urz uni-heidelberg.de]

Steven Vaitkus is currently Senior Research Scholar at the Marianne Weber Institute, Oerlinghausen, Germany. He has previously taught at the University of Bielefeld, Constance, Poznan (Poland), and Toronto, and has a major interest in international classical theory and cultural experience. Some relevant publications along these lines include, *How is Society Possible?* (Kluwer, 1991); 'Phenomenology and Sociology' (in *The Blackwell Companion to Social Theory*, 2nd Edition, 2000), and with Ilja Srubar (eds.) *Phänomenologie und soziale Wirklichkeit. Entwicklungen und Arbeitsweisen* (Leske und Budrich, forthcoming)

Address Marianne Weber Institute, Postfach 100 111, 42001 Wuppertal, Germany [email stevenvaitkus@t-online.de]

Part II
Legal Form and Legal Rationality: Max Weber's Legacy

[2]

FORMAL AND SUBSTANTIVE RATIONALITY IN AMERICAN LAW: A WEBERIAN PERSPECTIVE

RONEN SHAMIR

University of Tel Aviv, Israel

INTRODUCTION

IN THIS essay I interpret the rise of American legal realism with a Weberian perspective in mind. The conclusion of this exercise, which I intend to clarify in the course of this article, is that (a) Weber's *conceptual* treatment of law in capitalist society provides useful analytic tools for understanding the transformations of American law, although (b), Weber's *general* theory of a progressive evolution of law in the direction of a formally-rational system is too narrowly conditioned by the particular legal–political reality that existed in turn-of-the-century Germany.

I show that Weber's concepts of formally- and substantively-rational law and his analysis of the tension between the two provide an analytic framework for studying the *political* conditions that facilitate the rise and decline of given legal orders. Also, I show that Weber's analysis of the relationship between legal modes of thought and the internal organization of the legal profession (that is, the relationship between law and its carriers) leads to an analytic orientation which reads legal history not only as a struggle of ideas but also as a struggle among segments of the legal profession in search for influence and power.

Applied to the case of American legal realism, I develop four specific propositions. First, the rise of legal realism marked a transition from a (false) formally-rational legal order to a substantively-rational one. Second, the realist movement in law might have remained marginal to mainstream legal thought if not for the ascendancy of the reform-minded New Deal administration in the 1930s. The ability of the realists to influence and shape the legal agenda of the state during the 1930s had to do with the particular political conditions that existed in this period of transition. Third, the struggle of ideas about the nature and sources of law which accompanied the ascendancy of legal realism was also a manifestation of a struggle for intellectual hegemony and authority of expertise between the corporate bar (defending the prerogatives of a common-law based judicial system) and academic law professors. Finally, I argue that legal realism as a legal–political force retreated and that formally-rational law reappeared as the New Deal administration grew beyond its 'experimental' stage.

These propositions entail a qualification of Weber's *general* theory of law. For Weber, formally-rational law could only develop where two conditions existed: first, a codified system of written laws (a particular political configuration), and, second, a well established group of free-floating academic legal experts who could develop law as an autonomous science without having to consider changing political and economic pressures (a particular professional configuration).

In contrast, I argue that at least in the United States, formally-rational law was developed from within a court-centered system which relied on analogies and precedents, rather than statutory rules, as a basis for its 'rationalization'. In this configuration, codified law was considered as the ultimate embodiment of substantively-rational law. The enemies of statutory legislation viewed it as a manifestation of arbitrary considerations, as the invasion and corruption of autonomous law, as the enemy of formal rationality. The advocates of the transition from a court-centered system to a system that relied more heavily on statutory legislation, on the other hand, advanced the consciously articulated claim that an enlightened law should be more responsive to social and political considerations and less self-protective by an illusion of an autonomous system of logical rules.

In short, I try to show that the legal realists led a movement in the direction of a 'German' legal system: one that relied on statutory rules, enacted by a strong federal state, and developed by academic legal experts at the direct and indirect service of the state. Unlike Weber's model, this movement was conceived by its carriers as a shift away from, rather than towards, formally-rational law.

The organization of this essay is as follows: first I briefly outline the general Weberian propositions concerning the distinction between formally-rational and substantively-rational law, the tensions that are inherent in both, and the relationship between legal ideas and their social carriers within the legal profession. Second, I employ the Weberian vocabulary to describe the rise of American classical legal thought as an emergent court-centered formally-rational law. Third, I discuss the relative marginality of American academics in a system that assigned appellate courts, and an autonomous practising bar, a leading role in legal development. With this theoretical and historical background in mind, I move to discuss the legal realist challenge to the hegemony of courts. After briefly describing the basic positions of the realists, I situate the realist challenge in the context of the pragmatic politics of the New Deal, and discuss it as an 'academic revolt'. Finally, I end the essay by elaborating on the relationship between legal and political changes and argue for a model of change which, following Weber, is bound to result in a reemergence of formally-rational law.

THE WEBERIAN CONCEPT OF FORMALLY-RATIONAL LAW

A formally-rational law, writes Weber, 'represents an integration of all analytically derived legal propositions in such a way that they constitute a logically clear, internally consistent, and, at least in theory, gapless system of rules' (1978: 656). One of the most important attributes of such a system is its closedness: legal decisions are rational to the extent that they are internally consistent and theoretically predictable, and formal to the extent that the judge does not have to look beyond the boundaries of the 'gapless' legal system in order to solve a given legal problem. The formality of a given legal system is thus also a measure of its 'systemic autonomy' (Trubek, 1972: 729) and its immunity from external 'interferences'.

A formally-rational legal system, says Weber, may be of two types. First, there is the rigid type in which process is preferred over substance and disputes are decided on the basis of some predetermined formal legal criterion ('the utterance of certain words, the execution of a signature' and so forth [Weber, 1978: 657]). A legal system that only adheres to this type of formalism essentially constructs law as a 'second-order normative structure; the real source of values comes not from the "science" of law but from the unrestrained choices of individuals' (Trubek, 1986: 588).

This rigidity, however is commonly softened by what Weber calls 'logical rationality' (1978: 657). This logical rationality provides for a mechanism of law-finding in which the 'legally relevant characteristics of the facts are disclosed through the logical analysis of meaning, and where, accordingly, definitely fixed legal concepts in the form of highly abstract rules are formulated and applied' (1978: 657). Thus, formally-rational law can give rise to general doctrines of, say, reasonableness, causation and consideration, which are consistently applied to concrete cases.

Either in its 'rigid' or 'soft' form, however, formalism is first and foremost an expression of *jurisdiction*: the creation of boundaries within which decisions over issues of substance are protected and legitimized by pointing at their consistency with formal methods (Stinchcombe, 1991). Formally-rational law, in other words, is based on a deliberate exclusion of 'irrelevant substantive noise' from entering the decision-making process.

The resistance of formally-rational law to considerations of substance is contrasted with other ideal types of law. In particular, Weber speaks of substantively-rational law, in which

> . . . the decision of legal problems is influenced by norms different from those obtained through logical generalization of abstract interpretations of meaning. The

norms to which substantive rationality accords predominance include ethical imperatives, utilitarian and other expediential rules, and political maxims, all of which diverge from the formalism [of the former]. (1978: 657)[1]

The relationship and tension between formal and substantive principles of justice occupied much of Weber's attention. Throughout his work Weber emphasized that the intrinsic nature of formally-rational law created an 'insoluble' and 'inevitable conflict' between formal legal meaning and utilitarian and ethical expectations (1978: 319, 811, 885). While formal rationality advanced in the name of greater consistency and predictability and hence in the name of greater freedom, it also created conditions of coercion that denied the realization of this very freedom. Formal justice, Weber stated, 'infringes upon the ideals of substantive justice' (1978: 813):

> Formal justice guarantees the maximum freedom for the interested parties to represent their formal legal interests. But because of the unequal distribution of economic power, which the system of formal justice legalizes, this very freedom must time and again produce consequences which are contrary to the substantive postulates of religious ethics or of political expediency. (Weber, 1978: 812)

It seems that Weber not only considered this tension as an inevitable result of a historical process but also as a lesser evil. He treated with suspicion movements which tried to reintroduce substantive considerations to the legal decision-making process (such as the Free Law movement), and seems to have shared a strong belief in the need (and possibility) to develop a high degree of certainty and predictability in law with the promulgation of carefully drafted statutory rules. Accordingly, Weber considered legal codification as a fundamental step in the direction of a fully developed formally-rational legal science which would prevent substantive criteria from entering the judicial mode of reasoning.[2]

This Weberian attitude led some observers to argue, either critically or approvingly, that Weber considered formally-rational law as the highest form of legal development (Parsons, 1967; Hunt, 1978; Habermas, 1984). On the other hand, Weber's theory had also been read as a relentless critique of formal rationality (Ewing, 1987; Feldman, 1991).[3] The realization of the 'inevitable conflict' between formal rules and substantive norms, and the attentiveness to the fact that 'formally rational law obscures the significant effects of economic power' (Feldman, 1991: 227), led Weber to emphasize the function of formally-rational law as a legitimation mechanism.

In the case of capitalism, formally-rational law functioned not only in the capacity of the 'great facilitator' of certainty and predictability but also as a normative order which tended to conceal the substantive inequality between formally equal parties (1978: 730). In the case of political domination, the belief in the legality of rules that were based on 'formally-rational grounds' provided political authorities with their most sound basis of legitimacy (1978: 215). These legitimation functions of formally-rational law had to do with the strong perceived affinity, that Weber himself helped to perpetuate, between the idea of formally-rational law and the idea of law as a science. The development of formally-rational law was entrusted to expert academic law teachers who emancipated legal thinking 'from the everyday needs of the public' (1978: 789). In turn, this legal arrangement helped to conceal the unequal distribution of economic and political power in society behind a veil of an objective science of law. As a legitimation mechanism, therefore, formally-rational law was considered by Weber as an essentially conservative force which best functioned as a protector of a given status quo (1978: 813).

A FORMALLY-RATIONAL COMMON LAW?

Weber's ideal type of formally-rational law, which may be justly considered as a brilliant theoretical abstraction, was nonetheless concretely rooted in the legal–political reality of turn-of-the-century Germany. The political unification of the German state under Bismarck in 1870 was accompanied by a growing demand for legal uniformity. The creation of a comprehensive codified body of law, in turn, was regarded by Germany's academic positivists as both the practical and symbolic embodiment of political unification. In 1900, the Burgerliches Gesetzbuch (BGB), a general code of laws for all Germany, took effect. For Weber, the BGB represented the ultimate manifestation of the correspondence between rational authority and rational law, and, moreover, was a living example of a law that obeyed the demands of a logically clear system of legal rules. Codification, in other words, became identical in Weber's mind with the idea of formally-rational law.

The fact that the BGB was to a large extent a product of academic legal thinking also seems to have influenced Weber's view that the creation of formally-rational law depended on the extent to which legal practice and legal learning were formally separated. In Germany, academic law schools enjoyed a monopoly over legal education and trained prospective lawyers according to academic standards. These standards, said Weber, enhanced the development of legal concepts that had 'the character of abstract norms which, at least in principle, [were] formed and distinguished from one another by a rigorously formal and rational logical interpretation of meaning' (1978: 789). The autonomy and formal rationality that Weber attributed to the German legal system were related to the domination of the profession by an elite of academic scholars, whose detachment from the practical imperatives of practice allowed them to develop law as a science. Wherever legal education has been in the hands of practitioners, asserted Weber, 'no rational system of law could emerge' (1978: 787).

Having the above postulates in mind, it is clear that Weber did not consider the English and North American common law as formally-rational systems. First, legal training for bench and bar was in the hands of practitioners who resisted the systematic and comprehensive treatment of the law. Legal apprenticeship produced 'law as a craft', and only academic training produced 'law as a science' (Weber, 1978: 787).

Second, decisions in the court-centered system of the common law were determined on a case-by-case basis. No formally-rational law could emerge without the application of abstract legal propositions 'logically derived from *statutory texts*' (1978: 890; emphasis added). Judgments that drew on analogies and on the application of precedents, said Weber, resembled a form of 'empirical art', somewhat corresponding to the category of substantively-irrational law (1978: 890, 976). On the other hand, Weber vaguely conceded that the common law was '"formalistic" to a considerable extent in [its] practical treatment' of legal problems (1978: 891). To the extent that this was the case, the common-law system was a formally-irrational system, one that rendered decisions on the basis of some formal criteria but without having a systematic basis from which to anticipate any given result. At any rate, the common-law system was described by Weber as one whose degree of rationality was at the very least 'essentially lower' than that of continental Europe (1978: 890).[4]

Yet it seems that Weber underestimated the ability of a common-law system to undergo a process of rationalization and formalization.[5] At least in the American case which is considered here, 'logical' formal-rationality did characterize legal thought and practice since the second half of the nineteenth century, in fact corresponding to the development of law as a science in Weber's civil law world. Indeed, Weber's 'mistake' may be directly attributed to his sociological orientation. In Weber's mind, formally-rational law became too much identified with particular institutional arrangements which in Germany consisted of a strong bureaucratic state with a stake in a comprehensive system of codified rules, and with an academic elite that advanced the idea of law as a science.

The fundamental difference between the United States and Germany was that the process of formalization and rationalization, in contrast to Weber's expectations, took place in a legal system that assigned federal appellate courts with the task of 'scientific' legal production. The results, however, were remarkably similar to those produced by the codified system of Germany.[6]

In contrast to Weber's model, it was the threat of statutory legislation as a primary source of law that gave a decisive push to the idea of formally-rational law in America. In the 1820s and 1830s, a 'codification movement' was high on the national agenda. The movement met the fierce resistance of bench and bar who feared that 'any special claims of the profession to determine the nature and scope of legal development [were] undermined' by this trend (Horwitz, 1977: 257). A scientific law, they argued, could only be grounded in a judge-made law which was based on distinct modes of legal reasoning. Legislation, on the other hand, was portrayed as a flow of arbitrary acts of power that exposed the law to an uneven development, unpredictable results and ultimately to what Weber would have called substantive justice. Thus, in response to the codification movement, the 'underlying conviction held by all nineteenth century legal thinkers [was] that the course of American legal change should, if possible, be developed by courts and not by legislatures' (Horwitz, 1977: 256).

That federal appellate courts stood at the centre of the American legal system had to do with unique political conditions. Compared to Germany, the American governmental structure in the mid-nineteenth century was 'so peculiar that many have refused to consider it a state at all' (Skowronek, 1982: 5). Early

America was a 'state of parties and courts'; the latter, writes Skowronek, were the only institutions capable of filling the governmental vacuum and providing a sense of legitimacy and coherence to the national system (1982: 27).

It was in this court-centred system that the idea of autonomous and 'scientific' law took shape and crystalized – from the mid-nineteenth century onwards – through what is often referred to as 'classical legal thought'. The rise of classical legal thought was marked by an effort to portray the legal system as an autonomous and scientific system. This was done by shifting the focus from the substantive aspects of law to its formal qualities. Law was portrayed as a gapless system of rules, concepts and norms, which determined legal results independently of substantive political and economic considerations (Kennedy, 1980; Horwitz, 1992; Mensch, 1990).[7] Classical legal thought, in other words, closely corresponded with Weber's notion of formally-rational law.

Further, similarly to Weber's arguments concerning the legitimizing functions of formally-rational law, Horwitz (1977) portrays a picture of law that underwent a process of objectification in tandem with the changing demands and expectations of the nation's economic elites. The interest of capitalist groups in finding a normative order that would 'freeze' their economic advantages in the market was highly conducive to ideas that rested the foundations of law on the values of science and formal impartiality:

> If a flexible, instrumental conception of law was necessary to promote the transformation of the post-revolutionary American legal system, it was no longer needed once the major beneficiaries of that transformation had obtained the bulk of their objectives. Indeed, once successful, those groups could only benefit if both the recent origins and the foundations in policy and group self-interest of all newly established legal doctrines could be disguised. (Horwitz, 1977: 254)

In the American case, as in Germany, therefore, the development of 'law as a science' provided a legitimation basis for a particular status quo.

SOCIOLOGICAL CONSEQUENCES OF A COURT-CENTRED FORMAL RATIONALITY

Weber argued that 'no rational legal training or theory can ever arise' where legal education had been in the hands of practitioners (1978: 787). This postulate, to some extent, also proved right in the American case. The rationalization of American law corresponded to the gradual abandonment of legal apprenticeship and its replacement with academic legal training. In 1800, fourteen of the nineteen jurisdictions in America required apprenticeship to enter the bar. By 1860, only nine out of thirty-nine jurisdictions required it. On the other hand, 'starting about the middle of the nineteenth century, law schools began to proliferate', and 'the number of law schools doubled in the twenty years between 1889–90 and 1909–10, while the number of law students increased more than fourfold' (Abel, 1989: 41).[8]

Yet there was a clear 'anomaly', from a Weberian standpoint, in the development of academic legal education in America. Academic education was coupled with the development of the case method as the embodiment of a scientific approach to law. Christopher Columbus Langdell and James Ames, Harvard's deans from 1870 to 1910, were the father-figures of the method (Sutherland, 1967). They viewed law as a science, but argued that all the available materials of that science were contained in the decisions of appellate courts. In other words, the new prominence of law schools and the corresponding ideas of formal and rational legal science did not threaten the centrality and authority of appellate federal courts as the producers of legal knowledge. On the contrary, academic learning provided further prestige to judicial decisions as 'scientifically' produced texts. The role of the academic legal expert, from this perspective, was to 'help' the judge in the process of finding an already existing rational law by elaborating, systemizing and distinguishing the formal criteria of legal decisions. In this scheme, law professors became an adjunct to the judiciary, one is even tempted to say that judges were the authors and academics the librarians. It was in such terms, for example, that Samuel Williston of Harvard spoke of the professor's role:

> The best service a professor of law can render the profession, aside from his work of teaching, is to state in treatises, or essays, the rules or principles that after collating legal decisions and using such general knowledge as he may possess he conceives to be sound. This he will do with full recognition that he is not thereby giving to the counsellor or to the court all that is necessary for the performance of their respective tasks. He is only giving them aid of the kind that his own work best fits him to give, in a matter that is vital for the successful prosecution of their functions, whatever else may also be needed. (Williston, 1933: 609)

This particular arrangement meant that American legal academics never enjoyed the status and influence of continental jurists. The centrality of courts in the American legal system, on the other hand, allowed lawyers in private practice to enjoy professional autonomy, power and prestige to a degree that was unknown to the civil law world (Rueschemeyer, 1973). The case-by-case development of law, coupled with elaborate judicial procedures, ensured that the exclusive competence of lawyers became indispensable and that they could play a significant role in determining the scope and pace of legal development.[9] Thus, the professionalization of lawyers in America was based on a core ideology that not only portrayed law as a science but also situated the judiciary as the producers of this scientific knowledge. The idea of judgeship as a symbol, says Botein, 'loomed large in the process by which lawyers articulated ideology to establish their professional authority in modern American society' (1983: 49).

In sum, while both the civil law and the common-law systems evolved towards formal rationality, they followed a different path. In each case, as Larson (1977) noted, the results benefited different strata of jurists: legal academics in continental Europe and bench and bar in America.[10] The adjunct role that the academia was to play in the development of law in America was a constant source of tension between academics on the one hand and the judiciary and practising lawyers on the other (Larson, 1977). As we shall see, these tensions reached an unprecedented peak in the New Deal years, when the legal realists systematically challenged this professional configuration.

THE CHALLENGE OF LEGAL REALISM

The construction of a relationship between legal realism and Weber's concept of formally-rational law calls for a distinction between the formally-rational law as the 'presentation of self' of a given legal system (the 'is') and formally-rational law as an aspiration (the 'ought'). Weber assumed the existence of the 'is' in the civil law world and at the same time recognized that it legitimized a particular substantive social order (hence the debate concerning Weber's own normative position in regard to the 'ought'). The legal realists, on the other hand, challenged both the 'is' and the 'ought'. Formally-rational law did not exist in fact, and the aspiration to simulate the conditions of formal rationality should be discarded anyway.

The realist movement in law began its ascent in the 1920s as a reaction against some of the fundamentals of classical legal thought.[11] The critique of the judicial process as inconsistent and arbitrary, and the challenge to the idea that law was objectively found and applied by judges, however, was by no means novel. The realists owed an acknowledged intellectual debt to the pragmatist philosophy of John Dewey, C.S. Pierce, William James, Oliver W. Holmes and John C. Gray, who formed Harvard's Metaphysical Club in the 1870s, and they both criticized and continued ideas which were developed by Roscoe Pound's sociological jurisprudence and by the German Free Law school (White, 1972; Herget and Wallace, 1987).[12]

Pragmatist thought, in particular, had a significant effect on the realists' thinking. 'Crudely put', wrote C. Wright Mills, '"pragmatism" denotes a doctrine and mood which looks to the "practical", to "consequences", which elevates the "actions" which come out of given ideas to the status of a philosophical category' (1966: 235). The pragmatist insistence on consequences and experience, in turn, stemmed from their principled sceptic posture towards the articulation of absolute values and ideals.

Holmes argued that the beliefs in the compelling force of precedent and in the objectivity of legal rules that determined the course of legal development were a myth; the life of the law, he said, was based on experience and not on pure logic (Holmes, 1897). Gray argued along similar lines in his 1909 *The Nature and Sources of Law*. Gray discredited the role of predetermined legal rules in judicial decision making and argued that legal rules 'do not preexist the judicial decision: they do not exist eternally in heaven for all time, to be discovered by the judge in an act of *a priori* thinking . . . rather, they are made by judges' ([1909] cited in Benditt, 1978: 6). Like Holmes, Gray conceived of law as a manifestation of what judges said it was, and 'nothing more than this'. Thus, pragmatism was first and foremost a revolt against formalist and deductive thought and for the replacement of these with 'experience, life, growth, process, context, and function' (Hart, 1983: 130).

The pragmatist legacy directed the realists to insist on a few basic principles: 'the conception of law in flux, of moving law, and of judicial creation of law', 'the conception of law as means to social ends and not as an end in itself', 'the conception of society in flux, and in flux typically faster than the law', and hence the need of constant adjustment of law to social change, 'the *temporary* divorce of Is and Ought for purposes of study' (a claim that was largely misinterpreted to imply that realists were ethical relativists), and the principled 'distrust of traditional legal rules and concepts' (Llewellyn, 1931; also Frank, 1930). All of the above principles challenged the idea of a self-contained and autonomous system that obeyed its own rules; a challenge to the effort of jurisprudence to provide the law with a scientific basis as 'a way of finding out the truth', and a critique of this effort as the 'shining but unfulfilled dream of a world governed by reason' (Arnold, 1935: 730).

In terms of the Weberian theory of law, the formal rationality of law has been challenged on two grounds. First, legal realism doubted the possibility of attaining a rational system of law, insofar as rationality informed the notion that legal decisions were based on the application of abstract and general rules to concrete facts. In this respect, the realists argued that 'insofar as adjudication is rational at all, it is substantively rational, not formally rational' (Feldman, 1991: 233). Second, this substantively-rational (or more likely irrational) element of the judicial process was attacked by the realists for its arbitrariness, for its being largely unconscious, and for its lack of direction. In exposing the tension between formality and substance in law, the realists also offered the corrective whereby law could only be justified if it corresponded to the substantive criteria of adaptation to social change.

Thus the realists not only discredited the notion of formally-rational law but also suggested their own constructive alternative. At least for some of the realists, theirs was a 'true' science, whereas traditional conceptions of law were 'false'. Classical legal thought 'promised' to reduce social and economic uncertainty through the construction of a self-contained and universally applicable system of formal rules. Legal realism envisioned a different strategy of uncertainty reduction, by making a scientific effort to treat law in its relation to 'things and people' and not to 'words alone' (Llewellyn, 1931: 1223), and by thinking of law in its relation to crucial questions in the sphere of administration (Yntema, 1934: 207; Cohen, 1935).

In other words, legal realism provided a legal basis for a constructive social reform agenda that legal historians, as Horwitz (1992) aptly observes, have largely ignored. The realists' premise that law was nothing more than what the judge said it was and their subsequent interest in what courts did in fact, led observers to focus on the realists' rule scepticism (Hart, 1983), on their behaviorist positivism and subsequent neglect of the normative character of law (Hunt, 1978; Summers, 1982), and, in general, to focus on the realists' court-centred approach.

The unfortunate result is that too little attention has been given to the study of legal realism as an attempt to escape the grip of such a court-centred legal system. The legal realists not only investigated and critiqued the judicial process but also advocated a greater reliance on statutory legislation and informal administrative decision-making processes as alternative sources of law. It was this aspect of the realist vision that created the most direct link between the legal realists and the reform-minded administration of the New Deal era. The development of administrative law during the New Deal, with the active guidance of many legal realists, was thus a culmination of the crisis of legitimacy that realist criticism produced (Horwitz, 1992). It is the realists' 'action' agenda and its relationship to the particular political conditions that existed in the United States in the 1930s, therefore, that receives attentive treatment in the next section.

LEGAL REALISM AND THE NEW DEAL: SUBSTANTIVE LAW TRIUMPHANT

The general affinity between the New Deal and legal realism is widely recognised yet receives little theoretical analysis. It was during the New Deal that many legal realists became part of the administration's inner circles and it was only during the New Deal that the realists were able to translate their academic respectability into concrete influence on the legal system (Auerbach, 1976; Irons, 1982; Ackerman, 1983; Kalman, 1986).

Nonetheless, legal realism has rarely been treated as the legal manifestation of the political New Deal. Legal historians have been mainly engaged in situating legal realism in the context of the history of jurisprudential ideas at the expense of reading jurisprudence in a broader socio-historical context. Too often, the effort to trace the intellectual roots of the legal realists created a sense of historical continuity that failed to capture the metanarrative (to the degree that we may invoke such notions in a postmodern era) of legal change. Summers's (1982) analysis of legal realism as part of a long tradition of 'pragmatic instrumentalism' in America, in particular, serves as an example of a scholarly tradition that in spite of its own recognition of the important relationship between law and politics almost completely ignored the New Deal as the most important stimulus to the rise of legal realism 'in action'.[13]

The rise and decline of legal realism, from this perspective, has too often been presented as a history of ideas without social carriers, in which 'winning' and 'losing' was determined by the strengths and weaknesses of arguments. The dynamic of change in jurisprudence, however, as in other forms of discourse, is not only a result of a progressive evolution of abstract ideas, but a 'sea of stories' that drifts in tandem with political and economic developments.[14] An important sociological question, therefore, concerns the social circumstances which allowed legal realism to prosper during the 1930s and, ultimately, to retreat from centre-stage in the following years. The answer to this question, in turn, has to do with the fact that during the 1930s the realists' ideas fell on fertile political ground. The pragmatism of the realists, in other words, corresponded to a pragmatist spirit in politics.

The severe economic depression that accompanied the 1929 collapse of the financial markets was followed by a profound crisis of legitimacy for laissez-faire capitalism. In 1933, riding on popular waves of disenchantment, Roosevelt's New Deal administration came to power, promising a commitment to social and economic reforms which would fundamentally alter the stagnant status quo. The New Deal marked the most significant shift in American history from a relatively 'weak' and abstentious federal state to the modern regulatory federal state. The New Deal administration, however, was not committed to a single political philosophy but was rather based on 'an amalgam of conflicting policies and programs' (Hawley, 1966). The underlying unifying theme of these policies was the commitment to economic recovery that required, as far as the administration was concerned, different, if not conflicting, pragmatic experiments.

In the legal sphere, the administration's activist policies required a reliance on statutory legislation as the means of social and economic change. The increased use of legislation, and the conscious articulation of statutes that were based on innovative constitutional doctrines, were justified in terms of the urgent need to provide solutions to dire economic problems. Thus a legislative 'frenzy', as some unhappy critics observed (Butler, 1934: 99), turned America into 'a nation governed by written laws' (Calabresi, 1982). The novelty of this legislative programme, Calabresi notes, was that

> . . . unlike earlier codifications of law, which were so general that common law courts could continue to act pretty much as they always had, the new breed of statutes were specific, detailed, and 'well drafted.' Again, unlike the codes, which were compilations of the common law, the new statutes were frequently meant to be *the primary source of law*. (1982: 5; emphasis added)

Further, many new statutes – like the National Industrial Recovery Act, the Securities Exchange Act and Wagner's Labor Act – only outlined general principles. The task of administering these laws and interpreting them was delegated to administrative bodies that were expected to put teeth into them through intensive regulation. These powerful administrative bodies, in other words, produced another source of law: administrative law. The reliance on primary legislation and administrative regulation as major sources of law marked an important departure from the previous mode of legal production and a shift towards substantively-rational law.

Statutory legislation marked a shift from 'cases' to 'causes' (Jackson, 1934) as the fuel of legal change, thus sidestepping the traditional centrality of a judicial system which operated on a case-by-case basis. Administrative law, at least in the early years of the New Deal, was conceived as a valid body of law which grew outside the jurisdiction of courts. Arthurs best captures the tension administrative law creates: 'For most lawyers, administrative law is not the law *of* the administration; it is the law directed *against* the administration, the law by which reviewing judges ensure that the administration does not overreach' (1985: 6). New Dealers and their realist allies perceived administrative law in the former sense, in contrast to the expectations and interests of bench and bar. Further, the administrative process of the early New Deal was consciously constructed along informal lines. Judicial rules of evidence and procedure were avoided and administrative hearings and adjudicatory methods were deliberately marked by their informal character. Consequently, as Radin noted, lawyers missed 'the air of the cock-pit, the *chaude-mêlée* of the tournament, the *strepitus judicili* which in all reformatory efforts, popes and emperors, philosophers and publicists, have always attempted to eliminate' (1935: unpublished).

These changes reflected a new legal philosophy and a changing attitude to the relationship between law and social change. The administration was clear in its message that solutions to the economic problems of the nation could only be provided by massive legislation and that the purpose of the various statutes was to serve specific social and economic purposes. Law was to become a functional and instrumental mechanism: 'To my mind', Attorney General Homer Cummings told the American Bar Association, 'the law is not a mere body of precedents. I visualize it as a living, vital, growing thing, fashioned for service and constantly being refashioned for further service. Its function is to serve' (Cummings, 1933: 578).

If established constitutional doctrines and traditional legal principles stood in the way, they had to be changed, reinterpreted or, sometimes, avoided. Such, for example, was the case when the Guffey-Snider *Bituminous Coal Conservation Act of 1935* was pending in Congress. A subcommittee of the Senate Committee on Interstate Commerce asked Attorney General Cummings to testify as to the bill's constitutionality. Cummings refused, and President Roosevelt, for his part, sent the subcommittee a letter in which he argued that

> no one is in a position to give assurance that a proposed act will withstand constitutional tests, for the simple fact that you can get not ten but a thousand differing opinions on the subject. . . . I hope your committee will not permit doubts as to constitutionality, however reasonable, to block the suggested legislation. (*United States Law Week*, 9 July 1935: 1)

In sum, the New Deal encouraged an instrumental approach to law. Whereas 'autonomous law' provided legitimacy to the political and economic order that preceded the New Deal, it became an obstacle once social change was required. The state-building process, in the name of economic recovery, challenged the idea of legal autonomy; laws had to reflect the general will, and the commands of the legitimate sovereign, in turn, embodied this will. In Weberian terms, therefore, the New Deal signalled a transformation from a formal-rational legal order to a substantive-rational one; a shift from a highly structured, closed, and 'gapless' legal system, to 'lay justice' mechanisms and an open and flexible system of rules.

It was legal realism which was intellectually equipped to provide the cognitive basis for the legislative policies of the New Deal. The scepticism of the realists helped to legitimize the treatment of the Constitution as a practical and flexible text, and the realists' own experimental orientation led them to articulate the legal foundation for the expansion of the administrative machinery of the federal state and its greater reliance on statutory law. The administration's readiness to 'experiment' in the social and economic spheres echoed the realists' own emphasis on the need to experiment with the law. Jerome Frank, for example, suggested that 'realistic jurisprudence be re-named "experimental jurisprudence" and that those who lean in that direction be called experimentalists' (1933: 101). He described those experimentalists as 'constantly skeptical of their own formulations', who repudiate fixed beliefs as to the eternal validity of any particular means for the accomplishment of desired ends, ever ready to admit that their own ideas were 'based upon partial and unavoidable ignorance', and, perhaps above all, 'devoted to action' (1933: 101). Frank, as Duxbury writes, was committed to the New Deal, considered it as 'an elaborate series of experiments', and approached it with a 'reformist zeal' (1991: 3).

In their devotion to 'action', one of the most important contributions of the realists was to provide a rationale for the administration's growing reliance on statutory law and, in particular, on the administrative law that grew from it. This, necessarily, went hand in hand with an attack on the merits of the judicial process and with calls for withdrawing whole classes of controversy from the courts. Thurman Arnold and Milton Handler, for example, critiqued the judicial process as an outmoded and narrow 'catch-as-catch-can' philosophy (Arnold, 1934) that failed to 'keep pace with the far-reaching and rapid changes occurring in the world today' (Handler, 1934: 138). Arnold, following a psychological approach which Jerome Frank had been known for, argued that the very insistence on a 'trial by combat' could be attributed to the mystifying and irrational jurisprudential belief that only a contest and a conflict could bring out the 'truth' in any given dispute. The reason for this belief, he said, was that society needed the drama of battle and courts, on their side, were willingly playing their part (Arnold, 1934: 935).

This critique was linked with the advocacy of new methods and means that could serve as legitimate sources of law. Some realists emphasized the merits of statutory legislation. James Landis, for example, argued that

> the legislative process, quite distinct from the judicial process, tries to reach a solution on the basis of political or social expediency. It reaches certain balances which the judicial process can't reach because of the limitations that are inherent in that process. . . . (1934: 124)

Others stressed the merits of the administrative process as a more efficient and comprehensive form of justice. 'Obviously', wrote Handler, 'the demand for administrative tribunals arises because of the breakdown of the legal system in particular fields. The demand for those administrative tribunals arises because the problems are too complex, too difficult to be handled by the average judge' (1934: 138). And Arnold described as inevitable and socially desirable the process whereby 'regulatory functions escaped into another system of courts, called commissions', where a technique of conference replaced judicial methods because of the inability of the latter to articulate rules and regulations that went beyond the particular contest between two parties (Arnold, 1934: 913–47; also Jackson, 1934).[15]

On a different yet complementary front, the realists facilitated the administration's new reliance on statutory and administrative measures by ridiculing and criticizing the Restatement Project which by the 1930s had made significant progress under the auspices of the American Law Institute. The Restatement Project sought to answer the concerns of many jurists who, since the first decade of the twentieth century, acknowledged the ever-growing uncertainties and inconsistencies of modern case law. The purpose of the restatements, therefore, was to save the system from becoming 'more confused and more conflicting' (Williston, 1933: 598) and to arrange legal decisions in a way that would have retained the 'gapless' and coherent appearance of the legal system. Legal realists, for their part, rejected as 'static' and 'useless' the attempt of conventional jurisprudence to overcome legal uncertainty from within the system (Yntema, 1934). Thurman Arnold, in his typical biting language, thus described the restatement effort:

> Out of the whole confused effort comes the belief that a unified body of rational principles must exist, or else learned men would not be hunting for them with such untiring diligence. Present confusion is explained by showing that the law is an uncompleted science. The analogy of evolution, including the outworn scientific notion of the survival of the fittest, is employed. (1935: 731)

The New Deal administration clearly benefited from the academic theoretical support for its policies. The interventionist state needed scientific expertise both in order to administer its policies and in order to justify policies in terms of class-free projects for the public good (Larson, 1977; Stryker, 1990). The legal realists brought precisely such new legal 'scientific expertise' to the service of the New Deal administration. The task that legal realists were invited to perform in the service of the New Deal had a dual character. First, they were invited to draft legislation, to run administrative bodies and to transform the administration's policies into legal language. Second, they were needed in order to legitimize the administration's policies by cloaking them in a new legal ideology. In this capacity, legal realists – both in the direct service of the state and from their academic posts – were also needed in order to delegitimize the authority of federal courts and the heretofore established constitutional and legal doctrines that they delineated.[16]

In this latter capacity, the legal realists defended the New Deal from a vocal opposition which criticized the New Deal in the name of protecting the autonomy of law and the authority of the judicial system. This opposition included some of the realists' own academic peers, part of the federal judiciary (including a majority of judges in the Supreme Court), and the leadership of the practising bar. For the latter, in particular, the legal agenda of the realists represented a direct threat to their own prerogatives in controlling the direction and scope of legal development and a direct challenge to their established position as the bar's leaders (Auerbach, 1976; Shamir, 1992). In defending the policies of the New Deal, in articulating a new legal paradigm and in countering the arguments of the opposition, therefore, the realists functioned as an antidote to those segments of the legal profession (including the judiciary) which sought to undermine the New Deal's legislative reforms.

Legal Realism as an Academic Revolt

Responding to the realists' critique of the Restatement Project, George Wickersham, the president of the American Law Institute, declared that the realists represented a school of thought that was 'absolutely foreign' to the principle that the American Law Institute stood for: 'The jurisprudence of a nation is not made by acts of legislatures or decrees of administrative bodies. . . . Laws come and go, but the jurisprudence of a people moves on from precedent to precedent' (1934: 634; see also 1933: 328).

It was no coincidence that these words came from Wickersham who, apart from being the president of the Institute, was also a practising corporate lawyer, a senior partner in the prestigious Wall Street firm of Cadwalader, Wickersham & Taft. In fact, although many prominent academic scholars took part in the restatements, it was people like Elihu Root and George Wickersham, two conservative corporate lawyers, who orchestrated the project. For lawyers like Wickersham and Root, whose ideas largely reflected the opinions of the bar's elite, the realists' vision represented an outright heresy. It represented a struggle, as James Beck put it, between pragmatists and moralists; 'the founders of the Republic were moralists while the men of our time are pragmatists', he lamented (1933a: 689).

Yet at stake was more than a struggle of ideas. For the leaders of the American bar, largely senior partners in corporate law firms, the realists' vision and its impact on the administration's policies also represented the rise of a new academic counter-elite with a dangerous claim to a hegemonic position within the legal profession. Thus Beck complained that 'in the faculties of our law schools there are now many professors who . . . pretend to sit in judgement not only upon the decisions of the Supreme Court but upon the relative merits of the judges' (1933b: 49). Others spoke of the realists as 'dangerous academic theorists' and 'demagogues', whose objective was a new and unacceptable order (Diggs, 1933: 130; Miller, 1934: 350), and William Ransom, the president of the American Bar Association, flatly described 'professors and teachers [who] refuse allegiance to our constitution and form of government' (Ransom, 1936: 23).

Both lawyers and academic realists spoke openly about a widening gulf between teachers and practitioners. Charles Clark of Yale, the president of the Association of American Law Schools and a leading realist, complained that the leaders of the bar distanced themselves from academics because the latter were 'suspected in this country' (1935: 74). Clark doubted, however, whether there was anything that could be done about it. Simply, academic legal realists indeed saw themselves in a new leading position. As much as the New Deal administration benefited from the inclusion of academic experts, the realists benefited from the willingness of the state to be attentive to their opinions. As much as elite lawyers in private practice had distinct professional reasons to be hostile to the New Deal and to the realist spirit that permeated it, legal realism gave expression to the professional aspirations of legal academics.

The New Deal, with its conduciveness to legal realists' ideas, allowed law teachers to escape, although only temporarily, from their marginal position within the legal profession (for a similar argument see Dezalay et al., 1989). As academics, the realists suffered from a 'dual marginality'. On the one hand, they were not fully rooted in the academic world because high prestige legal education was almost exclusively geared towards the training of future corporate lawyers. The result was that law teachers were often just that: teachers in a professional school, rather than an integral part of the academic intellectual community.

On the other hand, the centrality of courts in the American legal system, as we have seen, situated appellate judges and their allies in private practice, rather than legal academics, at the apex of professional power and prestige. Moreover, the almost exclusive focus of legal education on appellate cases left little room for academic innovation in law, a fact that further emphasized the marginality of legal academics in both the legal profession and the scientific community of the university.

Before the New Deal, the major effort of legal realists was to establish themselves as an integral part of the academic community. The will to escape their marginality in academia found expression in two interrelated trends. First, realists stoked a closer relationship with other disciplines and incorporated non-legal materials to the curriculum of law schools (Kalman, 1986). Second, realizing that the case method constrained them to the firm grip of judicial texts, legal realists snapped at the Langdellian case method as a system that 'has choked legal education' (Frank, 1933; Landis, 1934; Llewellyn, 1935). The realist critique of the case method, as part of their general critique of law-as-a-science, therefore, was another expression of their aspiration to become more than mere teachers.

Yet it was the arrival of the New Deal that provided legal realists with an opportunity to assert a role than went beyond their academic standing. The administration's reliance on legislation and administrative methods went hand in hand with the realist critique of the exclusive role of courts in producing legal 'knowledge'. This, in turn, enhanced the role of academic legal experts in shaping legal doctrine and gave expression to the legal realists' aspiration to assume a leading position within the legal profession. Legal academics, and first and foremost legal realists, were invited by the administration to put into practice what they had been preaching in the academia. In practical terms, this meant that law professors assumed positions of power and influence that they never before enjoyed. Key governmental and administrative positions were occupied by legal academics, many from the ranks of Yale and Columbia law schools and some others from Harvard.[17]

As law came to be seen as the 'science of the compelling power of government to intervene in the relations of human beings' (Parkinson, 1935: 293), legal realists could convincingly argue that they were best equipped to coordinate the multiple sources of law and to scientifically 'manage' the legal system. Felix Frankfurter, who was described at the time as 'the most influential single individual in the United States' (*Fortune Magazine*, January 1936: 63), enthusiastically spoke about a new breed of lawyers–civil servants who could compete in power and influence with the best minds in corporate practice (1936: 61); Charles Clark praised the contribution of academics to legal development and the 'even more spectacular' activities of academics in the service of the federal government (1933: 18), and Leon Green, the Dean of Northwestern Law School, described law professors as the 'Lawyers' Brain-Trust', who not only developed jurisprudence but were also pivotal in providing services to the general public (1934: 1032).

In sum, the clash between legal realism and traditional (formalist) approaches to law was more than a struggle of abstract ideas. The challenge to formal rationality in law was also a challenge to the leading position of courts in the American legal system and an assertion of the intellectual superiority and legal competence of academic experts.

SUBSTANTIVE-RATIONALITY AS A TRANSITORY PHASE: EPILOGUE AND CONCLUSION

Even in the heyday of legal realism in the mid-1930s, there were some lawyers who were insightful enough to suggest that the substantive-rational era in law could not last. Carl McFarland, for example, reminded lawyers that they were witnessing a period of transition in which, like in previous periods in the history of the common law 'administrative justice has been the trying ground . . . whereby the courts have avoided some of the embarrassments of experimentation in new fields of government' (1934: 620). Similarly, Leon Green asserted that 'periods of great scientific and governmental activity . . . [are] necessarily periods of administration, while periods of stabilization are periods of law' (Green, 1935: 708). Observers like McFarland and Green, therefore, predicted that with the passing of the 'transitory' period, the administration's new legal mechanisms would eventually be judicialized (that is, 'formally rationalized'). History proved them right.

Although legal realism affected jurisprudential thought in many implicit ways (Hunt writes: 'we are all realists now' [1978: 59]), legal realism as a *policy-oriented agenda of action* had all but vanished. The realist legacy is now being carried by the Critical Legal Studies Movement (Duxbury, 1991) which is far from having a substantial voice in spheres of political influence, and by the Law and Society Movement which is dominated by social scientists.[18] The realist retreat from the halls of political power, the 'reemergence of proceduralism' (Horwitz, 1992), the resurfacing of a 'process-oriented' approach (Feldman, 1991), and the intellectual decline of 'pragmatic instrumentalism' (Summers, 1982), however, were not the result of an objective and scientific process in the course of which the realist logic was discredited as inadequate; nor has it been the result of the realists' 'failure' to develop a comprehensive scientific agenda (for example, Summers, 1982; and to some extent Hunt, 1978). The explanation for the tendency to return to formally-rational law lies elsewhere, I believe, and is related to changing political conditions.

My basic argument here is that the decline of realism had to do with the fact that the realist version of substantive law only served the needs of the administration during a period of transition. By the end of the 1930s, the New Deal in general, and the administrative process in particular, had already become established facts. The stabilization of the political order created new political conditions under which the need to use law as an instrument had been gradually replaced with a renewed interest in 'objectifying' the new established order. Once the New Deal administration became established it turned to formally-rational law as a mechanism of legitimation for its now-established innovations.

Perhaps the best example of this process concerned the administrative field. Throughout the 1930s, the American Bar Association fought for the substitution of the informal and 'substantive' methods of administrative commissions for orderly judicial methods and traditional procedural rules. Through most of this period, these attempts were considered by the administration and their realist advisers as nothing more than attempts to sabotage the New Deal's experiments (Auerbach, 1976).

In 1939, a report of the American Bar Association that repeated previous calls for administrative procedural reform fell on more receptive ears. In 1941, some of the proposals of the 1939 report were incorporated into the Walter–Logan Bill which passed Congress but was nonetheless still vetoed by Roosevelt. Yet the growing demand for administrative reforms certainly became more effective with the fading away of the 'transitory' period. Following the Walter–Logan Bill, the office of the United States Attorney General released its own report on the need for an administrative procedural reform. Only a minority among the authors of the report called for a formal code of administrative procedures and for a formal separation between the prosecuting and adjudicatory functions of administrative bodies (Department of Justice, 1941).

Still, a few years later it was the minority opinion that resurfaced in a series of Congressional bills that ultimately led to the Administrative Procedure Act of 1946. The Administrative Procedure Act, which imposed procedural requirements that narrowed the space for administrative informal methods, was supported by both the American Bar Association and the administration, thus representing the return of 'reconciliation and relative agreement' between the two (Verkuil, 1978: 277; Harrington, 1983).

When the political pendulum swung back in the direction of stabilization, the legal pendulum followed suit. A process of judicialization, and a gradual return to formal and 'autonomous law', was again set in motion. In the long run, therefore, the true 'victors' in the struggle between formalists and realists were the former; perhaps not a victory of 'moralists' over 'pragmatists', as Beck saw it, but certainly a victory of the restatement adherents over realist suspicion and hostility towards them.

I wish to conclude this article, therefore, by rejecting the idea that law moves from one progressive stage to another and by replacing it with the suggestive formulation that the interplay between ideally formal and ideally substantive law corresponds to the interplay between periods of stability and reform in the political arena. Weber, to be sure, never clearly articulated such a model of legal change. Weber was overtly suspicious of movements which advocated substantively-rational law, arguing that such movements 'will not suffice to stop the continuous growth of the technical elements in the law' and hence its formally-rational appearance (1978: 895). Yet Weber's recognition of the relationship between formally-rational law and a formally-rational political authority, on the other hand, allows us to invoke Weberian concepts as guidelines for this inquiry. When we combine Weber's predictions about the inevitable progression of formally-rational law, his views concerning the tensions which are inherent in such law, and his views concerning the interplay of law and politics, the theory seems less determined by the force of reason and more by changing political conditions.

Weber's exposition of the inherent tensions that exist within both substantively- and formally-rational law help to explain the conditions for transformations in law. The tensions that are embedded within a formally-rational order invite an ongoing political struggle for change. The outcome of this struggle, in the particular case, cannot be predicted. Yet, under certain circumstances, most often in times of war or economic depression, previous arrangements and structures, with their formal and seemingly objective appearance, cease to provide legitimacy to the existing order and are perceived as outdated obstacles in the further (substantive) rationalization of society. Under such conditions, sufficient political forces may be unleashed to bring about a greater push in the direction of substantive rationality. Substantive rationality, in this context at least, is the voice and engine of change. If formal rationality insists on the insulation of the legal system, substantive rationality is marked by its call to 'open' the legal system to substantive and pragmatic social and political considerations. Because substantive rationality is a mechanism of change, it is bound to retreat once change becomes routine. In Weber's own terms, we can read a period of change as a charismatic period which is bound to be routinized in the due course of time. For periods of routinization, formally-rational law is at its best, for it is through the logic of closedness and formal calculability that a given order acquires an aura of transcendence.

This model is fundamentally different from the one envisioned by Nonet and Selznick in their *Law and Society in Transition* (1978). Nonet and Selznick advocate an evolutionist model in which law gradually evolves towards responsive law, a new enlightened stage of legal evolution in which law responds to social needs and aspirations, thus being 'a renewal of instrumentalism, but for more objective public ends' (1978: 14–15). Nonet and Selznick explicitly base their vision of responsive law on the legacy of legal realism (1978: 18), but they fail to mention that as an activist political agenda, legal realism faded away and lost its vigour. Nowhere in their work do Nonet and Selznick address the basic fact that legal realism was actually implemented during the early years of the New Deal and had its years of operational glory. This omission has to do with the basic flaw in Nonet and Selznick's evolutionist model. The model may have its 'inner dynamic', as Nonet and Selznick assert, but it lacks the dialectic perspective that allows us to understand the failure of legal realism to establish itself as a permanent orientation.

In other words, the idea of a fully established and institutionalized responsive law as a permanent feature, like the idea of a permanent revolution, is a contradiction in terms. Autonomous law is discarded when its internal tensions and inconsistencies can no longer be sustained. But in order to institutionalize and permanently root desired reforms, a reawakening of formal rationality, as a means of ensuring stability, security and predictability, is again called for. In the sphere of the economic market, this means that the same old capitalists may dominate again after such 'radical' changes as, say, the Wagner Labor Relations Act.[19] In the legal sphere, this means that legalistic orientations and strict formal procedures regain their power, albeit under new conditions. It is by invoking Weber's analysis that we may grasp the cycle of *formal rationality – internal contradictions – substantive rationality – routinization – formal rationality*. Social change and progress appear, when they do, in the form of a *spiral ascent*: important and radical changes are introduced through substantive rationality; once in place, formal rationality, albeit on a new 'progressive' level, reappears.

NOTES

1. This familiar typology also refers to either formal or substantive systems of law which are irrational. Substantively-irrational law leads to decisions which, while based on some observable ethical criteria, are nonetheless unpredictable beforehand; they are empirical findings which are based upon concrete cases. Formally-irrational law, on the other hand, is 'associated with prophetic decisions or revelation': there are formal ways for arriving at decisions but the results are not logically understandable and are unpredictable beforehand (Trubek, 1972: 729; see also Schluchter, 1981).
2. Consider, for example, his response to Article 1 of the Swiss Civil Code. The Article stated that where a statute failed to provide a clear rule, the judge had to promulgate the rule that he/she would have created as a legislator. Weber, who acknowledged the practical usefulness of this rule, nonetheless argued that 'a judicial system which would practise such ideals would, in view of the inevitability of value-compromises, very often have to forget about abstract norms and, at least in the case of conflict, would have to admit concrete evaluations, i.e., not only informal but irrational law findings' (1978: 887).
3. That Weber both elaborated on the merits of formal rationality and exposed its shortcomings and distortions had been interpreted as Weber's unresolved ambivalence. Accordingly, Weber was described as a 'liberal in despair' (Mommsen, 1974; Alexander, 1983), and a 'tragic modernist' who suffered from 'intellectual schizophrenia' (Kronman, 1983; Trubek, 1986). See also, in general, Geoffrey Hawthorn's *Enlightenment and Despair* (1976: 137–63).
4. This is, of course, the source of Weber's 'England Problem'. The 'Problem' stems from Weber's assumption that formally-rational law and the advance of capitalism are mutually related. In England, by Weber's own account, capitalism developed without a corresponding rationalization of law. The England Problem is a source for a lively debate about the general validity of Weber's theory concerning the relationship between capitalism and law and about Weber's understanding of English law. This debate extends well beyond the scope of this paper. For Weber's own solutions to the problem see *Economy and Society* (1978: 814, 891–2). See also Rheinstein (1966), Trubek (1972), Hunt (1978), Ewing (1987); and, in general, Sugarman (1983) and Sugarman and Rubin (1984).
5. Both Trubek (1972) and Hunt (1978) open the door for such interpretation. Trubek points in this direction at the end of his discussion of the England Problem, suggesting that Weber cultivated a 'false distinction between English and continental law' (1972: 748). Hunt also writes that English law went through

a process of internal rationalization, came to be conceived in terms of 'pure law', and developed certain characteristics which 'Weber would have considered possible only in a codified system' (1978: 124). A step in this direction is also taken by Ewing (1987), who draws a distinction between Weber's notion of 'logical formality' (as a mode of legal thought), and Weber's concept of 'formal justice' (the sociological aspect of formal rationality).

6. Consider, for example, the decision of the American Supreme Court in the case of *Coppage* v *Kansas*. At stake was the constitutionality of a Kansas law that prohibited employers from requiring their employees to sign 'yellow dog' contracts (contracts that denied employees the right to join labour unions). The state of Kansas defended its enactment by arguing that the common law recognized limitations upon the freedom of contract in cases of 'duress'. The Supreme Court rejected the argument on the basis of its finding that the formal definition of duress in the common law did not include economic pressure and that the Kansas law, therefore, infringed on the contractual freedom of the parties. This result, as Mensch (1990) accurately observes, had been reached not because the court failed to acknowledge the substantive economic inequality between employers and employees, but because legal reasoning 'compelled' it to apply formal legal criteria. The court took the side of employers not because it was substantively biased against employees; such a view of the court, says Mensch, 'trivializes the underlying power of the classical conceptual scheme' (1990: 20). The legal construction in *Coppage* was strikingly similar to the way Weber thought of contractual freedom in the formally-rational German law: 'The formal right of the worker to enter into any contract whatsoever with any employer whatsoever', Weber wrote, 'does not represent for the employment seeker even the slightest freedom in the determination of his own conditions of work' (1978: 729). Rather, contractual freedom best served owners of property and those who enjoyed 'power in the market' (1978: 730).

7. Also indicative of the drive towards rationalization was the spread of treatises, and later into the twentieth century, the Restatement Project about which I will have more to say later. On the proliferation of treatises, see Friedman (1973).

8. Abel argues that in the course of the shift from apprenticeship to academic legal training, legal practitioners 'lost' their ability to control the number of practising lawyers, hence losing one of the most valuable resources of any professional group. The loss of control over the number of new entrants to the bar, however, was somewhat compensated by the fact that lawyers were able to enjoy a more 'scientific' professional image and hence to advance successful claims to professional autonomy and exclusivity over ever-growing areas of practice (for a critique of Abel, see Kritzer, 1991).

9. Neither was it a coincidence, therefore, that along with the assertions of legal autonomy and along with the rise of the modern law school, American practising lawyers developed their own institutions from which they asserted their independence and impartiality. Between 1870 and 1878, Bar Associations were formed in many of the nation's commercial centres: New York City in 1870, Cleveland in 1873, Chicago and St Louis in 1874 and Boston in 1877. Finally, in 1878, elite practitioners established the American Bar Association that claimed to speak for the American bar as a whole.

10. Larson attributes this distinction to Weber himself, and in this, I think, she credited him with an insight he did not offer. Weber spoke about the struggle for professional hegemony between academics and practitioners in a different context, in connection with the criticisms by Geny in France and Ehrlich in Germany of the idea of legal 'gaplessness' (Weber, 1978: 889).

11. Hart pondered: 'But in what did the realism of the Realists consist? I find it very

difficult to say because this active group of jurists differed from as much as they resembled each other' (1983: 131); see also Cortner (1964: 34). There is no coherent sense in which we may speak of the realists as a group save for the fact that most were legal academics, many from elite universities. Llewellyn's list of twenty people whom he considered as true realists created much confusion and contributed to a false sense of group identity that Llewellyn himself later tried to deny. Thanks to the new findings of Hull (1987), however, we now know that Llewellyn also produced other lists, more general in scope, in which scholars like Frankfurter, Landis and Handler, for example, three major figures in the development of administrative law, were also included. Here, I suggest that a useful way to look at the realists is to invoke their own preferred criteria and to ask 'what did the realist in fact do?' rather than asking 'what did the realist stand for?'. Thus I use the term 'realists' in its most general sense to include not only 'official' figures like Llewellyn, Frank, Arnold, Clark, Corbin, Douglas, Moore, Sturges, Powell, Oliphant, Yntema and Green, but also Frankfurter, Landis, Handler and a handful of lawyers like Benjamin Cohen, Corcoran, Wyzanski and Robert Jackson who all shared some elements of the realist vision of the Constitution, the judicial process, legislation and the administrative process.

12. Hunt observed that 'the realist movement only took form and character in the process of sharply distinguishing itself from Poundian sociological jurisprudence. It is a common feature of intellectual movements that they develop in conflict with those that retrospectively they may be seen to have most in common with' (1978: 40–1). The realists and Pound shared the view that judges should take account of larger social values ('interests' in Poundian vocabulary) in their decisions. In this, both advocated a form of substantively-rational law. The fundamental difference between sociological jurisprudence and legal realism, to my mind, was that the former never really challenged the supremacy of the judicial process per se, as the realists did. For a general comparison between the two see White (1972), Hunt (1978). Also of interest is the similarity between realist ideas and the German Free Law school (*Freirecht*) which is considered as the German counterpart of American (and Scandinavian) realism (Herget and Wallace, 1987). The Free Law school criticized what it considered as the false premises of formally-rational law throughout the second half of the nineteenth century and the first three decades of the twentieth. Its advocates challenged the idea of a gapless system of rules and urged courts to develop a conscious judicial creativeness, sensitive to substantive demands of justice, in their interpretation of statutes and codes. The Free Law movement, however, never succeeded in penetrating and influencing the structure and content of the German legal system; its advocates stood in direct opposition to the German academic legal establishment and faced a hostile political climate. The ideas of the legal realists, in contrast, fell on fertile political ground. For general background, see Herget and Wallace (1987); Weber (1978: 897, note 20).
13. Also, see Hunt (1978). Of course, legal realism preceded the New Deal and began its ascent in the 1920s. Nonetheless, the argument is that legal realism only gained ground as an influential paradigm that contributed to the development of legal institutions with the coming of the New Deal.
14. I owe this metaphor to Salman Rushdie's *Haroun and the Sea of Stories* (1990).
15. On the development of administrative law as a manifestation of a paradigmatic approach that threatens established patterns in the legal profession, see Arthurs (1985). On the response of the American Bar Association and elite corporate lawyers to the development of administrative law during the New Deal, see Verkuil (1978), Harrington (1983).
16. Accordingly, the legal realists also exerted considerable pressure on the Supreme

Court which, since the early New Deal, had systematically blocked some of the most central legislative plans of the New Deal (Jackson, 1941; Irons, 1982). Following the Schechter decision, for example, legal realists led the attack on the judicial review powers of the court, an attack that ultimately led to Roosevelt's 'court-packing' plan. The Schechter decision concerned the constitutionality of the National Industrial Recovery Act (NIRA). The law, whose constitutionality was in serious doubt even by many of the administration's supporters, was one of the central pillars of the early New Deal. The NIRA was declared unconstitutional on several grounds, among which central was the court's ruling concerning the act's unconstitutional delegation of powers. The aftermath of the decision brought to the fore various suggestions to directly curb the powers of the court (see Alsop and Catledge, 1938; Leuchtenberg, 1969; Irons, 1982).

17. Kalman (1986) reports seven people from Yale: Howard Marshall in the Petroleum Administrative Board, Walton Hamilton in the National Recovery Administration, Harry Shulman in the Railroad Retirement Board, William Douglas in the Securities and Exchange Commission, Abe Fortas, Thurman Arnold and Wesley Sturges in the Agricultural Adjustment Board. To this we may add Jerome Frank (with a background in corporate practice) in the Securities and Exchange Commission, Milton Handler in the National Labor Board, Lloyd Garrison and Calvert Magruder in the National Labor Relations Board, Felix Cohen in the Department of the Interior, Herman Oliphant in the Department of Treasury, and a host of young Harvard graduates (known as Frankfurter's 'hot dogs') in numerous governmental agencies.

18. For the similarity between the basic position of the realists and the critical legal studies movement, see Kairys (1990). For the 'sociological movement in law' being the heir to realism see, for example, Hunt (1978). It is also of interest that scholarly attention is tuned to current attempts to develop informal, or substantive, arenas of justice, which stand *outside* the state, the best example perhaps being the literature on community justice alternatives: see Harrington (1992) and, in general, *Social & Legal Studies* 1(2), 1992.

19. This model of change and stability is also invoked in Block's (1977) analysis of the relationship between the state and the capitalist class. Block writes: 'Not every extension of state power will survive beyond those periods in which state managers have special opportunities to expand the state's role. After a war, depression, or period of reconstruction, the business community is likely to campaign for a restoration of the *status quo ante*. State managers in these new periods will be forced to make some concessions to the business community in order to avert a decline in business confidence' (1977: 26).

REFERENCES

Abel, Richard L. (1989) *American Lawyers*. New York: Oxford.

Ackerman, Bruce (1983) *Reconstructing American Law*. Cambridge, MA: Harvard University Press.

Alexander, Jeffrey C. (1983) *Theoretical Logic in Sociology Vol. 3 – The Classical Attempt at Theoretical Synthesis: Max Weber*. Berkeley, CA: University of California Press.

Alsop, Joseph and Turner Catledge (1938) *The 168 Days*. New York: Doubleday.

Arnold, Thurman W. (1934) 'Trial by Combat and the New Deal', *Harvard Law Review* 47 (April): 913–47.

Arnold, Thurman W. (1935) 'Apologia for Jurisprudence', *Yale Law Journal* 44 (March): 729–53.

Arthurs, Harry W. (1985) *'Without the Law': Administrative Justice and Legal Pluralism in Nineteenth-Century England*. Toronto: University of Toronto Press.

Auerbach, Jerold S. (1976) *Unequal Justice*. London: Oxford University Press.

Beck, James (1933a) 'Mr. Beck Speaks on Citizenship', *American Bar Association Journal* 19 (December): 689–700.

Beck, James (1933b) 'The NRA is Unconstitutional', *Fortune Magazine* 8 (December): 48.

Benditt, Theodore M. (1978) *Law as Rule and Principle*. Stanford, CA: Stanford University Press.

Block, Fred (1977) 'The Ruling Class Does Not Rule: Notes on the Marxist Theory of the State', *Socialist Review* 33: 6–27

Botein, Stephen (1983) '"What Shall We Meet Afterwards in Heaven": Judgeship as a Symbol for Modern American Lawyers', pp. 49–69 in G. L. Geison (ed.), *Professions and Professional Ideologies in America*. Chapel Hill: University of North Carolina Press.

Butler, Rush C. (1934) 'Assembly Proceedings', *Reports of the American Bar Association* 59 (August): 99.

Calabresi, Guido (1982) *A Common Law for the Age of Statutes*. Cambridge, MA: Harvard University Press.

Clark, Charles E. (1933) 'Law Professor, What Now?', *Handbook of the Association of American Law Schools and Proceedings of the 31 Annual Meeting* (December): 14–24.

Clark, Charles E. (1935) *Handbook of the Association of American Law Schools and Proceedings of the 33 Annual Meeting* (December): 74–5.

Cohen, Felix (1935) 'Transcendental Nonsense and the Functional Approach', *Columbia Law Review* 35 (June): 809–41

Cortner, Richard C. (1964) *The Wagner Act Cases*. Knoxville: University of Tennessee Press.

Cummings, Homer (1933) 'Modern Tendencies and the Law', *American Bar Association Journal* 19 (October): 576–9.

Department of Justice (1941) *Final Report of the Attorney General's Committee on Administrative Procedure*. Washington, DC: Government Printing Office.

Dezalay, Yves, Austin Sarat and Susan Silbey (1989) 'From Dissident Challenge to Meritocratic Knowledge: Elements For A Social History of American Legal Sociology', Unpublished.

Diggs, James (1933) 'Should the Constitution of Oklahoma Be Amended, If So In What Respect', *Oklahoma State Bar Journal* (October): 127–32.

Duxbury, Neil (1991) 'Jerome Frank and the Legacy of Legal Realism', *Journal of Law and Society* 18: 175–205.

Ewing, Sally (1987) 'Formal Justice and the Spirit of Capitalism: Max Weber's Sociology of Law', *Law and Society Review* 21: 487–512.

Feldman, Stephen M. (1991) 'An Interpretation of Max Weber's Theory of Law: Metaphysics, Economics, and the Iron Cage of Constitutional Law', *Law and Social Inquiry* 16: 205–48.

Frank, Jerome (1930) *Law and the Modern Mind*. New York: Brentano's.

Frank, Jerome (1933) 'What Constitutes A Good Legal Education?', *American Bar Association Journal* 19: 723–8.

Frankfurter, Felix (1936) 'The Young Men Go to Washington', *Fortune Magazine* 10: 61.

Friedman, Lawrence M. (1973) *A History of American Law*. New York: Simon and Schuster.

Green, Leon (1934) 'The Law Professor, the Lawyers' Brain Trust', *American Law Schools Review* 7: 1031–5.

Green, Leon (1935) 'The Administrative Process', *American Bar Association Journal* 21: 708–12.

Habermas, Jürgen (1984) *The Theory of Communicative Action*, Vol. 1. Boston, MA: Beacon Press.
Handler, Milton (1934) *Handbook of the Association of American Law Schools and Proceedings of the 32 Annual Meeting* (December): 132–9.
Harrington, Christine (1983) 'The Political Economy of Administrative Law Practice', Paper presented at the *Annual Meetings of the Law and Society Association*, June 2–5, Denver, Colorado.
Harrington, Christine (1992) 'Popular Justice, Populist Politics: Law in Community Organizing', *Social and Legal Studies* 1(2): 177–98.
Hart, H. L. A. (1983) *Essays in Jurisprudence and Philosophy*. Oxford: Clarendon Press.
Hawley, Ellis W. (1966) *The New Deal and the Problem of Monopoly*. Princeton, NJ: Princeton University Press.
Hawthorn, Geoffrey (1976) *Enlightenment and Despair*. Cambridge: Cambridge University Press.
Herget, J. and S. Wallace (1987) 'The German Free Law Movement as the Source of American Legal Realism', *Virginia Law Review* 73: 399–455.
Horwitz, Morton J. (1977) *The Transformation of American Law 1780–1860*. Cambridge, MA: Harvard University Press.
Horwitz, Morton, J. (1992) *The Overthrow of Legal Orthodoxy*. New York: Oxford University Press.
Hull, N. E. H. (1987) 'Some Realism about the Llewellyn-Pound Exchange over Realism: The Newly Uncovered Private Correspondence, 1927–1931', *Wisconsin Law Review* 6: 921–69.
Hunt, Alan (1978) *The Sociological Movement in Law*. Philadelphia: Temple University Press.
Irons, Peter (1982) *The New Deal Lawyers*. Princeton, NJ: Princeton University Press.
Jackson, Robert (1934) 'The Bar and the New Deal', *Handbook of the Association of American Law Schools and Proceedings of the 32 Annual Meeting* (December): 113–20.
Jackson, Robert (1941) *The Struggle for Judicial Supremacy*. New York: Vintage.
Kairys, David (1990) *The Politics of Law: A Progressive Critique*. New York: Pantheon.
Kalman, Laura (1986) *Legal Realism at Yale 1927–1960*. Chapel Hill: University of North Carolina Press.
Kennedy, Duncan (1980) 'Toward an Historical Understanding of Legal Consciousness: The Case of Classical Legal Thought in America, 1850–1940', pp. 3–24 in S. Spitzer (ed.), *Research in Law and Sociology*. Greenwich, CT: JAI.
Kritzer, Herbert M. (1991) 'Abel and the Professional Project: The Institutional Analysis of the Legal Profession', *Law and Social Inquiry* 16: 529–52.
Kronman, Anthony T. (1983) *Max Weber*. Stanford, CA: Stanford University Press.
Landis, James (1934) *Handbook of the Association of American Law Schools and Proceedings of the 32 Annual Meeting* (December): 122–31.
Larson, Magali S. (1977) *The Rise of Professionalism: A Sociological Analysis*. Berkeley, CA: University of California Press.
Leuchtenberg, William E. (1969) 'Franklin Delano Roosevelt's Supreme Court "Packing" Plan', pp. 69–115 in W. H. Droze, G. Wolfskill, and W. E. Leuchtenberg (eds), *Essays on the New Deal*. Austin, TX: University of Texas Press.
Llewellyn, Karl (1931) 'Some Realism About Realism', *Harvard Law Review* 44: 1222–59.
Llewellyn, Karl (1935) 'On What is Wrong With So-Called Legal Education', *Columbia Law Review* 35: 651–78.
McFarland, Carl (1934) 'Administrative Agencies in Government', *American Bar Association Journal* 20: 612–14.
Mensch, Elizabeth (1990) 'The History of Mainstream Legal Thought', pp. 13–37 in

David Kairys (ed.) *The Politics of Law: A Progressive Critique*. New York: Pantheon.

Miller, Nathan (1934) 'The Constitution and Modern Trends', *Reports of the American Bar Association* 59: 348–61.

Mills, C. Wright (1966) *Sociology and Pragmatism: The Higher Learning in America*. New York: Oxford University Press.

Mommsen, Wolfgang (1974) *The Age of Bureaucracy: Perspectives on the Political Sociology of Max Weber*. Oxford: Blackwell.

Nonet, Philippe, and Philip Selznick (1978) *Law and Society in Transition: Toward Responsive Law*. New York: Octagon.

Parkinson, Thomas L. (1935) 'Are the Law Schools Adequately Training for the Public Service?' *The American Law School Review* 7: 291–8.

Parsons, Talcott (1967) *Sociological Theory and Modern Society*. New York: Free Press.

Radin, Max (1935) 'The Courts and Administrative Agencies', *Minutes of the Judicial Section of the American Bar Association* (July): Unreleased version. Typewritten.

Ransom, William (1936) 'Which Road for the Legal Profession?', *American Bar Association Journal* 22: 21–3.

Rheinstein, Max (1966) *On Law and Economy in Society*. Cambridge, MA: Harvard University Press.

Rueschemeyer, Dietrich (1973) *Lawyers and Their Society: A Comparative Study of the Legal Profession in Germany and the United States*. Cambridge, MA: Harvard University Press.

Schluchter, Wolfgang (1981) *The Rise of Western Rationalism*. Berkeley, CA: University of California Press.

Shamir, Ronen (1992) *Managing Legal Uncertainty: Elite Lawyers in the New Deal* Unpublished doctorate dissertation, Northwestern University.

Skowronek, Stephen (1982) *Building a New American State: The Expansion of National Administrative Capacities 1877–1920*. Cambridge: Cambridge University Press.

Stinchcombe, Arthur L. (1991) 'An Essay on the Demand for Formality in Laws, Regulations, and Organizations', Unpublished, Northwestern University.

Stryker, Robin (1990) 'Science, Class, and the Welfare State: A Class-Centered Functional Account', *American Journal of Sociology* 96: 684–726.

Sugarman, David (1983) 'Law, Economy and the State in England, 1750–1914: Some Major Issues', in D. Sugarman (ed.), *Legality, Ideology and the State*. London: Academic Press.

Sugarman, David and Gerry R. Rubin (1984) 'Towards a New History of Law and Material Society in England 1750–1914', in G. R. Rubin and David Sugarman (eds), *Law, Economy and Society, 1750–1914: Essays in the History of English Law*. Abingdon: Professional Books.

Summers, Robert S. (1982) *Instrumentalism and American Legal Theory*. Ithaca: Cornell University Press.

Sutherland, Arthur E. (1967) *The Law at Harvard*. Cambridge, MA: Harvard University Press.

Trubek, David M. (1972) 'Max Weber on Law and the Rise of Capitalism', *Wisconsin Law Review* 3: 720–53.

Trubek, David M. (1986) 'Max Weber's Tragic Modernism and the Study of Law in Society', *Law and Society Review* 20: 573–98.

Verkuil, Paul R. (1978) 'The Emerging Concept of Administrative Procedure', *Columbia Law Review* 78: 258–329.

Weber, Max (1978) *Economy and Society*. Berkeley, CA: University of California Press.

White, Edward G. (1972) 'From Sociological Jurisprudence to Realism: Jurisprudence and Social Change in Early Twentieth-Century America', *Virginia Law Review* 58: 999–1028.

Wickersham, George (1933) 'Address to the American Bar Association', *American Bar Association Journal* 19: 327–9.

Wickersham, George (1934) 'Address to the American Bar Association', *American Bar Association Journal* 20: 634.

Williston, Samuel (1933) 'The Judge and the Professor', *Reports of the American Bar Association* 58: 598–611.

Yntema, Hessel E. (1934) 'Legal Science and Reform', *Columbia Law Review* 34: 207–29.

[3]

Process Rationality as Legal Governance

A Comparative Perspective

Wolf Heydebrand
New York University

abstract: This article offers a comparative sociological perspective on the transformation of law and legal rationality in the US and continental Europe during the 20th century. It takes off from Max Weber's categories of formal and substantive legal rationality and proposes to examine post-Weberian developments in common and civil law from a new perspective, namely the rise of negotiated process rationality and its variants as emergent modes of legal governance. Process rationality is embedded in social networks as structures-in-process. In contrast to conventional forms of institutional government, governance is a series of informal, flexible and expedient strategies of problem-solving and crisis management based on bargaining and negotiation. The incipient privatization, commercialization and denationalization of law are understood as consequences of the postwar transnational expansion of American common law in the wake of globalization and the growth of US economic and political influence. The theoretical and practical implications of the rise of process rationality for constitutional jurisprudence and adjudication are profound, but require a separate technical analysis and critical discussion.

keywords: globalization of law ✦ legal governance ✦ legal rationalities ✦ negotiated process rationality ✦ privatization of law ✦ proceduralization

---

The central argument of this article is that both the form and the substance of law that have dominated western legal systems during the 19th and

20th centuries are facing major challenges and are undergoing a significant degree of transformation and restructuring. Structural changes in the modern state and in the capitalist political economy figure prominently in this transformation. Max Weber, no advocate of economist interpretations of history, nevertheless recognized the intimate connections between material social and economic interests and legal change (Weber, 1966: 37).

One of the basic symptoms of the structural transformation of economy, law and state is the creation of a new type of rationality or mode of governance based on a logic of informal, negotiated processes within social and sociolegal networks. The significance of networks as sites of governance is that, unlike institutions, they are informal structures-in-process that, by definition, cannot be held accountable to elected, appointed or otherwise 'legitimate' structures of authority. The deconstruction and restructuring of the 19th-century institutional framework of law and jurisprudence can thus be seen as one consequence of the momentous shift of the capitalist political economy toward economic and financial globalization. As Weber anticipated in his analysis of the 'anti-formalistic tendencies of modern legal development' (Weber, 1966: 303–21), state-centered intervention and regulation would come to dominate much of the 20th century (1920–90) and pose serious challenges to formal law and liberal legalism. The current round of global–local interaction and crisis management (since 1990) permits the formulation of a new perspective on these historical trends, including the eclipse of regulation and the denationalization of state and economy (Heydebrand, 2000; for similar arguments involving law and economic globalization, see Sassen, 1996: 12–21; Scheuerman, 1994, 1999a, 1999b; for closely related political perspectives on globalization, see Hardt and Negri, 2000; Scherrer, 1999).

Legal formalism, in its 19th-century incarnation as the liberal, law-based state in continental Europe and 'classical legal thought' in the US, had a powerful impact on western jurisprudence (see also Shklar, 1964 on 'legalism'; Goodrich, 1983). Weber (1966: 64) summarizes this formalism as follows:

> Present-day legal science . . . proceeds from the following five postulates: viz., first, that every concrete legal decision be the 'application' of an abstract legal proposition to a concrete 'fact situation'; second, that it must be possible in every concrete case to derive the decision from abstract legal propositions by means of legal logic; third, that the law must actually or virtually constitute a 'gapless' system of legal propositions . . .; fourth, that whatever cannot be 'construed' legally in rational terms is also legally irrelevant; and fifth, that every social action of human beings must always be visualized as either an 'application' or 'execution' of legal propositions, or as an 'infringement' thereof.

In short, the formal conception of the rule of law requires that state action rests on legal norms that are '(1) general in character, (2) relatively clear, (3) public, (4) prospective, and (5) stable' (Scheuerman, 1999a: 4).

By the early 1900s, this formalist conception was beginning to be challenged and superseded by substantive state-centered conceptions of the rule of law in both Europe and the US. A major reason for the short-lived impact of legal liberalism was that the abstract idea of formal equality before the law not only constructively ignores substantive differences among people as it was originally designed to do, but also veils their substantive inequalities in the process of application. Substantive legal rationality, in turn, was designed to concretize the application of law to the solution of specific social and economic problems. But this concretization and particularization of law in the form of the regulatory welfare state and other social policies became too bureaucratic and cumbersome. It faced opposition because of its ties with particular ideologies and modes of justification such as statist and nationalist socialism as well as the New Deal.

Thus, there is no reason to assume a unilinear or necessary historical progression of law toward either formal rationality or a specific type of substantive rationality. If history is any guide, it can be argued that Weber's thesis about law being a necessary condition for the development of capitalism and bureaucracy is largely limited to state-centered regimes in 19th-century continental Europe. Whereas the state and national administrative rationality emerged comparatively late in the US, i.e. during the Progressive Period around the turn of the century (Wiebe, 1967; Skowronek, 1982), the operation of a strong government in many continental European nation-states predated the rise of capitalist markets and corporate organization and shaped their development (Polanyi, 1957; Chandler, 1980). Indeed, it can plausibly be argued that Weber's ideal types of bureaucracy and formal legal rationality never really fit the American mold. They clearly apply to European civil law and certain 19th-century continental governments, but they cannot easily be transferred to the political, social and economic context of the US where the 'administrative process' (Landis, 1938; Woll, 1963) and the 'administrative state' (F. Morstein Marx, 1957; Freeman, 1997) had successfully established themselves as cultural and political alternatives to Weber's 'bureaucracy' (see also Horwitz, 1992: Ch. 8).

The working hypothesis of this article, then, is as follows: while 19th-century formal legal rationality was largely bracketed and superseded by the substantive rationality of the 20th-century regulatory state, both are now being challenged by the rise of a new legal rationality, namely negotiated process rationality and the attraction it holds for the interests of corporate and transnational governance.

Process rationality in law can be defined as an interactive, participatory, negotiated, reflexive and informal model of collective deliberation in dispute-processing, legal decision-making, law-making and legal policy-making. Deliberation and negotiation may occur among the participants of a dispute, in the presence of a mediator, arbitrator, or judge, in congressional committees, and in the context of consultation among members of Congress, the judiciary, agencies of the executive branch (e.g. the Department of Justice), and any of the regulatory or administrative agencies, not to mention the material interests and power plays of a host of other corporate or governmental actors. Process rationality is typically associated with, or embedded in, a social network-like structure-in-process, although it may also occur in the shape of informal or deviant relations within and between legal and governmental institutions. Process rationality shares neither the rule-governed, proceduralist schemata of formal legal rationality nor the consensual goal-directedness of substantive rationality. Process drives substance, not the other way around. Colloquially, this is often interpreted as getting the 'right people' at the table, and one will get substance. Whatever goals are associated with process rationality tend to emerge dialectically from within the process itself rather than directing it from outside.

Legal process rationality is superficially similar to democratic process rationality in its emphasis on interactive, participatory, communicative and reflexive modes of self-constitution, self-determination and self-government based on participants' self-defined autonomy and identity (see, in particular, Cass Sunstein's [1999] argument that judicial minimalism is an intrinsic element of a 'democratic' constitutional jurisprudence). But can this self-legitimation based on negotiated process occur in the absence of independent normative grounds such as external substantive values? And if not, isn't democratic process rationality therefore a form of governance rather than true democratic self-government (on this distinction and the 'cosmopolitan conception of democratic governance', see Held, 2000: 394, 402–6; on the related notion of 'performative citizenship', see Albrow, 1997: 175–7)? Process control or decision control in procedural justice may be set in motion by conflicting claims and disputes, but the process typically has a dynamic of its own and tends to move forward independently of the explicit articulation of substantive goals or projected outcomes such as dispute resolution or problem-solving, agreements, pacts and contracts.

As a historically specific model of collective deliberation, then, process rationality is bipolar in that it has both reconstructive (reformist, creative) and deconstructive (deformalizing, deinstitutionalizing) consequences. It is part of its open-ended, indeterminate and pragmatic character that process rationality is responsive to different structural contexts and historical contingencies which are themselves marked by uncertainty and indeterminacy. For example, Albrow (1997: 123–8) identifies three main areas where indeterminacy is specifically linked to the new globality and where a need for managing global indeterminacy is arising: first, in international organizations (IMF, the World Bank, WTO) that deal with the operations of the world economy. A second area is transnational corporate governance, particularly in view of the vagaries of financial global dynamics (see also Brenner, 2002; Sklair, 2002). The third area of indeterminacy is the worldwide expansion of the new information and communication technology.

Crisis management and governance under conditions of indeterminacy are complicated and aggravated by power plays at the level of direct power (authority), indirect power (agenda-setting), and hegemonic power (ideology) (Lukes, 1974). Political and economic power plays, in turn, may introduce instrumental versions of process control and decision control, thereby subordinating the process to internal or external manipulation and constraints. Thus, while process rationality tends to dissolve the liberal legalism of formal rationality and deconstructs the bureaucratic rigidities of substantive rationality, it is vulnerable to the very qualities that make it attractive as an alternative to formal and substantive modes of government: its tolerance of diversity and indeterminacy, its interactive and negotiated character, and its normative autonomy and self-justification. My purpose, then, is to counterpose the notion of process rationality to Weber's fundamental categories of formal and substantive rationality and to argue that process-oriented legal practices have increasingly informed the American and European systems of justice in the 20th century and are now assuming the role of governance in legal garb (what Sassen [1996: 12–21; 2000: 380–2] calls 'new legal regimes' or 'legal innovations').

The Logic of Formal and Substantive Rationality

Weber's notions of rationality operate at three different analytical levels and are formulated as contrasting ideal types. At the cognitive level, Weber distinguishes between practical and theoretical rationality. At the level of social action, an orientation toward value rationality is distinguished from instrumental or strategic ('purposive') rationality. Finally, at the institutional level, which concerns us here, the central distinction is between formal and substantive rationality. Let me briefly elaborate on these three conceptual pairs.

Rationality at the Cognitive Level: Practical vs Theoretical Rationality

Practical rationality refers to all forms of cognition in which means and ends are related to each other in a practical and pragmatic fashion. The concept of practical rationality comes close to the tradition-bound notion of common sense, i.e. it is a kind of contextual 'natural logic' which, by its very nature, is culturally variable and hence, culturally relative. In contrast to practical rationality, theoretical rationality refers essentially to the abstract models of logical, mathematical and scientific thought that have become the dominant instruments of cognition and knowledge in the course of western historical development (see also Kalberg, 1980: 1151–5; Albrow, 1990: 114–34).

Rationality at the Level of Social Action (Orientation): Value Rationality vs Instrumental (Purposive) Rationality

At the level of modes of social action, Weber contrasted value rationality with instrumental rationality. In value rationality, social action is based on a normative frame or value choice. Social action is value rational insofar as a particular value orientation is consciously selected from a number of possible value choices. It is non-rational, however, insofar as the value orientation, once chosen, implies an absolute commitment and determines action independently of considerations of adequacy, costs, consequences, or chances of success.

Instrumental rationality, by contrast, refers to the modern notion of rationally weighing the costs and consequences of action, or of implementing decisions on the basis of formal criteria of efficiency, cost–benefit, or risk–benefit analysis. In contrast to Weber's broad concept of practical rationality defined earlier, instrumental rationality is a form of rational choice that is narrowly focused on strategies of social action in which specific, technically defined means are mobilized for the purpose of acting on one's specific preferences and achieving determinate objectives. This type of rationality, Weber notes, is inherently utility maximizing and success oriented.[1]

Rationality at the Institutional Level: Substantive vs Formal Rationality

Weber sees formal and substantive rationality as attributes of normative orders and politico-economic institutions rather than of individual actors. Formal rationality always involves the rules, methods and normative procedures that are intrinsic to a particular social domain. For example, in the economic sphere, formal rationality refers to 'the extent of quantitative calculation or accounting which is technically possible and which is actually applied'. By contrast, substantive economic rationality refers to the degree to which economic processes are shaped by 'some criterion (past, present, or potential) of ultimate values, regardless of the nature of these ends' (Weber, 1978: 85). This definition permits the distinction between different substantive concepts of efficiency, for example, capitalist and socialist efficiency (Gordon, 1976). While for Weber the 'normative orders' of law, economy and the state are analytically separate, his later work suggests that these spheres are characterized by relations of mutual causation as well as a host of historical forms of interaction and empirical interrelationships. Let us look at Weber's 'legal rationality' in more detail.

Legal Rationality

Weber (1966: 13) defines law as a set of legal norms and rules that are guaranteed by a coercive apparatus in which specialized personnel are prepared to apply and enforce the norms. Law-making (legislation) and law-finding (judicial decision-making) are rational to the extent that they are guided by general rules rather than ad hoc, case-specific reasoning. Substantive legal rationality is guided by the general principles of an ideological or normative system other than that of the law itself, for example, political, religious, economic or ethical values, or substantive notions of equity, fairness or justice. Formal legal rationality is based on general rules internal to the legal code itself and is, in theory, independent of all substantive values and external determinations. Weber specifies two types of formal legal rationality which may serve to discriminate, inter alia, between person and action. Formal rationality is *logical* to the extent that it expresses its rules 'by the use of abstract concepts created by legal thought itself and conceived of as constituting a complete system'. It is oriented toward the interpretation of the intrinsic meaning of acts. By contrast, formal rationality is *extrinsic* to the extent that it ascribes 'significance to external acts observable by the senses' (Rheinstein, 1966: L). This empiricist element in the extrinsic version renders Weber's ideal type of formal-legal rationality compatible with the formal procedures of English common law (for example, it asks, what did a person actually do in a given situation?), whereas the logical version of formal rationality shows an affinity with continental 'legal science', i.e. with the conceptual and analytical jurisprudence of civil law, (for example, it asks, what did a person intend or mean to do in a given situation?). The first case focuses on the discrete act, the second on the whole person.

Weber's categories and ideal types are constituted by the binary oppositions of form and substance (content) as well as rationality and non-rationality (affect, tradition). In Weber's institutional types (especially the normative orders of the economy or law), rationality is defined in terms of the operation of general norms rather than particular, concrete instances. The more general and abstract legal norms are, the more universalistic (rational); the more case-specific and concrete, the more ad hoc

International Sociology Vol. 18 No. 2

characteristic of a structure, an institutional sphere, a normative order, or a collectivity.

At least three critical issues must be raised about Weber's categories of legal rationality.

1. In spite of the cognitive and structural dualism constituted by these categories, their mutual boundaries are frequently blurred. For example, 'substantive non-rationality' is by definition 'guided by reaction to the individual case' (Rheinstein, 1966: L) within the context of substantive norms. According to Weber, the case-based structure and some procedural aspects of the common law (e.g. jury trials) are substantively non-rational even though the rule of *stare decisis* and precedent in the form of written decisions and opinions lend it a formal character (see also Ewing, 1987). Similarly, the 'substance' of common law may contain hidden economic and religious presuppositions even when it is 'formal' (Shamir, 1993; Likhovski, 1999). It is, therefore, not easy to apply the Weberian scheme without running into a host of definitional difficulties.
2. While Weber includes both law-making and law-finding in his definition of law, there is no explicit distinction between legislation and decision-making in the typology just discussed. Here, the differences between civil law and common law perspectives become crucial. In the continental European civil law which is Weber's empirical and biographical frame of reference, legislation (law-making) is clearly separate from law-finding, judicial decision-making and the 'application' of the law to 'facts', not to mention implementation and norm enforcement. In the context of the common law, however, law-finding and law-making are coterminous, i.e. they are part and parcel of the same process. The law is held to be what judges say it is and judges can mobilize enforcement through the powers of contempt of court as well as administrative implementation. On the other hand, the legal realism and creativity of judicial interpretation under the common law can render the legal process somewhat indeterminate, as both supporters (Holmes, 1897) and critics (Horwitz, 1992; Kennedy, 1998) have noted.
3. Formal legal rationality and different versions of substantive rationality tend to clash in concrete, empirical cases, as Weber himself observed, or they tend to develop into mixed forms (see also Levine, 1981). Thus, Weber's categories reveal certain historical and logical limits. The category of 'substantive rationality' is 'full of ambiguities' (Weber, 1978: 85) and, one might add, too inclusive to be of much analytical use. While it is true that versions of religious substantive rationality are surviving in some parts of the world (e.g. in Muslim-dominated

societies), and political substantive rationality under remnants of state socialism (e.g. in China), substantive rationality in North America, Japan and Europe is generally tending toward mixed forms or versions that no longer fit the Weberian label. By the same token, what is still taken as formal law or even as the resurgence of formalism and due process (Dobbin et al., 1988; Edelman, 1990) are really remnants of substantive administrative rationality of the 20th-century regulatory state. As Weber (1966: 45) put it, 'In the modern state, it is true, there exists a trend formally to assimilate adjudication to "administration" (in the sense of "government") [e.g. 'the right to resort to administrative tribunals'] . . . But none of these guaranties can eliminate the basic contradiction between adjudication and "government".' A similarly 'administrative' act of governance is the eclectic adoption of niches and islands of seemingly formal procedures in the otherwise stagnant waters of the substantive political rationality of state socialist legal systems such as East Germany and Russia before 1989 (Heydebrand, 1996) and contemporary China (Johnson, 2000: 150–6), even though some observers detect the infusion of formalism and proceduralism into the Chinese legal system (e.g. Guthrie, 1999). In short, the applicability of the distinctions and the status accorded to formal rationality is limited essentially to the late 19th and early 20th centuries. The concepts no longer speak adequately to the forms of legal practice emerging throughout the course of the 20th century, especially between 1920 and 1990.

The Logic of Process Rationality

Weber used the term 'formal' in the sense that an intelligible structure of something is valid independently of its specific content or subject matter and that it has only logical meaning or is independent of social or subjective meaning. The term 'substantive' retains its reference to content, but true to the idealist tradition, substantive content is interpreted as ideal rather than material and refers to absolute values and ultimate ends.

In contrast to the static and determinative connotations of form and substance, the concept of process is dynamic and interactive. It involves a series of joint deliberations, transformative interactions and decisions oriented toward the production of some practical outcome (e.g. understandings, agreements, arrangements and problem solutions), and it implies a systematic forward, sometimes even 'progressive' movement that has constitutive implications for consensus formation (see also Tamanaha, 1997). Process entails self-activity as a form of social construction and thus has potentially creative and emancipatory implications.

International Sociology Vol. 18 No. 2

Process rationality is based on a model of interaction, deliberation and decision-making among relatively autonomous participants and thus tends to approximate the notion of the self-legitimation of negotiated process, including self-constitution through 'studied trust', 'learning by monitoring', 'constitutional ordering' and other 'constitutional' experiments (Sabel, 1993a, 1993b, 1994; Dorf and Sabel, 1998) as well as organizational rights claims (Dan-Cohen, 1986: 55–119).

I want to be clear, however, about the fact that the contextual and situational advantages of process rationality come at a heavy cost, namely the emergent deconstruction of procedural and substantive rights, the dissolution of the normative legality that is historically embedded in formal justice, and the deformation of constitutional protections and safeguards. To the extent, then, that economic globalization engenders the privatization and informalization of law and justice at the expense of central constitutional tenets of the rule of law, it deinstitutionalizes law and transforms it into an expedient, flexible and efficient type of governance (Scheuerman, 1999a, 2000; Heydebrand, 2000).

Process Rationality as a Mode of Governance

Process rationality in law is a product of the growth of organized capitalism and big government, on the one hand, and the undeniable expediency of operating without formal rules that might constrain corporate and national state power, on the other. As economic concentration increased and corporations grew larger, they were among the first to recognize that formal rules and procedures which they promoted in the 19th century had come to constitute an obstacle to efficient and expansive strategies in the 20th (Neumann, 1957, 1986). This is, of course, a version of the sorcerer's apprentice dilemma: the former servant turns into the master, the demons called upon to work for the sorcerer gradually become fetters that are hard to overcome or to get rid of. While 19th-century legal rules (notably property and contract) offered the individual entrepreneur a protective shield against ruthless competition, these rules turned into shackles once it became opportune to cooperate with erstwhile competitors or to ask for their hand in merger. But during and after the New Deal, big government, too, rediscovered that formal rules constrained its power of policy-making and implementation more than it had bargained for. Government agencies and corporations alike welcomed the informalism, flexibility and expedience offered by the open-ended process of bargaining and negotiation.

Informalism, flexibility, bargaining and expediency are key ingredients of the concept of governance. Whereas the idea of government refers to political structures of legitimate rule in which a parliamentary or democratic sovereign exercises authority on behalf of a given population, territory, or society, governance constitutes a set of strategies of problem-solving and crisis management enacted in the interests of a political elite or the technical imperatives of a system. An ad hoc set of instruments of societal guidance, technocratic steering, or social engineering tends to replace legitimate institutional authority; governance 'governs' without government (Rosenau, 1992; Hirst and Thompson, 1999: 269; Therborn, 2000: 172–3). Whereas a politically accountable and responsible government has a relative degree of autonomy to make decisions on behalf of the political interests and social needs of the governed, governance signifies the practical and pragmatic exercise of control over 'reterritorialized' spatial units regardless of their previous status in terms of 'legitimacy', 'authority', or 'autonomy' (Cox, 1993; Brenner, 1999). Strategies of governance typically make use of any available cost-effective or risk–benefit based means to achieve political and economic goals regardless of legal or constitutional implications. Examples are the use of 'neutral' information and communications technology, economic incentives or coercion, and political pressure or military force, including preventive war. The use of such strategies is ideologically and legally justified in terms of technical or 'objective' constraints, the putative absence of alternatives, the 'national interest', exceptional danger and threats to security, the lack of resources and the 'economic state of emergency' (Scheuerman, 2000).

If the ascendance of governance signifies the depoliticization of government and the selective deregulation of the economy, the legal parallel is the deformalization of law and the deinstitutionalization of justice. Such deformalization is typically associated with the privatization and commercialization of the public sphere, i.e. the rise of negotiated law and private justice as well as the ascendance of institutional deviance and white-collar crime.[2]

Selective deregulation and the privatization of the public sphere have grown in the US in the wake of neoliberal policy-making and the rising distrust of government since the early 1970s. They include the shift from public to private means of policing (see the rising concern about security and the protection of property by private police, e.g. Henry, 1981, 1983; Jones and Newburn, 1998; Mandel, 2002); the shift from formal adjudication to informal methods of dispute resolution such as arbitration, mediation and bargaining; the consequent rise of informal justice (Abel, 1982) and 'negotiated justice' (Dezalay, 1994); the justification of plea-bargaining by the Supreme Court (*Santobello* v. *New York*, 1972); the Supreme Court's minimalist 'jurisprudence of uncertainty' (Sunstein, 1999; Bybee, 2001); and the movement to privatize prisons and other institutions of social control. While some of these processes emerged in the late 1960s and early

1970s, they began to flourish with the economic expansion since 1991 as part of the contemporary round of globalization.[3]

In what way can these institutional changes be said to amount to a process of deinstitutionalization in the legal arena? Economic interests and political power may be ideologically masked, but their justification and legitimation can no longer be fully taken for granted. Institutional power can no longer be exclusively exercised independently of the interests and power of the participants such as actors in social networks and critical or insurgent social movements. Adjudication is increasingly replaced by arbitration, mediation and direct – bilateral – negotiation. This cuts both ways: it increases the power of participants in the process, but it also weakens or removes formal, institutional protections and constitutional guarantees. The extreme situation is one of bilateral confrontation and negotiation among more or less unequal private interests. It could potentially be mediated by the presence of a third party (such as the presence of the media in the court room), which guarantees a degree of publicity, hence some measure of 'accountability' and 'legitimacy' (see also Walton, 1969; Black and Baumgartner, 1998: 95–124). But it would not necessarily guarantee the substantive goals of equity or justice. The point is that the implementation and/or enforcement of agreements arrived at under such conditions is no longer exclusively a function of legitimate governmental and legal authority or legal rules, but of an overriding economic interest in 'order' and 'stability', for example, the continuation of some form of relationship between the 'contracting' parties, or a political or neocorporatist interest in conflict management, 'security' and effective 'governance'.

In short, process-oriented thinking and its associated practices of 'legal governance' tend to deconstruct, delegitimize and deinstitutionalize the existing framework of a legal culture that was thought to be solid and unchangeable. This deinstitutionalization does not eliminate courts and judges from process rationality as much as it transforms and subverts their traditional roles as institutional guardians of the rule of law. Whatever the efforts used to explain and justify reflexivity, informalism and anti-formalism as reformist or progressive elements within the rule of law, they are definitely not merely versions of the rule of law and cannot be reduced to it. One may want to insist, in line with Weber's dualism, that if it is not formal rationality, it must be substantive rationality. But process rationality does not have the consensual goal-directedness and absolutism of substantive rationality. If anything, there is a chance that Weber's legal rationalities are being transformed by a version of 'success-oriented' instrumental and strategic rationality. 'Legal governance' thus is a contradiction in terms insofar as the core meaning of governance implies the deformation of law and, generally, the deconstruction of the constitutional promise of the rule of law.[4]

Heydebrand *Process Rationality as Legal Governance*

As the concept of process rationality in law is potentially broad and internally contradictory, I want to propose three reflexive and critical methodological strategies that can help to alleviate this potential problem of excessive generality and ambiguity.

1. First, the validity claims of the new category can be 'tested' (falsified) by the degree to which there is a continued operation of the older categories, as in hybrid or mixed versions like formal process and substantive process. The emergent process rationality is neither all-encompassing nor merely widely dispersed throughout the legal system like Foucault's 'power and discipline'. Elements of substantive rationality continue to operate in the shadow of modern law and state in at least two arenas: (a) in the national state's widely cast interest in, and domain assumption about, crime control and social control (Garland, 2001), and (b) in those arenas of administrative regulation of the economy that are surviving deregulation, and in areas where social policy and substantive rights protection remain relatively intact (see, for example, policies on equal opportunity and affirmative action, sexual harassment, maternity benefits, grievance procedures and personnel procedures emerging from labor law and, more recently, 'employment law' [Stone, 2001; Scheuerman, 2001b]). While these tendencies are sometimes seen as a resurgence of formal legal institutional rationality and due process (Edelman, 1990), they are merely systemic versions of state-centered substantive rationality with the more or less explicit substantive goals of viability, stability, security and systemic control. However, formalist elements have survived the 20th-century sea change as well, or have emerged in reaction to what some conservative, 'strict constructionist' critics (e.g. former judge Robert Bork) perceive as either constitutional drift or, worse, liberal judicial activism. Moreover, federal court decisions and the composition and style of leadership of the US Supreme Court as well as the majority/minority ratios in its decisions and opinions still provide valid indicators of the nature and direction of legal change in the USA. In continental civil law systems, too, the nature and activism of state policy or of decisions emanating from supranational entities like the European High Court may offer indicators of the relative balance between formal, substantive and process rationality (Gibson and Caldeira, 1993).
2. A second factor that helps to concretize and specify the concept of process rationality is that it has spawned a number of variants both in the US and in Europe. Process rationality in law is responsive to different contexts and contingencies and has, therefore, assumed different forms (see also Galanter's [1981] 'process pluralism'). In the US, there is now a respectable century-old tradition of process-oriented

legal rationality that builds on the informal, interactive, negotiated, responsive, dialogical, reflexive, privatized and constitutive characteristics of American common law. The constitution of social relations by law, also known as 'constitutive law' (Brigham, 1996) is, of course, not necessarily identical with process rationality, especially under the regime of analytical jurisprudence. There are also substantive versions of constitutive law which may span the political spectrum from left to right, e.g. they may represent deformalized 'law in action', but without the built-in guarantees of a liberal-democratic rule of law (see Maus, 1980: 85). However, insofar as law is informal, flexible, negotiated and reflexive law, it will tend to cast itself as a constitutive discourse and practice within society rather than in instrumental terms (Hunt, 1993: 15–16, 301ff.).

In Europe, some of the characteristics of process rationality are similar, but the terms are different. For example, there are various conceptions of law as auto-poietic (self-referential), reflexive, post-regulatory, relational, procedural, proceduralized, deformalized (and perhaps 'deformed', given the difficulty of separating fact and value). Some observers also note a trend toward the convergence or 'harmonization' between common law and civil law (for France, see Provine, 1996; for Germany, Wiegand, 1991; for Britain, Werro, 1996). On the whole, however, European approaches still tend to favor 'procedural' conceptions of process (e.g. Fox, 2000; Serverin, 2000), whereas versions of 'substantive' process appear to linger in the US (see, for example, Abraham, 1986; Atiyah and Summers, 1987: 127ff.).[5]

3. A third point of reflexive criticism must come to grips with the fact that process rationality is part of the current ascendancy of economic criteria in the evaluation of political and legal effectiveness, a trend known as the economic analysis of law (Posner, 1998, 1995; Mnookin et al., 2000; Williamson, 1996). This means that negotiated process rationality is, in effect, not just a going concern since the rise of realism and post-liberal democratic managerialism, but it provides a rapidly growing framework of regulatory governance, especially in the wake of the transitions of 1989–91 (Heydebrand, 2000: 6–21). Moreover, financial globalization has changed almost all of the parameters of comparison and criteria of evaluation in favor of economic principles of efficiency and effectiveness that claim to provide a new mode of 'regulation on a global scale' (Bairoch, 2000; Eatwell and Taylor, 2000: 180–207; Applebaum et al., 2001).

Discussion and Conclusion

This article seeks to transcend the remnants of Weber's categories of formal and substantive legal rationality and to reconceptualize post-Weberian legal thought in terms of the idea of process rationality as a mode of legal governance. It reinterprets some of the salient developments in American legal theory and legal institutions during the last century in terms of the dissolution as well as the restructuring of the legal categories of form and substance and identifies similar developments in the European, particularly the German context. The proximate causes of the rise of process rationality are the revolt against legal formalism as increasingly unrealistic and inflexible; the intermittent mistrust of substantive rationality in the shape of the activist and interventionist policies of the 20th-century regulatory welfare state; the contradictions of the legal system and the legal profession (e.g. Abel, 1989) in responding to the changing demands of business and government and their institutional weakness in 'processing' the social problems, conflicts and movements spawned by various transitions. I have in mind, for example, the historical transitions from competitive to corporate capitalism, from the 19th-century minimalist state to the executive-centered state of the 20th century, and from there to the denationalized state and the informal, privatized 'law' of the current round of globalization. Weber anticipated the 'anti-formal tendencies' of modern law, but he did not live to see their modalities, their deconstructive and reconstructive potential, and their various incarnations and manifestations in Europe and America during the regulatory 20th century.[6]

Among the tendencies and movements most strongly exhibiting the influence of process rationality (and thus supporting the argument of this article) are legal realism, which has come to be associated with the political tenets and the organizational revolution of the New Deal; the rise of negotiated rule-making in administrative law; the economic analysis of law or what I have called 'economic common law'; collective bargaining and labor law; the alternative dispute resolution movement and the rise of negotiation, bargaining, mediation and arbitration as models of dispute resolution that have all but replaced the conventional model of adjudication; the rising deformalization of law (especially contract, tort) and judicial administration (plea-bargaining and settlement) in the wake of newly emerging kinds of informal, pragmatic, contextual and situational justice; the corresponding privatization and commercialization of law; and the instrumentalization of law for political purposes, especially transnational dispute resolution and governance.

A number of tendencies and movements can be seen as *countering these trends* and as reaffirming substantive law and procedures (thus providing a kind of negative evidence against the argument that all law is turning into legal governance). One is the early 19th-century sociological and political jurisprudence movement which is a transition to realism. While clearly anti-formalist, sociological jurisprudence was still advocating a version of substantive rationality in the shape of social needs and interests. Similarly transitional are the early applications of the delegation of powers doctrine which empowered administrative agencies to act substantively on behalf of congressional mandates. Clearly substantive in their goal-orientation are the protest movements of the 1960s and 1970s such as critical legal studies, feminist jurisprudence, critical race theory, and movements on behalf of gay and lesbian rights. Indeed, rights-oriented activism tends to collide with certain tenets of critical legal studies insofar as the latter advocates substantive communitarian goals, participatory democracy and a legal culture of consensus which might be threatened by proliferating special rights claims. The New Public Law Movement, too, can be said to reaffirm certain public interest elements of substantive rationality, although it is tempered by an openness for bargaining and negotiation in the sphere of public–private interaction and partnership. By the same token, European forms of social democracy (Scandinavian, British, German, Mediterranean) have emphasized substantive goals and the need for substantive rationality in law-making and decision-making.

Among the tendencies and movements reaffirming certain forms of proceduralism or showing signs of reformalization are the legal process approach and the economic analysis of law. Legal process is conceived as a rule-governed process that privileges procedure over outcome. It is therefore closer to the notion of a regularized and institutionalized procedure than to the idea of a self-sustaining and self-governing, but relatively open-ended process in which the goals or outcomes are contingent on participation, intensive interaction, willingness to negotiate and readiness to work out tentative compromises and provisional agreements.

The bipolar case of the economic analysis of law is more complicated. Conceptions of individual preferences, subjective agency and the market, however, open economic common law to the impact of negotiated process rationality and the privatization of law and justice. Insofar as legal rules create incentives and 'bargaining endowments' which can be used in negotiations in the context of a system of legal-economic exchange, process rationality enters into what would otherwise be a closed system of fixed rational rules. It is for this reason that, in the context of American common law, I subsume economic analysis under the category of 'process rationality' in decision-making.

My conclusion about the European versions of process rationality is that they are generally more rule-oriented and closer to the proceduralist model of the legal process approach than to the more informal, flexible and indeterminate forms of American legal realism, collective bargaining and alternative dispute resolution. In the context of a Habermasian communicative rationality, it seems that procedural rationality, proceduralization and democratic deliberation are clearly rule-governed models. While they embrace the notion of anti-formalism or the transcendence of the 'materialization' of law in favor of proceduralization, they nevertheless do not favor the ambiguity and relative indeterminacy of a negotiated process rationality. The idea of a 'procedural natural law', in fact, fundamentally signifies a return to a type of formal rationality that seeks to ground local, democratic processes of law-making and adjudication in a substantively justified procedural rationality. It is here where the democratization of law-making and formal dispute resolution is conceptualized as a marriage of popular sovereignty and democratic rule-making, i.e. as a kind of substantively oriented process rationality. As some observers argue, 'the EU provides the richest model as well as the richest body of intellectual and pragmatic resources for thinking about issues of federalism involving sovereignty, subsidiarity, and internationalization' (Fox, 1998: 903). It is not yet clear, however, to what extent these normative conceptions will remain utopian visions, or else, can be realized and implemented in a concrete, empirical context. Democratic law-making and dispute resolution have certainly become more vulnerable under the current round of economic globalization.

The only process-oriented exceptions to this assessment are associated with the heirs to Luhmann's auto-poietic systems theory, especially the work of Teubner (1992, 2000) and Willke (1988). In recent years, Teubner has moved toward a model of corporate and democratic self-regulation, which envisages reflexive, post-regulatory law only as a framework, not as a direct instrumental constraint. As a jurist, Teubner (1993a, 1994) is concerned to demonstrate the reality and viability of reflexive law in specific circumstances and cases, for example, environmental law and corporate law. At the same time, however, Teubner's (1997: 13) vision of a 'self-organizing process of mutual constitution of legal acts and legal structures' appears to drift toward a governance-oriented form of constitutive and 'situational jurisprudence' that has rightly been criticized as 'fundamentally inconsistent with a minimally defensible conception of the rule of law' (Scheuerman, 1999a: 3; also Scheuerman [2001a] and Wells [1991] on 'situated decisionmaking'; and Minow and Spelman [1991] on the deformalizing role of 'context').

Willke's (1988) 'relational' systems model of law, too, has a certain affinity with social network theory and open systems theory. This model is applicable to the governance-oriented functioning of political systems: for example, the operation of the 'network state' (Castells, 1998: 310–34; Teubner, 1993b) in the contemporary context of the EU. On the other hand, however, the notion of a process rationality in the European context tends to have the connotation of the deconstruction and deformalization of legal categories that are still tied to the traditions of national sovereignty and the autonomy of law. Such processes of deformalization may therefore generate resistance at the level of the legal and governmental institutions of some member states. Moreover, European community law, even though it is constructed by the constituent member states, cannot yet be called a truly democratic community law. While the constitution of a European legal system, therefore, lacks a normative democratic foundation, it has definite constructive process characteristics that may in time transcend both substantive and formal limitations within a viable and normatively justifiable procedural framework.

Notes

This article was originally first presented at the joint ASA/LSA Conference on Comparative Historical Perspectives on Law, Panel on 'Transnational Perspectives on Law', ASA Annual Meetings, Washington, DC, 16 August 2000. For helpful comments on earlier versions, I am grateful to Saïd Arjomand, Vanessa Barker, Elizabeth Boyle, David Greenberg, Elizabeth Joh, Samantha McBride, Aaron Panofsky, Adina Schwartz and the participants in the NYU Crime, Law, and Deviance Workshop.

1. Rationally weighing the consequences of one's actions implies what Weber calls an 'ethics of responsibility' (in contrast to the more absolutist, value-rational 'ethics of conviction'). The basis of a 'responsible' rational-ethical choice may be a formal calculus such as probability theory, game theory, or risk–benefit decision-making in which actors seek to maximize gains and minimize losses or rationally seek to weigh the cost of investments. Instrumental rationality and strategic decision-making are, according to Weber, the dominant basis of conduct in modern capitalist society. A systemic version of this type of rationality comes very close to what Weber might have called 'governance' had he not held on to the principle that law, in its formal and substantive versions of rationality, was intrinsically related to the legitimacy of the nation-state. As Albrow (1997: 62) put it in the spirit of Weber, 'The idea of law, and hence rationality, are intrinsic to the state.'
2. Some observers refer to these processes as a 're-feudalization' of the public sphere, i.e. the neocorporatist growth of large-scale corporations and government agencies that secretly negotiate political compromises behind closed doors (Habermas, 1989, 1995; Maus, 1986: 11–82, 277–331; 1992: 34; Dan-Cohen, 1986: 176–9). The current disclosures of institutional deviance, corporate crime and professional conflict of interest in accounting and law further accentuate these highly problematic consequences of economic deregulation and the privatization of public institutions (e.g. Cain and Harrington, 1994; Calavita et al., 1997; Castells, 1998: 166–205; Strange, 1998; Soros, 2002).
3. In law, the eclipse of government and sovereignty by the mechanisms of governance occurs at a comparatively practical, concrete level of implementation and enforcement, but I stress that it has its conceptual counterpart at the level of jurisprudence, legal doctrine and case law. This 'informalist

scholarship' (Brigham and Harrington, 1989: 42) includes the decline or 'death of contract' (Gilmore, 1974; Atiyah, 1978, 1979); the evolution of 'relational contract' from classical and neoclassical versions (Macneil, 1978; Shapiro, 1998); the proliferation of non-contractual relations in business (Macaulay, 1963, 1986) and 'private interest government' (Streeck and Schmitter, 1985); the ideological appeal of 'legal pluralism' and 'process pluralism' (Galanter, 1981; Teubner, 1997); and the privatization of transnational legal sovereignty (Dezalay and Garth, 1996; Scheuerman, 1999b; Heydebrand, 2000; Applebaum et al., 2001). Among the 'implications for inequality of discarding traditional international law sovereignty', for example, Kingsbury (1999: 84–90) cites the 'diminished restraints on coercive intervention' and the 'diminution of state functions without effective alternatives'.

4. Max Weber famously anticipated this possibility in two rather pessimistic passages of his work. The first one appeared at the end of his *Protestant Ethic and the Spirit of Capitalism* (Weber, 2002: 124) and refers to the 'last humans' living in an 'iron cage' as ' narrow specialists without mind, pleasure-seekers without heart'. The other one appeared at the end of Weber's sociology of law where he invokes the inevitable impact of 'technical and economic developments' on the law and the 'continuous growth of the technical element of the law and hence of its character as a specialist's domain'. 'Inevitably the notion must expand', Weber predicts, 'that the law is a rational technical apparatus which is continually transformable in the light of expediential [*sic*] considerations and devoid of all sacredness of content' (Weber, 1966: 321). Again, the notion of law as a 'rational technical apparatus' that can be continually restructured by means of an instrumental rationality comes close to what Weber might have called 'governance'. Such a fate, Weber concludes, can be concealed, but not avoided.
5. Modern process rationality, as a creative frame of reference, a constitutive context, a generative and productive force, and an instrument of the privatized power of situational rule is not primarily an extension of Weber's categories as much as it is a transcendence, an overcoming of the fateful dualities that he imposed on the sociology of law. As Albrow puts it prophetically, '[Weber's] work is one of the most abiding legacies of modernity, but the Global Age obliges us to go beyond it' (Albrow, 1997: 6).
6. From a sociological perspective, the prominence of informal processes of bargaining and negotiation in legal practice has a wider significance if one considers the massive shift of the modern occupational structure from manufacturing to services since the early 1970s. Professional and service occupations are characterized by the fact that the process of providing a service constitutes the product of the service. Legal counseling, management counseling, advertising and other advanced producer services such as innovative web design in the new media all involve close interaction with, and the active participation of clients (Abel, 1989; Cain and Harrington, 1994; Sugarman, 1994; Seron, 1996; Heydebrand and Miron, 2002).

International Sociology Vol. 18 No. 2

References

Abel, Richard, ed. (1982) *The Politics of Informal Justice*, 2 vols. New York: Academic Press.

Abel, Richard (1989) *American Lawyers*. New York: Oxford University Press.

Abraham, Henry J. (1986) *The Judicial Process: An Introductory Analysis of the Courts of the United States, England, and France*, 5th edn. New York: Oxford University Press.

Albrow, Martin (1990) *Max Weber's Construction of Social Theory*. New York: St Martin's Press.

Albrow, Martin (1997) *The Global Age: State and Society beyond Modernity*. Stanford, CA: Stanford University Press.

Applebaum, Richard, Felstiner, William and Volkmar Gessner, eds (2001) *Rules and Networks: The Legal Culture of Global Business Transactions*. Oxford: Hart Publishers.

Atiyah, P. S. (1978) *From Principle to Pragmatism: Changes in the Function of the Judicial Process and the Law*. Oxford: Clarendon Press.

Atiyah, P. S. (1979) *The Rise and Fall of Freedom of Contract*. Oxford: Clarendon Press.

Atiyah, P. S. and Summers, Robert S. (1987) *Form and Substance in Anglo-American Law: A Comparative Study of Legal Reasoning, Legal Theory, and Legal Institutions*. Oxford: Clarendon Press.

Bairoch, Paul (2000) 'The Constituent Economic Principles of Globalization in Historical Perspective: Myths and Realities', *International Sociology* 15(2): 197–21.

Black, Donald with Baumgartner, M. P. (1998) 'Toward a Theory of the Third Party', in *The Social Structure of Right and Wrong*, Ch. 6. San Diego, CA: Academic Press.

Brenner, Neil (1999) 'Beyond State-Centrism? Space, Territoriality, and Geographical Scale in Globalization Studies', *Theory and Society* 28: 39–78.

Brenner, Robert (2002) *The Boom and the Bubble: The US in the World Economy*. London: Verso.

Brigham, John (1996) *The Constitution of Interests*. New York: New York University Press.

Brigham, John and Harrington, Christine (1989) 'Realism and its Consequences: An Inquiry into Contemporary Social Research', *International Journal of the Sociology of Law* 17: 41–62.

Bybee, Keith J. (2001) 'The Juriprudence of Uncertainty' (reviewing Sunstein), *Law and Society Review* 35(4): 943–56.

Cain, Maureen and Harrington, Christine (1994) *Lawyers in a Postmodern World: Translation and Transgression*. New York: New York University Press.

Calavita, Kitty, Pontell, Henry and Tillman, Robert (1997) *Big Money Crime: Fraud and Politics in the Savings and Loan Crisis*. Berkeley: University of California Press.

Castells, Manuel (1998) *End of Millennium*. Oxford: Blackwell.

Chandler, Alfred D. (1980) 'Government vs. Business: An American Phenomenon', in J. T. Dunlop (ed.) *Business and Public Policy*, pp. 1–11. Boston, MA: Harvard Business School.

Heydebrand *Process Rationality as Legal Governance*

Cox, Robert W. (1993) 'Structural Issues of Global Governance: Implications for Europe', in S. Gill (ed.) *Gramsci, Historical Materialism, and International Relations*, pp. 259–89. Cambridge: Cambridge University Press.

Dan-Cohen, Meir (1986) *Rights, Persons, and Organizations: A Legal Theory for Bureaucratic Society*. Berkeley: University of California Press.

Dezalay, Yves (1994) 'The Forum Should Fit the Fuss: The Economics and Politics of Negotiated Justice', in M. Cain and C. Harrington (eds) *Lawyers in a Post-Modern World: Translation and Transgression*, pp. 155–82. New York: New York University Press.

Dezalay, Yves and Bryant Garth (1996) *Dealing in Virtue: International Commercial Arbitration and the Constitution of a Transnational Legal Order.* Chicago, IL: University of Chicago Press.

Dobbin, Frank, Edelman, Lauren, Meyer, John, Scott, W. Richard and Swidler, Ann (1988) 'The Expansion of Due Process in Organizations', in L. Zucker (ed.) *Institutional Patterns and Organizations*, pp. 71–98. Cambridge, MA: Ballinger.

Dorf, Michael C. and Sabel, Charles F. (1998) 'A Constitution of Democratic Experimentalism', *Columbia Law Review* 98: 267.

Eatwell, John and Taylor, Lance (2000) *Global Finance at Risk.* New York: The New Press.

Edelman, Lauren B. (1990) 'Legal Environments and Organizational Governance: The Expansion of Due Process in the American Workplace', *American Journal of Sociology* 95: 1401–40.

Ewing, Sally (1987) 'Formal Justice and the Spirit of Capitalism: Max Weber's Sociology of Law', *Law and Society Review* 21: 487–512.

Fox, Eleanor M. (1998) 'Globalization and its Challenges for Law and Society', *Loyola University Chicago Law Journal* 29(4): 891–902.

Fox, Eleanor M. (2000) 'Antitrust and Regulatory Federalism: Races Up, Down, and Sideways', *New York University Law Review* 76: 1781–807.

Freeman, Jody (1997) 'Collaborative Governance in the Administrative State', *UCLA Law Review* 45: 1.

Galanter, Marc (1981) 'Justice in Many Rooms', *Journal of Legal Pluralism* 19: 1.

Garland, David (2001) *The Culture of Control: Crime and Social Order in Contemporary Society.* Chicago, IL: University of Chicago Press.

Gibson, James L. and Caldeira, Gregory A. (1993) 'The European Court of Justice: A Question of Legitimacy', *Zeitschrift fuer Rechtssoziologie* 14: 204–22.

Gilmore, Grant (1974) *The Death of Contract.* Columbus: Ohio State University Press.

Goodrich, Peter (1983) 'The Rise of Legal Formalism; or the Defenses of Legal Faith', *Legal Studies* 3: 248–66.

Gordon, David (1976) 'Capitalist Efficiency and Socialist Efficiency', *Monthly Review* 28(3): 19–39.

Guthrie, Douglas (1999) *Dragon in a Three-Piece Suit: The Emergence of Capitalism in China.* Princeton, NJ: Princeton University Press.

Habermas, Jürgen (1989) *The Structural Transformation of the Public Sphere*, trans. T. Burger. Cambridge, MA: MIT Press.

Habermas, Jürgen (1995) *Between Facts and Norms: Contributions to a Discourse Theory of Law and Democracy.* Cambridge, MA: MIT Press.

Hardt, Michael and Negri, Antonio (2000) *Empire*. Cambridge, MA: Harvard University Press.

Held, David (2000) 'Regulating Globalization? The Reinvention of Politics', *International Sociology* 15(2): 394–408.

Henry, Stuart, ed. (1981) *Informal Institutions: Alternative Networks in the Corporate State*. New York: St Martin's Press.

Henry, Stuart (1983) *Private Justice: Toward Integrated Theorizing in the Sociology of Law*. London: Routledge.

Heydebrand, Wolf (1996) 'The Dynamics of Legal Change in Eastern Europe', *Studies in Law, Politics, and Society* 15: 263–313.

Heydebrand, Wolf (2000) 'Globalization and the Rule of Law at the End of the 20th Century', *2000 European Yearbook in the Sociology of Law*, pp. 25–128. Milan: Giuffre.

Heydebrand, Wolf and Miron, Annalisa (2002) 'Constructing Innovativeness in New Media Start-Up Firms', *Environment and Planning A* 34(11): 1951–84.

Hirst, Paul and Thompson, Grahame (1999) *Globalization in Question: The International Economy and the Possibilities of Governance*, 2nd edn. Cambridge: Polity Press.

Holmes, Oliver W. (1897) 'The Path of Law', *Harvard Law Review* 10(1): 457–78.

Horwitz, Morton (1992) *The Transformation of American Law, 1870–1960: The Crisis of Legal Orthodoxy*. New York: Oxford University Press.

Hunt, Alan (1993) 'Law as a Constitutive Mode of Regulation', in *Explorations in Law and Society: Toward a Constitutive Theory of Law*, pp. 301–33. New York and London: Routledge.

Johnson, Chalmers (2000) *Blowback: The Costs and Consequences of American Empire*. New York: Metropolitan Books, Henry Holt Co.

Jones, Trevor and Newburn, Tim (1998) *Private Security and Public Policing*. New York: Oxford University Press.

Kalberg, Stephen (1980) 'Max Weber's Types of Rationality: Cornerstones for the Analysis of Rationalization Processes in History', *American Journal of Sociology* 85(5): 1145–79.

Kennedy, Duncan (1998) *A Critique of Adjudication (fin de siècle)*. Cambridge, MA: Harvard University Press.

Kingsbury, Benedict (1999) 'Sovereignty and Inequality', in A. Hurrell and N. Woods (eds) *Inequality, Globalization, and World Politics*, pp. 66–94. Oxford: Oxford University Press.

Landis, James M. (1938) *The Administrative Process*. New Haven, CT: Yale University Press.

Levine, Donald N. (1981) 'Rationality and Freedom: Weber and Beyond', *Sociological Inquiry* 51: 5–25.

Likhovski, Assaf (1999) 'Protestantism and the Rationalization of English Law: A Variation on a Theme by Weber', *Law and Society Review* 33(2): 365–91.

Lukes, Steven (1974) *Power: A Radical View*. New York: Macmillan.

Macaulay, Stewart (1963) 'Non-Contractual Relations in Business: A Preliminary Study', *American Sociological Review* 28: 55–69.

Macaulay, Stewart (1986) 'Private Government', in L. Lipson and S. Wheeler (eds) *Law and the Social Sciences*. New York: Russell Sage Foundation.

Macneil, Ian (1978) 'Contracts: Adjustments of Long-Term Economic Relations under Classical, Neo-Classical, and Relational Contract Law', *Northwestern University Law Review* 72: 854–906.

Mandel, Robert (2002) *Armies without States: The Privatization of Security*. Boulder, CO: Lynne Rienner.

Marx, Fritz Morstein (1957) *The Administrative State*. Chicago, Il: University of Chicago Press.

Maus, Ingeborg (1980) *Buergerliche Rechtstheorie und Faschismus; Zur sozialen Funktion und aktuellen Wirkung der Theorie Carl Schmitts* [Bourgeois Legal Theory and Fascism: On the Function and Actual Influence of the Theory of Carl Schmitt]. Munich: W. Fink.

Maus, Ingeborg (1986) *Rechtstheorie und Politische Theorie im Industriekapitalismus* [Legal Theory and Political Theory in Industrial Capitalism]. Munich: W. Fink.

Maus, Ingeborg (1992) *Zur Aufklaerung der Demokratietheorie* [On Enlightening Democratic Theory]. Frankfurt: Suhrkamp.

Minow, Martha and Spelman, Elizabeth V. (1991) 'In Context', in M. Brint and W. Weaver (eds) *Pragmatism in Law and Society*, pp. 247–73. Boulder, CO: Westview Press.

Mnookin, Robert H., Peppet, Scott and Tulumello, Andrew S. (2000) *Beyond Winning: Negotiating to Create Value in Deals and Disputes*. Cambridge, MA: Harvard University Press.

Neumann, Franz (1957) 'The Change in the Function of Law in Modern Society', in *The Democratic and the Authoritarian State*, pp. 22–68. New York: Free Press.

Neumann, Franz (1986) *The Rule of Law: Political Theory and the Legal System in Modern Society*. Dover, NH: Berg.

Polanyi, Karl (1957) *The Great Transformation*. Boston, MA: Beacon.

Posner, Richard A. (1995) *Overcoming Law*. Cambridge, MA: Harvard University Press.

Posner, Richard A. (1998) *Economic Analysis of Law*. New York: Aspen Law and Business.

Provine, Marie (1996) 'Courts in the Political Process in France', in H. Jacob et al. (eds) *Courts, Law, and Politics in Comparative Perspective*. New Haven, CT: Yale University Press.

Rheinstein, Max (1966) 'Introduction', in *Max Weber on Law in Economy and Society*, ed. Max Rheinstein. Cambridge, MA: Harvard University Press.

Rosenau, James N. (1992) 'Governance, Order, and Change in World Politics', in E. O. Czempiel and J. N. Rosenau (eds) *Governance without Government*. Cambridge: Cambridge University Press.

Sabel, Charles (1993a) 'Constitutional Ordering in Historical Context', in F. W. Scharpf (ed.) *Games in Hierarchies and Networks*, pp. 65–124. New York: Campus.

Sabel, Charles (1993b) 'Studied Trust: Building New Forms of Cooperation in a Volatile Economy', in R. Swedberg (ed.) *Explorations in Economic Sociology*. New York: Russell Sage Foundation.

Sabel, Charles (1994) 'Learning by Monitoring: The Institutions of Economic Development', in N. Smelser and R. Swedberg (eds) *The Handbook of Economic Sociology*, pp. 137–65. Princeton, NJ: Princeton University Press.

Sassen, Saskia (1996) *Losing Control: Sovereignty in an Age of Globalization*. New York: Columbia University Press.

Sassen, Saskia (2000) 'Territory and Territoriality in the Global Economy', *International Sociology* 15(2): 372–93.

Scherrer, Christoph (1999) *Globalisierung wider Willen?* [Involuntary Globalization?]. Berlin: Edition Sigma.

Scheuerman, William (1994) *Between the Norm and the Exception: The Frankfurt School and the Rule of Law.* Cambridge: MIT Press.

Scheuerman, William (1999a) 'Economic Globalization and the Rule of Law', *Constellations* 6(1): 3–25.

Scheuerman, William (1999b) 'Globalization and the Fate of Law', in D. Dyzenhaus (ed.) *Recrafting the Rule of Law: The Limits of Legal Order*, pp. 243–66. Oxford: Hart Publishers.

Scheuerman, William (2000) 'The Economic State of Emergency', *Cardozo Law Review* 21(5–6): 1869–94.

Scheuerman, William (2001a) 'Reflexive Law and the Challenges of Globalization', *Journal of Political Philosophy* 9(1): 81–102.

Scheuerman, William (2001b) 'False Humanitarianism?: US Advocacy of Transnational Labor Protecions', *Review of International Political Economy* 8(3): 359–88.

Seron, Carroll (1996) *The Business of Practicing Law: The Work Lives of Solo and Small-Firm Attorneys.* Philadelphia, PA: Temple University Press.

Serverin, Evelyne (2000) *Sociologie du Droit.* Paris: Editions La Découverte.

Shamir, Ronen (1993) 'Formal and Substantive Rationality in American Law: A Weberian Perspective', *Social and Legal Studies* 2: 45.

Shapiro, Martin (1998) 'The Globalization of Freedom of Contract', in Harry N. Scheiber (ed.) *The State and Freedom of Contract*, pp. 269–98. Stanford, CA: Stanford University Press.

Shklar, Judith (1964) *Legalism.* Cambridge, MA: Harvard University Press.

Sklair, Leslie (2002) *Globalization: Capitalism and its Alternatives*, 3rd edn. Oxford: Oxford University Press.

Skowronek, Stephen (1982) *Building a New American State: The Expansion of National Administrative Capacities, 1877–1920.* Cambridge: Cambridge University Press.

Soros, George (2002) 'Busted: Why the Markets Can't Fix Themselves', *New Republic*, 2 September: 18–21.

Stone, Katherine van Wezel (2001) 'The New Psychological Contract: Implications of the Changing Workplace for Labor and Employment Law', *UCLA Law Review* 48: 519–661.

Strange, Susan (1998) *Mad Money: When Markets Outgrow Governments.* Ann Arbor: University of Michigan Press.

Streeck, Wolfgang and Schmitter, Philippe C., eds (1985) *Private Interest Government.* London: Sage.

Sugarman, David (1994) 'Blurred Boundaries: The Overlapping Worlds of Law, Business, and Politics', in M. Cain and C. Harrington (eds) *Lawyers in a Post-Modern World: Translation and Transgression*, pp. 105–23. New York: New York University Press.

Sunstein, Cass (1999) *One Case at a Time: Judicial Minimalism on the Supreme Court.* Cambridge: Harvard University Press.

Tamanaha, Brian Z. (1997) *Realistic Social-Legal Theory: Pragmatism and a Social Theory of Law.* New York: Oxford University Press.

Heydebrand *Process Rationality as Legal Governance*

Teubner, Gunther (1992) *Law as an Autopoietic System.* Oxford: Blackwell.
Teubner, Gunther (1993a) 'Company Interest: The Public Interest of the Enterprise "In Itself" ', in R. Rogowski and T. Wilthagen (eds) *Reflexive Labour Law,* pp. 21–52. Amsterdam: Kluwer.
Teubner, Gunther (1993b) 'The "State" of Private Networks: The Emerging Legal Regime of Polycorporatism in Germany', *Brigham Young University Law Review* 2: 553–75.
Teubner, Gunther (1994) 'Unitas Multiplex: Corporate Governance in Group Enterprises', in D. Sugarman and G. Teubner (eds) *Regulating Corporate Groups in Europe,* pp. 67–104. Baden-Baden: Nomos.
Teubner, Gunther (1997) ' "Global Bukowina": Legal Pluralism in the World Society', in G. Teubner (ed.) *Global Law without a State.* Aldershot: Dartmouth.
Teubner, Gunther (2000) 'Hybrid Laws: Constitutionalizing Private Governance Networks', unpublished manuscript..
Therborn, Goran (2000) 'Globalizations: Dimensions, Historical Waves, Regional Effects, Normative Governance', *International Sociology* 15(2): 151–79.
Walton, Richard E. (1969) *Interpersonal Peacemaking: Confrontations and Third-Party Consultation.* Reading, MA: Addison-Wesley.
Weber, Max (1966) *Max Weber on Law in Economy and Society,* ed. M. Rheinstein. Cambridge, MA: Harvard University Press.
Weber, Max (1978) *Economy and Society,* 2 vols, ed. G. Roth. Berkeley: University of California Press.
Weber, Max (2002) *The Protestant Ethic and the Spirit of Capitalism,* 3rd edn, ed. and trans. Stephen Kalberg. Los Angeles, CA: Roxbury.
Wells, Catharine (1991) 'Situated Decisionmaking', in M. Brint and W. Weaver (eds) *Pragmatism in Law and Society,* pp. 275–93. Boulder, CO: Westview Press.
Werro, Franz (1996) 'Harmonization of the Rules of Private Law between Civil Law and Common Law Countries', in V. Gessner et al. (eds) *European Legal Cultures,* pp. 164–6. Aldershot: Dartmouth.
Wiebe, Robert (1967) *The Search for Order, 1877–1920.* New York: Hill and Wang.
Wiegand, Wolfgang (1991) 'The Reception of American Law in Europe', *American Journal of Comparative Law* 39: 229.
Williamson, Oliver (1996) *The Mechanisms of Governance.* New York: Oxford University Press.
Willke, Helmut (1988) 'Three Types of Legal Structure: The Conditional, the Purposive, and the Relational Program', in G. Teubner (ed.) *Dilemmas of Law in the Welfare State,* pp. 280–98. New York: de Gruyter.
Woll, Peter (1963) *Administrative Law: The Informal Process.* Berkeley: University of California Press.

Biographical Note: Wolf Heydebrand, MA, PhD in sociology, University of Chicago, is currently Professor of Sociology and Member, Institute for Law and Society, New York University. His main interests are in the effects of economic globalization on organizational innovation and legal change.
Address: Department of Sociology, New York University, 269 Mercer Street, New York, NY 10003, USA. [email: wolf.heydebrand@nyu.edu]

[4]

SOME FALSE PREMISES OF MAX WEBER'S SOCIOLOGY OF LAW

HAROLD J. BERMAN*

Max Weber's sociology of law has received an enormous amount of acclaim among American legal scholars during recent decades,[1] and

* Robert W. Woodruff Professor of Law, Emory University; James Barr Ames Professor of Law, *emeritus*, Harvard University. This essay is dedicated to Gray L. Dorsey on the occasion of his seventieth birthday.

1. In a perceptive review of one of the earliest English translations of Weber's writings, Samuel E. Thorne, then Associate Professor Law and Librarian at Yale Law School, noted that

many of his ideas have become very widely accepted even by people who have never studied his writings. His sharp distinctions between "charismatic," "traditional," "formal-rational" and "substantively rational" types of law, his characterization of modern Western law as formal-rational, capitalist, and bureaucratic, and more generally his identification of various types of law with various types of political domination — reflect theories of law which, when baldly stated, are controversial. Nevertheless, being embedded in the immense historical and legal scholarship which Weber commanded and in the complex and intricate analytical network which he elaborated, these theories have seemed to his numerous admirers to be validated almost beyond a doubt.

One reason for the acceptance of Weber's legal sociology is that few people have carefully reviewed his historical and legal scholarship, but instead have merely assumed that since it is so immense it must be sound. Another reason is that the subtle interconnections which Weber draws between his theoretical models ("ideal types") and historical reality give an aura of plausibility to the former. When the ideal type fails to account for important elements of historical reality, Weberians fall back on its "analytical" or "heuristic" value. The fact that a given legal system falls within two or more ideal types is not disturbing to them: the ideal type is, for them, as real as the historical reality.[2] This confusion is aggra-

Weber's sociological works "have received little direct attention from English readers." Thorne, Book Review 56 YALE L.J. 188, 189 (1946) (reviewing FROM MAX WEBER: ESSAYS IN SOCIOLOGY) (H.H. Gerth and C. Wright Mills eds. 1946). It was the appearance eight years later of MAX WEBER ON LAW IN ECONOMY AND SOCIETY (Max Rheinstein ed., 1954) that first stimulated a rash of writings about Weber by American legal scholars. In 1986 David Trubek, John Esser, and Laurel Munger produced a bibliography entitled PRELIMINARY, ECLECTIC, UNANNOTATED WORKING BIBLIOGRAPHY FOR THE STUDY OF MAX WEBER'S SOCIOLOGY OF LAW (University of Wisconsin Institute for Legal Studies). Today Weber is referred to as a "patron saint" of American legal thought concerning the relationship of law to society. *Cf.* Trubek, *Max Weber's Tragic Modernism and the Study of Law in Society*, 20 LAW AND SOCIETY REV. 573 (1986). In 1984 one writer called him "the premier social scientist of this century." Schwartz, *Max Weber's Philosophy*, 93 YALE L.J. 1386 (1984).

Weber's enormous influence extends, of course, to other countries as well. John Finnis wrote in 1985 that "[a]mong the hidden streams nourishing jurisprudence at Oxford during the past thirty years, the work of Max Weber is among the most significant." Finnis, *On "Positivism" and "Legal Rational Authority,"* 5 OXFORD JOURNAL OF LEGAL STUDIES 74 (1985).

2. Alexander von Schelting, in his authoritative work on Weber's sociology of knowledge, states that it is impossible to remove from Weber's concept of ideal types "all its inherent obscurities, contradictions, and ambiguities." A. VON SCHELTING, MAX WEBER'S WISSENSCHAFTSLEHRE: DAS LOGISCHE PROBLEM DER HISTORISCHEN KULTURERKENNTNIS, DIE GRENZEN DER SOZIOLOGIE DES WISSENS 329 (1934 & reprint ed. 1975). Schelting stresses that ideal types are by definition theoretical models which can exist only in the mind of the observer. Nevertheless, it would

vated by the fact that Weber does not always distinguish between an "ideal" type (like bureaucracy) and a "real" type (like the Protestant ethic).

A third, more important reason for the widespread acceptance of Weberian legal theory among contemporary legal scholars is the fact that underlying its central concepts, as Anthony Kronman has shown, are certain unstated philosophical assumptions which give it intellectual coherence;[3] and these assumptions are widely shared. First, Weber starts from a sharp distinction between fact and value: facts, in Weber's view do not have any inherent meaning or purpose, and the meanings and purposes (values) attached to them by those who observe them are chosen by an exercise of will of those observers. Kronman rightly calls this a "positivistic theory of value," which rests on a "will-centered conception of personhood."[4] Second, Weber treats law as a fact, not a value, and

---

seem that if they are to serve as useful models, they must correspond to some degree to that which is observed. In fact Weber illustrates his ideal types with a wealth of data which he purports to draw from the real history of diverse societies. He also admits, however, historical "deviations" from the ideal type. As my colleague Frank Lechner has put it, Weber's ideal types are intended in part to describe and in part to distort historical reality. This would bear out the statement in the text.

3. A. KRONMAN, MAX WEBER (1983). Kronman writes on page 3:

> In this book, I offer an interpretation of the *Rechtssoziologie* which is intended to show that it does have an overarching conceptual unity .... My interpretation ... elaborates and emphasizes the common philosophical assumptions underlying Weber's treatment of many different topics in the *Rechtssoziologie* .... All reveal an implicit commitment, on Weber's part, to a few simple philosophical ideas; it is these that provide the unifying link between what is otherwise likely to seem a jumble of sometimes brilliant but essentially unconnected insights.

Cf. Id. at 4:

> This book ... attempts to demonstrate that the unstated philosophical assumptions that underlie [the] central concepts [of Weber's *Rechtssoziologie*] give the work as a whole a significant degree of intellectual coherence.

I have quoted these passages to counteract the statement made by David Trubek that although Kronman

> does ... try to demonstrate the unity of Weber's thought ... [his] ultimate conclusion is that Weber's theory of law and his ideas about the nature of society and social science were contradictory and reveal his apparent 'intellectual or moral schizophrenia' ....

Trubek, *supra* note 2, at 575.

The consistency of Weber's "methodology" has been defended by CAIN, THE LIMITS OF IDEALISM: MAX WEBER AND THE SOCIOLOGY OF LAW (S. Spitzer, ed.), 3 RESEARCH IN LAW AND SOCIOLOGY 53 (1980) and by Ewing, *Formal Justice and the Spirit of Capitalism: Max Weber's Sociology of Law*, 21 LAW AND SOCIETY REV. 487 (1987).

Consistency in philosophical assumptions and in methodology does not necessarily lead, however, to consistency in factual and theoretical conclusions. As the present essay attempts to show, Weber's philosophical and methodological errors, consistently pursued, led him in some instances to contradictory results.

4. KRONMAN, *supra* note 4, at 36. Arnold Brecht has traced the emergence of the sharp

states further that the social scientist should study law without himself evaluating the normative commitments of those who attach value to it.[5] In other words, the values which a given legal institution or set of legal institutions expressly or implicitly reflects or pursues are not values that inhere in the institutions but are values attributed to them by those who make or apply or respond to them; the scholar should study them empirically but should attempt to exclude his or her own values from such study. Third, what Weber calls formal-rational legal authority, namely, a system of politics in which domination is exercised by means of a logically consistent system of consciously made legal rules, corresponds to Weber's theory of value, which asserts the positivity of all norms. As Kronman has shown, formal-rational authority is the one form of political domination whose fundamental principle of legitimation expresses what Weber considered to be the truth about values; therefore, he was inclined (Kronman says "bound") to make this form of authority the model against which he contrasted other types.[6]

Thus Weber's sociology of law is appealing to many contemporary legal scholars partly because it denies that the world, including the world of law, has an inherent meaning or purpose, that is, any value "that antedates the choices and commitments of individual human beings."[7] At

distinction between fact and value to the writings of Simmel, Rickert, Jellinek, and Max Weber in the late nineteenth century. Its first expression was the doctrine of the logical "gulf" (Brecht calls it "the Gulf Doctrine") between the Is and the Ought. *See* A. BRECHT, POLITICAL THEORY: THE FOUNDATIONS OF TWENTIETH-CENTURY POLITICAL THOUGHT 207-231 (1959). He states that this doctrine was reflected in the belief that values are essentially subjective and not capable of scientific proof or disproof. "Its inability morally to condemn Bolshevism, Fascism, or National Socialism in unconditional terms was to become the tragedy of twentieth-century political science, a tragedy as deep as any that had ever occurred before in the history of science." *Id.* at 8. Yet Brecht himself defends "Scientific Value Relativism" as itself logically unassailable. *Id.* at 488-90.

5. Weber wrote that scholarship and science should be "value-free" (*Wertfrei*). There has been some debate about what he meant by that. For a recent discussion, see CAIN, *supra* note 4. Cain's defense against critics of Weber goes so far as to raise the question whether he meant anything at all by "value-free" other than that the scholar should make his own values "explicit and public."

6. KRONMAN, *supra* note 5, at 55. Finnis, *supra* note 2, at 76-80, attacks Kronman's view that Weber "was bound" by a positivist theory of values to give a privileged position to legal rational authority. He agrees with Kronman, however, that Weber did in fact move from a positivist theory of values to a positivist theory of law. Finnis argues that a formal-rational model is also consistent with a theory of natural law. He points out (pp. 80-83) that Weber himself stressed the influence of "natural law dogmas" on lawmaking in the past and called attention to the dangers involved in the contemporary "unmasking" of law as a mere instrument of power. Yet Finnis confirms that Weber denied the objectivity of values and asserted that both values and law are essentially creatures of will.

7. KRONMAN, *supra* note 4, at 20-21. Kronman points out at 25 that "[a]ccording to Weber, there is and can be no such thing as a group idea, an idea grounded in something other than the consciousness of a single individual." This, of course, is consistent with, and perhaps essential to,

the same time, Weber interprets social action, including law, in terms of dramatic contrasts among different civilizations and different eras of Western civilization, leaving the impression that history, including legal history, does indeed have a pattern and possibly even a direction, and that law in the West did indeed at one time have a historical mission. Weber's belief in the "disenchantment" of contemporary law and his own tragic view of modern man[8] reflect a nostalgia that is appealing to those legal scholars who, although they may have little hope and even less faith, nevertheless find some comfort in the myths of an earlier age.

Finally, Weber's appeal is based in part on widespread acceptance of certain of his historiographical (as distinguished from philosophical) assumptions. Weber postulated that in the West, starting in the sixteenth century, an earlier "medieval" "feudal" "traditional" type of law was gradually superseded by a "modern" "capitalist" "formal-rational" type of law. To be sure, this conception was contradicted by some of his own historical insights (for example, the insight that the canon law of the "medieval" Roman Catholic Church was in fact "modern" and "rational" in his sense of those terms, and that the modern city — as we shall see below — also originated in the heyday of "feudalism"). Nevertheless, Weber associated the rise of capitalism and the rational bureaucratic state with Protestantism[9] and insisted on the "traditional" and "patrimonial" character of both feudalism and Roman Catholicism. This corresponded not only to the conventional historiography of the late

---

the positivist theory that values do not inhere in factual reality but are willfully imposed upon it. Schwarts, *supra* note 2, at 1387, incorrectly concludes that Kronman is arguing that Weber believes that each individual is entirely free to choose among existing values or entirely free to choose new values. She combats this view by pointing out that Weber also believed very strongly in the "givenness of things," and that "our choices are situated in interpretive contexts which are historically given." Schwartz misses the point that the givenness of *things*, for Weber, does not imply the givenness of the individual's own *values*, and that "interpretive contexts," for Weber, are only the values which numbers of individuals have attributed to things in the past. *Id.* at 1392.

8. At the end of World War I, Weber said, "[T]he fate of our times is characterized by rationalization and intellectualization and, above all, by the 'disenchantment of the world.'" "The ultimate and most sublime values," he declared, have "retreated" either into mystical experience or into intimate personal relations. Although he deplored this "disenchantment of the world" (including the world of law), Weber nevertheless rejected any role for scholarship other than that of maintaining "plain intellectual integrity" and of meeting "the demands of the day." *See* Max Weber, *Science as a Vocation*, in FROM MAX WEBER: ESSAYS IN SOCIOLOGY 155-56 (Gerth and Mills eds. 1958) [hereinafter FROM MAX WEBER]. This divorce between the vocation of science and the vocation of prophecy corresponds to the divorce between facts and values. It contributed to the defection of the German universities in the spiritual crisis of the 1920s and 1930s. *Cf. supra* note 5.

9. WEBER, GESAMMELTE AUFSATZE SUR RELIGIONSGESCHICHTE, Vol. 1, Part 1, translated by T. Parsons as THE PROTESTANT ETHIC AND THE SPIRIT OF CAPITALISM (1930).

nineteenth and early twentieth centuries but also to the left-wing socialist historiography of that era which postulated a historical evolution from feudalism to capitalism to socialism.

Respect for Weber is so great, and criticism of him has been on the whole, so subdued, that to state bluntly that his sociology of law is generally wrong and that his influence has been generally harmful will strike many readers as perverse. At the same time, his scholarship is so massive and so complex that it would take far more than a single essay to expose the fallacies in it. What I propose to do here is to analyze one portion of Weber's work, namely, his sociology of the city,[10] to criticize its historiography, and to show some of the connections between its weaknesses and the weaknesses of his legal sociology as a whole.[11]

Weber's urban sociology starts with an analysis of the structural unity of the Western city as a community at the time of its historical origin in the eleventh to thirteenth centuries. He wrote that although the rudiments of the Western type of city may be found occasionally in other cultures, "an urban 'community' in the full meaning of the word appears only in the Occident." "To constitute a full urban community," he stated, "a settlement had to represent a relative predominance of trade-commercial relations, with the settlement as a whole displaying the following features: (1) a fortification, (2) a market, (3) a court of its own and at least a partially autonomous law, (4) a related form of association, and (5) at least partial autonomy and autocephaly, thus also an administration by authorities in the election of whom the burghers participated."[12] Such a peculiar system of forces, according to Weber, could only appear under special conditions and at a particular time, namely, late medieval Europe.[13]

Although cast in historical terms, Weber's theory of the city fails even to mention, much less to explain, the most striking and distinctive characteristic of the Western city, namely, its historical consciousness — that is, its consciousness of its own historical movement from past to future, its sense of its own ongoing, developing character. Partly as a result of that omission, the constituent elements attributed by Weber to the "full

10. This analysis is drawn form BERMAN, LAW AND REVOLUTION: THE FORMATION OF THE WESTERN LEGAL TRADITION 399-403 (1983). The references to Weber are drawn chiefly from his book THE CITY (D. Martindale and G. Neuwirth eds. and trans. 1958).

11. *See also* Berman, *supra* note 11, at 546-554.

12. WEBER, *supra* note 11, at 54-55.

13. *Id.*

urban community" of the Occident reflect its structural integration but they do not account for its dynamic character, its development in time. They do not explain why or how the twelfth-century city developed into the city of the sixteenth and the twentieth centuries, many of whose characteristics are identical to, or at least continuous with, those of the twelfth-century city, but others of which are substantially different in degree if not in kind.

A typical twentieth-century city has the following characteristics: (1) it is a corporation, endowed with legal personality, with capacity to sue and be sued, hold property, make contracts, purchase goods and services, employ labor, borrow money; (2) it is a political entity, usually governed by a mayor or city manager together with an elected council, which may employ officials, levy taxes, exercise the right of eminent domain, and perform other governmental acts and functions; (3) it is an economic unit, which usually purveys or controls the purveyance of water, gas, electricity, and transportation, and regulates the construction and use of housing and the location of economic enterprises; and (4) it is an agency for the promotion of social welfare, including education, health protection, poor relief, and public recreation.[14] Like their twentieth-century progeny, the cities of twelfth-century Europe were also corporate, political, economic, and social entities; however, the range of their activities in each of these roles was much more limited than that of a present-day city. Much of what a city does today was done then within the city by guilds and by the church as well as by the extended family. Also the city today is much more integrated in, and much more representative of, the modern national state, an entity which was only beginning to come into existence in the twelfth century. Yet despite these differences, the present-day city developed, by a process of organic growth, out of the cities and towns that were created, or recreated, in the period of the Papal Revolution;[15] and that process of growth was part of its character as an urban community.

The process of growth of the Western city cannot be explained without reference to its historical self-awareness, its sense of its own historical continuity and development, its consciousness of its own ongoing charac-

14. *Cf.* WILLIAM BENNETT MUNRO, THE GOVERNMENT OF AMERICAN CITIES (1926).

15. The rise of the modern European city in the late eleventh and twelfth centuries, and its connection with other revolutionary social, economic, and political changes that accompanied the struggle of the Church under the papacy to free itself from imperial, royal, and feudal control, is described in Chapter 12 ("Urban Law") of BERMAN, *supra* note 10, at 356-403.

ter as a community, its own movement from the past into the future. Historically, this was connected, first, with the religious dimension of the Papal Revolution, and especially with the mission of the church gradually to reform and redeem the secular order. It was connected, second, with the political dimension of the Papal Revolution and especially with the belief in the coexistence of plural autonomous secular polities; it was this belief that made it both possible and urgent for citizens to form urban communes independent of royal, feudal, and even ecclesiastical authority — something that would have been unthinkable before the papacy desacralized kingship. It was connected, third, with the legal dimension of the Papal Revolution, and especially with the belief that the reformation and redemption of the secular order had to take place by the continual progressive development of legal institutions and periodic revision of laws in order to overcome the forces of disorder and injustice.

Strangely enough, Weber in a later chapter contradicted his own earlier statement of what constitutes the uniqueness of the medieval Western city. Without noticing the discrepancy, he attributed all five characteristics of a "full urban community" — which at first he had said "appears only in the Occident" — to the Asiatic and oriental city also. The latter, too, he stated, was a fortress and a market. It, too, contained farms held in socage (that is, in nonfeudal tenure) with land alienable without restriction, or hereditary in an unencumbered way or obligated only with a fixed land rent. It, too, had its own "autonomous constitution," which presumably meant its own form of association and at least partial autonomy and autocephaly.[16] In all these respects, the differences between the medieval occidental city and its Asiatic counterparts were differences — Weber stated — only in degree. What "absolutely" distinguished the Western city, he finally concluded, was the personal legal condition, that is, the *freedom*, of the citizen.[17] Serfs emigrating to the cities had a common interest, he stated, in avoiding the imposition of military or other services by their erstwhile lords. "The urbanites therefore usurped the right to violate lordly law. This was the major revolutionary innovation of medieval occidental cities in contrast to all others."[18] Weber went on to say that the "cutting of status connections with the rural nobility" had been connected with the formation of municipal corporations — legally autonomous communes. "Similar preliminary stages of the constitution

16. WEBER, *supra* note 11, at 91.

17. *Id.* at 92, 93.

18. *Id.* at 94.

of a polis or commune may have appeared repeatedly in Asia and Africa," he added. (Note the cautionary words "preliminary" and "may".) "However, nothing is known [in Asia or Africa] of a legal status of citizenship."[19]

Thus Weber eventually recognized, albeit obliquely, that there was something about Western law that was of critical importance in the rise of the Western city. Also, it appears, there was something critically important about Western religion as well — which Weber also dealt with only obliquely. He pointed out that in the Asiatic cultures, including China and India, it was impossible to bring all the inhabitants of a city together into a homogeneous status group. "Foremost among the reasons for the peculiar freedom of urbanites in the Mediterranean city, in contrast to the Asiatic," he wrote," is the absence of magical and animistic caste and sib constraints. The social formations preventing fusion of urban dwellers into a homogeneous group vary. In China it was the exogamous and endophratric sib; in India . . . it has been the endogamous caste."[20] Here Weber turned to Fustel de Coulanges' work to show that the ancient Greek and Roman cities did create a religious foundation of citizenship by substituting the city cult meal for the cult meal of the family. Yet Weber offered no explanation of the relationship of the religious factor to the legal and political factor; more particularly, he did not confront the fact that ancient Greek and Roman cities rested on slavery and lacked that "peculiar freedom of urbanites" which was, in fact, characteristic not of "the Mediterranean city" as such but of the Western European city of the late eleventh century and thereafter. Thus Weber stopped short of saying that the emergence of urban liberties in the West was part of a revolutionary *religious* change, in which, on the one hand, the ecclesiastical polity declared its independence from all secular polities, and, on the other, the very concept of secular polities was for the first time created and secular polities were said to be reformable and redeemable by law.

Why did Weber misjudge the role played by law and religion in the origin and development of the Western city? And why did he miss entirely the role of Western historical consciousness, including the Western belief in the organic growth of legal institutions over generations and centuries?

19. *Id.* at 96.
20. *Id.* at 97.

Karl Marx had attributed changes in social consciousness, including religious and legal consciousness, to changes in technologies for meeting economic needs (the mode of production), and in the class struggle to control those technologies (relations of production). Weber, on the other hand, believed that in addition to the economic forces that determine social consciousness there are also political forces — in other words, that the drive for political power is an independent objective force and not (as Marx had thought) merely a reflection of economic conditions ("relations of production"). For Weber, therefore, the rise of the Western city in the late eleventh and early twelfth centuries was due not merely to the development of a new mode of production (artisan and craft industry), which drew the serfs from the manor in opposition to their feudal lords, but also to the development of new political relationships. Weber could see that the nobility, too, had political reasons to favor the creation and development of cities. He also introduced other factors into the causal chain, including legal factors. But Weber, like Marx, believed that the idea of creating cities, the growth of communal consciousness within cities, and the development of urban legal and religious concepts which manifested such consciousness — that all these constituted "values" attributed to "factual" (economic and political) developments.

Western legal institutions cannot, however, be explained satisfactorily in instrumental terms as an ideology or a superstructure based on economic and/or political foundations; nor can they be explained as essentially factual phenomena to which people attribute values. They can only be satisfactorily explained in terms that encompass and go beyond both values and facts. Indeed, all given ("factual") legal institutions contain within themselves values, in the sense of meanings or purposes. They have, in other words, what Lon Fuller called their own internal morality.[21] This means that in interpreting a prevailing legal rule one cannot properly avoid treating the rule as both an "is" (it prevails, it has force) and an "ought" (it has a moral purpose, a *telos*). To take an obvious example, the legal requirement of a fair hearing cannot properly be understood as having either a "factual" content separate from the "values" it embodies or a "value" content separate from its "factual" existence.

Weber refuted Marxian historical materialism by showing that causal relations in history are more complex and more indeterminate than Marx and Engels had supposed. He wrote: "If we look at the causal lines we

21. *See* FULLER, THE MORALITY OF LAW (rev. ed. 1969).

see them run, at one time, from technical to economic and political matters, at another from political to religious and economic ones, etc. There is no resting point. In my opinion, the view of historical materialism, frequently espoused, that the economic is in some sense the ultimate point in the chain of causes is completely finished as a scientific proposition."[22] Nevertheless, Weber's fact-value distinction led him repeatedly to trace the derivation of legal institutions to political domination (*Herrschaft*). Both tradition and rationality were, for him, primarily sources of legitimation of political authority, whereby coercion could be more effectively exerted. His definitions of the state and of law were in terms of coercion. He defined the state as a "human community that (successfully) claims the *monopoly of the legitimate use of physical force* within a given territory,"[23] and he defined law as "an order . . .[which] is externally guaranteed by the probability that physical or psychological coercion will be applied by a *staff* of people in order to bring about compliance or avenge violation."[24] Thus, his belief in the objectivity of facts and the subjectivity of values led him, in his sociology of law, to a political (as contrasted with an economic) materialism.

Weber's emphasis on the political foundations of law is associated with his neglect of the creative role of historical consciousness in the development of new legal institutions. He defined a "traditional society" as one in which legitimacy is based on "the sanctity of age-old rules and pow-

22. Proceedings of the First Conference of German Sociologists (1910), *quoted in* MAX WEBER, I ECONOMY AND SOCIETY lxiv (G. Roth and C. Wittich eds. 1968). Weber's PROTESTANT ETHIC AND THE RISE OF CAPITALISM is sometimes cited as evidence of an idealist, as contrasted with materialist, interpretation of history. In it, however, Weber does not trace the effect of Protestant ideas and values on material economic and political developments as such. Instead, he traces their effect on capitalist ideas and values, arguing that Protestant "asceticism" contributed substantially to the development of a capitalist vocational ethic (*Berufskultur*). As Wolfgang Schluchter has said, "It is true that Weber's analysis can illustrate the general manner 'in which ideas become effective in history.' For this purpose he deals not only with the doctrines but also with their practical consequences. But this does not turn his analysis into a plea for a spiritualist or idealist interpretation of history." W. SCHLUCHTER, THE RISE OF WESTERN RATIONALISM: MAX WEBER'S DEVELOPMENTAL HISTORY 142 (G. Roth trans. 1981). Schluchter cites statements of Weber in which he repudiated both an idealist and a materialist interpretation of history as "foolish and doctrinaire" and argued that all culturally significant phenomena are subject to "both [ideal and material] causal relationships." *Id.* It should be noted, however, that Weber seems to identify materialism with economic materialism. His view of law as an instrument of political coercion, and of political coercion as part of an objective factual reality distinct from subjective values, may properly be called a form of political materialism.

23. Max Weber, *Politics as a Vocation*, in FROM MAX WEBER, *supra* note 9, at 78 (emphasis in original).

24. MAX WEBER, *supra* note 22, at 34 (emphasis in original).

ers," and "traditional law" as law "determined by ingrained habituation." He stated that innovations in traditional law can be legitimized only by disguising them as reaffirmations of the past. Thus tradition, for Weber, refers to some point or points in the past, not to an ongoing continuity from past to future. It is (in Jaroslav Pelikan's phrase) not tradition but traditionalism, not the living faith of the dead but the dead faith of the living.[25] It is historicism, not historicity.[26] It is partly because he neglected the dynamics of traditional law that Weber overlooked the role of law (and of religion) in the revolutionary formation and gradual evolution of the European city.

Not only traditional authority (based on historicism) but also the other three types of authority postulated by Weber — the charismatic (based on inspiration), the formally rational (based on logical consistency of rules), and the substantively rational (based on fairness and equity) — are defined narrowly, so that they appear to be mutually exclusive.[27] In fact, however, the Western legal tradition, as it existed from the late eleventh to the twentieth century, combined — and thereby transformed — all four of these "ideal types."[28] The Western city owes both its origins

25. *See* PELIKAN, THE VINDICATION OF TRADITION 65 (1984).

26. *See* BERMAN, TOWARD AN INTEGRATIVE JURISPRUDENCE, 76 U. OF CAL. L. REV. (July 1988).

27. Weber's definitions of his "ideal types" of law are summarized in MAX WEBER ON LAW AND ECONOMY IN SOCIETY (Rheinstein ed. 1966) at xxxviii - xliii. It should be noted that substantive rationality in law and economics, which emphasizes ethical considerations, utility, expediency, and public policy, does not, in Weber's concept, correspond to any historical type of society, although Weber saw it emerging in "the anti-formalist tendencies of modern legal development" and possibly in a future socialist society. MAX WEBER ON LAW AND ECONOMY IN SOCIETY, *supra* at 63-4, 303.

28. Weber's own formalism went so far that he denied the possibility of reconciling conceptualism ("formal rationality") and equity ("substantive rationality"). Thus he wrote that "the juristic precision of judicial opinions will be seriously impaired if sociological, economic, or ethical argument were to take the place of legal concepts." WEBER, 2 ECONOMY AND SOCIETY 894 (1978). He is right, of course, if his proposition is read literally, with emphasis on the words "take the place of." What is missing is the recognition that ethical argument, certainly, and only to a slightly lesser extent economic and sociological argument, are not only implicit but often explicit in the body of formal rules developed in all Western legal systems and especially in the body of case law that developed in the English and American systems. Ewing, *supra* note 4, defends Weber against the charge that he underestimated the adaptability of the English common law to the need for a legal system which would protect contracts and property and thus achieve justice in the capitalist sense. She neglects to say, however, as Weber neglected to say, that the doctrine of precedent which was developed in England and the United States in the seventeenth through nineteenth centuries probably produced *more* calculability than the system of codes and commentaries — the *Pandektenrecht* — of the Continental jurists. At the same time, the linking of formal rules with concrete fact situations, and thus the theoretical possibility of combining what Weber called formal and substantive

and its subsequent development to a considerable extent to this combination.

Weber's sociology of law has been generally harmful, in my opinion, because it has contributed substantially to the widespread belief that the basic reason for the existence of legal systems is to enable those who have "a monopoly of the legitimate use of physical force within a given territory" to effectuate their control over the people of that territory, and also because it has contributed substantially to the widespread tendency to label given legal systems in terms of specific ideological types, each associated with a specific type of political authority. Today, for example, it is common to characterize the American legal system as capitalist, individualist, and democratic, and to contrast it with the Soviet legal system, which is characterized as socialist, collectivist, and authoritarian — without recognizing that each of these legal systems combines all these characteristics and others as well. Weber's disenchantment, and his determination to distance his scholarship from the crisis of law which he saw coming, was reflected in his separation of legal systems into distinct and mutually exclusive "ideal" categories of the sacred, the historical, the logical, and the equitable. Both he and his followers were thus distracted from the constructive task of showing the ways in which, in any healthy legal order, these elements are made to interact.

rationality, and of combining both with tradition, is probably greater in the Anglo-American than in the nineteenth-century Continental system of legal thought.

Part III
Law, Experience and Belief: Durkheim, Durkheimians and Beyond

[5]

A Formal Restatement of Durkheim's "Division of Labor" Theory*

JACK P. GIBBS
Vanderbilt University

Despite frequent references in the sociological literature to Durkheim's theory about the division of labor, sociologists have made few attempts to test it. The paucity of attempts and the very debatable outcomes thereof are due largely to Durkheim's use of the traditional discursive mode of theory construction. A discursively stated theory's logical structure is likely to be obscure, and for that reason alone tests of it are difficult and controversial. Rather than perpetuate the exegetical tradition in sociological treatments of the subject, this paper restates Durkheim's theory in accordance with a particular formal mode. That restatement identifies the theory's shortcomings and problems. But the eight premises imply only one testable theorem, and the theorem's predictive accuracy appears minimal unless "population concentration" is substituted for "density" in the first axiom. Nonetheless, the restatement clearly shows how extension of the theory (additional postulates) could further its testability.

Frequent citations of Durkheim's *The Division of Labor in Society* ([1893] 1949) reflect its enormous impact on sociology; but sociologists have been content to comment on, refer to, criticize, or praise the theory, which is to say do everything short of attempting to test it (Clarke 1987, Krohn 1978, Land 1970, and Schwartz and Miller 1964 are salient exceptions). The rare attempts are not puzzling, nor are the controversial interpretations of test findings (especially Baxi 1974 and Udy 1965 disputing Schwartz and Miller 1964). Many sociologists are prone to assess theories in terms of preconceptions or presuppositions, rather than test outcomes and predictive power (more dimensions than testability and predictive accuracy). Such assessments are perhaps inevitable because so few sociological theories are testable, let alone such that there is effective consensus as to the defensibility of the tests. Why do sociologists so rarely state testable theories? Because they persistently use the discursive mode of theory construction, which is nothing more than the conventions of a natural language (French, English, etc.); and they resist any formal mode, meaning any set of rules for stating a theory, some or all of which transcend natural language conventions. That persistence and resistance manifest a reliance on a rhetoric of preconceptions or presuppositions (e.g., conflict, not consensus, is the basis of social order) when assessing a theory, rather than a concern with testability and test outcomes. Indeed, unless a sociologist is convinced that scientific theories should be assessed by exclusive reference to predictive power, it would be folly for her/him to adopt formal theory construction.

*Address correspondence to Jack P. Gibbs, Apt. 3-J, 1801 Lavaca St, Austin, TX 78701; e-mail: Gibbs7000@aol.com.

Consistent with the foregoing, this paper restates Durkheim's "division of labor" theory in accordance with a particular formal mode of theory construction.[1] The primary goal is identification of the theory's shortcomings and problems, especially with a view to testability.

DENSITY AND THE DEGREE OF DIVISION OF LABOR

Durkheim's theory is important if only because of its ostensible scope—the number and inclusiveness of variables (dependent variables, in the case of explanatory scope). Because of the theory's discursive form, its scope—a dimension of predictive power distinct from predictive accuracy—cannot be assessed precisely or confidently. Yet Durkheim surely made arguments about both the division of labor and certain features of law.

The First Premise: Axiom 1

Commentators commonly ignore the biotic character of one of Durkheim's arguments about the causes of the division of labor. It is introduced by this question: Given some area (e.g., a mountain range), how much animal life will it support? An animal ecologist might respond that it depends—the greater the variety of species, the greater the volume of animal life. Elaborating, given only one species—say, sheep—each animal makes the same demands on the environment. Such commensalistic competition permits less animal life than do combinations of symbiotic, parasitical, and predatory relations (as among insects, birds, deer, and cats).

In *The Division of Labor in Society* (hereafter referred to as *DOL*; unless otherwise indicated, all page numbers refer to it), Durkheim (266–75) extended such reasoning to the situation in which the density of hunter-gatherers or agriculturalists increases over several generations without any increase in the division of labor. The outcome would be, Durkheim suggests, lethal competition for land and food. So as population density increases, survival eventually requires a greater division of labor. Described in terms of illustrative occupations, symbiosis—rather than commensalistic competition—links a farmer, blacksmith, and baker. So we arrive at Axiom 1 in the formal restatement: *Among countries or for a country over time, density is the positive determinant of the degree of division of labor.*

Relational terms or phrases. Defined all too briefly, a scientific theory comprises at least two logically related generalizations. The mode of formulation may require that in each generalization there is a term or phrase signifying the kind of relation that assertedly holds between the constituent variables. Without a clear "relational" term or phrase, idiosyncratic tests of the generalization are virtually inevitable. Moreover, unless the terminology is consistent with explicit rules of deduction, purported derivations of theorems (or conclusions) are debatable. Fortunately, relational terms or

[1] The mode is set forth in Gibbs (1994:279–364). There are several contending formal modes in sociology's literature (see Gibbs 1990 for references), and their contrasts should alarm advocates of formal theory construction. Indeed, dissensus among the advocates may have doomed their common cause; but when assessing theories in terms of their predictive power *relative to that of contenders*, any formal mode offers more than the discursive mode. The latter reduces *testability* and makes it difficult to judge any of the other six dimensions of predictive power (Gibbs 1994:8–20, 386–87). Illustrating briefly, *parsimony* is indicated by the ratio of conclusions to premises. But it is difficult even to identify the premises and theorems in a discursively stated sociological theory, let alone determine how each conclusion was deduced.

phrases and deduction rules need not be devised for each theory; both should be given by the formal mode of theory construction in use.

The relational phrase in this restatement of Durkheim is "the positive determinant," "the negative determinant," or "greater ... greater." Those are not among the bewildering variety of Durkheim's terms. Examine this passage (257): "The division of labor develops ... as there are more individuals sufficiently in contact to be able to act and react upon one another. If we ... call this relation and the active commerce resulting from it dynamic or moral density, we can say that the progress of the division of labor is in direct ratio to the moral or dynamic density of society. But this moral relationship can only produce its effect if the real distance between individuals has itself diminished in some way. Moral density cannot grow unless material density grows at the same time, and the latter can be used to measure the former."

The immediate problem is that the relational terms are difficult to identify, much less interpret; and there are hundreds of others in the *DOL*.[2] So relational terms alien to Durkheim are necessary to restate his theory formally. However, the use of particular causal terms is an issue. Numerous scientists and philosophers call for a causal language in stating a theory, but they do so without recognizing that the language cannot be both simple and unambiguous. Consider an assertion in the form of "*X* causes *Y*." Even ignoring the need for evidential criteria, the assertion leaves four questions unanswered. First, is reciprocal causation denied? Second, does it mean that an increase in *X* causes an increase in *Y* (positive causation) or that an increase in *X* causes a decrease in *Y* (negative causation)? Third, is the causation bidirectional or unidirectional (if positive and unidrectional, an increase in *X* causes an increase in *Y* but a decrease in *X* does not cause a decrease in *Y*)? Fourth, which type of causation—partial, paramount, exclusive, and so on—is denoted by the term "causes"?

Although space limitations preclude elaborate rationales, all premises in this restatement assert asymmetrical (nonreciprocal), bidirectional, and paramount or exclusive causation. Should even paramount causation appear unrealistic, Durkheim rarely suggested partial causation. So, whatever Durkheim meant by "density," he regarded it as being at least the paramount cause of the division of labor. The bidirectional versus unidirectional distinction is perhaps even more controversial. Although Durkheim ignored the distinction, bidirectionality is assumed here for two reasons: first, it is more conventional than unidirectionality; and, second, assuming unidirectionality would make tests of the theory much more difficult. Alternative interpretations of causation types should be entertained (see Turner 1990), but the crucial question is, "How can a restatement further the theory's testability and predictive accuracy?" and not "What did Durkheim mean?"

Unit terms or phrases. The unit phrase in Axiom 1 and all other subsequent empirical generalizations is "among countries or for a country over time." Without an explicit unit term or phrase, any empirical generalization is ambiguous, because (1) it fails to signify the kinds of entities (classes of things or events) that should be compared when testing the generalization, and (2) there is no indication whether the generalization is a longitudinal assertion or a cross-sectional assertion or both. So a formal mode of theory construction should require an explicit and consistent unit

[2] Another problem is that of distinguishing synthetic statements (empirical generalizations in particular) from analytic statements (definitions in particular). The discursive mode blurs that distinction, but a formal mode can avoid the problem by requiring two explicit divisions of each theory: the *intrinsic* part for synthetic statements (axioms, postulates, etc.) and the *extrinsic* part for analytic statements (definitions, formulas, etc.).

term or phrase in each component generalization of a theory. Such a rule is needed all the more because sociology has an astonishing number of unit terms or phrases (e.g., societies, countries, organizations, age groups, cities, families, communities), and it is inconceivable that any sociological theory holds for *all* types of units, let alone equally well.

One likely objection is to the use of the term "country." The alternative—"society"—is more consistent with Durkheim; but that term's meaning is extremely vague, and numerous conceptual problems perhaps prompt sociologists—including Durkheim—to leave "society" undefined. In particular, should "country" and "society" appear to be synonymous terms, note that the latter term can be construed as designating types of social units *in addition to countries*, such as tribes. Yet, for reasons stated subsequently, the restatement does not apply to several types of social units (e.g., tribes, cities). So "country" is the unit term, not just to avoid ambiguity, but also to promote testability and predictive accuracy.

Another issue is posed by the unit phrase "Among countries." Durkheim took an evolutionary stance; hence, his generalizations predominantly pertain to *change* (i.e.,"longitudinal"), and that is the rationale for "over time" in the unit phrase. Yet some of his generalizations are cross-sectional, and the theory's "range" dimension of predictive power would be less if its unit phrase precluded those generalizations, a point ignored by Udy (1965) when criticizing Schwartz and Miller's use of cross-sectional data in testing Durkheim's theory.

The Second Premise: Postulate 1

The first variable in Axiom 1 is "density," but some interpretations of Durkheim describe social or moral density as being a cause of the division of labor (Land's 1970 version and Clarke's 1987 version use still another term—"dynamic density"). Divergent interpretations are inevitable, for Durkheim actually made *two* causal arguments. One identifies material density as causal, contending that lethal commensalistic competition ensues if material density increases without increases in the division of labor. Yet just a few pages previously (256–63), Durkheim described increases in moral or dynamic density as causing the division of labor. The contrast cannot be ignored by equating "moral/dynamic density" and "material density." Durkheim used the latter term in the sense of "residential population density," but the meaning of moral or dynamic density is obscure unless it is interpreted as pertaining to the *frequency of interaction* (see Turner 1981:382).

Durkheim's argument about material density has one major advantage; it suggests "how" the division of labor avoids the lethal commensalistic competition. By contrast, it is not clear how moral or dynamic density generates potentially lethal commensalistic competition. Indeed, if foragers or agriculturalists compete for land, they are competitors, regardless of their interactions. Nor is it clear how or why "active commerce" necessarily results from moral or dynamic density (257), even granting that commerce reflects a division of labor.

The construct-concept distinction. The only way to avoid the ambiguity in Durkheim's causal argument is to make "density" the causal variable in Axiom 1, meaning residential population density *and/or* interaction frequency. The definition's equivocation alone mandates identification of "density" as a *construct*.

A construct is a term that the theorist may not define (a "theoretical" primitive term); if it is defined, the theorist regards the definition as too ambiguous and/or incomplete to be empirically applicable. By contrast, a "concept" is a term that the theorist does define, and he/she regards the definition as unambiguous and complete. That is the primary basis for characterizing a concept as sufficiently empirically applicable.

A term, definition, formula, or research procedure is empirically applicable *to the extent* that independent investigators (1) regard it as intelligible, (2) consider it as feasible to apply, and (3) agree when applying it to identify particular things or events, possibly reporting values as attributes of those things or events. Should a concept denote a quantitative phenomenon, it is linked in the theory with a *referential*, an acronym that denotes a formula and stipulations of requisite data. The theorist expressly or implicitly identifies the formula as being *sufficiently* empirically applicable (i.e., such that the theory's predictive accuracy exceeds that of contenders).

The feasibility requirement takes on special significance in the case of moral or dynamic density. Again, the meaning of either term is hopelessly vague unless translated as "frequency of interaction," but it is pointless to contemplate counting interactions even in a small city, much less a country. Even ignoring requisite research resources, various technical or ethical problems would preclude it.

First postulate. Durkheim asserted that moral or dynamic density and material density are positively correlated, and (257) "the latter can be used to measure the former." So the second premise is Postulate 1: *Among countries or for a country over time, the greater the density, the greater the residential population density.*

The rational term (greater ... greater) signifies positive covariation, the reason being that "density" cannot be defined such as to identify its connection with residential population density as causal. Yet Durkheim (257) assumed that the association between the two variables—moral or dynamic density and material density—is positive and very close, even though it is "useless to try to find out which has determined the other."

The Third Premise: Transformational Statement 1

The conventional definition of residential population density is the number of residents of an area as a ratio to the number of square miles or kilometers in that area. That definition is regarded as complete and unambiguous. Hence, the term is identified as a concept, and it is linked with a referential in Transformational Statement 1: *Among countries or for a country over time, the greater the residential population density, the greater the RRPD at* T_{0-1}. The temporal quantifier (T_{0-1}) signifies "any point in any calendar year," and the initial "R" is needed to underscore the distinction between the designation of a formula (i.e., the referential RRPD) and the concept (residential population density, in this case) to which it is linked in the statement.

The referential formula is $RRPD = P/A$, where P is the number of residents of an area at some particular point in time, and A is square miles or kilometers in the area at that time. The data pertaining to P and A are to come from the official census reports (individual countries) or from the publications of international agencies, such as the United Nations Statistical Office.

THE DIVISION OF LABOR AND OCCUPATIONAL DIFFERENTIATION

At no point in the *DOL* does Durkheim explicitly define the division of labor; and although the term clearly pertains to a quantitative phenomenon, Durkheim merely suggests that variety of occupations is the criterion of the *degree* of the division of labor. There are three objections. First, because the notion of "an occupation" is largely alien to foragers (hunting-gathering bands) and even to some horticulturalists, Durkheim's criterion implies that what anthropologists designate as tribes or bands have no division of labor. Second, "variety of occupations" ignores the distribution of population members among occupations (see Clemente 1972; Gibbs and Poston 1975). Third, "variety of occupations" does not get at functional interdependence, though it is a component of the division of labor recognized by Durkheim himself.

This definition avoids the third objection: the degree of division of labor is the amount of contrast among population members as regards their sustenance activities *and* the related amount of functional interdependence. A sustenance activity is an expenditure of energy in the production of what an economist would identify as a good, product, commodity, or service, though not necessarily one for exchange. Functional interdependence refers to (1) the reliance of humans on the exchange of goods, products, commodities, or services, and (2) the coordination or synchronization of activities in collaborative production. As such, the definition is compatible with both Durkheim's "societal" conception of the division of labor and Adam Smith's ([1776]1952) "organizational" conception, even though those two conceptions diverge. Indeed, the definition is compatible with both Marx's "social" and "workshop" divisions of labor (see Rueschemeyer 1986:10). However, the definition is not compatible with Kemper's (1972:743), which encompasses some sustenance activities and all manner of other human "arrangements" (e.g., a marriage ceremony): "The division of labor is an arrangement of actors whose coaction is required to complete a common task or attain a common goal."

Although the definition of a sustenance activity proposed above is not alien to any social unit (e.g., a tribe, a family), there is no prospect of a feasible measurement procedure. So "degree of division of labor" must be treated as a construct, but the notion is not hopelessly vague. In particular, the definition obviously does not pertain to *bases* of the division of labor, meaning *correlates* of differentiation in sustenance activities, such as age and gender. That point contradicts Friedson's (1976:307) assertion that the "degree of division of labor is ... inseparable from the bases of the division of labor." Granted, there can be no basis without some division of labor, but even a high degree is logically possible without any discernible basis.

The Fourth Premise: Postulate 2

The discursive mode of theory construction is contrary to this principle: unless constructs appear *only* in the premises (i.e., *not* in the conclusions), the theory cannot be tested defensibly.[3] Nonetheless, Durkheim's allusions to the variety of occupations suggest a construct-concept link, as in Postulate 2: *Among countries or for a country over time, the degree of division of labor is the positive determinant of occupational differentiation.* Before considering a defense of the causal assertion, note that the deductive implications would not be altered by replacing the causal term with a covariational term (here, "greater ... greater").

The concept. Occupational differentiation is defined as the number of occupations in a population and the evenness or uniformity of population members among those

[3]The use of the discursive mode in sociology has scarcely declined since Durkheim. Moreover, many treatments of Durkheim's theory (e.g., Garnsey 1981; Krause 1982; Rueschemeyer 1986) are a far cry from restatements, but along with the seven papers in Issue 1, Vol. 9 of *Sociological Forum* 1(9), they have served to check what may be (judging from the literature) a decline of sociological interest in the subject.

occupations. Although Durkheim focused on the number (variety) of occupations, note again that the distribution of population members among occupations is also relevant.[4] Even if there are thousands of occupations, it would be possible for over 99.0 percent of those engaged in sustenance activities to be in *one* particular occupation (for elaboration, see Clemente 1972:33–34).

Because the definition of "occupational differentiation" is considered to be clear and complete, the term is a concept and subsequently linked with a referential. However, note again that the term "occupation" does not apply readily—if at all—to some nonliterate peoples. In such social units, the sustenance activities of individuals vary so much over time—perhaps even hourly—and/or differ so little among individuals that they cannot be said to have an occupation; rather, each active adult tends to be a jack-of-all-trades. So there is a justification for the terms "countries" and "country" in the unit phrase—the term "occupation" is not alien to that type of social unit.[5] It is also not alien to various types of *intranational* territorial divisions (e.g., cities, metropolitan areas). But at that level a relatively low degree of occupational differentiation may be indicative of territorial specialization and concomitant functional interdependence, rather than a low degree of division of labor, another justification for the unit terms "country" and "countries."

The causal assertion in Postulate 2. The postulate's causal character is best understood by recognizing, unlike Durkheim, that occupational titles reflect social recognition of contrasts in the sustenance activities of population members. As those contrasts increase, individuals specialize in some type of sustenance activities; and eventually those who specialize in the same type are labeled socially, meaning that the eventual consequence is a set of occupational titles (e.g., baker, carpenter, blacksmith). In brief, differentiation in sustenance activities—one of two components of the division of labor—*causes* social recognition of categories.

Far from expressing a purely logical relation, Postulate 2 entails two assumptions. The first assumption—a positive causal association between *contrasts* in the sustenance activities of residents of a country and corresponding occupational differentiation—cannot be tested, because there is no feasible way to measure the contrasts in question for the residents of even one country. The second assumption is that of a close positive association between occupational differentiation and functional interdependence. Because a feasible measure of the amount of functional interdependence in a country is wanting, the second assumption cannot be tested; but it is empirically contingent nevertheless. As for treating gross national product (GNP) as a measure of functional interdependence, GNP may reflect the volume of exchange, but it does not reflect the amount of behavioral coordination and synchronization in collaborative production, as on an assembly line. That objection extends to linking functional

[4] Durkheim occasionally also alluded to industries (e.g., manufacturing); and were it not desirable to simplify the restatement, another postulate would link the division of labor and industry differentiation.

[5] This argument is consistent with the long history of economic anthropology (e.g., Herskovitz 1940), and it is not contradicted by Watson's (1929) survey of the division of labor into 30 "tribes." Those social units did differ substantially as to principal means of subsistence (e.g., some foragers, others agriculturalists), but Watson equated the division of labor with the presence of different *types* of activities (Watson's "divided activities"), rather than *socially recognized differences* among individuals as regards sustenance activities. Watson's (1929:632) claim that specialization "by craft and occupation may be found in some form in every preliterate tribe" is not based on an explicit criterion; and surely "regular activities" (Watson 1929:638) does not mean social recognition of individual differences, occupational designations especially. As for Murdock's (1937) observations on the division of labor by sex, he used the terms "occupations" and "activities" as though they are interchangeable. A variety of sustenance activities occurs in perhaps *all* nonliterate social units, even those of foragers (see especially Maryanski and Turner 1992), but that variety cannot be equated with distinct occupations.

interdependence with input-output relations among industries (Ervin 1987). The general point: a measure of occupational differentiation is not a *measure* of the degree of division of labor (see references in the measurement section of Keon and Carter 1985).

The Fifth Premise: Transformational Statement 2

As used in the social and behavioral sciences—sociology in particular—the language of operational definitions or indicators is conducive to a premature termination of theory construction. The point is not just that a theorist should stipulate the research procedure for testing his/her theory rather than blithely leave it to others. Additionally, the procedure should enter into the deduction of predictions (hypotheses) about particular units from the theorems when testing the theory. The initial step has been indicated previously in connection with residential population density, and the next is Transformational Statement 2: *Among countries or for a country over time, the greater the occupational differentiation, the greater the ROD at* $T_{0\text{-}1}$.

The prescribed referential formula is $\text{ROD} = (1 - [\sum X^2/\sum X^2])/(1 - [1/Nc])$, where X is the number of members of some designated population in a particular occupational category and Nc is the total number of occupational categories. Data pertaining to X and Nc can be obtained from census reports or from publications of international statistical agencies (e.g., the United Nations Statistical Office).

The foregoing stipulation of data sources is not implied by the definition of occupational differentiation. Rather, it is dictated by a concern with the feasibility of application, and it reflects judgments about the quality of particular *kinds* of data. Why is the ROD formula designed so as to eliminate the influence of *number* of occupational categories? Because there is every reason to assume that international variation in that number in census reports is arbitrary and bears little if any relation to the variation in the *true* number.

The character of transformational statements. Whereas operational definitions and designations of indicators tend to blur the distinction between logical (conceptual) relations and empirical relations, transformational statements are not ambiguous: they implicitly assert empirical relations. As a case in point, Transformational Statement 2 implies this claim: if the true amount of occupational differentiation were known for each country and the stipulated referential formula has been applied correctly to the stipulated kind of data, there will be a substantial positive correlation between those true amounts and the ROD values (referents). The claim stands even if the theorist has doubts as to what formula and kinds of data would be ideal. For that matter, even when the specified formula obviously departs from the ideal, the claim is not invalidated. In the present case, whatever the ideal formula may be, it would express both number of occupations and distribution. Although the ROD formula reflects only distribution, the ROD values could be highly correlated (positively, internationally) with values representing the true amounts of occupational differentiation.

The foregoing applies to the RRPD formula as well as to the ROD formula. Even though the RRPD formula is totally consistent with the definition of "residential population density," in Transformational Statement 1 that concept refers to the values that would be computed if the RRPD formula were applied correctly to *absolutely reliable data* pertaining to P and A, meaning the true P values and the true A values. Just as those true values are unknowable, so is the true amount of residential population density in any country.

THE DIVISION OF LABOR AND NORMATIVE CONSENSUS

Unlike most versions of Durkheim's theory, the present restatement makes no use of "mechanical solidarity" and "organic solidarity," but the immediate justification for this is not the nebulous meaning of those terms. Instead, whereas Durkheim created the impression that the two terms denote causal variables, "mechanical solidarity" is merely the *label* that Durkheim used to identify a social solidarity based on likeness and normative consensus (see 70, 106, 109, 130), while "organic solidarity" is the label for a social solidarity based on functional interdependence (see, e.g., 129). Granted, although Durkheim (192) evidently thought that an increase in one basis of social solidarity is *necessarily* accompanied by a proportionate decrease in the other basis, neither term—neither "mechanical solidarity" nor "organic solidarity"—plays an essential role in his theory.

The Sixth Premise: Axiom 2

Durkheim suggested (see, e.g., 61, 129–31, 149, 283) that as the division of labor increases, normative consensus is eroded. So we have Axiom 2: *Among countries or for a country over time, the degree of division of labor is the negative determinant of normative consensus.*

Some possible objections. Although translations of Durkheim from French to English exclude the term "normative consensus" (yet see 152), his allusions to shared beliefs of a moral or ethical nature (e.g., 99–103) and his observations on the collective conscience (especially 70) justify the present use of the term. Indeed, whereas Durkheim frequently suggested the possibility of a moral or ethical belief being shared *throughout* a society (i.e., maximum normative consensus), it is realistic to assume that the principal difference among societies or over time is the *amount* of sharing within each society at any point in time.

Axiom 2 asserts at least paramount causation, and that quality may fuel suspicion that Durkheim has been distorted. Granted, the relation is far more complex than is suggested by the axiom (see, especially, Turner 1981:384–87), but the *DOL* does not contain an explicit assertion of other causes of *variation* in normative consensus (or shared beliefs). Moreover, the subsequent statement of a rationale makes the generalization more plausible.

The rationale. Durkheim never confronted this question: How does the division of labor determine normative consensus (meaning shared moral/ethical beliefs)? Three considerations are steps toward an answer. First, differentiation in sustenance activities is one of two dimensions of the division of labor. Second, sustenance activities are repeated and patterned rather than idiosyncratic. Third, moral/ethical beliefs are neither innate nor acquired through unique experiences. Those considerations suggest this relation: normative consensus reflects homogeneity of experience, the only paramount determinant of which that varies substantially among countries and over time is differentiation in sustenance activities. Activities associated with age and gender roles are also commonly repeated and patterned, but general observations suggest that age-sex composition does not vary internationally as much as does differentiation in sustenance activities.

The foregoing provides a rationale for Axiom 2 (see also Turner 1990:1095), one that is consistent with Marx's economic determinism. Yet Durkheim made only passing reference in the *DOL* to Marx (393), even though Marx's interest in the division of labor was almost as keen as Durkheim's (for a treatment of the Marx-Durkheim-Weber positions, see Rueschemeyer 1986). Nevertheless, Durkheim, Marx, and Weber shared a keen interest, not only in the division of labor, but also in "order" or "cohesion" (Sheleff 1997; Wrong 1994).

Conceptual problems. Virtually all definitions of a norm suggest a *qualitative* character; hence, a particular norm (e.g., the proscription of premarital sex) is either present or absent in any social unit. That character creates some insoluble problems (for elaboration, see Gibbs 1981), one of which is introduced by this "sufficient consensus" question: What percentage of social unit members must make or subscribe to an evaluative statement for it to be a norm? Any answer would be vague, arbitrary, or unrealistic if 100.

Because normative consensus is a quantitative phenomenon, the "sufficient consensus" question does not arise. So a feasible measurement procedure may appear to be the only problem. Unfortunately, feasibility is not the only difficulty. The only way to gather relevant data systematically is through surveys in which social-unit members are asked normative questions, such as: Do you approve or disapprove of smoking marijuana? The question illustrates four problems. First, whatever the social unit, innumerable normative questions could be posed, and there is no defensible procedure for a *random* sample. Second, both the *direction* (approval/disapproval) and the *intensity* of evaluations should be considered in measuring normative consensus, but the appropriate method—including the wording of normative questions—is very debatable. Third, the marijuana question does not identify any characteristic of smokers (e.g., age) or the situation (e.g., public versus private), but surely humans take such contingencies into account when evaluating conduct; and just as surely there is no way to recognize all possibly relevant contingencies when posing normative questions. Fourth, although the marijuana question pertains to the respondent's *personal evaluations* of conduct, what of *personal expectations, perceived evaluations* (what the respondent believes others believe), *perceived expectations*, and *punitive reactions* to particular acts? Elaborating on the fourth problem, while it would be arbitrary to exclude any of the five normative dimensions (especially if the ultimate concern is with the identification of the *normative* determinants of behavior), there is no feasible way to get at all dimensions, let alone combine them in one measure of normative consensus.

The foregoing problems indicate why there is no real prospect of an empirically applicable definition of a norm or normative consensus. Moreover, even if an ideal procedure for measuring normative consensus could be devised, the resources required for its application to even a few countries would be prohibitive. So there are myriad reasons for identifying "normative consensus" as a construct.

A Missing Postulate

Identifying a term as a construct poses no problem if it is linked with a concept. Unfortunately, Durkheim never came close to an explicit generalization that suggests a link between normative consensus and any concept. The immediate implication, as indicated by Figure 1, is the preclusion of what would be the third postulate. An imaginative social scientist may eventually formulate that "missing" postulate; and it will be an *extension* of Durkheim's theory rather than only a formal restatement of it, but the restatement identifies what is needed in that extension.

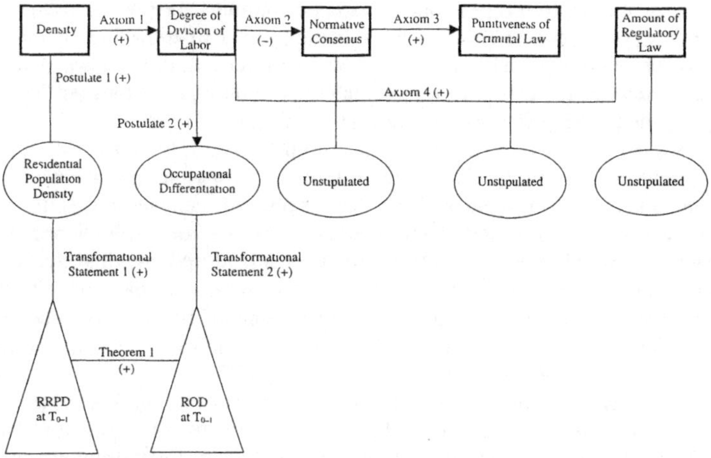

Significations: □ a construct; ○ a concept; △ denotes a referential forumla and instructions as to requisite data, both in the extrinsic part of the theory; (+) an increase causes an increase and a decrease causes a decrease, (–) an increase causes a decrease and a decrease causes an increase; (+ or –) a noncausal association

Figure 1. A diagram of a formal version of Durkheim's theory.

Although this paper's purpose is not to supply missing postulates or even survey possibilities, one illustrative *candidate* can be identified. At various points in *Suicide* ([1897]1951), Durkheim suggests that the suicide rate varies inversely with what is designated here as normative consensus. These suggestions are consistent with a long section in the *DOL* (246–49) where Durkheim elaborates on his claim that "suicide scarcely appears except with civilization" (246). However, those suggestions are made in connection with social integration, and it would be necessary to confront two of Durkheim's ([1897]1951) arguments: first, the suicide rate is supposedly a function of both social integration and social regulation; and, second, beyond some magnitude, social integration supposedly engenders "altruistic" suicides (Durkheim [1897] 1951:221).

NORMATIVE CONSENSUS AND THE PUNITIVENESS OF CRIMINAL LAW

Of all relations stated here, the least commonly recognized in versions of Durkheim's theory is that asserted in the seventh premise, Axiom 3: *Among countries or for a country over time, normative consensus is the positive determinant of the punitiveness of criminal law.*[6] Perhaps the relation is seldom recognized because ambiguities abound in Durkheim's statements about punishment and "collective sentiments" or "collective conscience." Beyond doubt, Durkheim held a consensual conception of crime and criminal law, as witness: "[W]e must not say that an action shocks the common conscience because it is criminal, but rather that it is criminal because it shocks the common conscience" (81). Yet earlier (77) he recognized that some acts are "an offense to collective sentiments," though not crimes (Durkheim refers to incest without

[6] Punitiveness is more explicitly the subject of Durkheim's "Two Laws of Penal Evolution" ([1899–1900] 1973), but that publication has less scope than his division of labor theory. See also Spitzer (1975).

acknowledging its criminalization in some jurisdictions), and later (82) he recognizes that some crimes do not offend collective sentiments (his example: fishing or hunting out of season). Moreover, his description of the state as an extension or embodiment of the collective conscience (or collective representations or collective sentiments) ignores the political, conflictive character of government (see Cotterrell 1999).

Despite some ambiguities, in various ways Durkheim suggests that (1) the punitiveness of a legal sanction varies directly with the extent of social disapproval of the type of crime and (2) social disapproval (or "the vivacity of the collective sentiments which are offended" [83]) and normative consensus are inseparable. However, that interpretation is disputable, because Durkheim admits that "[S]ome actions ... are more severely repressed than they are strongly reproved by general opinion" (82). But he then attempts to avoid the problem thus: "The extent of the activity which the governmental organ exercises over the number and the qualification of criminal acts depends on the force it receives" (85).

The foregoing notwithstanding, Axiom 3 is scarcely implausible; and Durkheim may have refrained from making the asserted relation explicit because of apparent isolated exceptions. Think of the matter in light of four generalizations. First, among types of crimes in a social unit or for any type over time, there is a positive association between the average gravity (perceived seriousness) of a type and the social disapproval of that type. Second, among types of crimes in a social unit or for any type over time, there is a positive association between the punitiveness of legal reactions to a type and the gravity of that type. Third, among social units or for any social unit over time, there is a positive association between the average social disapproval of all types of crime in a social unit and the amount of normative consensus in the social unit.[7] Fourth, a derived conclusion: among social units or for any social unit over time, there is a positive association between the amount of normative consensus in a social unit and the average punitiveness of legal reactions to crimes in the social unit.

Numerous statements by Durkheim (e.g., xiv, 77–81, 88–89, 99, 100–03, 108, 146, 152, 301) are consistent with the four generalizations. The following are illustrative. "Collective sentiments ... determine a reaction [to crime] of the same kind, which is as strong as they are intense" (xiv–xv). "They [penal reactions] are, in effect, more or less lively according to the vivacity of the offended sentiment, and also according to the gravity of the offense suffered. A strong state reacts more than a feeble state ..." (101).

The Punitiveness of Criminal Law

The term "punitiveness of criminal law" may refer to statutory penalties, to actual punishments, or to both.[8] Durkheim's statements scarcely provide a basis for a choice, and there is an insoluble problem regardless.

Punitiveness is a matter of degree, but there is no prospect of an empirically applicable referential formula. And feasibility of application is not the immediate problem. Consider "gang rape" as a reaction among some foragers to a woman condemned by public opinion for adultery. Now think of that reaction's punitiveness as compared to, say, 10 years in prison. The question is not just which is the more punitive, but also, how much more? The only obvious metric would be one of

[7] Normative consensus is defined, though not completely or clearly, as the amount of agreement among social unit members in their evaluations and expectations (personal and perceived) of acts in that social unit.

[8] Statutory and actual penalties are not exhaustive categories. Arrest and trial are perceived as punitive.

perceived punitiveness, but this question is then crucial: Whose perceptions? If the severity of a legal penalty in some territorial unit is to be judged by the residents only, an internationally comparable standard of punitiveness is a remote possibility at best. In any case, the difficulties in devising a feasible measurement procedure beggar description. All of the foregoing underscores the need to identify "punitiveness of criminal law" as a construct.

Another missing postulate. It is not the identification of "punitiveness of criminal law" as a construct that creates a problem. Rather, no statement in the *DOL* connects that or any similar term with a *concept*. Without the connection there can be no postulate in which the punitiveness of criminal law is a constituent variable. To make the situation worse, there is no obvious way to make the link that Durkheim failed to make.

Lest the problem be underestimated, consider a possible postulate: among countries or for a country over time, the greater the punitiveness of criminal law, the greater the statutory scope of the death penalty. The second variable can be defined as the proportion of all types of crimes for which execution is the prescribed penalty or one of the alternative penalties. That definition is so clear and complete that stipulation of a referential formula would appear redundant. Nevertheless, the generalization is objectionable for several reasons, one being the possibility of an identical death-penalty scope in two countries that differ radically as regards noncapital statutory penalties. The point is not that an extension of Durkheim's theory along the suggested line is impossible; rather, that it will require great ingenuity.

THE DIVISION OF LABOR AND THREE TYPES OF LAW

Durkheim's arguments about law expanded his theory's scope, but they are very narrow. Although Durkheim's interests in law were much broader, he treated law as an "external index" of social solidarity, a way of getting at a "moral phenomenon which, taken by itself, does not lend itself to exact observation nor indeed to measurement" (64).[9] So Durkheim's theory pertains to law only insofar as law "reproduces the principal forms of social solidarity" (68).

Two Types of Law

Durkheim's treatment of law is all the more narrow, not just because he recognized only two forms of social solidarity, mechanical and organic, but because he assumed that each form is manifested by only one of two types of law, repressive or restitutive. This part of Durkheim's theory—even his terminology—is unfortunate.

Repressive law. The repressive-restitutive distinction is couched in terms of sanctions. Durkheim said of repressive sanctions that they "consist essentially in suffering, or at least a loss, inflicted on the agent. They make demands on his fortune, or on his honor, or on his life, or on his liberty, and deprive him of something he enjoys. We call them repressive. They constitute penal law" (69). Given Durkheim's equation of

[9] Given the normative character of mechanical solidarity, Durkheim's allusion to it as a "moral phenomenon" is understandable; but the same characterization of organic solidarity reflects Durkheim's attempt to convince himself and the audience that organic solidarity is just as efficacious as mechanical solidarity (see, especially, Cotterrell 1999). For an extensive treatment of problems with the notion of solidarity, see Bayertz (1999:3–28), Kemper (1972), and Pope and Johnson (1983).

repressive law with penal law, it is puzzling that he did not use only the latter and far less esoteric term. Indeed, numerous statements in the *DOL* justify the present replacement of "repressive law" with "criminal law." Consider one illustrative statement: "The link of social solidarity to which repressive law corresponds is the one whose break constitutes a crime" (70).

Restitutive law. Durkheim defines restitutive law by reference to a distinctive kind of sanction: "[I]t does not necessarily imply suffering for the agent, but consists only of *the return of things as they were*, in the reestablishment of troubled relations to their normal state, whether the incriminated act is restored by force to the type whence it deviated, or is annulled, that is, deprived of all social value" (69). Because of its arcane terminology, the definition promises little agreement between independent investigators using the label "restitutive" to identify particular statutes. There are even doubts about entire major categories, such as Anglo-American tort law. It is debatable whether the administration of tort law "re-establishes troubled relations" in even the majority of cases, but Durkheim's aversion to psychological notions precludes reference to the intention of officials in enacting or administering statutes. Perception is also relevant in considering whether defendants "suffer" when paying tort damages, a possibility not negated by Durkheim's dismissal of Tarde's attempt "to find a sort of civil penalty in the payment of costs by the defeated party" (111).

Unfortunately, tort law is only one reason for doubting Durkheim's attempt to demarcate restitutive law. At various places, Durkheim suggests that restitutive law is a residual category—all laws other than criminal. Thus, he refers to it as comprising "civil law, commercial law, procedural law, administrative and constitutional law, after abstraction of the penal rules ... found there" (69).[10] Making restitutive law residual clarifies the notion, but generalizations about such a hodgepodge category strain credulity.

Regulatory law as the alternative designation. Although Durkheim specifically identifies (68) the division of labor as the cause of organic solidarity (actually, a conceptual rather than causal link), his characterization of restitutive law as an external index of organic solidarity does not even suggest an answer to this question: Why and how do increases in the division of labor cause increases in restitutive law? Durkheim's failure to confront the question directly reflects his reluctance to recognize human behavior's purposive quality. Hence, in Durkheim's view, laws are scarcely enacted to solve problems or, more broadly, realize goals. Rather, he writes—at least in the *DOL*—as though laws appear without conscious enactments. Contemplate these pronouncements:

> Punishment consists ... essentially in a passionate reaction of graduated intensity that society exercises through the medium of a body acting upon those of its members who have violated certain rules of conduct. (96)
>
> [A]lthough these rules [restitutive law] are more or less outside the collective conscience, they are not interested solely in individuals. If this were so, restitutive law would have nothing in common with social solidarity, for the relations that it regulates would bind individuals to one another without binding them to society. ... But society is far from having no hand in this sphere of juridical life. It is true that, generally, it does not intervene of itself and through its own

[10] Elsewhere, Durkheim added domestic law and contract law (122).

> movements; it must be solicited by the interested parties. But, in being called forth, its intervention is nonetheless the essential cog in the machine, since it alone makes it function. It propounds the law through the organ of its representatives. (113)

Durkheim's reifications and superorganicism led him to ignore law's instrumental quality (deterrence and incapacitation in the case of criminal law). And even his treatment of restitutive law reflects a seeming indifference to legislative actions to alleviate two problems created by the division of labor.[11] First, relations between producers and consumers become predominantly impersonal and anonymous, a condition conducive to fraud, hazardous products, and exploitation, in part because the transgressors have become invulnerable to extralegal sanctions (e.g., condemnation and ostracism). Second, the economy's components become extremely differentiated and functionally interdependent, thereby making the economy as a whole vulnerable to the malfunctioning of any component.[12] Unlike Durkheim's robots, real legislators—even dictators—are aware of such problems, though possibly unaware of their genesis in the division of labor. In any case, when officials undertake remedial action, it commonly takes the form of *regulatory law* (perhaps better designated as "regulatory/administrative" law). So whereas Durkheim's rationale for asserting a causal relation between organic solidarity and restitutive law is obscure, such is not the case when asserting a causal relation between the division of labor and regulatory law. An additional benefit of the terminological change is greater intelligibility; specifically, the meaning of "regulatory law" is clearer than that of "restitutive law," if only because the former has been a conventional term in Anglo-American jurisprudence for generations.

The proposed terminology appears contrary to Cotterrell's contention that "regulatory law is effectively left outside the scope of legal classification in *The Division of Labor*" (Cotterrell 1999:85). However, Cotterrell himself rightly recognized that Durkheim made "almost no effort to relate repressive and restitutive law precisely to familiar legal categories" (Cotterrell 1999:85).

The foregoing leads to Axiom 4: *Among countries or for a country over time, the degree of division of labor is the positive determinant of the amount of regulatory law.* As before, the causation is asserted to be asymmetrical (nonreciprocal), bidirectional, and paramount or exclusive.[13] However, even if the causation is bidirectional, it may well be that a decrease in the division of labor reduces regulatory law only if the decrease has been substantial over several generations. Durkheim notwithstanding, humans do not somehow uncritically solve problems, but they may cling to solutions for extinct problems.

The controversial exclusion of criminal law. At no point in the *DOL* does Durkheim suggest that criminal law disappears once the division of labor approaches the maximum. But he did not confront this question: If normative consensus should approach the minimum, why would criminal law continue? Perhaps it is necessary to preserve social order, especially as normative consensus declines. Yet that answer attributes an instrumental quality to law, something alien to Durkheim's theory. Moreover, although Durkheim displayed little interest in the absolute number of criminal laws, his statements suggest this generalization: as the division of labor increases, the ratio

[11] Durkheim wrote at length on the division of labor as a "problem" (especially 329–409), but the problem was always the maintenance of social solidarity.

[12] For a more extensive list of such problems and a more elaborate treatment, see Catton (1985).

[13] If only in light of the widely presumed contraction of regulatory law in the United States during the 1980s and no ostensible decrease in the division of labor, the causation asserted in Axiom 4 is surely debatable.

of restitutive law to criminal law increases. Two considerations prompted exclusion of that generalization from the restatement. First, the ratio would have to be treated as a construct, and linking it with a concept would be far more difficult than linking the construct "amount of regulatory law" with a concept. Second, for the generalization to hold, the division of labor must be positively associated with the amount of restitutive (regulatory) law but negatively associated with the amount of criminal law.

Elaborating on the second consideration, had Durkheim asserted a negative association between the division of labor and the volume of criminal law, the assertion would tax credulity.[14] Indeed, just the reverse possibility should be entertained: as the division of labor increases and normative consensus declines, criminal law expands to replace what were putative customs and mores as the only remaining basis for social order.

Still Another Missing Postulate

Although "regulatory law" is a more conventional term than "restitutive law," no one is likely to report some number as representing the amount of regulatory law in any legal system. Though all too real, problems in conceptualizing regulatory law are not the only consideration.[15] Unlike various kinds of law, the amount of regulatory law cannot be described in terms of number of statutes.

The enabling legislation that creates a regulatory agency (e.g., the U.S. Food and Drug Administration) is statutory, but the "laws" of that agency—if they can be so designated—take the form of directives and orders, rather than statutes. Hence, the very idea of counting "regulatory laws" is suspect.

AN ASSESSMENT OF THE THEORY'S PREDICTIVE ACCURACY

The use of a formal mode in *restating* a discursive theory reveals things about testability that may have been concealed. Thus, as already suggested (especially in Figure 1), only one testable generalization—the sole theorem—can be deduced from this formal version of Durkheim's theory; consequently, that version's predictive accuracy can be judged only by tests of that one generalization. However, it would be an illusion to suppose that the formal version somehow reduced the theory's testability. On the contrary, the formal mode only forces recognition of limited possibilities for *defensible* tests.

The Testability and Predictive Accuracy of the Sole Theorem

In accordance with the sign rule (Gibbs 1994:312–28), Axiom 1, Postulates 1–2, and Transformational Statements 1–2 imply this theorem: *Among countries or for a country over time, the greater the RRPD at T_{0-1}, the greater the ROD at T_{0-1}.*[16]

[14] Diamond (1965:12) and Seagle (1941:xiv–xv) have asserted that law is absent among some foragers, the very populations where, according to Durkheim, mechanical solidarity prevails and, hence, criminal law should flourish. Moreover, there is evidence (e.g., Land 1970) that the division of labor in the United States increased throughout the twentieth century, but there is no evidence of a decline in the volume of criminal law, federal or state. Indeed, Sheleff (1975:33) has commented on the *expansion* of criminal law as though universal.

[15] For a brief survey of the conceptual problems, see Gibbs (1989:405–06).

[16] Once each premise in a chain has been signed, a "+" (signifying positive causation or "greater ... greater") or a "−" (signifying negative causation or "greater ... less"), the conclusion's sign is negative if and only if an *odd* number of the premises have a negative sign. Erroneous arguments about the sign rule abound, and critics do not advance an alternative (for elaboration, see Gibbs 1994:325–27).

Because the referential formulas are empirically applicable, the theorem is testable.[17] The only doubt pertains to the temporal quantifiers, meaning designations of the relevant time periods. The causal character of Axiom 1 suggests that the empirical association would be closer if the ROD referents were lagged; but there is nothing in the *DOL* to suggest the lag's length, and the use of census data severely limits the alternatives. For many countries, because of census intervals, the lag must be exactly 10 years. Given that RRPD and ROD referents tend to change slowly, a 10-year lag probably would not make a substantial difference; hence, the two referents are to be for the same year, though the year may vary from one country to the next (e.g., 2000 for the United States but 2001 for Australia).

General observations on the theorem's predictive accuracy. Given the abundant opportunities to test the theorem, it is surprising that so few have been reported. That paucity probably reflects the traditional indifference of sociologists to testability and test outcomes when assessing a theory, but general observations are so *contrary* to the theorem that the paucity of tests is understandable. To illustrate, Australia, Canada, and the United States have much lower residential population densities than do China, Sri Lanka, and India, but occupational differentiation appears much greater for the *low*-density countries. Indeed, if there is any international association at all between population density *or* population size and occupational differentiation, it appears to be negative and, hence, completely contrary to the theorem (see Clarke 1987; Krohn 1978).

The evidence becomes complicated when general observations shift from cross-sectional to longitudinal comparisons (any country over time). In the longitudinal case, general observations are consistent with the theorem, meaning that increases in residential population density appear to accompany increases in occupational differentiation. Indeed, one of the few reports of research on the theory pertains to longitudinal data for the United States Land (1970) reported a substantial positive association for the United States over six decennial time points (1900 ... 1950) between occupational differentiation and three components of "dynamic density"—degree of urbanization, efficiency of the communication-transportation technology, and population size. Had he considered residential population density, he probably would have reported that it, too, is positively associated with occupational differentiation. Nonetheless, that finding would have been in stark contrast with general observation above on the cross-sectional (international) association between the variables. Moreover, although Land's research is perhaps the only way to salvage part of Durkheim's theory, there are two caveats. First, Land's independent variables depart from Durkheim in that the degree of urbanization pertains to concentration rather than to density, and Durkheim did not treat technological efficiency as a major variable (Turner 1981:384). Second, there is a need for a replication of Land's research for countries other than the United States (especially Ireland) and an extension of it to international (cross-sectional) comparisons.

An Interpretation of the Negative Evidence

Assume demonstration of a substantial positive association over time between residential population density and occupational differentiation. Then assume a

[17] Neither the premises nor the theorem imply the referential formulas signified in the theorem by RRPD and ROD. Accordingly, investigators are free to devise alternatives, but they will then have changed the theorem.

cross-sectional test of the restatement's theorem and an outcome consistent with general observations—no positive international association between the variables. Such *divergence* would not necessitate rejection of Durkheim's theory. The more constructive conclusion would be that a particular dimension of predictive power—intensity—is less for Durkheim's theory than for any contender that makes accurate predictions about *both types of relations* (longitudinal and cross-sectional) between occupational differentiation and some variable *other than* residential population density.

Durkheim's arguments about the relation between population (size and/or density) and the division of labor have no empirical support because of the functionalism that permeates much of his theory. Those arguments have a functionalist ring, because they depict the division of labor as meeting a "societal need"—avoidance of lethal competition and concomitant social disintegration as presumed consequences of increases in density. The very idea of societies having a "need" is a gross reification, and a functional explanation can be defended without invoking that idea.[18] Although functionalists in sociology ignore or deny it, a functionalist explanation couched in "latent" terms cannot be defended on empirical grounds if its explanatory mechanism is *other than* "selective survival," meaning that the pattern or uniformity in question (here, high density and high degree of division of labor) is explained by asserting that *exceptions* are eliminated (see Turner 1990:1091). However, support requires evidence that some minimum amount of the division of labor is necessary *as well as* sufficient for survival.[19] Should it be found that the amount is only sufficient, it would be evidence of *functional alternatives* (i.e., ways to meet the postulated "need"), and the explanation's predictive accuracy will suffer.

No imagination is required to identify possible alternatives to the division of labor as a means of avoiding lethal competition and concomitant social disintegration as possible consequences of increases in population density. Emigration is one; expansion of the population's boundary—perhaps through military action—is another (for elaboration, see Wallwork 1984:59). Those possibilities do not *necessarily* preclude a positive association between density and the division of labor, but there is nothing to prevent the operation of those alternatives independently of the division of labor; and the outcome could be a country having a high degree of division of labor but low density, a contradiction of the theorem.

Population concentration as the alternative causal variable. Several findings (e.g., Clarke 1987; Gibbs and Martin 1962; Krohn 1978; Land 1970) suggest that the predictive accuracy of the restatement's only testable theorem (Figure 1) would be substantial in *both* longitudinal comparisons and cross-sectional comparisons if "population concentration" were substituted for "density" in Axiom 1 and Postulate 1. The substitution is all the more desirable for two reasons. First, unlike Durkheim's "material density," the construct "population concentration" can be linked to the concept "degree of urbanization," which replaces "residential populations density" in Postulate 1; and that concept, in turn, can be readily linked with a referential formula. Second, unlike the case for moral or dynamic density, it can be argued that lethal competition and social disintegration will ensue if population concentration continues without increases in the division of labor.

[18] For elaboration on functionalism as a distinctive *kind of explanation*, see Gibbs (1989:chapter 9).

[19] Selective survival is not limited to mortality. To illustrate, divorce ends some marriages, and some occupations become extinct. Hence, the explanatory mechanism has wider application than it may appear.

The foregoing terminological change may be necessary to advance the predictive accuracy of Durkheim's theory.[20] Nevertheless, it would force recognition of this question: What would prevent a low degree of population concentration but a high degree of division of labor? If the answer is that a high degree of division of labor *requires* a highly concentrated population, it suggests a functional explanation in which population concentration, rather than the division of labor, meets some need. In any case, the causal direction of the relation between concentration and the division of labor would remain very debatable (see Kemper 1975).

General Observations Pertaining to Axioms 2, 3, and 4

Although general observations are a far cry from systematic tests, they are the only way in which Axioms 2, 3, or 4 can be assessed empirically. Anthropologists and historians commonly comment on features of sustenance activities in particular social units, and those commentaries suggest that some social units have a greater division of labor than others. Thus, no anthropologist is likely to question that prior to European subjugation, the division of labor was greater among the Yoruba than among the Comanche, and no historian would deny that the division of labor in Great Britain was greater in 1800 than in 1700. On the other hand, anthropologists might question any such judgment about the Aztecs (1500), Incas (1500), Haiti (2002), and Egypt (1000 B.C.).

The situation is worse when it comes to general observations on the amount of normative consensus. Even the common belief that normative consensus approaches the maximum in tribes or bands is debatable.

Ordinal judgments can be made about the difference between some social units as regards the punitiveness of criminal law, but appreciable agreement is a real prospect only if the criterion is the statutory scope of the death penalty. That criterion is debatable, if only because of the common contrast between statutory penalties and their administration. Then there is the problem of tribes and bands, where the presence of law—criminal or otherwise—is itself debatable (Diamond 1965; Seagle 1941). Accordingly, subsequent observations about the punitiveness of criminal law should be translated as "punitiveness of reactions to crime or deviance."

What has been said about judgments of the amount of normative consensus applies all the more to the amount of regulatory law. Indeed, judgments in that case are especially disputable because of problems in defining both law and regulatory law, such that independent observers could agree as to the presence or absence of those phenomena in particular social units, especially in nonliterate instances.

The ratio of restitutive laws to repressive laws. As indicated previously, at numerous points in the *DOL* Durkheim suggests this generalization: the greater the degree of division of labor, the greater the ratio of restitutive laws to repressive laws.[21] The generalization is less testable than is Axiom 4, if only because instances of two types of laws would have to be counted; nevertheless, more observations have been made on the generalization than on any other component of Durkheim's theory.

More than 60 years ago, Merton (1934:324) expressed doubts about the generalization. In the same year, Faris published a caustic review of the *DOL* in the *American*

[20] The change would be consistent with Durkheim's occasional references to population concentration (e.g., 257–58). However, if it is argued that he treated concentration as the principal causal variable, what of his more frequent references to density and some references to population volume (e.g., 262)?

[21] Because Durkheim never made the generalization truly explicit, it could be worded various ways, one being: a low degree of division of labor is associated with the preponderance of repressive law, and a high degree of division of labor is associated with a preponderance of restitutive law.

Journal of Sociology. Faris was no stranger to the anthropological literature, and he curtly dismissed Durkheim's arguments about "primitive" peoples. For that matter, numerous anthropologists have questioned Durkheim's arguments about mechanical solidarity (see, e.g., Pospisil 1971:134–35). As for Durkheim's statement about the preponderance of repressive laws in "mechanical" societies, consider Barnes's statement (1966:168): "[E]thnographic evidence shows that, in general, primitive societies are not characterized by repressive laws." Unfortunately, Barnes's statement is by no means atypical (see Cotterrell 1991, especially 925). Such statements were effectively ignored by McIntyre when she asserted that Durkheim "was almost certainly correct when he claimed that the *law* of these earliest societies was dominated by repressive and not restitutive law" (McIntyre 1994:78).

The criticisms of Durkheim's repressive/restitutive argument are debatable because they come only as general observations, some of which distort (e.g., interpreting Durkheim as asserting that all laws in "mechanical" societies are repressive). However, Schwartz and Miller's (1964) systematic comparison of 51 predominantly tribal social units went beyond general observations. They reported findings indicating an evolutionary sequence in the following "legal characteristics": mediation→police→legal counsel. On that basis, they questioned Durkheim's claim that the restitutive/repressive ratio increases with societal evolution (see also Schwartz 1974). In so doing, Schwartz and Miller (1964) ostensibly assumed that mediation reflects restitutive law and that police presence reflects repressive law, but the former appears to have preceded the latter (contrary to Durkheim). Wimberley's replication (1974) supports the Schwartz-Miller findings and appears even more contrary to Durkheim, for Wimberley concluded that there have been four evolutionary stages: mediation→judges and courts→police→legal counsel.

Udy (1965) questioned Schwartz and Miller's (1964) interpretation, alleging that an evolutionary sequence cannot be inferred justifiably from cross-sectional comparisons. However, neither Udy nor Schwartz (in reply 1965) recognized that an evolutionary sequence need not be assumed when assessing Durkheim's argument about the restitutive/repressive ratio. Rather, the argument can be interpreted as claims about *cross-sectional and longitudinal correlates* (causes or consequences) of the division of labor. In particular, the social units classified by Schwartz and Miller (1964: Table 1) as "mediation or without mediation but no police in either case" appear to have had less division of labor than those classified as "police but no legal counsel or police and legal counsel." So an evolutionary sequence need not be presumed to interpret the Schwartz-Miller findings (cross-sectional) as contrary to Durkheim's generalization about a particular correlate of the restitutive/repressive ratio. However, the suggestion is not that the issue is limited to the presumption or denial of an evolutionary sequence in the character of law. On the contrary, Durkheim's terminology and mode of theory construction made all manner of debates inevitable (see, e.g., Baxi 1974; Schwartz reply 1974).

Durkheim's generalization about the ratio has been excluded from the formal restatement, not just because of the empirical applicability of the notion of restitutive law but also because of negative evidence. Not even incontrovertible falsification of the generalization would corroborate Axiom 4, but neither would it invalidate that premise. Moreover, because Axiom 4 makes no reference to repressive (criminal) law, it poses less evidential problems than does the generalization about the restitutive/repressive ratio. But there is no denying the need for a postulate that links the construct "amount of regulatory law" with a concept.

An implied axiom. Of the four constructs in Axioms 2–4, plausible general observations can be made only on "degree of division of labor" and "punitiveness of criminal law." Consequently, a systematic empirical assessment of either Axiom 2, 3, or 4 is not possible. But general observations can be made in assessing this *implied* axiom: among countries or for a country over time, the greater the degree of division of labor, the less the punitiveness of criminal law. The axiom is implied by Axioms 2 and 3 (see Figure 1), and it is stated covariationally in recognition that the causation is indirect (i.e., through normative consensus).

As for the predictive accuracy of the *implied* axiom, it would be possible to make general but systematic observations on numerous "peoples" identified in Human Relations Area Files. Indeed, Spitzer (1975) came very close to such research, but because he focused on Durkheim's "Two Laws of Penal Evolution" ([1899–1900] 1973), the independent variables in his systematic comparisons of predominantly tribal social units do not include the degree of division of labor. Yet Spitzer's data do bear on Durkheim's distinction in his first law of penal evolution between "less" and "more" developed societies, and the distinction corresponds closely to "less" versus "more" division of labor. The findings indicate that the "intensity of punishment" (Durkheim's dependent variable) is much greater for those social units with *more* division of labor. That relation would hold, evidently, even among social units having more or less the same absolute character of central (political) power, the other independent variable in Durkheim's first law. That point is especially relevant when recognizing that Spitzer did not compare "countries." Even so, his findings generate doubts about the implied axiom.

Half right at most. Spitzer's comparisons should not be confused with Durkheim's survey (138–46) of various legal codes, from antiquity (e.g., Old Testament Israel, ancient Rome) to the Visigoths. The survey was undertaken to demonstrate that, over time, there has been an increase in the division of labor and a concomitant increase in the ratio of restitutive to repressive (criminal) laws.[22] That ratio has no necessary connection with the punitiveness of repressive (criminal) law, and Durkheim did not articulate a rationale for the implied assertion that, over time, the division of labor is correlated *negatively* with the number of repressive (criminal) laws but *positively* with the number of restitutive laws.

There are two reservations about Durkheim's survey. First, it remains to be seen whether independent investigators agree substantially in counting restitutive statutes and repressive statutes; and even if they should agree, statutes alone may not reveal the *true* volume of the two types of law in all legal systems.[23] Second, Durkheim merely assumed that the division of labor has increased *monotonically* since ancient times (Barnes 1966:168); but general observations on the Roman empire and Europe in the Dark Ages justify doubts.

Although Durkheim's survey is not directly relevant when assessing the implied axiom (the greater the division of labor, the less the punitiveness of criminal law), the same kind of survey might support that axiom. Thus, it appears that the death penalty's scope was much greater in, say, Babylonia, ancient Greece, or Imperial Rome than in any contemporary European country; and it also appears that the division of labor is much greater in contemporary Europe than it was in any

[22] Durkheim did not make the generalization explicit; and for an obscure reason he speaks of cooperative law rather than restitutive law, though indicating that the former is a subclass of the latter (139).

[23] The common-law tradition is alone sufficient to question an exclusive focus on statutory law.

antiquarian society. However, doubts about the relation are not limited to the possibility of a decline in the division of labor during the Dark Ages without an increase in the punitiveness of criminal law. As a case in point, the division of labor presumably increased in England during the 1700s; but capital offenses increased from about 50 in 1688 to over 200 in 1820 (Hay 1975:18).

Even if the historical trend has been consistent with the implied axiom, another kind of comparison indicates that, at most, Durkheim was only half right. He did not include foragers (hunters and/or gatherers) in his survey. Those populations are strategic because, of all commonly recognized types of social units (e.g., horticulturalists, peasant, feudal, industrial), foragers have the least division of labor.[24] Consequently, if the implied axiom is extended to social units in general, foragers should have the most punitive criminal law. Yet insofar as the Cheyenne (e.g., Llewellyn and Hoebel 1941), the Eskimos (e.g., Steenhoven 1962), the Ituri pygmies of Central Africa (e.g., Turnbull 1962), and the Kalahari foragers (e.g., Lee 1979) had criminal law prior to subjugation, punishments of offenders appear mild by any standard (see also various items in Lee's extensive 1992 bibliography of hunter-gatherer studies). In particular, it is disputable whether capital punishment prevailed in even the majority of foraging populations; and it is extremely questionable to identify instances of private vengeance as criminal justice.[25] So this pattern emerges: criminal law and/or reactions to deviance appear most punitive in social units where there is a *moderate* division of labor. Should systematic research confirm that possibility, the pattern will be a puzzle, and it will not do to say merely that Durkheim was half right. The implied axiom asserts a *negative monotonic* relation between the division of labor and the punitiveness of law; if that relation does not obtain, Axiom 2 and/or 3 must be abandoned or, at best, remain restricted to countries.

THE THEORY'S IMPORTANCE

For most policy purposes, an invalid theory cannot be important (though a valid theory is not necessarily important). Hence, if a formal mode promotes a theory's testability, it enhances the theory's potential importance; but a formal restatement may reveal negligible prospects for tests and thereby appear to diminish the theory's importance. The latter possibility is the case here, because the restatement indicates that three of the theory's four axioms cannot be tested directly or indirectly (Axiom 1 can be tested *indirectly* through tests of the sole theorem). Therefore, some comments on the importance of the untestable axioms are in order, if only to promote efforts to extend the theory in the form of additional postulates and thereby further its testability.

Goodbye to Normative Consensus

Barring some technological crisis (perhaps a *genuine* long-range energy shortage), the division of labor in the United States will continue to increase.[26] If so and if Axiom 2

[24] Note again that the degree of division of labor is distinct from its *bases* (e.g., age), even though there must be some degree for any basis to exist.

[25] Granted the difficulties of judging punitiveness, especially cross-culturally, hunters and gatherers have not commonly resorted to imprisonment, mutilations, or even severe corporal punishments. That claim is not undermined by the "poststructuralist crisis" in hunter-gatherer studies (see, especially, Lee 1992).

[26] It is unfortunate that Durkheim did not make technological complexity the prime mover of the division of labor (see Gibbs 1989:chapter 6; 1994:165–68).

of Durkheim's theory is valid, three outcomes are inevitable. First, all manner of interest groups (e.g., abortion foes, environmentalists, fundamentalists) will discover that it has become much more difficult to arouse public opinion by ethical/moral appeals. Second, the recent decline in the U.S. crime rate will prove to be short-run, and advocates of harsher legal punishments will be frustrated all the more. Third, social conflict will escalate, and legislative action (or inaction) will be increasingly influenced by lobbyists.

All three outcomes could be an effect of increases in the division of labor, because the greatest consequence of those increases may well be the diminution of normative consensus. To his credit, Durkheim was sensitive to that possibility, and at various points in the *DOL* he appears to doubt whether organic solidarity prevents social disintegration as effectively as mechanical solidarity supposedly once did.

The Triumph of Regulatory Law over Capitalism

The demise of Marxist regimes in Europe has lifted the spirits of apologists for capitalism and perhaps strengthened their determination to speak and write as though the 1930s never happened. For that matter, the resurgence of American capitalism commenced with the Reagan administration, and Reaganites have sought to preserve capitalism by reducing regulatory law. However, if the division of labor continues to increase and if Axiom 4 is valid, advocates of unregulated capitalism are fighting for a lost cause. Indeed, it is even debatable whether there was an overall reduction in regulatory law during the 1980s (see, e.g., Eisner, Worsham, and Ringquist 2000; Rabin 1986). Specifically, the triumphs of the free marketers may have been more than offset by myriad state and federal regulations designed (ostensibly) to protect consumers and the environment.

The point is not just that attempts of free marketers to deregulate are likely to be successful only in the short run, if at all. Regulatory law is also likely to expand far beyond the purely economic sphere. The repeal of Prohibition was a major step in that direction, though one commonly interpreted as decriminalization, rather than setting the scene for an expansion of regulatory law. Yet consider the multitude of boards and commissions that now control the production, distribution, and consumption of alcoholic beverages in the United States. Their existence alone is evidence of the expansion of regulatory law beyond the purely economic sphere.

Whatever the country, evidence that regulatory law increases proportionately with increases in the division of labor would lend support to a very important component of Durkheim's theory. His only mistake along that line was not recognizing that regulatory law is far more than an index of organic solidarity. It is a means by which legislators attempt to solve human problems, including the promotion of self-interest. Those problems appear infinite; and to the extent they are generated by the division of labor, they *are* infinite.

REFERENCES

Barnes, J. A. 1966. "Durkheim's *Division of Labor in Society*." New Series of *Man* 1:158–75.

Baxi, U. 1974. "Comment—Durkheim and Legal Evolution: Some Problems of Disproof." *Law and Society Review* 8:645–51.

Bayertz, K, ed. 1999. *Solidarity*. Boston, MA: Kluwer Academic.

Catton, W. R., Jr. 1985. "Emile Who and the Division of What?" *Sociological Perspectives* 28:251–80.

Clarke, C. J. 1987. "The Durkheimian Relationship Between the Division of Labor and Population: Cross-National Historical Evidence." *Sociological Focus* 20:13–31.
Clemente, F. 1972. "The Measurement Problem in the Analysis of an Ecological Concept: The Division of Labor." *Pacific Sociological Review* 15:30–40
Cotterrell, R. 1991. "The Durkheimian Tradition in the Sociology of Law." *Law and Society Review* 25:924–45.
———. 1999. *Emile Durkheim: Law in a Moral Domain* Stanford, CA: Stanford University Press.
Diamond, A. S. 1965. *The Comparative Study of Primitive Law*. London: Athlone.
Durkheim, E. [1893] 1949. *The Division of Labor in Society*. Translated by George Simpson. New York: Free Press.
———. [1897] 1951. *Suicide*. Translated by John A. Spaulding and George Simpson. New York: Free Press.
———. [1899–1900] 1973. "Two Laws of Penal Evolution." *Economy and Society* 2:285–308.
Eisner, M. A., J. Worsham, and E. J. Ringquist. 2000. *Contemporary Regulatory Policy*. Boulder, CO: Lynne Rienner.
Ervin, D. J. 1987. "Interdependence and Differentiation as Components of the Division of Labor." *Social Science Quarterly* 68:177–84.
Faris, E. 1934. "Review of Emile Durkheim on the Division of Labor in Society." *American Journal of Sociology* 40:376–77.
Friedson, E. 1976. "The Division of Labor as Social Interaction." *Social Problems* 23:304–13.
Garnsey, E. 1981. "The Rediscovery of the Division of Labor." *Theory and Society* 10:337–58.
Gibbs, J. P. 1981. *Norms, Deviance, and Social Control*. New York: Elsevier.
———. 1989. *Control: Sociology's Central Notion*. Urbana, IL: University of Illinois Press.
———. 1990. "Resistance in Sociology to Formal Theory Construction." Pp. 90–104 in *Formal Theory in Sociology*, edited by Jerald Hage. Albany, NY: State University of New York Press.
———. 1994. *A Theory about Control*. Boulder, CO: Westview Press.
Gibbs, J. P., and W. T. Martin. 1962. "Urbanization, Technology, and the Division of Labor: International Patterns." *American Sociological Review* 27:667–77
Gibbs, J. P., and D. L. Poston, Jr. 1975. "The Division of Labor: Conceptualization and Related Measures." *Social Forces* 53:468–76.
Hay, D. 1975. "Property, Authority, and Criminal Law." Pp. 17–63 in *Albion's Fatal Tree*, edited by Douglas Hay. New York: Pantheon Books.
Herskovitz, M. 1940. *The Economic Life of Primitive Peoples*. New York: Knopf.
Kemper, T. 1972. "The Division of Labor: A Post-Durkheimian Analytical View." *American Sociological Review* 37:739–53.
———. 1975. "Emile Durkheim and the Division of Labor." *Sociological Quarterly* 16:199–206.
Keon, T. L., and N. M. Carter. 1985. "Toward a Clarification of the Division of Labor Construct." *Human Relations* 38:1131–58.
Krause, E. A. 1982. *Division of Labor· A Political Perspective*. Westport, CT: Greenwood Press.
Krohn, M. D. 1978. "A Durkheimian Analysis of Crime Rates." *Social Forces* 57:654–70.
Land, K. C. 1970. "Mathematical Formalization of Durkheim's Theory of Division of Labor." *Sociological Methodology 1970* (annual):257–82.
Lee, R. B. 1979. *The !Kung San*. Cambridge, England: Cambridge University Press.
———. 1992. "Art, Science, or Politics? The Crisis in Hunter-Gatherer Studies." *American Anthropologist* 94:31–43.
Llewellyn, K. N., and E. A. Hoebel. 1941. *The Cheyenne Way*. Norman, OK: University of Oklahoma Press.
Maryanski, A., and J. H. Turner. 1992. *The Social Cage. Human Nature and the Evolution of Society*. Stanford, CA: Stanford University Press.
McIntyre, L. J. 1994. *Law in the Sociological Enterprise: A Reconstruction*. Boulder, CO: Westview Press.
Merton, R. K. 1934. "Durkheim's Division of Labor in Society." *American Journal of Sociology* 40:319–28.
Murdock, G. P. 1937. "Comparative Data on the Division of Labor by Sex " *Social Forces* 15:551–53.
Pope, W., and B. D. Johnson. 1983. "Inside Organic Solidarity." *American Sociological Review* 48:681–92.
Pospisil, L. 1971. *Anthropology of Law*. New York: Harper and Row.
Rabin, R. L. 1986. "Federal Regulation in Historical Perspective." *Stanford Law Review* 38:1189–1326.
Rueschemeyer, D. 1986. *Power and Division of Labour*. Cambridge, England: Polity Press.
Schwartz, R. D. 1965. "Reply." *American Journal of Sociology* 70:627–28.
———. 1974. "Legal Evolution and the Durkheim Hypothesis: A Reply to Professor Baxi." *Law and Society Review* 8:653–58.
Schwartz, R. D., and J. C Miller. 1964. "Legal Evolution and Societal Complexity." *American Journal of Sociology* 70:159–69.

Seagle, W. 1941. *The Quest for Law*. New York: Knopf.

Sheleff, L. S. 1975. "From Restitutive Law to Repressive Law: Durkheim's *The Division of Labor in Society* Revisited." *European Journal of Sociology* 16:16–45.

———. 1997. *Social Cohesion and Legal Coercion: A Critique of Weber, Durkheim, and Marx*. Atlanta, GA: Rodopi.

Smith, A. [1776] 1952. *An Inquiry into the Nature and Causes of the Wealth of Nations*. Chicago: William Benton.

Spitzer, S. 1975. "Punishment and Social Organization: A Study of Durkheim's Theory of Penal Evolution." *Law and Society Review* 9:613–37.

Turnbull, C. M. 1962. *The Forest People*. New York: Simon and Schuster.

Turner, J. H. 1981. "Emile Durkheim's Theory of Integration in Differentiated Social Systems." *Pacific Sociological Review* 24:379–91.

———. 1990. "Emile Durkheim's Theory of Social Organization." *Social Forces* 68:1089–1103.

Udy, S. H. 1965. "Dynamic Inferences from Static Data." *American Journal of Sociology* 70:625–27.

Van den Steenhoven, G. 1962. *Leadership and Law among the Eskimos of the Keewatin District, Northwest Territories*. Rijswijk, Z.H.: Excelsior.

Wallwork, E. 1984. "Religion and Social Structure in the Division of Labor." *American Anthropologist* 86:43–64.

Watson, W. T. 1929. "A New Census and Old Theory: Division of Labor in the Preliterate World." *American Journal of Sociology* 34:632–52.

Wimberley, H. 1974. "Legal Evolution: One Further Step." *American Journal of Sociology* 79:78–83.

Wrong, D. H. 1994. *The Problem of Order: What Unites and Divides Society*. New York: Free Press.

[6]

Durkheim on Collective Memory

BARBARA A. MISZTAL University of Leicester

ABSTRACT The paper argues that although Durkheim did not explicitly employ the notion of collective memory, his approach offers a very insightful understanding of the need for historical continuity. Durkheim's belief that every society displays and requires a sense of continuity with the past and that the past confers identity on individuals and groups allows us to see collective memory as one of the elementary forms of social life. The paper presents Durkheim's discussion of commemorative rituals in early societies, where he directly addresses the notion of social memory, which is seen as perpetuated by religious rites and as a means of ensuring shared morality and social cohesion. His conceptualization of the role of law and memory in sustaining organic solidarity is also considered. In conclusion it is discussed whether Durkheim's understanding of social memory provides us with relevant means to interpret social processes of remembering in today's societies.

KEYWORDS law, memory, morality, the past, religion, rituals

Introduction: the Durkheimian tradition

Watts Miller (1996) said that Durkheimian sociology is about mind-dependent yet at the same time will-independent things. Memory, for sure, fits this category. I will argue that although Durkheim did not explicitly employ the notion of collective memory, his approach offers a very insightful understanding of the need for historical continuity. Although it was his student, Maurice Halbwachs, who introduced the term 'collective memory' to sociology, Durkheim's input into the debate on the subject is rather worth discussing and preserving, particularly the importance that he attached to the revitalization of a group's social heritage for the reaffirmation of its bonds and the reinforcement of its solidarity. Such a reconstruction of Durkheim's approach can also assist recent attempts to rethink the notion of collective memory.

The question of what memory is and how it relates to the present has occupied many thinkers for centuries. Writers from the ancient Greeks to modern-day phenomenologists have been fascinated by the topic (Aristotle, Locke, Hume, Bergson). Although interesting, most such traditional accounts pay little attention to the collective nature of memory. The 'recent passion for memory' (Nora, 1996), which manifests itself in the increasing visibility and importance of memory narratives in social and political practice, and which has established memory as one of the main discourses in social science, tends to assume that memory is essentially social, that is, located in institutions in the forms of rules, laws, standardized practices and records. In this essentially Durkheimian orientation, memory discourse is used strategically not merely to explain the past but also to transform it into a reliable identity source for the present. Today's 'obsession with memory' (Huyssen, 1995), which was largely triggered by the commemorative fever of the 1980s and 1990s, further popularizes the Durkheimian tradition through its main research focus on political commemorative rituals.

Present-day memory discourse, while contributing to the development of a deeper and more insightful understanding of the workings of memory, still mainly relies on Maurice Halbwachs' (1950 [1926], 1992 [1941/1952]) description of the complexity of the process of social remembering. This revival of interest in Halbwachs, who asked how social groups retain, alter and reappropriate social memory, has resulted in the growing recognition of his claim that our belonging to a social group provides us with an essential memory aid. Halbwachs' conceptualization of collective memory as shared social frameworks of individual recollections follows Durkheim's belief that every society exhibits and requires a sense of continuity with the past. It also owes much to Durkheim's view of the past as the essential factor in creating solidarity, and to his argument that society is 'a complex of ideas and sentiments, of ways of seeing and feeling, a certain intellectual and moral framework distinctive of the entire group' (1973 [1912]: 277). At the core of the Durkheimian tradition, thus, is the insistence on the importance of a sense of collective identity, seen as being reinforced through links to the past. This tradition also stresses that the nature of group life shapes the way individuals think and remember and what they deem moral. Some representatives of this tradition (e.g. Connerton, 1989) explain how social memory is transferred through commemorative ceremonies and body practice and stress the way such memories are to be evoked and celebrated. Other researchers study how social solidarity is obtained through the cultural transmission of religious observance (Zerubavel, 1981) or how memory is institutionalized in legislation on government ethics (Schudson, 1992), or focus on the importance of tradition (Shils, 1981). The Durkheimian approach is, however, often criticized for being too vague and difficult to operationalize, for neglecting the question of the individual dimension of memory and for overlooking the interplay between individual and social memory. In order to evaluate its failures and strengths, it is necessary to go back to Durkheim's texts.

Early Societies: Morality, Religion and Memory

Durkheim addresses memory directly only in his discussion of commemorative rituals at the end of *Elementary Forms of the Religious Life*. However, despite the fact that his description of religious practices of the Australian Aboriginals lacks the explicit notion of social memory, it puts strong emphases on the importance of links to the past for group identity and solidarity. According to Durkheim, the societal need for historical continuity results in the crucial signification of periodic commemoration, which allows the society to 'renew the sentiment which it has of itself and its unity' (1971 [1912]: 420). The degree of group solidarity, created through remembering together, depends on the mythical properties of the group's memories, especially their ability to vitalize energy and arouse emotions.

Elementary Forms of the Religious Life presents how societies celebrate symbols of themselves in rituals that serve to sustain the vitality of a community's sacred beliefs and understandings and keep them to prevent them from being effaced from memory; in sum they 'revivify the most essential elements of the collective consciousness' (Durkheim, 1971 [1912]: 375). At the centre of what the community holds as sacred stands the collective imagined past, or the group mythical past, which refers to 'common beliefs, their common tradition, the memory of their great ancestors, the collective ideal of which they are incarnation' (1971 [1912]: 348). Rituals and their symbolism have significance as means of transmitting social memory, seen as the essential condition of the continuity of collective identity and social life. The mythology of a group expresses 'the way in which society represents man and the world; it is a moral system and a cosmology as well as a history' (1971 [1912]: 375). In shared celebration of the mythical past, 'the glorious souvenirs are made to live again before their eyes', and thus give them a feeling of 'strength and confidence; a man is surer of his faith when he sees to how distant a past it goes back and what great things it has inspired' (1971 [1912]: 375).

Seeing the myth of origin as one of the most powerful means of establishing a community's unity also assumes the existence of connections between collective memory and institutions guaranteeing collective beliefs and identity. In early societies, it is the role of religion to express and affirm the shared beliefs and understandings that characterize the society. Religion provides an all-embracing structure of beliefs, impresses on individuals a sense of the sacredness of something outside of them, and institutes a common destiny and identity not only with contemporaries but also with past and future generations. Sacred symbols and celebrations of past events help the recall of great events of the past that hold the community together, and, in turn, these ties to the past are cultivated by means of periodic commemoration rites. In other words, rites, through which the collectively imagined past receives an anchor and stability, serve 'the need of a community to resist change in the self-conception' (Hutton, 1988: 315).

To establish links between religion, the mythical past, rites and identity, Durkheim proceeds initially by examining the idea of the soul, seen as 'the cardinal idea of religion' (1971 [1912]: 50). He follows it up with the argument that rites are observed because they come from the ancestors and therefore their 'authority is confounded with the authority of tradition' (1971 [1912]: 371). Trying to establish how the soul, which is not a spirit, as it 'is attached to a body which it can leave only by exception', becomes the spirit and a cult object (1971 [1912]: 51), Durkheim points out that it is death that performs this transformation. 'When the body is once destroyed – and funeral rites have the object of hastening this destruction – the separation is taken as final' (1971 [1912]: 51). Thus, because the souls of ancestors become the first cult object, the first rites were funeral rites and the first altars were tombs. As the power of souls increased, people 'fall into dependence upon these spiritual forces, which they have created with their own hands and in their own image', hence came offerings, prayers, sacrifices, to satisfy the needs of the departed; 'in a word, all the apparatus of religious observances' (1971 [1912]: 52). In order to strengthen those sentiments, which, if left to themselves, would soon weaken, 'it is sufficient to bring those who hold them together and to put them in closer and more active relations with one another' (1971 [1912]: 210). Thus, in addition to funeral rites, ties to the past are cultivated by means of periodic commemorative rites, that is, ceremonies that relate to how the group represents itself, and promote a commitment to the collective ends and of affection for the group. As these rites solely consist of recollecting the past and making it present by means of representation, they 'act on the mind' to 'render the mythical past of the clan present to mind' (1971 [1912]: 375). In these ceremonies, the past is 'represented for mere sake of representing it and fixing it more firmly in the mind' (1971 [1912]: 376) in order to confirm the group identity and unity.

These rituals, because of their re-enactment of past persons or events through acts of performance, can be seen as mnemonic devices. Commemorative ceremonies are of cardinal importance for communal memory. Through their formalism and performativity, they are able to transmit and articulate memory non-verbally, 'encoded in set postures, gestures and movements, send a simple and clear message' (Connerton, 1989: 58). In this way, they entail a combination of cognitive and habit-memory. Moreover, the importance of bodily practices is reinforced further by the role of emotions in the process of celebration. As Durkheim noted, and others have subsequently confirmed (Nussbaum, 2001; Pennebaker and Banasik, 1997; Prager, 1998), emotions play an essential role in any recollection because they facilitate more intense and more prolonged affiliation. The more an event provokes an emotion, the more it elicits social sharing and distinctly vivid, precise, concrete, long-lasting memories of the event. On feast days, as the members of a group commemorate the past, their 'thoughts are centred upon their common beliefs, their common traditions, the memory of their great ancestors, the collective ideal of which they are incarnation; in a word, upon social things' (1971 [1912]: 348). As recent laboratory and field studies have both confirmed, the effect created by ritual experience – which can consist of arousal, ecstasy, loss of self and hallucinations, a state Durkheim recognizes as 'effervescence' – gets attached to the participants' knowledge structures (Marshall, 2002: 367).

As people, through memorized culturally specific postures, gestures and practices in the highly emotionally charged co-presence of others, enact their image of the past, their mutual bonds and feelings of belonging are reinforced. Thus, the other importance of these commemorative rites is connected with the fact that they bring individuals together and enhance moral consensus. Because to act morally means to act in terms of the collective interests, these ceremonies, by boosting people's feeling of belonging, reduce their egoistic orientation, which 'has no moral value' (Durkheim, 1961 [1925]: 65). Since morality 'must necessarily link man to goals that go beyond the circle of individual interests' (1961 [1925]: 65), the existence of moral consensus presumes the continuation of collective identity. Rites' function is to unite people and 'to multiply the relations between them and to make them more intimate with one another' (1971 [1912]: 348); thus, they focus people's identities and attach them to something greater than themselves. By vitalizing their common identity, ceremonies also reinforce the common consciousness that 'embraces all known reality; that is why it alone can furnish the minds with the moulds which are applicable to the totality of things and which make it possible to think them' (1971 [1912]: 444). The morality's authority, ensured by its connection with a power of religion, makes the collective memory into a source of stability and unity. In other words, in early societies, it is religion, closely associated with the mythical past, that plays the central role in providing the beliefs that justify morality, which then takes on the social function of religion and promotes and maintains solidarity. The religious ceremonies' authority is confounded with the authority of tradition, so when the members of a community strengthen their unity by ceremonial rituals in a state of effervescence, they put the myth into action' (1971 [1912]: 385), and 'celebrate it to remain faithful to the past' (1971 [1912]: 371). Religion, as a transcendental representation of the powers of society, through collective rituals that in turn create a social effervescence, maintains and revitalizes the social heritage of the group and helps transmit its values to future generations.

For Durkheim, periods of collective effervescence are moments during which groups and societies exhibit creativity and renewal. So collective effervescence, excitable gatherings and celebrations, which heighten people's energies and passions or, to use Randall Collins' (1998) language, 'charge' people's emotional 'batteries', are the seedbeds of human and social creativity. However, at least four major criticisms have been made of Durkheim's argument. First, it is criticized as being circular since his insistence on both the integrative and creative aspects of effervescent rituals means that he overlooks the point that their periodic return would not ensure creativity if there were no common bonds, for which strengthening ceremonial occasions are also essential (Nemedi, 1998). Second, Durkheim is also criticized for presenting routine rituals as extraordinary events, thus excluding from consideration many less intense and less formal ways of producing social solidarity. Third, his belief in the continuities of collective memory and in society as an entity *sui generis*, capable of self-generation and self-maintenance, underestimates the extent to which society's symbolic code, of which collective memory is one part, adapts to society's changing needs and tendencies (Schwartz, 2000). Fourth, Durkheim limits the re-creation of collective images of the past to periods of commemoration rites, during which, according to him, society ensures its renewal through ceremonies and celebration. Hence, the question remains how memory is preserved in ordinary periods and what binds people together in times of calm, when routine behaviour is the order of the day (Coser, 1992: 25).

Durkheim partially answers this question of how memory is stored in social relations in normal times by showing that the past endures in the present not only in formal commemorative practices but also in fundamental processes of social life. In addition to religious practices, which constantly renew group identity, we preserve the past by representing it to ourselves in words or through storing it in traditions and habitual conduct. 'We speak a language that we do not make, we use instruments that we did not invent; we invoke rights that we do not found; a treasury of knowledge is transmitted to each generation that it did not gather itself' (Durkheim, 1971 [1912]: 212). Language, seen as the social mechanisms guiding memories, bodily practices, habits and religious symbolic systems, is the vehicle for the past's influence over the present. According to Durkheim, it is to society that we owe these benefits of knowledge; society, which comprises past and present generations.

> When we start life we find already established and all around us a complex of ideas, beliefs and behaviors, which others have acknowledged and practiced before us. These are legacy of our forebears and will not change very much in the course of our lives.
>
> (1961 [1925]: 246)

By stressing our dependence upon knowledge that is transmitted from generation to generation, Durkheim opens up an opportunity for the conceptualization of memory as transmitted not only through performability of rituals but also through habit and as a communicative memory, that is, the residues of the past in language, which is a kind of knowledge/communication. Moreover, Durkheim's conceptualization of time and space as social constructions, that is, as objectively given social categories of thought produced within societies (categories that, while being fixed by the rhythms of collective life, ensure, in turn, the group's regularity and stability), makes it clear that collective memory requires 'the support of a group delimited in space and time' (Halbwachs, 1950 [1926]: 126). Durkheim's argument that 'the indispensable guidelines, in relation to which all things are temporally located, are taken from social life' (1971 [1912]: 10), in the context of his viewing society as the distinctive intellectual and moral framework, allows us not only to say that time is abstract, impersonal and common to the group but also that it is a 'veritable social institution' (1971 [1912]: 23) that is immobilized by the group memory. This point was further developed by Halbwachs (1950 [1926]), who pointed out that a group, through its tradition, seen as conveying an illusion of timelessness, colonizes time by ordering important dates within a commemorative sequence.

To sum up, according to Durkheim, the cohesion of early societies was generated by a shared morality that commanded general assent due to the integrative effect of group rites that evoked and celebrated the group mythical past. Religion, as a 'way in which societies become conscious of themselves and their history' (Durkheim, 1971 [1912]: 160), produces the superior authority of society and provides a manner of making sense of the world. In short, religion is closely associated with the mythical past, which holds a clue to collective beliefs, fears and knowledge. Despite the fact that Durkheim was not concerned with chronology or historical description, this connection between religion and memory offers rather an adequate picture of the status of memory in pre-modern times. For example, an examination of the nature of collective memory in the Middle Ages confirms the existence of a very close relation between memory and religion. The collective memory of this period is described as a circular liturgical memory rooted in religious beliefs, calendars and practices (Carruthers, 1990; Le Goff, 1992). This link between memory and religion was reinforced by the nature of Christianity and Judaism, both being 'religions of remembrance'. Moreover, memory, identified with prudence and rigorous discipline, was highly valued as the highest pursuit and 'the instrument for keeping in mind liturgies and saints, heaven, hell and purgatory' (Draaisma, 2000: 41). Durkheim, while showing how early societies solved the problem of cooperation by setting their foundation in religious beliefs rooted in the mythical past, assigns the same role and status to memory. In what follows, we examine his explanation of how modern societies ensure their solution to this dilemma.

Modern Society: Morality, Law and Memory

In early societies, morality, a matter of attachment, beliefs and rules, is intertwined not only with religion but also with law. This 'trinity' (Vogt, 1993: 71) is mainly sustained by the strength of the link between religion and law, which is due to the fact that both law and religion are a focus of willing allegiance, duty and commitment. Furthermore, in this type of society, law is mainly repressive and conveys religious guidelines as its 'role is to express and affirm the shared beliefs and understandings that characterize the society. And these beliefs and understandings are essentially religious' (Cotterrell, 1999: 51).

However, if in early societies morality is permeated with religion and expressed through law, the relationship between law and religion is less important in modern societies. Although Durkheim emphasizes the secularization of the content of the common consciousness and asserts that in modern societies shared beliefs and understandings are imbued in law and expressed by morality that is not necessarily rooted in religious sources, he never goes so far as to suggest that law replaces religion in modern society (Cotterrell, 1999). Rather, he points out that the collective consciousness in modern societies is less religious in its content due to the fact that the primary forms of collective sentiments originating from religious law are losing hold over individuals. He suggests that when the collective sentiments are divested of their religious content, 'little by little, political, economic and scientific functions free themselves apart by taking on a more acknowledged character' (1964 [1893]: 69).

As society develops with the progression of the division of labour, the importance of the collective consciousness is reduced because its scope becomes smaller and its intensity and determinateness decline. Durkheim asserts that in modern societies, the collective consciousness is narrower and refers mainly to a particular group and not to the whole of society, thus there is the growing importance of an occupational morality for each profession. Such societies – as they are faced with the fragmenting tendencies associated with industrial developments – are in danger of losing their cohesive morality. Yet modern society, according to Durkheim, is able to sustain social bonds sufficient to offset consequences of the division of labour due to a new role for intermediate occupational groups, which become a moral force capable of curbing individual egoism by invigorating a feeling of common solidarity. Since in order 'to commit ourselves to collective ends we must have above all a feeling and affection for the collectivity' (Durkheim, 1961 [1925]: 228), and since in modern societies there is an increasing emphasis on the group as the mechanism that bonds individuals to society, Durkheim, like Tocqueville, sees intermediary institutions, located between the individual and the state, as capable to act as an effective buffer against political domination and social fragmentation.

Yet, at the same time as the collective consciousness is reduced in scope, it becomes more abstract and generally closer to the human ideal. Consequently, the moral objectives of society become more and more generalized too.

> Nations grow upon the foundations of the small tribal groups of former times; then the nations themselves are joined in even greater social organizations. . . . Morality continuously disengages itself from particular

> ethnic groups or geographical areas precisely because each society, as it becomes larger, embraces a greater diversity of climatic and geographic conditions and all these differing influences mutually cancel themselves.
>
> (Durkheim, 1961 [1925]: 75)

Durkheim paints a rather complex picture of modern societies, where alongside the process of the maturing of the nation-state, which results in the moral objectives of society becoming more and more generalized, we see the occurrence of the process of fragmentation, which leads to the reduction in the scope of morality. The presence of these two trends, the generalization of national consciousness, which glorifies universalistic values and sustains the cult of individualism, and the fragmentation of social attachments, which provides for the plurality of moral meanings, introduces a need for pluralistic structures of regulation, which, as the basis of the normative integration, could, in turn, ensure social integration.

Thus, Durkheim's answer to the question that preoccupied him for a long time, namely what could replace religion as the basis of normative integration, stresses the role of secular morality. This raises the next dilemma, namely how this secular morality should be established and sustained. Durkheim's effort to find effective practical solutions to this problem led him to search for the conditions essential to the normal state of organic solidarity. While arguing that society is healthy and normal when it is able to adapt to particular conditions, he relies on the concept of normality to describe things as they are as well as how they should be. 'History has established that, except in abnormal cases, each society has in the main a morality suited to it, and that any other would not only be impossible but also fatal to the society which attempt to follow it' (1974 [1906]: 56). Durkheim's argument that society is 'the source and the end of morality', and his viewing the norm of health as providing the definition of social goals, allowed him to conclude that we 'cannot aspire to a morality other than which is related to the state of our society' (1974 [1906]: 59, 61). Consequently, in *The Division of Labor*, he rejects the enforced division of labour as a pathological type in which the habitualization of actions is solely due to the imposition of morality rules, and presents organic solidarity as a normal type of morality that arises out of understanding of a mutual interdependence. In other words, Durkheim seeks the morality of cooperation, which is

> . . . neither a compulsory morality imposed by rules nor voluntary agreement between subjects as to the conditions which appear acceptable to them for dealing with each other, but rather the product of an insight to be gained reflectively into functional equipments for egalitarian cooperation.
>
> (Joas, 1996: 59)

As he urges people to unite in a civic morality based on the recognition that we are interdependent and presents the question of emergence of a new morality as the issue of the emergence of new institutions, Durkheim privileges law. He asserts that individualism, the value system that unites modern society, has to be affirmed by law. Yet he fully realizes the complexity of law's relation with morality in modern societies: 'Law is no longer mainly an expression of the collective consciousness. It must somehow negotiate the diverse beliefs and understanding of diverse groups' (Cotterrell, 1999: 62). While religion, closely associated with the mythical past, was seen as playing a central role in mechanical solidarity, in organic solidarity it is law that stipulates how people must act. If secular morality under modernity, seen as the morality of interdependence, is authoritatively expressed by law, it raises the question of law's association with the past and the role of the continuity with the past in shaping shared values and sentiments.

Durkheim (1966 [1894]) asserted that the law and its rituals were essential for the creation and consolidation of the very specific sort of collective conscience required by a modern society. His approach assumes that in modern societies law is a conscious creation, whereas in earlier times the 'whole of law worked automatically in an unconscious way; it was a matter of custom' (1957 [1950]: 86). Legal judgment can foster social solidarity because in open debate the better argument prevails. In Durkheim's words, criminal prosecution, by allowing for confrontation of various memories, can serve the periodic need to reawaken and strengthen the public's feelings of moral outrage. For example, the Dreyfus Affair, which threatened to divide France in the 1890s, not only drew the nation's attention to the necessity of the re-evaluation of the basis of national unity, but has also marked France's collective memory for decades to come.

The Durkheimian idea that national solidarity is achieved through the sharing of liberal principles, and its assumption that the past is stored and interpreted by social institutions, or, more precisely, that memory is codified in law, can be translated into a statement that liberal law realizes its potential to construct solidaristic collective memory. The past endures in the present in legislation and groups' ethics, and therefore it is the essential element shaping the functioning of many institutions and of the national culture. Furthermore, according to Durkheim, one cannot understand political traditions by studying discourse alone. For him, discourse becomes tradition only if it succeeds in embodying itself in legal rules, codes and institutions. Such a conceptualization of the role of the past in the present, together with his viewing of criminal prosecution as serving the periodic need to strengthen the public's feelings of moral indignation, as well as his discussion of how legal judgment can foster social solidarity, provides us with an opportunity to see law as a mechanism of shaping collective memory.

The relationships between law and collective memory are at the foundation of many countries' original myths: for example, legal documents such as the

Magna Carta (UK) or the Declaration of Independence (USA) are essential for understanding their respective societies' beginnings and values. In all societies, to a considerable extent, courts, through their inputs into deciding historical questions, form collective memory. Memories that enjoyed the symbolic support of the law are not confined to the distant past. Post-war Europe, for example, saw many criminal prosecutions that aimed to influence national collective memories. Durkheim's assertion that the legal system is an enormously influential institution of collective memory is of a particular importance now, when in many post-authoritarian nations changes in collective memory are legally induced in order to reconstruct social solidarity. His hopes for liberal collective memory, combined with his belief in the importance of criminal law for the reconstruction of social solidarity on liberal foundations, provide us with a theoretical framework to argue that legal attempts to construct collective memory should necessarily aim for both truth and solidarity (Misztal, 2001).

Durkheim's concern with solidarity and his understanding of the importance of memory in holding societies together and in sustaining the transmission of values and desired patterns of behaviour offers us an interesting approach to situations in which both the right to historical truth and solidarity are at stake. According to Durkheim, social solidarity in modern societies does not mean uniformity, and the harmony of such societies depends upon the acceptance of difference. In other words, solidarity is best served by not denying the differences and not denying anyone the right to search for truth about his or her past. Yet truth about the past is only ensured by testing our memories against others' memories, while solidarity, as reconstructed on liberal foundations, means not a mechanical consensus and agreement on all questions but a recognition of mutual rights and willingness to work upon a common scheme. Hence liberal society does need a way of packaging shared history that allows for the diversity of memories and meets the truth claim. This can be illustrated by Durkheim's stand in the debate arising from the Dreyfus Affair. On the one hand, by providing the justification for the Dreyfusards, he constructed an argument in favour of the value of liberal individualism. On the other hand, while condemning the egoistical utilitarian version of self-interest, seen as a threat to solidarity, he stated that 'social life would be impossible if there did not exist an interest superior to the interests of individuals' (1990 [1898]: 72). For him, the value of the individual is at the centre of the modern *conscience collective*; nevertheless, demands for individual liberty cannot justify any attempts to undermine national unity and solidarity. Society has a duty to discover the truth, but how this truth is used should be dictated by society's need to preserve its integrity. In a sense, Durkheim argues that is up to us how much to remember and how much to forget, assuming that the truth is not denied and solidarity is not threatened. For the past to become a source of solidarity, the search for the truth about the past should be carried out under conditions of diversity and discourse, by relying not on 'a single narrator, but rather on a plurality of contending voices speaking to one another' (Sennett, 1998: 14). Durkheim's dual project of ensuring historical truth and solidarity in legal construction of collective memory faces, however, difficulties connected with the fact that memory can be used very selectively by various groups and is intertwined with imagination. It seems that his proposed solution to these problems resulting from the dilemmatic nature of memory points to the necessity for the state and its ability to impose a unitary and unifying framework of memory.

Durkheim implies that the state, as 'merely an instrument whose authority reflects the distortion of the *conscience collective*' (Jones, 2000: 243), has an important role in ensuring the authority of law, which is conceptualized as the more fundamental condition of social order. In other words, legal institutions are seen as mechanisms of systematizing remembering and forgetting, while the role of the state and its institutions is to sustain the authority of law, and, by the same token, ensure moral integration, as the precondition of social cohesion. In modern societies, writes Durkheim (1964 [1893]), alongside of an occupational morality and memory for each profession, seen as a result of the increasing complexity of society, which creates a competing source of morality, there is a separate national consciousness. Thus, the complexity and coherence in modern-day memory tend to correspond to complexity and coherence at the social level. Therefore what is now required is 'not just the authoritative expression of shared values and sentiments but also the creative art of government' (Cotterrell, 1999: 62). Since social solidarity is possible only to the extent that individuals share values and norms, the role of the state is to persuade people about the validity of such a common identity and value system by inducing both social remembering of certain events in specific ways and social forgetting of other events. This argument, more explicitly developed by many writers (Anderson, 1983; Hobsbawm and Ranger, 1983; Renan, 1990 [1882]), suggests that national myths and a national past are essential tools in the creative art of government.

The state's ability to construct an emotional attachment to the national heritage provides the framework for the moral authority of law and a sound secular morality, seen as the condition of national health. Moreover, the Durkheimian perspective, although it admits that there are as many memories as groups and that groups can use the past for various reasons, assumes that the past is highly resistant to efforts to reconstruct it. By arguing that we cannot wish for any morality other than that implied in the nature of our society, and by insisting on the persistence of what is remembered, Durkheim implies that the state and its institutions should ensure the representation of a national past that glorifies abstract values, not values of particular groups, and that, at the same time, can offer us something emotional and capable of arousing in us sentiments and attachments to traditions and beliefs. Learning what the elders define as good is the essential past of morality and collective identity.

> Without this feeling of the bond thus joining generation to generation – sense of continuity that makes of each generation a phase in the development of the collective being – social solidarity would be singularly precarious, since its life would not, perforce, outlast that of a single man, and since it would have to be renewed with each generation.
>
> (Durkheim, 1961 [1925]: 246)

While writing about moral education of children, Durkheim stresses that only by a means of the systematic exposure to their country's cultural heritage can children achieve a sense of identity and personal fulfilment, and therefore the child 'should be made aware of the legacy of those who preceded him' (1961 [1925]: 247).

Many scholars have commented on flaws in Durkheim's account of law (for example, that he overrated law's potential service to social solidarity, that his understanding of the role of law is naïve, that he could not see that law can be oppressive or insensitive: Cotterrell, 1999; Morrison, 1995; Osiel, 1997). Yet, despite Durkheim's inability to see law as a site of power and conflict, his understanding of collective memory provides us with an opportunity to grasp collective memories' peculiar ability to be 'simultaneously particularistic and universal' (Zelizer, 1995: 230) and to understand that some memories have constituted models for acting for the whole nation and as such 'embodied a universal cultural presence' (Schwartz, 2000: 255), while other memories are more particularistic. His approach also allows us to avoid many of the weaknesses of the 'invention of tradition' approach. *The Invention of Tradition*, a book edited by Hobsbawm and Ranger (1983), while pointing out that many traditions that appear to be old are actually products, at most, of the past couple of centuries, stresses the primary role of the state in shaping collective memory. According to Hobsbawm and Ranger (1983), invented traditions are used as a means of power, to establish or legitimize institutions, to symbolize social cohesion and to socialize individuals to the existing order. Unfortunately, the employment of this perspective to modern Western societies has become 'somewhat predictable' and repetitive (Confino, 1997: 1387). The 'invention of tradition' approach neglects to acknowledge that the past endures in the present not only through self-conscious commemoration rituals, that people can construct their own counter-memories from below, and that it is not always possible, particularly in democratic countries, to impose on people totally invented or fabricated traditions. As numerous examples from many countries show (Osiel, 1997), people tend to reject the vision of the past that contradicts their recollection and sense of truth. Some past events can be of such importance to people that they feel compelled to tell their stories; therefore a collective memory is not so easy to undermine or totally distort (Schudson, 1997: 5). The 'invention of tradition' approach also avoids the very interesting question of why some traditions but not others become popular and enjoy social support. What is remarkable about traditions is not that they are invented, as almost all of them, at least to some degree, are constructed, but why so many of them work and are accepted as 'real'. The growing recognition of the weaknesses of the 'invention of tradition' approach makes the Durkheimian perspective more attractive because, while recognizing that the essence of collective memory is always to confer the legitimacy of continuity, it still encourages us to see limits to the power of actors in the present to remake the past according to their own interest. In final remarks, I will exam Durkheim's overall contribution to the theory of social remembering.

Conclusion

Generally speaking, Durkheim's emphases on the persistence of the group past and its continuity come close to Tocquveille's (1968 [1840]) observation that when the past no longer illuminates the future, the spirit walks in darkness. Because he offers a broad and very imprecise notion of memory, many common negative evaluations of this term in general are also applied in his case, such as ones that point to its nebulousness and lack of clarity (Gedi and Elam, 1996), or criticize it for being a confusing or 'woolly' concept that lacks any explanatory power (Osiel, 1997: 18) or for coming close to 'the bad old Romantic notion of the spirit' or the 'inner' character of race or nation (Klein, 2000: 9). Nonetheless, Durkheim's contribution is valuable not only because it asserts that no memory can be isolated from its social context, from the language and other symbolic systems moulded by a society, but also because it points to 'the fact that permanent and changing visions of the past are part of one another' (Schwartz, 2000: 302). Therefore, Durkheim, who was among the first to develop the idea that collective imagined past is not only renewed, avoids any conceptualization of remembering as achieved monologically and instrumentally.

Some writers see the Durkheimian tradition, due to its focus on rituals, as containing elements of collective commemoration and placing collective memory 'at the heart of a society's system of rituals' (Pickering, 1998: 9). It is even argued, despite the fact that Durkheim addresses memory directly only in his discussion of commemorative rituals, that the notion of social memory offers 'the best way of interpreting Durkheim's social theory' (Pickering, 1998: 9). Durkheim's belief that every society displays and requires a sense of continuity with the past, and that the past confers identity on individuals and groups, allows us to define collective memory as one of the elementary forms of social life, or as part of society's intellectual and moral framework, and see it as the essential factor in creating solidarity. According to Durkheim, every 'state of conscience is a source of life', thus social memory can be seen as 'an essential factor of our general vitality' (1964 [1893]: 96). Anything that undermines the 'integrity of our conscience' is a threat to societal health as it fragments and weakens society

(Durkheim, 1964 [1893]: 96). Although Durkheim did not develop this idea explicitly, it can be asserted that seeing the myth of origin as one of the most powerful means of establishing a community's unity also assumes the existence of connections between collective memory and institutions guaranteeing the collective identity. In other words, since the connection between memory, collective consciousness and solidarity in early societies lies in the myth of origin, memory 'may be analyzed with the regard to the elementary forms of social life which we recognize as central characteristics of the *conscience collective*' (Gephart, 1998: 129).

Thompson (1998) generalizes the Durkheimian observation that societal unity depends upon the vitalizing power of memory and argues that social cohesion is provided by ideology. He claims that, for Durkheim, ideology, seen as a source of a mythical or imaginary representation of the underlying social structure, is a universal dimension of social life. However, it seems that Thompson's identification of collective memory with ideology overlooks the dualistic nature of Durkheim's concept of memory, or its ability to be 'simultaneously particularistic and universal' (Zelizer, 1995: 230). It also fails to notice Durkheim's concern with the links between memory and morality through their shared association with religion in early societies and with law in modern societies. While Durkheim allows for the sacred core to 'pass over into political structures of legitimation' (Joas, 1996: 64), this does not imply that it is social memory, rather than its institutional form, that takes on the role of an ideal. Furthermore, if we see Durkheim's theory of solidarity as theorizing collective memory, viewed as a social fact that bestows identity on individuals and groups, social memory cannot be seen as a substitute for ideology. This is because social facts, according to Durkheim, should be distinguished from ideas or ideologies because they always 'remain the same, however we look at them' (Craib, 1997: 28). Collective memory, as a social fact, is characterized by the persistence of what is remembered. Ideology, in contrast, is a designed version of the past, present and future of social order that reflects 'interest-based mobilizing culture that acts as a resource to mobilize movements, participants for change and resistance' (Platt and Williams, 2002: 353). Stressing the legitimation aspect of memory, which points to the fact that traditions can serve as a source of support for the exercise of power and authority, is the main characteristic of the 'invention of tradition' perspective rather than Durkheim's original concern.

Durkheim's approach, because of its focus on how the past endures in the present and concern with the question as to how a new morality can emerge, also differs from Halbwachs' perspective and other similar theories that try to comprehend how people use the past or deliberately designed it as a view of defining political realities and identities. According to Durkheim, the past survives in the present and tends to perpetuate itself into the future by making itself present in all practices: institutional, as it is transmitted through law and other institutions;

cultural, as it is transmitted through language and other symbolic systems; and personal, as in each of

> . . . us, in differing degrees, is continued the person we were yesterday, and indeed, in the nature of things it is even true that our personae predominate in us, since the present is necessarily insignificant when compared with the long period of the past because of which we have emerged in the form we have today. It is just that we don't directly feel the influence of these past selves precisely because they are so deeply rooted within us.
> (Durkheim, 1977: 11)

It is interesting to note similarities between Durkheim's statement above and Pierre Bourdieu's notion of habitus. Indeed, it is quoted by Bourdieu in his effort to explain his own term. Habitus is the system of durable dispositions to act that is produced by objective structures and conditions but is also capable of producing and reproducing those structures (Bourdieu, 1977: 72). It is 'embodied history, internalized as a second nature and so forgotten as history' (1977: 72) and it comprises strategies and practices through which social order 'accomplishes itself' and makes itself 'self-evident' and 'meaningful' (Bourdieu and Wacquant, 1992: 127–8). Memory, in the same way as habitus, organizes the manner in which individuals see the world and act in it. At the heart of both notions there is the dialectic between objective and subjective because our dispositions and frames of perceptions are seen as at once historical, social and individual. However, the Durkheimian view of memory, as providing a set of beliefs and patterns of action, differs from the notion of habitus because it strongly emphasizes the normative aspect of memory. In this perspective, memory, as the morality of remembering and forgetting, is seen to be securing a normative justification for practices and beliefs and providing people with some kind of direction when they are aimless, offering them 'some kind of anchor when they are adrift' (Schudson, 1992: 213).

Memory, as 'the normative transmission, which links the generations of the dead with the generations of the living in the constitution of a society' (Shils, 1981: 24), faces, however, new challenges in modern, fragmented and pluralistic societies. As the modern differentiation of social fields and institutions produces a differentiation of total social memory into a plurality of specialized circles of memory, the normative aspect of a societal memory can no longer be taken for granted. Furthermore, owing to the erosion of the state's ability to impose a unitary and unifying framework of memory (Nora, 1996), we witness, on the one hand, the cultural demise of authoritative memory or the collapse of comprehensive collective memory (Hervieu-Leger, 2000; Huyssen, 1995) and, on the other, the spread of community-based small memories, which absorb the need for identity, as well as the emergence of extra-territorial global memories, which are facilitated by 'the speed and imagery of the new global communications' (Levy and Sznaider, 2002: 91). In other words, the decline of comprehensive memory is accompanied by the spread of the process of denationalization of memory as well as trends towards its fragmentation and democratization. The growing significance of groups' memories and their politicization, as memory becomes a significant element in the development of social and cultural identities, often leads to the sacralization of memory, or memory becoming a 'surrogate' religion. Thus, the Durkheimian approach is still very relevant today as it can, better than any other perspectives, shed light on this new process of the enhancement of the sacrality of memory.

Durkheim can be accused of neglecting the question of how individual consciousness might relate to those of the groups and for putting too much emphasis on the collective nature of social consciousness. However, Halbwachs' (1950 [1926], 1992 [1941/1952]) more explicitly developed theory of collective memory is also criticized for disconnecting collective memory from the actual thought process of any particular individual (Fentress and Wickham, 1992). Furthermore, although Halbwachs tries to introduce psychology into the sociological enterprise, while Durkheim neglects the issue of individual consciousness, the former's more individualistic stand is less interesting not only because of its assumption that society's understanding of its past is always instrumental to the maintenance of present beliefs and that people use the past to give meaning to the present, but also because of its too positivistic definition of history and its over-rigid distinction between history and memory. In contrast to Halbwachs' strident disconnection of memory from historical reality, Durkheim's approach allows us to account for historical continuity and the complexities that arise from the intertwined workings of past and present. Even more importantly, despite the fact that Durkheim's social determinism is responsible for his failure to address the question of individual memory, his belief in the power of society to shape individual memory does not totally neglect the dialectical tensions between personal memory and the social construction of the past.

Nonetheless, Durkheim's focus on the emergence of institutions in the extra-ordinary experience of collective effervescence, his tendency to shift 'the weight of unresolved problems onto the level of politics' and to expect that organic solidarity can be smoothly produced by 'coordination between professional groups, the democratic state and individualistic ideal' (Joas, 1996: 61) mean that his idea of collective memory is not only underdeveloped but also reveals a discrepancy between 'is' and 'ought'. While this is consistent with his assertion that science is able to resolve all moral and political questions and to provide the justification for which single morality is required by society (in other words, what is 'normal' for a given society, where 'normal' means both things as they are and as how they should be), it does not necessarily fit our present-day intellectual culture with its broad pattern of explanatory pluralism. However, despite the fact that we reject Durkheim's aspiration for science to show the only possible set of moral judgements, we are still searching for a model that would move beyond mere description of social reality. Thus, Durkheim's concept of collective memory, with its links to the moral ideal and promises of solidarity and truth, retains some appeal.

References

Anderson, B. (1983) *Imagined Communities*. London: Verso.

Bourdieu, P. (1977) *Outline of a Theory of Practice*, trans. R. Nice. Cambridge: Cambridge University Press.

Bourdieu, P. and L.J.D. Wacquant (1992) *An Invitation to Reflexive Sociology*. Cambridge: Polity.

Carruthers, M. (1990) *The Book of Memory: A Study of Medieval Culture*. Cambridge: Cambridge University Press.

Collins, R. (1998) *The Sociology of Philosophies: A Global Theory of Intellectual Change*. Cambridge, MA: Harvard University Press.

Confino, A. (1997) 'Collective Memory and Cultural History: Problems and Method', *American Historical Review* December: 1386–405.

Connerton, P. (1989) *How Societies Remember*. Cambridge: Cambridge University Press.

Coser, L.A. (1992) 'Introduction', pp. 1–36 in M. Halbwachs, *On Collective Memory*, ed., introd. and trans. L.A. Coser. Chicago: University of Chicago Press.

Cotterrell, R. (1999) *Émile Durkheim: Law in a Moral Domain*. Edinburgh: Edinburgh University Press.

Craib, I. (1997) *Classical Social Theory*. Oxford: Oxford University Press.

Draaisma, D. (2000) *Metaphors of Memory: A History of Ideas about Mind*. Cambridge: Cambridge University Press.

Durkheim, É. (1957) *Professional Ethics and Civic Morals*, trans. C. Broookfield. London: Routledge. (Orig. pub. 1950.)

Durkheim, É. (1961) *Moral Education*, trans. E.K. Wilson. New York: Free Press. (Orig. pub. 1925.)

Durkheim, É. (1964) *The Division of Labor in Society*, trans. G. Simpson. New York: Free Press. (Orig. pub. 1893.)

Durkheim, É. (1966) *The Rules of Sociological Method*, trans. S.A. Solovay and H.H. Mueller. New York: Free Press. (Orig. pub. 1894.)

Durkheim, É. (1971) *Elementary Forms of the Religious Life*, trans. J.W. Swain. New York: Free Press. (Orig. pub. 1912.)

Durkheim, É. (1973) 'Forms of the Religious Life', pp. 269–97 in R. Bellah (ed.) *Durkheim, on Morality and Society*. Chicago: University of Chicago Press. (Orig. pub. 1912.)

Durkheim, É. (1974) *Sociology and Philosophy*, trans. D.F. Pocock, introd. J.G. Peristiany. New York: Free Press. (Orig. pub. 1906.)

Durkheim, É. (1977) *The Evolution of Educational Thought*, trans. D.F. Pocock. London: Routledge.

Durkheim, É. (1990) 'Individualism and the Intellectuals', pp. 62–73 in P. Hamilton (ed.) *Émile Durkheim: Critical Assessment*. London: Routledge. (Orig. pub. 1898.)

Fentress, J. and C. Wickham (1992) *Social Memory*. Oxford: Blackwell.

Gedi, N. and Y. Elam (1996) 'Collective Memory – What is it?', *History and Memory* 8(1): 30–50.

Gephart, W. (1998) 'Memory and the Sacred: The Cult of Anniversaries and Commemorative Rituals in the Light of the *Elementary Forms*', pp. 127–36 in N.J. Allen, W.S.F. Pickering and W. Watts Miller (eds) *On Durkheim's Elementary Forms of the Religious Life*. London: Routledge.

Halbwachs, M. (1950) *The Collective Memory*, trans. F.J. Ditter and V.Y. Ditter, introd. M. Douglas. London: Harper Colophon. (Orig. pub. 1926.)

Halbwachs, M. (1992) *On Collective Memory*, ed., introd. and trans. L.A. Coser. Chicago: University of Chicago Press. (Orig. pub. 1941/1952.)

Hervieu-Leger, D. (2000) *Religion as a Chain of Memory*. Cambridge: Polity.

Hobsbawm, E. and T. Ranger (eds) (1983) *The Invention of Tradition*. New York: Cambridge University Press.

Hutton, P. (1988) 'Collective Memory and Collective Mentalities', *Historical Reflections* 15(2): 311–22.

Huyssen, A. (1995) *Twilight Memories*. London: Routledge.

Joas, H. (1996) *The Creativity of Action*, trans. J. Gaines and P. Keast. Cambridge: Polity.

Jones, R.A. (2000) 'Émile Durkheim', pp. 205–48 in G. Ritzer (ed.) *The Blackwell Companion to Major Social Theorists*. Oxford: Blackwell.

Klein, K. (2000) 'On the Emergence of Memory in Historical Discourse', *Representations*, Winter: 127–53.

Le Goff, J. (1992) *History and Memory*, trans. S. Rendall and E. Claman. New York: Columbia University Press.

Levy, D.S. and N. Sznaider (2002) 'The Holocaust and the Formation of Cosmopolitan Memory', *European Journal of Social Theory* 5(1): 87–106.

Marshall, D.A. (2002) 'Behavior, Belonging, and Belief', *Sociological Theory* 20(3): 360–78.

Misztal, B.A. (2001) 'Legal Attempts to Construct Collective Memory', *Polish Sociological Review* 1(133): 61–77.

Morrison, K. (1995) *Marx, Durkheim, Weber: Formations of Modern Social Thought*. London: Sage.

Nemedi, D. (1998) 'Change, Innovation and Creation: Durkheim's Ambivalence', pp. 162–75 in N.J. Allen, W.S.F. Pickering and W. Watts Miller (eds) *On Durkheim's Elementary Forms of the Religious Life*. London: Routledge.

Nora, P. (1996) 'General Introduction: Between Memory and History', pp. 1–20 in P. Nora (ed.) *Realms of Memory*, Vol. 1, trans. A. Goldhammer. New York: Columbia University Press.

Nussbaum, M.C. (2001) *Upheavals of Thought*. Cambridge: Cambridge University Press.

Osiel, M. (1997) *Mass Atrocity, Collective Memory and the Law*. New Brunswick, NJ: Transaction Publishers.

Pennebaker, J.W. and B.L. Banasik (1997) 'On the Creation and Maintenance of Collective Memory', pp. 3–20 in J.W. Pennebaker, D. Paez and B. Rime (eds) *Collective Memory of Political Events*. Mahwah, NJ: Lawrence Erlbaum.

Pickering, W.S.F. (1998) 'Introduction', pp. 1–12 in N.J. Allen, W.S.F. Pickering and W. Watts Miller (eds) *On Durkheim's Elementary Forms of the Religious Life*. London: Routledge.

Platt, G.M. and R.H. Williams (2002) 'Ideological Language and Social Movements', *Sociological Theory* 20(3): 328–59.

Prager, J. (1998) *Presenting the Past: Psychoanalysis and the Sociology of Misremembering*. Cambridge, MA: Harvard University Press.

Renan, E. (1990) 'What is a Nation?', in H.K. Bhabha (ed.) *Nation and Narration*. London: Routledge. (Orig. pub. 1882.)

Schudson, M. (1992) *Watergate in American Memory*. New York: Basic Books.

Schudson, M. (1997) 'Lives, Laws and Language: Commemorative versus Non-Commemorative Forms of Effective Public Memory', *The Communication Review* 2(1): 3–17.

Schwartz, B. (2000) *Abraham Lincoln and the Forge of National Memory*. Chicago: University of Chicago Press.

Sennett, R. (1998) 'Disturbing Memories', pp. 10–46 in P. Fara and K. Patterson (eds) *Memory*. Cambridge: Cambridge University Press.

Shils, E. (1981) *Tradition*. Chicago: University of Chicago Press.

Thompson, K. (1998) 'Durkheim and Sacred Identity', pp. 137–61 in N.J. Allen, W.S.F. Pickering and W. Watts Miller (eds) *On Durkheim's Elementary Forms of the Religious Life*. London: Routledge.

Tocqueville, A. de (1968) *Democracy in America*, Vol. II, trans. G. Lawrence. London: Fontana. (Orig. pub. 1840.)

Vogt, W.P (1993) 'Durkheim's Sociology of Law: Morality and the Cult of the Individual', pp. 71–98 in S.P. Turner (ed.) *Émile Durkheim: Sociologists and Moralists*. London: Routledge.

Watts Miller, W. (1996) *Durkheim, Morals and Modernity*. London: UCL Press.

Zelizer, B. (1995) 'Reading the Past against the Grain', *Critical Studies in Mass Communication* 12: 214–39.

Zerubavel, E. (1981) *Hidden Rhythms: Schedules and Calendars in Social Life*. Chicago: University of Chicago Press.

Barbara A. Misztal is Professor of Sociology at University of Leicester . She is the author of *Theories of Social Remembering* (Open University Press, 2003); *Informality: Social Theory and Contemporary Practice* (Routledge, 2000); *Trust in Modern Society* (Polity, 1996) and co-editor of *Action on AIDS* (Greenwood Press, 1990).

Address: Department of Sociology, University of Leicester, Leicester LE2 7RH, UK. [email: bm50@le.ac.uk]

[7]

Constructing the Juristic Durkheim?

Paul Huvelin's adaptation of Durkheimian sociology

Roger Cotterrell

Introduction

It is well known that law was an important interest for Durkheim and for several of his closest followers and collaborators. But the nature and purposes of his engagement with law are less clear than might be wished and have often been misunderstood. Among writers on sociology of law, understandings of this engagement have usually been shaped by almost exclusive attention to the treatment of law in *The Division of Labour in Society* (1893b/1902b). Here, Durkheim seems to approach legal materials mainly for their capacity to provide, in the documentary form of ancient and modern codes, 'visible symbols' of social solidarity; an 'index' or measure of this elusive phenomenon. While *The Division of Labour* contains his most sustained discussion of legal doctrine from many societies and eras, the comparative and historical study of law is prominently presented in it as a methodological device for examining something that is, apparently, of greater sociological significance than law itself. Hence the sociological study of law appears on one familiar reading of this text as central and peripheral at the same time; a vital means to an end rather than an end in itself.

Durkheim's writings elsewhere (including his many reviews of books on legal subjects), as well as the approach and contents of the *Année sociologique* under his direction, make clear that, from a Durkheimian standpoint, law is far from being a secondary or derivative phenomenon. For Durkheim himself and several of his co-workers, it was a major topic for sociological study; an aspect of social life related (but not reducible) to morality, religion or the changing conditions of social solidarity. Matters are, however, complicated by the changing position of religion in Durkheim's sociology as it developed. In his early work, law appears sometimes to be 'a practical substitute for religion'[1] in modern society, as religion loses its regulatory power. But, in his later work, where the need even in modern society for something like religion is asserted (Durkheim 1912a), law's significance again becomes ambiguous or, at least, its function is harder to define. What balance, for example, is to be found between an idea of law as co-ordinating social functions in complex, diverse, modern societies, and an idea of law as expressing a value system or set of beliefs to underpin such complexity?[2]

This paper is concerned with law in the Durkheimian tradition: with Durkheim's approach to law and some ambiguities and limitations of this approach. What follows is part of an ongoing consideration of this subject centred on the way that Durkheim's ideas were adapted to serve the purposes of professional jurists who collaborated with him in the original project of the *Année sociologique*. Though several members of Durkheim's *Année* team had legal qualifications (Vogt 1983:177-178), only two, Paul Huvelin and Emmanuel Lévy, were actually professors of law. Colleagues in the law faculty of the University of Lyon for almost the whole of their academic careers, they were both active contributors to the journal. Lévy was in contact with Durkheim from 1896 and, as an editor and book reviewer, contributed to all volumes of the *Année*'s first series from its commencement in 1898. Huvelin, whom Lévy first put in touch with the Durkheimians, began his association (via Marcel Mauss) in 1899 and contributed from the sixth volume, published in 1903, until the end of the first series (1913).

It is clear that Durkheim valued highly the contribution of the two jurists from Lyon, telling Mauss that he would not know how to replace Lévy in the *Année* team (Durkheim 1998a:49). Huvelin, however, was a more prolific contributor than Lévy. He wrote one major article (Huvelin 1907), forty-one full book reviews and two short notes (Besnard 1983a:32). After Huvelin's premature death in June 1924, Mauss wrote, 'the loss of Huvelin is irreparable for us' (Mauss 1925a:497). Although these jurists have received relatively little discussion in Durkheimian literature, they were clearly much respected members of the team as far as Durkheim and Mauss were concerned.[3] And, recently, they have begun to attract attention among French intellectual historians.[4]

Both Lévy and Huvelin were sympathetic to central aspects of Durkheim's sociology and saw its powerful relevance for legal studies. Yet both felt a need to depart from Durkheim in important ways to make their scholarly work realistic and practically useful. I have discussed Lévy's contribution elsewhere (Cotterrell 2004). This present paper therefore concentrates on Huvelin's work as a response to, and adaptation of, Durkheim's sociology. I use a study by Huvelin to illustrate some problems which Durkheim's ideas posed for sympathetic jurists. The paper considers how one particular legal scholar tried to overcome these problems and to use elements of Durkheim's thinking to develop general sociological insights about law and its history.

Roger Cotterrell

Durkheim on law

When he began teaching sociology at Bordeaux, Durkheim made clear his wish to reach out to lawyers and welcomed law students to his lectures (Durkheim 1888a:108-109). Building bridges was surely a necessary strategy given the hostility that his ideas soon provoked from some law faculties. Many jurists were deeply sceptical of Durkheimian sociology. They often caricatured it as focusing on the social rather than the individual, on social forces rather than individual responsibility, and on an unrelenting questioning of traditions and established institutions (Cotterrell 1999:ch.3). Durkheim, for his part, advocated the reform of legal education to make law 'something other than conceptual games' and to show its cultural roots (Durkheim 1907d:244). But he also assumed that sociology could learn much from jurists and legal historians. In 1904, reviewing a book by the great comparative lawyer Édouard Lambert, Durkheim equated the study of comparative legal history with sociology of law, presumably emphasising in this context the 'genetic' rather than the 'functional' side of Durkheimian sociology (1904a(4):266). Comparative legal history could thus be a site of intimate cooperation between sociology and legal studies.

Durkheim's own thinking on law has to be understood as undergoing major changes during his career and leaving unresolved problems for those who have at various times attempted to construct a rigorous theory of law from his work. 'Moral ideas are the soul (*l'âme*) of law,' he writes (1909e: 150). But law is distinguished from morality by a degree of organisation, especially as regards the process of sanctioning breaches of social rules. Legal rules are 'instituted by definite organs and under a definite form and... the whole system which the law uses to realise its precepts is regulated and organised' (1900a(6):320-321). But the only organisation always found in relation to law is a court (*un tribunal*), which might be an assembly of the people as a whole, or an elite of judges (1893b/1902b:63/ t.52). So law's essence is adjudication and judgment, not legislation.

Compared with repressive law, restitutive law has much more extensive organisational needs. Modern law, mainly restitutive, is characterised by boards, administrative agencies, specialised officials, enforcement systems and detailed demarcations of jurisdictions. All of which seems to point towards the idea of law as an instrument of government and to a linking of law and politics. Indeed, Durkheim's early thinking in *The Division of Labour* suggests this. Ultimately, law is not just a reflection or index of moral bonds (of solidarity) but helps form them or even create them. The underlying morality of restitutive law might be considered a kind of official 'governmental morality', aimed at ensuring a good, integrated functioning of social life, rather than any popular morality or reflection of a collective consciousness (Cotterrell 1999:109-112). Law, in this image, is separated more and more from popular moral convictions insofar as these are society-wide. Modern law lives increasingly in regions remote from the heart of the collective consciousness (Durkheim 1893b/1902b: 81/t.69-70).

So it might appear that modern law is to be viewed as an active, powerful agent of governmental steering of society. But this seems not to be Durkheim's view. For him, law as a moral framework is hardly seen politically in any sense. Thus, a sociology of law and morals (these being intimately related) takes the place of a political sociology in the Durkheimian scholarly schema (cf. Favre 1983). Durkheim sees organic solidarity as the normal state of affairs for complex modern societies; anomie and the forced division of labour are abnormal forms. So law's task is not to arbitrate between dominant political interests but to fine-tune society, checking aberrations and freeing normal social processes of development when they become obstructed. Lawmakers, we might say, are like gardeners tending a plant. They do not make it grow and have limited knowledge as to why or how it does. They can only protect and nurture spontaneous processes of development over which they have relatively little control. Sociological laws, not juridical ones, produce solidarity. Social structure and the emergence of appropriate functional relations are the key to this process, not legal intervention as such.

In his work after the publication of *The Division of Labour*, Durkheim pulls back even more from the idea of law as a political force or a directive instrument of government. Two elements in his work, which contrast strongly with the approaches of his earlier writings, are central here. First is his reaffirmation of the value system of individualism as the unifying moral foundation of complex modern societies (Durkheim 1898c). Second is his implicit recognition that all modern law (not just surviving repressive or penal law) is an expression of the specifically modern individualistic content of the collective consciousness (Cotterrell 1999:ch.7). So law is seen eventually by Durkheim in modern (no less than simple or ancient) societies as deeply rooted in culture, in the sense of general beliefs, values, outlooks, attitudes and traditions of thought. The moral value system of individualism is implicit in modern social interaction and necessary to it as the differentiation of societies proceeds. But it is a contingent product of history in certain societies at certain periods. Law, it seems, has the general function of supporting and elaborating this value system; at least, this much is implicit in Durkheim's writings on contract, property, criminal and inheritance law (Cotterrell 1999:chs.5, 8 and 9). Hence law's task is, it seems, primarily an expressive one. Law is to be seen (in modernity as in earlier societies) as a distillation of moral values rather than a political instrument of governmental intervention in social relations. Where the latter use of law is appropriate it is as a derivation from the former.

Huvelin and Durkheimian sociology

For jurists wishing to import Durkheimian ideas into their legal scholarship a main problem has been how to find a significant, well-defined place for law in the edifice of social explanation and the general picture of modern society which Durkheim's sociology offered. The modern lawyer is typically concerned with using law to make things happen: to right wrongs, achieve justice, promote interests or secure rights. Many jurists in Durkheim's time, no less than now, would be dissatisfied with an image of law as a reflection of the established character of moral life or an index of social solidarity, or as explicable in its operations in terms of a long historical development of social structure (the shifting combinations of forms of social solidarity).[5] If they felt the need for a social theory of law at all, it would most likely be for theory that could recognise an active role for law in shaping society, engaging with power and intervening in or mediating political struggles. Durkheim's view of law might not seem to offer this possibility.

On the other hand, as has been noted, his work emphasises law's rootedness in values, its secure place in culture and its links with deep-rooted beliefs. These ideas, in some respects, elevate law to a place of great moral and cultural significance. Especially if their conservative aspects were stressed, they could be attractive to traditionally-minded lawyers. But since Durkheimian sociology advocated examining the social foundations of values that might be associated with law, it readily appeared threatening to conservative lawyers. It was to progressive, reformist jurists that it offered more attractions, insofar as it suggested that law, to be strong, must be rooted firmly in popular experience and understandings and could be understood as a social force only through empirical study of social change. The status of (conservative) jurists' doctrines might be usefully challenged by a sociological theory that saw the centre of gravity of law not in juristic disputes but in social conditions and popular belief systems.

Paul Huvelin's contact with, and eventual membership of, the Durkheim School may have been promoted initially as much by his restless intellectual curiosity and desire to challenge traditional ideas in his legal field (Appleton 1924:698), as by any wider sociological ambitions. Having obtained his doctorate in law for a thesis on an aspect of the history of commercial law (the law of markets and fairs), he joined the University of Lyon law faculty in 1899, aged 26, and stayed there for the rest of his career, becoming a full professor (of Roman law) in 1903.

Continental jurists were necessarily interested in Roman law as a primary historical foundation of European legal thought. Legal history, which Huvelin taught, was presented to French students largely as the reception, transmission and adaptation of Roman law into French civil law. But tracing the roots of current legal conceptions or traditions to distant sources such as the Twelve Tables of early Roman law (451-450 BC) could seem arbitrary unless one continued to ask where the concepts of this ancient law had come from. The whole approach of using history to expound legal tradition involved a kind of reading back from the ideas of the present to those of the past. So it could appear as a search for origins that might, for a curious and radical scholar, lie beyond the earliest documentary sources of Roman law themselves. Most cautious Roman law specialists would be likely to dismiss such ultimate inquiries as merely speculative. Huvelin, however, pursued them in a scholarly and imaginative way, using not just specifically legal materials but also information gleaned from other ancient literature. His work shows prodigious erudition combined with 'a pronounced taste for researches that give free flight to the imagination, where the ingenuity of conjectures can be given unfettered scope' (Appleton 1924:701).

He asks about the sources of Roman law itself in 'pre-legal' ideas, focusing on the field then designated as 'very ancient Roman law'; that is, the earliest conceptions of Roman law of which any evidence exists. These ancient legal conceptions are intermingled with religion, myth and magic. Early Roman legal procedures seemed to invoke magical elements (ritual being considered to produce specific effects on individuals' circumstances). To understand this ancient law required a process of imaginative reconstruction. Sketchy evidence of certain procedures and legal concepts was available, but often knowledge was lacking about the full meaning of the concepts or the significance of the procedures.

Huvelin was much impressed with the essay by Marcel Mauss and Henri Hubert on the nature of sacrifice, published in the *Année sociologique* in 1899. With the encouragement of Lévy, Huvelin wrote to Mauss in June of that year, explaining that he now saw the sociology of religion as a key to pursuing his studies. Sociological explanation of the nature of ritual seemed to him very relevant for an understanding of early legal procedures and he asked Mauss for guidance on relevant literature (Huvelin 2001). More generally, Huvelin thought that the work of the Durkheimian scholars might help in understanding how private law—especially the law of property, contract and civil wrongs (tort or delict)—emerged from the general religious matrix of early law which Durkheim had explained in *The Division of Labour*. For Huvelin, the interesting question was how, in societal development, private law (essentially the law of individual claims protecting private interests) became distinct from the general regulatory structures of the collective consciousness. What processes in history made this separate legal development possible?

Law and magic

It was the later essay by Mauss and Hubert, 'Outline of A General Theory of Magic', that gave Huvelin the clue he thought he needed. They saw religion and magic as having common sources in social belief but acting as opposing forces; magic rites do not unite society but are sometimes illicit and often secret, private activities. Magic is close to religion but turns away from the social cohesive function of religion and is a distortion and private appropriation. Magic becomes more individualistic and 'tends towards the concrete' and practical, while religion remains abstract and oriented to the collectivity. Magic is 'an art of doing things', a childish skill, the forerunner of techniques that would later discard all mystical elements. Belief in it is utilitarian, its value being only in its effects. Its kinship is with religion, on the one hand, and technology, on the other (Mauss and Hubert 1904:134-135/t.174-175). As a primitive technology, it shows how a collective phenomenon can assume individual forms.

Soon after Mauss and Hubert's essay was published in 1904, Durkheim invited Huvelin (who had been contributing to the *Année sociologique* since 1902) to write a full paper for the journal. Huvelin took the opportunity to produce an extremely learned piece on the origins of ideas of individual rights in magic (Huvelin 1907). He did not rely solely on Mauss and Hubert because he had already been exploring the idea that the procedures of early Roman law had magical elements and had published a long paper on the subject some years previously (Huvelin 1901). Nevertheless, Mauss and Hubert's idea of magic's technical power applicable to private ends, but closely related to religion, was of great importance. In 'Magie et droit individuel', Huvelin sees magic as distinguishable from religion by its purposes.[6] A social phenomenon becomes potentially illicit if it is turned to anti-social ends. Thus magic may or may not be illicit or anti-social, depending on how it is used. Huvelin's paper aims to show that one of its uses has been to provide various technical resources necessary for the earliest developments of private law.

First, magic gives individuals access to the power of spiritual forces that can be turned to their chosen private purposes. Second, magic can be a weapon of the wronged against the wrongdoer (for example, where the wrongdoer cannot be identified, magical rites allow some action to be taken against the unknown person). Third, magic can be harnessed as a guarantee of restitution. With the agreement of both parties to a transaction, a magic incantation or procedure provides for a sanction against one party which is to take effect only if that party defaults on undertakings given. Fourth, contracts can be enforced through the power of magical sanctions: future compliance with promises is guaranteed by the invocation of magical bonds between the parties. Fifth, through magic, writing assumes special importance in solemn procedures, the magical power of writing being well understood in many ancient civilisations. Huvelin's essay illustrates these processes and variants on them, with a wealth of detailed comparative examples from ancient history and the early legal (or law-like) practices of many civilisations.

In this way, 'in lending its own force to individual activity, magic prepared the way for legal sanctions' (Huvelin 1907:42). In early stages of legal development, magic allows individual activity to find a place in the purview of a law otherwise inspired by the collective sense of religion. Thereafter, Huvelin suggests, two possibilities present themselves. Sometimes, eventually, magical practices are prohibited once law becomes strong enough to do this. It becomes able to rely on its own resources of enforcement, which shed spiritual or magical elements. Otherwise, law coopts magic rites and rituals, as in the use of oaths, ordeals, formalities of writing and seals, symbolic transfers of property relying on precise rituals.

Huvelin's analysis is highly speculative, yet thoughtful and carefully documented. But is it Durkheimian? For Durkheim, law is social and moral in nature, not private and utilitarian. Yet these latter seem to be magic's characteristics in Durkheim's understanding (1912a:58, 61-62/t.42, 44-45). So how can society's law be built (in part) on magic? The thesis of 'Magie et droit individuel' is, in essence, Huvelin's effort to link restitutive law (indirectly) to religion and the collective consciousness in a way that Durkheim seemed unable to do in *The Division of Labour in Society*; Huvelin's argument is that the link is historical or developmental. He seeks to overcome what, in *The Division of Labour*, appears as the mystery of modern law's moral foundations (Cotterrell 1999:ch.7). For Durkheim (1893b/1902b: 81-83, 97/t.69-71, 82), restitutive law is not connected to the collective consciousness in any significant way. Huvelin claims that individual right (the foundation of all restitutive law) derives indirectly from religion or, more broadly, the matrix of beliefs and understandings that make up the collective consciousness. Over the ages this religious aspect is partly transformed into pure regulatory technique and magic is the medium that enables this to happen. Law distances itself from the religious matrix as technique, but the religious matrix itself makes possible a social evolution that gives rise to this freeing of law in the form of individual rights.

Huvelin seems to preserve what lawyers typically want to see in law: its power and freedom as a technique for providing security and facilitating projects, transactions and relationships. At the same time, he affirms Durkheim's view of law's origin in the religious matrix of early society. The approach was no doubt useful to him as a grounding for his researches on very ancient Roman law, helping to answer the questions: where did this law come from and how was it shaped? It might also have seemed appropriate for a modern jurist anxious to see law as somehow independent of broader aspects of social structure or social experience so as to be able to act on these.

Nevertheless, Huvelin's thesis is ultimately unstable. Is law a moral phenomenon or not? Durkheim (1893b: 276, 277) is clear that it is: law is entirely implicated with morality and inseparable from the conditions and needs of social solidarity; law is not a private resource. Huvelin's answer, however, seems to be both yes and no. On the one hand, law's moral nature is explicable ultimately in terms of its links to religion; on the other hand, private law's origins lie, it seems, in utilitarian technique. Magic provides the template for private law's mechanisms of control. It provides a model for law as a resource for private ends and as a privately appropriated technique. Law, it seems, takes on something of the utilitarian character of magic. This is surely something that Durkheim could not have accepted. For him, the utilitarian view of (a part of) law, implicit in Huvelin's explanation of its origins, would be incompatible with his essentially non-utilitarian conception of morality and with the assumption that law (inseparable from morality) must share morality's character in this respect.

Human bonds

A decade and a half later, just a few months before he died, Huvelin published his most striking effort to adapt Durkheim's thinking to a juristic outlook. He had planned to write an *Introduction to the Study of Law* that would draw on his sociological interests. In April 1923, he gave six lectures at the University of Brussels on 'The Spirit of French Law'. The sociological introduction to the course would have been incorporated into the planned book but ultimately it was the only part published, under the title 'Les cohésions humaines' (Huvelin 1923).

In this lecture, Huvelin tries to address in general sociological terms the question underlying his 'Magie et droit individuel' essay. What predates law? What, in sociological terms, provides the conditions for and shapes the social tasks of law? What gives rise to and makes possible human bonds (*cohésions humaines*)? And what is the place of law in securing and supporting these bonds? This is, of course, another way of posing Durkheim's question about the place of law in supporting or expressing social solidarity. But ultimately Huvelin answers this question in a very different way from Durkheim, whom he calls in the lecture 'my master'. Without Durkheim, declares Huvelin, there would be no sociology of law and, as regards method, 'we still rely on him, even when, as in my case, it is necessary to abandon some of his conclusions' (Huvelin 1923:137).

Huvelin tries to visualise the beginnings of civilization in his inquiry, just as he had in studying ancient Roman law. Law is not the source of social cohesion; something precedes it. The givens of sociological inquiry are (i) individuals in contact with each other, interacting and belonging to groups of many kinds, and (ii) societies. A society is the totality of individuals in a certain field of interaction, or encompassed by the same network of reciprocal influences (ibid.:134). The basis of all human bonds, Huvelin claims, is sympathy, a resonance that draws individuals together and produces positive feelings for another; not feelings of love (which seeks to possess or conquer the other) but of understanding, concern or liking. Sympathy expresses itself in sensitivity to the other and, to some extent (as a derivative characteristic) in imitation of others' ways or situations. It derives from two conditions, often interrelated: proximity and similarity. Thus, a moral unity often naturally arises among neighbours in frequent contact who become accustomed to each other, or among people who perceive themselves as having similar characteristics.

Solidarity, for Huvelin, is 'the totality of conscious and unconscious attractions deriving from sympathy' (ibid.:137). This is the basis of all social groupings in which people voluntarily link their individuality with that of others. Drawing such conclusions, he sees no problems with Durkheim's concept of mechanical solidarity, which he associates with the human bonds of attraction he describes. Yet it is clear that he understands the basis of this solidarity somewhat differently from the 'master', since sympathy provides for him an intermediate psychological element added to Durkheim's own association of similarity and proximity with mechanical solidarity.

As regards organic solidarity, however, Huvelin appears to break dramatically with Durkheim. He simply denies the existence of this kind of solidarity. The progress of the division of labour gives rise to individuality, which, for Huvelin, undermines solidarity based on sympathy. Remoteness and dissimilarity are sources of antipathy, not sympathy. The appearance of originality is often seen as a source of trouble or scandal; society acts against the innovator who is often seen as a heretic of some kind. But differentiation cannot be prevented; this tendency is just an incontestable fact. Organisation becomes more elaborate with societal development and takes the form of the creation and interrelating of specialised techniques or instruments (*outils*) to secure interdependence. Crucially, Huvelin insists, the division of labour does not produce sympathy and so cannot give rise to solidarity. The exchange of services leads rather to the effort to exploit others and dominate them.

Here then is the fundamental divergence from Durkheim. Durkheim notes that the division of labour can produce solidarity only if it is not forced (as in a master-slave relationship). But where, asks Huvelin, can we find authentic, voluntary specialisation or fully free vocations? 'One sees the birth and growth of originality, heresies, the spirit of invention, sectarianism. Sympathy born of similarity sees its scope curtailed by increasing differentiation. Antagonisms multiply' (1923:139). In such conditions, interdependence exists but specialisation creates an unstable environment, where reactions of antipathy may be dangerously unpredictable. So it is appropriate, in the context of a highly developed division of labour, to speak of *organic interdependence* but not organic solidarity.

In these conditions, according to Huvelin, law has precisely the powerful, directive role that Durkheim's sociology seems reluctant to accord it. Order is maintained in conditions of organic interdependence by two essential forces. The first is 'organised social constraint' (law), which requires a sovereign power to impose peace by means of a specialised force (ibid.: 141). As regards contracts, Huvelin denies that contractual relations create or express solidarity between the parties, who are likely to be concerned only with their own individual benefits. Law provides enforcement and 'a good number' of parties fulfil their contracts not through sympathy but fear (ibid.:142).

The other force maintaining the always precarious order of organic interdependence is that of common sensibilities or outlooks (*des états d'âme communs*) (ibid.). Interdependence can produce feelings of sympathy among individuals who exchange services in similar conditions. Similarity of situation and proximity may create spontaneous solidarity (perhaps Huvelin is thinking particularly of solidarity of classes, occupations or professions). In particular, common ideas and convictions can develop, even in conditions of elaborate division of labour. Some of these take on a 'religious veneer' as notions of justice, probity and honour (ibid.) and enter into law in various ways.

Indeed, law alone is not powerful enough to control the potential anarchy of the increasing division of labour. The 'religious imperatives' of justice, probity and honour, produced and strengthened in the enclaves of spontaneous solidarity in modern life, are necessary to support legal imperatives. Without them law would fail. It is vital to understand that law without moral support is 'almost nothing' (1923:143). Both moral and legal elements of order in modern society are indispensable. But the balance of attraction and constraint varies with the nature, history and conditions of social groups, and the direct roles of law and morals are inversely proportional: one compensates for the lack of the other. Huvelin calls this the 'law' of legal-moral compensations (*loi des compensations juridico-morales*) (ibid.).

Conclusion: Durkheim and Huvelin

Finally, therefore, Huvelin strongly affirms what is perhaps the central point to be gathered from Durkheim's legal theory as a whole: that law is inseparable from morality and that its function is to express and support this morality, which is the normative framework of solidarity in modern societies no less than earlier or simpler ones. But he departs from Durkheim in interesting ways. He wants to use a Durkheimian framework but (i) to avoid what he plainly sees as Durkheim's complacency about the nature and possibility of social solidarity in complex societies and (ii) to portray law as having a much more active role in fostering social cohesion than Durkheim explicitly recognises.

Reviewing 'Les cohésions humaines' in the *Année sociologique*, Mauss noted clear differences from Durkheim's positions but was sure that Huvelin's text would have interested Durkheim. Praising it warmly, he saw its framework as allowing interesting comparisons of societies in terms of their aptitude for organisation and spontaneous sociability (Mauss 1925b:27). And he thought that, had it been completed, Huvelin's book would have been an important contribution on the question of the state (Mauss 1931:12).

Yet comparison with Durkheim's positions shows the problematic features of Huvelin's ideas. In *The Division of Labour*, Durkheim treats the content and authority of law as given by the structural development of society. Law is tied to morality and expresses the conditions of solidarity. In this perspective, law is the moral structure of society expressed through particular organisational forms. In Durkheim's later work law is no longer discussed in terms of direct links between types of law and types of solidarity. Instead, the content of law (in modern and pre-modern societies alike) is considered in terms of the value system of the collective consciousness. In modern complex societies this value system is that of moral individualism. Law is thus a public expression of society's foundational values and central (officially promulgated) belief system.

By contrast, for Huvelin, law is influenced by morals but not derived from either the logic of the division of labour (creating the structural conditions of organic solidarity) or from popular morality. Law's function is not expressive but *corrective* of the sociologically 'normal' social order (which in complex modern societies is potentially one of chaos and disorder). Huvelin thus portrays law as a political force, somehow external to social life, that is available to control the natural tendencies of societal development, which are *away* from solidarity.

Huvelin, therefore, needs an 'independent' explanation—that is, an explanation outside the terms of the logic of Durkheim's sociology—of where law originates and gains its directive, controlling character. In 'Les cohésions humaines' he offers no such explanation. The earlier essay on magic and individual rights suggests, consistently with Durkheimian sociology, that law's origins are in the collective consciousness of early societal development, dominated by religion. Magic is the social phenomenon that eventually 'frees' law for future pragmatic development as a regulatory technique. Religion and magic thus provide the resources to support the development of legal ideas and institutions. Nevertheless, Huvelin's thesis does not actually explain the sociological origins of law, but rather the social phenomena that created conditions conducive to its emergence and development. Again, 'Les cohésions humaines' only suggests sociological reasons that make law necessary and give it its tasks. A sociological explanation of how law arises and develops is still missing.

Huvelin's effort to explain law's independent effectiveness and power is therefore unconvincing. Within the framework of Durkheimian explanation, law remains a cultural reflection and expression, rather than a sociologically intelligible instrument of societal guidance or control. This is not, however, to suggest that a Durkheimian view of law is unfruitful: far from it, because Durkheim's emphasis may be very important in highlighting law's interrelation with culture in many forms. It also properly insists on the significance of moral components in legal thought, practices and institutions, and in guaranteeing law's ultimate authority and defining its social functions.

But it is precisely what Paul Huvelin found missing in Durkheim's legal theory—an explanation of law's connections to power and politics in their historical settings—that later critics have almost always seen as its central problem. Mauss (1925a:497) admired Huvelin's 'taste for the practical and taste for ideas while being a master of legal dialectics' and he always saw the jurist as fully part of the Durkheim group. But the primary interest of Huvelin's work today lies in the fact that he tried, sympathetically and thoughtfully, to solve the fundamental problem of the place of power and politics in Durkheim's legal thinking and so to save the 'master' from himself.

Notes

1. The phrase is that of one of his followers, the jurist Emmanuel Lévy (1933:14, 35).
2. For detailed discussion of these and related matters see Cotterrell (1999).
3. See the effusive praise of Lévy in Mauss (1926). As regards Huvelin, Durkheim thought his ideas made him 'very close to us' and lost no time in enlisting his help for the *Année*. See Durkheim (1998a:319), and also his letter (1979:115) in support of Huvelin's Paris chair candidature in 1907.
4. On Lévy, see the symposium in *Droit et Société*, nos 56-57, 2004, the documentation in *Jean Jaurés cahiers trimestriels*, no 156, 2000, and Frobert (1997). On Huvelin, see the documentation in *Revue d'histoire des sciences humaines*, no 4, 2001, and Audren (2001).
5. It is significant that both Lévy and Huvelin were far more active in practical politics than Durkheim, though in Huvelin's case this activity was a late phase in his life and short-lived because of his early death.
6. Huvelin 1907:3. Cf. Durkheim's essential distinction: religion centres on a church, magic does not (1912a:58-65/t.42-47). Cf. Mauss and Hubert (1904:16/t.30).

References

Appleton, C. 1924 'Huvelin romaniste', *Revue historique de droit français et étranger*, 4e série, 3:696-704.

Audren, F. 2001 'Paul Huvelin (1873-1924): juriste et durkheimien', *Revue d'histoire des sciences humaines* 4:117-24.

Besnard, P. 1983a 'The "Année sociologique" Team', in Besnard 1983b:11-39.

____ ed. 1983b *The Sociological Domain: The Durkheimians and the Founding of French Sociology*, Cambridge: CUP.

Cotterrell, R. 1999 *Émile Durkheim: Law in a Moral Domain*, Stanford: Stanford University Press / Edinburgh: Edinburgh University Press.

____ 2004 'Emmanuel Lévy and Legal Studies: A View from Abroad' *Droit et Société* 56/57:131-141.

Durkheim, E. 1888a 'Cours de science sociale: leçon d'ouverture', in Durkheim 1970a:77-110.

____ 1893b Extract from Introduction, *De la division du travail social*, in Durkheim 1975b, II:257-288.

____ [1893b/1902b] 1986 *De la division du travail social*, Paris: PUF; 1984 *The Division of Labour in Society*, tr. W. D. Halls, London: Macmillan.

____ 1898c 'L'Individualisme et les intellectuels', in Durkheim 1970a:261-278.

____ 1900a(6)Review of Neukamp *Das Zwangsmoment im Recht...*, in Durkheim 1975b, III:319-321.

____ 1904a(4) Review of Lambert *La Fonction du droit civil comparé*, in Durkheim 1975b, III:266-271.

____ 1907d 'Sur la réforme des institutions judiciaires: l'enseignement du droit', in Durkheim 1975b, I:243-245.

____ 1909e 'Sociologie et sciences sociales', in Durkheim 1970a:137-159.

____ [1912a] 1985 *Les Formes élémentaires de la vie religieuse: le système totémique en Australie*, Paris: PUF; 1915 *The Elementary Forms of the Religious Life*, tr. J. W. Swain, London: Allen & Unwin.

____ 1970a *La science sociale et l'action*, ed. J-C. Filloux, Paris: PUF.

____ 1975b Textes, 3 vols., ed. V. Karady, Paris: Minuit.

____ 1979 Letter of 1907, *Revue française de sociologie* 20:115.

____ 1998a *Lettres à Marcel Mauss*, ed. P. Besnard and M. Fournier, Paris: PUF.

Favre, P. 1983 'The Absence of Political Sociology in the Durkheimian Classification of the Social Sciences', in Besnard 1983b:199-216.

Frobert, L. 1997 'Sociologie juridique et socialisme réformiste: note sur le projet d'Emmanuel Lévy, *Durkheimian Studies* (n.s.), 3:27-41.

Huvelin, P. [1901] 'Les tablettes magiques et le droit romain', in Huvelin 1929:219-271.

____ 1907 'Magie et droit individuel', *Année sociologique* 10:1-47.

____ [1923] 2001 'Les cohésions humaines: la place qu'y tiennent la contrainte juridique et l'attraction morale', *Revue d'histoire des sciences humaines* 4:131-144.

____ 1929 *Études d'histoire du droit commercial romain*, Paris: Sirey.

____ 2001 Letter of 1899 to Marcel Mauss, *Revue d'histoire des sciences humaines* 4:125-126.

Lévy. E. 1933 *Les fondements du droit*, Paris: Alcan.

Mauss, M. 1925a 'In memoriam: l'œuvre inédite de Durkheim et ses collaborateurs', in Mauss 1969, III:473-99.

____ 1925b Review of Huvelin 'Les cohésions humaines', in Mauss 1969, III:26-27.

____ 1926 'Emmanuel Lévy, juriste, socialiste et sociologue', in Mauss 1997: 729-732.

____ 1931 'La cohésion sociale dans les sociétés polysegmentaires', in Mauss 1969, III:11-25.

____ 1950 *Sociologie et anthropologie*, ed. C. Lévi-Strauss, Paris: PUF.

____ 1968-1969 *Œuvres*, 3 vols., ed. V. Karady, Paris: Minuit.

____ 1997 *Écrits politiques*, ed. M. Fournier, Paris: Fayard.

Mauss, M. and Hubert, H. 1899 'Essai sur la nature et la fonction du sacrifice', in Mauss 1968, I:193-307.

____ 1904 'Esquisse d'une théorie générale de la magie', in Mauss 1950: 1-141; 1972 *A General Theory of Magic*, tr. R. Brain, London: Routledge & Kegan Paul.

Vogt, W. P. 1983 'Obligation and Right: The Durkheimians and the Sociology of Law', in Besnard 1983b:177-198.

[8]

Emmanuel Lévy and Legal Studies : A View from Abroad

Roger Cotterrell *

Résumé

Emmanuel Lévy et les *legal studies* vus de l'étranger
Pratiquement inconnu dans le monde anglophone, Emmanuel Lévy, en raison de sa grande originalité, mérite pourtant d'être reconnu mondialement. Ses travaux sont comparables à la théorie juridique radicale qu'on trouve dans d'autres sociétés et sont plus nuancés que ceux d'autres juristes plus prestigieux à l'échelle mondiale. Ses analyses de la pratique politique du droit et sur l'impact social de la pensée juridique sont bien antérieures - de plusieurs décennies - aux idées similaires du mouvement des *critical legal studies* aux États-Unis. Sa compréhension du droit comme objet fondé sur des croyances potentiellement instables rappelle des thèmes des *legal studies* postmodernistes. S'il était parfois ambigu et vague dans ses travaux, cela s'explique par les éléments profondément contradictoires qui l'ont influencé.

Critique du droit - Croyance - Durkheim - Emmanuel Lévy - Postmodernisme - Réalisme juridique - Socialisme.

Summary

Emmanuel Lévy is almost entirely unknown in the anglophone world, yet his originality deserves international recognition. His work can be compared with radical legal theory in other societies but is more subtle than that of some internationally better known jurists. His ideas about the political practice of law and about the social significance of legal thought predated, by many decades, similar views of the American critical legal studies movement. His understanding of law as grounded in potentially unstable beliefs resonates with themes of postmodernist legal studies. Where Lévy is ambiguous and unclear, the cause often lies in the profoundly contradictory influences that shaped his thought.

Critical legal studies - Durkheim - Emmanuel Lévy - Faith - Legal realism - Postmodernism - Socialism.

L'auteur

Professeur de théorie du droit au Queen Mary and Westfield College, University of London.
Parmi ses publications :
- *Law, Democracy and Social Justice* (ed., avec B. Bercusson), Oxford, Blackwell, 1988 ;
- *The Sociology of Law : An Introduction*, London, Butterworths, 2nd ed., 1992 ;
- *Law and Society* (ed.), Aldershot, Dartmouth, 1994 ;
- *Law's Community : Legal Theory in Sociological Perspective,* Oxford, Clarendon Press, 1995 ;
- *Process and Substance : Lectures on Comparative Law* (ed.), London, Butterworths, 1995 ;
- *Émile Durkheim : Law in a Moral Domain*, Edinburgh, Edinburgh University Press, 1999 ;
- *Sociological Perspectives on Law* (ed.), 2 vol., Aldershot, Ashgate/Dartmouth, 2001 ;
- *The Politics of Jurisprudence ; A Critical Introduction to Legal Philosophy,* London, Lexis Nexis, 2nd ed., 2003.

* Queen Mary and Westfield College,
University of London,
Department of Law,
Mile End Road,
London E1 4NS.
<R.B.M.Cotterrell@qmul.ac.uk>

To be invited to contribute, as a writer from the common law tradition, to this symposium on a remarkable French legal scholar is an honour. Yet the task is daunting because vast intellectual distances must be bridged. Emmanuel Lévy's ideas, developed early in the twentieth century, are far removed from current tendencies in both Francophone and Anglophone legal scholarship and his work (none of it translated into English) is almost entirely unknown in English-language literature on law.

Until very recently, the only introduction in English to Lévy was in a translated adaptation of Georges Gurvitch's *Éléments de sociologie juridique* published in London as *Sociology of Law* in 1947. For theoretically-oriented researchers in England who, like the present writer, committed themselves to legal sociology in the 1970s, Gurvitch's book was essential reading to gain perspective on pioneer socio-legal theorists. But it criticised Lévy without explaining his ideas fully. Misleading translation of some key words (*e.g. valeurs, créances*) also made the discussion opaque.

At that time, Jean Carbonnier's *Sociologie juridique* (1978) surveyed the pioneers of sociology of law and briefly but intriguingly noted Lévy's originality and his socialist notoriety. Then André-Jean Arnaud's valuable *Critique de la raison juridique I : Où va la sociologie du droit ?* (1981) and some of Lévy's articles and pamphlets introduced me to his ideas and his unique style. Later I found copies of Lévy's *Les fondements du droit* and *La vision socialiste du droit*, dusty, fragile and yellowing in the basement of a London library. The books had clearly lain undisturbed for many years.

Learning more about Lévy over two decades, I realised that his situation and achievement had no parallels in the common law world, but his moral integrity and intellectual honesty seemed to shine like a beacon. The mixture of activism and scholarship in his career, and his apparently unquenchable idealism and personal tenacity, suggested that it would be good to know more about the details of his biography. A decade-long project of research on Émile Durkheim's legal sociology convinced me of Lévy's importance in radicalising aspects of Durkheimian legal thought, transforming it into a philosophy of political action by fusing and challenging it with other intellectual influences [1]. I felt that although Lévy's work had no direct relations with Anglophone legal scholarship, comparisons with « realist » and « critical » common law traditions were potentially worth exploring. This paper offers a few suggestions about possible directions for this exploration.

I. Between Marx and Durkheim

The main influences on Lévy's legal thought might be divided broadly into two clusters. One is the range of socialist thinking – related to but of-

1. Roger COTTERRELL, *Émile Durkheim : Law in a Moral Domain*, Edinburgh, Edinburgh University Press, Stanford, Stanford University Press, 1999, p. 188-194 and *passim*.

ten in tension with Marxism - that contributed to *socialisme juridique* in France and elsewhere in Europe at the beginning of the twentieth century [2]. The other is the sociological influence of Durkheim and the Durkheim school, of which Lévy was an active, committed and longstanding member. Neither of these intellectual movements seems to have left a living legacy for contemporary legal scholarship, so that the terrain in which Lévy worked might be thought to have become barren. But it would be far too negative and too unfair to his achievement to leave the matter at that.

He wrote : « *Au point de vue école, j'ai trouvé chez Durkheim confirmation de ceci : nous vivons de croyances* [3]. » In stressing the link between law and collective belief, Lévy focused on a matter that has become central to critical legal theory long after he wrote. The idea that we live by beliefs, and that law must be understood in its relation to collectively held convictions or understandings is an idea that is widespread in recent legal theories, though they explain that relation in many different ways.

Lévy's fusing of Durkheimian and socialist thought allows him to adopt a complex theoretical position. The path he traces runs between theories of ideology, on the one hand, and Durkheimian understandings of the nature of collective representations (*représentations collectives*), on the other. But these very different approaches to understanding the nature of shared beliefs or understandings suggest contrasting kinds of legal theory : on the one hand, theories of law as an instrument or reflection of ideology ; on the other, theories of law as a repository of social values, or as an expression of bonds of solidarity.

Theories of « law and ideology » tend to emphasise law's mystificatory functions or its contribution to the maintenance of dominant ideological currents. Legal doctrine and legal practice are seen as helping to promulgate broad systems of ideas and beliefs. The theoretical image of law is as a site of struggle for hearts and minds, a struggle between world-views, or between interpretations of the nature of social life. In Marxist terms, the conflict of ideas and beliefs is clearly part of class struggle. Law is both a prize and a weapon in this struggle [4]. The state is, in part, a mechanism through which ideological control is exercised [5].

Theories of « law and collective representations », derived from Durkheimian traditions, are likely to have a very different orientation. Law is not seen primarily as a site of struggle or a weapon but as an expression of

2. Nicole et André-Jean ARNAUD, « Le socialisme juridique à la "Belle Époque" : visages d'une aberration », in André-Jean ARNAUD (with Nicole ARNAUD-DUC), *Le droit trahi par la philosophie*, Rouen, CESPJ, 1977, p. 115-144.

3. Emmanuel LÉVY, *Les fondements du droit*, Paris, Alcan, 1933, p. 168.

4. Bernard EDELMAN, *Le droit saisi par la photographie. Éléments pour une théorie marxiste du droit*, Paris, Maspero, 1973, translated as *Ownership of the Image : Elements for a Marxist Theory of Law*, London, Routledge & Kegan Paul, 1979.

5. Louis ALTHUSSER, « Idéologie et appareils idéologiques d'État », translated as « Ideology and Ideological State Apparatuses », in Louis ALTHUSSER, *Essays on Ideology*, London, Verso, 1984, p. 1-60.

moral conditions. Law embodies the moral realities of social life. It represents collective convictions. Law's task is to define, rationalise and make explicit the currents of moral understanding and belief existing in society. Law expresses, in a public and codified form, social ideas that are otherwise inchoate and diffuse. The state is a mechanism for discovering, refining and expressing collective representations in a normative and institutional form, strengthening them and enabling them to foster social integration and solidarity [6].

The most serious ambiguities of Lévy's work arise from the fact that it uneasily combines the influences of these contrasting approaches to the relations of law and belief. But both approaches remain strongly present in current theoretical analyses of law. Certainly, in the Anglophone legal world, ideas about legal ideology, hegemony and the struggle of ideas conducted through law are now discussed in terms of critical legal studies (of many different kinds) [7] and rarely in terms of explicitly socialist legal thought or even less in terms of Marxism. Correspondingly, ideas about law's relation to morality, and about the importance of shared values expressed through law and serving as a foundation for solidarity, are rarely discussed at present in terms of Durkheimian sociology. But they are much debated in the language of communitarianism or republicanism [8].

The ambivalence in Lévy's approach can easily be noticed in his views on the state. On the one hand, he sees it as having the Durkheimian task of expressing and clarifying collective beliefs - especially those affecting credit, security, property and contracts. Where these beliefs are unstable, the state « *participe à l'instabilité des valeurs ; le droit devient perpétuellement en rupture* » [9]. Law and state reflect the shifting currents of collective belief. Law attempts to measure and reconcile conflicting representations. But Lévy sees the state itself becoming diffuse (even internationalised) [10] as it seeks to support a society that has become increasingly a regime of securities (*régime des valeurs*) depending entirely on unstable collective convictions (*croyances*) that cannot be contained within the borders of state jurisdiction.

Implicit in this view is the idea that changes in collective beliefs entirely determine the nature and function of the state and the role and content of law. Just as for Durkheim, « *les idées morales sont l'âme du droit* » [11], so for

---

6. Roger COTTERRELL, *Émile Durkheim : Law in a Moral Domain, op. cit.*, chs. 4 and 10.

7. See *e.g.* David KAIRYS (ed.), *The Politics of Law : A Progressive Critique*, New York, Basic Books, 3rd ed., 1998 ; Dan DANIELSEN and Karen ENGLE (eds.), *After Identity : A Reader in Law and Culture*, New York, Routledge, 1995.

8. See *e.g.* Philip SELZNICK, *The Communitarian Persuasion*, Washington D.C., Woodrow Wilson Center Press, 2002 ; ID., *The Moral Commonwealth*, Berkeley, University of California Press, 1992.

9. Emmanuel LÉVY, *Les fondements du droit, op. cit.*, p. 81.

10. *Ibid.*, p. 152.

11. Émile DURKHEIM, *La science sociale et l'action*, Paris, PUF, 2nd ed., 1987, p. 150.

Lévy « *la croyance crée le droit* » [12]. Law is rooted in belief : it is « *un substitut pratique de la religion* » and judges are its priests [13]. One senses that « *croyances* » might break law apart and force it into new forms. The state would have no option but to acquiesce in what might be called the social or cultural creation of law.

On the other hand, Lévy (citing Lassalle in support) suggests that law and rights *depend utterly* on the state. They are politically created and have no existence except through the state's directive force. « *Seul l'État assure ou enlève aux individus leurs droits [...]. C'est la loi qui donne, c'est la loi qui ôte, la loi, c'est à dire la volonté de l'État (législateurs, administrateurs, juges)* [14]. »

Thus, while one strand in Lévy's thought treats the state, as Durkheim did, as a deliberating « brain » distilling collective representations into legal form [15] and dependent on these representations, another strand treats the state as sovereign « will » without which collective representations cannot acquire legal force. The question is : is law ultimately dependent on the state which gives it force and authority, or is the state merely the servant of culturally or socially produced law ? Putting it more bluntly : are law's sources essentially political or moral ?

Lévy's ambivalence on the relations of law, state and society (the legacy of the conflicting theoretical influences on him) is unresolved because he leaves key ideas vague. His central concept of « *croyances* » is unclear, as Georges Gurvitch emphasised [16], and Lévy does not explain how collective beliefs arise, change and have effects. So their sociological character remains obscure : are they rooted in class interests (as ideology) or in conditions of social integration (as collective representations) ? How does law « measure » collective convictions ? By what processes are conflicts between them reconciled - by public deliberation (Durkheim) or by coercion or ideological mystification (Marx) ? How does law express « *croyances* » ? Does law alter them in the process because legal thought and doctrine have their own special qualities ? As a lawyer, Lévy could hardly be unaware of this issue, yet he has little to say about it. And these matters are not just of historical interest. Today the question of how far law reflects or mirrors collective understandings and how far it « constitutes » (defines and shapes) them remains a matter of debate [17].

12. Emmanuel LÉVY, *Les fondements du droit, op. cit.*, p. 96, 165.

13. *Ibid.*, p. 35-36 ; Emmanuel LÉVY, *La vision socialiste du droit*, Paris, Giard, 1926, p. 117-118.

14. Emmanuel LÉVY, *Les fondements du droit, op. cit.*, p. 53.

15. Émile DURKHEIM, *Leçons de sociologie*, Paris, PUF, 2nd ed., 1995, ch. 4 ; Roger COTTERRELL, *Émile Durkheim : Law in a Moral Domain, op. cit.*, ch. 10.

16. Georges GURVITCH, « Les fondements et l'évolution du droit d'après Emmanuel Lévy », in Georges GURVITCH, *L'expérience juridique et la philosophie pluraliste du droit*, Paris, Pedone, 1935, p. 190-191.

17. See *e.g.* Roger COTTERRELL, « Law as Constitutive », in Neil J. SMELSER and Paul B. BALTES (eds.), *International Encyclopedia of the Social and Behavioral Sciences*, Amsterdam, New York, Elsevier, 2001, p. 8497-8500.

Can law and morality be distinguished clearly ? For Lévy the distinction is that law provides a « measure » to limit, define and reconcile moral or other beliefs. But does morality not also « measure » (*i.e.* fix degrees of merit or responsibility) and address conflicts of beliefs or understandings ? Durkheim treats the difference between law and morality as only one of degree, legal rules being moral rules that have been institutionalised in certain vaguely defined ways [18]. Marx, by contrast, sees legal ideas and morality mainly as parallel expressions of ideology. Neither the Durkheimian nor the socialist traditions, on which Lévy draws, justifies any sharp separation of law and morality such as he seems to assume.

Despite its ambiguities, Lévy's work has enduring value for current legal studies. First, it stresses in a most striking way the *fragile* grounding of law's structures of meaning, and its *dependence* on social currents of belief and understanding that may combine (from the lawyer's standpoint) rational and irrational judgments. Secondly, Lévy's work is valuable for its provocative analysis of the conditions of stability and change in these social currents. It stresses that law is grounded in certain *faiths* that are not timeless, and that its legitimacy is never to be taken for granted.

Lévy's view of law is profoundly populist, asserting that law's strength lies ultimately not in the expertise of lawyers and judges who serve the state legal system but in the ideas of citizens at large. Eugen Ehrlich famously declared that the centre of gravity of law lies not in courts or legislation but in society itself [19]. Lévy goes much further : law's centre of gravity lies not just in « the social », understood as the patterns of social relations that make up society. It lies in the shifting social understandings and convictions of society's members : in collective psychology rather than observable patterns of social action.

Hence, in a striking radicalisation of legal thought, Lévy privileges, in every important respect, the understandings of non-lawyers over those of lawyers. Because he asserts that legal ideas depend for their legitimacy and ultimate meaning on the pre-legal convictions (*croyances*) of citizens, he cleverly turns on their head all traditional assumptions about the ultimate control of law. It is hardly surprising, then, that he should have provoked such antagonism to his theories among jurists ; and that he should have wanted primarily to address non-lawyers (socialist activists, industrial workers and, not least, the citizens of Lyon whom he served as deputy mayor) through his work.

---

18. Roger COTTERRELL, *Émile Durkheim : Law in a Moral Domain, op. cit.*, p. 60-61.

19. Eugen EHRLICH, *Fundamental Principles of the Sociology of Law*, Cambridge (Mass.), Harvard University Press, 1936, « Preface ».

II. Lévy and Critical Legal Studies

What connections exist between Lévy's ideas and modern legal thought ? Can there be points of contact with an international world of legal scholarship that has dismissed or, more often, simply been unaware of his work ?

Lévy can be regarded as a remarkable precursor of modern critical legal studies in some of its aspects. More than seven decades before the critical legal studies (CLS) movement came into being, initially in the United States, Lévy (with other adherents of *socialisme juridique*) emphasised the central CLS idea that legal concepts reflect broader social currents of thought and that as part of the process of challenging these broader currents, legal ideas themselves can be turned to new purposes and reinterpreted in new, more liberating and just ways. Long before CLS, Lévy saw legal argument as a form of political practice [20].

From the time of his thesis on *Preuve par titre du droit de propriété immobilière* (1896), he held the view that property rights existed only through the well-founded conviction of property owners in the soundness of their title. This conviction is made well-founded only by the general collective conviction as to what acts and circumstances are appropriate to give good proprietary title. Lassalle had argued that legal entitlements depend on and vary with collective belief in them : Lévy added to this the idea that these entitlements (or their value) could be destroyed by the *withdrawal of belief.*

Nearly a century after Lévy, CLS saw the political potential of forms of legal practice that aim to secure this withdrawal of belief in legal certitudes. CLS describes the establishment of these certitudes as the « reification » of legal ideas - their tendency to appear as solid, unshakeable and « thing-like ». To challenge reification involves a radical legal practice aiming to secure the withdrawal of belief in dominant interpretations of legal ideas. CLS describes this practice as one of attacking legal « hegemony ».

For CLS, legal ideas can potentially be turned upside-down by able, politically-aware, critical legal argument. Assumptions that underpin previous legal interpretations can be undermined and the possibility arises that judges might be forced to see legal ideas in radically new ways. Concepts of « property », « ownership », « contract », « responsibility », etc. might have to be reinterpreted in ways not foreseen by the court but brought forcibly to its attention. In the specific circumstances of a case, they might have to be broadened or narrowed to reflect changes in the social realities that the concepts presuppose.

As early as the beginning of the twentieth century, Lévy's prescription for radical legal practice in the service of the working classes was, in all es-

20. One of the clearest and fullest general accounts of CLS as a form of political practice focused on law is Robert GORDON, « Some Critical Theories of Law and Their Critics », in David KAIRYS (ed.), *The Politics of Law : A Progressive Critique, op. cit.*, p. 641-661.

sentials, the same as these CLS positions. To have thought through such ideas so long before American CLS scholars discovered and popularised them makes Lévy more than just a precursor. Even to call him a prophet seems inadequate. Although his analyses in simple class terms now seem archaic, his view of the social sources of the stability of legal ideas and his advocacy of a legal practice based in understanding those sources has striking contemporary resonance. His work in this respect is truly prescient.

Interestingly, Lévy's work also shows some similar faults to that of CLS. For all his proletarian sympathies, his political activism and his disdain for orthodox legal scholarship, Lévy's legal thought (like much CLS scholarship) is rooted in a law school environment. His analysis of the transformations of property and credit rights is in terms of juristic technicalities. Lévy devotes little attention to detailed social inquiry, despite his sympathy for sociology. The content of « *croyances collectives* » is largely assumed. He takes, from the socialist tradition and from Durkheimian sociology, broad assumptions about social change, using them as a generally unstated background for his juristic analysis. In a very similar way, American CLS writers cite the work of social theorists (*e.g.* Gramsci, Foucault, the Frankfurt School) often without engaging very much, themselves, in rigorous social analyses. In general, neither Lévy nor CLS recognises that a politics of law needs to be based on detailed empirical social inquiries about law's sources and effects and about the specific practices by which it is created, interpreted and enforced.

Lévy differs fundamentally, however, from CLS in the deterministic nature of his thought. This reflects both its Durkheimian and socialist origins. This determinism is perhaps the clearest marker of the decades that divide his thought from contemporary legal studies. CLS generally rejects any kind of social determination, any idea of history's inevitable movement in certain directions [21]. For Lévy, however, the movement from the traditional social regime of property rights to the modern social regime of credit rights and rights to securities is a structural movement, which he takes for granted as an historical process. Understood and interpreted correctly, this process guarantees, in Lévy's view, that the rights of labour will eventually absorb the rights of capital : the future is preordained [22]. Lévy's optimism about the role of law in ensuring the triumph of socialism is founded in his view that a historical transition in forms of wealth is occurring. In his analysis, this will inevitably benefit organised employees at the expense of capitalist employers. Whereas CLS insists that nothing is preordained and no laws of history make the future predictable, Lévy's theory is left in the dilemma that always haunted Marxist theory : how far is social change structurally

21. See *e.g.* Mark TUSHNET, « Critical Legal Studies : An Introduction to Its Origins and Underpinnings », *Journal of Legal Education*, 36, 1986, p. 505.

22. Emmanuel LÉVY, *Les fondements du droit, op. cit.*, p. 38-42.

determined and how far can it be produced by political initiative (for example, through law).

Lévy's work has disturbing implications for orthodox jurists not only because he turns the practice of law into a radical political practice. Perhaps more fundamentally, his idea that law rests only on subjective belief appears to *remove all objectivity* from juristic analysis. Legal edifices, on this view, are not just built on sand. A better metaphor would be that they float like hot-air balloons - and can collapse quickly if the thin fabric of belief is suddenly punctured. Otherwise, they can sink slowly if the air of conviction supporting them gradually cools. Similarly disturbing ideas about the radical « ungroundedness » of legal ideas were expounded during Lévy's lifetime (though after his main ideas were formed) by « legal realists » in the United States and other countries. More recently, in a different way, the idea has been associated with postmodern legal theory.

The American Felix Cohen wrote that any legal concept « that cannot pay up in the currency of fact, upon demand, is to be declared bankrupt, and we are to have no further dealings with it » [23]. It is nothing more than « transcendental nonsense ». The response of Cohen (and other legal realists) to the apparently ungrounded character of many legal ideas was, however, different from Lévy's.

For Lévy the convictions that underpin law are not entirely free-floating. In some way, they reflect structural conditions of society. As we have seen, Lévy's view of the nature and determinants of these conditions remains unclear (because of the ambivalence of his appeal to both Durkheimian and socialist traditions). A task of legal practice and legal analysis, however, is to help to bring law and the « *croyances* » it reflects more closely in touch with these structural conditions.

For American legal realists such as Cohen, legal practice and legal analysis must bring law into touch with « fact », meaning actual social behaviour. On the one hand, this involves discarding broad concepts and categories in favour of narrower ones that reflect distinctions in social practice (such as different kinds of contracting) [24]. On the other hand, bringing law into touch with facts involves focusing on judicial behaviour (what judges do, rather than what they say). It involves observing distinctions and categories employed by judges in deciding cases, even where these distinctions and categories are not recognised in orthodox legal concepts [25].

---

23. Felix S. Cohen, « Transcendental Nonsense and the Functional Approach » [1935], in Lucy Kramer Cohen (ed.), *The Legal Conscience : Selected Papers of Felix S. Cohen*, New Haven, Yale University Press, 1960, p. 48.

24. See *e.g.* the « Introduction » to Karl N. Llewellyn, *Cases and Materials on the Law of Sales*, Chicago, Callaghan, 1930.

25. See *e.g.* Karl N. Llewellyn, *The Common Law Tradition : Deciding Appeals*, Boston, Toronto, Little, Brown, 1960 ; Id., *The Case Law System in America*, Chicago, University of Chicago Press, 1989.

From a certain viewpoint, Lévy's theoretical approach to making law « realistic » is much more sophisticated than that of some American realism in his era. Instead of requiring that legal ideas « pay up in the currency of fact », Lévy asks that these ideas be attuned to theoretically explicable tendencies of social change. Though he offers no sociology himself, Lévy's legal theory presupposes a need for sociological interpretation of the environment in which law exists. In general, American legal realism made no such connections to social theory. Instead, its strength lay in its focus on the judicial function understood in behavioural and institutional terms.

III. Faith in Law

Lévy makes the dramatic claim that law is grounded in faith and that it has no substance beyond this. His legal theory, indeed, was sometimes called *fidéisme* [26]. This position may give him a limited affinity with aspects of postmodernist writing on law. Contemporary postmodernist scholars devote much attention to showing law's lack of ultimate foundations, and that its authority resides in myth or circular reasoning [27]. Some scholars are much concerned with the theoretical dependence of law on faith [28].

Here, Lévy may even offer useful correctives to recent tendencies in postmodernist thought about law. He sees law as grounded in (sometimes irrational) faith but he sees this grounding in the same constructive way that Durkheim does. Faith in law, if it is to be a living faith, must reflect the requirements of solidarity in society and must demand that these requirements be met through law.

In one sense, as some postmodernists claim, law is empty, supported only by fragile beliefs. Legal statuses may be masks to disguise the lack of more solid or meaningful bases of social relations [29]. It is as though a puff of wind could blow away the whole edifice. On the other hand, postmodernist legal writing often suggests that despite (or even because of) its lack of foundations, law is *strong*. When all social knowledge has been revealed as lacking foundations and the age of « grand narratives » has passed, law's transience, disposability and infinite adaptability seem congenial. Its moral emptiness makes it a form of knowledge entirely appropriate to a morally empty world.

26. Paul ROUBIER, « Emmanuel Lévy (1871-1944) », *Annales de l'Université de Lyon, 1943-1944*, fascicule spécial (Lyon, Imprimerie Bosc), 1945, p. 62.

27. Jacques DERRIDA, « Force of Law : The "Mystical Foundation of Authority" », in Drucilla CORNELL, Michel ROSENFELD and David Gray CARLSON (eds.), *Deconstruction and the Possibility of Justice*, New York, Routledge, 1992 ; Peter FITZPATRICK, *Modernism and the Grounds of Law*, Cambridge (UK), New York, Cambridge University Press, 2001.

28. See Peter OLIVER, Sionaidh DOUGLAS SCOTT and Victor TADROS (eds.), *Faith in Law : Essays in Legal Theory*, Oxford, Hart, 2000.

29. See Peter GOODRICH, *Languages of Law : From Logics of Memory to Nomadic Masks*, London, Weidenfeld and Nicolson, 1990, p. 295-296, 299-301.

For Lévy too, law can be morally empty, a mere shell, supported only by a lingering faith in its rationality or its elusive authority. This is how he sees the credit rights (*droits de créance*) of capital, when finally confronted by the credit rights of labour [30]. As law continues to ignore the social conditions of solidarity it must become ever more empty. One might even imagine that Lévy would not have been surprised at postmodernism's picture of the barrenness of contemporary law, a law that so often flies in the face of moral demands for just social relations.

Against the implications of much postmodernist writing, however, Lévy insists that law does not have to be like this. Something has to stand behind the mere faith that supports legal ideas as legitimate. Law need not be morally empty. Indeed, for Lévy, following Durkheim, law's vitality depends on it being morally rich. And this means that law should express the normative requirements of social solidarity, in the various social relations of community that law is called on to regulate. Lévy's tragic failure was that he thought this process was predetermined : that the movement of history would eventually ensure that law would reflect the conditions of solidarity. One can only imagine his anguish as experience (perhaps especially the experience of two world wars) surely eventually made him realise his mistake.

The legacy of Lévy's work for current legal studies is in its fertile suggestiveness more than in its specific positions. He reminds us of law's dependence on faith and belief. He stresses that the conditions of its legitimacy are ultimately moral. He emphasises that law's vitality depends on its contribution to social solidarity, and he insists that legal practice as a form of political practice should promote that contribution. Lévy suggests (through his own theoretical ambivalence, noted above) the problematic relation of law and the state. Very importantly, he stresses that the social forces shaping law now increasingly escape limitation by national boundaries. All these orientations in his work are highly relevant to current legal theory.

As is so often noted by those who read Lévy's writings, they are frustratingly allusive, unclear and ambiguous : full of rich but undeveloped observations. We can regret, as Durkheim did [31], that Lévy, « *plein de dispositions* », did not write more and complete his projects more satisfactorily. Yet, given the still profoundly stimulating qualities of many of his ideas, this fascinating French jurist surely deserves to find some of the international recognition that has eluded him for a century.

30. Emmanuel LÉVY, *Les fondements du droit, op. cit.*, p. 29-30, 38-39.
31. Émile DURKHEIM, *Lettres à Marcel Mauss*, Paris, PUF, 1998, p. 253.

[9]

GEORGES DAVY AND THE ORIGIN OF CONTRACT

GEOFFREY MACCORMACK*

Whereas the views of Sir Henry Maine on the relationship between status and contract are sufficiently well known in Anglo-American jurisprudence, those of Georges Davy, one of the group of scholars inspired by and associated with Emile Durkheim, appear by and large to be unknown. This is unfortunate as Davy, while accepting Maine's thesis in outline, produced the most detailed account of the development of "contract" from "status" that has yet been attempted. The reasons for the lack of knowledge of his work are that his principal essay, *La foi jurée,* has never been translated into English and that even the French original is hard to find (*1*). In France his work is cited with approval but I have not seen a full discussion or criticism of it (*2*). In comparing the views of Maine and Davy, I have restricted myself to those features of the latter's reconstruction which can still be said to possess some degree of plausibility. He himself subscribed to theories which have now been discredited, such as the assumptions that all primitive societies have a totem through which the members are mystically and magically bound together (*3*), and that they have followed a particular course of evolution marked by a transition from matrilineal to patrilineal succession. Elements of this kind in his account I have on the whole disregarded.

In maintaining "that the movement of the progressive societies has hitherto been a movement from Status to Contract" (*4*), Maine asserted the following propositions. The individual in a primitive or archaic society derived his rights and duties from his position in the family to which he belonged. Not only did his particular position, as a son, for example, require a certain mode of behaviour, but generally he was bound to obey the commands of the head of the household. It was not open to him either to modify his position by agreement with other members of the family, or to conduct independent transactions with persons outside the family.

*Professor of Jurisprudence, University of Aberdeen.

(*1*) It was his doctoral thesis published in Paris (Alcan, 1922). I am grateful to Professor G. van den Bergh of the University of Utrecht for supplying me with a photocopy. A summary of Davy's views is given in a collaborative work that has been translated into English: A. Moret and G. Davy, *From Tribe to Empire* (1926). This contains a useful account of the theory of social evolution which underlies his treatment of contract. For an account of his life and work—he died in 1976—see A. Girard, *L'Année Sociologique* 27 (1976), 5.

(*2*) Cf. M. Mauss, *The Gift,* translated by I. Cunnison (1954): J.-C. Rouveyran, "Contribution à une sociologie des contrats", *L'Année Sociologique* 28 (1977), 115.

(*3*) Davy is here following the thesis of E. Durkheim. See the latter's *The Elementary Forms of the Religious Life,* translated by J. W. Swain (1915).

(*4*) *Ancient Law,* with introduction and notes by Sir Frederick Pollock (1906), 174.

Only the head of the household might engage in transactions with the head of other households. He can be said to "contract", but only in the sense that he attracted obligation by completing the formalities prescribed for the transaction. Even in this case no obligation flowed from mere agreement. Contract proper comes into being only when three conditions are fulfilled: the individual members of the family acquire the power to enter into transactions in their own right with other people, the element of consent or promise becomes disengaged from the formalities expressing it, and obligations arising from agreement are regarded as distinct from those arising from the alienation of property (*5*).

Davy, while accepting some of Maine's generalisations, in particular the historical priority of status over contract (*6*), proposes a rather different scheme for the evolution of the notion of contract. Maine had relied heavily on Roman Law for his account of the development of contract, whereas Davy utilised primarily anthropological accounts of some North American Indian peoples which had not been available to his predecessor. On the basis of the anthropological evidence Davy singled out marriage and the institution of the potlatch (competitive gift-giving) as the two most important factors in the development of contract. As was the practice with members of the sociological school founded by Durkheim, Davy considered marriage and the potlatch not in isolation but as aspects of the totality of social life and change. To some extent I have disregarded the general social context which he constructs as a setting for the specifically "contractual" institutions, since it is in this area that his propositions are most questionable.

Like Maine, Davy held that recognition of the obligatory force of a promise or an agreement was the product of a long period of evolution. The essential feature of this process is that obligations originally derived from "status" come, through a series of complex developments, to be derived from promises or agreements. The process is divided by Davy into three main stages which may be denominated that of the family, marriage and the potlatch. Strictly, these stages are all "pre-contractual", that is, contractual functions are accomplished through means other than contract. This appears to be a way of saying that the basis of transactions in primitive societies is the status of the parties, whereas in advanced societies it is agreement. With the third stage, characterised by the institution of the potlatch, the beginnings of contract proper can be recognised.

In the most primitive societies obligations are derived from membership in a family and alliance by marriage. The way in which a member of a family is to behave with respect to other members is prescribed for him by the position which he occupies in the family. "Family" is here to be understood in a sense wider than that of the household. It comprises the

(*5*) Maine, *op. cit.*, 172 ff., 325 ff.
(*6*) *Foi jurée*, 6 n. 1.

largest unit, for example, the clan, within which obligations arising from blood relationship are recognised (7). The problem for primitive man is to devise a means by which he is able to enter into a relationship with outsiders, people who do not belong to his family. Contract, the means adopted by modern man, is not available to him. Instead, he has either to incorporate the stranger into his own family or create an analogous relationship through marriage into the latter's family. The principal institution by which incorporation into the family is achieved is the blood covenant. Through a rite by which the stranger mingles his blood with that of a member of the family, he is incorporated into the family as a brother (8). The same effect may be achieved through the sharing of food. Only by the change of status brought about through incorporation into the family by such means is the stranger able to enter into a relationship with it and so change the content of his rights and duties (9).

Marriage, which is in practice far more important than the blood covenant, operates in a similar fashion by modifying the rights and duties of the members of the families of the bride and groom through the production of a change of status. It achieves this in two different ways. First, it brings about a "communion" between the families through the introduction of the bride into the household of the groom and the resulting sexual union. From this point of view, marriage operates in a manner analogous to the blood covenant and may be seen as a "pre-contractual" means by which the enmity between the families is removed. The rule of exogamy forces an individual to take a wife from a group not related by blood to his own. Hence he has to look for her in a rival, naturally hostile group. Linking of the two groups through marriage contains or controls the natural enmity without necessarily removing it altogether. Marriage thus operates as a "pre-contractual" instrument, producing the same result as agreement produces in more developed societies.

Second, the marriage sets up a relationship of collaboration between the wife-giving and the wife-receiving groups marked by the reciprocal performance of services and the making of gifts. It functions both as a "contract" by which the rights and privileges of the bride's father are enabled to pass to his daughter's children through the medium of his son-in-law (contrat successoral), and as a "contract" which makes possible a recurrent exchange of goods and services between two groups (contrat d'échange). Again Davy's essential point is that results deriving in modern society from agreements or declarations of intention (trans-

(7) For Davy what is important is the mystical not the physiological aspect of kinship, that is, the belief that a certain group is descended from a certain ancestor where the relationship cannot be effectively traced but is symbolised by "la communauté de totem" (34-5). He adds: "le lien de parenté, au sens large que nous venons d'indiquer, est le modèle et le prototype de tout lien juridique" (35).

(8) I have disregarded Davy's treatment of the blood covenant as a sacrifice and his emphasis on the need for the stranger to "participate" in the family's totem.

(9) See, generally, ch. I of *Foi jurée*.

mission of rights and privileges, exchange of goods and services) can be achieved in the simplest societies only through a change in the status of individuals.

As a "contract of exchange", marriage exhibits several important features. It is a mechanism—and, indeed, the earliest known—by which different groups of people are enabled to acquire goods from each other. Within the general sphere of exchange set up by the marriage one finds the first examples of specific obligations attached to specific individuals, that is, particular members of the one family are under an obligation to perform specific services for, or transfer specific goods to, particular members of the other. Marriage also permits a solution to what Davy describes as "le gros problème du contrat" *(10)*: how to establish an interval in time between the creation of an obligation and its fulfilment? What he means may be illustrated from his account of marriage among the Kwakiutl, a North American Indian people.

A Kwakiutl bridegroom makes a payment to the man whose daughter he wishes to secure for his wife. This is only part of what he owes. The other, essential part of his obligation to be fulfilled in the future is the production of children. The initial cash payment may be regarded as arra, the birth of children representing the final discharge of the obligation incurred on marriage. On the other side, the father-in-law, in return for the arra, gives his daughter. She, too, can be regarded as arra, since the father's obligation is only finally discharged on the birth of a child. When this occurs he surrenders his titles and badges of rank to his son-in-law (through whom they pass to the child), and makes him a payment representing a return for the arra together with enormous interest. The purpose of the marriage was to secure transmission of the titles and badges of rank held by the wife's father to her children. Since this purpose could be achieved only at a time subsequent to the conclusion of the marriage, one had a situation in which the obligation (to surrender the titles) arose at the time the father gave his daughter as a bride, but could be fulfilled only later when a child was born. The giving of the daughter as arra is what ensures the later fulfilment of the obligation *(11)*.

Although marriage, on Davy's analysis, permits a solution to one of the fundamental problems of contract, namely, how to postpone the fulfilment of an obligation to a time subsequent to its creation, the solution is still derived from the status of the parties to the transaction. It is the status of an individual as daughter given in marriage by her father which enables her to function as arra with respect to the obligations created by the marriage. Contract has not yet been emancipated from status. This decisive step is accomplished through the institution of the potlatch. Davy bases his account of the potlatch principally on studies of certain North

(10) *Foi jurée*, 109.
(11) See, generally, ch. II of *Foi jurée*.

American peoples, although he cites some Melanesian data as well. Its most obvious characteristic is a widescale distribution of property by a group or individual to members of another group to the accompaniment of feasting and ceremony. The distribution may take place on a number of different occasions and fulfil a number of different functions. In all cases the recipients are under an obligation to make a return at an appropriate time. Should they fail to return more than they have received, they lose prestige and standing in the community. Hence one of the most important functions of the potlatch is the acquisition of titles and rank through success in the process of competitive gift-giving (*12*).

So varied and complex are the facts subsumed under the name potlatch that Davy suggests sense is to be made of them only if two basic types of potlatch are distinguished. The first and most primitive operates only between two groups who are in some way connected, as by marriage. Members of the one group on certain set occasions, in particular, funerals, marriages, initiations and births, perform certain services for, or make certain payments to, members of the other. The latter now incur the obligation to make a return as and when appropriate. This form of potlatch is still bound to the notion of status, since the occasions on which the services and payments are due are precisely those in which a change of status is brought about.

The other more developed form of potlatch is not bound to status in this way, even though it may have the effect of changing the status of those who participate in it. Davy describes it as a "simple contrat commercial de prêt dont le fonctionnement est absolument libre" (*13*). By this he means that the most striking features of the arrangement are the obligation imposed upon the recipient of the property to repay the equivalent with interest, and the fact that individuals as well as groups may distribute property to others whenever they wish; the distribution is not limited to occasions on which a particular change of status has occurred, such as a death, a marriage or a birth. However, even this developed form of potlatch is not yet a purely juridical instrument, since it possesses also economic and social aspects. It is a means for both the circulation of goods and wealth within the community and the acquisition of prestige, titles and rank by the most successful participant.

Although the developed potlatch is an economic and social as well as a juridical instrument, its juridical features are not only clearly identifiable, but are such that it may legitimately be described as a contract, even though the stage has still not been reached in which agreement in itself is held to produce legal rights and duties. These are the distinction between, and the identification of, separate parties, the creation of a relation between those parties and the fact that acceptance of the initial distribution produces an obligation to make a return with interest. The

(*12*) See, generally, ch. II of *Foi jurée*.
(*13*) *Op. cit.*, 170.

relationship between the parties is that of creditor and debtor and "cette constitution de dette c'est bien l'essence du contrat" (*14*).

On Davy's analysis it is the potlatch which contributes an essential condition for the emergence of contract, that of individualism. In societies which know only the primitive potlatch, individuals make payments to members of other groups, but the payments are made on account of the group and are given to individuals in their capacity as members of their group. The position begins to be different once a society has acquired the more sophisticated potlatch. One of the main functions of this potlatch is to allow individuals, through the distribution and display of wealth, to assert and maintain superiority *vis-à-vis* other individuals. In consequence, two important changes occur. Certain individuals come to be recognised as chiefs, as persons possessed of greater authority and power than others in the community. They acquire this position not in virtue of their birth, that is, in virtue of inheriting a particular position within a group, but through the wealth which they are able to control. In other words, they owe their status to their capabilities and merits as individuals (*15*). The emergence of chiefs in a society transforms it from one based broadly on a relationship between equals to one characterised by relationships between superiors and inferiors. The "feudal" structure of society is shown both by the relationship between a chief and his "vassals" or "clients" and the relationship between chiefs themselves. A chief deals with his own supporters on the basis of superior to inferior. He is under an obligation to distribute to them part of what he receives in potlatches, but they are under an obligation to help him in the acquisition of wealth for his own potlatches. Under this relationship the chief appears as "creditor" and his "vassals" as "debtors". Nor does a relationship of equality obtain between chiefs. Their success in the giving of potlatches determines their rank *vis-à-vis* each other. The one who manages to amass and distribute the greatest amount of property is accorded the highest prestige. He is the "creditor" and the inferior chiefs are his "debtors". The result of a potlatch is to rank the participants as "creditor" or "debtor" *vis-à-vis* each other (*16*).

The point Davy wishes to make is that the potlatch in its developed form paves the way for, but does not finally accomplish, the emergence of contract. Through the mechanism of the potlatch it is possible for persons in their capacity as individuals to engage in exchanges of property with each other. But they do not meet as equals. Each has a status of inferior or superior in relation to the other. One cannot say that contract proper has been achieved until the "feudal" stage of society has given way to the stage in which individuals transact with each other as equals.

(*14*) *Op. cit.*, 238-9.

(*15*) Davy represents the process of individualization as one in which the power originally diffused throughout the group comes to be concentrated in an individual as chief.

(*16*) *Op. cit.*, ch. V.

Although Davy's detailed interpretation of the ethnographic data can be questioned, as can the background of social evolution upon which he relies, I propose to leave aside this aspect of his work and consider instead what seems to me to be the more important (and defensible) theoretical issues suggested by his discussion *(17)*. In the first place, one can accept the proposition, which is now indeed something of a truism, that there are or have existed societies (often called "primitive") in which the relationships of kinship and marriage are the most important source of rights and duties. What this means is that a person's behaviour *vis-à-vis* another is determined for him by the positions they respectively occupy in the network of kinship and marriage. Nevertheless, one should not assume that in such societies there is no room at all for transactions between individuals based purely on elements of utility and bargaining powers.

More difficult to assess and, possibly, more contentious is Davy's assertion that societies in their earliest manifestations attach rights and duties to groups and not individuals. The problem of the definition of a group is not one that can be ventilated here. Usually, by a group in this context is meant a family (household) or lineage or clan, that is a number of persons connected by blood where the relationship is acknowledged by the members of the group. The statement that obligations inhere in groups and not individuals is ambiguous and may yield different meanings. If one observes the manner of life of a "primitive" group, one may find that individual members rarely perform any act entirely on their own. The basic routines of work and play are carried out collectively, though there may be some division of labour within the group either between men and women or adults and children. Such collective behaviour becomes marked when it is necessary to have dealings with another group, for example, one related by marriage. On such occasions one might find that all the members of both groups come together and feast and exchange gifts. In so far as the making of gifts can be described as the fulfilment of an obligation, one might say that the obligation rests upon the group, in the sense that all its members meet and carry it out collectively. But, in the absence of further evidence, one would not be justified in concluding that the group itself was to be conceived as a legal entity (or corporation) to which the obligation attached. Nor should one overlook the fact that sometimes important obligations are carried out individually and not collectively. A well known example from Malinowski's studies of life in the Trobriand Islands is the obligation resting on the husband to supply his wife's brothers with a large proportion of his crop *(18)*.

(17) For what follows see further my contribution to *Essays in Honour of Julius Stone* (forthcoming): "Gift", "Exchange" and "Contract".

(18) B. Malinowski, *Soil-Tilling and Agricultural Rites in the Trobriand Islands I*, second edition (1966), 188 ff. Even here the "individual" aspect should not be pressed too far, since it is expected that a brother-in-law will be helped by his younger brothers in the production of the harvest to be given to his sister's husband.

There is another sense in which "group" can be distinguished from individual obligation. If an obligation attaches to an individual in virtue of the status or position which he has within or *vis-à-vis* a group, one might wish to describe the obligation as belonging to or derived from a group, in order to distinguish it from an obligation which an individual might incur freely through his own act in respect of a particular transaction into which he has entered. From this point of view, the obligation on the Trobriand husband to supply his brothers-in-law with produce is a "group" not an individual obligation, because it is derived from his position or status in relation to his wife's family.

Group obligation in both of the senses which I have distinguished can be said to be historically prior to, or even more primitive than, individual obligation. Indeed, the second sense corresponds to what is normally meant by the historical priority of status over contract. But such a generalization should be understood in the sense of "what is predominantly the case" or "what is most likely to be found". In other words, one cannot assume that even in the most "primitive" or "simple" societies all obligations are "group" or derived from "status". There may be some transactions, especially of the trafficking or bargaining variety, which are concluded between individuals on the basis of their utility, and not because they are required by the positions occupied by the parties in their respective groups. This view of the "status" and "contract" question has an important consequence. Although it does not deny an historical progression from status to contract, in the sense that the latter notion has a far greater part to play in "developed" societies than the former, it rejects the idea of a logical or necessary connection between the two notions and hence the argument that contract has evolved or is some way derived from status.

Davy's isolation of the potlatch as the most significant factor in the development of contract can be viewed as drawing attention to three distinct types of phenomena. There is, first, the potlatch proper, known from some North American Indian peoples. At the risk of considerable over-simplification this may be described as a feast, given for the purpose of acquiring prestige, at which large quantities of valuables are given away or destroyed. Second, there is the obligation upon the members of one group to distribute property to, or perform services for, the members of another group on certain set occasions, in particular, marriage, birth, initiation and death. Finally, there is the general practice of exchange of gifts, which includes, but goes beyond, the other two classes of phenomena. Davy himself places the greatest emphasis on the potlatch as a means by which rank and titles are transferred and on the obligatory "prestations" associated with marriage, birth, initiation and death. He does not overlook gift-exchange, but considers it as the economic aspect of the potlatch and the other prestations. However, the practice merits closer attention than he accorded it. Gift giving, considered as a universal phenomenon, is more relevant to the development of contract than its more particular manifestations in the potlatch and the payments that become due on certain ritual occasions.

Most transactions found in simple societies under which property passes from one person (or collection of persons) to another may be analysed as gifts (*19*). What this means is that the property is handed over with the apparent intention of conferring a benefit on the recipient. Normally, there is no bargaining and no explicit reference to the expectation of a return. In fact, both parties understand that a return will be made. Yet, it is important not only that the pretence of pure gratuity be maintained, but also that there should be no undue haste in the offer of property by way of return. One of the reasons, possibly the most important, for the concentration on the notion of benefit is the nature of the relationships between individuals in simple societies. Normally, people have dealings with other people to whom they are related by blood or marriage. The relationship itself requires them to be in contact. Hence, it is best maintained through transactions which emphasise an element of friendliness and co-operation. Where people enter into a relationship for the first time, that is, they are not already related in any significant sense through blood or marriage, it is contemplated as lasting over a considerable period of time. Hence, it is again important that the elements of friendliness and co-operation should be to the fore. This is so even where the relationship has been formed for the purpose of trading. Many societies know the institution of the trading partnership, in which a person from one community trades with a person from another, thereby enabling each community to acquire goods which it does not produce itself. For example, it was a common practice for an Eskimo living near the coast to form a trading partnership with one living inland so enabling an exchange of inland and coastal produce. Not only do the partners make each other gifts which are not part of the trade as such, but the produce which they exchange is given in the form of a gift. The relationship is characterised by the trust of each partner in the generosity of the other (*20*).

The prevalence of gift-exchange suggests another point. Although the most important factor in the obligation to make a return is the relationship between the parties, one should not overlook the possibility that the receipt of property is, in itself, considered to impose an obligation to make a return. Certainly, there appear to be sound psychological reasons for arguing that acceptance of a present normally makes the recipient feel inferior to the donor. Furthermore, there is an instinctive recognition, not always easily distinguishable from the feeling of inferiority, that one should not benefit from a gift without making some return. This is the feeling which underlies notions of fairness and doctrines of unjust enrich-

(*19*) I leave aside payments made avowedly as recompense for a wrong, though even here analysis as gifts may not be inappropriate.

(*20*) See R. F. Spencer, *The North Alaskan Eskimo* (1959), 167 ff.

ment. From a combination of such feelings and attitudes arises an explicit obligation, accepted within a community, that an equivalent should be returned for what has been given.

One need look no further than the gift to find the solution to what Davy calls the problem of deferred fulfilment of an obligation. There is no need to resort to the particular instance of marriage among the Kwakiutl and impose upon it an artificial construction. The notion of gift itself furnishes the most satisfactory explanation. Someone who has received a gift is under an obligation to make a return. The obligation itself arises both from the acceptance of the property and the relationship between the parties. It is the latter fact which explains the necessity for deferring fulfilment of the obligation. The parties stand in a relationship characterised, at least overtly, by friendliness and co-operation (*21*). Hence, it is necessary to avoid the appearance of a purely economic or utilitarian transaction. What is important is the conferring of a benefit, not the effecting of a bargain demanding a swift return.

It is also the nature of the relationship between the parties which supplies the key to the understanding of the distinction between gift and contract. If property is transferred by way of a gift, the overt intention of the transferor is to confer a benefit on the transferee, and to provide tangible evidence of the friendly nature of their relation and the importance he attaches to it. The relationship itself is based on some element distinct from the need or wish to acquire particular property. On the other hand, the relationship between two contracting parties is determined by the terms of the contract and generally ends once its obligations have been fulfilled. The parties may stand in some relationship independent of the contract which they have concluded, but the relationship set up by the contract is distinct from any other that might exist. The objective of the contract may be described as economic or utilitarian. Each party wishes to obtain something of value from the other. Their agreement is based on their measurement of the values, and hence it is often the result of a process of bargaining (*22*).

The relationship between gift and contract is complex. All that will be attempted here is one or two generalizations. Two propositions appear incontrovertible. It is not the case that contract has evolved from gift, in the sense that the latter is the "source" or "origin" of the former. Even in a simple society one may discern transactions which would qualify as contracts in accordance with the criteria suggested above. On the other hand, one can affirm both that gift plays a much greater role in simple societies than contract and that in developed societies the reverse holds true. The reason for this lies in the change in social relationships which

(*21*) It is precisely in this respect that the potlatch constitutes an exception since the relations between the competing and rival chiefs may not be friendly.

(*22*) Elements of utility may also be present in gift exchanges. The point is that the emphasis is on generosity and the desire to confer a benefit.

very gradually takes place in a society's development. As soon as relationships cease to be restricted to those derived from kinship and marriage, people may deal with others on a temporary basis and restrict their relationship to the particular transaction. They no longer need to enter into or maintain a relationship emphasising friendliness and co-operation over a long period of time. It is in this environment that contract is able to flourish. Provided one understands the statement with a proper degree of caution, one may state that in a developed society contract fulfils the same function as gift fulfils in simple societies, that is, it provides the medium for the exchange of property between people. What in modern societies is achieved by contracts of sale, loan or hire was achieved in simple societies by exchanges of property viewed as gifts. Of course, even today contracts are often made between people who are related or who are friends. The relationship created by the contract is distinct from, but nevertheless influenced by, the other, more enduring relationship. There will probably be a reluctance on the part of either side to take the final step of seeking to enforce the contract by legal action. Such a step, if taken, marks the end of any real relationship between the parties.

There is much to criticise in Davy with respect both to the general theories he adopted and the detailed interpretations he proposed of the ethnographic data. Nevertheless, he had a better perception than Maine of the ways in which relationships of kinship and marriage determined an individual's rights, obligations and expectancies. This is not surprising since he had at his disposition a far wider range of anthropological studies than had Maine. Possibly his most important insight was his grasp, albeit in a distorted fashion, of the significance of gift for the history of contract. He placed too much emphasis on one particular type of gift (that associated with the potlatch) and erred in supposing that contract evolved from it. Yet, underlying his account was an awareness of the fact that in simple societies the making of gifts achieved many of the purposes that in modern societies are achieved by contract (*23*).

(*23*) I would like to thank Professor F. Lyall for his helpful comments on a draft of this note.

[10]

Integrating Reciprocal Perspectives : On Gurvitch's Theory of Immediate Jural Experience

Reza Banakar *

Prologue

> What are the roots that clutch, what branches grow
> Out of this stony rubbish ? Son of man,
> You cannot say, or guess, for you know only
> A heap of broken images, where the sun beats,
> And the dead tree gives no shelter, the cricket no relief,
> And the dry stone no sound of water...
>
> T. S. Eliot, *The Waste Land*

One cold February morning in 1990, a team of Council workers arrived at Arne Ekholm's cottage, a few miles outside the city of Ystad in southern Sweden. A storage depot was set up, and lorries and excavators were driven up to the cottage, shortly after which a complete destruction of the garden in front of the cottage began. This garden, now being stripped of its plantation, had been designed and built by Arne Ekholm's parents some seventy years earlier. It took three working days to lay waste Ekholm's family garden. The top soil was shovelled away together with the winter sleeping herbs, rare plants, three bee-hives with living colonies and anything else which happened to be in the garden at the time.

A few weeks later, Arne Ekholm — who, due to old age, stayed mostly at a care centre for the elderly — received a bill from the Council for 40,544 Swedish Kronor ($5,800) for the work done on his garden, which he subsequently refused to pay on the grounds that it was done against his expressed wishes. As a result, the Council sued him at the Ystad's Lower Court, and secured a ruling which required Ekholm to pay not only the bill, but also the interest on the amount he owned, plus the Council's litigation fees. Ekholm appealed against the ruling, claiming 140,000 Kronor in damages, and for the restoration of his garden from the Council. His appeal, however, was turned down.

According to Chapter 3 paragraph 17 of the *Swedish Planning and Construction Act* (plan-och bygglagen), gardens are to be kept "well-pruned" so that they do not cause significant inconvenience to the surroundings and to the traffic in the vicinity, creating the risk of accident. In Ekholm's case, some of his neighbours had complained about the state of his

* *Paul Dodyk Research Fellow* at the Centre for Socio-Legal Studies and Senior Research Fellow in Law at Harris Manchester College, University of Oxford.

garden to the Council, and the Council's Chief-Gardener, having inspected the garden, found it badly in want of care. It had run wild and was cluttered with what he judged to be scrap. Subsequently, the Council had urged Ekholm to put his garden in order and when Ekholm failed to comply, it had, in accordance with Chapter 10 paragraph 18 of the *Planning and Construction Act*, taken measures to improve Ekholm's garden, at his expense. This is usually done using an electric saw, but in Ekholm's case heavy machinery was employed, as if to teach him a lesson.

Ekholm's garden did not have the finely cut lawns, hedges, straight pathways or plants which one "normally" finds in "proper" gardens. Instead, there were a number of rare and old garden plants, growing amongst scraps, suckers and weeds. Ekholm regarded his garden not as a wilderness, but as a place where plants could grow freely. Moreover, according to some of the neighbours, the garden did not cause obstruction or danger to the traffic. One of Ekholm's neighbours even described it as a "blooming grove," telling the local newspapermen that it was a "magic garden." However, Ekholm's next-door neighbour, a sausage-dealer who owned seven hot-dog stands, did not share Ekholm's philosophy. He used the part of his own garden, which faced Ekholm's, for parking his vehicles and keeping petrol-containers, several garbage cans and a workshop for carrying out repairs. The sausage-dealer had tried several times to convince the old man to sell his house and garden to him and it was, in fact, he who had filed the complaint. It also happened that he was on friendly terms with the Council's Chief-Gardener.[1]

Ekholm, his neighbours, the Council and its inspectors, and finally the courts, all played a role in the creation of this case. They did so independently of each other and yet in relation to one another. How is the interface of their perspectives, values and interests, which are incidentally manifested at various levels of social reality ranging from spontaneously formed values to formally made court decisions, actually realised ? How is this "heap of broken images" transformed into one single event, captured in the destruction of a seventy-year-old garden ? Finally, what sense of justice flows out of this event ? In the following pages I shall initiate a quest for a theoretical framework capable of producing some answers to such questions. I shall attempt to do this by revisiting the works of Georges Gurvitch, which contains a systematic effort to devise a theory capable of capturing social life in its totality by exploring the interrelationship between various levels of social reality. Interestingly enough, to achieve this Gurvitch employs the notion of law as the cornerstone of his theory.

Georges Gurvitch (1896-1965) was born in Norworossisk in Russia, but spent a significant part of his professional life in France, where he succeeded to Durkheim's Chair in Sociology at the Sorbonne. Gurvitch was an exceptionally prolific writer with a wide range of interests and a remarkable

---

1 For background information on Ekholm's personal traits, his relations with the neighbours, the Council, etc., see Lotta Möller, "Brottet mot en trädgårdkultur" (1993) Sydsvenska Dagbladet, 4 juni; and Jesus Alcala, "Hovrätten som fastighetsmäklare" (1993) Sydsvenska Dagbladet, 15 juli.

scope of knowledge.[2] He distinguished himself from his predecessors by his systematic reflections upon the status of the sociology of law as an academic discipline, and by grappling with the problems posed by the multiplex reality of law. He was intrigued by the fusion of what he considered to be the simultaneous manifestation of the law in various forms and at various levels of social reality. Gurvitch's reflections on the status of the subject engaged him in the sociology of the sociology of law, while his attempts to grasp the multifaceted nature of law drove him to a quest for the "real" basis of the law, as a result of which he developed the concept of "social law," elaborated in *L'idée du droit social*, first published in 1932. Although reminiscent of Petrazycki's "intuitive law" and Ehrlich's "living law," Gurvitch's "social law" is an integral part of his gestalt sociology and, thus, a theoretical construct in its own right.

With a few exceptions, such as Pauline McDonald's essay, which celebrates Gurvitch's legal sociology, commentaries on Gurvitch's work have been sceptical of its empirical validity and theoretical rigour, suggesting that its underlying ideas are over-complex, fanciful, confusing and obsolete.[3] Most commentators acknowledge the depth and originality of Gurvitch's ideas and analysis, but argue that the positive aspects of his work are diminished by a host of factors, ranging from his personal traits to methodological and theoretical shortcomings.[4] Alan Hunt goes so far as to describe Gurvitch's labours as an ultimately fruitless journey, characterised by continuous lapses into metaphysics.[5]

Gurvitch's language admittedly is vague and fanciful, and his presentation is complex and abstract, but, these are not the only reasons for the lack of interest shown in his work in socio-legal circles. His concept of "social law" challenged and disturbed the traditional juristic notion of law which was founded on a state-centralistic ideology.[6] At the same time, it found itself at odds with the general direction of the sociology of law of the time, which was struggling to make a place for itself in the academic world by demonstrating its usefulness to policymakers and legislators, whose understanding of law was often limited to legal rules. However, during the last two decades, many of the prevailing assumptions within legal theory and the sociology of law which impeded the reception of Gurvitch's ideas, have been challenged by a range of radical schools such as feminism, postmodernism and legal pluralism. This has brought into question some of

---

2 For detailed presentations of Gurvitch's life and work, see Phillip Bosserman, *Dialectical Sociology : An Analysis of the Sociology of Georges Gurvitch* (Boston : Porter Sargent, 1968), and Pauline McDonald, "The Legal Sociology of Georges Gurvitch" (1979) 6 British Journal of Law and Society 24-52.

3 See McDonald, *supra* note 2.

4 See Alan Hunt, "The Sociology of Law of Gurvitch and Timasheff : A Critique of Theories of Normative Integration" (1979) 2 Research in Law and Sociology 169-204, Jean-Guy Belley, "Georges Gurvitch et les professionnels de la pensée juridique" (1986) 4 Droit et Société 353-70, and Jean Carbonnier, "Gurvitch et les juristes" (1986) 4 Droit et Société 347-51.

5 Hunt, *supra* note 4 at 189.

6 See Pierre Noreau and André-Jean Arnaud, "The Sociology of Law in France : Trends and Paradigms" (1998) 25 Journal of Law and Society 258-83.

the strongly held views on law and legal behaviour. Hence the need to revisit Gurvitch in an attempt to salvage what we can from his work.

Gurvitch's Work

Micro-sociology

Gurvitch's general approach is informed by radical empiricism with an institutional basis, a double-edged tool applied for analytical and methodological purposes, assisting him in identifying "reality" in experience and in institutions growing out of experience. According to Gurvitch, social reality exists on a number of "depths" or "levels" : the morphological level of physical characteristics and institutions, organised superstructures, patterns of collective conduct, spontaneous social conduct, social symbols, values/collective ideas and, finally, collective mentality or "noetic" mind.[7] The depth-levels express the degree to which social life is organised. Gurvitch developed this approach partly under the influence of phenomenology, in particular that of Edmund Husserl, Max Scheler and Henri Bergson. Hence his emphasis on (levels of) depth analysis of social reality, inspired by "method of inversion" or "phenomenological reduction."[8] This method tries to capture the phenomenon which is most directly experienced in social reality. The ideas and insights borrowed from phenomenology are also responsible for developing his concern with immediate social experience and his interest in the study of "noetic mind" or "human spirit" through the levels of depth analysis of social reality.

At the deepest level of social reality — *i.e.* below the material surface of society, organised superstructures, patterns of organised and unorganised collective conduct, the level of social symbols and the realm of values and collective ideas — Gurvitch identifies the collective mind. This deepest level generates symbols, ideas and values, which interpenetrate and interconnect all levels of social reality (though they are never completely absorbed by these levels). The values generated spontaneously at the deepest level constitute the whole when they are transformed by the totality into transpersonal values, *i.e.* when they reveal themselves in what Gurvitch calls "normative facts." Expressed differently, "normative facts" are "the collective acts of recognising spiritual values as embodied in social facts in which they are realised" which, as we shall see, may be identified by studying "immediate jural experience."[9]

The integration of the "depths" is mediated through 27 forms of "sociality" which are, in turn, defined as the "microscopic elements of which each real collective unit is composed."[10] These elements are not individuals or group structures but "social electrons," "the ways of being bound to the whole by the whole." They are the relationships through which the essence

---

7 Georges Gurvitch, *Sociology of Law* (London : Kegan Paul, Trench, Trubner & Co. Ltd, 1947).
8 *Ibid.* at 9.
9 *Ibid.* at 41.
10 *Ibid.* at 156.

of the human condition of being social is expressed. These "social electrons" contain an element of spontaneity and tend, in varying degrees, to be unstable and indeterminate. Every "form of sociality" produces its own corresponding "kind of law." Kinds of law are independent of types of group, society or State, but linked to the forms of sociality and layers of depth, *i.e.* they are in effect directly geared to micro social mechanisms. Gurvitch elaborates this further by describing how the kinds of law which compete within the same jural framework or legal system are "horizontally" and "vertically" differentiated. Horizontally, they consist of forms of sociality located on the same layer of depth, realising an aspect of the ideal of justice. Vertically, they are functions of the superimposed layers of depth in jural reality corresponding with a particular kind of law.

Horizontally, law is generated either by direct/spontaneous sociality (giving rise to the unorganised forms of law), which is manifested in the immediate states of collective minds and behaviours, or by organised/reflected sociality (giving rise to the organised forms of law), which is to be found in deliberately constructed superstructural patterns. Spontaneous sociality is partial social integration through collective intuition and symbolic communication in the spirit of the "We," as opposed to sociality by simple interdependence between me, you, him, them, *i.e.* relations with others. In short, two main kinds of law emerge out of this horizontal microsociological classification : social law (corresponding to sociality by partial fusion) and inter-individual law (corresponding to sociality by interdependence). Social law is the *rigid* law of integration in the "We" or in the totality and cannot be imposed from without. It is based on mutual trust, aid and cooperation, and permits the subject to participate directly in the whole and, thus, in jural relations. In contrast, inter-individual laws are *elastic* and *mobile* laws of co-ordination based on distrust, separation and conflict. Furthermore, they are, unlike social law, dependent on external pressure and sanctions.

Each kind of law, which was described above in terms of its *horizontal* qualities, unfolds itself *vertically* through three superimposed layers of law or jural reality. These layers are described as 1) law which is fixed in advance, *i.e.* law understood in its everyday sense of legal rules, decisions, courts, etc., 2) flexible law formulated *ad hoc*, *i.e.* discretionary exercise of law and 3) intuitive law, which is the direct recognition of the justice of the case. In Gurvitch's scheme, the horizontal and vertical classifications of kinds of law criss-cross. In this sense, the study of the "forms of sociality" becomes linked to, and inseparable from, the study of "kinds of law" as functions of layers of depth, creating the basis for Gurvitch's micro-sociology.[11]

It should be noted here that, in effect, Gurvitch lays the foundation for a theory of legal pluralism by positing that "a plurality of different kinds of

---

11 For a detailed presentation of "kinds of law" and "layers of law" see Gurvitch, *supra* note 7 at 166-181. For a diagram demonstrating how the types of law (organised/unorganised sociality) are correlated to "levels of depth" and layers of law, *i.e.* law fixed in advance, flexible law and intuitive law, see Hunt, *supra* note 4 at 187.

law may be in operation simultaneously within the overarching social framework of a single global society."[12] More importantly, these kinds of law are not defined in terms of their legal functions, as is the case with most legal scientific concepts of law, but in terms of the intensity and the form of social interaction of the social framework/context out of which they emerge. According to this position, law is, firstly, manifested in different forms at different levels of social reality; secondly, it is not confined to rule-systems emanating from the state, but to be found also at levels below the official legal system and its institutions; thirdly, these spontaneous manifestations of law — or "social law" — are not reflections or functions of the positive law or its official institutions; fourthly, social law is ultimately brought on through social interaction and underpins official law and its dependent institutions.

From the deepest level of social reality arise spontaneous values which are transformed into normative facts when they succeed in penetrating, and being moulded by, various levels of sociality. This deepest level can be accessed through a fruitful combination of philosophy (primarily methods of phenomenological investigation) and sociology, and by exploring the collective immediate experience, *i.e.* collective acts of recognising spiritual values manifested in the social facts through which they are realised. Whether logical, jural, spiritual, aesthetic or religious, these require "an integral experience involving spiritual as well as sense data."[13] Philosophy should be employed to determine the formal structure of immediate jural experience and the universal characteristics of jural values.[14] Sociology should be used to study, on the one hand, "the kinds of law as functions of different forms of sociality" and, on the other, "the kinds of law as functions of layers of depth which can be found within every form of sociality when it becomes normative fact."[15]

It is worth noting that Gurvitch's "social electrons" — which he also describes as the "agency" of social action producing social organisation — resemble the more modern notion of "agency" in social theory.[16] Also, spontaneity attributed to "social electrons" potentially provides a sociological basis for the "reflexivity" of agency, *i.e.* the dialectic of structure and agency.[17] Reflexivity is regarded by modern social theory as a tool which enables agency to reflect upon, and change, structures by unveiling the unthought categories which mould our more self-conscious practices. I am not suggesting here that there is a Kantian legacy of reflexive critique to be found in Gurvitch's work, of the type one finds, for instance, in Habermas's communicative ethics.[18] Nevertheless, his theory has received, by borrowing ideas from phenomenology, many neo-Kantian

12 McDonald, *supra* note 2 at 39.
13 Gurvitch, *supra* note 7 at 39.
14 *Ibid.* at 41.
15 *Ibid.* at 159.
16 *Ibid. op. cit.*
17 See Ulrich Beck *et al.*, *Reflexive Modernisation* (Cambridge : Polity Press, 1994).
18 Jürgen Habermas, *The Theory of Communicative Action*, vol. I (Boston : Beacon Press, 1984).

impulses, making them prone to reinterpretation and reconstruction with reference to modern social theory. Another possibility of such a reinterpretation is to be found in his notion of collective mind. Gurvitch's level of collective mind bears a resemblance to Habermas's "lifeworld," *i.e.* the sphere of spontaneously generated intersubjectively shared values, norms and worldviews, which are taken for granted by social actors, and out of which "system" is born. Habermas too has borrowed this notion from phenomenology and employed it as the basis for his micro social analysis. Even Gurvitch's layers of sociality show some similarity with Habermas's spheres of discourse, which arise out of "speech-acts" to deal with specific problems and, thus, are oriented to specific forms of "validity claims." It also resembles Sally Falk Moore's concept of semi-autonomous social fields, which have a rule-making capacity and the ability to bring about compliance to their rules within their own boundaries.[19]

An important difference between Habermas's spheres of discourse and Gurvitch's forms of sociality is that the former is not set up as an over-complex typology and predefined and limited analytically to a number of categories and subcategories. One might, indeed, view the empirical potential of the notion of sociality favourably, when its dimensions are broadly defined in terms of "spontaneous" and "organised sociality," on the one hand, and "sociality by partial fusion" and "sociality by interdependence," on the other. However, it is doubtful if Gurvitch's sub-categorisation of sociality into 27 forms is of much practical use to empirical researchers, particularly when we realise that it leads him to construct an even more complex typology of "social law" consisting of no less than 162 subcategories. Gurvitch seems to struggle in vain to make up for empirical shortcomings of his scheme by further theorising and analytical categorisation.

On the positive side, Gurvitch's forms of sociality are, unlike the other similar theoretical constructs, conceptualised specifically in terms of their jural properties, making them analytically apt to socio-legal interrogations.

Macro Concerns

The other factor of importance in Gurvitch's intellectual development is demonstrated by his preoccupation with the dialectical tradition of Marx and Fichte, which he utilised to further develop and transform the above-mentioned phenomenologically inspired method into the underlying philosophical theme of his work, which he then described as "hyperempiric dialectics" (the dialectical method grounded in reality). Thus, this later model not only incorporated the phenomenological insight into the relationship between meaning and reality, but also criticised Hegel and Marx for recognising only one form of dialectics. In contrast, Gurvitch's model identified a five-dimensional form of dialectics : complementarity (in which two apparently distinct elements are part of a distinct whole); mutual involvement, in which elements interpenetrate each other; ambiguity and

[19] See Sally Falk Moore, *Law as Process* (London : Routledge and Kegan 1976).

ambivalence, where there is both attraction and repulsion; polarisation of opposites (as in the Hegelian dialectics); and reciprocity of perspectives, or differentiation between parallel manifestations of the same elements.

The ultimate aim of this elaborate model of dialectics was to devise a conceptual framework capable of capturing social life in its totality, without losing sight of its highly fluid and ever-changing process of structuration, restructuration and destructuration.[20] This perpetually changing social "whole" is, at the same time, a balanced system which gains its equilibrium through "a fusion of reciprocal perspectives," *i.e.* by synthesising the basic elements of diversity and unity, individual and universal.[21] Integration (which defines the domain of social law) is mutual participation in the "whole," in the spirit of "We" (rather than in relationships of oppositions, *i.e.* "me," "you," "him"), in such a way that the "whole" becomes part of each individual element (social electron) without reducing the social reality into a monolithic unity. In this way, Gurvitch potentially safeguards the indeterminacy of his micro-sociological units (which potentially provides a basis for the reflexivity of his agency) without losing sight of the force of society which is manifested in the cohesion of social groups. A group's social cohesiveness, which incidentally provides its source of authority, is linked to the micro level through spontaneous transpersonal values, *i.e.* the "normative facts," from which social law derives not only its obligatory force, but also its legitimacy. Gurvitch's theory interpreted in this sense is, potentially, a macro-micro theory of law and society.

Latent Concern with the Micro-Macro Link

Gurvitch endorses Durkheim's structural functionalism and belief in collective consciousness (which is more than the sum of the consciousness of all individuals), and uses it to underpin his view that society and social structures must be studied as a whole. However, Gurvitch does not follow Durkheim all the way and rejects the assumption that the collective consciousness transcends the individual consciousness, thus resisting the Durkheimian tendency to reduce social life to structural factors existing independently of the individual's social psychological condition. Gurvitch achieves this by borrowing ideas from phenomenology, which "views consciousness as consciousness of something, whether this something is an object, another person, or an aspect of one's own physical and mental being."[22] This helps Gurvitch to argue that although consciousness is essentially an attribute of the mental operations of individuals, it can also have a collective dimension. In this way Gurvitch takes the first step towards connecting the individual's state of mind (the individual consciousness) with the level of social structure (the collective consciousness). This idea was hardly unfamiliar to Durkheim who, unlike Gurvitch, deliberately focused on the study of "social facts" to delimit the scope of his sociological

---

20 Georges Gurvitch, *L'idée du droit social* (Paris : Recueil Sirey, 1932) and *Dialectique et sociologie* (Paris : Flammarion, 1962).

21 *Ibid.* at 17.

22 McDonald, *supra* note 2 at 32.

investigation to what was empirically accessible to him. Armed with his phenomenological insight Gurvitch felt that he could transcend this limitation of Durkheimian sociology. Thus, he embarked on a path which ultimately leads to one of the central problems of modern social theory, namely, the link between the micro and macro levels of social reality.

A point is made here that Gurvitch's attempt to study the totality of social phenomenon, without losing sight of the fundamental role of the micro-level reality, is a latent recognition that micro and macro features of social life are inter-connected and inter-dependent. This idea is also supported by Gurvitch's realisation that he could not reach his objectives by employing one form of sociology. As a result he developed a "microsociology" to study forms of sociality, a "differential sociology" to study group dynamics and a "genetic sociology" to study the development of total social systems. Crystallised in Gurvitch's ambition are issues and questions which were raised by the micro-macro and structure-agency debates some twenty years after his death, as the result of the attempts to uncover the link between micro and macro or structure and agency, through grand synthesising.[23]

Interestingly enough, there are very few attempts within the sociology of law to develop a general theory capable of integrating the micro and macro levels, and also there are few researchers who employ integrative theoretical models of this kind. My suggestion is that Gurvitch's theoretical work should be re-examined in the context of modern sociology's concern with the integration of micro and macro (or structure and agency) levels. Gurvitch's work is, arguably, not as sophisticated as some recent attempts, but it has, in contrast to other attempts, the notion of law as one of its cornerstones.

On Immediate Jural Experience

Gurvitch argued that the sociology of law was to study "jural facts" which are the incarnation and realisation of "jural values." These were to be distinguished from "those social facts ... which, being equally related to spiritual values, are most closely akin to the facts of law, *i.e.* moral religious, aesthetic and similar facts."[24] In order to distinguish jural facts from other facts and values, Gurvitch borrowed Petrazycki's definition of law in terms of its imperative-attributive properties. Rules constituting the law have, therefore, a multilateral characteristic in a sense that they regulate behaviour on the basis of the link between claims and duties. This helps to distinguish jural facts from, for example, moral values which have a unilateral and intrinsically imperative character. This also allowed Gurvitch to develop his concept of justice without making references to moral ideals, and free from

---

23 See Ralf Dahrendorf, "Out of Utopia : Toward a Reorientation of Sociological Analysis" (1958) 64 American Journal of Sociology 115-27; Peter Berger and Thomas Luckmann *The Social Construction of Reality* (London : Allen Lane, 1967); and Anthony Giddens, reprint *The Constitution of Society : Outline of the Theory of Structuration* (Cambridge : Polity Press, 1986).

24 Gurvitch, *supra* note 7 at 41.

the influence of natural law, as a kind of balance or equilibrium — a temporarily stable condition among social relations — which is achieved between social values. Law therefore becomes, for Gurvitch, the attempt to realise justice. In short, Gurvitch defines law in terms of justice which ultimately regulates the relationships between persons and groups, by balancing social facts and spiritual values. Law seeks this justice by trying to bring the duties and claims of all the members of a collectivity into equilibrium. Most importantly for our purposes here, the establishment of this balance involves not a normative, but a factual judgement. Hence, through its attempts to bring about justice, law ultimately causes the collective realisation of spiritual values in fact.[25]

At the same time, true to his phenomenological learning, he defines the sociology of law in terms of the sociology of "noetic mind" or the human spirit, underlining the importance of "internal meanings." Thus, the specific properties of law were, according to Gurvitch, to be identified and described by examining what he called the "immediate jural experience," which he defines in the following way :

> Immediate jural experience consists in collective acts of recognising spiritual values as incarnated, embodied in social facts in which they are realised. It is that incarnation and realisation of values in fact which is the most profound datum of jural experience... Moreover, the most immediate data of jural experience are "normative facts" and the "justice" which governs them. These two data are closely interlinked and represent two abstract aspects of the same datum. Jural immediate experience as an act of recognition is essentially intermediate between an emotional-volitional experience of values and an intellectual experience of logical ideas. It diminishes the direct warmth of the experience of values by interposing the coolness of intelligence in order to reconcile them.[26]

"Immediate jural experience" is embodied in a variety of social forms, many of them taking place outside the institutional settings of the law. They range from the mundane experience of completing a form required by an authority to paying for the television license, from complying with the terms of a contract to the acts of legislators. In this sense our everyday life is permeated by forms of jural experience. These are, however, concealed from us by the complexity of our social relations. Gradual reduction and "inversion" have to be applied before identifying and exposing such experience to sociological examination.

The Dichotomy of Jural Facts and Values

The Dichotomy as an Impediment

As suggested previously, Gurvitch's work contains systematic reflections on the disciplinary status of, and problems intrinsic to, the sociology of law. The problems which this new discipline was experiencing were, according to

[25] *Ibid.* at 41-41.
[26] *Ibid.* at 41-42.

Gurvitch, brought on by the fact that it had to fight for its existence on two fronts, challenged as it was by sociology and legal science (or legal positivism).[27] Here, Gurvitch touches on a difficulty which is experienced in various forms by many socio-legal researchers as an epistemological tension rooted in the need to integrate sociological and legal visions of law and society. At the risk of exaggeration and over-simplification, one might say that the tension is caused by the difficulty to integrate the sociologist's "experience-distant" understanding of the law, which prioritises the study of the interaction between the law and its social environment, thus providing an outsider's view of the law, with the legal practitioner's "experience-near" perception of his/her field of activity, which is based on an insider's view of the law.[28]

This type of epistemological tension between external and internal factors, or between the perspectives of "outsiders" and "insiders", is indeed only to be expected in interdisciplinary fields of research. However, it takes on a special significance for the sociology of law because of its outward resemblance to a dichotomy intrinsic to all studies of law.[29] In its most basic form, this dichotomy, or shared duality, is expressed as the distinction between attributive facts and prescriptive norms. It is also discussed in terms such as legality (the system of legal rules and formal decisions) and right (or the law behind laws). Moreover, we find parallel forms of it in Durkheim's "restitutive" and "repressive law"; in Malinowski's distinction between social order independent of coercion or political institutions and order based on coercion; in Timasheff's paradigm of law which is constructed on the polarisation of ethics and power; in Weber's distinction between formal and substantive justice; in Pound's identification of the "gap" between "law in books" and "law in action,"[30] not to mention Gilligan's distinction between "the ethics of care" and "the ethics of justice," which provided the basis for a feminist critique of the law.[31] These dual manifestations of the law are not sociologically identical, or necessarily reducible, to each other. They do, nonetheless, have their roots in the functional differentiation of society, which was first expressed in the Enlightenment's intellectual and

27 *Ibid.* at 1.

28 See C. Geertz, "From the Natives point of View : on the Nature of Anthropological Understanding" in Russell T. McCutcheon, ed., *The Insider/Outsider Problem in the Study of Religion* (Cambridge : Polity Press 1999). For Geertz (*op. cit.* at 38-50) the perspectives of the insider (or the subject) is "experience-near" and different from that of the outsider (an analyst) which is "experience-distant." However, the difference between these two perspectives is one of degree, *i.e.* they are not polar opposites (*op. cit.* at 51).

29 See Alan Hunt, *Explorations in Law and Society : Toward a Constitutive Theory of Law* (New York : Routledge, 1993). Hunt is one of the few socio-legal scholars who have addressed the role played by forms of this dichotomy (or what he also calls "shared dualism") in the theoretical studies of law. According to Hunt contemporary theoretical studies of law exhibit a parallelism by conceptualising the law with a help of "a shared dualism" the general form of which is to be found between "coercion" and "consent." Hunt points out that the conceptualisation of this shared dualism may take "a variety verbal forms" (Hunt, *op. cit.* at 62).

30 Roscoe Pound, "The Limits of Effective Legal Action" (1917) 27 International Journal of Ethics 150.

31 Carol Gilligan, *In a Different Voice : Psychological Theory and Women's Development* (Harvard University Press, 1996). Orig. publ. 1982.

institutional separation of humans from nature, individuals from groups, facts from values, reason from belief, etc.[32] More importantly, they are not exclusive, in the sense that they can coexist simultaneously, if at different levels of social reality.

The dual descriptions of law also draw our attention to the multiplex reality of the law, to the fact that law is generated, perceived, experienced and presented in disparate forms at various levels of social reality. However, despite the dissimilarities inherent in these manifestations — Gilligan's dual description of the law has ostensibly little in common with, for instance, Malinowski's or Weber's descriptions — the dualities tend to express themselves along the separation of facts and norms. One facet is cognitively produced, the other is normatively contrived. Perhaps with the exception of Luhmann's theory of autopoiesis,[33] which regards the normative closure of the legal system as a condition for its cognitive openness, sociological theories of law have often emphasised one aspect of this dichotomy at the expense of the other, subsequently leaving the relationship between the internal and external, which generates the epistemological tension mentioned above, unexplored. An example of this one-sided emphasis can be found in Black's assertion that "law consists in observable facts, not in rules."[34] Alternatively, as in the case of the early sociology of law which was inspired by social engineering, socio-legal scholars investigated the gap between "law in books" and "law in action" neglecting the importance of the interface of these two facets of law. In this sense, the dichotomy imposes a theoretical and, thus, empirical limitation on the sociology of law.

This last point can be further illuminated by taking a closer look at the studies of the "gap" problem, which remains one of the main concerns of the sociology of law.[35] As Tamanaha has showed, the investigations of the gap are to be found in at least two forms.[36] The earlier forms, an example of which can be found in Ehrlich's study, highlight the differences between the rules of law, as introduced and enforced by the state, and the rules which are

32 See Thomas D. Barton, "Troublesome Connections : The Law and Post-Enlightenment Culture" (1998) 47 Emory Law Journal 163-236.

33 Niklas Luhmann, "The Self-Reproduction of Law and its Limits," in *The Dilemma of Law in the Welfare States*. Edited by Günther Teubner (Berlin : Walter de Gruyter,1986).

34 Donald Black, "The Boundaries of Legal Sociology" (1972) 81 Yale Law Journal 1086-1100 at 1091.

35 The investigation into the gap between the ideal and the reality of the law gave rise to a number of original empirical studies of contractual relations. See Vilhelm Aubert *et al.*, *En lov i søkelyset* (A Law In the Searchlight), (Oslo : Akademisk forlag, 1952), Stewart Macaulay, "None-Contractual Relations in Business" (1963) 28 American Sociological Review 55-67, and Jacek Kurczewski and K. Frieske "Some Problems in the Legal Regulation of the Activities of Economic Institutions" (1977) 11 Law and Society Review 489-505. Theoretically sophisticated enquiries into this problem are to be found in David Trubek, "Complexity and Contradiction in the Legal Order" (1977) 11 Law and Society Review 524-569, and R. M. Unger, *Law in Modern Society : Toward a Criticism of Social Theory* (New York : Free Press, 1976).

36 Brian Z. Tamanaha, *Realistic Socio-Legal Theory : Pragmatism and a Social Theory of Law* (Oxford : Clarendon Press 1997) at 101-3 and 117-8. Also see David Nelken, "The Gap Problem in the Sociology of Law : A Theoretical Review" (1981) 1 Windsor Yearbook of Access to Justice 35-61.

de facto followed by ordinary people in the course of their everyday life.[37] Other studies of the gap problem address the disparity between the rules of law and the practices of legal institutions. Both of these studies are important parts of the development of the sociology of law. Even today a large number of sociological studies of the law still address the gap issue. The inquiries into the gap problem depart from the assumption that the gap between law in books and law in action can and should be closed. As a result they neglect the dual character of the law. This paper suggests that the focus of attention should be directed away from "how and why is the gap created ?," a question which is already amply investigated, to the examination of the interplay between the law in books and the practices of people and institutions. To put it differently, having investigated the "gap" problem, the next step for the sociology of law is to examine the interaction between prescriptive norms and attributive facts, between law in books and law in action, between legal rules and social rules (living law), or legal rules and institutional practices. The objective of such examination should be to determine how and why the interaction between legal rules and social rules (or institutional practices) is realised as part of the larger reproduction of society.

Alan Hunt, who defines the dichotomy in narrower terms of coercion/consent, reaches a similar conclusion :

> The general deficiency inherent in dichotomous conceptions of law is that they have, as a necessary effect, a tendency to result in an unstable analysis that lurches between the polarities set up. They produce an "either-or" effect in which each theorization is reduced unavoidably to emphasizing "either" the element of consent "or" the element of coercion.[38]

Such studies neglect the fact that both sides of the dichotomy are necessarily and always present in different manifestations of the law. Law is simply not reducible to either one of the two elements.[39]

Transcending the Delimiting Effects of the Dichotomy

As it happens, sociology is best equipped, and strategically placed, to observe and analyse law's interaction with its social environment, while jurisprudence is best equipped to explore its internal operation and realities. However, as pointed out by Gurvitch, neither of these two is on its own adequately equipped to provide a proper description and analysis of the law. Sociology of law and philosophy of law, without mutual contact, are, according to Gurvitch, doomed to "sterility, dogmatism, and impotence."[40] Hence, "their reciprocal dependence and maximum possible collaboration

---

[37] Eugen Ehrlich, *The Fundamental Principles of the Sociology of Law* (Cambridge : Harvard University Press 1936). Orig. publ. 1913.

[38] Hunt, *supra* note 29 at 64.

[39] *Ibid.*

[40] Gurvitch, *supra* note 7 at 241.

would seem indispensable."[41] About half a century later we find Habermas arriving at the same conclusion :

> The philosophical discourse on Justice misses the institutional dimension toward which the sociological discourse of law is directed from the outset. Without the view of law as an empirical action system, philosophical concepts remain empty. However, insofar as the sociology of law insists on the objectivating view from the outside, remaining insensitive to the symbolic dimension whose meaning is only internally accessible, sociological perception falls into the opposite danger of remaining blind.[42]

Habermas, as Gurvitch before him, draws attention to the need to integrate the view from the inside with the view from the outside. This in turn requires a theoretical device capable of containing the internal-external dichotomy inherent in sociological studies of law. Hence, I suggest here that our attention should be directed away from the social functions of the dichotomy, such as the purported incommensurability of sociological and legal knowledge, the conflicts of views between sociologists and lawyers, and the gap-problem, towards the dual character of the law, and to the fact that law manifests itself differently at various levels, generating many forms of reality. Some features of law's reality emanate from its recursively sealed internal operations (*i.e.* the hermeneutical search for legal meaning predicated on substantive rules of law), which together with its inner institutional practices lay the basis for what we may call its "internal realities."[43] Other aspects of law's reality are born out of its interplay with other social factors and institutions, creating its "external realities." Both the external and internal realities can manifest themselves in disparate forms simultaneously at various "depth" levels. At one level, this might be best described in terms of the tension caused by searching for a balance between "rights" and "legality," while at another, it might be perceived as the tension between "formal" and "informal" regulation.

The law consists of prescriptive norms and descriptive facts; to put it differently, it consists of ought and is or, to use Gurvitch's terminology, "spiritual" and "sensible data." One of the greatest potentials of Gurvitch's work lies precisely in laying a conceptual foundation for a sociological theory of law capable not only of acknowledging the duality of the law, but also embracing it in a way which takes us beyond the limits of the dichotomy. Gurvitch accomplishes this task by defining law not in dual terms, but as the realisation of justice which is achieved by striking a balance between jural facts and values. This definition incorporates within it the interdependence of claims and duties, which owes much to Petrazycki's insight into the law's imperative-attributive character, and which may be

---

41 *Ibid.*

42 Jürgen Habermas, *Between Facts and Norms* (Cambridge : Polity Press, 1996) at 66.

43 See David Nelken, "Blinding Insights ? The Limits of a Reflexive Sociology of Law" (1998) 25 Journal of Law and Society 407-26, and Reza Banakar, "Reflections on the Methodological Issues of the Sociology of Law" (2000) 27 Journal of Law and Society 273-95.

expressed in three forms : integrative (social law), coordinative (formal positive law) and subordinative (non-democratic).

What endows Gurvitch's view with a unique sociological character is his recognition of the diversity of social life, as expressed in various layers of social reality. These layers, which contain the elements of multiplicity, are interconnected through their interdependence and the fusion of reciprocal perspectives into a balanced dynamic system. The integration of the diversity of social life is achieved with the help of "normative facts," *i.e.* the transpersonal values generated spontaneously by the deepest level of social reality, but realised through forms of sociality in social facts. These are manifested in immediate jural experience, which, in my somewhat free interpretation, amounts to empirical manifestation of spontaneous negotiation between facts and values. It is, to use Habermas's terminology, the reconciliation of values generated by the lifeworld with system imperatives. It is the bringing together of the micro and macro realities of the law and society, which enables us to transcend the dichotomies imposed by the dual nature of the law on socio-legal research. Finally, it is the basis for developing a theoretical framework capable of empirically studying the interconnectedness of internal and external realities of the law. Gurvitch's work can in this way make an important contribution to advancing one of the basic concerns of the modern sociology of law.

Empirical Relevance of Gurvitch's Theory

To demonstrate the potential inherent in Gurvitch's theory to transcend the dichotomy of facts and norms, or the inside and outside of law, we need to apply his ideas to empirical data. To this end, I have selected three studies highlighting three distinct features of law and legal behaviour, which will be presented and re-examined below with the help of Gurvitch's conceptual apparatus. The first study which I have chosen is John Flood's *Barristers' Clerks*,[44] which is one of the more exciting empirical studies of the practitioners and institutions of English law. I have also chosen this study because of its descriptive character and because its data is not extensively burdened by theoretical analysis. The second study, by Vilhelm Aubert *et al.*, focuses on the impact of legislation on social behaviour.[45] I have selected this study both for its emphatically empirical orientation, and because it is regarded as a classic attempt in the Scandinavian tradition of socio-legal research. Aubert's study also helps us to bring into focus some of the recent work on law and gender. The third example deals with dispute resolution and is based on my own research experience.[46] The use of this study is justified for two reasons : it examines an aspect of the law not covered by the other two studies, and I have greater control over the extent to which its underlying empirical material lends itself to reinterpretation.

---

44 John A. Flood, *Barristers' Clerks : The Law's Middlemen* (Manchester : Manchester University Press, 1983).

45 Aubert *et al*, *supra* note 35.

46 Reza Banakar, *The Doorkeepers of the Law* (Aldershot : Dartmouth; Brookfield, Vt : Ashgate, 1998).

I should point out that such an examination will necessarily suffer from certain limitations. No matter how descriptive the empirical data used in this part might be, they are still collected with the help of certain theoretical assumptions. Hence, there is a theoretical bias in their composition, which might or might not be conducive to an examination of Gurvitch's ideas. I shall try to minimise such unwarranted theoretical side-effects by using Gurvitch's theory only for further theoretical analysis and for critical reflection on the results of these studies. This might not do justice to the real potential of Gurvitch's theory, and will certainly not provide us with a basis to examine the validity of all its claims, but it will nonetheless give us a general idea regarding its applicability to empirical material and whether or not it may be employed to conduct empirical research.

The Legal System, its Practitioners and Institutions

A barrister's clerk is traditionally seen as the barrister's secretary, servant, dresser, guide, stopwatch, auditor, treasurer, council and friend.[47] The clerks' general manner and, in particular, their well-defined, deferential and controlled behaviour towards barristers appear to confirm the view that they are socially inferior even to the most junior barrister in a chamber. In his study of barristers' clerks, which is now almost twenty years old, John Flood uncovers some of the hidden aspects of the clerk-barrister relationship, depicting a new picture of the clerk as a manager with expert knowledge of the "by-ways and labyrinths of the law,"[48] a gatekeeper with organisational leverage and a broker quietly manipulating unseen strings and restraining his governors' behaviour. He steers "his barrister through a welter of conflicts, creating an environment in which they can perform efficiently, to the benefit of both the chambers and the clerk."[49] One clerk, for example, describes his relationship with his barristers as one of patience, tolerance and understanding, all of which are the prerequisites for the delicate operation of "moulding of a barrister,"[50] for which the clerk sees himself largely responsible.

Many of the decisions made by clerks concern the allocation of cases. These decisions are based on the clerk's evaluation of his barrister's experience and ability (or shortcomings and weaknesses) in legal practice. As Flood explains, the barrister, to a great extent, hands over the responsibility for his welfare to his clerk.[51] In a sense, clerks acquire and apply a working knowledge of one feature of the judicial system. Through first-hand personal experience of working in chambers, they gain an insight into how the system of courts function as a socio-legal institution. The barristers' legal practice and, in fact, their whole career, not to mention the ordinary citizen's access to justice through effective legal representation, is in a sense influenced by clerks' legal know-how. Finally, the clerk's views

47 Flood, *supra* note 44 at 37.
48 *Ibid.* at 131.
49 *Ibid.* at 55.
50 *Ibid.* at 54.
51 *Ibid.* at 55-56.

on admitting new members to the chamber carry considerable weight, strengthening his function as a gatekeeper.[52]

Although Flood's study shatters the traditional popular views of clerks' relationship with their barristers by revealing their organisational expertise, knowledge and the extent to which they influence the working of the judicial system, it nonetheless stops short of attributing full legal status to clerks. In Flood's view, they stand in the "no-man's-land" of the English legal system, *i.e.* they are of the law, but not in the law. Flood defines clerks as "the law's middlemen" and "gatekeepers," ignoring the fact that, although these "gatekeepers" find themselves in what appears to a lawyer as a "no-man's-land," they nonetheless constitute an integral and indispensable part of the legal system. Indeed, an important part of this system relies heavily on the clerks' knowledge of listing procedures and fee-fixing, and on their capacity for dealing with the personnel of the legal profession, which in view of their gatekeeping function, requires closer scrutiny.

The clerks' gatekeeping function stands in stark contrast to the "no-man's-land" status attributed to them. Not only do they decide whether or not to admit clients, but they also play an important role in admitting new members. As pointed by Flood, the clerks are often the only persons to have spent any time observing potential tenants during their pupilage.[53] All such gatekeeping decisions involve balancing values and facts concerning the organisation of chambers, and have a bearing on the practice of the law at all levels. They involve distinguishing between "insiders" and "outsiders" to the law at various levels of legal organisation. This highlights the role played by clerks in organising the everyday running of the legal system. The clerks' efficacy in this regard is dependent on their working knowledge of the institutions of the law and legal procedure rather than substantive law.

What confuses the issue of the clerks' legal status in this study is that their "depth" of reality is not recognised as having any jural value or as legally relevant data. Instead it is viewed as, if not inferior to, certainly dependent on the jural reality of the barrister. Gurvitch would argue that the barristers' jural reality pertaining to the chambers is generated by the organised fixed body of procedural and substantive rules of the law, which arguably constitutes the most rigid and superficial level of jural reality, while the clerks' reality belongs to a more profound jural depth, and is more in tune with "intuitive spontaneous law" and based on their spontaneous perception of normative facts (or immediate jural experience). Gurvitch could help us to re-evaluate the clerks' legal standing in terms of the "no-man's-land," which in essence denies their vital role in the judicial system.

It is equally important to point out what Gurvitch's approach omits. Gurvitch tends to belittle the level of organised formal law and lawyers' immediate jural experience, which he regards as "superficial." This tendency is neither sociologically justifiable, nor theoretically constructive, for it conceals the importance of power in socio-legal relations. Thus, although

52 *Ibid.* at 132-133.
53 *Ibid.* at 132-133.

Gurvitch's ideas bring the clerks into the legal domain, they tell us little about why they were initially labelled as outsiders. This can, in turn, easily lead us to neglect the role played by the legal profession in its attempts to preserve and enhance its own status by safeguarding its monopoly of legal knowledge, which is defined in terms of making decisions on the basis of substantive law.[54]

Therefore, applying Gurvitch's theory, we can argue that the clerk is not an outsider to the law, to the legal system, or to the practice of the law for that matter. He possesses a considerable amount of training in, and working knowledge of, the law and its institutions. However, his knowledge, training, and actions are realised primarily within a level of social reality which is different from, but interconnected and sociologically primary to, that of the barristers. The so-called "no-man's-land" of the clerk, which suggests that the clerk is ultimately an outsider to the law, is, indeed, firmly established within the boundaries of the English judicial system, but at a "depth" which makes it more susceptible to spontaneously generated values of the collective consciousness. Hence, the clerks described by Flood tended to react strongly against all deviations from their preconceptions of the "normal", the most common of which concerned women and ethnic minorities. They regarded women as physically or emotionally unsuited to the Bar, and if they employed them it was only to "add a bit of glamour to the chambers."[55] At the same time many of them avoided the "ethnic problem' by not admitting members of ethnic minorities to chambers. These practices are simply in tune with the values prevalent in England at the end of the 1970s. The barristers do not and cannot — perhaps they even need not (again note the importance of power and authority) — reflect these values publicly in their legal practices simply because their actions are regulated and monitored formally at a more organised (legally formal) depth than the clerks. Again, we must bear in mind that Gurvitch's theoretical tools tell us nothing about the forms of gender, ethnic and cultural domination which operate through the customary practices ("social law") of chambers.

How the layers of sociality independently, but simultaneously and in relation to each other, create the reality of the chambers and affect the English justice system, are demonstrated, in a theoretically undeveloped form, in Flood's account of the disagreement between a clerk and his barrister, who had argued with a stipendiary magistrate over a procedural point where the barrister felt the magistrate was quite wrong. The barrister decided to write to the magistrate, formally registering a complaint, and to send an explanatory note to the solicitors. The clerk questioned the wisdom of this, lest the barrister "loses face,"[56] which would by implication damage the standing of the chambers. This disagreement constitutes the confrontation of two types of jural fact : one emanating form the surface level of organised law (manifested in the barrister's complaint) in terms of

[54] Terence C. Halliday, *Beyond Monopoly : Lawyers, State Crises, and Professional Empowerment* (Chicago : The University of Chicago Press, 1987).

[55] Flood, *supra* note 44 at 50.

[56] *Ibid.* at 47.

"he," "you," "them," the other reflecting the social law underpinning the organisation of the courts and chambers (stated in the clerk's concern about the impact of the barrister's complaint on the common interest of all members of the chambers) expressing the notion of "We." Such incidents could provide us with an empirical basis for determining the existing layers of jural reality and exploring the mechanisms through which these realities become interrelated. This would then allow us to examine their degree of fusion. It would allow us to examine the clerk's social position as a mediator linking social law and formal law. The study of these mediatory and integratory functions would guide us towards a new concept of law which is capable of transcending the dichotomous understanding of the law and legal behaviour, which was described in the second part.

The Impact of Legislation on Patterns of Behaviour

The 1948 *Housemaid Act* was introduced in Norway to improve the working conditions of domestic helps by protecting their interest through precise provisions regulating their working hours, termination of contract, wages, days off, vacations, etc. The *Act* limited the freedom to contractually set the law aside. The effects of this *Act* on the working conditions of housemaids was investigated in 1952 by Aubert, Eckhoff and Sveri, who examined its impact on the behaviour of housemaids and their employers. This was done by interviews aimed at evaluating the knowledge of the provisions of the *Act* among a representative sample of housewives and housemaids in Oslo. The choice of research questions was justified by the assumption that the law could not have any effect if those to whom it was addressed had no knowledge of its content. Thus, to assess the impact of the law one needs to take into account those variables which "intervene between the promulgation of the law and the behaviour of the public ... the most important of these is the level of information among the recipients of the legal communication."[57]

The study established that only one tenth of the sampled relationships showed complete conformity to the rules of the law. Moreover, the main requirement of the law, *i.e.* the ten-hour working day, was set aside in approximately half of the 233 households, which provided the basis of the investigation. In short, most rules laid down by the law were frequently violated, although there were considerable variations between the different clauses.[58] This result was then correlated with the housewives' and housemaids' knowledge of the law. Only three housewives and three housemaids mentioned the law as a cause for possible recent changes in the working conditions :

> But as soon as the Housemaid Law was mentioned, 80 per cent of the housemaids and 81 per cent of the housewives claimed to have at least heard about the law. Although less than one fifth of the respondents were completely unfamiliar with the law, 36 per cent of the housemaids and 26 per cent of housewives were unable to

57 Vilhelm Aubert, *Sociology of Law* (London : Penguin, 1977) at 117.
58 *Ibid.* at 116-117.

> mention a single clause in the law. The ten-hour working day seems to have been the most publicised and most widely known part of the new law ... A fair amount of information exists with respects to the norms regulating termination of hire, days off and vacations. But the norms on the length of working hours, and especially on overtime and periods of wage payment, seem to be "law in books' rather than "law in action'.[59]

Aubert interpreted this result with the help of Sumner's hypothesis that law grows, or should grow, out of mores,[60] and concluded that the rules which are fairly well known are those where the law corresponds to the existing customs. Similarly, the less known rules are those where the law tries to reform behaviour without the sanction of custom. However, contrary to Sumner's assumptions, Aubert noted that his data also indicated that those who were relatively well aware of the norms of the new law were people who had some contact with the law.

Using Gurvitch's theory we can elaborate on Aubert's first conclusion pointing out that the rules which are known correspond to "social law," the law of integration. This draws our attention to the fact that the Act is introduced at the surface level of social reality, *i.e.* at the level of societal organisation, and as such is most effective in co-ordinating co-operation and relations of interdependence ("you," "her," "them"). The fact that there is a level of "social law" at work also means that there is a level of social integration characterised by relations of fusion ("We" relations), into which the housemaids are drawn. This conclusion is supported by another empirical study, by Tone Sverdrup, which demonstrates that women employed in domestic work in Norway,[61] through the nature of the work they perform, are drawn into relationships characterised by family bonds, which exist on a more personal level and involve trust. These relationships are formed by what Gilligan described as "the ethics of care," which, in contrast to the "ethics of justice" which express male experiences through abstract rules and principles, display the experiences of women through a holistic approach to morality and a concern for others.[62]

Neither Aubert nor Gurvitch take into account the gender bias of the law. Yet, I would argue that Gurvitch's theory is receptive to gender analysis. The relationship between housemaids and their employers tend to shape and develop, not only out of interdependence and co-operation, but also, to use Gurvitch's concepts, by a form of social fusion ("We" spirit), which is specific to family life. Making formal contractual claims is ill-suited to the form of sociality of this level of reality, which is permeated by "the ethics of care." To understand the efficacy of the Housemaid Act, or for that matter,

---

59 *Ibid.* at 118.

60 W. Graham Sumner, *Folkways* (New York : New American Library Edition, 1960) (First ed. 1906).

61 Tone Sverdrup "Mellom ektenskapskontrakt og lønnskontrakt" *Rapport fra nordisk forskerkurs i kvinnerett*, Skrift nr 3 från Institut for offentlig rett (1982), cited and discussed in Thomas Mathiesen, *Rätten i samhället* (Göterborg : Bokförlaget Korpen, 1985).

62 See Gilligan, *supra* note 31.

any other law which aims to regulate exchanges involving trust and personal relations, one necessarily has to approach and analyse the law and its effects in a totality. This totality is reminiscent of the "holistic" approach adopted by many feminists.

Following Gurvitch we can start by stating that the question of legislation always involves more than one level of social reality. Those to whom the law is addressed are engaged in various forms of sociality and fusion and thus, in various degrees, access information and are exposed to new legal rules. However, although knowledge of the law is a necessary prerequisite, it does not by itself provide sufficient grounds for compliance with the rules. There will inevitably be some degree of tension between the official legal norms, which are the law of the levels of organisation and co-operation expressing "the ethics of justice," and the jural facts of the lower levels of sociality, which in this study incorporate "the ethics of care." Our investigation could gain valuable insights by exploring if and how a balance is struck between these two types of jural facts. Thus, Gurvitch's micro-sociological theory invites us to pay attention to the *horizontal* interaction between inter-individual and social law. At the same time, his differential sociology draws our attention to a *vertical* form of interaction between the State law (the *Housemaid Act*) and the social law of domestic relations. These two forms of social interaction take place simultaneously. To do these, we should study the immediate jural experience of those involved in the process of interfacing these types of perspectives. To strike such a balance is, for Gurvitch, to realise justice and to achieve the fusion of reciprocal perspectives, thus integrating various levels of social life. Aubert's investigation tells us nothing about the interface (or possible fusion) of jural facts emanating from various levels of social reality. As a result, we know nothing about how the parties to the relationship made use of the different forms of jural facts available to them to promote their own positions or safeguard their interests. Such an approach will also bring into focus the link between agency and structure, on the one hand, and the tension between internal and external realities of the law, on the other. To expand on these aspects of Gurvitch's ideas we need to use a form of data which is collected with the interface of perspectives in mind.

Dispute Resolution

The third study, this time based on the author's own research experience, consists of a sociological examination of the Swedish Ombudsman against Ethnic Discrimination.[63] By comparing a number of cases processed by the Swedish Ombudsman against Ethnic Discrimination in 1990 and 1995, I tried to describe how the 1994 *Swedish Act against Ethnic Discrimination* (AED) functioned in practice. The cases which I used as the basis of my empirical investigation revealed the existence of two distinct sets of perspectives on, and subsequently realities of, the AED : that of the Ombudsman, which was constrained by the terms of reference of its office

[63] See Banakar, *supra* note 46.

and the existing body of legal rules and doctrines, which urged him to act primarily as an impartial investigator of complaints, and that of the complainants' view of the Ombudsman as the champion of their cause and a legal bulwark against racism, discrimination and social injustice. The complainants' perspectives were, however, rooted in different levels of social reality. Some complaints emanated from the unorganised everyday interactions between ordinary people (a shop assistant treating a customer in a way the latter perceived as discriminatory). Other cases concerned the more institutionalised levels of cooperation (an employee complains against her employer's prohibiting her to wear a shawl). Yet another category was to be found in complaints against authorities' alleged discriminatory treatment of individuals or groups (an applicant for a job files a complaint against the police claiming that his application for a position as immigrant officer was rejected because of the police's discriminatory approach).

Although these two sets of perspectives (the Ombudsman's and the complainants') were distinct in their empirical manifestations or, to put it differently, were generated independently of each other, they were nonetheless formed in relation to, and through interaction with, one another. The outsider's view of the AED expressed in the complaints which were lodged with the Ombudsman, were often based on personal and subjective experience of ethnic discrimination. They often neglected the importance of providing evidence of unlawful discriminatory practices which could stand up in court. This outsider's view constituted the point of departure for the Ombudsman, whose actions were constrained by the imperatives of the law, its institutions and culture. The complaints also represented attempts to challenge jural facts of various levels of sociality by using official law to demand justice, *i.e.* they sought a new form of equilibrium in a relationship. As a result, they often reflected the rationale of that level of sociality which is ill-suited to the logic of official law.

This study demonstrates that the social functions and efficacy of the AED are geared to the interface of relevant perspectives. A model is needed which can answer "if', "how', and "to what extent' a fusion of perspectives (those of the complainant, the alleged perpetrator, and the Ombudsman) is achieved. Which types of value and jural fact are used in various cases and what kind of a balance is struck ? Such an approach helps not only to acknowledge the diversity of values in social life, but also to relate this diversity to forms of sociality, which generate their own social law, treating official law as one important factor in the social equation of the AED. It also indicates that the study of the link between the internal and external realities of the law can be assisted by investigating the micro-macro (or structure-agency) link. Both the Ombudsman and the complainant are empowered by structural legal and political factors, yet they employ the reflexive ability of the agency intrinsic to their social positions to affect and alter the structural relationships. This insight is, in a latent form, inherent in Gurvitch's emphasis on the fusion of reciprocal perspectives by synthesising elements of unity and diversity.

Values generated spontaneously at the level of the collective mind interpenetrate, to various degrees, the more patterned and organised levels of social life interconnecting them. Their successful penetration of one or more levels elevates their status to that of transpersonal values. At the same time they are transformed by the forms of sociality prevailing in each "depth" level, that is to say, the values become moulded by the specific intensity and quality of interaction of the level which they happen to penetrate. Another interpretation of this Gurvitchian idea, which incidentally finds empirical support in the three studies above, is that the values generated through everyday interaction are reshaped and employed by the agency in structuration and re-structuration of social life. As a result of this transformation the values are changed into normative facts, *i.e.* the spontaneous source of the positivity of law, of its validity, what Gurvitch calls "source of sources." The normative facts are flexible and dynamic revelations of collective beliefs. As such they belong to the exterior of the legal system, yet (as illustrated by Aubert *et al.*) they ascertain the limits of the efficacy of the formal rules of the judicial system. They also provide the basis for Gurvitch's notion of justice. If normative facts are the realisation of spiritual values in facts (reflected in immediate jural experience and mediated by the recognition of such values), then justice is the employment of normative facts to achieve a temporary equilibrium between social values and in social relations. The interface of various perspectives in the study of the Swedish AED is a complex revelation of the search for this equilibrium, a search which is empirically accessible through the study of "immediate jural experience."

Epilogue

The ravaging of Ekholm's family garden embodies an "immediate jural experience." It is a "jural fact" *per se* in the sense that it incarnates and realises "jural values" of the community where Ekholm lived. It is the indication of a collective realisation of specific values in facts. It also captures a snapshot of an attempt to balance specific claims and duties intrinsic to the social setting of Ekholm's life. Since this process is realised at various levels, one can easily mistake it for being no more than a random collection of disconnected and fragmented actions, accidentally thrown into one single frame. Ekholm's case shows how justice is realised and how temporary social fusion is achieved when a plurality of different kinds of law, indicating layers of sociality, come into simultaneous interaction. In a sense, the event is born out of the fusion of reciprocal perspectives, values and interests. Ekholm's values and beliefs, expressed in his philosophy of gardening and his eccentric personality, comes into confrontation with the expectations of some his neighbours. Ekholm's values seek the deeper meaning of life, while his neighbours' values aspire towards a sense of collective normality and conformity. Ekholm's values fail to transform themselves into normative facts, a fact which provides an insight into the power dimension of this case, while those of his neighbours are recognised institutionally in the response of the Council, which is, in turn, underpinned by the court decision.

All such attempts to strike a balance between facts and values provide temporary and transitory relief. None of the states of equilibrium created by seeking justice in this manner survive the passage of time. All structural manifestations of values (whether they are jural or moral or religious) in facts are constantly under re-evaluation, deconstruction and reconstruction by the reflexivity inherent in agency. Ekholm illustrates this when he refuses to surrender to his neighbours' successful re-structuration of relationships, by appealing for a second time, this time to the High Court, as a result of which the High Court quashed the ruling of the Lower Court in his favour. The High Court's ruling does introduce a new level of social reality into the social equation of this event, questioning not only the validity of the decision made by the Lower Court, but also the social law of the community. This new decision is as much a product of the internal reality of the law as the reflexive potential inherent in Ekholm's social position. Two perspectives are, thus, confronted here to legally produce a social message, crystallised in which are some aspects of the values manifest in Ekholm's gardening. The process is hardly concluded by this new legal ruling. In fact, this ruling indicates the birth of a new conflict, threatening the precarious unity of the layers of social life. It neither restores Ekholm's garden nor changes the fact that his immediate community established its values by destroying his garden against his wishes. The destruction of the garden is an image of the transformation of jural values into facts, but also a clear manifestation of a form of domination.

When applying Gurvitch's theory one needs to keep in mind that "social law" does contain forms of domination. Moreover, the formal law of the surface "depths" deserves more attention than it receives in Gurvitch's theory. It, too, can embody forms of domination affecting the formation of levels of sociality (those who administer the chambers and, thus, influence the citizens' access to justice, still remain the barristers' clerks), yet, paradoxically, it plays a vital role in the establishment of democracy. When applying Gurvitch's concepts, one can easily neglect the fact that formal law is the only means by which the mutual recognition of face-to-face interactions ("spiritual values" in Gurvitch's jargon) may be transmitted into interaction among strangers.[64]

Having said that, Gurvitch's theory of immediate jural experience has still much to offer socio-legal research. It contains *inter alia* ideas concerning the possibility of integrating the diverse manifestations of "spiritual and sense data."[65] Through its attempt to grasp the "full reality of law"[66] it links two sets of dichotomies : the structure-agency within social theory and the internal-external (or experience-distant and experience-near) realities of law in socio-legal studies. His notion of justice brings together

---

64 See Habermas, *supra* note 42.
65 Gurvitch, *supra* note 7 at 241.
66 *Ibid.*

facts and norms, linking claims and duties, while providing a theoretical device to describe the fusion of the levels of social reality (linking agency and structure). At the same time, it creates a common basis for integrating the sociology of law, the philosophy of law, jurisprudence and legal dogmatics. In this sense, Gurvitch's concept of justice becomes the social cement that temporarily holds the "heap of broken images" together.

Résumé

Cet article suggère que plusieurs idées de Gurvitch, présentées à l'origine de manière abstraite, ont gardé leur pertinence pour l'analyse socio-juridique. Sous une forme révisée qui permettrait leur application, elles seraient utilisables en recherche empirique. À cette fin, je réinterprète quelques une des principales approches théoriques de Gurvitch à la lumière de la recherche socio-juridique des dernières décennies. Je les applique par la suite aux données empiriques recueillies personnellement ou par d'autres chercheurs dans des études variées. Il s'agit de savoir si les perspectives théoriques de Gurvitch peuvent approfondir leur compréhension et ainsi ouvrir de nouvelles voies à la recherche socio-juridique.

Abstract

This paper suggests that many of Gurvitch's ideas, which were originally presented in an abstract fashion, are still highly pertinent to socio-legal analysis. They may be employed in empirical research in a revised form, which would make them receptive to operationalisation. To this end, I focus on some of the main theoretical ideas developed by Gurvitch, reinterpreting them critically and in the context of the socio-legal research of the last few decades. Then, I apply them to empirical data collected through the author's personal research experience and some other empirical studies. The question prompting this examination is whether Gurvitch's theoretical insights could enhance our understanding of such data and thus open new avenues of socio-legal enquiry.

Reza Banakar
Centre for Socio-Legal Studies
Wolfson College
University of Oxford
Oxford, Great Britain OX2 6UD

Part IV
Law as Discourse, System, Field: Habermas, Luhmann, Bourdieu

[11]

CAN RIGHTS, DEMOCRACY, AND JUSTICE BE RECONCILED THROUGH DISCOURSE THEORY? REFLECTIONS ON HABERMAS'S PROCEDURALIST PARADIGM OF LAW

*Michel Rosenfeld**

Introduction

There are different images or paradigms of law which correspond to different conceptions of justice and different sources of legitimacy. Moreover, in the context of complex, pluralistic contemporary societies, the relationship between law, justice, and legitimacy has become acutely problematic as competing conceptions of the good cast legal relationships as relationships among strangers,[1] and as justice according to law[2] seems irretrievably split from justice against or beyond law.[3] In the face of these difficulties, one could simply abandon the quest for justice beyond law and settle for a combination of democracy and legal positivism which would reduce political legitimacy to majority rule and confine the role of law to the stabilization of expectations among legal subjects. However, if fearful of tyrannical majorities and dissatisfied with the prospect of predictable but unjust laws, one could opt for justice beyond law and embrace human rights as a shield against the abuses of legislative majorities and the inequities of positive law. In short, in a contemporary pluralist society, law's legitimacy seems to require sacrificing either democracy or justice.[4]

---

* Professor of Law, Benjamin N. Cardozo School of Law.

1 *Cf.* Max Weber, Economy and Society 637 (Guenther Roth & Claus Wittich eds., 1968) (greater differentiation characteristic of modern legal systems was prompted by the advent of the market which brought strangers together to exchange goods and which had to be regulated by universal laws transcending the biases of intracommunal norms).

2 "Justice according to law is achieved when each person is treated in conformity with his or her legal entitlement." Michel Rosenfeld, *Autopoiesis and Justice*, 13 Cardozo L. Rev. 1681, 1681 (1992) (footnote omitted).

3 "Justice against law, on the other hand, is the justice that makes it plausible to claim that a law is unjust (even if it is scrupulously applied in strict compliance with the entitlements which the law establishes)." *Id.*

4 Recent debates in American constitutional law offer a salient example of the split between democracy and justice. Some have advocated restrictive interpretations of constitutional rights, for fear of unduly trampling on the will of legislative majorities, while others have not hesitated to promote enlarging the scope of antimajoritarian constitutional rights in the name of "fundamental justice" and "basic fairness." Compare, e.g., the ma-

Being relegated to either democracy or justice is bound to be frustrating, in as much as majoritarian rule cannot be purged of all arbitrariness and justice cannot shed all intracommunal roots to rise above the reach of partial communities.[5] There is, however, an apparent way out of the vicious circle circumscribed by arbitrary democracy and parochial justice. That way out is through proceduralism, or, more precisely, through the kind of proceduralism that is capable of yielding what John Rawls calls "pure procedural justice."[6] It bears emphasizing that most kinds of proceduralism will not do. After all, democratic lawmaking can be viewed as a form of proceduralism based on universal suffrage and majority rule. Nonetheless, it is conceivable that there could be some kind of proceduralism capable of overcoming the residual arbitrariness of democratic lawmaking while, at the same time, maintaining a neutral stance toward the diverse and often conflicting conceptions of the good found throughout the polity.

Habermas's proceduralist paradigm of law has all the makings of a most attractive candidate for the purpose of establishing the legitimacy of law through pure procedural justice. Indeed, Habermas's proceduralist approach based on communicative action deals with the residual arbitrariness of democracy by relying on dialogical consensus as the source of law's legitimacy. On the other hand, Habermas's proceduralism provides fundamental rights a legal grounding that seemingly obviates any need to justify such rights in terms of any conception of the good not equally shared by all the members of the polity. Moreover, not only does Habermas's proceduralist approach to law offer a way to resolve the conflict between democracy and justice, it also aims at estab-

jority, concurring, and dissenting opinions in cases such as Planned Parenthood of Southeastern Pa. v. Casey, 112 S. Ct. 2791 (1992); Roe v. Wade, 410 U.S. 113 (1973); and Griswold v. Connecticut, 381 U.S. 479 (1965).

5 Justice beyond law cannot achieve complete impartiality toward all strangers in the relevant class of legal subjects. Therefore, it must, at least in part, rely on a vision of the good that has intracommunal roots, thereby favoring members of the relevant intracommunal group over the remaining legal subjects. Thus, even the most basic and fundamental human rights embodied in numerous international covenants have been criticized as being somewhat parochial or culturally biased. *See generally* Burns H. Weston, *Human Rights, in* Human Rights in the World Community: Issues and Action (Richard P. Claude & Burns H. Weston eds., 1989) (focusing on western liberal origins of modern human rights conceptions); *see also* Will Kymlicka, Multicultural Citizenship 4 (1995) ("Traditional human right standards are simply unable to resolve some of the most important and controversial questions relating to cultural minorities.").

6 According to Rawls, pure procedural justice is achieved when any outcome is justly provided because a fair procedure was properly followed. John Rawls, A Theory of Justice 86 (1971).

lishing an internal connection between popular sovereignty and human rights, thus providing a normative underpinning for a legal regime that is poised to satisfy both democracy and justice.

In the last analysis, the value of proceduralism and the possibility of achieving pure procedural justice depend on the background assumptions and the material conditions surrounding the insertion and deployment of the relevant procedural devices and practices. Consistent with this, I will argue that Habermas's proceduralist paradigm of law ultimately fails to generate pure procedural justice and that it falls short of furnishing a comprehensive resolution of the conflict between democracy and justice. Habermas appears to have taken proceduralism as far as it can go, and through his discourse theory has made great progress over the proceduralism that has emerged from the works of his major predecessors, namely, Hobbes, Kant, and Rawls. But, as I shall endeavor to indicate in what follows, even Habermas's more nuanced and versatile proceduralism ultimately confronts the need to embrace contestable substantive normative assumptions in order to contribute to the resolution of conflicts that divide the members of the polity.

In order to be in a better position to provide a principled assessment of Habermas's proceduralism, I shall first attempt to put it in context. Accordingly, in Part I, I briefly examine some of the most salient general features of proceduralism as a means to establish its normative legitimacy. In Part II, I concentrate on the background assumptions, material conditions, and tasks which give shape to Habermas's proceduralism and I provide a critical assessment of certain problems it raises. In Part III, I take a close look at a type of feminist objection which seems to go to the heart of Habermas's discourse-theoretical justification of law. Finally, in Part IV, I conclude that Habermas's discourse-theoretical approach to law, while incapable of generating pure procedural justice, nonetheless can play an important constructive role in determining the normative legitimacy of contemporary law.

I.

Procedural justice—of which pure procedural justice is a limiting case—is a necessary component of any complex system for dispensing justice. Procedural justice, moreover, has an essentially twofold role in a contemporary constitutional legal system: first, to insure the just application of substantive norms belonging to the realms of distributive, corrective, or retributive justice; and second, to protect the worth and dignity of persons whose legal entitlement and obligations are subject to determination or modification by instrumentalities of the state. While these two roles of procedural justice are often intertwined in practice, they remain conceptually distinct. Thus, for example, in the context of the United States's adversarial criminal law system, the defendant's right to counsel and right to cross-examine witnesses can be viewed in two ways. These rights can be seen as both an important tool in the pursuit of the truth—which is essential to the fair application of the substantive norms embodied in the relevant criminal statues—and as a means of recognizing the defendant's inherent dignity by guaranteeing his or her right of participation in a proceeding that may result in a drastic change in his or her legal status. Conceptually, however, procedural justice as a means of application is generally parasitic on the substantive norms which it is designed to implement. Accordingly, the adversary system's suitability as a vehicle of procedural justice depends on whether it provides a reliable means to ascertain the guilt or innocence of the accused. Providing such a means is essential to the implementation of the relevant substantive norms of justice embodied in the criminal code. In contrast, procedural justice as a means to vindicate the dignity of the accused is largely independent from, though it cannot squarely frustrate the application of, the above mentioned relevant substantive norms. Consistent with this reasoning, even when the evidence against a criminal defendant is so overwhelming that guilt is obvious beyond any reasonable doubt, the defendant is still entitled to have "his day in court."[7]

Accordingly, procedural justice simultaneously depends on and transcends particular substantive norms of justice.[8] It does not follow from that, however, that by virtue of transcending a particular substantive norm, or a particular set of substantive norms, procedural justice transcends all substantive norms. In fact, even when procedural justice vindicates human dignity, it depends on

7 Furthermore, to the extent that its ability to ferret out the truth is what makes the American adversary system of criminal justice procedurally just as a means of applying relevant substantive norms of retributive justice, some of its key features as a guarantor of human dignity—such as the Fifth Amendment's privilege against self-incrimination, which allows the criminal defendant not to testify against him or herself—seem somewhat at odds with its role as a procedural vehicle for the application of substantive justice.

8 Actually, the dependence between procedural justice and substantive norms of distributive, corrective, or retributive justice is mutual rather than one sided. Indeed, if a substantive norm is not capable of being applied in a procedurally just manner, it is altogether not suitable as a legitimate legal norm, although it may still qualify as a legitimate moral norm.

substantive norms. However, the norms on which procedural justice depends, in that instance, operate at a higher level of abstraction than the particular substantive norms sought to be applied in a just manner. Furthermore, because it is likely that there would be a greater consensus regarding the substantive norms operating at higher levels of abstraction (compared to the less abstract substantive norms sought to be applied in a just manner), the more abstract norms may appear to be universal or beyond conflicting conceptions of the good. In other words, from the perspective of the level of abstraction at which the conflict of particular substantive norms unfolds, the more abstract norms may be perceived as remaining beyond dispute.

To illustrate this last point, let us consider the following example. Suppose that a state guarantees a certain minimum standard of living to every citizen; everyone who can prove that he or she cannot reach this standard through his or her own means is entitled to receive public assistance. To implement this policy, the state erects a welfare administration charged with the responsibilities of processing applications for public assistance, determining whether to award public assistance to particular applicants, and determining whether to terminate such assistance upon a finding that a particular recipient no longer needs it. Suppose, further, that the state's constitution requires that each citizen be given an opportunity to be heard before the revocation of any statutory entitlement.[9] To assess the administrative procedures designed to carry out the state's public assistance program, reference must be made to the following two norms: each citizen has a right to a state-guaranteed minimum standard of living; and every citizen is entitled to be treated with dignity and respect—which in this case requires that he or she be afforded an opportunity to be heard before the termination of public assistance payments. Although both of these norms are substantive and contestable, the first, which is more concrete, is much more likely to generate controversy than the second. Thus, whereas libertarians, utilitarians, and egalitarians would undoubtedly all endorse the second norm, they would most certainly disagree concerning the legitimacy of the first norm, with the libertarians strongly objecting against welfare rights.[10] Also, from within the trenches of the conflict over welfare rights, the equal

[9] *Cf.* Goldberg v. Kelly, 397 U.S. 254 (1970) (Due Process Clause of the Fourteenth Amendment requires a hearing prior to the termination of welfare payments).

[10] *See, e.g.*, Robert Nozick, Anarchy, State, and Utopia (1974).

dignity norm may be perceived as universally valid or at least settled beyond dispute.

The importance of procedural justice for modern legal systems and the importance of its structure enabling it to fulfill the twofold role identified above are no accident. Given modern law's strong tendency to cast relationships among legal subjects as relationships between strangers, it is hardly surprising that matters of procedure should be brought to the forefront often predominating over matters of substance.[11] Perhaps less obvious, but equally important, is the fact that this flight to procedure can never be completely successful, since matters of substance persist although they are often either concealed or displaced. A particularly important example of how substantive norms can be concealed by procedural ones emerges through a closer look at pure procedural justice.

Rawls suggests gambling as an example of pure procedural justice. In his own words, "If a number of persons engage in a series of fair bets, the distribution of cash after the last bet is fair, or at least not unfair, whatever this distribution is."[12] In other words, *any* distribution resulting from a series of fair bets is just, so long as the bets remain fair. If there is no tampering with the betting procedure, such as there would be in the case of cheating, then the outcome of the betting is purely procedurally just (or purely procedurally not unjust). Moreover, since gambling is a means to distribute or redistribute money or goods, gambling which consists exclusively of a series of fair bets produces, in a purely procedural manner, outcomes which further, or at least do not contradict, the requirements of distributive justice.

If we look more closely at the proposition "any distribution resulting from a series of fair bets is just," we can discern two different plausible interpretations: one narrowly focused on gambling as a procedure, the other more broadly focused on gambling as a distributive device. Under the narrow interpretation, fair gambling, in contrast to unfair gambling, is just to the extent that all participants in fair gambling obtain everything which they are enti-

11 An extreme example of the uses of procedural issues to mask conflicts between parties with widely divergent conceptions of the good is provided by the protracted discussions concerning the shape of the negotiating table at the onset of certain peace talks. *See, e.g.*, Thomas L. Friedman, *Third Round of Mideast Talks Closes with Scant Progress*, N.Y. TIMES, Jan. 17, 1992, at A1; Jackson Diehl & David Hoffman, *Participants Gather for Mideast Peace Talks*, WASH. POST, Oct. 29, 1991, at A16.

12 RAWLS, *supra* note 6, at 86.

tled to expect, namely an equal opportunity[13] (in the sense of an equal probability) to become the winner. From the broader perspective, however, fair gambling can only be just—or, much more likely, not unjust—if certain material conditions and certain normative assumptions are present. Thus, if fair gambling only involves individuals who risk small amounts of discretionary income, in the context of a normative setting where random allocations of discretionary income would not contravene prevailing norms of distributive justice, then any outcome of fair gambling is not unjust. If, on the other hand, fair gambling were to involve large sums of money, including what for some gamblers would be considered sums necessary for purposes of their subsistence, and if the gambling were to take place in a setting in which, according to prevailing substantive norms of distributive justice, redistributions of income that cause any one to fall below the subsistence level are deemed to be unjust, then even such fair gambling would clearly be (distributively) unjust.

As the example of gambling indicates, pure procedural justice depends on substantive norms of justice as much as the other forms of procedural justice. Pure procedural justice differs only in that under the confluence of certain material conditions and certain substantive norms of justice, application of a given procedure is bound to produce a just (not unjust) outcome or one of many equally just (not unjust) outcomes. Moreover, the perception that pure procedural justice remains independent from substantive norms of justice is made possible by a twofold abstraction. First, the legal subjects who avail themselves of the relevant procedure are abstracted from (in the sense of being lifted out of) the lifeworld of their daily existence. Second, the relevant procedure is abstracted from the concrete material conditions and particular substantive norms on which it depends for its ultimate justification. The second abstraction would be performed through lifting the relevant procedure from its broader legitimating factual and normative context, and then focusing on this procedure so narrowly as to leave its factual and normative setting out of the resulting picture.

The processes of abstraction present in both procedural and purely procedural justice, while operating somewhat differently, are ultimately relied upon to perform largely similar tasks. On the one hand, abstraction is supposed to sufficiently detach legal subjects from the totality of their concrete trappings in order to place

---

13 *See* Michel Rosenfeld, Affirmative Action and Justice: A Philosophical and Constitutional Inquiry 42 (1991).

the spotlight on similarities among such subjects, while downplaying the differences that set them apart. Accordingly, in the example of gambling, the individuals involved are considered in relation to their placing bets and not in terms of their differing wealth, education, social class, or family status. Similarly, in the context of the economic marketplace or of contract as a legitimate tool of procedural justice, individuals are considered in their capacities as producer, buyer, seller, or consumer rather than as men or women, rich or poor, or members of an ethnic majority or minority.

In addition to lifting legal subjects out of their concrete sociopolitical circumstances, abstraction serves to minimize or to conceal reliance on contestable substantive norms when attempting to settle conflicts among legal subjects. Moreover, these two different tasks performed by abstraction are not independent from one another, but rather, are closely connected. As already mentioned, the principal normative function of law in complex modern societies is to provide for just intersubjective dealings among legal subjects who relate to each other as strangers. And, as between strangers, justice would seem to require, above all, that all those involved be treated as equals and that the customs, normative beliefs, and ethical commitments of some not be favored over those of others. Also, because one is most likely to perceive a stranger in terms of the ways he or she differs from the members of one's own group, justice among strangers seems to require conceptualizing the realm of intersubjective transactions at a level of abstraction that optimizes awareness of what strangers have in common.

Where legal subjects relate to each other as strangers, procedural justice becomes extremely important and promotes a brand of equality that clusters around similarities. Genuine equality, however, requires taking into account relevant differences as well as relevant similarities.[14] Accordingly, procedural justice seems prone to overemphasize similarities, while underemphasizing differences. Because of this, from the standpoint of achieving global justice, every move in the direction of the greater abstraction required by procedural justice should be paired with a move in the opposite direction in order to prevent the eradication of relevant differences. This latter move, moreover, may either be set in motion automatically, in the context of pure procedural justice operating under propitious material conditions and normative

14 Inequality results as much from treating those who are different as inferior as it does from imposing treatment as equals onto those whose relevant differences have been disregarded or suppressed. *See id.* at 222-24.

assumptions, or it may be triggered by the application of substantive norms that counter the flight toward abstraction promoted by procedural justice. In short, the task of justice is to account for and reconcile relevant identities and relevant differences. Viewing law as a medium, the above proposition means that the formal equality derived from law, which conforms to procedural justice, must be reconciled with the substantive equality that properly incorporates differences. Furthermore, substantive equality can be promoted through the content of legal norms.

Before turning to an examination of Habermas's proceduralist paradigm, in light of the preceding observations, there are two further points about proceduralism in general which must be briefly mentioned. First, it does not necessarily follow that although proceduralism cannot do away with the need to embrace substantive norms, pure procedural justice is impossible. Clearly, proceduralism cannot rise above substantive norms or appeal to universally valid substantive norms. However, this does not preclude reliance on contestable substantive norms to the extent that such norms must be implicitly or explicitly embraced by all those confronted with the necessity of interacting with others, as legal subjects having to relate to each other as equals and as strangers. In other words, proceduralism may be acceptable in the context of contestable substantive norms. This is true provided that the latter norms cannot be legitimately contested by those who come under the sweep of the background assumptions and material conditions underlying the proceduralism under consideration.

Second, a distinction must be drawn between what may be called "primary proceduralism" and what may be referred to as "derivative proceduralism." Under primary proceduralism, deployment of the relevant procedure is both indispensable to and determinative of any outcome that may be considered legitimate. However, under derivative proceduralism, outcomes are ultimately determined and legitimated by something more fundamental than, or logically antecedent to, the relevant procedure. Consequently, the relevant procedure is relegated to an auxiliary or essentially rhetorical role. As an illustration, one can cite the difference between "pure" or "primary" social contract theory and derivative social contract theory:

> Pure social contract theory posits that the ultimate justification of all legitimate social and political institutions lies in the mutual consent of the individuals affected by such institutions. . . . Derivative . . . social contract theories, on the other hand, recognize the social contract device, but do not rely at the deepest level on

> mutual consent as the source of the legitimacy of social and political institutions.[15]

Consistent with this distinction, Hobbes is an exponent of pure social contract theory, whereas Locke is an exponent of derivative social contract theory.[16] In Locke's theory, the ultimate source of legitimacy is not the social contract itself, but rather the natural right to property. This right to property both prompts the passage from the state of nature to civil society and delimits the scope and function of the social contract.[17]

More generally, pure procedural justice requires primary proceduralism and is ultimately inconsistent with derivative proceduralism. Therefore, derivative proceduralism is not genuine proceduralism but rather substantive theory in procedural garb.

II.

Habermas's proceduralism, rooted in his discourse theory, emerges against the background of Hobbesian as well as Rawlsian contractarianism. Hobbesian contractarianism satisfies the requirements of primary proceduralism yet remains morally arbitrary; Rawlsian contractarianism incorporates the standpoint of Kantian morality, but proves ultimately to belong to the realm of derivative proceduralism.[18] In Hobbesian contractarianism, the contractual device both shapes and legitimates the contract of association, which marks the passage from the state of nature to civil society.[19] The contractual device, moreover, performs a critical intersubjective task both by mediating between the conflicting wills of individual contractors and yielding a common will, which differs from every individual will involved, yet is nothing but the product of a voluntary compromise among all the contractors.[20]

---

15 Michel Rosenfeld, *Contract and Justice: The Relation Between Classical Contract Law and Social Contract Theory*, 70 Iowa L. Rev. 769, 857 (1985).

16 *See id.*

17 *See id.* at 857-58.

18 *See* Jürgen Habermas, Between Facts and Norms: Contributions to a Discourse Theory of Law and Democracy 449-50 (William Rehg trans., 1996).

19 For a more detailed discussion of Hobbes's social contract theory, see Rosenfeld, *supra* note 15, at 849-50, 852-55, 858-59.

20 In a paradigmatic contract between a buyer who wishes to obtain a coveted good as cheaply as possible, and a seller who wishes to sell that good as expensively as possible, the contract price will be set at a level that is higher than what the buyer wishes, but lower than that wished for by the seller. Moreover, the contract price has to be such that neither the buyer nor the seller prefers to walk away from the contract rather than entering into it. Thus, the conflict between the will of the buyer and that of the seller is settled upon agreement on a contract price, which becomes the joint (intersubjective) will of buyer and seller but which transcends each of their (initial) individual wills.

Also, in the context of Hobbesian contractarianism, the state of affairs resulting from implementation of the contract may comport with the requirements of pure procedural justice, provided certain material conditions and normative assumptions are satisfied. Those conditions and assumptions are the ones that underlie Adam Smith's conception of a market society in which the "invisible hand" of competition transforms the clash of private interests into a realization of the public interest.[21] In the context of the kind of atomistic competition envisaged by Adam Smith, contract serves to transform the products emanating from the arbitrary wills of individuals into building blocks for the emergence of the public interest.

Absent atomistic market competition, and upon rejection of the Smithian conception of the relationship between the pursuit of private self-interest and promotion of the public interest, contract alone cannot serve to bridge the gap between private and public interest. Accordingly, contract loses its ability to produce pure procedural (distributive) justice. Furthermore, while still a medium for mediation of conflicting wills, contract no longer serves as a means to transcend the arbitrary wills of individual contractors. Finally, in the context of atomistic competition, each contractor presumably has an equal opportunity to influence the shaping of the common will through joint and mutual contract, whereas in the absence of rough material equality among contractors, the superior bargaining power of some contractors allows them to have significantly greater influence than others on the configuration of the intersubjective will produced through contract.[22] In short, cut loose from its Smithian moorings, Hobbesian contractarianism in the end is both morally arbitrary as well as partial toward some of the contractors.

---

21 For a more extended discussion of the relationship between Adam Smith's conception of a market society and the achievement of pure procedural justice through the implementation of contracts, see Rosenfeld, *supra* note 15, at 873-77.

22 Whereas it is obvious that the mere *fact* of contracting tends to lose its legitimating role in the context of a legal contract between two contractors with widely different bargaining power, it is not immediately apparent that an analogous change takes place in the context of the social contract. Upon reflection, however, the analogy seems to hold to the extent that once the "invisible hand" premise is dropped, all the different conceptions of the good are not likely to fare equally well when subjected to the social contract device. Thus, for instance, communitarian and feminist conceptions of the good are much less compatible with the ideology of contract than are individualistic and atomistic conceptions. *See, e.g.*, Carol Pateman, The Sexual Contract 2, 108 (1988) (social contract establishes a "fraternal patriarchy" through which men rule over women). Accordingly, if differences had to be settled through a contractual agreement, atomistic individualists would have a built-in advantage over communitarians or feminists.

Rawlsian contractarianism proposes to resolve both of the defects which plague its Hobbesian counterpart. To overcome moral arbitrariness, Rawls infuses his social contractors with Kantian moral universalism. Whereas Hobbesian contractors are motivated to enter into the social contract to secure indispensable social cooperation on terms most favorable to the furtherance of their own arbitrary will, Rawlsian contractors seek to establish principles of justice upon which they could all equally agree.[23] Moreover, to avoid the pitfalls caused by differences in power among contractors and by partiality, Rawls places his hypothetical contractors behind a "veil of ignorance." This is designed to make it possible for contractors to agree upon principles of justice without taking into account either their social position or their conception of the good.[24]

The veil of ignorance secures equality by allowing strangers to ascend to a higher level of abstraction. At this level they can discover the core of their common identity, unhampered by the power struggles and the clashing differences of their daily existence. Based on that new-found equality predicated on their common identity, strangers, through reciprocal recognition, can discover fair principles of justice to govern all of their intersubjective dealings. However, Rawls's use of the contract device at a higher level of abstraction comes at too high a cost. Indeed, in the course of establishing abstract equality behind the veil of ignorance, Rawls has sacrificed difference, has reduced the social contract from a dialogical to a monological device, and has unwittingly paved the way for the predominance of some perspectives which cannot be justified as being superior to those against which they compete.[25]

Rawls's abstract equality behind the veil of ignorance is objectionable to the extent that it drastically downplays difference in its search for a solid common core of identity. Genuine equality requires taking into account relevant differences as well as relevant similarities. Rawls's contractors have been deprived of the means to perceive diversity, and are thus unable to factor relevant differences into their elaboration of fair principles of justice. Differences are also essential to the proper functioning of the institution of contract, as only contractors with different needs, desires, motivations, and resources are likely to seek out one another to negotiate a contractual exchange. Ultimately, Rawls's contractors behind

23 *See* Rawls, *supra* note 6, at 11-12.

24 *See id.* at 11.

25 For an extended discussion of these shortcomings of Rawls's contractarianism, see Rosenfeld, *supra* note 13, at 233-37.

the veil of ignorance are reduced to the position of mere abstract egos.[26] And since abstract egos are interchangeable, as identically constituted and uniform in perspective, individual conclusions would not differ from those reached in concert concerning legitimate principles of justice. Under these circumstances, the contract device seems altogether superfluous, rendering Rawls's principles of justice monological rather than dialogical,[27] and his brand of contractarianism derivatively proceduralist at best.

The most serious defect of the Rawlsian process of abstraction is that it ultimately makes it possible, under the guise of remaining neutral among different perspectives, for some perspectives to gain the upper hand over others. This results from the very means of abstraction that Rawls sets into motion in order to transform the totality of everyday individuals embedded in their particular sociopolitical norms, institutions, customs, and practices into a collection of pure abstract egos acting as social contractors behind a veil of ignorance. Looking closely at this process of abstraction, a distinction can be drawn between physical differences and differences in perspective. For example, there is a difference between racial identity as a function of skin pigmentation and racial identity as the product of a distinct historical and cultural-based perspective. Now, we can accept that the veil of ignorance conceals differences based on skin pigmentation just as we can readily imagine a society that is not comprised of differences in skin color. However, if historical events such as slavery and racial apartheid have created distinct perspectives, which by and large correspond to differences in skin color, then how can we go beyond these differences in perspective while discarding differences in skin pigmentation? If there is a universal perspective that transcends all particular perspectives, proceduralism would be entirely superfluous or merely trivial. Absent such a universal perspective, however, the abstract egos behind the veil of ignorance would have to adopt either a racial minority or a racial majority perspective in order to arrive at any common principles sufficient to sustain fair principles of jus-

26 [Under] Rawls'[s] original position . . . common principles emerge only after all differences in life plans and in natural and social assets have been set aside. Under these circumstances, common principles are reached, not from a diversity of perspectives that incorporates the multitude of existing differences, but from the mere abstract identity that equalizes all individual perspectives after having neutralized all the possible sources of individual differences.

Id. at 234-35.

27 This analysis is consistent with Habermas's assessment of Rawls's theory. *See* Jürgen Habermas, Moral Consciousness and Communicative Action 66 (Christian Lenhardt & Shierry W. Nicholsen trans., 1990).

tice. Under these circumstances, a racially influenced perspective becomes a material condition that is bound to have an impact on the selection of principles of justice, yet it remains concealed behind the erasure of differences relating to skin pigmentation.[28]

Habermas's discourse-theoretical proceduralism provides the means to overcome the particular limitations of both Hobbesian and Rawlsian contractarianism. By relying on communicative action—action oriented toward reaching understanding[29]—as a means to generate consensus, Habermas provides a procedural approach that makes for a clear demarcation between the *generation* of intersubjective norms and their *use* to one's own advantage. Consistent with this demarcation, and as a consequence of excluding "strategic action"[30] from the process designed to lead to the consensual adoption of intersubjective norms, Habermas provides a way to surmount the arbitrariness and lack of impartiality inherent in Hobbesian contractarianism. Indeed, contract is, above all, the institution of choice to channel peaceful and orderly interaction among strategically oriented social actors. Accordingly, the use of contract to generate intersubjective norms seems destined to subordinate the perspective of the rulemaker to that of the strategic actor who wishes to press his advantage as far as the rules permit. However, from the standpoint of communicative action, where the focus is on reaching a consensus, both arbitrary will and the strategic actors' thirst for success seem sufficiently isolated and neutralized to move beyond the constraints inherent in Hobbesian contractarianism.

Communicative action also provides the means to overcome the two principal defects of Rawlsian contractarianism—namely its inability to properly account for differences and its unintentional privileging of certain perspectives over others. Not only is everyone supposed to participate in Habermas's discursive procedure for generating and validating intersubjective norms, but there is no

[28] For a more extended discussion of the role of race in shaping different perspectives in the context of American society, as well as the relation between such perspectives and norms of justice, see ROSENFELD, *supra* note 13, at ch. 9.

[29] For a comprehensive discussion of communicative action, see 1 JÜRGEN HABERMAS, THE THEORY OF COMMUNICATIVE ACTION (Thomas McCarthy trans., 1984) [hereinafter 1 HABERMAS, THE THEORY OF COMMUNICATIVE ACTION], and 2 JÜRGEN HABERMAS, THE THEORY OF COMMUNICATIVE ACTION (Thomas McCarthy trans., 1987).

[30] According to Habermas, in strategic action, "the actors are interested solely in the *success*, i.e., the *consequences* or *outcomes* of their actions, [and] they will try to reach their objectives by influencing their opponent's definition of the situation, and thus his decisions or motives, through external means by using weapons or goods, threats or enticements." HABERMAS, *supra* note 27, at 133.

veil of ignorance and everyone is free to introduce any matter of concern for discussion. Accordingly, differences are not eliminated *ex ante*, but are taken into full account; the ultimate decision as to which differences to count as relevant to be reached by consensus after full and uninhibited discussion. Moreover, Habermas's dialogical approach, unlike Rawls's contractarianism, is not reductive when it comes to taking different perspectives into account. Indeed, not only does Habermas envisage taking all different perspectives into account, but he insists that his discursive procedure calls for the complete reversibility of the perspectives of all participants in communicative action.[31] In other words, Habermas's proceduralism requires, as a prerequisite to reaching a legitimate consensus, that conflicts presented for discursive resolution be considered by all participants from each and every perspective involved.

Having thus set the procedural path free from unwarranted Hobbesian and Rawlsian constraints, Habermas proposes his proceduralist paradigm. According to this paradigm, the legitimacy of law is to be gauged from the standpoint of a collectivity of strangers who mutually recognize one another as equals and jointly engage in communicative action to establish a legal order to which they could all accord their unconstrained acquiescence. By means of communicative action, a reconstructive process is established through which the relevant group of strangers need only accept as legitimate those laws which they would all agree both to enact as autonomous legislators and to follow as law abiding subjects.

In accordance with this proceduralism, legal subjects can construct a perspective that enables them to view themselves simultaneously as the authors and the addressees of law. From that perspective, moreover, they may jointly determine which laws would be acceptable to them in their capacities as both authors and addressees. And, consistent with this proceduralism based on communicative action, democracy and rights not only can be reconciled but also apprehended as internally connected and mutually dependent.[32] Indeed, absent the safeguards built in through communica-

---

31 *See id.* at 122.

32 As Habermas states,

> a legal order *is* legitimate to the extent that it equally secures the co-original private and political autonomy of its citizens; at the same time, however, it *owes* its legitimacy to the forms of communication in which civic autonomy alone can express and prove itself. This is the key to a proceduralist understanding of law.

Jürgen Habermas, *Paradigms of Law*, 17 CARDOZO L. REV. 771, 777 (1996).

tive action, democracy and rights remain at loggerheads since the only guarantee against oppression by legislative majorities would come from antimajoritarian rights limiting the scope of legitimate democratic lawmaking. However, from the standpoint of communicative action, the same rights, which those in the minority would otherwise grasp as shields against the majority, would loom as part of the same bundle of rights and freedoms which enables each member of the legal community to become integrated with every other member of that community.

In addition to reconciling rights and democracy from the standpoint of communicative action, Habermas's proceduralist paradigm of law also offers innovative means to pursue the purely procedural achievement of justice. Indeed, as Habermas indicates, the principal task of the strangers who relate to each other as equal consociates under law is to reconcile the requirements of legal equality with those of factual equality.[33] In other words, through communicative action, legal actors are supposed to reach agreement among themselves as to which factual similarities and differences ought to be taken into account by the law. As we have seen, Hobbesian contractarianism shortchanges the demands of justice to the extent that its proceduralism favors recognition of the identities and differences dear to the most powerful. Likewise, Rawlsian contractarianism also proves inadequate because, among other things, its removal of certain differences *ex ante* renders it only derivatively procedural. Finally, substantive resolutions of the problem of justice necessitate recourse to justice beyond law, which compels favoring certain conceptions of the good over others. In light of these alternatives, Habermas's procedural proposal seems particularly attractive for at least two important reasons: first, it allows all identities and differences to be considered while weeding out strategic uses of them; and second, it requires subjecting all of the identities and differences to every one of the perspectives represented by participants in communicative action. Accordingly, Habermas's proceduralism promises to reconcile legal and factual equality in a way that not only accounts for all existing identities and differences, but that also takes into consideration the importance of every asserted identity and difference for each of the different perspectives represented in communicative action.

The reconciliation of legal and factual equality is a paramount task for postmetaphysical justice. As Habermas notes, however, the two postmetaphysical legal paradigms—namely the liberal-

33 *See id.* at 778-79.

bourgeois paradigm and the social-welfare paradigm (which he seeks to replace with his proceduralist paradigm)—have not satisfactorily dealt with the nexus between legal and factual equality.[34] The liberal-bourgeois paradigm reduces justice to the equal distribution of rights, thus basically ignoring factual equality.[35] The social-welfare paradigm, on the other hand, seeks to remedy this deficiency by zeroing in on the eradication of factual inequality, and in so doing reduces justice to distributive justice.[36] As a consequence of this, in order to achieve factual equality, the dignity and autonomy of those who must be clients of the welfare state become substantially undermined.[37]

The material conditions underlying the emergence of Habermas's proceduralist paradigm of law thus include both the successive existences and failures of the liberal-bourgeois and social-welfare paradigms. The liberal-bourgeois paradigm relies primarily on a formal conception of equality that clearly places identity above differences.[38] The social-welfare paradigm, in contrast, fosters a material conception of equality that places differences and the need to account for differences in the forefront, leaving equality as identity in the background.

From the broader perspective of the struggle for equality, originating in the repudiation of the feudal order, one can observe an intertwining dialectic between identity and difference as well as between equality and inequality. A brief look into this dialectic is warranted at this point in order to place the struggle to reconcile legal and factual equality, and the three paradigms of law discussed thus far, in a broader context. This should make for a more thorough picture of the background and normative assumptions and of the material conditions surrounding Habermas's proceduralist paradigm of law.

In the struggle against feudal hierarchy, equality as identity achieved predominance, as clearly evinced in the American Declaration of Independence's famous phrase, "All men are created equal." Moreover, the emergence of equality as identity being a rallying point for eighteenth century bourgeois revolutionaries is

34 *See id.* at 776-80.

35 *See id.*

36 *See id.*

37 *See id.*

38 In other words, in the liberal-bourgeois paradigm, rights are distributed equally to everyone since every individual is considered identical to every other individual as a being who is inherently entitled to have rights. But if (material) differences among individuals tend to be downplayed, inequalities in the capacity to exercise rights will be disregarded.

set against the feudal order's association of difference with hierarchical relations between superiors and inferiors. In other words, in this particular setting, equality goes hand in hand with identity whereas inequality is coupled with difference. Consistent with this view, the pursuit of equality as identity is to promote the establishment of equal dignity of citizens regardless of status or birth.

There are, however, other contexts in which equality as identity can be used as a weapon against treating all members of society as equals.[39] This occurs when equality has to be purchased at the price of giving up cherished differences; for example, when equal membership in a polity is conditioned on the adoption of an official religion which may require repudiating or suppressing one's own religious preferences. More generally, in terms of the dynamics between identity, difference, equality, and inequality, whether equality as identity ultimately contributes to, or frustrates, treating every member of society as an equal depends on whether equality as identity is pursued in a setting that is best characterized by the metaphor of the master and the slave or by that of the colonizer and the colonized. Indeed, the master treats the slave as inferior because he is different, whereas the colonizer offers the colonized equal treatment provided that the latter give up his own language, culture, and religion and adopt those of the colonizer.[40] Accordingly, in a master-slave setting, equality as identity is a weapon of liberation whereas in a colonizer-colonized setting, it is a weapon of domination.[41]

The dialectic between equality as identity and equality as difference unfolds in the context of the struggle for equality against the backdrop of commitment to prescriptive equality—that is, accepting, as a normative proposition, that all persons are inherently equal autonomous moral agents. Moreover, a discrepancy exists

---

39 Following Dworkin's distinction, equal treatment—that is, giving to each the same thing—must be contrasted with treating persons as equals—that is, as possessors of the same inherent worth and dignity. *See* RONALD DWORKIN, TAKING RIGHTS SERIOUSLY 227 (1977).

40 For a more extended discussion of these issues, see ROSENFELD, *supra* note 13, at 222-24.

41 A clear example of this contrast is furnished by the constitutional treatment of racial differences in the United States. At the time when racial apartheid was constitutionally sanctioned, the slogan "the constitution is colorblind" was a weapon used against the denial of equal dignity to African-Americans. *See* Plessy v. Ferguson, 163 U.S. 537, 552 (1896) (Harlan, J., dissenting). In the context of modern day claims to entitlement of affirmative action, as a remedy against the lingering effects of past discrimination, however, "the constitution is colorblind" has become the rallying point for those who refuse to redress continuing inequities against African-Americans. *See, e.g.*, Paul C. Roberts, *The Rise of the New Inequality*, WALL ST. J., Dec. 6, 1995, at A20.

between the ideal of prescriptive equality, which requires a reconciliation of legal and factual equality accounting for all relevant identities and differences, and the conception of equality embraced by active combatants in the struggle for equality. As long as the full realization of the ideal of prescriptive equality remains elusive, combatants struggling for equality seem bound to embrace positions more tilted toward identity or difference, according to whether they wage their fight against particular inequalities grafted upon particular differences or, on the contrary, against inequalities maintained through exploitation of certain identities. In as much as the tilt required to combat inequality unduly sweeps ideally relevant identities or differences, the struggle for equality forces its protagonists to temporally forgo the acknowledgment of certain identities or differences that ultimately must figure in any legitimate reconciliation between legal and factual equality. Finally, the dialectic between identity and difference assuredly compensates for deviations that tilt too far toward identity or difference, without ever reconciling the path of the struggle for equality with the one carved by the ideal of prescriptive equality.

Regardless of whether questions of justice can ultimately be determined independently from questions concerning conceptions of the good, from the standpoint of those engaged in the struggle for equality, *how much* equality there should be and *for whom* is always embedded within the limited horizon of a concrete conception of the good. To the extent that the struggle for equality is likely to involve more than two protagonists, a protagonist's tilt toward identity or difference in dealing with one antagonist may come back to haunt that protagonist when confronting another antagonist. Thus, for example, from the perspective of the generation that carried out the American Revolution and adopted the Constitution, their tilt toward identity, reflected in the phrase "all men are created equal," was undoubtedly useful in the struggle against Britain's monarchy. That same tilt, however, proves to be a nuisance if not a downright obstacle in the context of establishing a constitutional democracy that recognizes the institution of slavery as lawful.[42] This example is admittedly extreme in that the per-

[42] It is noteworthy that the United States Constitution of 1787 implicitly recognizes the legal validity of slavery. *See, e.g.*, U.S. Const. art. I, §§ 2, 9. Neither does the Constitution contain equality rights, thus remaining at odds with the 1776 Declaration of Independence. It would not be until after the Civil War that the Constitution would be amended to repudiate slavery, and establish equality rights. U.S. Const. amends. XII, XIV. For a thorough and enlightening discussion of these issues, see David A.J. Richards, *Revolution and Constitutionalism in America*, 14 Cardozo L. Rev. 577 (1993).

spective embraced by America's founding generation leads to a blatant contradiction, unless one is prepared to proceed as if slaves were less than human.[43] Even in more mundane cases, however, there is likely to be a tension, if not a contradiction, between the tilt one is forced to assume in one's struggle for equality and the optimal amount of interplay between legal and factual equality consistent with one's perspective grounded in one's own conception of the good. In sum, considering that the struggle for equality is waged from multiple perspectives and against many differently positioned antagonists, the dialectic between equality and inequality generates tilts, either in the direction of identity or difference, which require correction. Overly sweeping claims are also generated, which require adjustment to become better (without ever becoming fully) reconciled with the comprehensive perspective from which they are made. Thus, the interplay between identity and difference must be treated as though it were a dynamic process affecting both the configuration and the scope of equality at any given time and place.

Consistent with the preceding analysis, from the standpoint of every perspective shaped by a particular conception of the good (which is compatible at the highest levels of abstraction with prescriptive equality), the reconciliation between legal and factual equality must satisfy two distinct and, at least to some degree, incompatible requirements. First, such reconciliation should satisfy the optimal relationship between identity and difference within the conception of the good espoused by the relevant perspective. Secondly, such reconciliation should level the playing field between the existing tilts and excesses that result from the ongoing struggle for equality among representatives of different perspectives. If the desired balance is not achieved, the optimal mix between identity and difference could not properly be set in motion in order to become effective. On the other hand, achievement of the desired balance requires reliance on certain identities and differences that are bound to upset, or at least postpone, the implementation of the optimal mix.

The three paradigms of law discussed by Habermas can now be put in context, both in terms of the dynamic struggle for equality, and in terms of competing perspectives on equality and justice. In terms of the struggle for equality, there is a dynamic progression from the tilt toward identity of the liberal-bourgeois paradigm, to

---

43 Shamefully, this is what the United States Supreme Court did in its infamous *Dred Scott* decision. Dred Scott v. Sandford, 60 U.S. (19 How.) 393 (1857).

the tilt toward difference of the social-welfare paradigm, and finally to the attempt to incorporate, reconcile, and balance the virtues of liberal identity and social-welfare difference within the proceduralist paradigm proposed by Habermas. Therefore, as against the two paradigms which it seeks to replace, Habermas's proceduralist paradigm appears to have significantly levelled the field on which the battle for the optimal reconciliation of legal and factual equality must be fought. This, however, does not necessarily imply that Habermas's paradigm levels the field sufficiently as between the competing perspectives it encompasses, or that it can yield any reconciliation of legal and factual equality that would be acceptable to all the encompassed perspectives.

Focusing on the issue of the perspectives encompassed within Habermas's proceduralist paradigm, three important questions arise. First, does Habermas's proceduralist paradigm, by the very nature of communicative action, effectively exclude certain perspectives? Second, does the proceduralist paradigm provide a workable means of achieving a genuine consensus among the competing perspectives it encompasses regarding the optimal mix of identities and differences, in relation to the legitimate reconciliation of legal and factual equality? And, third, does the proceduralist paradigm provide an adequate means of leveling the field on which the perspectives it encompasses compete for justice and equality? Phrased somewhat differently, these three questions can be restated as: (1) *which* perspectives can expect justice under Habermas's proceduralism?; (2) can such proceduralism produce justice *among* different perspectives?; and (3) can such proceduralism yield equal justice as gauged from *within* each of the encompassed perspectives?

Consistent with Habermas, in answering the first question it is clear that some perspectives are effectively excluded from the discursive resolution of questions concerning justice. Thus, all perspectives that could be broadly characterized as metaphysical perspectives—including those framed by religious dogma and ideology—would effectively be excluded or, more precisely, would effectively exclude themselves from any dialogical process designed to resolve issues of justice. To be sure, this is not problematic for Habermas's proceduralist paradigm since he makes it clear that his paradigm is designed for postmetaphysical conflicts over justice. The exclusion of metaphysical perspectives is noteworthy. It underscores that communicative action is not neutral as between all conceptions of the good, even if in the final analysis it remained neutral among the different conceptions of the good that are not incompatible with it.

Communicative action effectively excludes not only metaphysical perspectives but also nonmetaphysical ones that reject adherence to prescriptive equality. Indeed, there seems to be little point, from the standpoint of nonmetaphysical perspective adherents (who maintain that some are inherently superior), to submit their views concerning justice for discussion with those whom they do not consider as equals. Even if convincing the unworthy is not deemed futile, communicative action by its very structure would still remain manifestly unfavorable toward blatantly inegalitarian ideologies that altogether reject prescriptive equality. In short, it remains to be seen whether Habermas's proceduralism is neutral as between the perspectives it encompasses. However, the exclusion consistent with Habermas's proceduralism of metaphysical and nonmetaphysical hierarchical perspectives indicates that it is ultimately tied to certain substantive normative assumptions, albeit negative ones.

The answer to the second question—namely, whether communicative action can carve out a common ground for justice encompassing all of its perspectives—depends on the nature of the procedural devices involved in communicative action as well as on the existence of material conditions making it plausible for the reversal of perspectives (undertaken by actors engaged in communicative action) to generate fruitful consensuses or compromises. As conceived by Habermas, communicative action requires each participant to have an equal opportunity to present claims for consideration and a universal commitment to be swayed only by the force of the better argument.[44] Thus, the only legitimate normative regulations under Habermas's proceduralist paradigm would be those which have been assented to by all the participants in rational discourses who might be affected.[45] Moreover, in the context of legal as opposed to moral norms, Habermas stipulates that assent could be based on bargaining and compromise as well as on consensus.[46] Finally—and an important advance over Rawlsian contractarianism—the needs, wants, and interests of participants in communicative action are not taken by Habermas to be immutable; rather they are subject to evolution and transformation pursuant to dia-

---

44 For a comprehensive discussion of communicative action, see 1 HABERMAS, THE THEORY OF COMMUNICATIVE ACTION, *supra* note 29, at 273-337.

45 *See* HABERMAS, *supra* note 18, at 459-60.

46 *See id.* at 460.

logical exchanges. Because communicative action, as conceived by Habermas, can contribute to the formation of opinions and wills,[47] it is not simply relegated to finding overlapping interests; it is also equipped to harmonize interests through dialogical transformation.

In view of the characteristics of Habermas's proceduralism, there are at least three significant impediments to the goal of achieving an accord on justice among representatives of the diverse perspectives engaged in communicative action. First, the reconciliation of perspectives might ultimately prove to be a purely contingent matter. In that case, Habermas's proceduralism would prove inadequate because under many plausible circumstances it would fail to lead to any legitimate reconciliation of legal and factual equality.

One way to avoid this latter possibility is by emphasizing the requirement of rationality. Indeed, if rationality is called for by communicative action in the selection of ends, in dealing with the means toward one's ends, and in dealing with conflicts that exist among persons who pursue different ends, then attaining an accord on justice may no longer be contingent. But that leads to the second problem. If the requirement of rationality is strong enough to foreclose the contingency of an accord, then that accord is dependent on the operative norm of rationality rather than on dialogical reciprocity. Consequently, Habermas's proceduralism would become essentially derivative.

Relying upon bargaining and compromise, as well as on consensus coupled with emphasis on the transformability of needs, provides an alternative way to minimize the chance that the proceduralist paradigm will fail to yield an accord. This last alternative, however, leads to the third problem. If the pressure to reach an accord is intense, then bargaining and compromising—even if they remain free of strategic action—may favor certain perspectives over others (as contrasted with certain individuals over others). If that were the case, Habermas's proceduralism would fail to remain neutral as between the perspectives which it encompasses (much like Hobbesian contractarianism proved unable to remain neutral as between all contractors).

The preceding observations fail to identify any definitive answer to the second question. However, they raise significant doubts whether Habermas's proceduralism alone, unsupported by

---

47 *See id.* at 461-62.

substantive norms, can reliably lead to an accord on justice among different perspectives without favoring some of those perspectives.

The last of the three questions—namely, can the proceduralist paradigm level the field on which competing perspectives vie for justice—as with the second, cannot presently be given anything nearing a definitive answer. To the extent that proceduralism's search for an accord on justice leads to the favoring of some perspectives, the third question would seem to require a negative answer. However, assuming an accord could be reached without having to favor any of the relevant perspectives, the success of Habermas's proceduralism to level the playing field would appear to depend on whether the requisite leveling could be achieved through dialogue, or whether it calls for predialogical or extradialogical adjustments. To further clarify these matters, I now turn to an important feminist objection to Habermas's proceduralism.

III.

The feminist challenge to Habermas's proceduralism is particularly serious since it is launched from a perspective that is neither metaphysical nor hierarchical in nature. Moreover, the feminist challenge attacks Habermas's proceduralism on at least two different levels. On one level feminists can argue, even assuming communicative action remains neutral between feminist and male-oriented perspectives,[48] the respective needs, wants, and interests of each are given such disparate interpretations that it is not realistic to expect any general agreement on how to reconcile legal and factual equality. On another level, feminists can argue that discursive proceduralism cannot level the playing field which has traditionally heavily tilted toward male-oriented perspectives. Additionally, feminists could press the more radical claim that by its very structure communicative action favors male-oriented perspectives over feminist ones. Consequently, no purely dialogical determination of the relation between legal and factual equality could ever prove genuinely acceptable to feminists.

Habermas agrees with the feminists that both the liberal-bourgeois and the social-welfare paradigms evince biases against wo-

48 It is important to remember that what distinguishes feminist perspectives from male-oriented ones are primarily gender-related differences. These differences are largely sociocultural constructs rather than differences merely based on sex. Furthermore, while feminist perspectives may more likely be embraced by women than by men, certain men are genuinely feminists just as certain women side with antifeminists.

men.[49] However, he disagrees with the feminists when it comes to the proceduralist paradigm. Essentially, Habermas's response to the feminist challenge is that since gender differences are constructed and not pre-established, conflicts between feminist and male-oriented views should be amenable to dialogical resolution just as other interperspectival conflicts.[50]

To determine whether Habermas's proceduralism can successfully overcome the feminist challenge, it is first necessary to take a closer look at some of that challenge's principal characteristics. Moreover, since there is by no means unanimity among feminists, I shall take a reconstructive approach and combine various elements that have figured in feminist critiques, while advancing the most effective good faith feminist challenge possible. Also, as gender-related issues may vary among cultures, I will only refer to gender-related issues as they arise in the United States.

The feminist challenge in the United States is premised upon a constitutional, legal, cultural, and social tradition that has repeatedly used and/or constructed differences between men and women to the detriment of the latter, in order to perpetuate a male dominated society. In that society, with its male-oriented institutions, the best women can hope for is that gender differences will not be used against them. In other words, women's only realistic escape from being subordinated has required them to settle as being colonized[51] in a male run colony. From the standpoint of the relationship between legal and factual equality, women have generally experienced two different regimes during the course of American history. Initially, the relationship between legal and factual equality unfolded in a setting tilted toward difference, with differences being, for the most part, weighted against women.[52] More recently, the tilt has shifted toward identity, but women still have been significantly disadvantaged, in as much as identity has essentially meant conformity with male identity.[53]

It is against this background of exploited differences and coerced identities that feminists may construct a comprehensive per-

---

49 *See* Habermas, *supra* note 32, at 781-82.

50 *See id.* at 783-84; *see also supra* pp. 796-98.

51 See the distinction between master/slave and colonizer/colonized relationships, *supra* notes 40-41 and accompanying text.

52 *See, e.g.*, Bradwell v. Illinois, 83 U.S. (16 Wall.) 130 (1873) (state refusal to allow women to practice law held constitutional on grounds that a woman's proper role was that of a wife and mother).

53 *See* Martha Minow, *Justice Engendered*, 101 HARV. L. REV. 10 (1987) (arguing that Supreme Court adjudication on sexual discrimination and pregnancy has posited men's experience as the "norm" against which women are measured).

spective, with a vision of the good based upon a recasting of identities and differences in ways that are likely to be liberating and enriching for women. Inspired by Carol Gilligan's vision, feminists might construct a conception of the good stressing intimacy, attachment, interdependence, care, concern, responsibility, and self-sacrifice.[54] Such a feminist conception of the good would sharply contrast with its typical male-oriented counterpart, emphasizing separation, competition, and achievement.[55]

Now, let us suppose that representatives of the above-sketched feminist perspective (to whom I shall refer as "the feminists") confront representatives of the typical male-oriented perspective (to whom I shall refer as "the masculinists"), and that they jointly endeavor to reach a dialogical consensus on a mutually acceptable reconciliation of legal and factual equality. Let us suppose, further, that from the outset the feminists stipulate that they concede that the proceduralist paradigm is neutral as between masculinist and feminist perspectives. Under these circumstances, the feminists will start the confrontation by recounting the history of sex discrimination and will argue for the adoption of legal norms that would enhance care, responsibility, and meeting the needs of concrete others.[56] The masculinists, on the other hand, while acknowledging past inequities, will propose legal norms emphasizing autonomy and fair competition which would preclude gender-based discrimination.

Assuming that no legal norm capable of equally satisfying the masculinists and the feminists were to emerge at that point, our protagonists could proceed to engage in a reversal of perspectives. This would allow them not only to achieve greater empathy toward their antagonists' plight, but also to become aware of the relative importance of each particular claim from within the comprehensive perspective it originated. Awareness of the relative importance of

---

54 *See* CAROL GILLIGAN, IN A DIFFERENT VOICE: PSYCHOLOGICAL THEORY AND WOMEN'S DEVELOPMENT 12, 73-74, 132 (1982). Gilligan is concerned with morals, not law. Her views, however, have influenced feminist legal theorists. *See e.g.*, Ellen C. DuBois et al., *Feminist Discourse, Moral Values, and the Law—A Conversation*, 34 BUFF. L. REV. 11 (1985). For a critique of Gilligan by a feminist legal theorist, see Jeanne L. Schroeder, *Feminism Historicized: Medieval Misogynist Stereotypes in Contemporary Feminist Jurisprudence*, 75 IOWA L. REV. 1135, 1141 n.12 (1990).

55 Habermas has rejected the validity of Gilligan's challenge relating to issues in the theory of moral development. *See* HABERMAS, *supra* note 27, at 175-84. That controversy, however, has no direct bearing on the use of Gilligan's work to outline the contours of a plausible feminist conception of the good.

56 *Cf.* GILLIGAN, *supra* note 54, at 11 (contrasting men's tendency to focus on "the generalized other" with women's draw toward the "particular other").

conflicting claims within their respective perspectives might prove quite helpful—it would be rational to sacrifice a claim of lesser importance within one's own perspective to accommodate a claim that within another perspective is much more important. Such a sacrifice would be rational (in the sense of rationality of means rather than rationality of ends) considering the potential for reciprocal gestures that would ultimately inure to the benefit of all those involved.

Now, let us assume that after ranking all wants and interests and abandoning the pursuit of those which rank lower in the hierarchy, in order to facilitate the realization of those which rank higher, the masculinists and the feminists still have not been able to settle on equally acceptable legal norms. At that point, it is possible that each would try to convince the other to change their needs and wants. Thus the feminists would argue that competition is not everything and greater connectedness could enrich the lives of the masculinists. The masculinists would try to impress upon the feminists that competition is not as bad as they think, particularly if it is scrupulously rid of all vestiges of gender discrimination.

At that point in the dialogue, it is possible that a consensus regarding legal norms might be reached. But it is equally possible that a consensus on equally acceptable legal norms might never be reached. The inability of reaching a consensus would not occur because of any strategic behavior, but simply because the honestly held divergent conceptions of the good, even after accounting for all the concessions and adjustments mentioned above, would remain too far apart.

Thus far I have assumed that the feminists do not challenge the proposition that the proceduralist paradigm is neutral as between the feminist and the masculinist perspectives. There are, however, several plausible reasons which would lend support to such a challenge. Furthermore, the feminists could bring either a moderate or a radical challenge against the proposition regarding proceduralist neutrality.

For the moderate challenge, feminists would argue that the procedural guarantees afforded by dialogical proceduralism are insufficient to level the playing field since public discourse has historically been heavily tilted toward masculinist perspectives, as have the liberal-bourgeois paradigms and the social-welfare paradigms and most existing legal norms. Given that masculinist views are so entrenched in the ideology and the institutional structures of the polity, to have an equal opportunity to present one's claims and to attempt to transform existing needs, wants, and interests, seems fairly unlikely to balance the conflicting positions. This is true not because of any strategic conduct by the masculinists, but rather because they are so deeply set in their ways.

Even assuming its validity, the moderate challenge may not be fatal to proceduralism, since even deeply entrenched positions could change over time. However, time is not a trivial matter when it comes to legitimating legal norms. If meaningful changes in opinion- and will-formation can be expected to take several generations, then exclusive reliance on dialogical proceduralism would seem undesirable and inadequate.

Much more threatening to discursive proceduralism is the radical feminist challenge. That challenge takes as its first point of argument Gilligan's view that men's ethics are oriented toward rights, equality, and fairness, while women's are oriented toward responsibilities, equity, and the recognition of differences in need among concrete others.[57] Suppose the masculinists and the feminists incorporate, as part of their conceptions of the good, the views that Gilligan ascribes respectively to men and to women. Feminists could then launch the following attack. By its very structure—which is designed to lead to justice, equality, and rights—the proceduralist paradigm is inherently biased in favor of masculinist perspectives, against feminist perspectives. Ironically, because it provides for a reversal of perspectives, the proceduralist paradigm does not exclude expression of the needs, interests, or desires of feminists and even allows for masculinist empathy toward feminist claims. But those virtues are eventually nullified, in that, by its very nature, the proceduralist paradigm channels all intersubjective conflicts toward resolutions that must comport with justice, equality, and rights. Although the proceduralist paradigm gives the impression of treating feminists as full partners in the dialogical process, the very structure of that process forces feminists to suppress their most fundamental differences in order to obtain a measure of recognition that does not seriously threaten the hegemony of masculinist perspectives. In short, the proceduralist paradigm makes it possible for an individual feminist claim to be given priority over a competing masculinist claim, but it forecloses something much more fundamental from a feminist perspective—the replacement of "the hierarchy of rights with a web of relationships."[58]

[57] *See id.* at 164.

[58] *Id.* at 57.

In defense of the legitimacy of the proceduralist paradigm, it could be argued that if the radical feminist challenge proves anything, it proves too much. Because its targets include justice, equality, and rights as such, rather than any particular conception of them, the radical feminist challenge implies that law itself cannot possibly be justified as a medium for legitimate intersubjective interaction. Therefore, the radical feminist challenge would ultimately lead to a social universe devoid of law, in which feminists would either forcibly convert those who would oppose the implementation of their conception of the good, or their antagonists would go their own separate way.

Feminists, however, could argue that their radical challenge does not necessarily have the dire implications mentioned above. Viewed more closely, the radical feminist challenge is not against law itself, but against a paradigm of law which is buttressed by a particular conception of law and rights. Following this line of reasoning, a brief focus on Habermas's conception of rights reveals that while he is open as to the content of legal rights, he clearly embraces a "static" rather than a "dynamic" conception of law as a medium of intersubjective interaction.[59] In Habermas's view, legal rights (as opposed to moral rights) are above all entitlements, which are logically prior to the duties they trigger.[60] Therefore, such rights carve out boundaries which tend to separate the rightholder from those who must assume a duty as a consequence of his or her entitlement. In the context of a dynamic jurisprudence such as the common law, however, because of the presence of greater flexibility, open-endedness, and indeterminacy, rights and duties become the product of interaction among legal actors; thus, they are always susceptible to further perfection through cooperation.[61]

---

59 *See* Arthur J. Jacobson, *The Idolatry of Rules: Writing Law According to Moses, With Reference to Other Jurisprudences*, 11 CARDOZO L. REV. 1079, 1125 (1990); *see also* Arthur J. Jacobson, *Hegel's Legal Plenum*, 10 CARDOZO L. REV. 877, 889-90 (1989) [hereinafter Jacobson, *Hegel*]. For present purposes, the key distinction between these two jurisprudences is that dynamic jurisprudences are open-ended and primarily concerned with the realization and development of legal personality. Static jurisprudences are primarily concerned with instituting legal order and, accordingly, draw sharp lines between legal relationships and other intersubjective relationships which remain essentially beyond the reach of law.

60 In Habermas's own words, "[w]hereas in morality an inherent symmetry exists between rights and duties, legal *duties* only result as consequences of the protection of *entitlements*, which are conceptually prior." HABERMAS, *supra* note 18, at 451.

61 *Cf.* Jacobson, *Hegel*, *supra* note 59, at 890-91 (in the common law system persons cannot interact without generating rights and duties, yet cannot know what those rights and duties are until after they have interacted).

With the distinction between static and dynamic jurisprudences in mind, the feminists can argue that their radical challenge does not demand the abolition of law, justice, equality, and rights—it calls only for the replacement of the proceduralist paradigm and its static conception of rights with an alternative paradigm creating a dynamic conception of rights. This alternative paradigm would alter the importance of justice, equality, and rights, by balancing them against normative standards designed to enhance promotion of the "web of relationships." Moreover, any alternative paradigm of law designed to be consistent with the radical feminist challenge, could neither be exclusively dialogical nor merely procedural. It would have to press substantive feminist norms against masculinist objections, thus having to rely on predialogical or extradialogical sources of legitimacy.

Proponents of legal proceduralism may object to any alternative feminist paradigm which would countenance the imposition of feminist norms over masculinist objections arguing the paradigm would be arbitrary or inconsistent with a commitment to prescriptive equality. Feminists however could counter, arguing that their proposed alternative paradigm would neither be arbitrary nor in violation of the dictates of prescriptive equality. Focusing on the dialectics between identity and difference, and between equality and inequality, feminists could claim that progress toward an optimal reconciliation of legal and factual equality has always been achieved through a series of thrusts that overshoot their intended target, thereby tilting legal paradigms toward certain conceptions of the good to the detriment of other conceptions. This state of affairs requires compensation which necessitates generating a tilt toward the opposite direction. Therefore, the feminist alternative paradigm, with all its bias, is a logical moment in the ongoing struggle to reach an optimal reconciliation of legal and factual equality. Consequently, such an alternative feminist paradigm is neither arbitrary nor contrary to prescriptive equality.

Based on the above examination of the feminist objection to Habermas's proceduralist paradigm of law, it is now possible to give a more complete answer to the two questions left open at the end of the Part II. First, unaided by additional substantive norms, legal proceduralism cannot be expected to produce justice among different perspectives within its domain. Second, proceduralism alone fails to yield equal justice as gauged from *within* each of the encompassed perspectives.

IV.

Considering that pluralism implies a lack of agreement regarding substantive norms, it would seem to be the most promising ally of pure procedural justice. Ideally, proceduralism should save pluralism from the embarrassment of having to choose among the various competing conceptions of the good it encompasses. However, pluralism and pure procedural justice are ultimately incompatible. Conversely, whereas a community that shares the same substantive norms may seem to have no use for mere procedural justice, pure procedural justice can assume a legitimate role in the context of shared substantive norms, as indicated by the gambling example discussed earlier.[62] If these observations are correct, then Habermas's legal proceduralism may be vindicated to the extent that it is confined to contexts regulated by shared substantive norms. Moreover, while such vindication may fall quite short of pluralist expectations, it is by no means trivial.

Before looking into the relationship between pluralism and pure procedural justice, a distinction concerning pluralism must be briefly addressed. Pluralism may either be methodological or comprehensive. Methodological pluralism can be characterized as a tool designed to prevent any substantive conception of the good from achieving a dominant position in the public sphere. Comprehensive pluralism, on the other hand, is a full-fledged substantive perspective encompassing a particular conception of the good which requires the inclusion and protection of different substantive perspectives that can be accommodated peacefully within the polity. The distinction between these two kinds of pluralism raises the following question: Since comprehensive pluralism relies on shared substantive norms, is it not then compatible with pure procedural justice? As we shall see, the answer to this question is eventually negative, even though comprehensive pluralism reserves an important but limited role for proceduralism.

To get a better understanding of the relationship between pluralism and proceduralism, it is useful to refer back to the image of transcommunal market relationships among strangers.[63] At first, one can assume that the market where strangers came to exchange goods was an important yet occasional focus for intersubjective dealings. Under these circumstances, the market required transcommunal laws to regulate dealings among strangers and to stabi-

---

62 *See supra* pp. 796-98.

63 *See supra* notes 20-27 and accompanying text. For a more extended discussion, see Rosenfeld, *supra* note 2, at 1689-94.

lize the latter's expectations. Aside from the occasional forays into the market, intersubjective dealings also took place intracommunally, where they were regulated primarily by common religious and ethical norms or by laws conforming to such norms. Given that everyone returned to his or her own community except for limited market exchanges, it makes sense that the legal norms regulating market transactions would be procedural in nature. Although one cannot properly speak of pluralism in this scenario, it would be fair to speak of a proceduralism bound by a plurality of distinct communities.

At the next stage, one can imagine that the market has become more important, and that all the bordering communities sending people to the market will associate into a loose confederation. In this situation, pluralism and proceduralism co-exist, but their respective spheres of operation remain completely separated from one another.

As the market encroaches ever more on communal life, however, proceduralism and pluralism enter a collision course. On the one hand, the market increasingly expands onto the terrain formerly reserved for communal ethical and religious life, forcing substantive communal norms to spill over into the sphere of market interactions for lack of another suitable outlet. On the other hand, since markets are not perfect, the more pervasive market relations become, the greater the need to bring in substantive norms in order to channel market transactions toward the common good.

To the extent that market self-regulation is no longer satisfactory, proceduralism must give way or become subordinated to substantive norms. Methodological pluralism may be used in an effort to prevent proponents of certain conceptions of the good from subjugating proponents of other conceptions, but it is merely a limited tool with restricted potential. Comprehensive pluralism, on the other hand, provides a full-fledged perspective and therefore deserves a closer look.

The ideal underlying comprehensive pluralism is to create a society in which all conceptions of the good are equally encompassed, but in which none is dominant (or superior). However, this ideal cannot possibly be realized. It is obvious that the entire pluralist project will collapse unless comprehensive pluralism itself is given priority over the remaining conceptions of the good. Therefore, to survive, the project of comprehensive pluralism must split and proceed at two distinct levels. Furthermore, this split must take place in two logically, though not necessarily temporally, different moments. In the first moment, comprehensive pluralism must be detached from other perspectives in order to ascend to the requisite position of primacy. Yet to survive, pluralism cannot remain detached because it is ultimately parasitic on other perspectives. Indeed, if all other conceptions of the good were to disappear, pluralism would become meaningless. Accordingly, a second moment must follow.

In the second moment, pluralism must be reconnected with the perspectives from which it had been detached. However, the reconnection must allow pluralism to retain its primacy while allowing the other perspectives to remain equal among themselves. To be viable, pluralist norms must occupy the place of a second order of norms, while the norms which emanate from other substantive conceptions of the good would operate as first order norms.

If the equal subordination of all first order norms to the second order norms of pluralism were possible, then comprehensive pluralism could in principle go hand-in-hand with proceduralism. However, this is not possible since equal subordination requires detachment as well as reintegration. Indeed, detachment of pluralism as a second order norm is realized through a process of negation that is embraced by all comprehensive pluralists and deals equally with all first order norms. Hence, in its negative work, comprehensive pluralism could rely on purely procedural devices.

However, with respect to the positive task of reintegrating subordinated first order norms, neither equality nor unanimity can be achieved by comprehensive pluralism. Because, when it comes to reintegrating into a comprehensive pluralist framework, some first order norms—such as those of crusading religions—will prove altogether incompatible with pluralism and therefore have to be suppressed. Other first order norms—such as those of noncrusading religions—will have to be displaced but they will not have to be suppressed. For example, while such norms will be expelled from public places, they will be given a protected place in the private sphere.

Even among those first order norms which should be granted full reintegration into the comprehensive pluralist polity, some will fare better than others. This seems inevitable since the second order norms operating alone cannot determine the configuration of a pluralist society's legal and political institutions. Since all fully admitted first order norms are not likely to coalesce into a harmonious whole, institutional norms and practices are bound to rely more heavily on some than on others.

In sum, comprehensive pluralism is a dynamic system that depends on the concurrent work of a thrust and counterthrust which is propelled by the permanent tension generated by the friction between its negative and positive work. In such a setting, proceduralism has an important negative role to play—it can be vital in pluralism's struggle against the permanent entrenchment of any particular set of first order norms that it encompasses. However, proceduralism can also play a limited, but nonetheless crucial, role on the positive front. By exposing particular inequities through its leveling mechanisms and by revealing concealed inequities through the reversal of perspectives (in the case of Habermas's dialogical proceduralism), proceduralism can channel pluralism's need for contested first order norms toward more encompassing, widely shared, and less oppressive alternatives. Although this would not solve the problem of reconciling legal and factual equality, it might significantly alleviate existing inequities.

To be sure, this seems to be a far cry from what Habermas seems to expect from his proceduralist paradigm of law. All the same, while Habermas may not have reconciled democracy, rights, and justice through proceduralism, he has certainly shown us creative and fruitful new ways to approach these elusive subjects, and has afforded us new means to sharpen our grasp of them.

[12]

Habermas on Nationalism and Cosmopolitanism*

PABLO DE GREIFF

Abstract. After drawing a distinction between a cosmopolitan attitude and institutional cosmopolitanism, this paper reconstructs Habermas's account of the relationship between morality and law in order to argue that this account can be the basis of a cosmopolitan attitude which, although insufficient, on its own, to ground cosmopolitan institutions, can, nonetheless, motivate interest in institutional cosmopolitanism. The paper then examines Habermas's proposal for institutionalizing a system of cosmopolitan governance. It distinguishes and explores the reach and limitations of three arguments in favor of institutional cosmopolitanism not always adequately differentiated in Habermas's work: (a) an argument from the weakness of the nation state, (b) an argument from the democratic deficit of nationalism, and (c) an argument from the state's incapacity to guarantee human rights.

Although it is (still) premature to talk about the demise of the nation state, there is no question that the conditions that led to the entrenchment of the nation state beginning with the Treaty of Westphalia in 1648 have changed considerably (see, e.g., Lyons 1995 and Zacher 1992). Changes in the military, in technology, in international trade, in cultural diffusion, and in internal and external politics, in addition to increased migration and renewed pressure for the recognition of particular identities within existing nation states, give an idea of the magnitude of the difficulties associated with theorizing about international political organization. In this respect, it might represent a significant advantage to reflect upon questions of nationalism from the standpoint of a broad social and political theory that already encompasses the factors listed. Jürgen Habermas's recent writings on nationalism and cosmopolitanism reflect such an advantage. They are part and parcel of an

*My gratitude to Thomas McCarthy, Ciaran Cronin, Newton Garver, and Jerome Slater, who read an earlier draft of this paper and offered valuable suggestions. I also appreciate the questions and comments I received after presenting a shorter version of this paper at the Department of Government of the University of Texas at Austin, in April 1999. David Braybrook and Benjamin Gregg deserve special thanks. I am also grateful to the participants in the VII Critical Theory Roundtable, held at the University of Toronto in October 1999.

ambitious theory of democratic society, and can therefore deal in a systematic way with a greater variety of concerns than the occasionally illuminating but often opportunistic thoughts on nationalism so popular today. Although, as I will argue, Habermas's defense of cosmopolitanism still requires some work, it at least has three desirable characteristics: First, it does not rest on a repudiation of the achievements and merits of the nation-state; second, it is sensitive to difference; and, most importantly, it emphasizes the importance of democratic rights even at the cosmopolitan level.

The focus of this paper will be on the normative arguments in defense of cosmopolitan political organization either adduced by Habermas or that can be constructed on the basis of his work, rather than on the concrete details of his institutional proposal. In section 1, I argue that Habermas's account of the relationship between morality and law afforded him an opportunity to make a case in favor of a cosmopolitan attitude that he surprisingly missed. In section 2, I provide a brief sketch of the institutional dimension of Habermas's cosmopolitanism, and in section 3, I distinguish and engage three normative arguments in favor of cosmopolitanism.

1. A Preliminary Consideration: On the Relationship between Morality and Law

Before examining in detail Habermas's recent arguments concerning cosmopolitanism, I would like to suggest that an argument in favor of a cosmopolitan *attitude*, if not of cosmopolitan institutions, can be constructed on the basis of his earlier work. A cosmopolitan attitude consists of an obligation to assess the morality of one's acts at least in part in light of the acceptability of their consequences by everyone affected by them, regardless of borders, territorial or otherwise. While this constructed argument has no institutional implications of its own, it is nevertheless helpful in providing a motivation for cosmopolitan organization. Cosmopolitan institutions can then be justified as the best means of institutionalizing moral requirements, thus unburdening individuals of moral obligations that might be difficult for them to observe on their own.

The core of the argument in favor of a cosmopolitan attitude lies in Habermas's analysis of the relationship between a universalistic conception of morality and the notion of legal validity. Habermas offers two different accounts of this relationship, one in works prior to *Between Facts and Norms* (Habermas 1996) and the second in that book and in his latest essays. In essence, both accounts support the same general point: Given a post-traditional world in which metaphysical or religious justifications of morality and law are no longer sufficient, one can still make use of the notion of justification in a universalistic sense by articulating the notion of validity in terms of discursive acceptability. The crucial insight behind this position is that in a culture such as ours, the only forms of rationally acceptable justification for binding norms is, precisely, the ability to stand up to critical scrutiny and prove acceptable to those who have to live by them, in a discursive situation in which all are treated as free and equal participants.

In works that precede *Between Facts and Norms*, Habermas provides an account of the validity of norms in general without distinguishing between moral and legal norms. According to this account, norms are valid if and only if they satisfy a moral principle of universalization. This principle (U) states that every valid norm of action has to fulfill the condition that

> [*a*]*ll* affected can accept the consequences and the side effects its *general* observance can be anticipated to have for the satisfaction of *everyone's* interests (and these consequences and interests are preferred to those of known alternative possibilities for regulation). (Habermas 1990, 65)

The failure to distinguish between moral and legal norms in addition to the requirement that all norms satisfy a moral principle of universalization suggests that in his earlier work Habermas subordinated legal legitimacy to the universalistic principle of morality (U). Although this imposes on the law demands that will be seen to be inappropriate, given that there is no territorial closure to a universalistic moral principle, it should be plain that the subordination of legal legitimacy to such a principle of morality leads to the conclusion that the legitimacy of laws depends upon their consequences for all those who are substantially affected by them, not only within national borders, but wherever those affected reside. This position, then, could constitute the basis of a radically cosmopolitan argument; since Habermas argues not only for a universalistic principle of morality, but for the thesis that universalizability can only be tested through real dialogues and not through Kantian thought experiments, then one would have the premises of an argument in favor of deliberative forums, and possibly of political representation within electoral districts whose membership should not be defined in terms of a territorial criterion, but of being affected by a given norm, regardless of traditional political—national or international—boundaries.

In summary, as long as morality is understood in universalistic terms, and provided that legitimacy is subordinated to morality, this introduces a universalistic requirement into law-making. Whether this requirement is best satisfied by supranational institutions would take further elaboration, but, at a minimum, the argument suggests a moral obligation which legislators in particular bear, an obligation that requires them to assess the impact of their law making in terms that go beyond considerations of national expediency. This is what I call a cosmopolitan attitude.[1]

[1] I tried to put this argument to use in the context of discussions about drug policy in De Greiff 1999.

In *Between Facts and Norms* and succeeding works, Habermas changes in significant respects his account of the relation between morality and law, and he does it in a way that seems to threaten the defense of a cosmopolitan attitude just sketched, for the new argument is specifically intended to overcome the subordination of legality to morality. I will argue that despite the changes, a defense of a cosmopolitan attitude can still be constructed, but that this requires helping Habermas out of a confusion.

As part of a more comprehensive discourse theory of democracy, Habermas introduces in his later works a higher degree of differentiation between morality and law and a modified account of their relationship. Instead of arguing that *all* norms are valid if they satisfy a universalistic moral principle, he now argues that moral and legal norms satisfy different principles of validity. The principle of moral validity remains the same, namely (U), but now a separate principle of democratic legitimacy is introduced:

> only those judicial statutes may claim legitimacy that meet with the agreement of all citizens in a discursive law-making process that is itself legally constituted. (Habermas 1996, 110, 135)

So, what is the relationship between the principles of moral validity and of legal legitimacy? Given that the core discourse-theoretic position that validity ought to be understood in terms of rational acceptability remains unchanged, Habermas now argues that both (U) *and* the principle of legal legitimacy are specifications of a general principle of validity according to which

> [j]ust those action norms are valid to which all those possibly affected could agree as participants in rational discourses. (Ibid., 107)

This general principle merely explicates the impartial standpoint from which questions of the validity of norms should be assessed, without discriminating yet between moral and legal norms of action. It can, though, be specified for both, yielding the two different principles of moral validity and democratic legitimacy. The principle of moral validity (U), then, is supposed to specify what the notion of impartiality which is at the core of validity entails when the norms at issue are moral norms. Similarly, the principle of democratic legitimacy specifies what discursive, impartial validity amounts to when the norms in question are legal norms.

The key idea behind linking legitimacy and morality as nothing more than specifications of the very same principle of validity (understood in terms of rational acceptability) is that both legitimacy and morality—as all other forms of validity—hinge on what is rationally acceptable for all. On the other hand, the motivation for distinguishing between them is twofold: In the first place, it is only once the two principles have been distinguished that their relation can be properly spelled out. The earlier conflation of legitimacy and morality had led to the subordination of the former to the latter, and this subordination, Habermas now argues, obscures the relationship between legitimacy and democracy. If it were held that coincidence with morality is a sufficient condition for the legitimacy of laws, as natural law theorists used to maintain, there would be no legitimating role left for democratic procedures to play. To think that legitimacy derives directly from morality leads to a paternalistic foisting of rights to citizens, whereas according to Habermas's more thorough recent constructivism, citizens ought to be able to see themselves as authors of the rules they live by (see Habermas 1996, 120–1, 127–8, and secs. 3.1.4, 3.3).

An additional argument adduced by Habermas for reconsidering the subordination of law to morality is that such relation rests on an insufficient differentiation between these two spheres. Shortly before the publication of *Between Facts and Norms*, Habermas spelled out his rendition of the old distinction between pragmatic, ethical, and moral reasons. He distinguishes between ethics and morality by arguing that ethics answers the question What ought I/we to do?, on the basis of considerations of personal or collective identity. By contrast, morality interprets the same question as one that should be answered on the basis of considerations of justice or rights (see Habermas 1993; 1996, 15–52, 95–9). Following Kant, Habermas holds that what makes moral norms distinctive is that they raise a universal validity claim, and so differ both from pragmatic discourses, the validity of whose conclusions—Kant's "imperatives of skill"—is contingent on the commonality of particular ends, as well as from ethical discourses, whose claims—"counsels of prudence"—are valid only for members of a community which already shares a tradition and its strong evaluations (Kant 1968, 415–16).

Part of Habermas's point in introducing the distinction between pragmatic, ethical, and moral reasons in the context of the discussion of legal legitimacy was to address the charge that discourse ethics could not provide an adequate account of legitimacy, for it ignored the importance of ethical, and especially of pragmatic, reasons in the justification of laws (see, e.g., Tuori 1989). In *Between Facts and Norms* Habermas has now opened up room for such teleological dimension of valid law: He now specifically argues that in the justification of laws, pragmatic and ethical considerations rightly play a role.

What happens to the cosmopolitan consequences of the account of the relationship between morality and law once the account of legitimacy is expanded in this manner? Oddly, Habermas talks as if legitimacy became a purely internal, national issue. This may converge with traditional legal theory, but it conflicts with his own position on the relationship between morality and law, and, incidentally, leads him to miss a possible justificatory ground for his later interest in cosmopolitanism. Habermas now holds that the scope of the legitimating constituencies, what he calls the "reference system," the group of people whose consent has to be secured in the legitimation of a norm, is a function of the type of norm in question. Specifically, he argues that only moral norms refer to a group whose scope encompasses humanity in general, whereas the reference system of legal norms is a particular legal community:

> With moral questions, humanity, or a presupposed republic of world citizens constitutes the reference system for justifying regulations that lie in the equal interest of all. In principle, the decisive reasons must be acceptable to each and everyone. With ethical-political questions, the form of life of the political community that is "in each case our own" constitutes the reference system for justifying decisions that are supposed to express an authentic, collective self-understanding. In principle the decisive reasons must be acceptable to all members sharing "our" traditions and strong evaluations. (Habermas 1996, 108)

The cosmopolitan consequences of the earlier account of the relationship between morality and law, seem, indeed, to be under threat. It is worth spending some time considering the reasons that led Habermas to settle the scope of the reference systems for morality and law in the way he did. The first reason has to do with the positivity of law, the fact that legal norms are enacted, and this means that they always emanate from a particular community. Habermas puts the point as follows: "Unlike moral rules, legal rules do not norm (*normen*) possible interactions between communicatively competent subjects *in general* but the interaction contexts of a concrete society. This follows simply from the concept of the positivity of law, that is, from the facticity of making and enforcing law. Legal norms stem from the decisions of a historical legislature; they refer to a geographically delimited legal territory and to a socially delimitable collectivity of legal consociates, and consequently to particular jurisdictional boundaries" (ibid., 124).

The second reason for determining the scope of the legitimating community of law in less than cosmopolitan terms has to do with the importance of ethical and pragmatic reasons in the process of legitimating laws. The point here is that the irruption of these reasons introduces a contextualist element in processes of legitimation, for, after all, pragmatic and ethical reasons owe whatever force they have to the contingent fact of sharing some particular ends or evaluations.

Are these reasons convincing? To allow the positivity of the law to determine the scope of the relevant legitimating community seems to betray a degree of "state-centricity" that is incompatible with other strains of Habermas's position. Moreover, this move is question begging, for part of the issue that needs to be decided is, precisely, who should be included as a participant in discourses in which the legitimacy of laws is at issue. The fact that historically these discourses have been territorially bounded leaves open both the normative question of whether these discourses ought to be more cosmopolitan, as well as the practical question of whether they can be organized effectively in such a fashion.

Thus, the whole weight of the argument for narrowing the scope of legitimating discourses rests on the second reason, the fact that legal discourses involve ethical and pragmatic considerations which are contextual in nature. Were this factor sufficient to determine the extent of the consideration we owe others, then particular jurisdictions would be absolutely free to adopt whatever laws they wanted, regardless of the consequences of those laws beyond their own borders. But then it would not be clear what Habermas means by insisting that "a legal order can be legitimate only if it does not contradict basic moral principles" (ibid., 106). Indeed, the necessary coherence of legitimate laws with the requirements of morality is a point that Habermas reiterates repeatedly, and that figures in the very definition of legitimacy (see Habermas 1996, 152, 154, 156).

If the validity of law were simply contingent on the law achieving certain goals and on embodying a shared community identity, Habermas's legal theory would collapse into a form of communitarian positivism. While with the positivists Habermas wants to distinguish between morality and law, against positivism, he insists that legitimacy imposes moral constraints on the law. Legitimate laws, therefore, can express a community's sense of identity, and reflect its evaluative and practical priorities as well, *so far as the laws' compatibility with the universalistic requirements of morality has been established*.

Since it is apparent that Habermas articulated his account of the legitimacy of law in a traditional state-centric manner, perhaps he would like to argue that the satisfaction of the principle of morality associated with legal legitimacy is exhausted once it is guaranteed that the law in question is in the equal interest of *all*, where the "all" refers merely to all the members of a particular legal community. This does lead to the settling of the relevant legitimating constituencies in the way Habermas suggests, and explains the meaning of the assertion that "whereas moral norms are directed to every person, legal norms address only the members of the legal community" (ibid., 156; see also 112). However, whereas the restriction of universality to the members of a particular legal community might make perfect sense in a world of isolated nation states, or in those cases in which laws have no substantial spill-over effects across national borders, the world is no longer so fragmented, and the number of laws that do generate significant spill-over effects is increasing. Moreover, Habermas himself sometimes argues about the requirements that morality imposes on the law in a way that is incompatible with his talk about the territorial closure of the legitimating constituency:

> By their very structure laws are defined by the question of which norms citizens want to adopt for regulating their common life. To be sure, discourses aimed at achieving self-understanding are *also* an important component of politics. In such discourses the participants want to get a clear understanding of themselves as members of a specific nation, as members of a local community, as inhabitants of a region, and so on; they want to determine which traditions they will continue; they strive to determine how they will treat one another and how they will treat minorities and marginal groups; in short, participants in such discourses (or in identity politics)

> hope to become clear about the kind of society in which they want to live. *But* [...] *these questions are subordinate to moral questions* [...]. The question that has *priority* in legislative politics is how a matter can be regulated in the equal interest of all. The making of norms is primarily a justice issue, subject to principles that state what is equally good *for all*. Unlike ethical questions, *questions of justice are not related at the outset to a specific collective and its form of life. The law of a concrete legal community must, if it is to be legitimate, at least be compatible with moral standards that claim universal validity beyond the legal community*. (Ibid., 282)

There are then two possible readings of the argument. On the *stronger reading*, exemplified by the quotation above, there is a universalistic moral constraint inherent to the notion of legitimacy itself. Even this stylized argument would entail serious changes in our understanding of sovereignty. A universalistic requirement would make countless present laws illegitimate not because they fail procedural prerequisites, or because they are unfair to some citizens within a particular legislative community, but because of the ill-effects these laws might have on citizens of *other* countries. Legislative sovereignty, as it was classically understood, would be severely curtailed. Legislators would be free to frame laws on the basis of pragmatic and ethical reasons as long as these laws do not conflict with moral norms—and these moral norms, as explained before, are derived not just from the community served by them, but from the community affected by the proposed legislation, regardless of conventional borders, national or otherwise.

On the *weaker reading*, legitimacy really imposes no extraterritorial concerns. Whatever obligation we have to countenance the effects of our laws on those beyond our national border is a moral rather than a legal obligation. But this would also be sufficient to generate the basis for a cosmopolitan attitude. Although laws that might be unacceptable to those beyond a particular jurisdiction might still be legitimate, they would fail a moral requirement which legislators stand under the obligation to satisfy, an obligation which requires assessing the validity of norms with an eye to their acceptability to all who are affected by them.

In my view, the stronger reading of the argument is not only the correct one, but would also be useful for justifying a cosmopolitan attitude. Habermas, however, writing in response to critics of the implications of his earlier views on morality and law, emphasizes in *Between Facts and Norms* the contextualist rather than the universalistic import of this relationship. Hence an opportunity to motivate the later institutional form of cosmopolitanism was not taken up.

It is important, however, to be clear about the nature of the missed opportunity. It is not that a justification for cosmopolitan *institutions* can be constructed on the basis of moral premises alone. This will require an explicitly political argument, as we will see in section 3, part (c) below. Nevertheless, an opportunity to motivate concern for cosmopolitanism has been wasted. I am trying to retrieve it.

Now it is time to move from a defense of a cosmopolitan attitude to institutional cosmopolitanism. In the next section I will sketch Habermas's institutional proposal, and in section 3 examine the merits of its backing.

2. The Institutional Proposal

Very briefly, the following is what Habermas provisionally defends: (1) the establishment of supranational institutions with executive, legislative, and judicial powers, and (2) the creation of appropriate representative democratic procedures at the supranational level. Concerning Europe, for example, he defends "[n]ew political institutions such as a European Parliament with the usual powers, a government formed out of the Commission, a Second Chamber replacing the Council, and a European Court of Justice with expanded competencies" (Habermas 1998c, 156). In short, Habermas advocates "a transition of the European Community to a democratically constituted, federal state" (ibid.). More broadly, Habermas follows those who defend transforming existing international institutions, using them, nonetheless, as the basis for the formation of a supranational democratic regime. He is thus sympathetic towards the strengthening of the executive functions of the United Nations, giving this body the authority to act in defense of human rights even if such decisions violate the present understanding of state sovereignty and its associated principle of non-intervention (see Habermas 1998b, sec. iv; 1998d, sec. iv). Additionally, since effectiveness in the real world is not only a matter of authorization but of power, Habermas supports the institutionalization of the judicial power of the UN. This includes support for a permanent International Criminal Tribunal with competence to initiate prosecutions and to hear both cases between individuals and cases between an individual and a state.[2] It also includes advocating the formation of a neutral armed force capable of enforcing UN resolutions for those cases in which "preventive and non-violent" interventions fail to work. These proposals would give flesh to the notion of humanitarian intervention. The general idea is to form an international legal order that at the very least would bind individual governments to respect the basic rights of their citizens, if necessary through the threat or the implementation of sanctions (Habermas 1998b, 129–32; 1998d, 179ff.).

Habermas, though, is aware that, given how past and present inequalities of power have affected existing international institutions, augmenting the executive and judicial role of those institutions is risky from the standpoint of justice. The main risk, of course, is that relaxing the principles of sovereignty and non-intervention can easily lead to unfair uses of international force. Even ostensibly defensible UN interventions have teetered on the brink of illegitimacy, for the objector has plenty of instances to offer as warrant for a

[2] I expressed some of my reservations about international courts under the present inequalities of the system of states in De Greiff 1998.

charge of selectivity (Habermas 1998d, 180). In order to meet this problem, at least procedurally, Habermas also argues in favor of the democratization of international institutions. In particular, regarding the UN, he supports adding a second chamber to the General Assembly turning it into a World Parliament whose members would be elected by popular vote. The aim of this addition is to overcome this body's character as a "mere assembly of government delegations" becoming instead a "parliament [in which] peoples would be represented as the totality of world citizens not by their governments but by elected representatives" (ibid., 187). Regarding the Security Council, Habermas backs motions to extend membership to other powerful countries (Japan and Germany) and to regional groups (e.g., the European Union). Similarly, and also with the idea of democratizing the executive power of the Security Council, Habermas defends replacing the veto power of the permanent members of the Council with a suitable form of majority rule (ibid.).

3. The Backing

Depending on one's preferences, Habermas's cosmopolitan proposal constitutes either a wish list, or a catalogue of follies. Here, my aim will be to engage Habermas's defense of the proposal sketched above. I distinguish three arguments which Habermas does not separate clearly, and which I differentiate here for analytical purposes. They are meant to be mutually supporting, rather than independent trains of thought.

a. The Argument from the Weakness of the Nation State

Clarifying the first line of defense of this proposal will allow me to highlight at the same time one of the virtues of Habermas's defense of cosmopolitanism, namely, that it rests not on a simplistic repudiation of the nation state or of nationalism, but rather, on an analysis of their accomplishments and their limitations. Briefly, according to Habermas, functionally speaking, the nation state arises in order to remedy a dual legitimation and integration crisis that appears with the demise of the old European feudal order and which deepens with the acceleration of processes of modernization. After the wars of religion and the emergence of creedal pluralism, authority needed to be legitimated in secular terms. The processes of modernization left in their wake isolated individuals and dislocated communities (see Polanyi 1944). The achievement of the nation-state consists precisely in addressing both problems at once. By becoming states and incorporating democratic, constitutional procedures, communities gain a measure of legitimacy for their authoritative political institutions. Furthermore, it is precisely the adoption (in most cases deliberate) of the idea of a nation which creates the bonds of mutual solidarity among former strangers, that motivates the extension of democratic citizenship, addressing thereby the problem of disintegration (see Habermas 1998a, 1998b).[3]

But it is precisely this integrative, solidaristic achievement of the nation which is presently under threat, and whose preservation, Habermas argues, will be possible only at a higher level of political organization, namely, supranationally. He appeals here not only to familiar considerations concerning the weaknesses of nation states in the face of global ecological problems, inequality, organized crime and the denationalization of the economy, considerations which one might call pragmatic. Instead, he gives a normative twist to these well-known apprehensions by calling to mind the following scenario: What is noteworthy about processes of economic denationalization is not merely the increased magnitude of economic activity across national borders, but the rapid mobility of capital and the consequent competition for it among different states, which can lead to a race among countries to dismantle their welfare systems in the search for competitive advantages. This international "race for the bottom" might accelerate the formation of underclasses even in developed countries, with three possible important consequences: first, an increased appeal to repressive policies in a vain attempt to contain the existence of a large underclass; second, the decay of the infrastructure of increasingly large areas, especially of the urban centers, and third, as the combined outcome of these two consequences, the collapse of the bonds of social solidarity and of political legitimacy, bonds which were, precisely, the two great achievements of the democratic nation state (see Habermas 1998a, sec. v).

The general position being defended, then, is that only expanded coordination can stem the tide of social disintegration and allow us to meet global environmental and social problems. There is of course an important pragmatic component to this position, but it is not just an argument based on expediency, for more is being said than that our present standard of living will decline unless we shift focus towards cosmopolitan institutions; the important claim is that the weakness of the nation state undermines the social and economic conditions of solidarity, and that the normative bases of law and legal-political institutions will be undermined as well, because processes of legitimation become less representative and hence less democratic. Democracy, then, has to be saved by institutionalizing it at the cosmopolitan level as well.

But there is in this argument a leap between the diagnosis of the present and the cosmopolitan prescription. Even if we agreed not only with the descriptive part of the case, but also, with its predictive part—that is, with the account of the formation of the underclass, the rise of repression, the decay of infrastructure, and finally, the erosion of solidarity and legitimacy —this argument does not univocally support the formation of transnational

[3] Habermas is by no means alone in thinking about the achievement of the nation in terms of forging bonds of solidarity. Some of the recent defenders of nationalism focus on this aspect of life within nations. See, e.g., Miller 1987–88, Weiler 1997, Tamir 1993.

political structures. It might be that Hobbesian realists take the same point of departure in order to argue for the strengthening rather than the weakening of the structures of national sovereignty (see, e.g., Enzensberger 1994; Brown, Lynn-Jones and Miller 1995). This sobering critique maintains that given that developed democratic countries cannot solve all the world's problems, the least—and perhaps the most?—they can do is to make sure that their own conditions of legitimacy are preserved, even if the price to be paid is the implementation of exclusionary policies.

One need not be a realist of the kind just mentioned in order to have qualms about this first line of defense of cosmopolitan structures. After all, it is still an open question whether supranational arrangements would be more or less effective than nation states at adopting policies that would foster solidarity and legitimacy. Here the evidence is ambiguous: While it can be argued that economic transfers within the European Union, and, even more so, measures to prevent a race to the bottom, have effectively helped sustain the conditions of social solidarity and legitimacy within and across European countries, the weight of competitive economic imperatives in the recent trend towards globalization warrants some doubts.

b. The Argument from the Democratic Deficit of Nationalism

There is one further problem that needs to be addressed at this point. According to Habermas's own analysis, the nation state was instrumental in giving rise to bonds of solidarity, which in turn were essential for the establishment of democracy. As he puts it, the "invention of the people's nation (*Volksnation*) had a catalyzing effect on the democratization of state power. A democratic basis for the legitimation of domination would not have developed without national self-awareness, because it was the nation that first created solidarity between persons who until then had been strangers to each other" (Habermas 1997, 171). But if this is so, it must then be asked whether democracy can survive independently of the nation. Examining this issue will allow me to broach one of the many ways in which Habermas is sensitive to questions of difference—the second great virtue of his position—and at the same time, raise questions that remain outstanding.

Despite the historical importance of the convergence of democracy and nationalism in the creation of the modern nation state, Habermas insists that the link between them is merely contingent. Indeed, he argues that there is a tension between nationalism and democracy, that the tension is coming to a head, and that this is another reason to start thinking about forms of political organization that would allow us to preserve democracy beyond the framework of the nation state. The inherent tension stems from the fact that the idea of the nation is usually understood in terms of ascriptive criteria like ethnicity, or a common language, or a shared culture, whereas democracy is founded on the ideal of voluntary association and universal human rights.

Habermas wants to argue that democracy can shed its dependence on nationalism now, and that it is urgent to do so, for the twentieth century has manifested grotesquely the dangers of clinging to this relationship. This implies that he disputes the communitarian claim that the effective operation of a constitutional democracy has as a necessary condition a culturally or ethnically homogeneous population. In framing this argument Habermas makes use of a pair of related distinctions that is becoming important in discussions not just about nationalism, but more generally about political justification in multicultural contexts. He distinguishes between a civic and an ethnic sense of the nation, and between a political and a majority culture. The idea, of course, is to restrict the object of politics so as to make political agreement more feasible. A functioning democracy does not require agreement over cultural practices in general, but rather, a still demanding but more modest agreement about abstract constitutional principles and more concrete legal-political practices. Nationalism, according to this view, may have played an instrumental role in extending the notion of citizenship rights to previously disenfranchised groups, transforming thereby the *Adelsnation*, the nation of the nobility, into the *Volksnation*, the nation of the people (Habermas 1998a, 110). But in this transformation it is the civic and not the ethnic sense of the nation that is crucial, according to Habermas. The content of the rights that were extended remained firmly tied to abstract principles such as equality and democracy. We now find ourselves, he claims, in a situation in which solidarity need not be mediated by identification with a concrete and particularistic majority culture, but one which expresses a shared *legal-political* culture: "[I]n complex societies the citizenry as a whole can no longer be held together by a substantive consensus on values but only by a consensus on the procedures for the legitimate enactment of laws and legitimate exercise of power" (Habermas 1998e, 225). In other words, modern democracies are integrated not by old fashioned patriotism, but by what Habermas and others call "constitutional patriotism," a reflexive and abstract form of identity which is manifested in the "readiness to identify with the political order and the principles of the Basic Law" (Habermas 1989, 257). One might call this a form of civic patriotism, which does not eliminate but merely subordinates regional, inherited loyalties.

It should be apparent why this is a useful concept in this context. In the first place, this form of social integration is meant to accommodate the inevitable pluralism of contemporary societies. It is meant to express an abstract agreement about basic norms rather than cultural convergence on substantive matters of the good or productive life. In the second place, to the extent that different constitutional traditions embody the same set of rights, it is plausible to think, according to Habermas, that the same sort of constitutional patriotism could accommodate a new, supranational form of integration. If for example, the Basques, the Catalans, the Danish, the Greeks, and so on, all think that attachment to constitutional, democratic principles lies at the core of their political identity, it is easier to envisage their coming together in some form of political organization than if each persists in subordinating their political ideals to their specific cultural identities (see Habermas 1996, chap. 3, sec. 3; 1998a, 117–19).

The foregoing seems to me to merely express a hope, however. Whereas it is clear how nationalism played an integrative role in the emerging democracies of the eighteenth and nineteenth centuries, or, more apropos here, whereas it is clear why the notion of rights had to be complemented by nationalism, it is not so obvious that constitutional patriotism, on its own, can integrate supranational entities. It is possible to cull from Habermas's work two responses to this doubt: The first is an account of the role of legal institutions in the formation of the modern identity of citizens. This account reminds us that modern political consciousness is not simply a result of membership in prepolitical ancestral communities based on kinship. Rather, national identity is at least in part a function of politics, of the active enjoyment of the status of citizen within a political community. Legal structures help to constitute identity. So, for instance, the identity of the French is bound up not merely with a shared cultural identity, but with the shared legal-political institutions that are part of the legacy of the Revolution. Legal-political institutions have what Habermas calls a catalytic or inducing effect on the formation of identities (see, e.g., Habermas 1998c).

This might be helpful initially, but I do not think that it addresses the objection fully. Nationalism, as Habermas himself argues, was useful for it was a means of determining membership of a particular political community. Nationalism, that is, attempts to provide an answer to the question that Robert Dahl posed so clearly: "To say that all people [...] are entitled to the democratic process begs a prior question. When does a collection of persons constitute an entity—'a people'—entitled to govern itself democratically?" (Dahl 1989, 183). The idea of the nation provides an answer to the question of the scope of particular legal institutions, a question that constitutional principles themselves do not answer. Something prior to constitutional principles determines who falls under their authority. Constitutional patriotism, like the very idea of republican government, begs this question.

Let me illustrate the point. Habermas has plausibly defended the idea that emerging European institutions will have the mentioned catalytic effect, that is to say, that they will help precipitate the formation of a European identity (different from, but not eliminating, rather overlaying, the identity of French, German, Danish, and so on). But of course, constitutional patriotism does not, on its own, integrate the citizens of the European Union. After all, this is still a *European* Union. Something else helps determine membership and solidifies integration, and this is a shared history, shared traditions (and, the Turks would add with chagrin, a shared religion). The account of the impact of legal-political structures cannot, by itself, do this. In other contexts it would be even less unreasonable to doubt that constitutional patriotism is a sufficiently strong integrative force for supranational integration. The experiences of many nation states do not provide strong grounds for optimism: Legal institutionalization has failed to lead many post-colonial countries—even some highly culturally and ethnically homogeneous ones—to the requisite degree of integration, in some cases after decades or centuries of constitutionalization. The history of Latin American countries, for instance, provides plenty of examples of the many ways in which constitutionalization may fail to lead to political integration, let alone to its supranational version.

Habermas's second response to the doubt about whether there is a sufficiently strong functional replacement for the integrative force of nationalism, one that would lead to supranational integration, is the argument according to which the growing awareness of the globalization of present dangers (environmental disasters, the proliferation of arms, organized crime, etc.) "has long since united the world into an involuntary community of shared risks" (Habermas 1998d, 186; 1998b, 150). But there is a significant difficulty with this last suggestion. Although it might very well be true that these risks are shared, since they do not impact equally on different countries, and, especially, since different countries have greatly different possibilities of responding to them, it is plausible that the threats, rather than leading to increased cooperation will lead to increased protectionism and friction. Even in the environmental arena, the evidence supporting increased cooperation is less than unambiguous (see, e.g., Shue 1997). Regarding international crime, a restricted problem about which one would expect unproblematic cooperation, the difficulties in establishing international tribunals or indeed a European police task force (let alone a world-wide force), the constant acrimony surrounding judicial evidence-sharing, and the general inequities in the treatment of criminals and in the distribution of the burdens of fighting them, raise questions about whether an awareness of common risks is a sufficiently strong integrative force to lead to cosmopolitan institutions.

c. The Argument from Lack of Guarantees

Given the ambivalent results of the first two lines of defense, a strong position in favor of cosmopolitan structures cannot rest solely upon these foundations. Habermas offers another familiar defense of cosmopolitanism, this one more straightforwardly normative in character. Part of the argument is presented as a response to Kant's essay of 1795 on *Perpetual Peace* (Kant 1983b) in which Kant trims the transnational sails that he had unfurled eleven years earlier in his *Idea for a Universal History with a Cosmopolitan Intent* (Kant 1983c). In *Perpetual Peace*, as is well known, Kant argues that perhaps his earlier support for a world government might lead to a form of oppression, and defends instead a federation of sovereign states. Indeed, Kant introduces a distinction between a "universal state" (*Völkerstaat*) "based upon public laws backed by force and submitted to by every nation," (Kant 1983a, 89) and a "federation of nations" (*Völkerbund*) a more modest structure whose aim is not to constitute a legal order to increase welfare and justice, but rather to abolish war (Kant 1983b, 115–20). Kant was trying, as so many people have since then, to reconcile national sovereignty with the goal of maintaining peace in the long run.

Habermas, by contrast, gives up on this aspiration. For him, Kant's dual aspiration is ridden with tension. The concern to leave intact the sovereignty of the members of the federation will predictably conflict in hard cases with the need to oblige unruly members to subordinate their own *raison d'etat* so that peace may be perpetuated (see Habermas 1998d, 166–71). Since Kant's federation is eminently dissolvable—so as to respect the sovereignty of its individual members—there is nothing that obligates unruly members to preserve peace. Kant's "voluntary association" does not give rise to any actionable rights, and hence, its permanence and effectiveness remains unexplained. For Habermas, the promotion of peace requires that states be under the obligation to act in harmony with the principles of the federation, and this entails a right of intervention in defense of this obligation on the part of other member states.

The core of Habermas's third defense of cosmopolitanism, then, lies in the worry that the nation state is not a reliable guarantor of human rights. Habermas acknowledges that international law took a great leap forward after the Nuremberg trials established the principle that individuals are proper subjects of international law, and therefore that they can be held accountable for deeds committed within the borders of their own nation and under the authority of their own state. And yet, the present international system remains a hybrid that resembles Kant's federation in its desire to give a role both to individual rights and to the rights of nation states implied by the notion of national sovereignty. The present UN-based system is an association not of peoples but of nation states. As such, the organization defends the principles of mutual respect, non-intervention, and consent as the basis of obligation to comply with international law.[4]

Leaving aside practical difficulties with Habermas's proposal—no small concession—I want to concentrate on the normative aspects of this third defense. Supporters of the nation might object to Habermas's proposal by pointing out that it is not obviously clear that a commitment to a universalistic conception of rights, on its own, requires a commitment to cosmopolitan structures. At least conceptually, they will argue, moral universalism is in principle compatible with a world organized into a system of states. Liberal political theory has traditionally asserted this position. The demands of universalism could be met "distributively": Assuming that the different nation-states in the world system respected individual rights, each state would articulate and exercise its power in accordance with a legal system that embodies the same fundamental rights and obligations found in all the

[4] See Laberge 1998, for an interesting comparison between Kant's federation, the UN, and NATO.

other legal systems. So, if the objection holds, a further set of steps would be needed to go from this abstract argument about individual rights to a conclusion in favor of cosmopolitan political organization.

Charles Beitz has spelled out a distinction between moral and institutional cosmopolitanism which a critic might use as the basis of an objection to this line of defense: *Institutional* cosmopolitanism "holds that the world's political structure should be reshaped so that states and other political units are brought under the authority of supranational agencies of some kind." *Moral* cosmopolitanism "concerns itself, not with institutions themselves, but with the basis on which institutions, practices, or courses of action should be justified or criticized. Its crux is the idea that each person is equally a subject of moral concern, or alternatively, that in the justification of choices one must take the prospects of everyone affected equally into account" (Beitz 1994, 124). Armed with this distinction, Beitz writes:

> The doctrine of universal human rights is cosmopolitan in its foundations without being cosmopolitan in its institutional requirements. That is, the most natural foundation of human rights doctrine lies in the related cosmopolitan ideas that conceptions of individual well-being are not fundamentally relative to culture or geographical location and that, in the assignment of responsibility for satisfying basic individual needs, national (or cultural or ethnic) boundaries do not necessarily play a limiting role. At the same time, however, human rights doctrine does not prescribe any particular institutions (or set of institutions) for the world as a whole. Instead, it specifies minimum conditions that any institutions should satisfy. Accordingly, human rights doctrine does not rule out the possibility—indeed it trades on the hope—that its institutional requirements can be satisfied within a political structure containing nation-states more or less as we know them today. (Beitz 1994, 127)

But this objection misses its target. Understanding why it does is an important part of understanding the distinctiveness of Habermas's approach to cosmopolitanism. I consider it a great advantage that Habermas, unlike other commentators, has developed his views on cosmopolitanism as part of a wide-ranging theory of democracy and rights. Of course, one could say that in this way his views about this concrete issue are freighted with the difficulties that may afflict the theory as a whole. But if the theory is a strong one, the problem is ameliorated, and the end result is that the link between cosmopolitanism and democracy is explicitly established. This interest in democracy I take to be the most salient feature of Habermas's take on cosmopolitanism.

So, the crucial point at this juncture is that Habermas's theory of rights is not a moral, but a *political* theory of rights. In other words, the objection misses the target because Habermas is not arguing that moral premises lead directly to institutional consequences. Moral premises, as I argued in section 1 above, can motivate the adoption of a cosmopolitan attitude, but they cannot by themselves ground cosmopolitan institutions. Platonism is dead. In highly differentiated and complex societies, one does well to be suspicious of efforts to derive institutions from moral considerations alone.

One might say that cosmopolitan institutions, rather than being derived from morality, follow from the requirements of politics themselves. Let me explain. According to Habermas, despite the fact that rights can be justified by appealing to moral reasons, that is, to reasons that can be universalized, human rights are not moral but legal in character. As actionable claims, rights are structurally part and parcel of legal orders (Habermas 1998d, 189–93; 1996, sec. 3.3). This account of the nature of rights, of course, does not answer which rights people should have.

This question is answered from a discourse-theoretic perspective as part of a prior, more general political question, namely which rights must persons grant one another if they want to legitimately regulate their life in common by means of positive law (see Habermas 1996, 118, 122, 126, 129). Consistent with the procedural aims and with the discursive character of his project, Habermas argues that in answering this question nothing must be presupposed other than the discourse principle—which ultimately follows from the presuppositions of communication—and the notion of law—which is implied in the formulation of the question itself (ibid., 127–9). Now, it turns out that each of these elements is pregnant with consequences. Of particular relevance in this context is that according to Habermas, the form of law itself presupposes some rights. Laws per force refer to legal subjects, and these in turn are constituted by means of the attribution of certain rights and obligations. In his words, "there is no law without the private autonomy of legal persons in general" (Habermas 2002, 201). This private autonomy is secured by means of rights which include "the right to the greatest possible measure of equal individual liberty," the rights which secure "the status of a member" in an association under the rule of law, and the rights that guarantee legal protection (Habermas 1996, 122).

However, the legitimacy of law is not exhausted in the mere respect for individual rights to autonomy. Habermas proposes two reasons to explain why this is so. First, limiting rights to autonomy rights involves blocking the self-understanding of citizens as the authors of their own laws. In the absence of political rights, no matter how liberal a regime of autonomy rights might be, citizens would at best enjoy a paternalistically imposed set of rights. Second, without political participation the equality of rights is always under threat. Consequently, in addition to autonomy rights, *political* rights are necessary as well. On the other hand, political rights, by themselves, are not sufficient for the exercise of popular sovereignty either. The correct way of thinking about the relationship between legal legitimacy and democracy, Habermas maintains, presupposes the realization that citizens participate in the political process as legal subjects, which, again, presupposes the rights to private autonomy. As he summarizes his position,

> [t]he internal relation between democracy and the rule of law consists in this: on the one hand, citizens can make appropriate use of their public autonomy only if, on the basis

of their equally protected private autonomy, they are sufficiently independent; on the other hand, they can realize equality in their enjoyment of private autonomy only if they make appropriate use of their political autonomy as citizens. (Habermas 2002, 202)

The broader aim of Habermas's theory is to establish that human rights and democracy presuppose one another. Although the theory is originally framed in terms of the sorts of rights that members of the same nation-state ought to grant one another, the hypothetical question that it answers does not predetermine the scope of the political unit for which the answer remains valid. In other words, any community, local, national, regional, or global, whose members want to norm their interactions by means of legitimate positive law, ought to institutionalize the same set of rights. After all, the aim of these rights is to attempt to secure the rational acceptability of decisions taken by means of legitimate law. Since law can be appealed to in order to regulate the mutual interactions of different sorts of subjects in a variety of contexts, this means that the hypothetical procedure of a mutual conferring of rights can be performed at different levels of political organization, beyond the level of particular nation-states, and it would require, all the same, the institutionalization of all the relevant rights, this time across national borders. While the basic human rights that must be conferred in order to establish a legitimate constitutional regime are essentially the same in each case, the political institutions required for their implementation would have to reflect the different scope of the practical matters to be regulated and the different composition of the populations subject to the laws enacted. Thus Habermas's general theory of human rights points to a global political order in which sovereignty, which in the modern state system resided more or less exclusively in the nation state, would be divided and dispersed among local, national, and regional regimes, with a global regime taking responsibility for the implementation of human rights at the global level. This argument, then, seeks to justify cosmopolitan rights from the standpoint not of a moral theory but of a (normative) political theory of rights that seeks to answer which rights individuals ought to grant one another if they want to regulate their interactions by means of legitimate positive law. An objection based on a distinction between moral and institutional cosmopolitanism leaves the argument untouched. Of course, this line of defense makes the justification of cosmopolitanism contingent on the acceptability of the theory of rights, itself a substantive consideration, but one which I cannot take up here.

Conclusion

Different arguments in favor of cosmopolitanism are offered in, and can be constructed on the basis of, Habermas's work. None proves with deductive force that cosmopolitan political structures ought to be adopted, but that is no fault in the position. The days of a science of politics understood in this way are long over. Just as it seems correct to argue that the justification of particular laws involves the full range of reasons, practical, ethical, and moral, it makes sense to think that in the justification of legal orders in general—including a cosmopolitan order—practical, ethical, and moral considerations will play a role. No single kind will be decisive. This makes the justification of cosmopolitanism messy. Habermas's is certainly complex, and, as I have pointed out, it needs revisions at different junctures. But at least it has the virtues of acknowledging the virtues (as well as the limitations) of the nation state, of being sensitive to difference, and of emphasizing the importance of democratic rights even at the cosmopolitan level.

State University of New York at Buffalo
Department of Philosophy
Buffalo NY 14260
USA
E-mail: degreiff@acsu.buffalo.edu

References

Beitz, Charles R. 1994. Cosmopolitan Liberalism and the States System. In *Political Restructuring in Europe. Ethical Perspectives*. Ed. Chris Brown. London: Routledge.
Brown, Michael E., Sean M. Lynn-Jones, and Steven E. Miller, eds. 1995. *The Perils of Anarchy: Contemporary Realism and International Security*. Cambridge, Mass.: MIT Press.
Dahl, Robert. 1989. *Democracy and Its Critics*. New Haven: Yale University Press.
De Greiff, Pablo. 1998. International Tribunals and Transitions to Democracy. *Public Affairs Quarterly* 12: 79–99.
———. 1999. Drugs, National Sovereignty, and Democratic Legitimacy. In *Drugs and the Limits of Liberalism*. Ed. Pablo De Greiff. Ithaca: Cornell University Press.
Enzensberger, Hans Magnus. 1994. *Civil Wars: From L.A. to Bosnia*. New York, NY: New Press.
Habermas, Jürgen. 1989. Historical Consciousness and Post-Traditional Identity. In *The New Conservatism*. Trans. Shierry W. Nicholsen. Cambridge, Mass.: MIT Press.
———. 1990. Discourse Ethics: Notes on a Program of Philosophical Justification. In *Moral Consciousness and Communicative Action*. Trans. Christian Lenhardt and Shierry W. Nicholsen. Cambridge, Mass.: MIT Press.
———. 1993. On the Pragmatic, the Ethical, and the Moral Employments of Practical Reason. In *Justification and Application*. Trans. Ciaran P. Cronin. Cambridge, Mass.: MIT Press.
———. 1996. *Between Facts and Norms*. Trans. William Rehg. Cambridge, Mass.: MIT Press.
———. 1997. *A Berlin Republic: Writings on Germany*. Trans. Steven Rendall. Lincoln: University of Nebraska Press.
———. 1998a. The European Nation State: On the Past and Future of Sovereignty and Citizenship. In *The Inclusion of the Other*. Ed. Ciaran Cronin and Pablo De Greiff. Cambridge, Mass.: MIT Press.
———. 1998b. On The Relation between the Nation, the Rule of Law, and Democracy. In *The Inclusion of the Other*. Ed. Ciaran Cronin and Pablo De Greiff. Cambridge, Mass.: MIT Press.

———. 1998c. Does Europe need a Constitution? Remarks on Dieter Grimm. In *The Inclusion of the Other*. Ed. Ciaran Cronin and Pablo De Greiff. Cambridge, Mass.: MIT Press.

———. 1998d. Kant's Idea of Perpetual Peace: With the Benefit of Two Hundred Years. In *The Inclusion of the Other*. Ed. Ciaran Cronin and Pablo De Greiff. Cambridge, Mass.: MIT Press.

———. 1998e. Struggles for Recognition in the Democratic Constitutional State. In *The Inclusion of the Other*. Ed. Ciaran Cronin and Pablo De Greiff. Cambridge, Mass.: MIT Press.

———. 2002. Legitimation through Human Rights. In *Global Justice and Transnational Politics*. Ed. Pablo De Greiff and Ciaran Cronin. Cambridge, Mass.: MIT Press.

Kant, Immanuel. 1968. Grundlegung zur Metaphysik der Sitten. In *Kants gesammelte Schriften. Akademie Ausgabe*. Ed. Gottfried Martin. Berlin: De Gruyter. (1st ed. 1785.)

———. 1983a. Theory and Practice. In *Perpetual Peace and Other Essays*. Trans. Ted Humphrey. Indianapolis, IN: Hackett. (1st ed. 1793.)

———. 1983b. Perpetual Peace. In *Perpetual Peace and Other Essays*. Trans. Ted Humphrey. Indianapolis, IN: Hackett. (1st ed. 1795.)

———. 1983c. Idea for a Universal History with a Cosmopolitan Intent. In *Perpetual Peace and Other Essays*. Trans. Ted Humphrey. Indianapolis: Hackett. (1st ed. 1784.)

Laberge, Pierre. 1998. Kant on Justice and the Law of Nations. In *International Society*. Ed. David Mapel and Terry Nardin. Princeton: Princeton University Press.

Lyons, Gene M. and Michael Mastanduno, eds. 1995. *Beyond Westphalia: State Sovereignty and International Intervention*. Baltimore: Johns Hopkins University Press.

Miller, David. 1987–88. The Ethical Significance of Nationality. *Ethics* 98: 647–62.

Polanyi, Karl. 1944. *The Great Transformation*. Boston, MA: Beacon.

Shue, Henry. 1997. Eroding Sovereignty: the Advance of Principle. In *The Morality of Nationalism*. Ed. Robert McKim and Jeff McMahan. Oxford: Oxford University Press.

Tamir, Yael. 1993. *Liberal Nationalism*. Princeton, NJ: Princeton University Press.

Tuori, Kaarlo. 1989. Discourse Ethics and the Legitimacy of Law. *Ratio Juris* 2: 125–43.

Weiler, Joseph. 1997. Does Europe Need a Constitution? Reflections on Demos, Telos, and Ethos in the German Maastricht Decision. In *The Question of Europe*. Ed. Peter Gowan and Perry Anderson. London: Verso.

Zacher, Mark. 1992. The Decaying Pillars of the Westphalian Temple: Implications for International Order and Governance. In *Governance without Government: Order and Change in World Politics*. Ed. James Rosenau and Ernst-Otto Czempiel. Cambridge: Cambridge University Press.

[13]

DE COLLISIONE DISCURSUUM: COMMUNICATIVE RATIONALITIES IN LAW, MORALITY, AND POLITICS

*Gunther Teubner**†

I.

At the end of the seventeenth century, Johan Nikolaus Hert, a German legal scholar of Roman private law, wrote the treatise *De Collisione Legum*. He was dealing with one of the most disturbing experiences in his epoch of the emerging nation states—the experience that on earth there was more than one law, more than one justice.[1] Hert stood in stark contrast to his more famous French contemporary, the brilliant Blaise Pascal, who reacted to the same problem with critique, deconstruction, and irony: "A funny justice that ends at a river! Truth on this side of the Pyrenees, error on that."[2] Invoking systematic construction and elaborate casuistry, Hert was the first and only German to date to make a serious and thorough attempt to resolve nagging questions of conflict of laws.[3] To work out collision rules was the solution. Hert complexified the so-called statutist method according to which collision rules determined jurisdiction by analyzing the nature of the statutes involved. Developing a complex rule system for the collision of laws, Hert felt compelled to distinguish the incredible amount of sixty-three different casuistic constellations in order to fight Pascal's paradox. For this scholarly exercise he became famous, and rightly so. But his immortality in legal circles is based on the desperate sigh which he hove while drawing his tortured distinctions: "*quam sudent doctores*." How the doctors are sweating!

De Collisione Discursuum, the collision of discourses, is a variation on this theme which makes modern and postmodern doctors sweat. It is no more the fragmentation of universal justice in different national laws that haunts us, but the fragmentation of universal rationality into a disturbing multiplicity of discourses. And today,

---

* Professor, London School of Economics.

† The translations in this Article are those of the author.

1 *See* GERHARD KEGEL, INTERNATIONALES PRIVATRECHT VI § 3 (C.H. Beck ed., 7th ed. 1995).

2 BLAISE PASCAL, PENSÉES 151 (1964).

3 For details, see HERRMANN, JOHAN NIKOLAUS HERT UND DIE DEUTSCHE STATUTENLEHRE (1963).

we are faced with a similar alternative of a deconstructive and a reconstructive answer: Blaise Pascal or Johan Nikolaus Hert? Funny rationality that ends at the boundary of discourse? Or a tormented casuistry of collision rules for interdiscursivity?

Jürgen Habermas's earlier work,[4] as he himself concedes, could still be understood as constructing one and only one communicative rationality which integrated discursivity and morality.[5] If, in a plurality of social situations, we raise the question of validity of norms, we enter into a discourse which, under certain procedural conditions and under the guide of the universalization principle, leads us to a consensus about valid norms which we can call rational. Various institutionalized patterns of practical argumentation, like the procedures of legal or political deliberation, are certainly historically contingent. However, their bewildering multitude can be measured against the one ideal of rational discourse which serves as a regulative idea and a standard of critique.[6] In a somewhat different interpretation of Habermas's theory, legal argumentation could be seen as a "special case" of a rational discourse on practical questions which develops its own peculiarities. But the hierarchical relation between general discourse and legal discourse makes sure that there is one—and only one—communicative rationality.[7]

Now, in *Faktizität und Geltung*, Habermas makes a decisive move towards a plurality of discourses—and their concomitant rationalities.[8] Modern plurality, he argues, does not result one-dimensionally from social differentiation as theorists in the Durkheim tradition would have it. Habermas reconstructs several historical processes of differentiation in which various communicative practices emerge with highly peculiar procedures, logics of argumentation, and internal rationalities.[9] Not only do different system rationalities appear, but the lifeworld itself becomes auton-

---

4 *See, e.g.*, JÜRGEN HABERMAS, LEGITIMATIONSPROBLEME IM SPÄTKAPITALISMUS [LEGITIMATION CRISIS] (1973); JÜRGEN HABERMAS, ZUR REKONSTRUKTION DES HISTORISCHEN MATERIALISMUS [COMMUNICATION AND THE EVOLUTION OF SOCIETY] (1976) [hereinafter HABERMAS, REKONSTRUKTION].

5 *See id.*

6 *See* HABERMAS, REKONSTRUKTION, *supra* note 4, at 265.

7 *See* ROBERT ALEXY, THEORIE DER JURISTISCHEN ARGUMENTATION: DIE THEORIE DES RATIONALEN DISKURSES ALS THEORIE DER JURISTISCHEN BEGRÜNDUNG 261 (1978).

8 JÜRGEN HABERMAS, FAKTIZITÄT UND GELTUNG: BEITRÄGE ZUR DISKURSTHEORIE DES RECHTS UND DES DEMOCRATISCHEN RECHTSSTAATS 140 (1992). For the English translation, see JÜRGEN HABERMAS, BETWEEN FACTS AND NORMS: CONTRIBUTION TO A DISCOURSE THEORY OF LAW AND DEMOCRACY (William Rehg trans., 1996).

9 *See id.* at 77.

omous as against functional systems (politics, economy). Moreover, the lifeworld in its turn differentiates internally into diverse spheres—personality, culture, and societal community. Finally, culture develops into several autonomous fields of knowledge, each of them following a specific *Eigenlogik*.[10]

This complex reconstruction enables Habermas to separate autonomous argumentative practices along different dimensions, among others morality from legality,[11] morality from ethics,[12] law from politics, and discourse from negotiation.[13] At the very end, Habermas observes the interplay of five distinct "types of discourse and negotiation."[14] Moral discourses specialize around the principle of universalization; ethical discourses aim at individual and collective identity; pragmatical discourses relate purposes to means and set priorities among collective goals; legal discourses care for the internal consistency of legal rules; and negotiations develop a culture of fair compromise between nongeneralizable interests.

With this move toward discursive plurality, Habermas does not merely render his theory analytically richer and moves it closer to institutional realities. In addition, he systematically brings together two separate intellectual traditions, so that they considerably profit from each other: social differentiation and fragmentation of discourses. Sociologists have observed that modern society has become divided into several social systems and autonomous spheres of rationality. Philosophers have observed language to become fragmented in different language games, logics of argumentation, and apparently incommensurable discourses. Habermas's theory integrates these two traditions and relates them to each other in the interplay of external and internal, in the "double perspective" of functional analysis and rational reconstruction.[15]

But there is a decisive difference. Theories of systemic and discursive plurality tend to stress separation, incommensurability, and nonreconcilable difference. As for interdiscursivity, if these theories recognize it at all, they observe mainly closure and indifference, perhaps structural coupling, at best a certain elective affinity. The most radical position toward the collision of discourses can be found in Lyotard's "victimology," which is comparable to Pascal's "funny justice" in the conflict of laws. For Lyotard, dis-

10 *See id.* at 107, 124-35.
11 *See id.* at 135-38, 286-91.
12 *See id.* at 127, 188.
13 *See id.* at 192.
14 *See id.* at 196-207.
15 *See id.* at 57-60.

courses are hermetically closed; if they "meet" they can only do "injustice" to each other; one discourse is the other discourse's "victim."[16]

Habermas's insistence on practical reason and communicative power makes him opt for the opposite: for unity, not for difference; for integration of discursive plurality, not for their sheer fragmentation. Therefore, discursive plurality, taken seriously, creates a much more dramatic challenge for Habermas's theory that relies ultimately on discursive reason and does not content itself playing around with social differentiation or with linguistic diversity. After the move to pluridiscursivity, the success of Habermas's theory now depends on a plausible solution to the collision of discourses. If Habermas's "proceduralization" of reason is supposed to make sense it needs now to be developed in a double direction: rational procedures for various discourses and rational meta-procedures for interdiscursivity. If practical reason were not to disintegrate into a Pascalian "funny rationality" of discourses, then we are today again in the situation of Johan Nikolaus Hert. Complex rules of collision need to be worked out, tortured distinctions have to be made, even if the doctors are sweating. But here, Rudolf Wiethölter,[17] an erudite scholar in both legal theory and conflict of laws, warns us, predicting not only sweat, but sweat, blood, and tears in the desperate search for a meta-discourse that resolves the conflict of discourses. He calls it a "*Rechtsgottesgericht*": Where is the forum, who sets the standards, which are the procedures?

II.

Habermas is well aware of the collision problem.[18] His answer in *Faktizität und Geltung*: No hierarchy of discourses—especially no superiority of morality over legality—but discursive compatibility! For the conflicts between pragmatic discourses, procedurally regulated negotiations, ethical-political discourses, and moral and legal discourses, he concludes: the universal concern demanded by the discourse principle finds its guarantee in the compatibility of all discursive programs with what can also be morally justified.[19]

---

16 JEAN-FRANÇOIS LYOTARD, LE DIFFÉREND [THE DIFFEREND: PHRASES IN DISPUTE] 21, 42, 43 (1983).

17 Rudolf Wiethölter, *Zum Fortbildungsrecht der (richterlichen) Rechtsfortbildung: Fragen eines lesenden Recht-Fertigungslehrers*, 3 KRITISCHE VIERTELJAHRESZEITSCHRIFT FÜR GESETZGEBUNG UND RECHTSWISSENSCHAFT 1, 22 (1988).

18 *See* HABERMAS, *supra* note 8, at 141.

19 *See id.* at 206.

On several other occasions, Habermas insists on "complementarity,"[20] "double perspective,"[21] "congruence,"[22] "noncontradiction," "mediation," and "commensurability."[23] These are all variations of the same theme: If we have to take seriously the diversity and the autonomy of discourses, then the unity of practical reason needs to be replaced by discursive compatibility. But, obviously, with compatibility Habermas does not offer a solution. At best, he formulates a problem.

What does compatibility of discourses mean? I have distinguished at least five versions of discursive compatibility—all of which can be traced in Habermas's book.

A. *Indifference?*

Habermas refers to Kant's famous formulation that law needs to be indifferent to devils and angels.[24] The results of legal reasoning should be indifferent to the motives and reasons of moral angels and rational choice devils. In general, this could mean that discourses are free in developing their idiosyncratic argumentation, and need not care about external consistency with reasons of other argumentation practices if ever their results fit together.

B. *Smallest Common Denominator?*

Some of Habermas's formulations seem to point in the direction of the famous "ethical minimum" of the law, especially when he demands that law should be compatible with morality, and should not contradict moral reasoning.[25]

C. *Ad-hoc Conciliation?*

The idea of an "application discourse" apparently points in this direction.[26] The conflict of moral principles, ethical identities, political values, and legal rules cannot be resolved *in abstracto*. Rather, it is the richness of the concrete case-constellation, the "situational reference" that allows one to identify "adequate" criteria for their mutual delineation.[27]

---

20 *Id.* at 137, 145.
21 *Id.* at 107.
22 *Id.* at 128.
23 *Id.* at 206.
24 *See id.* at 144.
25 *See id.* at 193.
26 *See id.* at 266; *see also* KLAUS GÜNTHER, DER SINN FÜR ANGEMESSENHEIT: ANWENDUNGSDISKURSE IN MORAL UND RECHT (1988).
27 *See* HABERMAS, *supra* note 8, at 267.

D. *Mutually Exclusive Jurisdictions?*

Discourses would claim exclusive areas of competence within the boundaries of their symbolic territories and would mutually respect their sovereignty.[28]

E. *Moral-Legal Superdiscourse?*

Although the discourse principle is too abstract to resolve practical questions, at least on the meta-level it can develop procedures and criteria able to be universalized to resolve conflicts of jurisdiction between moral, legal, and political discourses.[29]

Although Habermas experiments with all of these different versions of compatibility, his sympathies are with a combination of versions D and E, with a philosophical superdiscourse that delineates exclusive areas of jurisdiction. Discourse theory has the legislative competence to enact collision rules. The method is similar to the above-mentioned old statutists, Bologna's famous conflict-of-law school that distinguished criteria of jurisdiction according to a correspondence of the nature of the *statuta* and the cases involved: *statuta realia, statuta personalia, statuta mixta*.[30] In his "process model" of colliding discourses, Habermas distinguishes various areas of jurisdiction according to the nature of the discourse and the nature of the "issue" involved. "Various types of discourses and forms of negotiation," he asserts, "correspond to the logic of these issues."[31] Thus, the logic of issues determines discursive jurisdiction in five areas: pragmatic, ethical, moral and legal discourses, and procedures of fair negotiation. He systematically defines the nature of these discursive *statuta*: purpose/means relation, collective identity, universalization principle, normative coherence, and fair compromise. He even begins to elaborate a complex casuistry which attributes concrete issues of political life to abstract logics of discourses: abortion and social policies are under the jurisdiction of the moral discourse; in contrast, protection of animals and urban policies are under the jurisdiction of the ethical discourse, and so on.[32] This is where we begin to sweat. The distinctions become tortured. Greetings from Johan Nikolaus Hert!

But at this point we feel a certain hesitation in Habermas's thinking. After having dethroned the moral superdiscourse in

---

28 *See id.* at 196-207.
29 *See id.* at 201-07.
30 *See* KEGEL, *supra* note 1, at III § 3.
31 HABERMAS, *supra* note 8, at 196.
32 *See id.* at 204.

favor of a "*Gleichursprünglichkeit*," an original equality, of relative discourses, Habermas hesitates to subsequently crown the philosophical discourse king which would now be hailed to possess the competence of competences. Habermas himself does not seem to believe in the distinguishing power of his rules of discursive jurisdiction. After all, moral and legal questions refer certainly to the same problems. In the vocabulary of a collision doctrine, we would call this the "transdiscursive" character of most concrete political issues that does not allow us to plausibly identify a *sedes materiae* in a one-to-one correlation of issue to discourse. And it is not by chance that Habermas stops short of speculating about how to identify concrete institutions in which separate spheres of discursive jurisdiction are exclusively represented.[33] Only tentatively he searches for a certain temporal institutionalization of these differences in a "process model"[34] which, however, he hastens to relativize again by introducing manifold feedback-relations between different phases.[35] And when it comes to existing institutions of political legislation and legal adjudication, the five discourse types remain there in an undifferentiated mix.[36] What seems possible, at best, is to reconcile them ad hoc.

Thus, facing the conflict of discourses, Habermas is oscillating between two positions: leaving it to the heterarchy of relative discourses versus erecting the hierarchy of a superdiscourse. He is confronted with a somewhat uncomfortable alternative. Either practical reason is limited to only one of the five partial aspects—moral justice, collective identity, choice of collective goals and means, fair compromise, and legal consistency—whose interrelation remains unclear. Or there is a superdiscourse which has the legislative capacity to set rules in case the discourses collide.

III.

Perhaps there is something wrong with the clear-cut alternative of heterarchy versus hierarchy, relative discourse versus superdiscourse. Can legal history teach us here a lesson in its century-old and down-to-earth experience with conflict of laws? Indeed, the doctrine of conflict-law did develop a third position between heterarchy and hierarchy which is worthwhile to be looked at more closely. The turning point was the territorial differ-

33 *See id.* at 207.
34 *Id.* at 201-07.
35 *See id.* at 207.
36 *See id.* at 191.

entiation of European society in autonomous nation states. Before this point, Bologna's statutists were successfully governing conflicts between local jurisdictions and a universal *jus commune.* However, the more national laws were gaining in autonomy, historicity, and uniqueness, the less convincing became an international *jus commune* of collision rules which maintained the unity of law—at least at a meta-level—deciding about national jurisdictions. With the nation-state and its claim for sovereignty, territorial domination and exclusive jurisdiction, a strange entangling of the norm-hierarchy occurred among particular substantive rules and universal collision rules. The ground-level became indistinguishable from the meta-level, but, paradoxically, remained distinguishable at the same time. What happened was a historical process in which even international collision rules became nationalized. As a clear *contradictio in adiectu*, international private law became national in its character. Instead of one international private law that decided jurisdictional conflicts, there emerged a national multitude of international private laws. Every nation-state developed autonomously its own, idiosyncratic law of conflict between legal orders. Funny justice: The party to a legal conflict became judge in her own cause!

Many international lawyers deplore this "tangled hierarchy"[37] and attribute the (con)fusion of levels to the weakness or the non-existence of a global legal order. For them, lack of globality is the reason why we do not have a truly international law of conflict which, institutionally, would keep rules and meta-rules apart. I think there is a deeper reason for the strange asymmetry. I find it in Habermas's concept of "*Gleichursprünglichkeit*," in the original equality or equal originality of discourses, and, in our case, of laws of nations. If the *diversitas legum* is no longer seen as emanating from the unity of divine or natural law, in any case, from one *jus commune*, if national laws are seen as separate chains of legal distinctions each having its own irreversible history, each stemming from an obscure national filiation, each provided with a myth of origin, then universally applicable collision rules do violate the unique "spirit" of each of these autonomous laws. If the unique characteristics of a cultural identity defines the idiosyncracies of a national law, then such law must also have the power to define the perception of its outside world from its unique perspective. Na-

[37] *See* DOUGLAS R. HOFSTADTER, GÖDEL, ESCHER, BACH: AN ETERNAL GOLDEN BRAID (1979); *see also* Douglas R. Hofstadter, *Nomic: A Self-Modifying Game Based on Reflexivity in Law*, *in* METAMAGICAL THEMES: QUESTING FOR THE ESSENCE OF MIND AND PATTERN 70-86 (Douglas R. Hofstadter ed., 1985).

tional laws claim the right to a domestic construction of foreign law, literally, to its incorporation in the body of the *lex fori*. Ago gives an especially purist version of this view claiming that collision rules do not deal with the question "Should we apply foreign or domestic law?"[38] Rather, national meta-rules produce themselves national substantive law by using outside rules as material and reconstructing them anew in the context of domestic law: "*l'ordre juridique est toujours nécessairement exclusif dans le sens qu'ils exclut le caractère juridique de tout cequi ne rentre pas en lui-mème.*" (the legal order is always necessarily exclusive in the sense that it excludes the legal character of everything that does not enter into itself.)

In more abstract terms, the strange paradox of self-justice in the conflict of domestic and foreign law—the peculiar asymmetry of a law that decides its own conflicts with other laws, and thus violates flagrantly the principle of impartiality—can be reformulated with the concept of re-entry. Once an original distinction has been drawn, it reproduces itself in a subsequent chain of distinctions which builds on the original distinction (legal/illegal). The chain distinguishes itself from the outside world through its very reproductive operations (legal operations/rest of the world). It integrates itself with the outside world neither by reaching into the world outside its own distinctions nor by appealing to a higher authority (be it of divine or natural law, be it of the doctors of Bologna). Rather, it repeats in itself the difference between two symbolic spaces by distinguishing between its self-perceived identity and a constructed outside world (domestic/foreign law). This is re-entry: a chain of distinctions reformulates its difference to the outside world in the language of its own distinctions (national rules on international collisions). It cannot connect itself to other chains of distinctions except by re-entry, by a reconstruction of these other chains in its own terms. The main effect of this re-entry: If, for an outside observer there was incommensurability of different sorts of distinctions, after the re-entry, there is comparability and compatibility. An internal meta-level can be constructed that transforms the former external heterarchy into an internal hierarchy (substantive rules versus meta-rules of rule collision).

If Habermas takes his idea of discursive *Gleichursprünglichkeit* seriously, then "re-entry" seems to offer itself as a formal model of how to deal with interdiscursivity. Due to *Gleichursprünglichkeit*, none of the partial discourses—neither

---

[38] KEGEL, *supra* note 1, at X § 3.

morals, ethics, law, nor philosophy—is a natural candidate for a superdiscourse. Otherwise, we would have to admit, all of these original equals actually are superdiscourses. The moral discourse reformulates the conflict of different discourses in terms of generalizable interests, the ethical discourse reformulates in terms of individual and collective identity, the legal discourse reformulates in terms of treating norm-case-relations equally or nonequally, and so forth. Each of these discourses has an internal dynamics that propels its chain of distinctions not only for substantive questions, but also for questions of discourse collisions. Discourse collisions search in vain for one central meta-discourse. There is only a plurality of decentralized meta-discourses that reformulate collisions in their own idiosyncratic language. After all, Lyotard seems not so wrong with his assertion that in the conflict of discourse no *litige* takes place, but rather a *différend*: By reconstructing foreign rationalities in its own domestic language, each discourse necessarily does "injustice" to the inner essence of the others.

"Justice" would then take on a specific meaning. Under modern conditions, it would not be rendered meaningless, as Kelsen asserted. Nor would justice be identical with the partial and highly specialized rationality of the moral discourse, applying nothing but the stern and rigorous universalization principle, as Habermas suggests today. Rather, justice would have to be reformulated as a relational concept. However, at the same time, this justice is nonhierarchical and asymmetric. Justice relates discursive identity and discursive otherness not from "above," but from the unique perspective each discourse has to the rest of the world of discourses. Legal justice then becomes a matter of degree, not a binary choice. Justice can be realized to the degree as a concrete historical legal discourse is simultaneously able, externally, to incorporate the rationalities of other discourses and, internally, to observe its own requirements of legal consistency. Denoting the richness of the idiosyncratic world construction of the legal discourse, legal justice would be universal and particular at the same time. This is more than "adequate complexity" of the legal system that looks exclusively to the question of how, under the condition of extreme social differentiation, internal legal consistency can still be achieved.[39] Justice will be realized to the degree a concrete legal order is able to respond at the same time to an additional question. Not only to

[39] *See* Niklas Luhmann, Ausdifferenzierung des Rechts: Beiträge zur Rechtssoziologie und Rechtstheorie (1981); Niklas Luhmann, Rechtssystem und Rechtsdogmatik Stuttgart (1974).

what degree does law justice to its own requirement of legal equality, but also to what degree does law justice to the *Eigenlogik* of other discourses. This results in a third question: If law increasingly gives justice to outside discourses, is it capable of changing the internal criteria of coherence accordingly? And Michael Walzer's *Spheres of Justice* would take on a different meaning. Not only would a multitude of specific social and professional contexts develop a multitude of specialized moralities. But specialized argumentation practices would reflect discourse specific norms in their relation to norm projections of other spheres of life.

IV.

If "re-entry" is the third position that marks the difference to Habermas's treatment of interdiscursivity, what are the consequences for legal argumentation? Does the distinction make a difference when moral, ethical, pragmatic, and interest-oriented arguments actually enter the legal discourse? My answer in a nutshell: "enslavement." Indeed, Habermas rightly stresses the point that despite the profound differentiation of morality and legality, moral and ethical arguments do reappear frequently, and legitimately, in legal reasoning. And he overcomes the obvious contradiction between autonomy and reappearance by the metaphor of "translation." Moral contents, Habermas argues, do not enter law as such; they are "translated" into the "legal code," whatever this means.[40] Thus, he can reject pure legalism *à la* Windscheid, the (in)famous German pandectist who maintained that political, moral, and economic arguments were irrelevant to the "lawyer as such," as being hopelessly out of step with argumentative reality.

In his turn, Habermas constructs legal decisionmaking as a process model in which pragmatic, ethical, moral, and interest-oriented arguments are freely interchanged; only at the end does the result need to go through the filter of legal argument: a test of coherence with established legal norms, especially constitutional norms. This ultimately makes judicial review necessary in which the new programs are examined for their ability to fit into the existing legal system.

Similarly, in the application discourse of judicial adjudication, Habermas identifies a plurality of pragmatic, ethical, moral, and interest-oriented arguments which again are disciplined by the legal requirement of "conditions of decisional consistency."[41]

40 *See* HABERMAS, *supra* note 8, at 250.
41 *Id.* at 268.

Legal consistency appears in both cases as a screening method that filters out some of the solutions that have been found in the free interplay of discourse types and negotiations. In the collision of discourses, it is an excluding device that rules out certain extravagant results.

To my mind, Habermas underestimates in both cases the "legal proprium." Legal consistency is not only a filtering device. It is the very productive mechanism that opens the gates for a whole cascade of distinctions. "Treat equal cases equally and unequal cases unequally" should not be seen as the *Grundnorm*, the static basic norm but the *Grundverfahren*, the dynamic basic procedure of the legal discourse that opens a self-propelling process of a chain of distinctions. It deals not only with the problem of normative coherence, as Habermas suggests—if and how a consented rule fits into a system of rules. Rather, it triggers a generative mechanism, a "historical machine" as von Foerster would say,[42] when it asks the *question directrice* if a new case should be treated "alike or not alike" to a historically given relation between rules and cases. And in this context, it is not so much "stare decisis" which is of interest, the binding effect of precedents, of treating equal cases equally. Rather it is "distinguishing" and "overruling," treating unequal cases unequally, that unleashes law forces.[43] It is legal unequality that opens a definite conceptual framework for the infinite search for alternative rules and facts, principles and values, and that produces innovations which in their turn reproduce for the next chain of cases the dialectics of "alike or not alike."

And it is this historical machine that legal discourse, on its own territory, uses to "enslave" other discourses. Relentlessly searching for criteria of equal/unequal, the legal discourse freely borrows ideas, rules, and principles from other discourses, exploits moral, ethical, pragmatic, and strategic arguments, but subdues them to the very basic procedure of determining legal equality/inequality. There is no free interplay of arguments, but rather the stern discipline of a legal search procedure that defines, on the basis of its historical configuration, which aspects are relevant and which not, which arguments are admitted and which not, how priorities have to be set, and how conflicting perspectives have to be resolved. For moral philosophers, it is one of the most frustrating experiences when their eloquent suada is brusquely interrupted by a lawyer's argument: "Legally, this is irrelevant." And this inter-

42 *See* HEINZ VON FOERSTER, OBSERVING SYSTEMS 201 (1981).

43 *See* NIKLAS LUHMANN, DAS RECHT DER GESELLSCHAFT 110-17 (1993).

ruption is not merely due to arbitrary *auctoritas* of the judge, but equally to the *ratio* of legal doctrine and procedure. It is the present state of the law—*die gegenwärtige Rechtslage*—in its historical evolution that decides about production, admission, and the foundation of unequality. Disposition about unequality is the privilege of the law in the interplay of discourses; the dynamic realization of the "legal proprium" which dictates also the legitimate/nonlegitimate use of nonlegal arguments.

This enslavement of foreign arguments under the basic procedure of law expresses, I submit, a different aspect of the proceduralization idea. Habermas tends to reserve the idea of "proceduralization" for the very general procedural requirements of an ideal discourse on practical questions. Legal procedures, he contends, do not interfere with the "inner logic of argumentation."[44] But is this really true? "Treating new cases alike/not alike" is a procedure that determines the scope and quality of admitted arguments, the sequence of equality tests, and the criteria of what equality in this context means. As a basic procedure for the legal discourse, it interferes deeply with the inner logic of argument, be it legal argument or the legal assimilation of moral, ethical, or pragmatical arguments. It would have as its counterparts other autonomous discourses—the "universalization procedure" of morality in its Kantian, Rawlsian, or Habermasian version, or an "identity search procedure" in ethical discourses, or the utility calculus of "rational choice"—which in their turn typically proceduralize argumentation and incorporate, but thereby enslave foreign arguments, among them legal concepts, rules, and principles.

V.

But how should such a mundane enterprise like the law be able in its tormented casuistry to "incorporate" the vast multitude of high-culture discourses such as morality, ethics, and pragmatics on the one side and powerful economic and political arguments on the other? Why should the legal discourse be able to make highly diverse aspects compatible, a feat that a philosophical superdiscourse was not supposed to be able to accomplish? Let us have a closer look—with empathy and compassion—at the victims of this semantic slavery. "Alike or not alike—that is the question" which attracts other discourses to law. Once selectively admitted, they

44 *See* Habermas, *supra* note 8, at 288.

suffer a peculiar transformation. Moral maxims, ethical self-realization, pragmatic recommendations, and policy requirements—to use Habermas's very typology—lose their specific identity. They all reappear now in the guise of sheer legal norms, rights, and duties, principles, and values—simple components of the legal discourse. Habermas uses the metaphor "translation" to analyze this transubstantiation of morality into law.[45] As long as the differences of languages is maintained, the immigration of moral contents into law does not signify any immediate moralization of law.[46]

Indeed, it signifies the very opposite, a juridification of morality with the result of leveling out discursive differences. Originally, there were incommensurable rationalities directed into different dimensions of meaning. Now their legal enslavement makes them commensurable, comparable, and decidable—only within the boundaries of law, of course. Here, we find the reason for the shameless eclecticism of law that treats moral maxims and economic policies equally as "values" among which the law can establish priorities according to prior legislative or judicial decisions. Here, we find the reason why high culture is inevitably trivialized whenever lawyers begin to incorporate it in their briefs, as German lawyers tend to say self-critically: *zu kleiner Münze verrechtlicht* (juridified into small coins).

With high sensitivity Habermas analyzes this transformation from moral rules into legal rules: moral contents are translated into the legal code and are endowed with a different mode of validity.[47] This leads him to an informative typology of differentially "moralized" legal norms. However, he seems to underestimate the simplifying effect of this translation when he, in his polemics against Alexy's theory of balancing goods, insists that within legal practice, the difference between deontological principles and teleological values needs to be respected. In my view, this is a paradigmatic case. It shows how the legal discourse deals with fundamental differences between other discourses. Certainly, Habermas is right:

> Norms and values are different, first in their reference to obligatory versus teleological action; second, in their binary versus gradual coding of their validity claims; third in their absolute versus relative oligartoriness; and fourth in the criteria which are applied to the coherence of rule systems or value systems.[48]

---

45 *See id.* at 250-53.

46 *See id.* at 253.

47 *See id.* at 252.

48 *Id.* at 311.

There are many legal theorists who would support this distinction and base whole systems of legal theory on it (deontological versus consequentialist theories). Legal practitioners, however, show no interest at all to respect these distinctions; they are determined to resolve collision issues and to transform them into a decidable form. Thus, the argumentative practice of law decides about collisions of discursive logics by leveling out their fundamental differences. For lawyers, their method of *Abwägung* (balancing) has exactly the same structure, be it balancing between principles, between values, or even between interests. They identify them in terms of the case at hand; they determine the degree to which they collide, they evaluate them as legitimate, they weigh them against each other and find the criteria for this weighing in legislative and judicial decisions. Worse, the trivialization of different logics enables them to treat incommensurable things alike and balance—*horribile dictu*—principles, values, and interests against each other. Pears and apples! Justitia is blind!

Maybe Habermas effectively points to the limits of solving discursive collisions by legal trivialization. Maybe he signals an overload of the traditional way in which discourse collisions are translated first into one-dimensional conflicts between legal norms, principles, and values, and then decided via legal doctrine and the hierarchy of courts. This should make us sensitive to other ways—less hierarchical and doctrinal, yet more decentral and processual—in which law deals with the collision of different worlds of meaning.

VI.

Fight fire with fire! Increasingly, law's response to the fundamental collision of discourses seems to be to fight fragmentation by fragmentation! This is the opposite strategy to mapping external conflicts within the uniting conceptual framework of one and only one legal doctrine and relying on the hierarchical unity of the court system to decide doctrinal conflicts.

Now, instead of relying on the unity of law, there are tendencies to translate external discourse collisions into internal conflicts between specialized legal fields. And, in their turn, substantive legal fields find again an asymmetrical, self-referential way of resolving their conflicts. We could call this a "double re-entry." The distinction between different discourses reappears first in legal assimilation of other discourses and reappears a second time in the asymmetric collision rules in the conflict between different legal fields.

Internal differentiation of law can be seen as a response to the fragmentation of society in various systems and discourses. As is well known, internal differentiation of law has long since moved beyond the traditional broad distinctions between public law, private law, and criminal law. For example, the fragmentation of private law into a multitude of special fields (*Sonderprivatrechte*) has destroyed the conceptual-dogmatic unity of private law.[49] What is important for our context of discursive plurality, is that this internal differentiation lead to a close symbiosis between discursive domains outside the law and special fields within the law. Joerges puts responsibility on "the prevailing conditions in the social domain concerned which entail the specific differentiation of private law and lead to the fragmentation of the private law doctrine and legislation."[50] And this internally differentiated law looks more and more like a Russian doll that contains in itself ever smaller dolls. Even key areas within private law, such as tort law, can no longer be integrated by means of unified normative principles. The "compartmentalization of the classic 'general' law of tort into a law of specialized torts," for example, seems an irreversible state of affairs, to which the law reacts by providing differentiated "solutions for specific interests and social fields."[51] Nowadays, legal doctrine develops different theories of tort for different social fields, and this is no accident.[52] The practice of the courts has destroyed the old unity of law guaranteed by doctrine and has replaced it by a multiplicity of fragmented legal territories that live in close contact with their neighboring territories in other social practices.

Demands for restoring the "unity of the legal order" are, of course, merely rhetorical in character, or are used tactically when the occasion arises.[53] Attempts to establish a conceptual or axio-

---

49 *See* CHRISTIAN JOERGES, VERBRAUCHERSCHULTZ ALS RECHTSPROBLEM: EINE UNTERSUCHUNG ZUM STAND DER THEORIE UND ZU DEN ENTWICKLUNGSPERSPEKTIVEN DES VERBRAUCHERRECHTS (1981); Christian Joerges, *Quality Regulation in Consumer Good Markets: Theoretical Concepts and Practical Examples*, *in* CONTRACT AND ORGANIZATION: LEGAL ANALYSIS IN THE LIGHT OF ECONOMIC AND SOCIAL THEORY 142-63 (T.C. Daintith & Gunther Teubner eds., 1986).

50 Christian Joerges, *Die Überarbeitung des BGB-Schuldrechts, die Sonderprivatrechte und die Unbestimmtheit des Rechts*, 20 KRITISCHE JUSTIZ 166, 166-82 (1987).

51 GERT BRÜGGEMEIER, DELIKTSRECHT: EIN HAND-UND LEHRBUCH 82-89 (1986).

52 *See id.* at 313-463.

53 *See, e.g.*, HORST JAKOBS, WISSENSCHAFT UND GESETZGEBUNG IM BÜRGERLICHEN RECHT (1983); Ernst Wolf, *Kein Abschied vom BGB*, 15 ZEITSCHRIFT FÜR RECHTSPOLITIK 1-6 (1982).

logical unity through legal dogmatics are doomed to failure.[54] This is as true for private law as it is for the law in general.

How to deal with these internal conflicts that represent larger discursive collisions is still an open question. The idea of the "relative autonomy of legal fields"[55] seems to be both realistic and normatively acceptable. Explicitly, this idea uses concepts developed in the international private law for the collision of legal fields. Prominent among them figures the conflict-of-law principle of *ordre public*. *Ordre public* excludes the domestic application of foreign law in case that foreign law violates fundamental legal principles of domestic law. In its application to intralegal collisions, the starting principle is that doctrinally and procedurally specialized legal fields are essentially independent, and are only subject to limitations in situations where *ordre public* happens to be relevant. Each legal field will develop its own doctrinal structures according to the demands of the social practice involved, but in cases where problems of *ordre public* arise, the particular legal field would have to respect the fundamental principles and policies of the other legal fields. It would have to incorporate them into its own autonomous doctrine as a limitation on its activities. This seems to be a realistic way of reformulating the old idea of the unity of the legal order. In modern legal systems characterized by a high degree of internal differentiation, a close integration is no longer possible, neither through concepts and values nor through the court hierarchy. This is the revenge of the slaves! Certainly, they are enslaved by legal trivialization. But they still have the power to destroy the doctrinal unity of law from the inside. They compel the legal discourse to give up the goal of legal unity. Instead, what can be achieved, at best, is only a measure of compatibility between the doctrines of autonomous legal fields and the mutual reflexive adoption of their fundamental principle.

---

54 *See* Wolfgang Zöllner, *Zivilrechtswissenschaft und Zivilrecht im ausgehenden*, 188 ARCHIV FÜR DIE ZIVILISISCHE PRAXIS 86, 100 (1988).

55 *See, e.g.*, RAINER WALZ, STEUERGERECHTIGKEIT UND RECHTSANWENDUNG: GRUNDLINIEN EINER RELATIV AUTONOMEN STEUERRECHTSDOGMATIK (1980); Rudolf Wiethölter, *Materialization and Proceduralization in Modern Law*, *in* DILEMMAS OF LAW IN THE WELFARE STATE 221-49 (Gunther Teubner ed., 1985); Rudolf Wiethöler, *Social Science Models in Economic Law*, *in* CONTRACT AND ORGANIZATION: LEGAL ANALYSIS IN THE LIGHT OF ECONOMIC AND SOCIAL THEORY 52-67 (T. Daintith & Gunther Teubner eds., 1986); Rudolf Wiethöler, *Proceduralization of the Category of Law*, *in* CRITICAL LEGAL THOUGHT: AN AMERICAN-GERMAN DEBATE 501-10 (C. Joerges & D. Trubek eds., 1989).

VII.

Let me try a final analogy. Frequently, private international law decides against domestic law and opts for the application of foreign law. Such an "externalization" happens when the case at hand seems to have a "closer relation" to the foreign legal order than to the domestic one. In the conflict of discourses, there is an equivalent to this externalization. The legal discourse resolves the collision by externalizing certain normative questions from its domain and delegating them to other normative practices. *Boni mores* and *bona fides* are the classical examples of resolving a discursive collision by referring it to morality, whatever this meant to be. More modern examples are references to "reasonable man," "public policy," "commercial practices," and "professional standards." Here is a remarkable difference from what we had called "enslavement." There, the law did simulate other argumentative practices by reconceptualizing them in terms of legal norms, principles, and values. Here, the law delegates its norm-creating task to other on-going argumentative practices. And it reads the result of such practices and then tries to assimilate them into legal rules. To be sure, the law plays quite an active role in this assimilation. But the fact remains that it is the ongoing argumentative practice outside the law that has an upper hand in determining the normative result.

How should we interpret this externalization? We might say that the collision of discourses is resolved by a mutual influencing of two argumentative practices that actually take place. In this case, two discourses are simultaneously reading and misreading their results. And in this process, certain *eigenvalues* emerge that have proven themselves in the practice of two discourses. These *eigenvalues* have greater plausibility and greater stability than the above mentioned results of legal trivialization or internal differentiation.

To conclude, I ask why employ these somewhat counter-intuitive tendencies toward asymmetry, re-entry, internal differentiation, and re-externalization? Why opting against a superdiscourse, against unity of law, against central court hierarchy? My tentative answer is: historicity. It is the accumulated experience of institutionalized argumentative practices that is rich enough to develop concrete criteria of relevance, to determine the sequence of distinctions, and to suggest topics of evaluation in order to cope with the disquieting reality of conflicting discourses.

[14]

The Ambitious Modesty of Niklas Luhmann

MICHAEL KING* AND ANTON SCHÜTZ**

> *There are no solutions for the most urgent problems but only restatements without promising perspectives . . . success seems highly improbable. On the other hand, we can see fascinating possibilities of arriving at a higher level of intelligibility. It requires at present a kind of stoic attitude to stay on the job and 'do the formulations'.*
>
> Niklas Luhmann, *The World Society as a Social System* (1985)[1]

INTRODUCTION

Nothing is more in keeping with the spirit of Niklas Luhmann's work than to entitle this article with an apparent paradox: the simultaneous presence of ambition and modesty. What Luhmann offers is a theory of society, a 'grand theory' in the European tradition, but one which runs directly contrary to the claims for universal competence and exhaustive accounts of reality associated with 'grand theories'. It is a theory which acknowledges modestly that it cannot answer many of the important questions that face modern societies.

In his introduction to a glossary of his theoretical terminology,[2] Luhmann places his theory in an historical context. He writes:

> At the end of this century we find ourselves facing new kinds of tasks. The society that we observe today is no longer that of Marx, Weber or Durkheim. And even more so, it is not that of the Enlightenment or the French revolution. More than ever before, the past has lost its binding force and this is also true in regard to the value criteria which once formed the basis for the search for rationality. And perhaps for these reasons knowledge about the future is more riddled with uncertainty than in any previous period. In this situation we can change almost nothing with those instruments specific

* *Centre for the Study of Law, the Child and the Family, Brunel University, Uxbridge UB8 3PH, England*
** *Department of Law, Birkbeck College, Malet Street, London WC1E 7HX, England*

We should like to thank Andrew Goldsmith, James Penner, and Peter Beyer for their comments on earlier versions of this article. We are also grateful to the Law Department of the Australian National University for enabling Michael King to work on this article through his appointment as a Visiting Fellow earlier this year.

to science: explanation and prognosis. It must be possible, however, to describe adequately what we find ourselves facing.

Luhmann's theoretical scheme attempts to deal with failures in explaining and predicting by placing the emphasis on observation rather than explanation and prediction. The way that Luhmann achieves this is by limiting his analysis of society to what he, in his theoretical scheme, brings to the concept of society and not even attempting to discuss 'society', in the way that it is understood by others. Problems of consciousness, for example, which most other writers see as central to 'society' do not even appear in his version of society. The Luhmannian version of society, therefore, does not depend upon any political programme, whether socialism, liberalism or compromises between the two. The notion of a utopian past or future society against which the present may be compared does not feature in Luhmann's scheme.

Just as society for Luhmann is not, therefore, what most people would consider society to be, so Luhmannian sociology is not what many contemporary sociologists would consider to be sociology. Yet Luhmann is quite aware of the identity problems of contemporary sociology, but still insists that his theoretical scheme should be considered as sociology in that it attempts to analyse society as an essentially social phenomenon and not deal with societal issues merely at the level of abstraction. Indeed, the project that Luhmann sets himself in his writings represents the very summit of sociological ambition, while never allowing his readers to forget that his theory does not recognize summits or privileged panoramic viewpoints.

Unlike many social theories Luhmann's scheme does not depend upon the kind of reductionism that one finds in biological, psychological or economic models which transform society or societal events to 'facts', whether biological, psychological or economic, rather than treating them as uniquely 'social'. In another sense, however, Luhmann's theory is reductionist. Indeed, reduction is the very subject of the theory, its starting point.[3] In Luhmann's scheme 'reality', the external world, is inaccessible. Gathering or obtaining knowledge about it is *constructing* it. Construction, in turn, is simplifying and choosing among possible simplifications. All system are agents of and for reduction. Where Luhmann's theory differs intrinsically from other reductionist observers, however, is in the fact that it makes reduction one of its deliberate choices. The theory selects problems that are reducible to components capable of yielding results and questions capable of being answered according to their own theoretical terms.

OBSTACLES TO UNDERSTANDING LUHMANN

Understanding Luhmann is not easy, even if one reads German fluently or has access to translations of his major works. The difficulties are largely not ones of words or language but of concepts. Luhmann's basic unit for analysis is *the system* and not individuals, social groups, ideologies, culture, and so on. Systems relate to each other and to their environments through *observation*, which reconstitutes everything observed in the system's environment into a *distinction*.[4] 'Society' consists, therefore, not of a single social system, but of many: one for law, one for economy, one for science, one for Luhmannian theory, and so on, each of which constructs itself and its environment according to its distinctive operations. Each system represents an entity, existing within an environment which it itself constructs from its operations. Furthermore, it reproduces its own identity within that environment. In this sense the parts are more important than the whole. One could even say that the whole is *less* than the sum of its parts. Luhmann thus emphasizes the inadequacy of all totalizing concepts, such as 'man' or 'nature'.

Before moving on to look at these important parts of Luhmann's scheme, we shall examine what we see as four of the major obstacles to an appreciation of Luhmann's theory of autopoiesis or operationally closed systems, which may arise from certain strands of past social theory. These are: (1) the need for causality; (2) the unified individual; (3) functionalism; and (4) social reality.

1. *The need for causality*

As long as one maintains that the aim of social science is to study objectively chains of causality which connect social phenomena and that this aim is realizable, as long as one holds on to the belief that it is possible to produce a definitive explanation for any social event, it will really not be possible to enter into the spirit of Luhmann's approach to society and the social world. Yet Luhmann in his theory makes no attempt to reform the philosophical notion of causality. His focus is rather on the *improbability* of the elusive phenomenon which we call society and which incorporates so much meaningful activity and offers such a range of possibilities.

For Luhmann, to conceive of the possibility of a sociology which is able to predict accurately social behaviour is to deny the problematic and contingent nature of society. He rejects the belief that sociology should define itself as a producer of causal explanations or that science, including social science, should take on the role of generating norms, that is, all those 'ought' statements which are based on political, moral or religious beliefs, or on causal theories founded ultimately on such beliefs. Since there can be no ultimate observer, any causal accounts produced by sociology are limited in their application or are bound to lead to disappointments. Where causality is concerned, Luhmann's starting point is the disappointing results of causal explanations and the lessons derived from these disappointments rather than the explanatory theories themselves. As we shall see, functionally differentiated social systems are functional to society in the sense that they provide the conceptual means (such as notions of causality) whereby things that appeared improbable are transformed into probabilities. This is not simply a matter of masking the truth or giving things a rationalistic or convincing appearance; rather, the very evolution of society depends upon these improbable-into-probable transactions in such a way that what was improbable actually *becomes* probable. In this way, Luhmann then begins where causal explanations fail by converting questions of causality into questions of probability and contingency.

2. *The unified individual as the preferred unit of sociological analysis*

In a general way, social theories have tended to reduce societies to collections of individuals. Individuals differ because they exist within different cultures, different political ideologies, different *epistèmes*, and so on. These theories differ from one another in the way in which they interpret the relations between individual and society. Psychoanalytic, social, psychological, and many sociological theories construct society as the sum of relations between individuals. These see social institutions as projections of individual needs and interests. 'Common sense' interpretations also tend to present an implicit version of society as something constructed by people and of different societies as reflecting differences in cultural or racial characteristics, which in turn are a product of individual diversity. According to Luhmann, this portrayal of the individual as the prime mover, principal actor and, therefore, preferred unit for the analysis of the social world may well have been useful at some moment in history when:

> [s]ocial status (*condition*, *quality*, *état*) was the most stable characteristic of an individual's personality. This is no longer possible for a society differentiated with respect to functions, such as politics, economy, intimate relations, religion, sciences, and education.[5]

The functionally differentiated nature of modern society thus disqualifies 'the individual' as a useful unit of sociological analysis. 'Nobody can live in only one of these [functionally differentiated] systems.' This is not to deny that individuals exist as minds, brains, conscious systems. Nor, according to Luhmann, is it 'to deny that we are all human. But to want to be human has no scientific basis. It amounts to sheer dilettantism'.[6]

Luhmann's concerns, therefore, are very much those of a sociologist who wishes to avoid what he claims are the severe limitations that arise from conceiving societies in other than sociological terms. In the first place, for Luhmann there must be a clear conceptual distinction between what people *think* (consciousness) and what they *communicate* to other people (communication). According to his theoretical approach, the way to approach an understanding of society is through their communications, which in modern societies are organized into functionally differentiated systems. Secondly, Luhmann believes that sociological theories that apply a society-as-individuals approach to modern societies will inevitably give priority to one functional system to the exclusion of others or to the interpretation of others from the perspective of one observing system only. It could be argued, therefore, that theories based upon the power inequalities between races or genders are essentially political theories and not sociological in the sense that they cannot describe social phenomena in societal terms, but are obliged invariably to return to explanations founded on differences (whether biological or socially constructed) between individuals or groups of individuals.

3. *Functionalism*

In Luhmannian theory the notion of functionalism is completely reformed from previous sociological ideas of what is and what is not functional for society. In order to grasp the full sense of this modification, we need to identify the two major concepts that characterized functionalist thought prior to Luhmann. These were:

(a) The organismic image or body corporate

Society, like the body, was seen as consisting of many different organs each contributing to the well-being of the whole in ways which are specific to that *organ*. Within this version of functionality is an implicit notion of causality. The *organs* of society are the *cause* of its healthy functioning. Malfunction or inefficiency in one system causes poor performance and possible failure in other systems. This eventually results in social disorder and ultimately in the complete collapse of society.

(b) Perfection

According to this fundamental notion of medieval theological and philosophical thought, society was part of creation and as such was naturally perfect. Where imperfections existed, they could be attributed to precise events or to guilty culprits, external to society itself. So that for each evident imperfection in society a precise external cause could be identified as its source, such as the plague, a bad harvest, or an invasion by the Tartars. After Kant, the concept of perfection was replaced by that of *conditions-of-possibility*, according to which the plague was no longer seen as the result of, for example, celestial vengeance for the desecration of the Host, but was rather an improbable outcome of the combination of rats and microbes. Thus, the 'imperfection' in society was not external to nature but part of nature itself. This meant that nature was not naturally good or, in other words, that reality was not composed of naturally 'best solutions', but instead of fragile and transient outcomes of contingent conditions.

Luhmann's concept of functionalism frees the notion of function from its links with both the organic image and the notion of perfection. It considers society as the ongoing result of its own capacity to reproduce its own conditions of possibility. Functionalism in this new Luhmannian sense is not compatible with the idea of agencies 'being functional' to society, performing part of the task of the whole. Anything that is considered as a task of society must first be *produced* by society and this production depends upon conditions that could be otherwise. Functions are not given entities. They emerge from selections which could have been made differently. In this way, according to Luhmann, what *sociology*, as an observer of society, identifies as functional to modern society (for example, law, the family, the economy, science, religion, and so on) are the result of the evolution into increasing differentiation which characterizes these societies. Their functionality is, therefore, a result of selections which have permitted social systems to see society (and, in some cases, themselves) in terms of functionality (see 'Societies and Social Systems' below). Criticisms directed against Parsonian functionalism, therefore, have little relevance to Luhmann's theory with its emphasis upon the contingent nature of social functions and its problematization of the very notion of functionality.

4. *Social reality*

Within contemporary sociology, the idea that people construct their own social world has by now become banal. As a theoretical orientation, it focuses attention on the social activities, such as science or politics, through which versions of social reality are constructed. In its normative form, social constructionism is used in a critical way in order to demonstrate how the 'reality' constructed by institutions such as courts, scientific laboratories or political parties falls short of, distorts or provides only a partial account of what the writer is able to identify as 'reality' or, at least, a more realistic or valid 'reality'. What Luhmann tells us is rather different. Following George Spencer Brown,[7] he claims that 'there is an external world, which *results* from the fact that cognition, as a self-operated operation, can be carried out at all, but that we have no direct contact with it'.[8] At the psychological level, therefore, there is a system (consciousness) which 'knows' the world through its selection or coding of external stimuli followed almost instantaneously by its internal operations upon them.

For Luhmann, as we have seen already, it is not *people* who determine social reality by constructing the world around them. Social reality is not produced by individual or collective consciousness nor are societal institutions simply a translation of human needs into social form. In addition to this, however, Luhmann – much like Foucault, and in certain respects for the same motives – criticizes structuralist accounts of society.[9] He also rejects language as the starting point for a theory of society. Even if language may be the consequence of biological or psychic structures,[10] to analyse society in terms of language is to deny society as an independent phenomenon worthy of scientific analysis in its own right. As we shall see, society, for Luhmann, consists only of communications, which are selections produced from choices that have historically become available.[11] Language may be, and often is, an important mode of communication, but communications are neither produced nor pre-programmed by language.

Without people and their capacity to use language there could, of course, be no communications and no society at all. In this sense and only in this sense (and not as conscious entities or starting points for any sociological analyses), people and language are indispensable to contemporary society. In order to understand Luhmann's theory of society, therefore, one needs to go beyond social constructionist and linguistic approaches to social reality, while at the same time retaining the notion of the phenomenal nature of society and the possibility that many versions of social reality may exist alongside one another at any one time. The central problem which has to be confronted is that of a reality which exists but which is inaccessible. There can be nothing other than observation, no universal 'truth' without reference to a particular system and no ultimate observer, meaning an observer which could not itself be observed. When Luhmann writes about society, he is writing exclusively about what he refers to as 'world society', that is to say, a society limited by the boundaries of what is communicable (or more precisely, communicated) and by no other boundaries.

COMMUNICATIONS, SOCIETY (*GESELLSCHAFT*), AND SOCIAL SYSTEMS

'Societies are encompassing systems, in the sense that they include all events which, *for them*, have the quality of communication.'[12] For sociology, they represent simultaneously the subject matter and the great Unknown, the sum total of all possible meanings. In Luhmann's words, society is 'the closed system of connectable communications, reproducing communication by communication'.[13] One arrives, therefore at a typical Luhmannian circular description, in that anything which can be understood through communications as belonging to society forms part of that communicative universe which is called society. Society, it must be emphasized, exists quite independently of people or consciousness and will continue to exist and to reproduce itself just as long as communications, that is, speaking, gesturing, writing, acting or omitting to act continue.

Society is 'world society' in the sense that it represents the boundaries of what is 'known' and communicable. It is the whole world of communicable meaning among human beings. It 'cannot be the subject of communication because we cannot distinguish it from anything that it does not encompass'.[14] For Luhmann, therefore, society cannot be limited by national identities, such as English, French or American society, since today all three, along with all other national entities, form part of a communicative whole which relate to one another politically, economically and in other ways, existing for one another within one society. Within different contexts society, however, may be as small as an isolated village or tribe or as large as 'the global system of the world society'. It may consist of many different communicative subsystems which are organized in different ways, according to nature of the society. The operations of these sub-systems produce communications.

Society, unlike social subsystems, is unable to communicate with its environment,[15] as it itself consists of all that is communicable. Yet, this is not to say that the environment is identical for all societies. For example, the environment for an 'isolated tribe', that is, a tribe that does not know of and is unknown to the rest of the world, does not extend beyond the rain forest and the sky. Obviously, this does not mean that the trible is incapable of imagining gods and supernatural causes for earthly events. Such gods, however, are able to manifest themselves to the tribe only in ways that are known and, thus, form part of the tribe's environment. Once it has been discovered by explorers, the environment for the tribe soon becomes the whole world. Consumer goods and diseases arrive giving the tribe not only a knowledge of the world society outside the rain forest, but also a dependence on the social systems of that world: health, economics, law, and so on. The tribal leaders may still try to retain an identity for the tribe as autonomous, existing within a closed communicative world, but perturbations from the tribe's environment – the death of its members from 'white man's diseases', the attraction of industrially manufactured goods – make such an identity impossible to sustain. The tribe has become part of world society.

Building on Durkheim's distinction between societies based on mechanical and organic solidarity, Luhmann sees pre-modern societies as either organized into equivalently structured sub-systems (*segmentary differentiation*), such as religious clans or families among which there was relatively little interdependence or structured according to an unequal distribution of wealth and an hierarchical architecture of power (*stratificatory differentiation*). Modern societies, for Luhmann, have the unique quality of being divided into *functionally differentiated* subsystems.[16]

In the broad theoretical tradition of the division of labour,[17] from which Luhmann's idea of functional differentiation is a direct descendent, these diverging practices are seen as resulting from choice, learning and rational preferences. By contrast, Luhmann, as we have already mentioned, sees these functions simply as having happened, not through conscious choice or rational decisions, but through selections in the way that events in the environment were observed, which gave rise to the possibility of further selections, and so on. Systems become functional for society because, through a process of *evolution* (see below), they have come to be seen and understood as functional for society.

Luhmann sees the functional differentiation present in modern and contemporary society as having evolved as a result of the increasing complexity of the society combined with the absence of any transcendent authority, such as God's law or the sovereign's rule. Furthermore, and of particular importance for the development of his theory, he attributes to these functionally differentiated subsystems, not only labour divisions, but the *organization of meaning* through the production of communications using their unique binary coding of the external environment. These functionally differentiated systems are diverging practices, spheres of activity, a collection of autonomous but interdependent process each derived from its exclusive use of one of what Talcott Parson called *symbolically generalized media* and Luhmann refers to as *the Symbolically Generalized Media of Communication.* Economy, for example, uses the medium of money, law of legality, politics of power, science of truth, religion of faith, sexuality of love. Although these media have meaning for the whole of society, they are developed within subsystems as a binary code by which the system 'understands' or 'reproduces' society, the environment and its identity or self-image. The code for science, for example is true/false, for law, legal/illegal, for medicine, healthy/unhealthy, and so on.

The limited access to the external environment creates serious problems of communication between systems. In the functionally differentiated conditions of modern society these systems are operationally closed in terms of their uniqueness of their function. Law, for example, can only perform its own functional operations, such as holding trials and making legal judgments. It cannot replace the functional operations of the economy, nor can religion replace politics. The meanings that they produce through their communications are also closed in the sense that communications generated by one system, using its unique coding is able to be 'understood' by other systems only by being reconstituted within those systems. Moreover, each system observes other systems within its environment, but is unable to observe the world in the same way as other systems, since there is no way that coding can be shared. Since each social system with its unique coding of the environment also constitutes a part of that environment for other systems, it follows that any communications emerging from one system require to be reconstituted, using the coding of the other system before they can be understood by another system.

The closure of functional social systems in modern society is the result of the enormous success that these systems have achieved through their respective codings. These success stories put each system in the position of observing other systems as part of its own environment.

Any exchange of information between systems through the process of reconstruction using the system's unique code would not be possible, were it not for the existence of 'generalized media' which have meaning in different systems. Ironically, however, as well as solving the problems of non-communication across systems, these generalized media also create more problems of their own by giving the illusion of communication, whereas in fact the same terms are understood in different ways within different systems.[18]

The *autopoiesis of social systems* which we have briefly described, does not stretch its inherent constructionism to the point of claiming that systems are autonomous or independent in the sense of possessing immunity from the effects of each other's operations.[19] On the contrary, they are interdependent in that the effective operations of each of them depends upon the effective operations of others, but they are also autopoietic or self-referential. Interdependence here does not refer to the need of one system to sustain another in any organismic way, for this would not be consistent with their autopoietic nature. It relates, rather, to the fact that communicative events may well have repercussions not only for the social institution in which the events formally occur, but in many or all other systems. A court's decision that it is not willing to uphold certain contractual rights is clearly a legal communication (legal/illegal) which alters the structure of the legal system. In addition, it is also likely to have repercussions within the economic system, changing the expectations and perhaps undermining the confidence of businesspeople in the value of entering into formal contractual relations. The resultant changes in business practices could in turn affect the political system, education, health, art, the family, and so on.

Although Luhmann's theory may be unable to predict the precise nature of such changes, since they depend upon the contingent reconstruction of events within different systems or offer categorical causal explanations for their occurrence, it is able to describe the social condition which have made such events possible. Luhmann describes society as being in a constant state of adjustment, with irritations or perturbations in the environment of one system setting off changes in that system which could have a ripple effect throughout all segments of the social system. What Luhmann emphasizes in his work is not the stability of modern societies, but their fragility and improbability and the need to increase, where possible, the conditions for stability. At the same time, as the opening quotation of this article reveals, there is unprecedented scope for expansion and development offered by a phenomenal world of possibilities limited only by what is knowable through communication.

MEANING, CONTINGENCY, AND SELECTION

For Luhmann, things happen because selections are made and the phenomenal world changes accordingly. He deliberately leaves unanswered the question which preoccupies much contemporary social theory: why should one version of reality be preferred or privileged over others? The answer to such questions lies in the notion of causality that one chooses to explain society's selections. What Luhmann gives us is an account of the processes whereby selections become available and, once made, give rise to other selections progressively accumulating complexity.

It is because social and conscious systems, unlike nature and biological systems, need to operate within the realm of meaning that they are faced with this problem of making selections. Selections involve the bringing into conceptual form (the giving of meaning) the capacity to operate conceptually. War and peace, power and love, money and art, religion and science are not the outcomes of chance happenings, but of choices that have been made. The notion that Luhmann uses to describe this process by which selections are made and meanings attributed and developed is *contingency*.

In its philosophical sense, contingency represents the simultaneous exclusion of necessity and impossibility. The concept of contingency indicates the position of a given outcome, while directing attention to possible alternatives. It indicates, first, that which exists – and is, therefore, demonstrably not impossible – and, secondly, that which has possible alternatives – and is, therefore, not believed to be necessary.[20] Contingency indicates the possibility that things could be different. As regards the functioning of a system, the fact that one thing is selected implies the possibility that other possibilities exist which were negated, or not selected even if they could have been. Something is contingent when it is observed as having been selected from a range of diverse possibilities, which still remain as possibilities notwithstanding the fact that they have not been selected and notwithstanding that it may now be too late to select them.

In Foucault's theory, the attention directed to contingency resulted in a new evaluation of history. History, according to the Foucauldian conception, focuses on the contingent – that which demonstrably has happened against the background of the absence of any necessity or probability that it should have happened. For Luhmann's sociological theory, the concept of contingency is essential in so far as the theory deals with selections made by social systems which give meaning to the external environment. Luhmann's theoretical scheme relies upon the assumption that these selections are contingent. In other words, when a system attributes meaning, it could have selected some other meaning and these other meanings still remain as possible interpretations, despite the fact that they have not been selected. Contingency is thus the starting point for all those problems of co-ordination and transmission of what Luhmann calls the system's *selectivity*.

A social system's selectivity refers to the process by which the external environment is reduced to communicative events amenable to the system's internal operations through the negation of other possible meanings. The important issue for Luhmann's theory is not the fact that those meanings which were not selected may have been more effective in predicting outcomes, but that they still exist. In their selectivity, social systems, therefore, necessarily involve the risk of disappointed expectations, of other possibilities occurring that were not predictable from the system's limited selectivity. Yet, this risk is unavoidable as the system cannot do otherwise than to access reality using its own specific coding. In the observation of one social system by another these issues of possibility and necessity which characterize the nature of contingency take on their specifically social form of *double contingency*.

Double contingency

The concept which has its origins in the social theory of Talcott Parsons[21] describes the way in which contingency manifests itself in the social field. Where two social systems encounter one another, each selection of system A depends not only upon its own selectivity (that is, its selection of meanings from those available to it), but also upon the selectivity of the other system, B. The problem is that the only way that system A can observe (or 'understand') system B is through its own (A's) selectivity. The same is true for B's observation of A. Each system therefore constructs its relationship to the other from meaning that is available exclusively to itself. For each of them the other is 'a black box', not only in so far as the other's criteria for selection cannot be observed, but also because any attempt by B to protest against or to correct A's constructions makes sense to A only in so far as A treats them as part of its constructions. There is no alarm-clock which is able to drag you up and out of your constructions – at least no alarm-clock which you would be able to hear. Restricted by its own selectivity, A can only see the inputs and outputs of the other system and not the self-referential observation taking place within that system. In other words, all that is visible for one system (A) is the way that the other system appears to deal with the external environment. What is invisible to A is the selectivity of the other system (B). It has no way of seeing the way that B interprets the external environment (including A itself) except by the use of its (A's) own selectivity.

As we have seen, whatever selections are made by one social system, other possibilities existed and were negated by the system (the concept of *contingency*). The same thing is true of any other system (social or psychic) which the system observes and this gives rise to the phenomenon of *double contingency*. In order to cope with double contingency, each system observes the other as a system-in-an-environment, without being able to observe the internal operations of the other system or that system's selectivity, without 'understanding' its way of 'understanding' external reality. Since neither is able to 'get inside the head' of the other, this means that A's selections from its range of possible meanings are dependent upon B's selection from its range of possible meanings and vice versa. The result is that feeling of uncertainty well known to everyone as the reason why so many communications are never realized, why the probable does not become reality. The development of functionally differentiated social systems, each with its own increasingly complex ways of interpreting the external environment, has arisen, according to Luhmann, in direct response to the problem of double contingency. These systems operate in ways which attempt to govern uncertainty and risk, notwithstanding the indeterminacy of the selections of different systems and their interdependence on each other's selections. This accounts both for the autopoietic nature of social systems and for their tendency towards increasing complexity in the face of uncertainty. The way that systems deal with uncertainty is by creating from their communications structures which make uncertainty appear certain or, at least, more certain. In becoming part of the environment that A constructs, B's selections become reduced to those available to A. B's meanings become '*B's meanings within system A*'. This enables A to avoid uncertainty and to cope with the problem of disappointed expectations arising from B's behaviour by constructing everything that B does in terms of meanings provided by A. Only by communicating about its own communications is system A able to offer the semblance of certainty and provide some rational explanations for disappointed expectations.

THE LEGAL SYSTEM

Towards the end of his book, *Public Law and Political Theory*,[22] Martin Loughlin offers his readers an account of Luhmann's approach to law drawn from Luhmann's book, *A Sociological Theory of Law*.[23] Loughlin offers this account as an attempt to open the way to a new approach to thinking about public law, distinguishing the legal from the political. In order to illustrate how, according to Luhmann, there are two ways of dealing with disappointed expectations, Loughlin gives the following example:

> If . . . I habitually bump into lamp-posts, as a result of an expectation that they will move out of my way, . . . I am soon likely to learn and adjust my expectations of the behaviour of lamp-posts. If, on the other hand, I expect officials to treat citizens with equal respect regardless of the colour of their skin, I am unlikely to adjust my expectation even if I regularly encounter officials who act contrary to it.[24]

The example conveys well part, and only part, of Luhmann's distinction between cognitive and normative learning – that of learning from experience. I am indeed likely to 'learn' from bumping into lamp-posts. After a specific number of bumps, dependent upon such personal attributes as my indifference to pain and my obstinacy, I am likely to learn from my experience or, at any rate, more likely than the lamp-post is to learn from me. One does not need autopoietic theory to confirm this.

A more serious limitation in Loughlin's account lies in the overly limited use he makes of the lamp-post experience. He misses the opportunity of contrasting how encounters with lamp-posts may result in normative 'not learning' as well as cognitive 'learning'. He could, for example, have pointed out that, while in the light of my experience I would *not* be likely to stick to my expectation that lamp-posts will get out of my way, I could well do so if others' expectations concerning lamp-posts were not met. Take, for instance, my expectation that lamp-posts should provide light. Even if several lamp-posts disappoint my expectation, I would be unlikely to change that expectation. I would even believe myself entitled to complain to the appropriate highway authority that my expectation had not been met. In the first case I would deal with my disappointment in a cognitive or 'learning' manner, while in the second, in a 'non-learning', that is, a normative manner.

The second problem arises from Loughlin's counter-example of racist officials. This is symptomatic of a certain lack of clarity which not uncommon in recent discussions by legal scholars of autopoietic theory's explanation of the difference law makes to society. In numerous accounts the important issue of law's influence on personal commitment (or individual morality) takes precedence over attempts to explain the way in which the legal system operates at the social level. This leads to confusion between ethical commitment and normativity. Normativity is an attribute of *communications*. Ethical duties or commitments are linked to *people*. Antigone's determination to bury her dead brother despite Creon's law is not related to communications that have taken place or to disappointed expectations, but to what she regards as her duty to her brother, to herself, and to the gods. A more correct way to present Luhmann's distinction between cognitive and normative ways of dealing with disappointed expectations would be to imagine two comparable situations concerning a legal official. In those countries where racial discrimination by officials is illegal, one could then offer the following example of the difference between normative (non-learning) and cognitive (learning) ways of dealing with disappointments. As a plaintiff to legal proceedings, I am likely to drop my case if a judge refuses to accept my writ on the ground that it has been issued out of time. I am not, however, likely to give up my claim if the judge turns it down for reasons concerning the colour of my skin.

This brings us to the third flaw in Loughlin's example, the difference between psychic and social systems. Unlike social systems, psychic systems are able through their internal operations to evaluate events on the basis of sense, probability, moral rectitude, illegality, 'political correctness', aesthetic value, and so on, an asset which is entirely absent from social systems. The horizon of meaning for a psychic system is determined only by its consciousness. Loughlin's 'I' is a conscious system. It is quite able to maintain for himself a belief in the immorality of racist officials and a commitment not to tolerate such behaviour. This commitment, as we have seen, is ethical; it is not contingent upon the question as to whether or not the racism of the official is illegal or conforms to the law. These questions of commitment occurring at the level of consciousness and psychic systems are indeed, as Loughlin, quoting from Luhmann, points out, 'institutionalized' and 'enforced by a degree of consensus'.[25] They are open to resolution by what is regarded as acceptable behaviour and what is not in a particular context. As we have seen, Antigone stands firm against the 'institutionalized consensus' expressed through Creon's commandment. But at the level of society, of social systems, communications, on the level of what is communicable in society (and what is not), there is no way for one social system, such as law, to proceed other than through its own selectivity. In other words, racism is an ethical issue; it becomes a normative issue when law declares racism to be illegal. Having failed initially to make unambiguous this distinction between psychic and social, it is little wonder that the only way that Loughlin can deal with the resulting problem of double contingency between subsystems is to avoid it altogether.

Loughlin's brief excursion into Luhmann's world does, however, emphasize clearly that what makes *law* functional for society, is *specifically* related to the problem of managing disappointed expectations, of 'living with disappointment'. According to Luhmann, ethical and sociological traditions have in the past attempted to solve the problem of explaining how societies cope with disappointment by evoking universal norms and values which arise either from the nature of human relations or from some consensus or from some 'tautological circumscription'. These are the traditions that Loughlin follows, mistakenly believing that he is providing an account of Luhmann's approach. In contrast to these traditions, however, Luhmann's explanation is sociological, relying on the notion of double contingency which typifies relations between social systems:

> [I]f we relate the function of oughtness to the problem of surprise and disappointment inherent in double contingency we can work out a functional definition. There are two (and only two) possible ways to react to disappointments: by learning and adapting expectations and by maintaining expectations contrary to fact. The decision as to the way to settle the issue may be made in advance and then [it] colors the expectation.[26]

In Luhmann's scheme, the function of the legal system is not, however, that of universal moral entrepreneur cleverly converting consensually-based beliefs into norms for individuals, who otherwise would rely upon learning from experience. Some people, as psychic systems, may wish to treat law in this way, but law as a social system operates quite independently of their behaviour. It makes available to society a selective version of the world produced by its lawful/unlawful, legal/illegal coding.[27] Of course, the expectations generated by law itself may not be met. Officials may well behave in an unlawful way but this does not affect law's internal operations, because, according to these operations, they will be lawfully sanctioned for such behaviour. Law and not the individual is able normatively to maintain its expectations, even where they are counterfactual.

Within the legal system's selected environment, events in the external environment are explicable in legal terms and only in legal terms. Law itself determines from a range of possible options, laid down by its own limited vision of the world, the features of the particular situation that it recognizes and, among those features, which of these are relevant to the legal issue. What does it mean to say that law does not learn from experience? It means that for law, illegal acts do not become legal *because they are committed.* Theft from cars, smoking marijuana, or racial discrimination are interpreted by law as illegal acts despite the factual evidence that a large number of people engage in them. Their widespread commission is not sufficient to convince the legal system that they are now lawful or that their existence can now be accepted as an object for cognitive expectations or learning by experience, no longer subject to law's coding. Obstinately disregarding the evidence of experience, law continues to maintain their illegality. It is in this sense, therefore, that law's social function is to avoid the necessity of learning from experience, from disappointed expectations.

If we go back to Loughlin's 'I', the *psychic* observer, we can place law in its social context by comparing its selectivity with those generated by other systems, which are not in general free from the constraint of 'learning from experience'. I may choose to interpret the official's behaviour in other than legal terms, preferring other meanings to those produced by law. If I select an economic interpretation, I might well observe the official's behaviour as being motivated by the profit he makes from discriminating against black people. Perhaps, for example, black people appear to be in a less favourable position than white to engage with the official in an exchange of favours which will benefit the official. Alternatively, I may choose to interpret the official's actions in political terms – he could be trying to curry favour with those who have power to dismiss or promote him. If we take the expectations produced by these other (non-legal) functional subsystems, it is clear that these expectations *are* subject to learning from experience. Economic and political expectations may well need to be changed if, for example, the official is known to have rejected bribes from white people or if it transpires that his superiors have in the past sacked other officials for discriminating against black people. While always existing as political and economic 'facts', this same behaviour, considered within the legal system, results in the disappointment of legal expectations which in turn can be expected to result in legal sanctions. What the legal system is able to guarantee is that the racist official's behaviour, being illegal, remains illegal.

CLOSURE AND UNITY: THE AUTOPOIESIS AND IDENTITY OF LAW

The apparent paradox whereby social systems are described as being open to external information (*cognitive openness*) but closed in their operations (*normative closure*) is the inevitable outcome of each system's autopoietic nature, its unity. What is meant here by the unity of a system? As we have already explained in the section on 'Social Systems', each system extracts information from the environment through the process of selection. It is able to operate on that information only as communications, which are exclusive to itself. The system's communications both constitute itself, defining its role, boundaries, relations with the environment and other systems, and so on, and represent the environment in terms of its own selection or coding. Taking law again as our example, the legal system exists only through its communications. Law's communications both constitute the law and present the environment in legal terms. This is by no means a sterile or unproductive process. What it means, however, is that the legal system is able only to communicate in legal terms and that the environment that it constructs within the operations of the legal system is likely to consist increasingly of legal complexity, of legal communications about communications, and of legal communications about legal communications:

> The practice of jurisprudence calls for knowledge of the world. But within this sphere of relevance there exists the core of legally valid action which changes the legal position, engenders legal consequences, and thereby makes possible new normative expectations which would not have acquired a legal quality without this action of engendering. The legal system itself determines what kind of events have this effect. It is impossible to identify these events without a knowledge of the legal system.[28]

As Luhmann puts it succinctly, '[O]nly the legal system can bestow legally normative quality on its elements and thereby constitute them as elements'.[29]

As a direct result of functional differentiation, the communications of one social system are exclusive to that system. Try, for instance, solving legal problems using unmodified economic principles, medical treatment, political axioms, conflicts or religious dogmas and it becomes clear how important functional differentiation has become for modern societies, where no universal or pervading reference such as the god of the middle ages or the sovereign of early modernity exists.[30]

It is both functionally and operationally impossible for law to communicate in political, economic, religious or medical terms, because, as we have seen, it is bound to constructs its external environment according its binary code of lawful/unlawful. But each system also creates and develops its own unique internal complexity. This consists of structures which allow it to 'understand' the complexity of the external environment, by reducing that environment to its own terms. Within the legal system, for example, specialized courts, procedures, and conceptual devices are continually being developed to enable law to deal with new problems emerging from the increasingly complex ways in which modern society defines itself and its operations. Since no system can go beyond the boundaries set by its binary code, the internal complexity of the system must necessarily be limited by its selectivity – in the case of law, its coding of lawful/unlawful (legal/illegal).

Among critical lawyers this notion of *normative closure* is probably the best known and the most misrepresented and misunderstood of all Luhmann's theoretical concepts. In fact the legal system is no more 'closed' in the sense of keeping something out than the ear is closed to noise or the eyes closed to sights. The concept of 'closure' is an attempt to express the fundamental fact, which is difficult to articulate and, therefore, frequently ignored, that social systems, like ears and eyes, cameras, tape-recorders, and many other items, are *characterized* by the fact that they do only what they do and nothing else.[31] Closure, for Luhmann, is nothing more or less than a necessary consequence of functional differentiation. This means, first, as we have already indicated, that the business of one social system cannot be undertaken by another. Secondly, closure exists because that is the way that, in the communicative universe, modern societies and the relationship between society and social systems have evolved. It does not, therefore, refer to some specific defect of law – its blindness or its failure to keep up-to-date – or to some deliberate policy on the part of the courts, for example, to maintain the status quo regardless of the consequences for individuals or for society. The implications of this evolutionary process are that the state of functional differentiation in modern societies cannot be replaced by measures that might have brought about such changes at other moments in history, whether a decree, order, Act of Parliament, general election or papal pronouncement, and so on. Today, there is no longer any overriding power able to enforce such measures. It can be changed only through further evolution in the phenomenal constitution of society, through events at the interface of subsystems.

Thirdly, closure implies that information from the environment is available to the system only through the communicative process or synthesis of information, utterance, and understanding.[32] Although each system must depend for its continued existence upon information obtained from the external environment (law, for example, depends upon a constant stream of social dilemmas and conflicts which society expects it to solve and resolve), '[I]nformation is not something that the system takes in from the environment. Information does not exist "out there" waiting to be picked up by the system.'[33] Social systems are, therefore, cognitively open (that is, open to information), but operationally closed (the information cannot be imported directly into the system). In Luhmann's words, autopoietic closure:

> does not mean isolation; *nor even that internal causes are more important than external ones.* Such evaluations are left to observations of the system' ... The thesis of operative closure merely says that for any system only what is accessible for its own operations is accessible ...[34]

Much of the concern in the legal literature concerning Luhmann's concept of closure is entirely misplaced. Critical lawyers usually mistake the idea of law as a closed system as being formalist and legal positivist, with the legal system (meaning the courts, judiciary, lawyers, and so on) being presented as existing in a world of their own, where they are at liberty to make laws, decide cases, and develop a network of rules and principles free from any political influence or economic or social 'realities'. This is clearly not what Luhmann is saying, although it may well be that this is the image that the legal system projects of its own operations. In Luhmann's scheme, law is not only open to influence from outside; its very existence and continuing evolution and the schematic evolution of society depends upon such influence. However, direct influence in the input-output terms of power relations between systems is not possible. Any external perturbation in the system's environment is 'recognized' and constituted only in terms of the system's selectivity and must necessarily be subjected to the system's limited capacity for operating. This means that political attempts to use law to achieve its own policy objectives may often backfire or produce unintended outcomes. The same is true of law's claims to be able to regulate the operations of other autopoietically closed systems.

Autopoiesis refers to the way in which systems in their operations are able to use only those concepts derived from their own communicative structures and the fact that they alone may engage in communications of this functional variety:

> Only the law can say what is lawful and unlawful and in deciding this question it must refer to the results of its own operations and the consequences for the system's future operations.

But the term, 'autopoiesis' relates also to the self-identity (*Identität*) of the system. Each system constructs from its own structures an image of society, of itself and of its place and role in society, including the limits and extent of its own operations. Hence, law presents itself not merely with a self-image which defines its own role within society, and the limits of its own operations (what should and what should not be subjected to law's operations) but also with the role of deciding issues of legality for society. In constructing their self-image systems may ' "identify" themselves with a simplified image of themselves'.[35] It is not surprising, therefore, to find English judges going out of their way to communicate that their decision-making activities are quite distinct from those of politicians or administrators. As Jeffrey Jowell reports, in an article on administrative law in Britain:

> Today's commentators and judges go to extraordinary lengths to demonstrate that the judiciary does not in practice interfere with the executive task of governing. It is said, therefore, that administrative law deals only with process and not substance.[36]

Furthermore, particularly in those communications destined for external consumption, law may offer heroic versions of itself. James Boyd White in his book, *Justice as Translation*,[37] for example, describes the favourable and self-enhancing way in which judges present themselves and their social role in their judgements.

In constructing its self-identity, law is unable to use communications other than those derived from its own structures, that is, structures derived from the coding lawful/unlawful. One cannot, therefore, expect legal communications to ascribe political motives to judicial decisions or to be concerned about the cost of legal operations.[38] Other observing systems, such as politics and economics, will, of course, be able to analyse the legal system from the point of view of its unequal distribution of power or its cost-effectiveness. These observing system will also, however, be restricted by their own autopoietic nature both as to what they select as relevant to their analysis and the way that the analysis is conducted.

PARADOXES IN SCIENCE AND LAW

A paradox exists whenever a proposition appears to entail its own negation. 'This statement is false' is, for example, clearly paradoxical. In Luhmann's scheme, paradoxes occur for systems during their observation of themselves and the environment. Luhmann sees systems as constituted in a paradoxical manner. They may construct their own identity as a system only by distinguishing themselves from their environment, but the environment may only be distinguished from the system by means of that system's internal operations. This means that the act of *denying (Negation)* that it is part of the environment can only be achieved through the system's own operations. This situation is paradoxical because the system is bound to distinguish itself from an environment that does not belong to it, observing at the same time that such an environment is nothing other than a product of its own operations.[39]

This paradox of self-observation becomes particularly problematic for contemporary society when it occurs in functional systems. Take, for example, science, which, since modernity, has tended to assume the function of determining 'truth' for society. The code, which governs its internal operations and by which science constructs the external environment, is that of 'true/false' or 'true/not true. Science, therefore, distinguishes itself from its environment by the specificity and uniqueness of its identity, yet since any communication is subjected by science to science's coding (or selectivity), how can science be sure that its claim to be capable of distinguishing truth from falsehood is in fact 'true'? The claim rests entirely on science's construction of an environment in which it itself appears as capable of making such judgments of truth and falsehood.

The legal system, which claims to operate on the basis of just/unjust, in a similar manner finds itself confronting a paradoxical situation in which law poses the problem of its own justice or, at least, applies that distinction to its own observations of external reality.[40] Law's functional identity based on its ability to 'do justice' is itself subject to the legal system's coding of legal/illegal, lawful/unlawful. Justice may, therefore, be either lawful or unlawful with the resultant paradoxes of 'lawfully unjust' or 'unlawfully just.' Within the environment constructed by law, the paradox of justice/injustice is resolvable only by transforming it into the distinction, lawful/unlawful – distinction that may be made by law, and law alone.[41]

Paradoxes represent a problem for the observer *but not necessarily for the system which operates on the bases of them*. The fact that science, for example, operates in a paradoxical mode appears problematic only to the observer of the system. The operations of a system proceed blindly in so far as it is unable to look at itself 'as if from outside itself'.[42] To observe an operation you need, in fact, a separate, second operation, one that can see the paradoxical constitution of the first and, as Luhmann observes, you cannot do both at the same time. But your observer, who is able to observe what you are doing is subject to the same restrictions as you in observing himself or herself. He or she in turn proceeds in a blind manner. One might say that each system's selectivity, or binary distinction creates a blind spot which prevents it from seeing the paradoxes within its own operations.

If law, in observing its own operations, would observe current operations of conflict resolution notions of justice which were not based on its lawful/unlawful distinction, society would be completely different from what it is. The present level of differentiation which it has achieved would collapse. In order to maintain its distinctive identity the legal system is, as Luhmann points out, in constant need of 'deparadoxification', that is, of ongoing repairs to the constant appearance of just/unjust paradoxes which occur when law is observed by other systems and the results of the observations are observed by the legal system and translated into legal terms. These observations are transformed within law's environment into distinctions and, far from inhibiting law's internal operations, this process of deparadoxification, the substitution of distinctions, is a particularly rich source of creativity, obliging law to find ever more inventive ways of masking the appearance of paradoxes. Yet it does this without ever finding a 'natural' or transhistorically adequate position.[43] To take a topical example, the externally observed injustice of wrongful criminal convictions gives rise to the paradox of lawful, but unjust, to which law's operations are blind, being able only to apply the coding lawful/unlawful. In order to deparadoxify the paradox, law must transform it in ways which make it amenable to a distinction based on lawfulness/unlawfulness. It is not surprising, therefore, to find the Court of Appeal inventing new ways to overturn its previous decisions in order to convert injustice into unlawfulness making what was previously lawful, but unjust, appear unlawful and giving its present decision the appearance of both lawfulness and justice.

It should not be imagined that law is unique in its capacity for creative deparadoxification. To a greater or lesser degree, it occurs in all functionally differentiated systems. For science, for example,the paradox created by the functional identity of producing true/false communications is transformed into the binary distinction, scientifically proved/scientifically unproved, or into attempts, such as Karl Popper's, to distinguish what is 'scientific' from what is 'unscientific' or as yet lacking the conditions for recognition of scientific truth. Through this device, science is able to maintain its functionally differentiated identity, creating within its own internal operations a distinction which avoids the paradox of simultaneous truth and falsehood.

TIME, COMPLEXITY, AND EVOLUTION

In Luhmann's scheme time, and not causality, is the key to the evolution of social systems and the relationships between them. The only certainty is that in modern societies evolution is generally in the direction of increasing complexity. This has been made possible through the change in the organization of society from hierarchical stratification to functional stratification. The differentiation of systems on the basis of functionality in modern societies allows for ever-increasing complex differentiations to be made and these system differentiations provoke in turn increasing structural complexity within social systems, which enables each system to reduce the external environment to terms that can be 'understood' through its own selectivity. Yet, even the move towards increasing complexity is not necessarily irreversible.

Social systems become linked to one another, not through deliberate or even unconscious motives to influence or dominate one another (for, as we have seen , social systems unlike conscious beings are unable to 'think' in this way) but, rather, they relate through temporal association and through the disposition of each system to differentiate itself from the environment and so preserve its distinct identity.

Time, past, present, and future are all essential elements in Luhmann's account of the evolution of systems and society. Luhmann in his analysis of time goes far beyond the obvious point made by G.H. Mead and other phenomenologist writers that communication defines time for the actors.[44] What he proposes is that social systems construct concepts of time for society and for their own operations. They then exist within the temporal constraints that they themselves have constructed. One example is religion, which in Jewish, Christian, and Islamic notions of the creation and the last judgement not only provided society with the framework with which to conceptualize the past, present, and future, but also created the sense of continuity between these. In general, social systems, through their communications, construct for themselves a past which can only be known in terms of the present and an unknown future exists on the assumption of the continuation of the present. The phenomenon of risk, for instance, is analysed according to the distinction, present future/future present. 'Present future' equals the content of on-going expectations and predictions while by 'future present' Luhmann refers to the ex-post-analysis, the analysis that will be possible only *then*.[45]

ELEMENTS IN AN EVALUATION OF LUHMANN

When the expectations of social theories founded upon ideological beliefs concerning 'society' or implicit models of 'human nature' suffer the disappointment of failed predictions, the tendency is for the theories to go out of fashion. Other theories, equally ideological or dependent upon notions of human nature, take their place as the widely accepted mediators of social knowledge, only to be replaced in time often by the old, discarded theories returning modified or in a new guise. Whatever the theoretical ambitions of Luhmann's theoretical scheme, it turns its back on those practical ambitions expressed through predictions. Instead he analyses current predictions, asking the question: what *at present* is known about our prediction making, our prediction believing?

This is not, of course, to suggest that Luhmann's theory is itself value-free in its attempts to evaluate society's operations and beliefs. It is quite legitimate for political theorists, for example, to observe Luhmann's ideas as political ideology and to criticize it as such. Luhmann, is reported to have described himself, tongue in cheek, as a 'bourgeois Marxist'! In Germany, it has been Habermas and representatives of the Frankfurt critical school of law who have sought to label Luhmann's ideas as conservative. This, as we have seen, is not entirely untrue, but perhaps it is true in a different way from that claimed by his critics. Luhmann is indeed guilty of a kind of conservatism, but his conservatism takes the form of a belief in the importance of functional differentiation in modern societies and a belief in the dangers of what he calls '*dedifferentiation*'. This occurs when systems no longer differentiate themselves from the environment on the basis of their selectivity. Politics, for example, may construct law as a system capable of answering economic, or child welfare questions, not on the basis of lawfulness/ unlawfulness, but according to some notions of economics, science or health reconstituted as legal issues. This damages system identity through what Teubner refers to as a 'loss of epistemic authority'.[46] In law, it is likely to lead to confusion and to undermine the legal system's social function of 'avoiding the necessity of learning from experience'. Similar confusion and loss of functionality may occur when other systems are observed as reconstructing notions of lawfulness/unlawfulness as the basis of their own communications.[47] This is not, one need hardly add, a proscription against social change as such, but it does lay down boundaries, albeit of a general nature, for the performance of social systems by pointing out the risks involved when one system constructs others in a way which threatens their selectivity.

To mount a criticism of Luhmann's theoretical scheme is a difficult enterprise, much like the problem that philosophers have in criticizing Hegel. You may chose to reduce it to a mere caricature. If, however, you want to tackle it at the level of social theory and not at that of moral philosophy or political ideology, you will need to proceed rather differently. Danilo Zolo,[48] for example, does criticize the theory at this level, arguing that a general theory of social systems which presupposes self-referential systems means that it is necessary to give up any idea of non-circular theoretical constructions and with it the very notion of progress through 'normal science.' Luhmann has responded by denying that this is the case, stating that 'the general theory of social systems limits itself to convert usual *premises* of scientific research into functions'.[49] Within the functional system of science, those scientific tools and procedures associated with normal science have every right to exist.

From the point of view of a positivist social scientist who wishes above all to get out into the social world and test hypotheses, Luhmann's theory presents, therefore, a quite hopeless case, the only cure for which amounts to forgetting that it ever existed. For them, there is no way of knowing within the canon of positive science whether Luhmann is right or not. It would be a pity, however, for those socio-legal scholars who have committed themselves to mapping out, through the methods of empirical sociology, the operations of the law and its effects in society, to dismiss Luhmann's scheme as having no relevance to their work. Of course, they might well ask the question: how fruitful are these abstractions which attempt to make sense of the whole of the phenomenal world by imposing upon it to concepts of 'system', 'communication', 'double contingency', 'functionality', 'self-reference', and so on? Luhmann's answer is that in a world where many different theories compete to explain the natural processes of knowledge, 'physicalist (materialist) . . . biological and sociological', 'the theoretical goal will surely not be attained by means of new interpretations of the classics of sociology or the clarification of single concepts'. What is needed is some general theory that 'claims to be valid for all social phenomena'.[50] But this answer can be questioned in turn.

Luhmann's theory of autopoiesis may be seen primarily as a theory about theories, a theoretical schema which describes and analyses the relationships between the many and varied attempts to make sense of the world and the functions of these 'systems' for modern society. Its application to particular sociological research projects must, therefore, be seen in terms of general orientations rather than detailed research processes or methodologies. The theory cannot be reduced to a shopping list and anyone who wishes to make use of Luhmann's ideas, whether in empirical projects or in relating them to socio-legal issues should first make themselves familiar with the theoretical orientation set out in the selected list of his texts which follows.

A SELECTION OF LUHMANN'S WORKS IN ENGLISH

'The Future Cannot Begin: Temporal Structures in Modern Society' (1976) 43 *Social Research* 130–52.

'Generalised Media and the Problem of Contingency' in *Explorations in General Theory in Social Sciences: Essays in Honour of Talcott Parsons*, eds. J. Loubser, A. Effrat, and V. Lidz (1976) 507–32.

'Differentiation of Society' (1977) 2 *Canadian J. of Sociology* 29–54.

The Differentiation of Society (1982).

'The World Society as a Social System' (1982) 8 *International J. General Systems* 131–8.

'The Self-Description of Society: Crisis, Fashion and Sociological Theory' (1984) 25 *International. J. of Comparative Sociology* 59–92.

Trust and Power (1984).

'The Autopoiesis of Social Systems' in *Sociocybernetic Paradoxes: Observation, Control and Evolution of Self-Steering Systems*, eds. F. Geyer and J. van der Zouwen (1986) 171–92.

'The Individuality of the Individual: Historical Meanings and Contemporary Problems' in *Restructuring Individualism: Autonomy, Individuality and the Self in Western Thought*, eds. T. Heller et al. (1986) 313–25.

'Society, Meaning, Religion – Based on Self-Reference' (1986) 46 *Sociological Analysis* 5–20.

Love as Passion. The Codification of Intimacy (1986).

'The Theory of Social Systems and its Epistemology: Reply to Danilo Zolo's Critical Comments' (1986) 16 *Philosophy of the Social Sciences* 112–31.

'The Representation of Society within Society' (1987) 35 *Current Sociology* 101–8.

'Closure and Openness: On Reality in the World of Law' in *Autopoietic Law. A New Approach to Law and Society*, ed. G. Teubner (1988) 335–48.

'The Sociological Observation of the Theory and Practice of Law' in *European Yearbook of the Sociology of Law*, ed. A. Febbrajo (1988).

'The Third Question: The Creative Use of Paradox in Law and Legal History' (1988) 15 *J. of Law and Society* 153–65.

'The Unity of the Legal System' in *Autopoietic Law: A New Approach to Law and Society*, ed. G. Teubner (1988) 12–35.

'The Cognitive Program of Constructivism and a Reality that Remains Unknown' in *Self-Organization, Portrait of a Scientific Revolution. Sociology of the Sciences Yearbook*, eds. W. Krohn et al. (1990) 64–85.

Essays on Self Reference (1990).

Political Theory in the Welfare State (1990).

'Operational Closure and Structural Coupling: The Differentiation of the Legal System' (1992) 13 *Cardozo Law Rev.* 1419–41.

Risk: A Sociological Theory (1993).

NOTES AND REFERENCES

1 (1982) 8 *International J. General Systems* 137.

2 C. Baraldi et al., *Glossario dei Termini della Teoria dei sistemi di Niklas Luhmann* (1990). p. 5.

3 Stefan Rossbach writes:

> 'It is the first theory that problematizes the notion of problem, that reduces the scope of possible or empirically given (posed) problems to specific systems possibilities, to what can be done about it, and what can be done is nothing else than what can be reduced. ('Beyond Undecidability', unpublished paper presented at the European University Institute, Florence, March 1992.)

4 G. Spencer Brown, *Laws of Form* (1971).

5 N. Luhmann, 'The Individuality of the Individual: Historical Meanings and Contemporary Problems' in *Restructuring Individualism: Autonomy, Individuality and the Self in Western Thought*, eds. T. Heller, M. Sosna, and D.E.Wellbery (1986) at 318.

6 id., p. 323.

7 Spencer Brown, op.cit., n. 4.

8 N. Luhmann, 'The Cognitive Program of Constructivism and a Reality that Remains Unknown' in *Self-Organization, Portrait of a Scientific Revolution. Sociology of the Sciences Yearbook*, eds. W. Krohn et al. (1990) 64–85 at 64 (emphasis added).

9 See Luhmann's discussion of Lévi-Strauss's *Mythologiques* (1964,1966,1968,1972) in N. Luhmann, *Soziale Systeme* (1984) at 377–489.

10 See, for example, A.N. Chomsky, *Syntactic Structures* (1957) and *Language and Mind* (1968).

11 N. Luhmann, *Essays on Self Reference* (1990).

12 N. Luhmann, 'The Self-Description of Society: Crisis, Fashion and Sociological Theory' (1984) 25 *International. J. of Comparative Sociology* 59–92 (emphasis added).

13 N. Luhmann, 'Operational Closure and Structural Coupling' (1992) 13 *Cardozo Law Rev.* 1419.

14 This is the way that Peter Beyer describes 'the immanent', but it applies equally to Luhmann's concept of society. See P. Beyer, *Religion and Globalization* (1994) 5.

15 The environment for society consists of an infinite list of elements including people, fauna, flora, the atmosphere, climate, and geological features.

16 This does not mean that segmentary and stratificatory differentiation, which characterized the way in which meaning in pre-modern societies, were organized play no part at all in modern societies (Luhmann, op. cit., n. 1, p. 135). Economic systems may still rely, for example, upon stratification 'to order the relations of persons . . . to the production process' (P. Beyer, 'Introduction' to N. Luhmann, *Religious Dogmatics and the Evolution of Societies* (1984) xxii) while segmentation may still operate in political and religious systems.

17 E. Durkheim, *The Division of Labour in Society*, trans. W.D. Halls (1984).

18 See the confusions arising through the use of the term 'consent' in law and in mediation described in M. King and C. Piper, *How the Law Thinks about Children* (1990) ch. 5.

19 R. Lempert, 'The Autonomy of Law: Two Visions Compared'; D. Nelken, 'Changing Paradigms in the Sociology of Law', both in *Autopoietic Law: A New Approach to Law and Society*, ed. G. Teubner (1988).

20 Baraldi, op. cit., n. 2.

21 T. Parsons, *The Structure of Social Action* (1937); *The Social System* (1952); *Structure and Process in Modern Societies* (1960); *The System of Modern Societies* (1971).

22 M. Loughlin, *Public Law and Political Theory* (1992).

23 N. Luhmann, *A Sociological Theory of Law* (2nd ed., 1985) trans. by E. King and M. Albrow.

24 Loughlin, op. cit., n. 22, p. 251.

25 id.

26 N. Luhmann, 'Generalised Media and the Problem of Contingency' in *Explorations in General Theory in Social Sciences: Essays in Honour of Talcott Parsons*, ed. J. Loubser et al. (1976) 507–32 at 509.

27 The coding or programming of the environment selects both what may be considered as a legal question (pertaining to law/not pertaining to law) and also which side of the distinction lawful/unlawful should be applied to an event.

28 N. Luhmann, 'The Unity of the Legal System ' in Teubner, op. cit., n. 19, pp. 12–35 at p. 17.

29 id., p. 20.

30 N. Luhmann, *Political Theory in the Welfare State* (1990) at 236.

31 See M. King, 'The "Truth" about Autopoiesis' (1993) 20 *J. of Law and Society* 1–19; R. Lempert in Teubner, op. cit., n. 19.

32 Luhmann, op. cit., n. 11, at pp. 3–4.
33 id.
34 N. Luhmann, 'Closure and Openness: On the Reality in the World of Law' in Teubner, op. cit., n. 19, pp. 335–48 at p. 336 and 339 (emphasis added).
35 Luhmann, op. cit., n. 1, pp. 131–8 at p. 135.
36 J. Jowell, 'Courts and Administration in Britain: Standards, Principles and Rights' (1988) *Israel Law. Rev.* 409 at 415.
37 J. Boyd White, *Justice as Translation* (1990) ch. 4.
38 When critical legal academics analyse law in terms of the power structures underlying legal judgments, therefore, they are producing political, not legal communications. Similarly, judges or lawyers or legal administrators concerned that cases should be settled so as to avoid costs are producing economic, and not legal, communications.
39 Baraldi, op. cit., n. 2.
40 N. Luhmann, 'The Third Question: The Creative Use of Paradox in Law and Legal History' (1988) 15 *J. of Law and Society* 153-65.
41 id., p. 160.
42 Baraldi, op. cit., n. 2.
43 Luhmann, op. cit., n. 40. See, also, N. Luhmann, 'The Sociological Observations of the Theory and Practice of Law' in the *European Yearbook of the Sociology of Law* (1988).
44 N. Luhmann, 'The Future Cannot Begin: Temporal Structures in Modern Society' (1976) 43 *Social Research* 130–52 at 146.
45 N. Luhmann, *Religious Dogmatics and the Evolution of Societies* (1984). See, also, M. King, *Muslim Families in Europe: A new Identity for Islam* EUI Working Paper ECO (1993).
46 G. Teubner, 'How the Law Thinks: Toward a Constructivist Epistemology of Law' (1989) 23 *Law and Society Rev.* 727–57.
47 M. King, 'Law's Healing of Children's Hearings. The Paradox Moves North' (1994) *J. of Social Policy* (forthcoming).
48 D. Zolo, 'The Epistemological Status of the Theory of Autopoiesis and its Application to the Social Sciences' in *State, Law, Economy as Autopoietic Systems: Regulation and Autonomy in a New Perspective*, ed. by G. Teubner and A. Febbrajo (1992).
49 N. Luhmann, 'The Theory of Social Systems and its Epistemology: Reply to Danilo Zolo's Critical Comments' (1986) 16 *Philosophy of the Social Sciences* 112–31.
50 id., at p. 132.

[15]

Economics of Gift – Positivity of Justice

The Mutual Paranoia of Jacques Derrida and Niklas Luhmann

Gunther Teubner

I. System versus *Différance*

NIKLAS LUHMANN and Jacques Derrida have made the same diagnosis of the sober world of lawyers and economists.[1] Where other people observe rational decisions based on cost/benefit calculations and on rule/fact subsumptions, their diagnosis is: madness of decision. In contrast to all analyses of rational choice, games theory and decision theory, and all promises of normative argumentation and discursive rationality, the protagonists of autopoiesis and deconstruction insist that the everyday routines of legal and economic decisions contain a component of madness, irrationality, mystery and even sacredness. The irrational is not to be viewed as a negligible remainder in a process of increasing rationalization but as the driving force of the decision. According to Luhmann:

> The mystery of the decision and the mystery of the hierarchy respectively support each other. Both exhibit an unspeakable (dare one say, religious) element, which makes them into what they are. (Luhmann, 1993c: 287)

According to Derrida law and justice work:

> . . . without calculation and without rules, without reason or without rationality . . . we can recognise in it, indeed accuse, identify a madness. And perhaps another sort of mystique. And deconstruction is mad about this kind of justice. Mad about this desire for justice. (Derrida, 1990: 52)

The deconstructive consensus held by the opponents goes even further. The irrational not only occasionally breaks into ecstatic moments of the calculation of decisions but reaches the foundations of formal rationality. Derrida and Luhmann are in agreement that arbitrariness, inconsistencies, antinomies, paradoxes and even violence, lie at the bottom of the most refined constructs in economic and legal action. However, exposing the irrational is not the end of analysis in the spirit of Carl Schmitt's (1985, 1996) decisionism but, instead, constitutes its very beginning. Both theories are not at all aimed at denouncing the detailed practices of justification and calculation in economics and law as mere ideological mystification of power constellations.[2] On the contrary, Derrida and Luhmann raise drastically the expectations of the quality of economic and legal calculations – despite their paradoxes. Exposing the irrationality of a decision does not, according to both authors, mean suspending the claims concerning social justice but, on the contrary, it means taking the normative requirements of justice even more seriously.[3]

However astonishing the convergence of autopoiesis and *différance* may be, the crucial point is not to uncover isomorphisms, analogies and selective affinities.[4] Usually, systems theorists prefer a selective incorporation technique.They decorate the facades of their autopoietic palaces with deconstructive fragments of *différance*, of *itération*, of *trace*. This is certainly attractive for theory building but ultimately leads only to an involution of the architectonics without altering the foundations. If 'wit' means the connection of remote ideas, then this decorative incorporation is as irrelevant as the rigorous confrontation of deconstruction and autopoiesis preferred by Derridists which ends only in reciprocal immunization.

By contrast, I would prefer a reading of a reciprocal paranoia in Derrida's and Luhmann's writing which exposes a dynamic of mutual persecutions between the theories. Indeed, it begins with a common analysis of foundational paradoxes in law and economy which binds the theories together. But then incompatible reality constructs come in which render the theories blind and distrustful to each other. We ought to dispense with all hope of restoring sight to the blind and trust to the distrustful. Rather, we should exploit the paranoiac dynamic itself which is, by definition, a 'form of delirium characterized by convictions which, despite being apparently similar, are in reality conflicting and are not capable of being altered either through logic or through experience, e.g. delusions of grandeur or fears of persecution' (Felice, 1987: 1432). Autopoiesis and deconstruction – what do we gain from their reciprocal fears of persecution which end in a hectic whirl of deconstructive moves and systemic counter-moves, in an ascending relation of stabilizations and destabilizations, in a dance of reciprocal plagues? This reading of paranoia becomes productive when the closed world of fictions of one theory reappears in the other's fictitious world. Thus: autopoietic systems as Jacques Derrida's nightmare, the gift of justice as Niklas Luhmann's redemption.

II. Foundational Paradoxes

First, it is amazing how radically they depart from common assumptions revoking the consensus on the foundations of legal and economic institutions. Not only courage but extravagance are necessary, if, like Derrida (1992: ch.1), one does not wish to ground a social theory of the economy on exchange and reciprocity, but instead wishes to see the foundations of economic action in the structure of the gift. The pure gift relation, according to Derrida's conceptualization, is totally asymmetrical: it means giving without gratitude. It exposes a radical non-reciprocal generosity which is destroyed if only trace elements of symmetry, reciprocity and even recognition, not to speak of the social bond of gratitude, exist. Such courage is also necessary if, like Luhmann (1988a, 1993d: 545), one refuses to conceive of law's foundation in terms of a *Grundnorm*, an ultimate rule of recognition, substantive and procedural principles of legal validity, or in terms of its socio-political legitimation, but in terms of the extreme borderline case of the pure self-referentiality of legal operations, which fall into paradoxical confusion through their self-application. It is precisely Luhmann's and Derrida's radicalism which offers a new view on the foundations of legal and economic institutions, a view which until now was seen to be based on a flaw of reasoning (Fletcher, 1985: 1279). Legal and economic institutions, Derrida and Luhmann insist, are not based on rational principles but on dangerous antinomies and paradoxes which not only destroy their legitimacy but also paralyse each operation and calculation through their self-contradictory structures.

As regards the founding paradox of law, however, despite their consensus over the initial analysis, our opponents' views are suddenly reversed into being completely incompatible with each other. Both commence with a critique of law's violence which is informed by Walter Benjamin (1977: 179–203) to the extent that the customary critiques of law which refer to ideology and power and which expose law as the expression of economic or political interests are rejected as being superficial. At a deeper level, both authors view law as caught in the paradoxes of its own self-referentiality.[5]

> Since the origin of authority, the foundation or ground, the position of the law can't by definition rest on anything but themselves, they are themselves a violence without ground. Which is not to say that they are in themselves unjust, in the sense of 'illegal'. They are neither legal nor illegal in their founding moment. (Derrida, 1990: 943)

Luhmann (1988a: 154) identifies the same phenomenon; he sees at the bottom of legal rule hierarchies 'the paradox of the binary code applied to itself'. For both authors, all attempts to ground law on legitimate normative foundations or even on a concept of justice are, in the end, useless. They are all confronted with the violence of the primordial distinction between legal and illegal which in itself cannot be revealed as legal, legitimate or just, but merely as violent arbitrariness.

The foundational paradox is the point where the bifurcation of deconstruction and autopoiesis begins. Derrida does not shy away from the precipice of law's paradox and attempts to enter the dark worlds of the paradox with a bold interpretation of the original violence of law which leads him to a mysterious distinction of various legal forces (Derrida, 1990: 1027 ff.). Reinterpreting Benjamin's famous essay on law and violence, he distinguishes between a mythical foundational violence which establishes the positivity of the state and the law only through bloodshed, and a divine foundational violence establishing a different justice which is destructive and even annihilating but which is life-supporting and without bloodshed. It is at this stage that Derrida formulates the most provocative paradox: the distinction between positivity and justice is itself indecipherable; there are no criteria which might distinguish between mythical and divine violence, not only before the decision but also after the decision. The question is merely postponed to an indeterminate future which is, in effect, a delegation to an infinite responsibility.

Luhmann detests such precipices; for him, these results of deconstructive analysis further confirm the paralysing effects of the paradox which gather strength the more one attempts to shed light on the darkness of the legal paradox. The results are merely Derridean 'verbal acoustics', obscurities of speech and the typical deconstructive gestures to shock people with dark paradoxes: 'a mixture of arbitrariness and paralysis' (Luhmann, 1990b: 134).[6] Luhmann explicitly proceeds in the opposite direction: while it is fruitless to develop a theory which only repeats the inconsistencies, the unruliness, the darkness of the legal paradox in a different language, a creative use of the paradox becomes possible once one inquires into the social techniques of de-paradoxification. De-paradoxification means to invent new distinctions which do not deny the paradox but displace it temporarily, and thus relieve it of its paralysing power. This leads Luhmann to detailed historical and sociological analyses of how, in European legal history, institutionalized distinctions between natural and positive law or, currently, distinctions between legislation and adjudication, have produced their impressive cultural achievements despite or precisely because of the legal paradox.[7]

Thus, contrary to first appearances, the foundational paradox of law is not Derrida's and Luhmann's common object of analysis but is merely their common runway which they then, however, use for a take-off in opposite directions: the autopoietic escape from and the deconstructive search for the paradoxes of law. If one then takes a closer look at the foundational paradox of the economy, the different way they treat it indicates that it is not yet sufficient to identify their difference of paradoxification and de-paradoxification as merely a difference in cognitive interests, analytical directions and conceptual apparatus. Already their formulations of the economic paradox are so different that their common starting point is barely recognizable; rather, a more fundamental difference between autopoiesis and deconstruction comes into view.

For Luhmann, the circulation of the economy is made possible at the historical moment when economic institutions circumvent successfully the paradox of scarcity, according to which the richer supply of the one is the greater need of the other, more abstractly: every access to scarce goods which serves the lessening of scarcity increases scarcity. Only by rendering this blockage invisible can the paradox be overcome and the circulation of the economy be commenced. This occurs when the effects of access to rare resources are bifurcated and effectively institutionalized as a binary code in economic action.

> For he who acts quickly, the access to scarce resources lessens. For all others, it increases . . . condensed scarcity appears then as the difference to have/not to have. (Luhmann, 1988b: 181)

Derrida determines the conditions of possibility of economic circulation from a different starting point, not from the paradoxes of access to scarce goods, but from the impossibility of the pure gift. The gift relation is the exact opposite of the exchange relation of the economy but, at the same time, provides the stimulus for the circulation of the economy. The founding paradox of the economy arises in the moment when the pure gift relation, which exists before any reference to subjectivity, constitutes the subject:

> One would even be tempted to say that a subject as such never gives or receives a gift. It is constituted, on the contrary, in view of dominating, through calculation and exchange, the mastery of this hubris or of this impossibility that is announced in the promise of the gift. (Derrida, 1992: 24)

And yet, both versions of the economic paradox coincide in the concept of property. The bifurcation of the effects of access, the coding of property as the difference between to have/not to have, and the attribution to semantic artefacts of property owners and non-property owners leads, according to Luhmann, away from the blockades of the scarcity paradox and into the dynamics of the economy. According to Derrida, the constitution of the subject as an offerer and receiver destroys the purity of the gift and renders the calculations of the economy possible through the recognition of the property of the subject.

But Derrida's interest in the circulation of the economy is not orientated to Luhmann's social techniques of de-paradoxification, to the socially constructed order of the property code, later the money code, and economic programmes. Instead he analyses how the continual production of the gift permanently interrupts economic circulation, how the irrationality of the gift does indeed transcend economic rationality. We do not therefore have two competing social theories on the economy before us which illuminate the same subject matter from different perspectives and with different cognitive interests. Rather, two opposite worlds clash whose opposites can no longer be understood only as the competition of different methods, theories or paradigms. Luhmann's ambitious attempt to construct a theory of society as the phenomenology of communication – based on a strict analogy with Edmund Husserl's phenomenology of consciousness – stands in stark contrast to Derrida's explicit refusal to develop a scientific theory. Theory, Derrida insists, would be incapable of thinking the gift. Instead, he attempts to revitalize the analogy concerning the opposites of thought and epistemology, the opposites of noumenal and phenomenal, in order to conceive of a 'transcendental illusion of the gift' which 'exceeds the limits of experience, knowledge, science, the economy and even philosophy' (Derrida, 1992: 30).

Thus, although they initially agree on the paradoxical foundation of law and economy, both schools of thought have in fact nothing to say to each other. Luhmann asks the question of how de-paradoxification techniques construct the immanence of social institutions and build a world of autopoietic social systems, their coding and programming. By contrast, Derrida's thought aims at the transcendence of social institutions through their re-paradoxification and proposes a counter-world of *différance* in which the deconstructive double movement permanently exposes the founding antinomies of social institutions as well as the paradoxical paralysis of concrete decisions in law and economy. Luhmann's world and Derrida's counter-world stand orthogonally against each other and cannot directly influence the other. It is, however, precisely their mutual closure that makes them threaten, persecute and haunt each other.

III. Derrida's Nightmare: Autopoietic Social Systems

Why can indifference, however, not prevail? Why should Niklas Luhmann stalk Jacques Derrida, following his deconstructive movements step by step? And why should systems theorists continuously be intellectually harassed by deconstructionists? While the opposing features of de-paradoxification and re-paradoxification, of empirical institutional analysis and transcendental illusion, of the immanence of social systems and their transcendence by *différance*, can render plausible the way in which they exclude each other, they do not explain how and why they haunt each other.

There is, however, a different linkage of autopoiesis and deconstruction. The linkage lies in their basic concepts, or rather in their *distinctions directrices*. Derrida's distinction between writing and speech is drawn in such a way that it is necessarily blind toward Luhmann's distinction between consciousness and communication, but is, at the same time, continuously provoked by it. On another level, precisely the opposite happens. Luhmann's autopoiesis is permanently provoked by Derrida's *différance* but is at the same time unable to conceptualize it. This mutual blindness of their *distinctions directrices* is reponsible for their perception of the social and thereby for their views on the possibility of justice.

Derrida and Luhmann start with the same question, namely, why Edmund Husserl's phenomenology of consciousness cannot do justice to social institutions. Their concern to wipe out Husserl's blind spot concerning society is shared by other contemporary theories on 'Justice towards the

Other' – Lyotard, Habermas, Levinas.[8] There is a general agreement that Husserl's attempts to integrate society into the philosophy of consciousness – the (in)famous *Monadengemeinschaft* – has failed (Husserl, 1950: 125, 137, 157). His distinction between consciousness and the outer world leaves no place for the social, and the mere phenomenal construction of the world of consciousness is the reason for the principal inadequacy of the theory with regard to social institutions. Society, let alone a multiplicity of conscious individuals, cannot be conceived adequately by Husserl's phenomenology. Since Husserl describes communication as a mere declaration of signs, meaning is produced exclusively in consciousness. This does not do justice towards the other: the other practically only conducts a phenomenological (consciousness-dependent) existence. The distinction between transcendental/empirical (ideal/psychological) serves only as a poor compensation. While it makes a universal, objective and ideal sphere of meaning beyond a single consciousness possible, it has, however, inherited all the difficulties associated with transcendentalism: it is ahistorical, a priori, unempirical, undynamic, highly abstract, 'pure', etc.

Lyotard's phenomenology of language games attempts the exact opposite which, however, is bound to repeat and thereby to mirror Husserl's problems. Here, the world is constituted by mere constructs of language games (Lyotard, 1987). Consciousness, inner discourse, introspection are thereby made taboo. Since language games are self-referentially constituted, this theory cannot deal adequately with the inner infinity of consciousness. Actors are mere pale linguistic constructs of language games. Lyotard's blind spot is to be found at precisely the same place as Husserl's; however, Husserl and Lyotard find themselves at the opposite sides of the distinction between inner/outer respectively – consciousness on the one hand and discourse on the other. Husserl's exclusion of the social is paralleled by Lyotard's exclusion of consciousness. The issue of justice is not, according to Lyotard, a problem of being fair to the originality, the infinity and depth of the other, but merely a problem in the conflictual relation between different closed discourses. The *différend* can never become a *litige.* The *différend* necessarily ends up in injustice, in the violence of one language game to another.

Now, Derrida and Luhmann both attempt to overcome the alternatives of consciousness/discourse as monopolists in the production of meaning. With the primacy of writing over speech and the polemic against the philosophy of consciousness, Derrida (1978, 1998) specifically aims at the blind spot between consciousness and speech. Writing is supplementary to this distinction; it undermines the difference between 'inner' and 'outer' processes of meaning which leave a trace. And here is the point where Derrida's *distinction directrice* interlocks with Luhmann's. In order to circumvent the sterile juxtaposition of the philosophy of consciousness and the theory of language games, Derrida deconstructs the hierarchy of speech and writing in a double way, into a tangled hierarchy and into a secret reversal of the hierarchical relation.[9] This ingenious idea matches the originality of Luhmann's conceptual move. Luhmann (1995c: ch. 7) intends to overcome the

Husserlian *Monadengemeinschaft* by duplicating the process of sense-making: consciousness and communication are producing separate, independent and autonomous worlds of meaning which cannot be reduced to each other. However, the two *distinctions directrices*, Derrida's writing/speech and Luhmann's communication/consciousness, are mutually exclusive. The one distinction 'sits on' the blind spot of the other. They cannot be integrated into a synthesis. What remains, for the outside observer, is a continuous 'switching' from one distinction to the other resulting in an almost simultaneous observation of the world which contains two contradictory but at the same time supplementary perspectives. A condition of this supplementarity, if it is to become productive, is that the distinctions are capable to shed light on their respective blind spots.

Derrida's writing/speech difference exposes an unavoidable blind spot when it comes to the peculiarities of social institutions. The distinction is responsible for the (in)famous asociological character of deconstruction. Because it imposes writing upon the difference of consciousness and speech as the impossible third party, it excludes society from intertextuality. Deconstruction cannot grasp the autonomy of the social. At the same time, it cannot do justice to the precipices of the individual consciousness, given that writing cannot distinguish communication and consciousness. As a compensation, deconstruction draws from Levinas's philosophy of alterity which, however, constitutes only another correction of the Husserlian blindness to the social. Levinas (1979) juxtaposes the totality of meaning with the infinity of transcendence and places the reality of the other in the realm of infinity. This amounts to a 'premature' sacralization of the social which makes disappear any experience of society in the blind spot of the distinction between totality and infinity.

This is where Derrida's nightmare begins. Social systems operate in the blind spot of his *distinction directrice.* He can deconstruct economic and legal institutions but only as texts and intertextualities, not as social systems. Their restless autopoietic self-reproduction haunts him continuously, despite all attempts at deconstruction. It is the secret of autopoiesis that social systems are no longer threatened by the paradoxes of their deconstructive reading. Autopoietic self-reproduction means that in routine operations they are constantly de-paradoxifying their foundational paradox. Thus, they are capable of deconstructing deconstruction, of course not in the sense that they can exclude it on a long-term basis but in the sense that they shift, displace, disseminate, historicize deconstruction itself, which drastically changes the conditions of its possibility (Luhmann, 1993b: 490, 1995b). Luhmann's concepts are Derrida's non-concepts, autopoietic monsters in the world of deconstruction, which constantly stalk paradoxifying efforts with their relentless de-paradoxification. This is particularly true for Luhmann's central concepts of social autopoiesis, polycontexturality and second-order cybernetics.

What is the paradox that is dealt with by social autopoiesis? It is the paradox of alterity, the paralysing self-contradictions that occur in the primordial encounter with the other. Action is paralysed whenever Ego makes her action dependent on Alter and vice versa. The encounter with the other and the precipices which arise here are, of course, Derrida's continuous theme in his philosophy of gift and in his philosophy of justice (Derrida, 1990: 959, 1992). In Luhmann's theory they appear in the paradox of double contingency (Luhmann, 1995c: ch. 3). But their treatment makes the decisive difference. In Luhmann's account, the paradox of the encounter with the other is resolved by the emergence of autopoietic social systems. Social systems do not abolish the original paradox but they transfer it to a new sphere of meaning, namely, that of communication. Double contingency of two self-referential systems in their inner infiniteness is made bearable when communication emerges as an autonomous system of sense-production. Communication makes the paralysing effects of the paradox vanish because 'the self-referentiality of social systems presumes an immanent duality so that a circle emerges whose interruptions are able to give rise to structures' (Luhmann, 1997: 333).

To be sure, the paradox of alterity remains. But it changes its form; it is reconstructed and homogenized within the sphere of communication. Now it no longer paralyses two self-referential systems that are reconstructing each other in an infinite and unresolvable circularity, and it reappears as the precarious but manageable social interdependence of two communicative constructs, ego and alter. The paradoxical effects of their encounter are, so to speak, rendered harmless when they are reconstructed in communication. But there is a price to pay. While the paradoxes of the encounter with the other disappear, the foundational paradoxes of social systems emerge. Rendering them invisible in their turn becomes then the permanent problem of communication.

While Derrida does relentlessly enquire into the paradoxes of constituting subjectivity and intersubjectivity, the instruments of deconstruction are designed in such a way that they cannot thematize the crucial transformation of the paradox of alterity into the foundational paradoxes of worlds of communication, among them the paradoxes of law and economy. Thus, deconstruction remains hostage to the orginal paradoxes of alterity. This points again to Derrida's deficit of historical and sociological analyses. *Specters of Marx* is very strong on all kinds of spectrologies, but very weak when it comes to concrete analyses of contemporary society.[10] A deconstructive analysis that took account of the transformation of the paradox of double contingency into the foundational paradoxes of emerging social systems, would need to become historical, especially to recognize its own transformations. While the basic structures of the paradox remain the same, social processes of their invisibilization and the threatening moments of their re-emergence depend on historical contingencies. The paradox itself is 'necessary knowledge, a transcendental necessity, the "successor of the transcendental subject" ' (Luhmann, 1997: 755). By contrast, the distinctions which are used for de-paradoxification, are dependent on historical-societal conditions of plausibility, of acceptability, are contingent on binding knowledge in particular societies. This is how the social construction of systems, their continuous deconstruction and their recurrent reconstruction become subjects of the sociology of knowledge. What kind of society makes particular de-paradoxifying distinctions plausible? What kinds of *choques exogènes* expose again the paradoxical foundations of a social institution? The deconstructive obsession is thereby thoroughly socialized and historicized. To exorcize the paradox of alterity always remains a possibility but, remarkably, it has 'no consequences' (Fish, 1989), whilst the successful re-paradoxification of a concrete social system which must transform itself under concrete historical conditions establishes the actual threat.

The next autopoietic monster – polycontexturality[11] – gives rise to other deconstructive nightmares because it again changes the historical situation drastically. The emergence of a multitude of autonomous spheres of meaning within society, the establishment of their own codes and programmes, and, particularly, their operational and observational closure against each other produce a new anti-deconstructive immunity. They become resistant to the paradoxes of other spheres of meaning. The legal system, for example, deals extensively with economic conflicts but remains indifferent towards the economic paradox of scarcity, the resolution of which is declared an economic problem, not a problem of law. To give another example from law – when constitutional lawyers construct self-referring rules, actually a logical impossibility, they do not care about the Cretan paradox that haunts logicians. With cool indifference, they apply self-referring rules in legislative and judicial practice.[12] Deconstruction counts in law only if it touches upon the legal paradox itself and threatens legal practice in its application of the binary code legal/illegal. Then, and only then, do the conceptual machineries of legal doctrine begin their relentless search for 'saving distinctions'. At the beginning of the modern age it was the collapse of natural law and today it is the effect of globalization which amounts to a real threat to the operations of the legal system (Teubner, 1998). While natural law hierarchies have been safely replaced by the institutionalized practices of legal positivism, the threats of globalization are still provoking modern law and, so far, there are no saving distinctions in sight.

Here also, however, polycontexturality has the effect of deconstructing deconstruction. Polycontexturality makes it possible for social systems to externalize their foundational paradoxes by shifting them to other social systems. When they are displaced from one social system to another, they lose their paralysing power. The politicization of the legal and the economic paradoxes are striking historical examples. Both social systems successfully externalized the problems when they institutionalized a differentiation between 'levels' of decision-making (between the level of adjudication and legislation in law, between decisions concerning allocation of money and the actual amount of money in the economy) and defined the 'higher level' no longer as a problem for legal or economic action but as a problem for the political system (legislature and central bank as political institutions).[13]

The highest degree of deconstruction resistance, however, is attained when second-order cybernetics, the difference of operation and self-observation, is firmly institutionalized in social systems. The operations of legal systems (judicial precedents, legislative decisions, contracts) then establish an autonomous network of decisions, the validity of which is not necessarily dependent on legal self-observations, i.e. on legal argumentation (concepts, doctrines, principles, policies), but is merely loosely connected with them. Such an institutionalized insulation of self-observation and operation creates problems for deconstructive practice given that it does not systematically distinguish texts from social institutions, i.e. materialized, long-lasting normative structures which are based on presumptions of consensus. Contradictions, antinomies and paradoxes, which regularly arise in the line of legal argumentation, do not necessarily have an effect on the operational decision-making of law. Only when deconstructive moves affect the validity of legislative, judicial or contractual decisions, something which recently appeared as a consequence of the globalization crisis of law, then the hectic search for new bases of normative validity begins (Heller, 1985: 185; Wiethölter, 1986: 53).

Taken together, autopoiesis, polycontexturality and second-order cybernetics have the effect of successfully immunizing social systems against their deconstruction. To be sure, their immunization works only temporarily, given that they are time and again overtaken by their own paradoxes. The result of this almost rhythmical play of paradoxification, de-paradoxification, re-paradoxification is an evolutionary dynamics in which deconstruction, permanently provoked by its autopoietic subversion, is bound to change its character continuously. Variation, selection, retention – should the evolutionary mechanisms that give rise to the proliferation of monkeys and social systems also direct the hectic iterational movements of *différance*? But deconstructive Darwinism would not be its worst nightmare but would instead be the amazing productivity in the interplay of deconstruction and autopoietic reconstruction. Paradoxes not only threaten the structures of social systems (legal rules, economic routines), against which they must defend, separate and protect themselves; more importantly, paradoxes provoke economic and legal institutions into the relentless production of new rules and routines. The actual deconstructive obsesssion is not with defensive, conservative, systems maintaining their original structures but with their insatiable impulse for the invention of new differences. The birth of autopoiesis from the spirit of deconstruction?

IV. Luhmann's Redemption: The Gift of Justice

It is often asserted that the blind spot in Luhmann's systems theory is where other people see the person, the individual, the subject (e.g. Frankenberg, 1989: 336). The assertion is plainly wrong. Destruction of the subject, personless systems, anti-humanism – this critique can be successfully levelled at discourse theories as well as at deconstruction (which, for its part, can be criticized for a re-subjectification of *différance*) but not at systems theory.

Luhmann explicitly attributes the dynamic of autopoiesis not only to society but also to consciousness. As said above, he circumvents the complementary failures of philosophy of consciousness and language theory by duplicating the sites of meaning-production. In contrast to Derrida, who silences the distinction mind/society with his comprehensive concept of writing, Luhmann separates communication and consciousness and constructs both as autonomous worlds of meaning. In a sense, Luhmann combines Husserl with Wittgenstein: he combines the phenomenology of language games with that of consciousness, however, without merging them (as Derrida's *différance* or Habermas's intersubjectivity attempt to do) into one. The blind spot of autopoiesis lies somewhere else, not in the absence of a subject but precisely in the distinction between two 'subjects', in the distinction between communication/consciousness, society/individual, outer/inner, system/system.

One ought not to view this as a flaw in the theory. Rather, it is its greatest achievement. Up to now it is Luhmann who has offered the most plausible construction of the autonomy of the social. Society is a web of recursive communications, nothing else; human beings are in the environment of society. Its greatest achievement, however, necessarily makes it blind to the symbolic space where the *monades* of communication and consciousness meet each other. This is the weak point which Habermas has successfully attacked as the 'artificial' separation of psychological and social systems (Habermas, 1987: ch. 12). Of course, Luhmann has continuously worked on the blind spot of his theory, and attempted again and again to compensate for the violence of the mind/society separation. Emotionally loaded concepts such as 'structural coupling' or 'interpenetration' were introduced to reconnect psychic and social systems. But the inner logic of the theory forces him time and again to locate the linkages exclusively within the participating systems themselves. True, Luhmann submits, systems are irritated by their outside world, but irritation is a self-achievement of the irritated system in its internal reconstruction of the outside world. With such conceptual manoeuvres, Luhmann tries to minimize, if not to eliminate, the interaction, the translation, the interrelation between consciousness and communication.

Relation, according to Luhmann, is a non-concept, not only as regards intersubjectivity but also intersystemicity, which can only be dealt with through compensatory observations through the sychronization of actions and their mutual reconstruction. The same compensatory mechanism also works in the super-theory's holy of holies – in the distinction of system/environment. Autopoiesis theory is not able to conceptualize the relation between system and environment, which is then compensated for through secondary constructs of structural coupling (Luhmann, 1997: 92ff.). And it is precisely in the holy of holies where autopoiesis is haunted by deconstruction. The unity (!) of *différance* begins to afflict the unrevisable multiplicity of autopoietic systems. According to Derrida, the constitution of meaning does not appear in separate parallel processes of mutually closed systems – not to speak of a separation of psychic and social systems. Rather, the Derridean *différance* exposes a differential, transformational, context-dependent, continuously contingent but interconnected dynamics which resists a clear separation of its legal, economic, political, religious aspects, interactional and organizational patterns, social and psychic components, not to speak of their systemic closure (Derrida, 1982). The thesis is that while such a concept of *différance* is incompatible with autopoiesis, it is at the same time its necessary supplement. The open dance of heterogeneous operations, the infinite network of relations, the interplay of various aspects which occurs continuously without transferring them to a closed system – these are dangerous supplements to autopoietic closure. This understanding of *différance* cannot be systematically integrated into autopoiesis, it comes from outside as a threatening affliction of closed systems.

The necessary blindness of the system/environment distinction has important consequences for a concept of justice. In contrast to popular prejudice, Luhmann does not dispose of justice as a hackneyed old-European idea but places it in a central position in his theory of law. But, under modern conditions, justice can no longer serve as a criterion for the decision of individual cases. Nor is justice the highest internal norm of law, nor an external political or moral value which positive law must comply with. Instead, justice serves as law's contingency formula, problematizing the relation between law and its social environment. As compatibility between adequate social complexity of law and its internal consistency of decisions, justice mediates internal and external requirements (Luhmann, 1974: 23, 1981: 274ff., 1993b: 214ff.). But here again systems theory cannot deal with the environmental relation 'as such', but only asymmetrically, either from the inner perspective of the legal system or from the external perspective of an observer. The interrelations between law and society, the processes of translation from one system into the other, disappear again in the blind spot of the system/environment distinction. To be sure, this formulation of justice reflects adequately the internal requirements of modern positivized law. Under conditions of extreme functional differentiation, the internal decision-making consistency of law is strained by polycontexturality – a precarious problem to which the contingency formula of justice reacts. Luhmann's concept of justice is less adequate when it comes to institutions in law's environment, as they appear only as external disturbances of law, that endanger consistency, to which one can do justice only through a new kind of consistency.

Most importantly, however, this concept of justice is not commensurate to the relation of law and 'world', defined as the unity of difference of law/non-law, the unity of the difference of system/environment. This is the most difficult issue for an autopoietic theory of justice. Despite the fact that Luhmann concedes that:

> . . . the intention of the observation of unity of difference remains possible and makes sense in the world of meaning. But this sense takes on the form of a paradox, the form of the basic paradox of identity of difference. (Luhmann, 1996: 16)

Under this premise, the unity of difference of law and non-law, for Luhmann, can never be a suitable theme of justice, nor a theme for the contingency formula of any social system. But it is precisely at this vulnerable point that Derrida (1990: 959) places his difficult and unstable distinction between justice and positive law:

> . . . a distinction between justice and *droit*, between justice (infinite, incalculable, rebellious to rule and foreign to symmetry, heterogeneous and heterotropic) and the exercise of justice as law or right, legitimacy or legality, stabilizable and statutory, calculable, a system of regulated and coded prescriptions.

Derrida's conception of justice distinguishes itself from Luhmann's:

> . . . just because of this infinity and because of the heteronomic relation to others, to the faces of otherness that govern me, whose infinity I cannot thematize and whose hostage I remain. (Derrida, 1990: 959)

This conception of justice – which draws from Levinas's philosophy of alterity – is, parallel to Luhmann's, neither an internal legal norm, nor an external social, moral or political condition of law, but aims – now in strong contrast to the case of Luhmann – at the transcendence of law, which is unattainable to legal operations but whose demands they are continuously subject to. To the extent that deconstruction emphasizes the irreconcilable difference between positive law and such a form of justice, it formulates the transcendent dimension of law. Ironically, this would, precisely in Luhmann's sense, constitute an observation of law and world as unity of the difference of law/non-law which necessarily ends in paradoxes.

This is Derrida's central thesis: justice as transcendence in an irreconcilable contrast to the immanence of positive law which, however, is haunting law constantly. And it is here that parallels to the relationship of gift to the circulation of the economy become visible. The gift is not only, as in Marcel Mauss's *Essai sur le don*, an ethical or political counter-principle to the cold economic logic of capitalism. The gift transcends every social relation and provokes it – as in the metaphor of the beggar – as an unconditional demand of the Other (Derrida, 1992: Ch. 2). The gift is not pure transcendence without any connection to the circulation of the economy, but in a self-contradictory relation of unrevisable separation and permanent provocation. Thus, Derrida's repeated calls for political engagement, which are provoked by the unsatiated demands of a transcendent justice and gift (Derrida, 1990: 933).

Luhmann's sociology does not address this question. Instead, it is solely concerned with the immanence of law, the positivity of legal acts, legal rules and law's relation with the social environment. Luhmann goes further in only one instance. When the law is confronted with its own paradox, then indeed it is – also and particularly from the perspective of systems theory – exposed to its own transcendence. But systems theory, with its insistence on de-paradoxification of law, strictly prohibits this exposure. If one is to avoid blockages of law's decisions, then one needs to make the paradox invisible, not to confront it. Social autopoiesis, for the sake of self-continuation, needs to suppress the relationship of social systems to transcendence. There is only one social system where this issue is legitimately addressed. Only religion as an autonomous social system is entitled to thematize explicitly social paradoxes. Religion and no other social system deals with the symbolization of the third which is excluded by the difference between system and environment (Luhmann, 1984, 1990a, 1996).

By contrast, Derrida's gift of justice poses uncomfortable questions to autopoietics. Most embarrassing is one question: is there a particular experience of the transcendence of law? In this perspective, the legal paradox is no longer exclusively observed from the standpoint of its avoidance but is observed under the question of whether legal language has the capacity to symbolize what lies beyond law as the utopia of law (Blecher, 1991). While it remains correct that positive law can only arise out of the invisibilization of the legal paradox, a concept of justice, separate from positive law but connected to it, would then directly confront the paradox of law and no longer deal only with law's internal consistency or with its environmental adequacy. Instead of being the formula for law's contingency formula, justice would be the formula of its transcendence. Questions of justice would not merely be concerned with esoteric law or with theoretical speculations, but with the practical experience which comes about when criteria of justice are considered. One should not deny that it makes an important difference in the practice of law if one is exposed to 'deconstructive justice', to extreme demands of a justice that can never be realized, to the almost unbearable experience of an infinite responsibility, to a sense of fundamental failure of law, even a tragic experience that whatever you decide in law will end in injustice and guilt. The symbolization of transcendence would then no longer be limited to religion, as a specialized social system, but would be an authentic experience for the legal system itself, as it would also be for the economic and other social systems whose contingency formulas are based around their specific experiences of paradox. Why should the transcendence formulas of social institutions be exclusively dealt with in the system of religion and not within these institutions themselves? Justice is too important to be left up to priests (let alone to lawyers). Should one not view – and this is the question I shall end with – Derrida's profound and demanding analyses of the commonalities and the differences of gift and justice, the transcendence formulas of the economy and the law, as a new, original and actual historically adequate form of religious experience in a time of extreme polycontexturality?

Notes

1. Luhmann's and Derrida's most relevant texts on law and economy are Derrida (1990, 1992, 1994) and Luhmann (1985, 1988b, 1992a, 1992b, 1993d, 1995a).

2. Derrida is quite explicit on this point, e.g. Derrida (1990: 933).

3. Derrida (1990: 1004) in his analysis of the precarious relation between positive law and justice, asks explicitly for a 'compromise between two incommensurable and radically heterogeneous dimensions'; cf., on the same issue, Derrida (1993: 73–5). Luhmann (1993d: 225ff.) argues for a difficult balance within contemporary justice, rendering 'adequate complexity of law . . . compatible with internal decisional consistency'.

4. For the ongoing debate between deconstruction and systemism, see Berg and Prangel (1993), Cornell (1992), Hahn (1996), Koschorke and Vismann (1999), Stäheli (1995).

5. On paradox and self-reference in general, see Dupuy and Teubner (1990). On the paradoxes of legal self-reference see Teubner (1993: ch.1).

6. Luhmann's most explicit critique of Derrida's work can be found in Luhmann (1993a).

7. On various social practices of de-paradoxification in general, see Luhmann (1995b, 1995d); on the institutional history of de-paradoxification in law, Luhmann (1988a).

8. Lyotard (1987), Habermas (1996), Levinas (1979).

9. On this double movement see Dupuy (1990).

10. Derrida, 1994: ch.3, where more or less journalistic impressions of globalization are meant to revitalize the ambitious claims of Marx's social theory.

11. On this concept, see Günther (1976).

12. On the legal and logical problems of self-referring rules, especially in constitutional law, see Hart (1983), Hofstadter (1985), Ross (1969), Suber (1990).

13. For this externalization technique in law, see Luhmann (1990c); in the economy, Luhmann (1988b: 100).

References

Benjamin, Walter (1977) 'Zur Kritik der Gewalt', in Walter Benjamin, *Gesammelte Werke*, Bd. 2. Frankfurt: Suhrkamp. [English translation: Walter Benjamin, 'Critique of Violence', in *Selected Writings, Volume 1 1913–1926*, ed. M. Bullock and M.W. Jennings. Cambridge, MA: Belknap Press, 1997.]

Berg, Henkde and Matthias Prangel (eds) (1993) *Kommunikation und Differenz.* Opladen: Westdeutscher Verlag.

Blecher, Michael (1991) *Zu einer Ethik der Selbstreferenz oder: Theorie als Compassion: Möglichkeiten einer Kritischen Theorie der Selbstreferenz von Gesellschaft und Recht.* Berlin: Duncker and Humblot.

Cornell, Drucilla (1992) 'The Relevance of Time to the Relationship Between the Philosophy of the Limit and Systems Theory', *Cardozo Law Review* 13: 1579–603.

Derrida, Jacques (1978) *Writing and Difference.* Chicago, IL: University of Chicago Press.

Derrida, Jacques (1982) *Margins of Philosophy.* Chicago, IL: University of Chicago Press.

Derrida, Jacques (1990) 'Force of Law: The Mystical Foundation of Authority', *Cardozo Law Review* 11: 919–1046.

Derrida, Jacques (1992) *Given Time.* Chicago, IL: University of Chicago Press.

Derrida, Jacques (1994) *Specters of Marx.* New York: Routledge.

Derrida, Jacques (1998) *Of Grammatology.* Baltimore, MD: Johns Hopkins University Press.

Dupuy, Jean-Pierre (1990) 'Deconstructing Deconstruction: Supplement and Hierarchy', *Stanford Literature Review* 7: 101–21.

Dupuy, Jean-Pierre and Gunther Teubner (eds) (1990) *Paradoxes of Self-Reference in the Humanities, Law, and the Social Sciences.* Stanford, CA: Anma.

Felice, Lucio (1987) *Il grande dizionario Garzanti della lingua Italiana.* Milano: Garzanti.

Fish, Stanley (1989) *Doing What Comes Naturally: Change, Rhetoric, and the Practice of Theory in Literary and Legal Studies.* Oxford: Oxford University Press.

Fletcher, George P. (1985) 'Paradoxes in Legal Thought', *Columbia Law Review* 85: 1263–92.

Frankenberg, Günter (1989) 'Down by Law: Irony, Seriousness, and Reason', pp. 315–52 in C. Joerges and D. Trubek (eds) *Critical Legal Thought: An American-German Debate.* Baden-Baden: Nomos.

Günther, Gotthard (1976) 'Life as Poly-Contexturality', pp. 283–306 in G. Günther, *Beiträge zur Grundlegung einer operationsfähigen Dialektik I.* Hamburg: Meiner.

Habermas, Jürgen (1987) *The Philosophical Discourse of Modernity.* Boston, MA: Beacon Press.

Habermas, Jürgen (1996) *Between Facts and Norms: Contributions to a Discourse Theory of Law and Democracy.* Cambridge, MA: MIT Press.

Hahn, Marcus (1996) 'Vom Kopfstand des Phonozentrismus auf den Brettern der Systemtheorie oder: Luhmann und/oder Derrida – einfach eine Entscheidung? Anmerkungen zu "Die Form der Schrift" von Niklas Luhmann', *Soziale Systeme* 2: 283–306.

Hart, Herbert L.A. (1983) 'Self-referring Laws', pp. 170–8 in H.L.A. Hart (ed.) *Essays in Jurisprudence and Philosophy.* Oxford: Clarendon Press.

Heller, Thomas C. (1985) 'Legal Discourse in the Positive State: A Post-Structuralist Account', pp. 173–199 in G. Teubner (ed.) *Dilemmas of Law in the Welfare State.* Berlin: de Gruyter.

Hofstadter, Douglas R. (1985) 'Nomic: A Self-Modifying Game Based on Reflexivity in Law', pp. 70–86 in D.R. Hofstadter, *Metamagical Themas: Questing for the Essence of Mind and Pattern.* New York: Bantam.

Husserl, Edmund (1950) *Husserliana.* The Hague: Martinus Nijhoff.

Koschorke, Albrecht and Cornelia Vismann (eds) (1999) *Widerstände der Systemtheorie: Kulturtheoretische Analysen zum Werk von Niklas Luhmann.* Berlin: Akademie.

Levinas, Emmanuel (1979) *Totality and Infinity: An Essay on Exteriority.* The Hague: Nijhoff.

Luhmann, Niklas (1974) *Rechtssystem und Rechtsdogmatik.* Stuttgart: Kohlhammer.

Luhmann, Niklas (1981) *Die Ausdifferenzierung des Rechtssystems.* Frankfurt: Suhrkamp.

Luhmann, Niklas (1984) *Religious Dogmatics and the Evolution of Societies.* New York: Mellen.

Luhmann, Niklas (1985) *A Sociological Theory of Law.* London: Routledge.

Luhmann, Niklas (1988a) 'The Third Question: The Creative Use of Paradoxes in Law and Legal History', *Journal of Law and Society* 15: 153–65.

Luhmann, Niklas (1988b) *Die Wirtschaft der Gesellschaft*. Frankfurt: Suhrkamp.

Luhmann, Niklas (1990a) 'Society, Meaning, Religion – Based on Self Reference', pp. 208–33 in P. Colomy (ed.) *Neofunctionalist Sociological Theory*. Aldershot, Hants: Brookfield.

Luhmann, Niklas (1990b) 'Sthenography', *Stanford Law Review* 7: 133–7.

Luhmann, Niklas (1990c) 'Verfassung als evolutionäre Errungenschaft', *Rechtshistorisches Journal* 9: 176–220.

Luhmann, Niklas (1992a) 'The Coding of the Legal System', pp. 145–85 in A. Febbrajo and G. Teubner (eds) *State, Law, and Economy as Autopoietic Systems: Regulation and Autonomy in a New Perspective*. Milano: Giuffrè.

Luhmann, Niklas (1992b) 'Operational Closure and Structural Coupling: The Differentiation of the Legal System', *Cardozo Law Review* 13: 1419–41.

Luhmann, Niklas (1993a) 'Deconstruction as Second-Order Observing', *New Literary History* 24: 763–82.

Luhmann, Niklas (1993b) 'Observing Re-entries', *Graduate Faculty Philosophy Journal* 16: 485–98.

Luhmann, Niklas (1993c) 'Die Paradoxie des Entscheidens', *Verwaltungsarchiv* 84: 287–310.

Luhmann, Niklas (1993d) *Das Recht der Gesellschaft*. Frankfurt: Suhrkamp.

Luhmann, Niklas (1995a) 'Legal Argumentation: An Analysis of its Form', *Modern Law Review* 58: 285–98.

Luhmann, Niklas (1995b) 'The Paradoxy of Observing Systems', *Cultural Critique* 31: 37–55.

Luhmann, Niklas (1995c) *Social Systems*. Palo Alto, CA: Stanford University Press.

Luhmann, Niklas (1995d) 'Why Does Society Describe Itself as Postmodern?', *Cultural Critique* 31: 37–55.

Luhmann, Niklas (1996) 'Die Sinnform Religion', *Soziale Systeme* 2: 3–33.

Luhmann, Niklas (1997) *Die Gesellschaft der Gesellschaft*. Frankfurt: Suhrkamp.

Lyotard, Jean-François (1987) *The Differend: Phrases in Dispute*. Manchester: Manchester University Press.

Ross, Alf (1969) 'On Self-Reference and a Puzzle in Constitutional Law', *Mind* 78: 1–24.

Schmitt, Carl (1985) *Political Theology: Four Chapters on the Concept of Sovereignty*. Cambridge, MA: MIT Press.

Schmitt, Carl (1996) *The Concept of the Political*. Chicago, IL: University of Chicago Press.

Stäheli, Urs (1995) 'Latent Places of the Political in Luhmann's Systems Theory: Towards a Politics of Deparadoxification', *Working Papers 5*. Colchester: Centre for Theoretical Studies.

Suber, Peter (1990) *The Paradox of Self-Amendment: A Study of Logic, Law, Omnipotence and Change*. New York: Peter Lang.

Teubner, Gunther (1993) *Law as an Autopoietic System*. London: Blackwell.

Teubner, Gunther (1998) 'The King's Many Bodies: The Self-Deconstruction of Law's Hierarchy', *Law and Society Review* 33: 763–88.

Wiethölter, Rudolf (1986) 'Social Science Models in Economic Law', pp. 52–67 in T. Daintith and G. Teubner (eds) *Contract and Organization: Legal Analysis in the Light of Economic and Social Theory*. Berlin: de Gruyter.

Gunther Teubner is Professor of private law and legal sociology at the University of Frankfurt and Centennial Visiting Professor at the London School of Economics. His research fields are social theory of law and comparative private law. His recent publications include *Paradoxes of of Self-Reference in the Humanities, Law, and the Social Sciences* (1991), *State, Law, Economy as Autopoietic Systems* (1992), *Law as an Autopoietic System* (1993), *Droit et réflexivité* (1994), *Environmental Law and Ecological Responsibility* (1995), *Entscheidungsfolgen als Rechtsgründe* (1995), *Global Law Without A State* (1998), *Il diritto policontesturale* (1999) and *Die Rückgabe des Zwölften Kamels* (2000).

[16]

On Pierre Bourdieu's Legal Thought

Mauricio García Villegas *

Résumé

Commentaires sur Pierre Bourdieu et le droit
Dans cet article, l'auteur analyse la contribution de Bourdieu à la sociologie du droit à partir d'une perspective comparée. L'hypothèse développée est la suivante : les analyses de Bourdieu sur le droit se comprennent mieux si on les examine en ayant à l'esprit l'opposition entre sociologues et juristes en France. De même, l'auteur montre que cette approche du droit par Bourdieu liée à sa théorie de la domination politique est influencée par une vision étato-centrée fortement en relation avec l'histoire politique de la France et qui ne prend pas en compte les mutations actuelles de la régulation juridique. Riche théoriquement, la sociologie du droit de Bourdieu est néanmoins marquée par le contexte dans lequel elle a été produite.

Débats disciplinaires - Droit et politique - Histoire du droit - Pierre Bourdieu - Sociologie comparative du droit - Théorie socio-juridique.

Summary

This essay discusses Bourdieu's contribution to the sociology of law from a comparative perspective. It argues that Bourdieu's ideas about law may be understood through an explication of the disciplinary debates among sociologists and lawyers in France. The paper is divided into three parts. The first section discusses fundamental ideas in Bourdieu's legal thought. The second part locates his thinking within the theory of law and in social theory. Finally, the third part discusses the disciplinary squabbling among French sociologists and jurists, comparing their situation to that of colleagues in other countries, and explains how these misunderstandings had a significant influence on Bourdieu's work.

Comparative sociology of law - Disciplinary debates - Law and politics - Legal history - Pierre Bourdieu - Socio-legal theory.

L'auteur

Professeur de droit à l'Universidad Nacional de Bogotá, Colombie, et *Research Associate* à l'Institute for Legal Studies, University of Wisconsin-Madison. Ses travaux de recherche portent sur la sociologie du droit comparé et la théorie du droit constitutionnel.
Parmi ses publications :
- *La eficacia simbólica del derecho*, Bogotá, Ediciones Uniandes, 1994 ;
- *El caleidoscopio de las justicias en Colombia* (avec B. de Sousa Santos), Bogotá, Ediciones Uniances, Siglo del Hombre, 2001 ;
- *Sociología jurídica*, Bogotá, Universidad Nacional de Colombia, 2001 ;
- *Derecho y sociedad en América Latina* (sous la dir., avec C. Rodríguez), Bogotá, ILSA Universidad Nacional, 2003.

* Facultad de Derecho, Universidad Nacional, Ciudad Universitaria, Bogotá, Colombia.
<mvillegas@facstaff.wisc.edu>

M. GARCÍA VILLEGAS

Pierre Bourdieu showed remarkably little interest in the study of law. His thought in this area is fragmentary and incomplete. Disciples, followers, and commentators of Bourdieu manifest the same lack of interest regarding the legal phenomena. In the United States, for example, although references to his work are common in studies of law and society [1], in depth analyses on Bourdieu's legal thought by either sociologists or jurists are absent. In France, scholars interested in his legal contributions are no more than a handful of academics, who try to apply his theory to the study of specific legal areas in a somewhat hit-and-miss fashion [2]. Should we then conclude that Bourdieu's ideas are not important to the study of law ? I think not. The fact that the law is a marginal topic in Bourdieu's work can better be explained by the uncertain nature of the communications amongst French sociologists and jurists and the relative marginality of the sociolegal perspective in France than by the importance of Bourdieu's legal ideas to the two disciplines. Bourdieu himself recognized on several occasions that he had not dedicated the time and effort to this subject that its importance warranted.

In this essay I propose to discuss Bourdieu's contribution to the sociology of law from a comparative perspective, taking advantage of my position as an external observer to the French sociolegal debate. The principal idea that I wish to develop here is the following : Bourdieu's contribution to theorizing legal phenomena needs to be understood through an explication

1. Above all in those that take a cultural approach : this is the case of Legal Consciousness Studies (on this see Mauricio GARCÍA VILLEGAS, « Symbolic Power Without Symbolic Violence ? », *Florida Law Review*, 55 (1), 2003, p. 157-189 ; ID., « Symbolic Power Without Symbolic Violence ?, Critical Comments on Legal Consciousness Studies in USA », *Droit et Société*, 53, 2003, p. 137-161). It is significant, for instance, that in the 2004 Law and Society Association annual meetings, not one paper was presented on Bourdieu's legal thought out of more than seven hundred papers read.

2. In the United States, Patricia EWICK and Susan SILBEY, *The Common Place of Law : Stories from Everyday Life*, Chicago, University of Chicago Press, 1998. In theoretical studies of sociology of law, Bourdieu is frequently cited to justify a theoretical framework (see for instance : Ruth Margaret BUCHANAN, « Context, Continuity, and Difference in Poverty Law Scholarship », *University of Miami Law Review*, 48, 1994, p. 999-1062 ; Michael W. MCCANN, *Rights at Work : Pay Equity Reform and the Politics of Legal Mobilization*, Chicago, University of Chicago Press, 1994 ; Sally Engle MERRY, *Getting Justice and Getting Even : Legal Consciousness among Working-Class Americans*, Chicago, University of Chicago Press, 1990). For a general assessment see Mauricio GARCÍA VILLEGAS, « Symbolic Power Without Symbolic Violence ? », *op. cit.* In France, perhaps the best known repository of the ideas of Bourdieu on the legal field is Dezalay (Yves DEZALAY, Austin SARAT and Susan SILBEY, « D'une démarche contestataire à un savoir méritocratique. Élément pour une histoire sociale de la sociologie juridique américaine », *Actes de la recherche en sciences sociales*, 78, 1989, p. 79-90 ; Yves DEZALAY and David TRUBEK, « La reestructuración global y el derecho », *Pensamiento Jurídico*, 1, 1997 p. 5-41) ; other authors in France who have shown an interest in Bourdieu's work include : Alain BANCAUD and Yves DEZALAY, « La sociologie juridique comme enjeu social et professionnel », *Revue interdisciplinaire d'études juridiques*, 12, 1984, p. 1-29 ; Alain BANCAUD, « Une "constante mobile" : la haute magistrature », *Actes de la recherche en sciences sociales*, 76/77, 1989, p. 30-48 ; Alain BANCAUD, *La haute magistrature entre politique et sacerdoce*, Paris, LGDJ, 1993 ; Fréderic OCQUETEAU and Francine SOUBIRAN-PAILLET, « Champ juridique, juristes et règle de droit : une sociologie entre disqualification et paradoxe », *Droit et Société*, 32, 1996, p. 9-26 ; Francine SOUBIRAN-PAILLET, « Quelles voix(es) pour la sociologie du droit en France aujourd'hui ? », *Genèses*, 15, 1994, p. 142-153.

of the disciplinary debates amongst sociologists and lawyers in France ; these debates both locate his theory and enable us better to understand the scope and type of discourse that he employs. The paper is divided into three parts. In the first section, I discuss some ideas that I believe are fundamental to the writings of Bourdieu on law. In the second part, I try to locate his thought within the theory of law and in social theory and to show its sociological roots and its sociolegal limitations. Finally, I will discuss the disciplinary squabbling amongst French sociologists and jurists, comparing their situation to that of colleagues in other countries, and I will explain how these misunderstandings had a significant influence on Bourdieu's work.

I. Bourdieu and the Law

A complete exegesis of Bourdieu's legal thought would require the explication of a series of theoretical assumptions proper to his social theory that I lack the space to embark upon in these pages. I will limit myself to the explanation of one point that I consider essential to Bourdieu's conception of the legal field as well as better to understand the French debate that his thought on the question of law has provoked. This point concerns Bourdieu's attempt to construct a theory of legal practice that could transcend the subject/object dichotomy.

In Bourdieu, culture cannot be understood outside the economic conditions in which subjects act. Cultural tastes are never disinterested and can only be understood by starting from a theory of symbolic power [3]. Culture is a set of dispositions internalized by individuals through a process of socialization that constitute schemas of perception and understanding of the world. These internalized dispositions work only to the extent that there is a certain correspondence with the hierarchical order that they represent. According to Bourdieu, « *il existe une correspondance entre les structures sociales et les structures mentales, entre les divisions objectives du monde social - notamment en dominants et dominés dans les différent champs - et les principes de vision et division que les agents leur appliquent* » [4]. This correspondence fulfills essential political functions in society. Thus symbolic systems are not only tools of knowledge but, first and foremost, instruments of domination. A central objective of Bourdieu's work is to show how culture and social class correlate. In general terms Bourdieu's sociological theory asks the following question : how is it possible that hierarchically based systems of domination persist and reproduce themselves through social practices ? Bourdieu views society as a stratified and differentiated

3. According to Swartz, interpreting Bourdieu : « If his theory of practices extends the idea of interest to culture, then his theory of symbolic power extends culture to the realm of interest with the claim that all forms of power require legitimation » (David SWARTZ, *Culture and Power : The Sociology of Pierre Bourdieu*, Chicago, University of Chicago Press, 1997, p. 89).

4. Pierre BOURDIEU, *La noblesse d'État. Grandes écoles et esprit de corps*, Paris, Minuit, 1989, p. 7.

space in which individuals struggle to defend positions and interests. Now, domination, more than something linked to the use of physical violence, is articulated through, and experienced through, the use of symbolic violence. The ones who are dominant in society do not achieve that position merely through possession of economic capital. They also attain it thanks to the cultural capital that they possess and to the close connection between these two forms of capital. This articulation operates in such a way that the symbolic systems - through which we establish classifications and determine the essential categories of social inclusion and exclusion - have both a cognitive/social organization function [5] and also a political function of domination. The law is a good example of symbolic system.

The law is a social field - set of objective and historical relations between positions of social actors who struggle for power or capital - in which participants struggle over the appropriation of the symbolic power that is implicit in legal texts [6]. Thus, the law becomes a form *par excellence* of symbolic power - and of symbolic violence - given the possibilities possessed by its practitioners to create institutions and with them historical and political realities through a simple exercise of naming [7]. The internal dynamic of the field is associated with the question of domination. The potential of the law to establish classifications that are essential to the social order - legal/illegal, just/unjust, true/false - entails enormous political power. Legal authority is the privileged form of power, especially in terms of legitimate symbolic violence - monopolized by the State - which the State both produces and practices [8]. The use of the symbolic is an inherently violent practice to the extent to which it imposes meaning on the world and on social relations in which economic and political power lose their original arbitrary and exclusive connotation and appear as something normal and acceptable.

But the law can not be reduced to a tool for political domination. In understanding the symbolic force of law or its legitimizing effect, we must avoid both those materialistic accounts that see only power relations in the explanation of law, as well as idealistic ones that explain it through the general recognition of the universal values expressed in its norms. « We can no longer ask whether power comes from above or from below », says Bourdieu with reference to the debate between critical and doctrinal expla-

5. The cognitive structures which social agents implement in their practical knowledge of the social world are internalized « embodied » social structures (see Pierre BOURDIEU, *La distinction : critique sociale du jugement*, Paris, Minuit, 1979).

6. Pierre BOURDIEU, « The Force of Law : Toward a Sociology of the Juridical Field », *Hastings Law Journal*, 38 (5), 1986, p. 814-853 (p. 817-818) ; French original : « La force du droit. Éléments pour une sociologie du champ juridique », *Actes de la recherche en sciences sociales*, 64, 1986.

7. *Ibid.*, p. 839.

8. This idea of symbolic power is also usefully explored by Georges BALANDIER, *Le pouvoir sur scènes*, Paris, Balland, 1992 ; and Harry PROSS, *Violencia social de los simbolos*, Barcelona, Anthropos, 1989.

nations of law [9]. Bourdieu counters the materialistic accounts, acknowledging the existence of an autonomous social universe capable of the production and reproduction, by the logic of its specific functioning, of a legal corpus relatively independent of external constraints [10]. However, he also recognizes that, the legal field has a smaller degree of autonomy than others, such as the artistic or the literary fields, given the essential role it plays in social reproduction.

Since the law is a social field in which a great deal of social and symbolic capital resides, it is not surprising that inside the field there are fierce clashes among its members for the possession, and distribution, of this capital. From this point of view, the theoretical debates inside the legal academy - for instance between formalists and anti-formalists in the early 20th century in United States, or between *iuspositivism* and *iusnaturalism* in 20th century-Europe - seek to consolidate a specific possession-position-distribution of the symbolic capital that is at play both inside and outside the field. Inside the legal field, actors located in different positions and endowed with different dispositions, fight for the chance to pronounce the final word about the meaning and ultimate scope of the law. Such a struggle is not only intellectual but also political, given the fact that the most legal debate has direct implications for the distribution of power and goods that occurs in the political field. Controlling the law is important to social control [11]. This is why the struggle also takes place outside the field.

The conventional idea that the legal culture of countries, with its debates, its authors, its schools and internal movements, is sufficient to explain the origin, evolution and actual status of the legal traditions and legal practices found therein is seen to be problematic. That explanation ignores the strong connections that exist between the culture and the social and material conditions in which it prospers. « *Il n'est pas trop de dire qu'il* fait *le monde social, mais à condition de ne pas oublier qu'il est fait par lui* [12]. » Structures limit and mold perceptions, discourses, and practices from which social reality is constructed. The subject is as much of the world as the world is subjectivized, says Bourdieu. In short, the internal struggle among legal actors for the appropriation of symbolic power has not been independent of the political context in which it has taken place. Connections between the political and the legal field are multiple and mutually constitutive.

This does not mean, as some theories of the law have led us to believe, that knowledge of the material conditions in which the legal discussion takes place is sufficient to know the outcome. The legal field in its majesty,

9. Pierre BOURDIEU, « The Force of Law : Toward a Sociology of the Juridical Field », *op. cit.*, p. 841.
10. *Ibid.*, p. 816.
11. So, for example, the legal delimitation of the right to property is also a response to poverty and social marginality.
12. Pierre BOURDIEU, « La force du droit. Éléments pour une sociologie du champ juridique », *Actes de la recherche en sciences sociales*, 64, 1986, p. 13 ; English version, p. 839.

its rites, and its shrines is not amenable to being reduced merely to existing economic forces. It is not just a reflection of the material world [13]. Neither is the law pure erudition that can be detached from the social conditions in which it is found. These extremes ignore the existence of law understood as a social field that is relatively independent of external demands - the logic of which is determined, according to Bourdieu, by two factors :

> [...] *d'une part, par les rapports de force spécifiques qui lui confèrent sa structure et qui orientent les luttes de concurrence ou, plus précisément, les conflits de compétence dont il est le lieu et, d'autre part, par la logique interne des œuvres juridiques qui délimitent à chaque moment l'espace des possibles et, par là, l'univers des solutions proprement juridiques* [14].

II. Social Theory and Legal Theory in the Writings of Bourdieu

The core concepts of Bourdieu's conception of law are found in his text « La force du droit », published in 1986 [15], although elements appear scattered throughout his entire output [16]. One of the difficulties with this article is derived from the fact that in it Bourdieu utilizes critical arguments against legal theorists and sociologists alike, with the aim of making his diatribe against the jurists and the legal system more effective. In the course of outlining his legal conception, Bourdieu attacks both sociological and legal theories of law, and both conservative and progressive legal approaches. As a result it is difficult neatly to classify his thought. No legal perspective is privileged in the discussion : Felix Cohen and the realists appear in opposition to Kelsen and the positivists just as Kelsen and Luhmann are opposed to Althusser, and to E. P. Thompson, and that in a presentation of the juridical debate that seems to render all of them inadequate. This suggests that his theory both distances itself from the sociolegal currents or traditions, and also tries to attain a broader scope than that of a simple sociological critique of the legal science of jurists.

What Bourdieu terms a « rigorous science of law » (*une science rigoureuse du droit*) as opposed to a « legal science » (*science juridique*) is a critical explication of law from the field of sociology, that is to say, a *critical*

13. Evgeny PASHUKANIS, *Law and Marxism : A General Theory*, London, Ink Links, 1978.

14. Pierre BOURDIEU, « La force du droit », *op. cit.*, p. 3-4 ; English version, p. 816.

15. See note 12.

16. Above all in some chapters contained in Pierre BOURDIEU, *Choses dites*, Paris, Minuit, 1987, especially : « De la règle aux stratégies », « La codification » and « Espace social et pouvoir symbolique » ; Pierre BOURDIEU, « Habitus, code et codification », *Actes de la recherche en sciences sociales*, 64, 1986, p. 40-44 ; and ID., « Les juristes, gardiens de l'hypocrisie collective », in François CHAZEL and Jacques COMMAILLE (sous la dir.), *Normes juridiques et régulation sociale*, Paris, LDGJ, 1991, p. 95-99.

sociology of law [17]. Above all, Bourdieu distances himself from the critical or progressive currents of legal thought that dominated France over much of the 20th century. Here I am referring basically to two : materialist perspectives, whether of a marxist (Althusser) or anthropological (Levi-Strauss) cast, and « social » or « communitarian » perspectives. Materialist approaches in large part found a home in the movement *Critique du droit*, created at the end of the seventies. The second, which I may term « social », found initial expression in the *Free Law Movement* represented by Eugen Ehrlich and Kantorowitz in Germany, and later in the work of Gurvitch in France [18]. According to this perspective, the law should be an expression of the interests and the existing patterns in communities ; the official law then should be constructed « from below, » out of the social realm.

The fact that Bourdieu's ideas on law could have some influence on the legal thought of lawyers, or so-called *science juridique* (legal science) could be important but it does not seem to be the essential point. It is true that very often, when Bourdieu refers to the law, he treats specific problems of legal theory - such as legal interpretation - but this does not mean that his aim is to construct a theory of law. Bourdieu wanted above all to construct a sociological explanation of law that was consistent with his theory of social fields, and particularly with his concept of *habitus*. Therefore, Bourdieu's theory should not be read, or at least not exclusively, from the starting point of legal science but rather from a sociological perspective. Stated more specifically, jurists who become interested in Bourdieu's work should first immerse themselves in his social and critical theory of rules and habitus, and from there explain subjects such as symbolic violence and the « hypocrisy » of jurists [19]. Only in this way can his pejorative statements about law and lawyers be assessed in their correct proportions. So, for example, Jacques Caillosse - in the article published in this journal - questions the coherency of Bourdieu's discourse in the following passage : « *Si l'opposition entre règles et régularités dont Bourdieu fait gros usage n'est en tant que telle en rien discutable, jusqu'où est-elle totalement compatible avec la réflexion qu'il esquisse par ailleurs sur la fatalité de l'interprétation juridique ?* » There would be, according to Caillosse, « *une représentation démiurgique du Droit et du Législateur, totalement incompatible avec la théorie*

17. In the sociology of law it is important to distinguish between at least two types of approaches. Some authors attempt to integrate law as one aspect of the general explication of the workings of society. This view was adopted by the classical sociological theorists and may be termed *sociology of law*. The second approach sets itself the task of explicating the law from a sociological perspective. The authors who are mining this vein generally consider themselves to be working in a current that is critical of formalist legal dogma. This second approach can be called *sociolegal theory*. On this see the classic distinction made by Renato Treves between « sociology in law » and « sociology on law » (Renato TREVES, « Two Sociologies of Law », *European Yearbook in Law and Society*, 1977).; see also Jacques COMMAILLE, « Sociologie juridique », in Denis ALLAND and Stéphane RIALS (sous la dir.), *Dictionnaire de la culture juridique*, Paris, PUF, 2003.

18. See Pierre BOURDIEU, « La force du droit », *op. cit.*, p. 14, footnote 36 ; English version p. 84.

19. Speaking of an article of Bourdieu (Pierre BOURDIEU, « Les juristes, gardiens de l'hypocrisie collective », *op. cit.*).

M. GARCÍA VILLEGAS

de l'interprétation ». Similarly, Violaine Roussel - essay also published in this volume - considers that Bourdieu's idea of formalization of the norms supposes a rigidity in legal practice that does not actually exist and thus should not be contrasted to the flexibility of habitus. It seems to me that the problem with these interpretations lies in the fact that they do not start from Bourdieu's social theory : they do not take into consideration the different meanings that Bourdieu gives to the word *norm* or *rule* : as social regularity or as legal norm.

The meaning of concepts such as rule, norm and habitus in Bourdieu's *théorie de la pratique* is a central point in his work, and for this reason it merits a detailed treatment. Let's begin by examining the following passage from *Choses dites* :

> *Le jeu social est réglé, il est le lieu de régularités. Les choses s'y passent de façon régulière ; les héritiers riches se marient régulièrement avec les cadettes riches [...]. Je peux dire que toute ma réflexion est partie de là : comment des conduites peuvent-elles être réglées sans être le produit de l'obéissance à des règles ?* [20]

Bourdieu's idea was to construct a « model of the game which will not be the mere recording of explicit norms or a statement of regularities [...] ». His purpose was to account for socially regular actions which cannot be explained, either as the result of obedience to rules, or as brute causality. Bourdieu rejects the notion of norm - understood as legal or moral commandment - with the intention of « *échapper aux naïvetés les plus grossières du juridisme qui tient les pratiques pour le produit de l'obéissance des normes* » [21]. Frédéric Ocqueteau and Francine Soubiran-Paillet are correct in suggesting that the rejection of rules - understood as commands that produce obedience - as an explanation of certain social regularities is a rejection that ought to be interpreted in the context of the ethnological debate that Bourdieu unleashed during the 1970s in his *Esquisse d'une théorie de la pratique* [22], and in which the concept of habitus was central [23]. In other terms Bourdieu's solution for this intermediate model between rules and norms was the concept of habitus. The habitus is

> [...] *un système de dispositions durables, structures structurées prédisposées à fonctionner comme structures structurantes, c'est-à-dire en tant que principe de génération et de structuration de pratiques et de représentation qui peuvent être objectivement « réglées » et « régulières » sans être en rien le produit de l'obéissance à des règles, objectivement adaptées a leur but sans supposer la visée*

20. Pierre BOURDIEU, *Choses dites, op. cit.*, p. 81.

21. Pierre BOURDIEU, *Esquisse d'une théorie de la pratique*, précédé de *Trois études d'ethnologie kabyle*, Genève, Droz, 1972, p. 171.

22. Pierre BOURDIEU, *Outline of a Theory of Practice*, New York, Cambridge University Press, 1977.

23. According to Ocqueteau and Soubiran-Paillet, in this debate Bourdieu attempts to differentiate his position from those of Radcliffe-Brown and Malinowski. For Radcliffe-Brown norms are what ensures order in society, and Malinowski's interest lay in individual choices and the way individuals act to achieve their own interests (Frédéric OCQUETEAU and Francine SOUBIRAN-PAILLET, « Champ juridique, juristes et règle de droit : une sociologie entre disqualification et paradoxe », *op. cit.* ; chapters published in English in *Outline of a Theory of Practice*).

consciente des fins et la maîtrise expresse des opérations nécessaires pour les atteindre et, étant tout cela, collectivement orchestrées sans être le produit de l'action organisatrice d'un chef d'orchestre [24].

The concept of habitus then - always viewed within this sociological perspective of explication of social practices and their regularities - is intended to move beyond the institutionalized epidermis that makes up the legal rules by which persons behave or do not behave in a certain manner. As Jacques Bouveresse wrote : « As the habitus is not necessarily of a mental nature (there are forms of habitus which are simply corporeal) it is independent of any distinction between the conscious or unconscious, and it is not less independent of distinctions like that between the product of a simple causal constraint and an action that is "free" in that it escapes any constraints of this nature [25]. » The habitus is then an intermediate concept between rules - in the legal sense - and causality or rules in a physical sense.

The pejorative sense in which Bourdieu often uses terms such as rule or norm finds its explanation in his structural theory of practice (*théorie structurelle de la pratique*) where he attempts to connect culture, structure, and practice. Norms are accorded this treatment, in the first place, because they are seen as obstacles to real knowledge of social practices, or in Bourdieu's own words for the knowledge of « the immanent principle to practice » that is to say, habitus. In the second place, the meaning and scope of norms is generally monopolized by jurists, the owners par excellence of symbolic violence in the society, through the so-called *science du droit.* For this reason Bourdieu speaks more disparagingly of lawyers than, for example, sports figures.

However, as outlined above, Bourdieu himself was careful not go too far in his condemnation of the legal sphere : « *La réaction contre le juridisme en sa forme ouverte ou masquée ne doit pas conduire à faire de l'habitus le principe exclusif de toute pratique, bien qu'il n'y a pas de pratique qui n'ait l'habitus à son principe* [26]. » The legal rules are a type of substitute that intervenes when the habitus is incapable of fulfilling its regulatory functions. The law is, then, the exception whereas habitus is the rule [27]. Exceptions arise in moments of crisis in the habitus : « *On peut poser en loi générale que plus une situation est dangereuse, plus la pratique tend à être codifiée. Le degré de codification varie comme le degré de risque* [28]. » Here we see the virtue of codifying a rule which is that it allows, like all rationalization,

24. Pierre BOURDIEU, *Esquisse d'une théorie de la pratique, op. cit.*, p. 175.

25. Jacques BOUVERESSE, « Rules, Dispositions, and the Habitus », in Richard SHUSTERMAN (ed.), *Bourdieu : A Critical Reader*, Oxford, Blackwell, 2000, p. 53.

26. Pierre BOURDIEU, *Esquisse d'une théorie de la pratique, op. cit.*, p. 25.

27. This of course is particularly clear in those societies in which there is no developed legal order, such as, for example, among the Kabyle people.

28. Pierre BOURDIEU, *Choses dites, op. cit.*, p. 96.

« *une économie d'invention, d'improvisation, de création* » [29]. But the form or the codification does not operate simply through its technical efficiency in clarifying or rationalizing, according to Bourdieu :

> *Il y a une efficacité proprement symbolique de la forme. La violence symbolique, dont la réalisation par excellence est sans doute le droit, est une violence qui s'exerce, si l'on peut dire,* dans les formes, *en mettant des formes. Mettre des formes, c'est donner à une action ou à un discours la forme qui est reconnue comme convenable, légitime, approuvée [...]. La force de la forme [...] est cette force proprement symbolique qui permet à la force de s'exercer pleinement en se faisant méconnaître en tant que force et en se faisant reconnaître, approuver, accepter, par le fait de se présenter sous les apparences de l'universalité - celle de la raison ou de la morale* [30].

Hence, for Bourdieu, the law is not reducible to a question of interests - as Weber or Marx thought - just as interests are not reducible to law. Hence, the first lines in his article « La force du droit », in which Bourdieu tries to construct a relatively autonomous legal sphere between the positivist formalism of Hans Kelsen, in which the subjective view dominates, and the materialism of Louis Althusser, in which the objectivist perspective does. As I said before, we are here assessing Bourdieu's challenge to construct a theory of legal practice that could transcend the subject/object dichotomy. It is :

> [...] *un univers social relativement indépendant par rapport aux demandes externes, à l'intérieur duquel se produit et s'exerce l'autorité juridique, forme par excellence de la violence symbolique légitime dont le monopole appartient à l'État et qui peut s'assortir de l'exercice de la force physique* [31].

While Bourdieu is interested in the law as a social field in which an important part of the mechanisms of social production and reproduction are defined and executed, Caillosse is interested in the law itself and the possibilities of constructing a science of law. In his analysis of Bourdieu, Caillosse emphasizes, among other points, one that, in my view, is somewhat secondary : his pejorative view of lawyers and of their claims to possess their own rational and politically neutral truth. Caillosse could be correct in his complaint about Bourdieu's negative bias in that it is true that the law is something more than a symbolic pantomime maintaining the political power of certain social interests. However, in my view Bourdieu's emphasis is more rhetorical than analytical ; Bourdieu is trying to deconstruct the myths of the so-called *science juridique,* insofar as the law is a bastion of symbolic violence that allows the reproduction of the structure of social domination and the perception of the legitimacy of that process.

The above does not mean that Bourdieu's conceptualization of the law is invulnerable to criticism. The theory of Bourdieu can be challenged either as a critical theory or as a flawed critical theory. My reservations, which I

29. *Ibid.*, p. 103.

30. *Ibid.*

31. Pierre BOURDIEU, « La force du droit », *op. cit.*, p. 3 ; English version p. 816.

think I share with Professor Caillosse, address the second point ; that is, they refer to the inadequacies of its critical proposition. Although as stated above, the sociological theory of Bourdieu on law has great explanatory power and represents a significant advance over both materialist and communitarian critical theories, it has also important limitations. The emphasis on symbolic efficacy of law as an expression of legitimated state violence gives one the impression that the law is part of a hegemonic monolithic institutional order and that the fissures in this order are insignificant. This view of the state and of law has obscures the emancipatory potential which occasionally arises in the discourse on rights [32].

This statist and monopolistic outlook on the law is closely linked to French history and to the relationship of law and political power in that history. Since the French Revolution the law is conceived of as a matter of legislation, a fact which led to a clear separation between, on the one hand, legal doctrine aiming at being formalistic and « scientific, » and on the other hand, legal critique or sociolegal perspective, being political and ideological. Critical or anti-formalistic perspectives in France, and to a lesser extend on the European continent, usually dismiss legal autonomy and overestimate the sociological and political dimension of law.

In the Anglo-Saxon tradition, the role of the judge encouraged an interpretivist and political understanding of law. Whereas, in England and USA the term *law* relates to political power and does not necessarily include a concept of *right* - see for instance John Locke or the American Declaration of Independence -, in Europe terms like *droit, recht, diritto, derecho* had a larger meaning, including what was right. This is why critical view in Europe tends to get rid of the *law* in order to highlight rights as social rights not legal rights.

For anti-formalists and socio-legal movements in France - as well as in Latin American countries - law was seen as *political power* that ought to be denounced and replaced by another power and another law. This conception is part of a long European tradition rooted in the beginnings of the absolute monarchy in France at the dawn of the 17th century [33]. According to this, the law is the expression of state sovereignty embodied in the monarch. The French Revolution did not break with this tradition. On the contrary, it accentuated it by proposing the idea - initially put forward by Sieyès and later by Robespierre - of popular sovereignty. The writings of Rousseau, interpreted by Sieyès, did not leave much room for political critique through law.

32. See Michael McCann and Tracy March, « Law and Everyday Forms of Resistance : A Socio-Political Assessment », in Austin Sarat and Susan Silbey (eds.), *Studies in Law, Politics, and Society*, London, JAI Press, 1995 ; Michael McCann, « Resistance, Reconstruction, and Romance in Legal Scholarship », *Law and Society Review*, 26 (4), 1992, p. 733-749 ; Boaventura de Sousa Santos, « Oppositional Postmodernism and Globalization », *Law and Social Inquiry*, 23 (1), 1998, p. 121-139.

33. On this point, see for instance Jean Van Houtte, « La sociologie du droit ou les limites d'une science », *Droit et Société*, 3, 1986, p. 171-186.

In short, Bourdieu's critique of law should be understood as an attack on a particular type of political domination through law that had a particularly successful moment in French political and institutional history. That model, nowadays, is in crisis, in France and throughout the world, or at least it no longer has the force that it once had. This does not necessarily mean that domination is less effective ; simply that it utilizes multifaceted and frequently opposed conditions. In the specific case of the law, Bourdieu's theory does not enable us to understand the intricate problems of inter-legality and legal pluralism that occur in contemporary societies as an outgrowth of the confluence of national, local and transnational orders that can be and often are mutually exclusive. Bourdieu had a view of the legal field that was too nationally rooted, as authors like Dezalay and Garth have assumed the task of disproving through their own Bourdieu's theory of social fields.

III. Bourdieu's Approach to the Disagreements between Lawyers and Sociologists

One of the first surprises for researchers new to the sociolegal debate in France is the enormous importance that disciplinary differences between jurists and sociologists assume in this country. In general terms, these disagreements have been fueled by political-cultural factors : opposing perceptions of the world owing to the social and institutional emphases of the two profession ; differentiation between lawyers and sociologists in terms of hierarchal social status which leads to conflicting political opinions, etc. [34]. Of course this does not happen only in France ; different cultural and political sensibilities characterize the legal and sociological communities in other countries as well. However, what in other countries is a difference in the focus, in France is almost antipathy. I will use Bourdieu's social theory to assess this point.

The clash between lawyers and sociologists in France may be associated with the type of legal doctrine created out of the French Revolution, and the strength with which lawyers exert the monopoly of legal interpretation inside this legal doctrine. Let me explain. In each legal tradition different protagonists of the legal debate - judges, legislators, and professors - have attained different positions and amount of power. The contrast between Common Law and Civil Law jurisdictions is rooted in the political and social history of England and the continent. Since 1200 England has possessed a unified legal system called, for this reason, common law. This is even more important if we take into consideration the fact that France reached the stage of one code of laws for the whole realm just before the Revolution of

34. André-Jean ARNAUD, *Le droit trahi par la sociologie*, Paris, LGDJ, coll. « Droit et Société. Recherches et travaux », 1998 ; Jacques COMMAILLE, « La sociologie du droit en France. Les ambiguïtés d'une spécialisation », *Sociologia del diritto*, 16 (2), 1989, p. 19-42.

1789 and Germany accomplished the same task in the 19th century [35]. Codification on the continent was the response, brought about by the Enlightenment, to a great need for rationalization and organization. English lawyers never felt such a need. Since feudal times the King of England had been able to organize and centralize judicial practice so the local jurisdiction and feudal courts diminished in importance.

In France, efforts aiming at the consolidation of a unified legal system came about with the creation of the absolutist state in the 16th century [36]. But the French legal system was not really unified until the end of the Revolution, when the Civil Code was put in place. Since the Revolution, legislation is alleged to be the source of the legal system whereas the role of the judiciary is relegated to the task of mechanical application. Not only did the law acquire a great deal of formality and rationality but also there was a clear separation between the political function of creation - corresponding to the legislators - and the technical function of adjudication, which was supposed to be driven by free value judgment [37]. This is why the legal mainstream never accepted the limitation on the autonomy of the law vis-à-vis social facts and political powers. The main debate vexing legal scholars pitted scholars supporting legal positivism against those advocating natural law. It was framed to answer the question of whether or not the legal system was autonomous from fundamental values, not from social values or constitutional values.

In short, the dominance of professors and lawmakers in the process of fostering autonomy in the French legal system favored a formalistic type of legal science, divorced from practice, and self-sufficient. This in turn accentuated the importance of the symbolic capital earned by protagonists in the legal field, individuals whose fate was closely tied to that of the dominant interests. This particular historical formation not only created a type of legal critique that reduced law to political manipulation, as explained above, but also established epistemological barriers to communication between sociologists and lawyers. It is important to bear in mind that Bourdieu writes in this very particular French context, and therefore it is also important to understand his theory from that context.

Conclusion

In this essay I have tried to bring a historical and comparative perspective to the debates on law and society in France and particularly to the as-

35. R. C. van Caenegem, *Judges, Legislators and Professors : Chapters in European Legal History*, Cambridge, Cambridge University Press, 1987, p. 94.

36. Perry Anderson, *El Estado Absolutista*, Madrid, Siglo Veintiuno Editores, 1979.

37. A different development took place in America over the course of the 19th century, with the consolidation of the idea that judges make a significant portion of the law. The explanation of this trend had to do with the history of judges in America and their relation to political power. On this point see R. C. van Caenegem, *Judges, Legislators and Professors, op. cit.*

sessment of Bourdieu's conception of the legal field within this debate. My first point has been that such an assessment should be contextualized in the disciplinary disputes and prejudices reigning between sociologists and lawyers, which have been determined by the history of legal doctrine and legal formalism in France. Because Bourdieu's view of the law did not escape this disciplinary dustup, it is useful to put his thought in context, beginning from the particular features of the legal field that he had in mind.

In the second place, criticisms of Bourdieu's thought on law are often launched from the theory of law (*jurisprudence*) and thus tend to underestimate the importance of his social theory and especially his idea of habitus, to the comprehension and correct appraisal of his contribution on legal phenomena.

In the third place, the sociolegal debate in France frequently hides a deeper and more fundamental debate between *consensus* and *conflict* theories, which likewise implicates a division between progressive and conservative theories. Generally speaking, the true debate on the sociological meaning of law - and this is what Bourdieu's work takes up, and not a science of law - is determined by theoretical presuppositions on social theories, *i.e.* the author's position on a theoretical spectrum on which these two theories are at the extremes [38]. So, for example, lawyer's reservations about the idea that the law is a particularly efficient form of symbolic violence exerted legitimately by the state, originate - mostly unconsciously - in a sort of consensus, or liberal, conception of society rather than in a legal conception.

Finally, the critical and disciplinary emphasis in Bourdieu's thought on the law obscures the political complexity of law in contemporary society and, particularly, the ambiguous nature of rights as tools for social emancipation. Although they generally operate to bolster state legitimacy (symbolic efficacy) they also have the potential to be appropriated by social movements and to serve as a political weapon against hegemonic power. Bourdieu's lack of acknowledgment of this complexity is closely linked to the French history of rights and the political role that they have filled. Nevertheless, Bourdieu's critical theory represents an advance in comparison to other critical theories, which, in France, have basically been related to the work of Durkheim or Marx. Pierre Lascoumes, for example, has argued that those countries in which legal sociology developed under the influence of Durkheim - such as France, Belgium, and Spain - created a positivist legal sociology that little by little lost its independence from law [39]. On the other hand, the countries influenced by Max Weber's legal sociology - Anglo-Saxon countries, Germany, and Italy - put more stress on interpretation and were more flexible in epistemological terms, which facilitated its develop-

38. On the concept of theoretical presupposition see Jeffrey ALEXANDER, *Twenty Lectures*, New York, Columbia University Press, 1987.

39. Jacques COMMAILLE, « The Law and Science : Dialectics Between the Prince and the Maidservant », *Law and Policy*, 10 (2/3), 1983, p. 253-265.

ment [40]. The scholarly work of Pierre Bourdieu may represent a third path - closer perhaps to Weber than to Durkheim - with the potential to move the studies of law and society ahead. But of course these ideas deserve more time to be developed [41].

40. See Pierre LASCOUMES, « Le droit comme science sociale. La place de E. Durkheim dans les débats entre juristes et sociologues à la charnière des deux derniers siècles (1870-1914) », in François CHAZEL and Jacques COMMAILLE (sous la dir.), *Normes juridiques et régulation sociale*, Paris, LGDJ, 1991, p. 39-49 ; also Évelyne SERVERIN, *Sociologie du droit*, Paris, La Découverte, 2000, p. 46, and Michael POLLAK, « La place de Max Weber dans le champ intellectuel français », *Droit et Société*, 9, 1988, p. 189-203. In the French context the underestimation of Weber's sociology of law lies also in the political opposition between two French sociologists : Raymond Aron - defending Weber's ideas - and Georges Gurvitch drawing upon Durkheimian social theory (Michael POLLAK, « La place de Max Weber dans le champ intellectuel français », *op. cit.*), the latter being the most important representative of French sociology of law in the mid-twentieth century.

41. I would like to thank Director Jacques Commaille for his invitation to participate in this discussion on the work of Pierre Bourdieu and its implications for the study of law.

Part V
Foucault, Discipline and Regulation

[17]

*Between Governance and Discipline: The Law and Michel Foucault**

VICTOR TADROS†

Abstract—This article attempts to re-establish the importance of Foucault's work for an understanding of the way in which modern law operates. This argument has two stages. Firstly, there is a critique of the interpretation of Foucault's work by legal and sociological thinkers. It is argued that by reading the term 'juridical' as synonymous with the term 'law' in Foucault, people miss the substance of Foucault's argument. The term juridical describes an arrangement and a representation of power rather than the law. This is made clear through a critique of J. S. Mill's *On Liberty* which is shown to make a juridical distinction between power and a free space of action which is unsustainable. Secondly, Foucault's genealogy of power relations is recast from the perspective of a legal theoretician. Foucault's history of power relations is constructed from historical differences in the mode of operation of power and discourse. By analysing these differences and their relationship to the mode of operation of law, an account of the place of modern law in Foucault's genealogy is established. Modern law operates between Foucault's concepts of government and discipline. It provides a key way in which government decisions can adjust the relationships between disciplinary institutions. This introduces the idea that law begins to operate in the perspective of the complete lives of individuals rather than just to prevent certain actions. Law, then, operates in accordance with what Foucault calls 'bio-power'.

1. *Introduction*

A number of scholars whose approach is within the Critical Legal Studies movement have recently expressed scepticism about Michel Foucault's understanding of law. In turn, in this article, I would like to express scepticism about their understanding of Foucault's work in general and in particular his argument about the decline of the juridical matrix of power. In the first part of the article I would like to show some of the inadequacies of recent jurisprudential scholarship on Foucault. Briefly there are two different claims which have been raised against Foucault's understanding of law. The first is developed by Hunt and Wickham in their book *Foucault and the Law*[1] and is shared by Peter Fitzpatrick. They

* Many thanks go to Costas Douzinas, Gunther Teubner, Kenneth Campbell, John Gardner and Adam Tomkins for their instructive comments on an earlier draft of this paper.

† School of Law, King's College London.

[1] *Foucault and the Law: Towards a Sociology of Law as Governance* (London: Pluto Press, 1994). Hereafter referred to as Hunt and Wickham (1994).

argue that in contrasting 'juridical power' and 'disciplinary power' he reduces the law to simple formulae which do not adequately describe its nature in the modern world. In this reading 'juridical power' is equated with 'legal power', an equation which I would resist. The second criticism of Foucault, which is slightly more sophisticated, is argued for by Boaventura de Sousa Santos in his book *Toward a New Common Sense.*[2] He suggests that although Foucault is correct in highlighting the role which disciplinary power has played in modern society, he underestimates the extent to which disciplinary power is intertwined with juridical power. Again Santos equates 'juridical power' with 'legal power'. In failing to appreciate the contrast which Foucault makes between disciplinary power and the juridical matrix I would argue that the potential of Foucault's work to position modern law[3] is lost.

Both Hunt and Wickham and Santos attempt to find in Foucault's work an answer to the question 'what are the minimum conditions for a statement or system of statements to be considered as law?'. By concentrating on this kind of question both the originality of Foucault's approach and the challenge which such an approach provides are lost. Foucault's genealogical method analyses the political structures of power relations in different periods, bringing out their particularity through the historical *changes* that take place. In line with this, it is the *differences* between the modes of operation of law that characterize a Foucauldian approach rather than what they have in common. That is not to say that one *could not* find the minimum conditions for a discourse to be considered as law but this is just not Foucault's question. Furthermore, his studies *do not* rely on any particular answer to this question. For Hunt and Wickham and Santos the term 'juridical' refers directly to law and thus, for them, it is by analysing this term that one could discover the answer to this question. But a careful reading of Foucault shows that it is not his intention to equate the terms 'juridical' and 'law'. The term juridical, as we shall see, refers to the *conception of power relations* which one might call Austinian. It is neither the case that all law is necessarily 'juridical' in Foucault's understanding of the term nor that the only way in which juridical power manifests itself is legal.

What is at stake in the different interpretations of the term 'juridical'? Once this term is understood correctly, the position of the law in Foucault's work becomes an open question. This leaves us with two problems which this article is designed to address. Firstly, if it is the case that law, for Foucault, is not necessarily juridical and that the juridical does not always find its expression in law the question remains as to the relationship between this juridical conception of power relations and the law. But secondly, and more importantly, if Hunt and Wickham are mistaken about the relationship between the juridical and the

[2] *Toward a New Common Sense: Law, Science and Politics in Paradigmatic Transition* (London: Routledge, 1995). hereafter referred to as Santos (1995).

[3] Foucault's work, until the end of the 1970s, distinguishes between three periods; the Middle Ages, the Classical Age, and the Modern Age. Roughly, the Middle Ages extends from the twelfth century to the middle of the seventeenth, the Classical Age runs from the middle of the seventeenth until the end of the eighteenth century and the Modern Age begins at the beginning of the nineteenth century.

law, a re-evaluation of the relationship between the *other* mechanisms of power and the law is called for. For Foucault the juridical conception of power relations no longer adequately describes the way in which power predominantly operates in modern society; as Foucault has famously written, 'in political thought and analysis, we still have not cut off the head of the king';[4] the ancient conception of power as a possession which is wielded to deny certain forms of action is still in place but it no longer effectively describes the various ways in which power manifests itself. If the law is not necessarily juridical in its operation, and I would argue that in modern society it is not even predominantly juridical in Foucault's sense, then the relationship between the law and the modern forms of power (that is discipline and government) needs to be re-evaluated. The criticism that Foucault reduces *law* to the Austinian conception of 'rules + sanctions' cannot, then, be levelled at Foucault as, for him, this is the very mode of operation of power which has been superceded. And this supercession has resulted not only in the proliferation of disciplinary power but also in the transformation of law. Whilst jurisprudential scholarship since Hart has not failed to perceive the changing character of law it has failed to situate it historically and politically. That is to say, by considering the analytical question 'what is law?' in isolation, jurisprudential scholarship has not accounted for the *historical differences* in law's evolution. The rich history of *critique* which is associated with this philosophy of difference is thus lost to the Anglo-American tradition. By attempting to bring this question of the *nature* of law back to Foucault, Hunt and Wickham also miss this vital element of Foucault's genealogical method.[5]

On a more general level, a Foucauldian account of the law should help to show some weaknesses in the liberal position on law. Foucault's work shows that the liberal understanding of power which opposes the areas controlled by social and state power to a space of freedom is inadequate when seen against the background of the multiplicitous operations of power. The liberal conception sees power as operating predominantly on a field of acts. The primary question for liberal theory is 'which acts ought to be permitted and which acts ought to be prohibited? Foucault's account of power relations, however, shows that power is involved in the construction of the *lives* of individuals and, in modern society at least, is exercised on the field of lives. Power is not only preventative, it is also creative or as Foucault would put it, it is not only deductive, it is also

[4] Foucault, *The History of Sexuality* Vol. 1 (trans Hurley, London: Penguin, 1978) Introduction at 88–9. Hereafter referred to as *HoS*.

[5] Whilst Hunt and Wickham are aware of Foucault's 'anti-subjectivist' view of history, they do not recognize the implications of this position. For Foucault, as for Heidegger, man is thrown into a historical frame which he inherits and which does not evolve according to the intentions of a rational animal that lies outside this evolution and directs it. The paradigm shifts in different historical periods, in Foucault, consist not just of an alteration of the subject, then, but of an alteration of the 'frame' of social phenomena themselves. By showing how the subject is constructed within the social frame, then, Foucault's predominant purpose is not to criticize traditional historical methodology (though this is one implication of his work). His predominant purpose is to provide a critique of modernity through a thorough analysis of the social frame in which the subject is immanent. The juridical conception of power provides one way in which the subject is constructed (as a transgressor) and it is to this that Foucault contrasts 'bio-power' whereby man is not seen predominantly through his transgression but with regard to his 'complete life'.

productive. But this creative or productive form of power does not take the spectacular form of legal or social interdiction. It operates through successive, trivial moments of exercise. Foucault makes this clear by using the concept of discipline. The succession of disciplinary forces, however, results in a dominating form which both constructs the subject and subjects him to subtle forms of control. As a result of Foucault's analysis, liberal theory, which still dominates legal philosophy, seems directed towards an archaic vision of society which was displaced more than 200 years ago. The dominant and dominating form of modern power which is characterized by discipline evades the liberal attack. As the law is complicit in this modern regime of power, the consequences of a Foucauldian account of the relationship between law and power provides a fundamental challenge to liberal jurisprudence. This can be shown most clearly against the background of Foucault's genealogy of power relations. Consequently, in the second part of the paper, I would like to try to re-establish Foucault's schema in order to discover the position of modern law in the continuum of power relations. To do this I will show how the juridical matrix has been replaced by the two poles of bio-power: the disciplinary network and techniques of governance. A brief summary of my argument would be as follows. The juridical conception defines power in relation to a series of acts. It defines which acts transgress and which are permitted. Law is not the only way in which the transgressive threshold is defined nor is it the only way in which it is enforced. As John Stuart Mill, who might be called a typically juridical thinker, makes clear in *On Liberty* both social power and legal power can define the transgressive threshold. Hence what Foucault calls 'the juridical' is not equivalent to legal power. It describes any form of power which attempts to prevent a certain type of action through the threat of legal or social sanctions.

Foucault argues that this is not the predominant way in which power is exercised in the Modern Age. Rather, he suggests, modern power can be described by the term 'bio-power'. Bio-power does not operate in relation to a series of acts but rather in relation to the lives of individuals. Bio-power has two poles; discipline and governmentality. Discipline operates on particular individuals in a particular space. It collects information about an individual and acts according to that information. In the Classical Age it occurs in schools and workshops. In the Modern Age it spreads to families and hospitals and begins to be exercised by marginal religious groups, psychiatrists, psychologists, and social workers. Governmentality, on the other hand, operates on particular groups of individuals. It receives information through statistical analyses, financial reports and population registers. Its techniques of power are directed to making adjustments in the population and their economic condition. Legislation is one technique which is used to make these adjustments. It works alongside the other governmental devices which, in the eighteenth century, were collected under the name of the police.

Once we have developed the mode of formation and operation of these two poles of bio-power we will be in a position to consider the role of modern law.

Law, in my understanding operates as a field through which techniques of governance can intervene in the disciplinary network. Law, then, acts as an interface through which governmental decisions can take effect by adjusting the operations and arrangements of the disciplinary mechanisms. But by connecting itself to both of the poles of bio-power law, in justifying itself, it masks the need of each of these forms of power to legitimate themselves.

2. *Critique Misses the Target*

In *Foucault and the Law* Hunt and Wickham state that Foucault's understanding of law does not take into account the variety of roles which law plays in modern society. Their argument is based on two related claims. The first is that Foucault regards the law as equivalent to rules backed up by power and the second is that he equates the law with sovereignty. Of the former they write; 'the formula "law = rules + sanctions" lies at the heart of the positivist tradition in jurisprudence. It is thus pertinent that Foucault chooses to direct his fire against this widely held and influential conception of law, but fails to engage with any more sophisticated conceptions which seek to explore the connection between legal regulation, legal rights and constitutionalism' (Hunt and Wickham, 1994: 41). Hence they suggest that Foucault's conception of law falls to the same criticism which H. L. A. Hart famously made of Austin in *The Concept of Law.* To equate the law with criminal law, they argue, simply excludes too much. If regulation is one of the primary modes of power in modern western society then the law has an important role to play in the exercise of this form of power. In arguing for the latter the authors claim that Foucault equates law with pre-modern forms of power. They suggest that Foucault regards the law as emanating at every instance from sovereignty. They write that 'the strict association which Foucault makes between sovereignty and law is at best unhelpful and at worst simply perverse in denying the self-evident truth of the intimate connection between modern forms of power and legal mechanisms' (Hunt and Wickham, 1994: 62–3).

By formulating their argument in this way Hunt and Wickham have made clear a fundamental misunderstanding about Foucault's project as a whole. Foucault, as they themselves suggest, does not have a theory of what law, in all its different manifestations, *is*. Foucault was anything but a closet positivist. The law, in Foucault's account, operates in a number of different ways and within a number of different relationships of power. Hence François Ewald, who was a close colleague of Foucault, has written that we must 'imagine a history of law that would give meaning and function to the law's varying modes of formal expression'.[6] *The* Law does not operate in the same way and in the same structures over history. And both its role and its formal

[6] Ewald, 'Norms, Discipline and Law' in Post (ed.), *Law and the Order of Culture* (University of California Press, 1991) at 139. Hereafter referred to as Ewald (1990).

expression are at least partially governed by the predominant ways in which power is exercised.

Hunt and Wickham derive their argument about law from a number of statements which Foucault has written concerning 'the juridical'. Hence they quote Foucault from *The History of Sexuality* Vol. 1 where he writes 'we shall try to rid ourselves of a juridical and negative representation of power, and cease to conceive of it in terms of law, prohibition, liberty and sovereignty' (*HoS*: 90–1; Hunt and Wickham, 1994: 40). But whilst Foucault is arguing that power must not be understood in terms of the juridical, Hunt and Wickham seem to be suggesting that law must not be understood in terms of juridical power. Whilst they are clearly correct in not seeing law in this way, their argument would seem to have little relation to Foucault's understanding of the juridical. In his essay *Norms, Discipline and the Law* Ewald has already warned against lawyers equating juridical power and real law itself. We must, he writes, be careful to 'distinguish law and its formal expression from the juridical' (Ewald, 1990: 139). This is what Hunt and Wickham fail to do. In failing to provide an analysis of what Foucault means by 'the juridical', the nature of Foucault's argument is lost.

A similar criticism can be levelled at Boaventura de Sousa Santos. Santos argues that whilst disciplinary power is an important part of modern society, it has not replaced but only supplemented juridical power. For Santos, juridical power and disciplinary power are compatible with each other. There is, he writes, 'a deep interpenetration' between the two, which allows the 'isomorphic transformation of the former into an alter-ego of the latter' (Santos, 1995: 4). It is the possibility of these transformations, Santos suggests, that allows defendants to be at once legal and medical subjects and hence to be disposed of either to prisons or psychiatric institutions from the courtroom.

Again, this account seems to equate juridical power with the law. Furthermore, in *Discipline and Punish* Foucault provides us with a more than adequate account of the 'isomorphism' of which Santos writes. He suggests that the colonization of the punitive technology by the disciplinary mechanism has resulted in a continuum which operates between the hospital and the prison as well as including schools, the military and even social services. The possibility of alternative methods of disposal, in an account compatible with Foucault, would arise from the fact that *both* the prison and the psychiatric hospital are disciplinary institutions. The law, in this account, operates as a relay between the police and the disciplinary institutions, an idea which I hope to develop later.

The whole issue of the relationship between law and the different manifestations of power, which is probably the central theoretical advantage which can be provided by a Foucauldian account of law, is obscured if the term 'juridical' is read as synonymous with the term 'law'. The shifting structure of power relations provides the background against which the evolution of law can be understood. Even the criminal law, which has often been seen as the sole justification for an Austinian conception of law, can be understood as operating as a part of a disciplinary regime against which its gradual transformation can be better appreciated. The psychiatrization of the modern criminal law, which has been well recognized, can best be understood as a disciplinary phenomena. It is not, I would argue, an example of the law bowing to the pressure of 'scientific knowledge'. Rather it is the law bowing to a disciplinary necessity:[7] discipline requires more than just a legal transgression to impose a punishment. It requires that punishment *serves a purpose* in the context of the complete life of the individual or the particular group of which he or she is a part. Whilst the criminal law, to a certain extent, retains its juridical justifications and operates in a juridical way (punishing according to the nature of the transgression alone to deny that transgression) it also begins to evolve according to the disciplinary network of which it is a part. As we can see, and this should become clearer later, in modern society there is a complex relationship between the juridical justifications of law and the disciplinary network in which it takes its place in modern society.

3. *What is the Juridical?*

Perhaps a first step towards a more rigorous understanding of Foucault would be to consider more carefully the term 'juridical'. I have already suggested that for Foucault the juridical is not equivalent to law in all its manifestations. What, then, does the term refer to?

The term 'juridical', in Foucault's work, is somewhat difficult to pin down. He seems to use the term both to describe a discursive understanding of power, which could be either Modern or Classical and to describe a particular network of power; a real set of power relations which are connected together in a particular form. Ewald suggests that when Foucault uses the term he is referring merely to the discourse through which power articulates itself. The juridical, for Ewald, is a ' "code" that enabled monarchical power to constitute itself' (Ewald, 1991: 139). This is a little misleading. In *HoS* Foucault, in talking of 'the juridical system of law', suggests that 'law cannot help but be armed, and its arm, *par excellence*, is death' (*HoS*: 144). The juridical system, then, is not merely a discourse: it is armed. We must, however, be careful in interpreting this statement by Foucault. It is clear that Foucault is not talking about law as it manifests itself in the Modern Age. As he writes later, when bio-power grows in importance at the expense of the juridical 'the law operates more and more as a norm' (*HoS*: 144). The modern form of law, in Foucault's understanding is not juridical. Foucault contrasts modern law itself with juridical law. In order to capture the

[7] On the one hand this results in extreme sentences being given to offenders who commit a series of minor 'social nuisances' (see, for example, *Dawn Clarke* (1975) 61 *Cr App R* 320). On the other it results in extremely light sentences for offenders who seriously transgress but for whom there is no purpose in punishing; a vivid example of this can be seen in the infanticide legislation. In both cases psychiatric concepts, which are at best scientifically dubious, are used to justify these legal decisions. In the former it is the concept of psychopathy, in the latter it is the psychiatric conditions following birth (see the Infanticide Act 1938). The former has been shown, by Baroness Wootton amongst others, to be circular whereas the latter, as Seabourne Davies notes in an article written at the time at which the Infanticide Act was passed, was never the basis upon which that Act was passed: see 'Child Killing in English Law' (1937) 1 *MLR* 203.

heterogeneous nature of 'the juridical' in Foucault's work, then, we must understand the term as referring both to a code which is used to describe power (a juridical discourse) *and* as a real network of power relations that was once in place.

This becomes a little clearer in Foucault's *Two Lectures*.[8] In the second lecture, Foucault talks of the disjunction between the operations of disciplinary power and the juridical code that masks them. He suggests that power has maintained a way of describing itself which has little relation to the actual operations of power in modern society. Foucault calls the code by which power is described juridical whereas the actual mechanisms of power are known as disciplinary. However, in making this distinction he also suggests that the juridical code was originally articulated along with a particular arrangement of power relations that we might call a network or matrix. That is not to say that *power itself* can ever be described according to a juridical configuration but rather that individual power relations were once linked together in a network which can be so described. It is the whole system of connected power relations in the Middle Ages that we might call juridical rather than any particular exercise of power.

Hence we must consider three different phenomena if we are to understand the sophistication of Foucault's argument about law; firstly there is the law itself (which may take a number of different forms), secondly there is the network of power relations (which, at different times, may be either juridical or disciplinary, for example) and finally there is the code by which power presents itself (which for Foucault is consistently juridical).

We are now in a position to consider some of the elements of the juridical code itself. To do this I would like to consider the work of John Stuart Mill, a typical juridical thinker. I would like to show how Mill attempts to make a distinction between power and the free space which it maintains and how this distinction, in Mill's own work, collapses.

4. *What is in the Libertarian Space?*

> 'One still believes in good and evil and experiences the triumph of the good and the annihilation of evil as a task (that is English; typical case: the flathead John Stuart Mill)'.[9]

As the juridical discourse would have it, the series of acts form the field on which power is exercised. The law or morality traditionally defines, more or less precisely, the series of possible actions, certain of which are prohibited and certain of which are left within the free space. The liberalism of John Stuart Mill

[8] Foucault, *Two Lectures in Power/Knowledge*, C. Gordon, (ed.) (Hemel Hempstead: Harvester/Wheatsheaf, 1980). Hereafter referred to as *TL*.

[9] Nietzsche, *The Will to Power*, Kaufmann and Hollingdale (trans) (New York: Vintage, 1968) at 21. Many thanks go to Adam Tomkins for drawing my attention to this quote.

is a good example of this juridical trend and by considering his essay *On Liberty*[10] I hope to bring out the shift which Foucault traces from the juridical matrix to the modern forms of power.

In *On Liberty* Mill argues that there are two forms of power; the power of the state and social power. The former operates through the threat of legal punishments whereas the latter operates through social mandates. Both of these utilize sanctions in order to discourage the individual from committing certain acts. In general, Mill continues, independence needs to be defended against both of these forms of power. Mill therefore writes that 'there is a limit to the legitimate interference of collective opinion with individual independence' (Mill, 1859: 9). The role of good politics, for Mill, is to discover that limit. However, Mill suggests, the very possibility of benefiting from a free life depends on limiting certain actions by others. 'All that makes existence valuable to any one,' Mill writes, 'depends on the enforcement of restraints upon the actions of other people' (Mill 1859: 9). Therefore some rules of law and some forms of moral or social mandate must be imposed in order to restrain these undesirable, liberty-limiting, actions. It would seem, then, that it is freedom itself that legitimizes or authorizes the exercise of power. One could, Mill thought, decide whether a particular action ought to be restrained according to the principle of harm; it is those actions which are significantly harmful to others that need to be prevented through legal and social power. He writes: 'the only purpose for which power can rightfully be exercised over any member of a civilized community, against his will, is to prevent harm to others' (Mill, 1859: 14). This argument would seem to be in line with his famous utilitarianist doctrine of which I need say no more.

If Mill's *On Liberty* can be regarded as a typical example of juridical thinking, then, it would seem that the juridical understanding of power is only articulated against a series of acts that it helps to define. In the juridical system acts must be distinguished according to what Luhmann calls a binary code; legal/illegal, or moral/immoral. And it is against this background of acts that its success or failure becomes visible. Hence, if we consider Mill's scheme in terms of law alone, we might find a 'loophole in the law' within which the law allows one to commit a harmful act. This would be an example of legal inadequacy. Alternatively, we might find the law overextending itself; the law might exercise its power to prevent a certain act which is not harmful.[11] Hence the problem of

[10] J. S. Mill, 'On Liberty' in *On Liberty and Other Essays* (Oxford: Oxford University Press, 1991). Hereafter referred to as Mill (1859).

[11] The case of *R* v *Brown* has been argued along these lines. In that case the defendants were convicted of sado-masochistic activity with full consent. On the one hand the case has been regarded as a substantial infringement on the liberty of the defendants, who did no harm to anyone outside their circle. Hence Lord Lowry states the case for the defence as follows; 'So far as I can see, the only counter argument is that to place a restriction on sado-masochism is an unwarranted interference with the private life and activities of persons who are indulging in a lawful pursuit and are doing no harm to anyone except, possibly, themselves' *R* v *Brown* [1993] 2 All ER 75 at 100; see also Lord Mustill's dissenting judgment in which he states that although the acts are morally repulsive, they are within the sphere of private morality and hence should not be punished by the law. On the other hand the decision to convict was defended on just this basis. Hence Lord Templeman stated that 'society is entitled and bound to protect itself against a cult of violence. Pleasure derived from the infliction of pain is an evil thing. Cruelty is uncivilized'—ibid at 84.

legitimacy unfolds only on the basis of which acts are to be prevented and which are to be allowed. Whether power is exercised socially or legally, it defines a threshold of transgression; to act 'against' the predominant mechanisms of power in this scheme is not to resist; it is to transgress, to cross the threshold which marks the limit of the legal or social free space.

The absolute difference between this free space of legitimate action and the acts on which power could legitimately be exercised is the core distinction of *On Liberty* and of liberal thought in general. Through the liberal discourse, then, rules are articulated onto a series of acts and these rules are general and impersonal. As Anne Barron has put it; 'General rules therefore delineate spheres of autonomy within which individuals may pursue ends of their own choosing absolutely free of state interference'.[12] General rules are directed at acts and not at individuals; they are not specific to a class or to an individual. The paradigm of power, in this reading, is law.

As we have seen, at the beginning of *On Liberty*, Mill defines his problem in terms of the extent to which power can legitimately limit action; 'some rules of conduct', he writes, '... must be imposed, by law in the first place, and by opinion on many things which are not fit subjects for the operation of the law. What these rules should be, is the principal question in human affairs' (Mill, 1859: 9). But in Section IV of *On Liberty* there is a slippage of this distinction and this slippage undermines it. It arises because Mill becomes aware that juridical power cannot go to the heart of individual action. Power, in Mill's scheme, can only prevent the most disordered action from occurring. It cannot encourage ordered or advantageous action. But we cannot be expected not to interfere with the actions of another in any way at all unless these acts are harmful. Mill is aware of this difficulty and he hopes to overcome it with a further distinction. And this distinction can be read as superceding that between the sphere of power and the 'autonomous spheres' which help to legitimate it. It is worth quoting the relevant passage in full.

> 'It would be a great misunderstanding of this doctrine to suppose that it is one of selfish indifference,' Mill writes, 'which pretends that human beings have no business with each other's conduct in life, and that they should not concern themselves about the well-doing or well-being of one another, unless their own interest is involved. Instead of any diminution there is a need of a great increase of disinterested exertion to promote the good of others. But disinterested benevolence can find other instruments to persuade people to their good than whips and scourges, either of the literal or the metaphorical sort' (Mill, 1859: 84).

The new difference which emerges, then, is the difference between 'whips and scourges' (that is the social and legal power that Mill defined at the beginning of his essay) and 'other instruments' of persuasion, the 'disinterested exertion to promote the good of others'. But it is difficult to see how this difference is

[12] Barron, 'Legal Discourse and the Colonisation of the Self in the Modern State' in Carty (ed.), *Post-Modern Law* at 110.

anything more than the difference between two ways of exercising power. The term 'exertion' itself is nothing more than a synonym for the exercise of power. Furthermore, the distinction between the social power of Part I and these 'other instruments' is barely intelligible. 'Human beings,' Mill writes, 'owe to each other help to distinguish the better from the worse, and encouragement to choose the former and avoid the latter'. And yet he suggests that 'neither one person, nor any number of persons, is warranted in saying to another human creature of ripe years, that he shall not do with his life for his own benefit what he chooses to do with it' (Mill, 1859: 84). But Mill provides us with no way of distinguishing between the 'encouragement' of the first quote and the 'saying to another creature ... that he shall not do' of the second.

The precise meaning of this 'shall' in Mill's sense of social power is unclear. When one uses the word 'shall' there is an imperative to act or not to act. But this imperative, like encouragement, can always be resisted. The 'shall' does not have legal force behind it but only social sanction. But it is unclear how the 'encouragement' of the first quote is anything other than a force which can be resisted itself. If there is a distinction in the quality of such a force, Mill does not make it clear precisely what that distinction is. The more likely solution is that it would be a distinction in quantity. In that case, though, it would be difficult to support the assertion that the imperative of the 'shall' is always stronger than the exertion of the encouragement.

This distinction which is indistinct, or rather difference to which we are indifferent, becomes, for Mill, the touchstone of legitimation. It is only the 'shall' which, in *On Liberty*, is subject to the requirements of legitimation. It is only in the cases of social sanction that we must decide whether interference is justified according to the principle of harm. There is an absence of legitimation in the free space, which itself is filled with the power of the 'encouragements'. This absence is itself legitimized by reference to 'nature'. Hence he writes;

> though doing no wrong to anyone, a person may so act as to compel us to judge him, and feel to him, as a fool, or as a being of an inferior order ... We have a right in various ways, to act upon our unfavourable opinion of any one, not to the oppression of his individuality, but in the exercise of ours ... We may give others a preference over him in optional good offices, except those which tend to his improvement. In these various modes a person may suffer very severe penalties at the hands of others, for faults which directly concern only himself; but he suffers these penalties only in so far as they are the natural, and, as it were, spontaneous consequences of the faults themselves, not because they are purposely inflicted on him for the sake of punishment. (Mill, 1859: 85–6).

However, the nature of these 'natural consequences' remains ambiguous. Mill avoids speculation about how these supposedly natural consequences are constructed, how they organize themselves and what relationship they have with the principles of ethics, truth, and justice themselves. It is not until one investigates the organization of the free space and the devices of power that are located there that one can consider the question of liberty at all. For the distinction between liberty and power upon which Mill relies and which underpins the whole discussion about the legitimacy of power turns out to be merely a distinction between one arrangement of power relations and another; in other words, there is a background to the question of legitimacy upon which it rests and which, in itself, cannot be the subject of legitimation. One cannot even raise the discussion about legitimacy without the social distinction between different forms of power.

Foucault's genealogy of power relations can be seen as tracing the background against which ethical decisions are made. This background is masked by the juridical contest between liberty and power. There is, for Foucault, no free space in which 'spontaneous' and 'natural action' occurs. The 'free space' is overdetermined by disciplinary power which partitions its gaps and which eventually colonizes the traditional site of juridical power as well. In what follows I would like to attempt a brief exegesis of this genealogy.

5. *State, Law, Sovereignty*

In order to trace this genealogy of power relations we must attempt to consider the juridical network at the time of its emergence in the Middle Ages. The law evolved in a particular way and it associated itself with particular mechanisms of power. By considering the form of law as it emerged in the Middle Ages I hope to show why it was that the juridical understanding of power came to establish itself so firmly as the way in which power was to be described.

Prior to the solidification of the state, according to Foucault, one finds a certain amount of disorganization in the field of power. Territory, more often than not, governed power relations; vassalage, suzerainty, and serfdom were common manifestations of this power. However, this disorganization gave rise to certain conflicts whose resolution could not be guaranteed. Without a hierarchy to unite them, the different territorial powers could only resolve conflicts through the sword. The principle of hierarchy was accepted as a solution to this violence. So long as every potential conflict could be solved at the pinnacle of the hierarchy, society would always be moving towards a state of order. Hence Foucault writes that if the states 'were able to gain acceptance, this was because they presented themselves as the agencies of regulation, arbitration, and demarcation, as a way of introducing order into the midst of these [prior] powers' (*HoS*: 87).

This is not to say that hierarchy was the way in which power was *exercised*. Hierarchy was a way of understanding power; it was, Foucault writes, 'by no means adequate to describe the manner in which power was and is exercised, but it is the code according to which power presents itself and prescribes that we conceive of it' (*HoS*: 88). The concept of the state achieved the codification of power. One could say that the codification of power responded to the urgent need for order. The power relations through which this hierarchy was constructed were already more or less in place. In achieving the codification of these power relations the state in Foucault is equivalent to what Deleuze and Guattari call an 'assemblage of capture'.[13] And perhaps the most important mechanism in this operation of capture was the law.[14]

The introduction of a more or less complete system of law, then, should not be thought of as a force wielded by the monarch to ensure compliance through the threat of a violence which he holds. The law succeeded not by exerting violence but by unifying through the alliance of power relations that were already in place. By the beginning of the Classical Age the codification of power relations was sufficiently established to have converted the prior mechanisms of power into a legal mechanism. The law, then, co-ordinated the pre-existing relationships of power and reduced the potential for conflict between the structures that they formed. In order to do this the law presented itself as a threshold of transgression and as the right of the Sovereign to use violence where the laws that constituted his sovereignty were violated. Law's *symbolic representation* was as a monopoly of the *right to violence*, primarily exercised by a Sovereign. Power was symbolically represented as a possession which is ultimately given to the Sovereign by God but which he could divide up as he saw fit, thus constructing hierarchies. However, as I have suggested, this does not adequately represent the way in which law actually operated. Whilst the law maintained the appearance of force, it actually worked, at least partially, by a co-ordination of pre-existing powers; trust law was a residue of this operation. The symbolic representation of law as the sovereign right to violence was a condition for the law's acceptance as well as a method for co-ordinating the form which the legal structure took. However, at least in a Foucauldian account, law operated as much through co-ordination as it did through violence.

This symbolic manifestation of law did, however, have its effects. It resulted in a juridical mechanism of law which had two parts which together produce truth and which together help to legitimize the operations of law today. The first part of the mechanism was the *investigation*. Through the investigation the court attempted to establish the truth of the act. It introduced into the law what Foucault calls 'an authoritarian search for truth'. The mechanism of power through which it functioned was the confession. Through confession the individual introduces into the law the truth about himself; where previously he had been authenticated by the ties of alliance and the truth of his crime had been established through the ordeals, in the confession he was 'authenticated by the discourse of truth he was able or obliged to pronounce concerning

[13] Deleuze and Guattari, *A Thousand Plateaus* (trans Massumi) (London: Athlone, 1988) at 437. Hereafter referred to as Deleuze and Guattari (1988).

[14] Deleuze and Guattari make the argument that the territorial powers already anticipated the form of the state, which they at once instituted and resisted. They write that 'there exist collective mechanisms that simultaneously ward off and anticipate the formation of a central power. The appearance of a central power is thus a function of a threshold or degree beyond which what is anticipated takes on consistency or fails to, and what is conjured away ceases to be so and arrives' (Deleuze and Guattari, 1988: 431–2). Foucault's account seems to be consistent with that of Deleuze and Guattari. Unfortunately there is not space to consider their rigorous account of state formation here.

himself' (*HoS*: 58). Hence by introducing the confession the law appropriated an advantage previously exercised solely by the Church: the ability to stimulate the power relationships which an individual had with himself for its own ends. The power relation which an individual had with himself became coupled to the law. The investigation also had the advantage of making the interdictions articulable to the law. When the method of establishing the truth was the ordeal, there was no need to specify the particular nature of the crime, the precise mode of its commission. However, once the confession was introduced it became possible to distinguish precisely one crime from another both in terms of its gravity and its type. The more the law required offences to be articulated by the defendant, the more it could respond to its own language and thus reproduce and regulate its own development.

The second part of the juridical network was spectacular punishment. In the Middle Ages a public and spectacular violence was guaranteed in cases of transgression. The aim of the execution, Foucault writes, 'was to make an example, not only by making people aware that the slightest offence was likely to be punished, but by arousing feelings of terror by the spectacle of power letting its anger fall upon the guilty person'.[15] But this form of punishment, unlike the modern penal system, also served as an articulation of the law itself. This articulation took two forms. Firstly the punishment was regarded as the final extraction of the confession. Hence Foucault writes that 'in the eighteenth century judicial torture functioned in that strange economy in which the ritual that produced truth went side by side with the ritual that produced the punishment' (*DP*: 42). But secondly this public violence expressed the force of the sovereign which was temporarily diminished by the crime. As the sovereign was the public embodiment of the law, the ritual of the scaffold was itself an articulation of the power of the law. In turn, although the law was not confined to its punitive form, the symbolic representation of law took a juridical form.

It is easy, then, to see why the juridical understanding of power became predominant in political theory in the Middle Ages and the Classical Age. Through the form of the confession the law effectively articulated a series of carefully defined acts which it would not tolerate. In order to discourage the public from committing these acts it utilized the threat of violence. By defining a series of acts the law defined a threshold beyond which it would not interfere. Hence the problem of legitimacy, towards the end of the Classical Age, was articulated in terms of where to draw this threshold. The problem remains the same for Mill and he answers it according to the principle of harm.

By the end of the Middle Ages, then, there was a juridical network of power that consisted of a hierarchy that was supported by the confession and spectacular punishments. To this was attached a juridical theory of power that articulated both the justification of sovereign power (which was at this stage more or less religious) and its form (which was hierarchical; power was held at the top of a

[15] Foucault, *Discipline and Punish* (trans Sheridan) (London: Penguin, 1979) at 58. Hereafter referred to as *DP*.

hierarchy and exercised downwards). That is not to say that there were not laws and other forms of power which operated above the juridical threshold. However, prior to the Classical Age, these forms of power were not symbols for the law; they consisted mostly of the ancient feudal and religious rights and the relationships of familial alliance that were already beginning to decline. Eventually, as the law took the juridical structure as its form, these ancient rights began to lose if not their effect then their coherence. Furthermore, because of the visibility of the punitive technology, there developed a symbolic equivalence between the criminal law and law which was, until very recently, maintained by political and legal theory. As a result of this symbolic equivalence law was seen as the Sovereign's right of force rather than the mechanism for a politics of direction.

6. *Discipline: Partitioning the Gaps*

'The disciplines,' writes Foucault, 'established an "infra-penality"; they partitioned an area that the laws had left empty; they defined and repressed a mass of behaviour that the relative indifference of the great systems of punishment had allowed to escape' (*DP*: 178). In order to understand the development of modern law it is necessary to be specific about the differences between this disciplinary form of power and the juridical form of which there are four.

1. *Discipline Intensifies as well as Represses.* The juridical, as we have seen operates by means of interdiction. It controls action by denying. Discipline, on the other hand operates in two directions at once. It discourages undisciplined action but it also encourages disciplined action. The encouragement may take a number of forms, not least of which is repetition; by encouraging the individual to repeat the same action over and over he attains what might be called a norm of behaviour; he becomes *normalized.*
2. *Discipline Homogenizes through Activities.* Juridical power operated by defining a threshold between two fields of activity. Either one had crossed the threshold or one hadn't. Discipline, on the other hand, prescribes a norm which one may hope to attain or a maximum which one may hope to achieve. There is no absolute difference between the space of the transgressive and the space of freedom for discipline. One does not transgress in discipline, one deviates or underachieves. Consequently, discipline does not describe spaces into which it cannot enter. It has the density of a 'perpetual penality that traverses all points and supervises every instant in the disciplinary institutions' (*DP*: 183). This precise quantification and qualification of behaviour allows a series of comparisons from which one can develop a hierarchy of values: a table.
3. *Discipline Acts in the Production of Subjects.* If the juridical network permanently presented itself to the subject in a spectacular form, its effect on the subject and his understanding of himself was difficult to direct. It was only the defendant, he who transgresses, that was encouraged to investigate

himself through the confession. Discipline, however, is more direct in the production of subjects. Through a homogenous application on a number of different subjects, discipline produced a norm. Deviation from this norm should not be seen as a minor transgression, it should be seen as defining the place of the individual amongst a series of other individuals. The most prominent example of this 'placing' occurs in the form of the examination of which, Foucault writes, 'each individual receives as his status his own individuality' (*DP*: 192). For Foucault, then, discipline does not just control or prevent particular acts, it produces particular subjects who will not just do what one wishes but who will always act in a particular manner, in the way one wishes.

4. *Disciplinary Power is Ideally Invisible in its Application.* The juridical network was attached to a visible exercise of power through which, as we have seen, it became effective. In doing so, the individual himself only became visible to the extent to which he transgressed; only as a site of transgression and a site upon which the power of the sovereign can be exercised. Disciplinary power, on the other hand, attempts to cast light away from itself and onto the individual. Panopticism is the predominant example of this principle. The principle of Panopticism is to see without being seen; to exercise power through observation alone. By making the individual constantly observable to itself, discipline exercises power with the minimum of violence and is, as a result, more difficult to resist; disciplinary power is less apparently present in its exercise.

Disciplinary power, then, filled the gaps which the juridical network treated with 'indifference'. It organized the actions of individuals in a productive manner where the juridical network could only be deductive. But, during the Classical Age, it operated alongside the juridical network. At least until the beginning of the eighteenth century, the methods through which the state and the law exercised power remained more or less the same as in the Middle Ages. The disciplinary mechanism was contained within the spaces left free by juridical power. This is what Foucault calls the 'discipline-blockade'. As a result of their containment within institutions, and despite the differences in their mode of operation, disciplinary techniques could exist alongside the law, organizing power relations within the spaces left by the juridical network. And yet, because of their unspectacular symbolic manifestation, these disciplinary techniques escaped the juridical necessity of legitimacy. In contrast to the very public violence of the juridical network, disciplinary controls were symbolized as a 'gentle' operation of power. Discipline, unlike juridical force, is exercised through *the love of man* rather than the spirit of revenge. Consequently they were not exercised as of right, to be granted by God, but as of care and expediency. The survival and proliferation of the disciplines, unlike juridical law, did not depend on their justification. It is this that allows these disciplinary forces to pass unnoticed in Mill's account. Discipline appeared symbolically as the 'natural order of things';

a form of power to which no right needed to be attached. Whilst political theory debated the right of the Sovereign to exercise his power, discipline evolved in the gaps which Sovereign power left, constructing its edifices in these 'natural spaces'. The continuing trend of liberal thought that chants the right to freedom against the law remains blissfully unaware of this development in the field of power relations.

Towards the end of the Classical Age, however, the mechanisms of the State and the law themselves began to evolve. Whilst the spectacular forms of punishment were still in place, the way in which the law was used began to be transformed. This transformation is described by Foucault as the concept of *governmentality*, a concept which sits more comfortably with the *modus operandi* of the disciplinary institutions. Together, the two poles of discipline and governmentality constitute what Foucault calls 'bio-power'.

7. *The Regulation of Populations*

Towards the end of the 1970s Foucault gave a series of lectures on the political technology of the Classical Age. The title of the most famous of these lectures is *Governmentality*.[16] In that lecture the concept of governmentality is connected to the economy and the population. Governmentality defined as its object the population on which it acted through the field of the economy. I will go on to consider each of these elements

A. *The economy*

According to Foucault, in *Governmentality*, the word 'economy' was originally used in the sixteenth century to designate a form of government whose aim was 'the correct manner of managing individuals, goods and wealth within the family ... and of making family fortunes prosper (*G*: 92). When the sovereign acted economically he acted with the same diligence 'as that of the head of a family over his household and his goods' (*G*: 92). In the eighteenth century the aim was still the correct management of goods and wealth. However, the object of control was altered from the family to the population. The family was still important but only as a segment of the population rather than as a model of the state. Hence the word 'economy', in the eighteenth century, was used similarly to the way in which it is used today. It was articulated in relation to 'the perception of new networks of continuous and multiple relations between population, territory and wealth' (*G*: 101). As we shall see, with this new object the economy provided a field of analysis and a field of intervention for government.

B. *The population*

A whole new set of targets emerged by making the population the primary object of government and economics. I will limit myself to two examples. Firstly the

[16] Foucault, 'Governmentality' in Burchell, Gordon and Miller (eds), *The Foucault Effect: Studies in Governmentality* (Hemel Hempstead: Harvester/Wheatsheaf, 1991). Hereafter referred to as *G*.

size of the population became important. Hence the control of the birth rate became a function of government. This created the conditions for sex to become an object of political science; sex was directly related to the size of the population (*HoS*: 26). Secondly the relationship between the wealth of the nation and the size of the population became a political target. Through the new statistical sciences the average wealth of the population became calculable. An important aim of government was to maximize average and/or total wealth and, perhaps, also to distribute wealth effectively.

C. *Government*

The method through which these aims were to be achieved was through what Foucault calls the 'disposal' of things. By disposal he means an arrangement of things through which one can achieve certain ends. But the things are not just objects. They are 'a sort of complex composed of men and things' (*G*: 93); that is, men in relation to objects and events in the world. Government was utilized to make adjustments in the relationships between men and things which became available to it through the economy.

Foucault, then, describes a three-tier network of government. The population was the object for analysis and alteration; for disposal. The government was the political technology which performs this alteration and the economy was a field of action which connected the two together. The economy both provided a description of the population and a place where governmental decisions could be organized. Government could intervene tactically into the economy by utilizing laws but it could also do so by adjusting taxation, prescribing standards for education, by building an infrastructure as well as by directing moral and religious education.

8. *Government and the Law*

The law did not itself fade from view as a result of this new political technology. However, the law no longer provided a model which described or unified the State. Although there was an increase in the quantity of legislation, this legislation was not only used in order to describe a threshold of transgression. It was also used as a tactic amongst other governmental tactics for disposal. 'With government,' Foucault writes, 'it is a question not of imposing laws on men, but of disposing of things: that is to say of employing tactics rather than laws, and even of using laws themselves as tactics—to arrange things in such a way that, through a certain number of means, such and such ends may be achieved' (*G*: 95). No doubt some of the juridical technology still remained (and still remains today) but the predominant use of legislation was altered through governmental technology.

This change altered the relationship between man and the State. Prior to the eighteenth century man had been seen by the State more or less as a juridical subject. He was understood only as a site of action which was legal or illegal or at least transgressive or legitimate. Other than that he was constituted through a feudal hierarchy. However, government began to see each man as a complete individual with a particular way of living. Men could be grouped, divided and controlled according to their function in the population as determined by the economy. Foucault describes the difference thus: "feudal power consisted in relations between juridical subjects insofar as they were engaged in juridical relations by birth, status, or personal engagement, but with this new police state the government begins to deal with individuals, not only according to their juridical status but as men, as working trading, living beings'.[17] For Foucault this is nothing less than the 'entry of life into history' (*HoS*: 141).

We can now begin to see the difference between modern law and the juridical understanding of power. Power, in the juridical understanding is predominantly exercised on acts. However, once the governmental technology was put in place, the law began to be exercised in order to adjust the relationships between individuals *qua* individuals. The primary aim of law was no longer to prescribe general rules which defined a level of transgression, it was to intervene into the relationships between particular groups of people according to information carefully collected and analysed in the form of the economy. By failing to see the difference between this new role of law and the juridical form of power, both Hunt and Wickham and Santos fail to appreciate the place of law in Foucault's scheme. The principle of harm, then, becomes inadequate to legitimize *all* law because government, towards the end of the Classical Age, could utilize law productively as well as deductively. Hence if one wanted to develop a relationship between Foucault and Hart it would be that Foucault situates Hart's critique of Austin historically. The 'positive' role of law, in a Foucauldian account, takes its place amongst a more general technical apparatus of governmental control which intervenes into the lives of individuals and groups in response to knowledge collected about those lives. Whilst legal theory has remained focused on the legitimacy of legislating on certain acts (pornography, civil disobedience, homosexuality, prostitution, and so on) the *way in which law operates* has shifted to the regulation of the lives. The modern regulatory aspect of law, then, ought not to be understood merely as 'power-conferring' but should be seen as intervening in the social construction and government of the modern subject.

However, our understanding of the role of law in Foucault's analyses is not complete until we have seen the shift in disciplinary power in the Modern Age and the relationship of law to this shift. We can then see how law is caught between the two poles of bio-power: discipline and government.

[17] Foucault, 'The Political Technology of Individuals' in Martin, Gutman and Hutton (eds), *Technologies of the Self* (London: Tavistock, 1988) at 156.

9. *Discipline and the Prison System*

At the beginning of the Classical Age, then, the legal machine combined two mechanisms; the investigation and the punitive technology. The investigative process, by making law articulable to itself, helped to create a unified legal code. The State or the sovereign could intervene into this legal code through legislation. Towards the end of the eighteenth century the traditional juridical form of legislation was at least supplemented by a governmental form. Laws were not passed just as general rules which applied to the juridical subject but as specific rules which were designed to intervene in the lives of particular groups of subjects and to 'dispose' their relationships differently. It was not until the beginning of the nineteenth century, however, that the punitive technology itself began to be transformed. One could call this transformation the colonization of legal punishment by the disciplinary mechanism. The architectural form which resulted from this colonization was the prison. In order to understand this development it is first necessary to consider Foucault's analysis of discipline in the Modern Age.

10. *Swarming Discipline*

As we have seen, discipline, in the Classical Age, was confined to what Foucault calls the 'discipline-blockade'. It was utilized within certain institutions for the ends of those institutions. In the nineteenth century, however, the disciplinary mechanism becomes dislodged from these institutions. This led to the free circulation of discipline within the social plane. In *Discipline and Punish* Foucault elegantly describes this process. 'While, on the one hand, the disciplinary establishments increase,' Foucault writes, 'their mechanisms [*mécanismes*] have a certain tendency to become "de-institutionalized", to emerge from the closed fortresses in which they once functioned and to circulate in a "free state"; the massive, compact disciplines are broken down into flexible methods of control, which may be transferred and adapted' (*DP*: 211[18]). This is what Foucault calls the 'swarming of the disciplinary mechanisms [*mécanismes*]' (*DP*: 211; *SP*: 246).

The delocalization of discipline resulted, for Foucault, in its 'democratic' application; that is, discipline, unlike the juridical network, was applied relatively homogeneously throughout the social field. This was achieved through the extension of disciplinary functions from the institutions to the community. The primary method by which this extension took place was surveillance. Two examples should suffice to show what Foucault means when he suggests that discipline was extended beyond the walls of the institutions. Firstly, the information collected about pupils in the schoolroom began to be seen as evidence of parental practice; by observing a child the school could indirectly observe its parents which, in severe cases, could lead to their investigation by social services.

[18] Foucault, *Surveiller et Punir* (Paris: Éditions Gallimard, Paris, 1975) at 246. Hereafter referred to as *SP*.

Secondly, the observation of patients in hospital and the statistical analyses carried out there began to make hospitals aware of the general health of their local communities. The hospital could thus monitor the rise of epidemics, give sanitary advice to the inhabitants of the region as well as advising state authorities of the health problems in that region. In each of these cases discipline was applied not only to the subjects within the institutions but to subjects outside its walls. This tended to stimulate the emergence of extra-institutional disciplinary sites. Families and even individuals began to discipline themselves.

The result of this extension of discipline from the institutions was the constitution of a delocalized mechanism or what Foucault calls a *dispositif*.[19] This *dispositif* becomes available for use in multiple settings and for a broad variety of functions. As we have seen, the disciplinary *dispositif* began to regulate its own operations outside of its institutional beginnings. The disciplinary regime of the school begins to monitor the disciplinary regime of the parents. But this relationship could always be reversed; the indiscipline of the child in the home can be monitored by the parents who can, as a result, monitor the disciplinary regime of the school. As a result a certain amount of homogeneity was created between the family and the school; their disciplinary regimes began to evolve together in a symbiotic fashion. And this analysis can be extended to the hospital and the military as well as the work place and also psychiatric institutions. Finally, the homogeneity of the different disciplinary sites results in what Santos calls 'isomorphism'; the ability to transfer a single subject between institutions for a variety of exercises and functions which, to a certain extent can be integrated in the individual. For example, the child is disciplined in the school. If the results of this regime are significantly bad he can be transferred to borstal. If this is unsuccessful he can be transferred to a psychiatric institution, or to the prison. Only once the subject becomes disciplined, or what Foucault calls 'docile' can he escape these corrective institutions. He does not, though, escape the disciplinary network; he is transferred to the work place where the disciplinary regime continues.

The disciplinary *dispositif*, then, reproduces itself by providing the solutions to its own failures. Discipline constructs observations of its own functions to which it can respond. For example, information can be developed in the school about the child which can be used to observe the parents. The parents can, in return observe the school. But the school can also produce information about its children in general in the form of statistical tables. By responding to this information, discipline begins to discipline itself.[20] This reflexive operation of discipline is used to redirect the operations of the school itself and, at a

[19] The term *dispositif* has been translated as mechanism, apparatus, device, grid of intelligibility and deployment. None of these terms does full justice to Foucault's notion of dispositif. What Foucault is getting at is the system of relations that can be established between a heterogeneous ensemble of discourses and power relations. For a general discussion of the term see 'Confessions of the Flesh' in *TL* above n 8 at 194–8. For the original see *Dits et Ecrits*, Defert and Ewald (eds) (Paris: Gallimard, vol III, 1994) at 298–30. Also see Gilles Deleuze, 'What is a Dispositif?' in Armstrong (ed.), *Michel Foucault: Philosopher* (London: Routledge, 1992).

[20] This self-observation is the equivalent of 'second-order observation' in systems theory. The ability of discipline to respond to self-observation with new disciplinary techniques can be called 'autopoiesis'.

governmental level, schools in general. Furthermore, the information produced directs decisions in the family. The family, rather than simply observing the operations of the school through the child, observes the school through the form of 'league tables'.

These techniques, however, are not limited to a particular discourse (in this case the educational discourse). Discipline exploits the differences between discourses. For example, observations can be passed from the prison to the psychiatric hospital. The techniques of one institution can be used to direct the operations of another. The psychiatric hospital tends to emphasize the desired end of cure whereas for prison it is control, deterrent, and rehabilitation that constitute the desired ends. However, the techniques that are used to achieve these ends are similar in each case. For example, each distributes its subjects in a similar way and each manages the individual's time in a similar way. Each observes, produces reports and adjusts its operations according to its observations. This creates the possibility for the transfer of information between the institutions. Each individual becomes a 'case' (*DP*: 191) about whom a *dossier* is produced. This dossier can be transferred from institution to institution to construct an integrated disciplinary regime which responds to the complete life of the individual. Furthermore, it allows the techniques of one institution to take effect in another institution; the role of the psychiatrist in the prison system provides one obvious example. Even the criminal law begins to play a part in this disciplinary regime; in deciding sentences the law must take into account all of the information with which it is provided. Rather than responding merely to the crime, the criminal law begins to respond to the life of the individual. In this sense, even the criminal law, in a Foucauldian reading, cannot be seen as conforming to an Austinian jurisprudence.

As a result of this integration between different institutions and discourses through the disciplinary *dispositif*, a certain homogenization is achieved between institutions. Even the functions of the different institutions become, to a certain extent, homogeneous. Hence the prison itself becomes utilized for diagnosis whereas the psychiatric hospital becomes a site for control.[21] Foucault's notion of discipline, then, has the advantage of explaining Santos's observation of 'isomorphism' whilst maintaining the potential for discursive differences between

[21] The nineteenth-century concept of moral insanity shows how the psychiatric discourse managed to combine these two ends. Moral insanity was a disorder which was characterized only by anti-social behaviour. Psychiatry, in developing this disorder, combined its therapeutic aims with the necessity to control certain individuals who 'could not manage their own affairs' but who were not subject to the criminal law. This psychiatric function still remains in the modern concept of psychopathy. In general it is used in cases where the individual commits a series of minor transgressions which do not necessarily break the law. The case of *Dawn Clarke* (see n 7 above) is one rare example when a 'psychopath' came to court. She had already been released from a psychiatric hospital by a Mental Health Tribunal and so could not be returned to such an institution by the Court. This resulted in a sentence of 18 months' imprisonment at first instance for the breaking of a flowerpot which was reduced to a fine of £2 by the Court of Appeal. Lawton LJ's judgment clearly shows that the Court was more concerned with responding to her undisciplined life than it was with the actual offence which it was considering.

institutions. It also helps to explain how these differences begin to break down in the twentieth century.[22]

11. *The Colonization of the Mechanics of Punishment*

In a relatively short time, Foucault suggests, the visible and violent technology of punishment was replaced by one that hides its operations, one that is intense but relatively unspectacular; the use of the scaffold declines and the prison is erected in its place. As a disciplinary regime, the prison system is distinguished from the discursive production of law. In the Classical Age, as we have seen, punishment was the final articulation of the law. The law was represented in punishment. In the Modern Age, however, punishment is fundamentally a part of the disciplinary regime to which the penal law is a party but of which it is not a part.

The only significant way in which penal law was involved in the techniques of the prison was that it determined the sentence. But eventually even the sentence was subject to alteration by the prison regime.

There are three related ways in which discipline functions within the prison.

- Discipline introduced the most rigorous regime of alteration into the prison. Whilst the prison had originally been intended as a punitive apparatus to deprive the individual of his liberty, it soon became an intense institution of transformation. The prison must, Foucault writes, 'assume responsibility for all aspects of the individual, his physical training, his aptitude to work, his everyday conduct, his moral attitude, his state of mind' (*DP*: 235).
- Discipline functions continuously on the individual. Every moment of the prisoners time is controlled by the regime. There is no interruption in its programme. When Foucault writes that the prison 'has no exterior or gap' (*DP*: 236) he means that the individual, for the time that he is in prison, has his whole mode of living accounted for.
- The continuity of the prison system led to a new target for punishment. The prisoner was not punished *qua* offender. He was punished *qua* delinquent. The delinquent is a source of crime, a dangerous individual. It is his life in general that is the target of punishment rather than the gravity of the act which he has committed.

But the prison, for Foucault, does not only function on the delinquency which it discovered. It actually produces this delinquency. By gathering together those

[22] In this sense Foucault's disciplinary *dispositif* can be seen as an example of non-systemic autopoiesis. Discipline is self-observing and self-reproducing but it does not form a system. Discipline consists of a series of techniques whereas systems consist of differences in codification. As Luhmann suggests, a system reduces complexity in its observations 'insofar as it announces a selection and thereby reduces possibilities'—Luhmann, *Social Systems* (trans Bernarz Jr) (Stanford, CA: Stanford University Press, 1995) at 68. A particular disciplinary institution also selects in this way. However, discipline exploits the differences between the codes; its self-evidence and hence its autopoiesis becomes possible through its potential for aligning different systems and making possible isomorphism not just in terms of subjects (Santos) but also in terms of information. Through the similarity of their disciplinary operations disciplinary institutions can translate information easily between different codes; it is easy to transform the dossier into the *curriculum vitae* through the subject herself, thus connecting the school to the work-place and so on.

who have transgressed the prison helps to form a community of delinquents; by leaving the family of the criminal without support the prison helps to encourage further crime and so on. This delinquency does, however, have the useful function of segmenting crime within a particular segment of the community.[23] This, for Foucault, is what makes it acceptable. Crime, through the concept of delinquency, is confined to a particular class and particular geographical locations rather than being dispersed amongst the community as a whole.

The delinquents which were produced in prison were soon returned to it by the police. What Foucault describes, then, is an autopoietic ensemble of the prison, the police and delinquency which is closed in upon itself. 'One should speak of an ensemble', Foucault writes, 'whose three terms (police–prison–delinquency) support one another and form a circuit that is never interrupted' (*DP*: 282). The system reproduces itself by creating a particular form of problem to which it is the only available solution. There is no other way to combat the rise of delinquency other than by imposing a stronger disciplinary regime in the form of the prison which then produces more delinquency. The law is merely a relay in this system.

Hence there are two reasons why the prison was so acceptable to modern society. Firstly, it utilized the disciplinary mechanisms that were already in place in the other institutions of the nineteenth century. And secondly it produced a problem to which it was the only solution. In doing so it segmented crime within an autopoietic cycle and thus made crime tolerable; so long as crime was located within a certain section of the community it could be controlled and regulated in such a way as did not disrupt the social order.

12. *Where is the Law?*

The problem for legal scholars after Foucault's analysis of the modern techniques of power is that the justification for the law appears quite distant from the way in which law actually operates. Both of the traditional juridical elements of the law have become captured by more modern techniques of power; governmentality and discipline. Consequently the analyses of juridical scholars such as Mill appear inadequate to legitimize modern law. This is so for two reasons. Firstly, the free spaces which law is supposed to protect have been filled by other techniques of power and secondly laws are no longer predominantly applied in order to prevent certain harmful transgressions but to dispose more efficiently the relationships between members of the population. Two questions then emerge. Firstly, what is the precise role of the courts in modern society? And

[23] Foucault suggests that the disorganization of criminal activity was particularly threatening to the social order of the late eighteenth century. The popular fear of crime that arose was one of the principle reasons why the prison system was acceptable. It created the impression of order amongst the disorder of crime. Hence Foucault writes that the prison system, despite its inability to reduce crime, 'does not miss its target; on the contrary it reaches it, in so far as it gives rise to one particular form of illegality in the midst of others, which it is able to isolate, to place in full light and to organize as a relatively enclosed, but penetrable, milieu', *DP* at 276.

secondly, why is it that the law and power have continued to justify themselves in a way which has little relation to their modern mode of functioning?

I have already alluded to Foucault's understanding of law as a relay in the autopoietic ensemble of police–prison–delinquency. Of course these comments are confined to the criminal law. Let us flesh out the way in which this works by relating a familiar narrative. The police capture an individual. He is tried in the court according to statute and common law. He is transferred to prison where he mixes with other prisoners in a disciplinary regime. On release he continues to be observed. But, having a criminal record he finds it difficult to return to work. He then utilizes the connections which he has established in prison in order to commit a further crime or series of crimes until he is returned to the prison. The legal system is, in Foucault's sense, a relay because it transfers an individual from the police to the prison which then produces or reproduces him as a delinquent. But there is another sense in which the legal system is a relay which has not been considered by Foucault; it is also a relay between governmental decisions and the disciplinary network.

The role of law which I want to suggest is similar to that which Foucault gives to the *dispositif* of sexuality in *HoS*. In the last chapter of that book Foucault considers the two poles of bio-power that developed in the Classical Age and which I have considered above; disciplinary power and governmentality. He goes on to suggest that in the nineteenth century these two forms became connected 'in the form of concrete arrangements [*agencements concrets*] that would go to make up the great technology of power in the nineteenth century' (*HoS*: 140). He suggests that the *dispositif* of sexuality would be one of the most important of these *agencements*. But the way in which this *dispositif* would operate to connect the two poles of bio-power is left unclear in *HoS* and as far as I am aware Foucault did not return to this problem.[24] I would like to suggest that alongside the *dispositif* of sexuality, it is the law, in modern society, which is the predominant institution through which this connection is made.

We can consider how this would work particularly effectively from the example of the criminal law. If we return to our example we can see that the modern criminal law effectively transfers delinquents from the police to the prison system. However, it does a little more than that. It also designates, at least to a certain extent, who will be so passed and for what term. This is done according to common law and statute. The code of law is thus connected to the disciplinary network through the mechanisms of the trial. Hence, by adjusting the code of law, adjustments are also made in the autopoietic system of police–prison–delinquent. As a result the modern governmental technology could dispose of the relationships between the police, the prison, and the delinquents by passing legislation, one of the most important governmental tactics. The proliferation of legislation governing police powers, the specific codification of minor crimes and the Mental Health Acts of the nineteenth and twentieth

[24] The volumes with which Foucault originally intended to follow *La Volonté de Savoir* were eventually abandoned and were replaced by two books on antiquity, *The Uses of Pleasure* and *The Care of the Self*.

centuries are all examples of the way in which governmentality has directed and adjusted relations established in the disciplinary network.

Hence Foucault's understanding of law as a governmental tactic (from *Governmentality*) and the incorporation of law into a 'continuum of apparatuses (medical, administrative and so on)' (*HoS*: 144) from *HoS* are compatible. Law is at once 'plugged into' the governmental pole and into the disciplinary network. This explains, in an account compatible with that of Foucault, why the law, despite losing its juridical foundations, has continued to develop as such an important device of power during the Modern Age. The law was 'enchained' between the governmental technology and the disciplinary network; these three elements combined together symbiotically, resulting in their mutual evolution.[25]

But although the position of law as a field of intervention between the two poles of bio-power is inconsistent with the juridical justification of law, this juridical justification has been maintained both in political theory and in the law itself. The question, then, which Foucault asks in *HoS* is 'why is this juridical notion of power, involving as it does the neglect of everything that makes for its productive effectiveness, its strategic resourcefulness, its positivity, so readily accepted?' (*HoS*: 86). The answer that he gives there is very brief; that 'power is tolerable only on condition that it mask a substantial part of itself' (*HoS*: 86). He expands upon this comment in the second of his *Two Lectures*.

In the second of these lectures Foucault suggests that the theory of sovereignty, in the eighteenth century, had two roles. The first was that the developments in this theory actually limited the power of the monarch. This in turn extended the spaces in which disciplinary power could develop, spaces which were still inscribed by the juridical network of power. The democratization of sovereignty in the work of Rousseau, for example, provided 'a permanent instrument of criticism of the monarchy and of all the obstacles that can thwart the development of disciplinary society' (*TL*: 105). In effect by grounding the notion of sovereignty in the will of the population, political theory articulated the idea of a legitimate libertarian 'free space' in which disciplinary power and the governmental technology could develop. A similar argument can be directed at Mill as I have attempted to show above.

Hence the second role of the theory of sovereignty was that it masked the operations of disciplinary power. As it was articulated in the eighteenth century, Foucault suggests, the theory of sovereignty was superimposed upon the disciplinary mechanisms, concealing their modes of operation and domination. And yet, for Foucault, the theory of sovereignty was also 'fundamentally determined and grounded in mechanisms of disciplinary coercion' (*TL*: 105). He explains this duality in the following way. When the rise of the disciplinary mechanisms became necessary in the Classical Age, it at once became necessary to mask their method of domination. The theory of sovereignty was incapable of legitimizing

[25] The law appears only to be a relay in one direction; it provided a way for the governmental pole to adjust the disciplinary machines. The transfer of information from the disciplinary network to the governmental pole is provided, for the criminal law at least, by the discourse of criminology.

disciplinary power but its democratization did suggest a public right which came out of a homogenous democratic society. But the homogeneity on which this public right depended was articulated at once through the disciplinary mechanisms that hierarchized the population and the governmental mechanisms which unified it through the notion of the economy.

But the theory of sovereignty did not just operate in political theory. It also operated in the law, resulting in substantial changes to the law.[26] And because the law was 'plugged into' both the disciplinary network and the governmental technology, the theory of sovereignty managed to legitimize both of these activities without effectively representing their mode of operation. The privileged locus of political criticism was cast in juridical terms; it was always a question of the overextension of political power. The actual points at which power was exercised were invisible to this theory even as they dominated the social field. Hence the success with which law covered up its own paradoxes[27] and articulated its legitimacy was not just a condition for its own evolution. It was also a condition for the masking of the governmental and disciplinary exercise of power. This is why, whilst both sides of the juridical machine have become infested with more productive operations of power, the juridical code has flourished, and nowhere has it flourished more than in legal discourse.

13. *Conclusions*

The consequences of Foucault's work for the law have still to be effectively evaluated. I hope that I have shown how some of the current scholarship underestimates the complexity and rigour of Foucault's position as well as providing some new directions in which a Foucauldian analysis of law could be developed. The implications of Foucault's analysis for legal theory are difficult to evaluate. Foucault was not primarily concerned with law and offered little analysis of the role which was played by law in different epochs. Nevertheless we can reach a few tentative conclusions concerning these implications.

By focusing on the question 'What is the Law?', Anglo-American legal theory has lost the richness of the historical differences in law's genealogy. By attempting to reduce the law to its ahistorical *minimum conditions*, Anglo-American scholarship has failed to engage with the question of the operation of *modern law* and its theoretical relationship to the institutions with which it interacts. Foucault, on the other hand, establishes the importance of historical difference in analysing phenomena. By examining the historical transformations of the institutions of

[26] One example of this was the introduction of proportionality in sentencing.

[27] For a forceful account of the covering up of legal paradoxes see Niklas Luhmann's, 'The Third Question: the creative use of paradoxes in law and legal history' (1988) 15 *Journal of Law and Society* 153. Luhmann argues that 'there are paradoxes everywhere, wherever we look for foundations. The founding problem of law, then, is not to find and identify the ultimate ground or reason which justifies its existence. The problem is how to suppress or to attenuate the paradox which an observer with logical inclinations or with a sufficient degree of dissatisfaction could see and articulate at any time' (Luhmann, 1988 at 154). Foucault would not, as Luhmann does, see the paradox as the main motivating factor behind legal discourse.

power, Foucault shows how transgressive acts have, in general, begun to decline as the focus of power to be replaced by a *field of lives*. The institutions of power are no longer predominantly concerned with preventing the most disordered acts from occurring. Rather they are concerned with the direction of the lives of individuals, groups and the population as a whole.

The rise of what Foucault calls 'bio-power' (that is, government and discipline) does not result in an annihilation of the law. It results in the at least partial transformation of its mode of operation. The criticism that Foucault sees the law according to the Austinian 'rules + sanctions' formula is misplaced. Foucault did indeed have a tendency to concentrate on the criminal law (as it was most closely associated with the institutions with which he was concerned) but even the criminal law, in Foucault's account, begins to respond to the complete lives of individuals in the Modern Age. As Foucault suggests in his article, *The Dangerous Individual*, there is a question which 'is essential in the Modern Tribunal, but which would have had a strange ring to it 150 years [previously]: "Who are You" '.[28] Foucault's point is that even in the criminal law it is the life rather than the act to which the law responds.

Whilst Foucault did not effectively consider the role of the other areas of law in his genealogy I believe that his account *encourages* rather than *precludes* an account of law which directs rather than forces. The modern law takes place within a field of powers for which it no longer provides the model but in which it plays an important part. Foucault's concept of governance seems to encapsulate something significant about the modern role of law. But this legal governance can only be effectively evaluated if it is seen as the result of a historical evolution in which the juridical structure of the State has been displaced by a mobile, flexible, and self-reproducing technology of power which responds to an entirely different field of knowledge; the field of lives as opposed to the field of acts. In this paper I have attempted to show how the law takes its place between the two poles of bio-power, allowing the governmental technology to adjust the disciplinary mechanisms. In doing so I have attempted to focus on the question 'How does law operate?' rather than the question 'What is law?' In doing so the law, in its modern form, appears in a new guise. Rather than the structure or fabric which constitutes our society, the law is a machine which oils the modern structures of domination, or which, at best achieves a tinkering on the side of justice.

Finally, an engagement with Foucault, displaces the liberal trend that opposes individual freedom to the law. By concentrating on the legal right to expression, the density of the modern operations of power and the creativity of its institutions is passed over. Mill's conception of power is too limited to be useful as a way of analysing modern society or modern law. Whilst, from Mill's perspective, we can construct a critique of the overextension of the criminal law into our private lives, we are incapable of understanding the way in which law regulates (and

[28] Foucault, 'The Dangerous Individual' in Kritzman (ed.), *Politics, Philosophy, Culture: Interviews and Other Writings 1977–1984* (London: Routledge, 1988) at 126.

thus legitimates) the operations of discipline. It is these operations, rather than juridically imposed interdictions that constitute the fabric of the modern subject. However, Mill's conception of power is still widely accepted by many Anglo-American jurisprudes (Hart and Dworkin to name but two of the most prominent) who fail to see that the opposition between freedom and the law is no longer adequate to ground jurisprudential thought. The law operates in a field of power relations within which it is only a directing force. Consequently, liberation from the blunt technology of the juridical does not prevent the individual being subjected to the loving force of bio-power.

[18]

From Discipline to Flexibilization? Rereading Foucault in the Shadow of Globalization

Nancy Fraser

Michel Foucault was the great theorist of the fordist mode of social regulation. Writing at the zenith of the postwar Keynesian welfare state, he taught us to see the dark underside of even its most vaunted achievements. Viewed through his eyes, social services became disciplinary apparatuses, humanist reforms became panoptical surveillance regimes, public health measures became deployments of biopower, and therapeutic practices became vehicles of subjection. From his perspective, the components of the postwar social state constituted a carceral archipelago of disciplinary domination, all the more insidious because self-imposed.

Granted, Foucault did not himself understand his project as an anatomy of fordist regulation. Positing a greater scope for his diagnosis, he preferred to associate disciplinary power with "modernity" *simpliciter*. And most of his readers, including me, followed suit. As a result, the ensuing debates turned on whether the Foucauldian picture of modernity was too dark and one-sided, neglecting the latter's emancipatory tendencies.[1]

Today, however, circumstances warrant a narrower reading. If we now see ourselves as standing on the brink of a new, postfordist epoch of globalization, then we should reread Foucault in that light. No longer an interpreter of modernity per se, he becomes a theorist of the fordist mode of social regulation, grasping its inner logic, like the Owl of Minerva, at the moment of its historical waning. From this perspective, it is significant that his great works of social analysis – *Madness and Civilization, The Birth of the Clinic, Discipline and Punish, The History of Sexuality*, volume one – were written in the 1960s and 1970s, just as the OECD countries abandoned Bretton Woods, the international financial framework that undergirded national Keynesianism and thus made possible the welfare state. In other words, Foucault mapped the contours of the disciplinary society just as the ground was being cut out from under it. And although it is only now with hindsight becoming clear, this was also the moment at which discipline's successor was struggling to be born. The irony is plain: whether we call it postindustrial society or neoliberal globalization, a new regime oriented to "deregulation" and "flexibilization" was about to take shape just as Foucault was conceptualizing disciplinary normalization.

Of course, to read Foucault in this way is to problematize his relevance to the present. If he theorized fordist regulation, then how does his diagnosis relate to postfordism? Is his account of the disciplinary society dépassé? Or does the regulatory grammar of fordism also subtend neoliberal globalization? In what follows, I shall examine such questions while steering clear of both of those hypotheses. Proposing a third, "transformationalist" interpretation, I shall maintain that while the emerging postfordist mode of social regulation diverges sufficiently from the fordist one to preclude simple extension of the Foucauldian analysis of discipline, that analysis can still serve to illuminate it. More precisely, it can inspire us to creatively transform Foucauldian categories to account for new modes of "governmentality" in the era of neoliberal globalization.

1. Conceptualizing Fordist Discipline

To conceptualize discipline as the fordist mode of social regulation is to bring together Foucauldian and Marxian categorizations. Whether or not Foucault himself would have countenanced the association is a question that could well be debated, as one can find textual support for both sides.[2] Here, however, I pass over that issue, as my intention is not to be faithful to Foucault. I seek, rather, to historicize him, just as he himself sought to historicize many others, not least among them Marx. In my effort, as in his, historicization means recontextualization, rereading texts in light of categories and problems not available to their authors. And so in this sense I shall be faithful to him after all.

So: discipline as the fordist mode of social regulation. Let me begin to unpack the meaning of that hypothesis by explaining what I mean by fordism. As I use the term, "fordism" covers the period of "the short twentieth century," from the First World War to the fall of Communism. In this period, capitalism generated a distinctive mode of accumulation, premised on mass industrial production, mass commodity consumption, and the vertically integrated corporation. But fordism was not simply a matter of economics. Rather, fordist accumulation mechanisms were embedded in, and dependent upon, a facilitating shell of social, cultural, and political arrangements. In the First World, one such arrangement was the family wage, which linked labor markets to emerging gender norms and family forms, while fostering an orientation to privatized domestic consumption. Another was a burgeoning consumer culture, adumbrated through advertising, mass media, and mass entertainment. Importantly, some of fordism's most characteristic first-world institutions did not fully develop until after World War Two: the "class compromise" that incorporated labor as a major player in national polities; the Keynesian welfare state, which stabilized national markets and afforded social entitlements to national citizens; and, as mentioned above, an international financial system that enabled national-state steering of national economies. Finally, as these last points suggest, fordism was an international phenomenon organized along national lines. Disproportionately benefiting the wealthy countries of the North Atlantic while depending on colonial (and later, postcolonial) labor and materials, it fostered national aspirations and institutional forms in the Third World, even as it stunted development of the economic and political capacities needed to realize them. Also central were anti-fascism and anti-communism. In a century of virtually unending hot and cold world wars, fordist states fatefully commixed private industry with publicly financed military production, while also creating international organizations pledged to respect their national sovereignty. The result was a multifaceted social formation. A historically specific phase of capitalism, yet not simply an economic category, fordism was an international configuration that embedded mass production and mass consumption in national frames.

Understood in this way, what does fordism have to do with Foucault? To establish the link, we must assume that fordism was not just a set of mutually adapted institutions. We must posit, rather, that subtending those institutions was a distinctive set of regulatory mechanisms which suffused them with a common ethos. Widely diffused throughout society, these small-scale techniques of coordination organized relations on the "capillary" level: in factories and hospitals, in prisons and schools, in state welfare agencies and private households, in the formal associations of civil society and informal daily interaction. The "micro-political" counterpart of fordist accumulation, these practices of "governmentality" embodied a distinctive "political rationality." Reducible neither to *raison d'état* nor to universal instrumental reason, the regulatory grammar of fordism operated far beneath the commanding heights. Yet it was equally far removed from "traditional" social regulation by customs and values. Organizing individuals, arraying bodies in space and time, coordinating their forces, transmitting power among them, this mode of governmentality ordered ground-level social relations according to expertly designed logics of control. The upshot was a historically new mode of social regulation – a *fordist* mode suited to nationally bounded societies of mass production and mass consumption.

So far I have sketched the idea of fordist regulation in the abstract. Now I must fill in its qualitative character. Exactly what sort of governmentality is proper to fordism? What constitutes the specificity of its characteristic ordering mechanisms and political rationality? The answers, I suggest, can be found in Foucault's account of disciplinary biopower. But this suggestion raises serious problems. What in Foucauldian discipline is specifically fordist? Moreover, what should we make of the fact that Foucault located many of discipline's defining moments long prior to the twentieth century – in Enlightenment medical reforms, Jeremy Bentham's Panopticon, and nineteenth-century uses of population statistics?[3] Finally, how shall we understand the fact that although Foucault never thematized the problem of scale, he nevertheless implicitly situated his analysis of discipline in relation to the national/international nexus?

To begin with the historical problem: it is certainly true that Foucault traced the origins of discipline to the eighteenth and nineteenth centuries. But he also claimed to be writing "the history of the present." Thus, we are justified, I contend, in reading his early material through the prism of genealogy (his word). In that case, the clinic and the prison appear as early and still isolated proving grounds for regulatory practices that became fully developed, operational, and hegemonic only much later, in the twentieth century. On this reading, for which one could cite textual support, the disciplinary society emerged in its own right only after the general diffusion of techniques that had been pioneered much earlier, in scattered discrete institutions.[4] Only then, with the advent of fordism, did discipline become generalized and emblematic of society at large.

Not only is this hypothesis historically plausible, but it also affords some clues to our two other questions: the qualitative character of fordist governmentality and the problem of scale. In particular, it suggests three defining features of that mode of social regulation, now interpreted as Foucauldian discipline: totalization, social concentration within a national frame, and self-regulation. Let me elaborate each in turn, drawing largely on US examples, construed in Foucauldian terms.

First of all, fordist discipline was *totalizing*, aimed at rationalizing all major aspects of social life, including many never before subject to deliberate organization. Animated by a passion for control, Henry Ford's managers sought to rationalize not only factory production but also the family and community life of their workers, on the assumption that work habits began in the home. In the teens and twenties, likewise, US reformers began to build municipal, state, and federal regulatory agencies aimed at ensuring public health and safety. The same period saw the proliferation of codified bodies of rationalizing social expertise: manuals of child-rearing, household management ("home economics"), social work (casework), psychotherapy (medicalized and lay-popular), and industrial psychology, to name just a few. Later came special age-targeted control agencies (juvenile justice) and body-regimens (sex manuals, nutrition programmes, and physical fitness schedules). Apparently, no social arena was off-limits in the campaign to subject everything to rational control. The fordist passion for planning even found expression in mass culture's utopian fantasies, especially the elaborate synchronized chorus lines of Hollywood films.[5]

If fordist discipline was totalizing, it was nevertheless – and this is its second defining feature – *socially concentrated within a national frame*. As the century unfolded, various previously discrete disciplines converged upon a new societal space within the nation-state. Called "the social" both by Hannah Arendt and the Foucauldian Jacques Donzelot, this was a dense nexus of overlapping apparatuses where institutions of social control became interconnected.[6] In the social, the fields of industrial relations, social work, criminal justice, public health, corrections, psychotherapy, marriage-counseling, and education became mutually permeable, each drawing from the same reservoir of rationalizing practices while elaborating its own variations on the common grammar of governmentality. In some countries, including Foucault's France, this disciplinary heartland was largely the province of the national state; in others, such as the United States, nongovernmental agencies played a larger role, supplementing state apparatuses. In all cases, however, the social was correlated with a national state. Although Foucault did not explicitly thematize the question of scale, his account assumed that disciplinary ordering was nationally bounded. From his perspective, the national-social was fordist regulation's ground zero, the zone of its densest elaboration and the launching pad for its wider diffusion. It was from this zone that fordist discipline radiated outward, imperceptibly spreading throughout national society. Yet social concentration did not entail vertical hierarchy, with commands flowing unidirectionally downward from the top of a traditional pyramid. Rather, disciplinary apparatuses subsisted side-by-side in the space of the national-social, their agents cooperating and competing on a par. Their milieu was one of middle-class professionalism, in which practitioners enjoyed considerable discretion, even as their activities were highly rationalized. The result was that disciplinary powers were socially concentrated yet horizontally arrayed within a national frame. Thus, as Foucault insisted, fordist discipline was simultaneously systematic and "capillary."

The third major feature of fordist discipline follows from the preceding two: this mode of social ordering worked largely through *individual self-regulation*. This was the original meaning of the phrase "social control," coined in 1907 by the American sociologist Edward Ross, as a democratic alternative to hierarchy and external coercion. As Foucault emphasized, advocates of social control sought to foster self-activating subjects capable of internal self-governance. Wagering that such subjects would be more rational, cooperative, and productive than those directly subordinated to external authority, fordist reformers devised new organizational forms and management practices. In offices, factories, and social-service agencies, supervisors were urged to listen to workers and clients, solicit their input, and increase their scope of autonomous action. On the supply side, meanwhile, child psychologists, educators, and child-raising experts proposed to reform practices for socializing children. Aiming to nurture future autonomous self-regulating citizens, they urged mothers to feed on demand, fathers to abjure corporal punishment, teachers to foster curiosity and to explain the rationales behind rules. Analogous desiderata informed practices as disparate as marriage counseling and open-ended sentencing of criminals. The overall thrust was to "subjectify" individuals, to encourage linguistification of their internal processes as a means of holding them responsible for those processes, thereby augmenting their capacities for self-policing. Effectively conscripting individuals as agents of social control while at the same time promoting their autonomy, fordist discipline sought to replace external coercion with internal self-regulation.[7]

In general, then, fordist discipline was totalizing, socially concentrated within a national frame, and oriented to self-regulation. The result was a form of governmentality that far transcended the bounds of the state, even as it remained nationally bounded. Widely diffused throughout national societies, productive as opposed to repressive, rational as opposed to charismatic, it mobilized "useful [if not wholly docile] bodies" in nationally bounded societies of mass production and mass consumption.

Certainly, many criticisms can be raised against this quasi-Foucauldian account of fordist regulation. For one thing, it is overly condemnatory of fordism, neglectful of the latter's progressive and emancipatory aspects. In particular, it is too dismissive of the individualizing, subjectifying moment of social control, too quick to reduce its autonomy-fostering orientation to a normalizing regimentation. Finally, it is embroiled in a performative contradiction, as it depends for its critical power on the very humanist norms, above all autonomy, that it wants simultaneously to unmask. Although I myself have raised such criticisms of Foucault in the past, and although I still consider them pertinent now, I shall not pursue them here. Here, rather, I address a different problem: the relation between discipline and *postfordism*. In so doing, I intend to problematize what I once called Foucault's "empirical insights," as opposed to his "normative confusions."[8]

2. From Discipline to Flexibilization?

The preceding account of fordist discipline assumes at least three empirical propositions that no longer hold true today. It assumes, first, that social regulation is organized nationally, that its object is a national population living in a national society under the auspices of a national state, which in turn manages a national economy. It assumes, second, that social regulation constitutes a nonmarketized counterpart to a regime of capital accumulation, that it is concentrated in the zone of "the social," and that its characteristic institutions are the governmental and nongovernmental agencies that comprise the (national) social-welfare state. It assumes, finally, that regulation's logic is subjectifying and individualizing, that in enlisting individuals as agents of self-regulation, it simultaneously fosters their autonomy and subjects them to control, or rather, it fosters their autonomy as a means to their control.

If these propositions held true in the era of fordism, their status is doubtful today. In the post-89 era of postfordist globalization, social interactions increasingly transcend the borders of states. As a result, the ordering of social relations is undergoing a major shift in scale, equivalent to *denationalization* and *transnationalization*. No longer exclusively a national matter, if indeed it ever was, social ordering now occurs simultaneously at several different levels. In the case of public health, for example, country-based agencies are increasingly expected to harmonize their policies with those at the transnational and international levels. The same is true for policing, banking regulation, labor standards, environmental regulation, and counterterrorism.[9] Thus, although national ordering is not disappearing, it is in the process of being decentered as its regulatory mechanisms become articulated (sometimes cooperatively, sometimes competitively) with those at other levels. What is emerging, therefore, is a new type of regulatory structure, a multi-layered system of globalized governmentality whose full contours have yet to be determined.

At the same time, regulation is also undergoing a process of *desocialization*. In today's hegemonic – neoliberal – variant of globalization, massive, unfettered, transnational flows of capital are derailing the Keynesian project of national economic steering. The tendency is to transform the fordist welfare state into a postfordist "competition state," as countries scramble to cut taxes and eliminate "red tape" in hopes of keeping and attracting investment.[10] The resulting "race to the bottom" fuels myriad projects of *de*regulation, as well as efforts to privatize social services, whether by shifting them onto the market or by devolving them onto the family (which means, in effect, onto women). Although the extent of such projects varies from country to country, the overall effect is a global tendency to destructure the zone of "the (national) social," formerly the heartland of fordist discipline. Decreasingly socially concentrated, and increasingly marketized and familialized, postfordist processes of social ordering are less likely to converge on an identifiable zone. Rather, globalization is generating a new landscape of social regulation, more privatized and dispersed than any envisioned by Foucault.

Finally, as fordist discipline wanes in the face of globalization, its orientation to self-regulation tends to dissipate too. As more of the work of socialization is marketized, fordism's labor-intensive individualizing focus tends to drop out. In psychotherapy, for example, the time-intensive talk-oriented approaches favored under fordism are increasingly excluded from insurance coverage and replaced by instant-fix pharma-psychology. In addition, the enfeeblement of Keynesian state steering means more unemployment and less downward redistribution, hence increased inequality and social instability. The resulting vacuum is more likely to be filled by outright repression than by efforts to promote individual autonomy. In the US, accordingly, some observers posit the transformation of the social state into a "prison-industrial complex," where incarceration of male minority youth becomes the favored policy on unemployment.[11] The prisons in question, moreover, have little in common with the humanist panopticons described by Foucault. Their management often subcontracted to for-profit corporations, they are less laboratories of self-reflection than hotbeds of racialized and sexualized violence – of rape, exploitation, corruption, untreated HIV, murderous gangs, and murderous guards. If such prisons epitomize one aspect of postfordism, it is one that no longer works through individual self-governance. Here, rather, we encounter the return of repression, if not the return of the repressed.

In all these respects, postfordist globalization is a far cry from Foucauldian discipline: multi-layered as opposed to nationally bounded, dispersed and marketized as opposed to socially concentrated, increasingly repressive as opposed to self-regulating. With such divergences, it is tempting to conclude that the disciplinary society is simply dépassé. One might even be tempted to declare, following Jean Baudrillard, that we should all "oublier Foucault."

3. Globalized Governmentality

That, however, would be a mistake. If contemporary society is postfordist and therefore post-disciplinary, it can nevertheless be profitably analyzed from a quasi-Foucauldian point of view. The key is to identify the characteristic ordering mechanisms and political rationality of the emerging new mode of regulation. The result would be a quasi-Foucauldian account of a new form of globalizing governmentality.

As I see it, this project has at least three major parameters. A first crucial task is to conceptualize the transnational character of postfordist regulation. A second task is to theorize its increasing reliance on dispersed and marketized modes of governmentality. A third task is to analyze its distinctive political rationality, including its characteristic objects of intervention, modes of subjectification, and mix of repression and self-regulation. For each task, fortunately, we can draw on some pioneering work that is already available.

The transnational character of contemporary governmentality is the explicit subject of a large body of literature on globalization. Under the heading of "governance without government," many scholars are mapping the contours of a new multi-layered regulatory apparatus which operates on a transnational scale. In this picture, social ordering is no longer nationally bounded, nor correlated with a national state, nor centered in any single locus of coordination. Rather, the locus of governmentality is being unbundled, broken up into several distinct functions, and assigned to several distinct agencies which operate at several distinct levels, some global, some regional, some local and subnational. For example, military and security functions are being disaggregated, relocated, and rescaled as a result of "humanitarian interventions," "peacekeeping operations," the "war on terrorism," and a host of multilateral security arrangements. Likewise, criminal law and policing functions are being unbundled, rebundled, and rescaled, sometimes upward, as in the case of international war crimes tribunals, the International Criminal Court, "universal jurisdiction," and Interpol; but sometimes downward, as in the case of tribal courts and the privatization of prisons. Meanwhile, responsibility for contract law is being rescaled as a result of the emergence of a private transnational regime for resolving business disputes (a revival of the *lex mercatoria*). Economic steering functions are being rescaled upward to regional trading blocs, such as the European Union, NAFTA, and Marcosur, and to formal and informal transnational bodies, such as the World Bank, and the IMF, and the World Economic Forum; but also downward, to municipal and provincial agencies, increasingly responsible for fostering development, regulating wages and taxes, and providing social welfare. In general, then, we are seeing the emergence of a new multi-leveled structure of governmentality, a complex edifice in which the national state is but one level among others.[12]

This new globalizing mode of regulation brings a considerable dispersion of governmentality. Unlike its fordist predecessor, the postfordist mode of regulation tends to "govern-at-a-distance," through flexible, fluctuating networks that transcend structured institutional sites.[13] No longer nation-state-centered, today's social ordering works through the powers and wills of a dispersed collection of entities, including states, supranational organizations, transnational firms, NGOs, professional associations, and individuals. At the country level, for example, QUANGOs assume regulatory functions previously held by the state; with the privatization of prisons, utilities, and schools, electoral accountability is supplanted by negotiations among "partners" on "community" boards.[14] At the international level, likewise, a motley and changing crew of unelected notables convenes annually for loosely institutionalized discussions at Davos, while legal regulation of transnational business gives way to new forms of ad hoc, informal arbitration, whose private and discretionary character insulates them from public scrutiny.[15] The result is a ruling apparatus whose composition is so complex and shifting that the distinguished international-relations theorist Robert F. Cox has named it "*la nebuleuse*."[16]

Its shadowy quality notwithstanding, postfordist governmentality evinces some recognizable qualitative traits. This mode of regulation relies far more heavily than its predecessor on marketized ordering mechanisms. In the guise of neoliberalism, it vastly expands the scope of economic rationality, introducing competition into social services, transforming clients into consumers, and subjecting expert professionals to market discipline. In this regime of "de-statized governmentality," substantive welfare policy gives way to formal technologies of economic accountability as auditors replace service professionals as the frontline disciplinarians.[17] Meanwhile, as vouchers replace public services and privatized "risk management" replaces social insurance, individuals are made to assume new levels of "responsibility" for their lives. Displacing fordist techniques of "social control," market mechanisms organize large swaths of human activity; even decisions about marriage and childbearing are entangled with market incentives and disincentives.

The result is a new, postfordist mode of subjectification. Neither the Victorian subject of individualizing normalization nor the fordist subject of collective welfare, the new subject of governmentality is the actively responsible agent. A subject of (market) choice and a consumer of services, this individual is obligated to enhance her quality of life through her own decisions.[18] In this new "care of self," everyone is an expert on herself, responsible for managing her own human capital to maximal effect.[19] In this respect, the fordist project of self-regulation is continued by other means.

Nevertheless, the postfordist mode of governmentality differs sharply from its predecessor. Fordist regulation implicitly aspired to universality, despite persistent social inequality. In Foucault's account, its object of intervention was not only the disciplined individual, but the "general welfare" and "the population" as a whole; disciplinary normalization was linked to "biopower," which projected national synchronization and standardization, albeit on the backs of subjugated colonials. In contrast, postfordist governmentality has burst open the national frame, as we have seen. In so doing, moreover, it simultaneously renounces the latter's universalist thrust, without, however, resorting to laissez-faire. Rather, postfordist regulation establishes new forms of (transnational) segmentation. Working largely through population profiling, it separates and tracks individuals for the sake of efficiency and risk prevention. Sorting the capable-and-competitive wheat from the incapable-and-noncompetitive chaff, postfordist welfare policy constructs different life courses for each. The result is a new kind of segmented governmentality: responsibilized self-regulation from some, brute repression for others. In this "dual society," a hypercompetitive, fully networked zone coexists with a marginal sector of excluded low-achievers.[20]

The preceding sketch is only that: a cursory overview of some of the ways in which postfordist governmentality is being envisioned. Much work remains to be done. Let me close by indicating two additional directions for further research.

One intriguing possibility concerns the ordering functions performed by "networks" in postfordism. A ubiquitous buzzword of globalization, the term "network" names both a form of social organization and an infrastructure of communication. The hallmark of networks is their ability to combine rule-governed organization with flexibility, open-endedness, decenteredness, and spatial dispersion. Thus, in business, we have the various transnational chains of firms – suppliers, contractors, jobbers, etc. – that comprise the lean, easily altered structure of niche-oriented "just-in-time" production. Likewise, in the peculiar intersection of politics, religion, and criminality that is so much on our minds today, we have terrorist networks: transnational, decentered, spatially dispersed, seemingly leaderless, and impossible to locate, at least by anything so clunky as a national state, yet capable of stunningly well-organized acts of synchronized massive destruction, enlisting McWorld in the service of Jihad, if not forever destabilizing the distinction between them.[21]

Seemingly more rhizomatic and Deleuzian than disciplinary and Foucauldian, networks may nevertheless be emerging as important new vehicles of postfordist governmentality. Critical theorists of globalization would do well to try to analyze them in Foucauldian terms. Above all, we might explore their articulation (both competitive and cooperative) with more familiar types of regulatory agencies.

A second candidate for a quasi-Foucauldian analysis of globalization is the related notion of "flexibilization." Another ubiquitous buzzword of globalization, "flexibilization" names both a mode of social organization and a process of self-constitution. Better: it is a process of self-constitution that correlates with, arises from, and resembles a mode of social organization. The hallmarks of flexibilization are fluidity, provisionality, and a temporal horizon of "no long term." Thus, what networks are to space, flexibilization is to time. So we have the flexible specialization of just-in-time production in the world of business. And we have the "flexible men" (and women) described by Richard Sennett, who frequently change jobs and even careers, relocating at the drop of a hat, whose collegial relations and friendships are trimmed to fit the horizon of no long term, and whose selfhood does not consist in a single meaningful, coherent, overarching life-narrative.[22] Such flexible selves seem more fragmented and postmodern than the subjectified, identitarian selves described by Foucault. Yet they may nevertheless be emerging as important new vehicles of self-regulation – at least for the "capable classes." And so critical theorists might subject them too to a quasi-Foucauldian analysis. Above all, they might try to determine whether the project of social control through self-governance and even personal autonomy might outlive fordism in some new guise.

In all such analyses, we should recall that discipline was Foucault's answer to the following question: how does power operate in the absence of the king? Today, of course, his answer is no longer persuasive, but that is not all. More disturbingly, the question itself needs to be reformulated: How does power operate after the decentering of the national frame, which continued to organize social regulation long after the demise of the monarch? In fact, it would be hard to formulate a better guiding question as we seek to understand new modes of governmentality in the era of neoliberal globalization. In my view, such an effort is the most fitting way by far to honor one of the most original and important thinkers of the previous century.

NOTES

1. See, e.g., the essays in *Foucault: A Critical Reader*, ed. David Couzens Hoy (Oxford: Blackwell, 1986) and *Critique and Power: Recasting the Foucault/Habermas Debate*, ed. Michael Kelly (Cambridge MA: MIT Press 1994).

2. See esp. Michel Foucault, *Power/Knowledge: Selected interviews and other writings, 1972–1977*, ed. Colin Gordon (New York: Pantheon, 1980) and *Language, Counter-Memory, Practice: Selected Essays and Other Writings*, ed. Donald F. Bouchard (Ithaca NY: Cornell University Press, 1977).

3. Michel Foucault, *The Birth of the Clinic: An Archaeology of Medical Perception*, tr. A.M. Sheridan Smith (New York: Pantheon, 1973), *Discipline and Punish: The Birth of the Prison*, tr. Alan Sheridan (New York: Pantheon, 1977), and "Governmentality," in *The Foucault Effect: Studies in Governmentality*, ed. Graham Burchell, Colin Gordon, and Peter Miller (Chicago: University of Chicago Press, 1991).

4. Foucault, *Discipline and Punish.*

5. Eli Zaretsky, *Secrets of the Soul: Psychoanalysis, Modernity, and Personal Life* (Knopf, forthcoming).

6. Hannah Arendt, *The Human Condition* (Chicago: University of Chicago Press, 1958); Jacques Donzelot, *The Policing of Families*, tr. Robert Hurley (New York: Pantheon, 1979).

7. Zaretsky, *Secrets of the Soul.*

8. Nancy Fraser, "Foucault on Modern Power: Empirical Insights and Normative Confusions," *Praxis International* 1, no. 3 (October 1981): 272–87.

9. Susan Strange, *The Retreat of the State: The Diffusion of Power in the World Economy* (Cambridge & New York: Cambridge University Press, 1996).

10. Phil Cerny, "Paradoxes of the Competition State: The Dynamics of Political Globalization," *Government and Opposition* 32, no. 2 (1997): 251–74.

11. Loïc Wacquant, "From Slavery to Mass Incarceration," *New Left Review* 13 (Jan.–Feb. 2002): 41–60.

12. Manuel Castells, "A Powerless State?" in *The Power of Identity* (Oxford: Blackwell, 1996); Cerny, "Paradoxes of the Competition State"; Stephen Gill, "New Constitutionalism, Democratisation and Global Political Economy," *Pacifica Review* 10, no. 1 (February 1998): 23–38; Michael Hardt and Antonio Negri, *Empire* (Cambridge, MA: Harvard University Press, 1999); Jürgen Habermas, "The Postnational Constellation and the Future of Democracy," *The Postnational Constellation: Political Essays*, tr. and ed. Max Pensky (Cambridge, MA: MIT Press, 2001); David Held, "Democracy and the New International Order," in *Cosmopolitan Democracy: An Agenda for a New World Order*, ed. Daniele Archibugi and David Held (Cambridge: Polity, 1995); James Rosenau, "Governance and Democracy in a Globalizing World," in *Re-imagining Political Community: Studies in Cosmopolitan Democracy*, ed. Daniel Archibugi and David Held (Stanford: Stanford University Press, 1999); Saskia Sassen, "The State and the New Geography of Power," *Losing Control? Sovereignty in an Age of Globalization* (New York: Columbia University Press, 1995); Strange, *The Retreat of the State*; and Wolfgang Streeck, "Public Power Beyond the Nation-State: The Case of the European Community," in *States Against Markets: The Limits of Globalization*, ed. Robert Boyer and Daniel Drache (London & New York: Routledge, 1996).

13. Hardt and Negri, *Empire*.

14. Nikolas Rose, "Governing 'Advanced' Liberal Democracies," in *Foucault and Political Reason: Liberalism, Neoliberalism, and the Rationalities of Government*, ed. Andrew Barry, Thomas Osborne, and Nikolas Rose (Chicago: University of Chicago Press 1996): 37–64

15. William E. Scheuerman, "Economic Globalization and the Rule of Law," *Constellations* 6, no. 1 (1999) and David Schneiderman, "Investment Rules and the Rule of Law," *Constellations* 8, no. 4 (2001).

16. Robert W. Cox, "A Perspective on Globalization," in *Globalization: Critical Reflections*, ed. James H. Mittelman (Boulder: Lynne Rienner, 1996) and "Democracy in Hard Times: Economic Globalization and the Limits to Liberal Democracy," in *The Transformation of Democracy?*, ed. Anthony McGrew (Cambridge: Polity, 1997).

17. Rose, "Governing 'Advanced' Liberal Democracies."

18. Ibid.

19. Colin Gordon, "Governmental Rationality: An Introduction" in *The Foucault Effect,* 1–51.

20. Robert Castel, "From Dangerousness to Risk," in *The Foucault Effect*, 281–98.

21. Manuel Castells, *The Rise of the Network Society* (Oxford: Blackwell, 1996); Hardt and Negri, *Empire*.

22. Richard Sennett, *The Corrosion of Character: The Personal Consequences of Work in the New Capitalism* (New York: Norton, 1998).

[19]

The death of the social? Re-figuring the territory of government

Nikolas Rose

Abstract

The social, as a plane of thought and action, has been central to political thought and political programmes since the mid-nineteenth century. This paper argues that, while themes of society and concerns with social cohesion and social justice are still significant in political argument, the social is no longer a key zone, target and objective of strategies of government. The rise of the language of globalization indicates that economic relations are no longer easily understood as organized across a single bounded national economy. Community has become a new spatialization of government: heterogeneous, plural, linking individuals, families and others into contesting cultural assemblies of identities and allegiances. Divisions among the subjects of government are coded in new ways; neither included nor excluded are governed as social citizens. Non-social strategies are deployed for the management of expert authority. Anti-political motifs such as associationism and communitarianism which do not seek to govern through society, are on the rise in political thought. The paper suggests some ways of diagnosing and analysing these novel territorializations of political thought and action.

Keywords: social; citizenship; risk; expertise; governmentality; community; exclusion.

In almost all advanced industrial countries, from Sweden to New Zealand, the old certainties of 'the welfare state' are under attack, and welfare systems are undergoing transformation.[1] One sees the privatization of public utilities and welfare functions, the marketization of health services, social insurance and pension schemes, educational reforms to introduce competition between schools and colleges, the introduction of new forms of management into the civil service modelled upon an image of methods in the private sector, new contractual relations between agencies and service providers and between professionals and clients, a new emphasis on the personal responsibilities of individuals, their families and their communities for their own future well-being and upon their own obligation to take active steps to secure this. At the level of 'governmentality' – in the sense that the term was used by Foucault: the deliberations, strategies, tactics and devices employed by authorities for making up and acting upon a population and its constituents to ensure good and avert ill – it seems as if we are seeing the emergence of a range of rationalities and techniques that seek to govern without governing *society*, to govern through regulated choices made by discrete and autonomous actors in the context of their particular commitments to families and communities (Rose 1993b, 1994). Of course, these changes, which are not confined to nations with right-wing regimes, may prove to be ephemeral. None the less, these shifts in policy appear to be paralleled in a shift within knowledge itself. The approaches often unified under the term 'post-modernism', together with a number of more local analyses, suggest that the object 'society', in the sense that began to be accorded to it in the nineteenth century (the sum of the bonds and relations between individuals and events – economic, moral, political – within a more or less bounded territory governed by its own laws) has also begun to lose its self-evidence, and 'sociology', as the field of knowledge which ratified the existence of this territory, is undergoing something of a crisis of identity.

While the destabilization of social theory has often been pioneered by those who think of themselves as progressives, the relation of those on the left to the transformations in the welfare state has been almost entirely negative. This is not surprising, given the intimate relations between socialism, as a rationality for politics, and the proliferation of social devices that made up welfare: the social state, social insurance, social service, the social wage, social protection and the rest. But perhaps we need to interrogate this opposition, in which the forces of progress seem obliged to take the side of the social against the forces of reaction which stand for individualism, competition, the market and the like. To begin such a task, we might usefully start by interrogating the notion of 'the social' itself. Are we witnessing not just a temporary shift in political and theoretical fashions but an event: 'the death of the social'?

Government from 'the social point of view'[2]

When, over a decade ago, Jean Baudrillard diagnosed 'the end of the social' (Baudrillard 1983), he offered his readers three propositions: That *the social has never existed*, but has always been a kind of simulation of a social relation that has now undergone a de-simulation, a disintegration of what was, in any event, an imaginary space of reference and play of mirrors; that *the social has really existed and now invests everything*, has extended from a process of the rational control of residues – vagrants, lunatics, the sick – to a state in which everyone is completely excluded and taken in charge for a project of functional integration sanctified by the social sciences; that *the social has existed in the past but has ceased to do so* – the sociality of the contract, of the relation of state to civil society, of the dialectic of the social and the individual has been destroyed by the fragmentations of the media, information, computer simulation and the rise of the simulacrum. Baudrillard concludes with a tender recollection of 'the unbelievable naivety of social and socialist thinking, for thus having been able to reify as universal and to elevate as ideal of transparency such a totally ambiguous and contradictory – worse, such a residual or imaginary – worse, such an already abolished in its very simulation "reality": the social' (Baudrillard 1983: 86).

This diagnosis undoubtedly catches something significant, despite its characteristically apocalyptic tone and opaque field of reference. It reminds us, if we should need reminding, that 'the social' is invented by history and cathected by political passions: we should be wary of embracing it as an inevitable horizon for our thought or standard for our evaluations. Gilles Deleuze, in his introduction to Jacques Donzelot's *The Policing of Families*, puts the issue in rather more sober terms: 'Clearly it is not a question of the adjective that qualifies the set of phenomena which sociology deals with: *the* social refers to a *particular sector* in which quite diverse problems and special cases can be grouped together, a sector comprising specific institutions and an entire body of qualified personnel' (Deleuze 1979: ix). 'The social', that is to say, does not represent an eternal existential sphere of human sociality. Rather, within a limited geographical and temporal field, it set the terms for the way in which human intellectual, political and moral authorities, in certain places and contexts, thought about and acted upon their collective experience. This novel plane of territorialization existed within, across, in tension with other spatializations: blood and territory; race and religion; town, region and nation. A host of lines of organization and intervention cast across most European nations and in North America over the nineteenth century and the first half of the twentieth intersected, connected and entangled in this hybrid zone of 'the social'.[3] Social statistics, then sociology, and all the social sciences, would play their part in stabilizing the social as a domain *sui generis*, whose reality could no longer be ignored. Simultaneously, political forces would now articulate their demand upon the State *in the name of the social*: the nation must be governed in the interests of social protection, social justice, social rights and social solidarity.

By the early decades of the twentieth century, politicians in different national contexts in Europe and North America had been forced to accept that government of at least some aspects of this social domain should be added to the responsibilities of the political apparatus and its officials. One sees a rejection of the totalizing claims of political economy to prescribe and delimit the legitimate means to be used for the government of economic life. Simultaneously, law can no longer be the sole and sufficient legitimate political means for achieving order and security; indeed law itself must answer to the demands of social government. The political rationalities that have played so great a part in our own century – socialism, social democracy, social liberalism – may have differed on many things, but on this they agreed – the nation must be governed, but one must pose the question of how to govern from 'the social point of view' (cf. Procacci 1989; for France, see Donzelot 1984; for England see Collini 1979; Clarke 1979). 'The social' became a kind of '*a priori*' of political thought: order would have to be social or it would cease to exist.

To speak of 'the death of the social' is undoubtedly misleading. Indeed 'social' policies are increasingly articulated at a supra-national level through international bodies such as the Organization of Economic Co-operation and Development, the World Health Organization, the United Nations and the European Union. But, despite the undoubted persistence of the theme of society and social cohesion in contemporary political argument, '*the* social' in the sense in which it has been understood for about a century is none the less undergoing a mutation. The conditions for this mutation, and the correlative emergence and proliferation of 'advanced liberal' programmes of government under a variety of different national political regimes, are heterogeneous and dispersed. Economic arguments have placed in question the idea of a national economy, whose formation in the nineteenth century was a key condition for the delineation of a social territory. Economic relations have come to be understood, not just as trans-national, not in terms of relations among discrete national economies, but as connecting up components of one national population with components of another – economic competition is between cities, between sectors, between specialized markets within economic relations that do not respect national political boundaries. The problem of national economic government is now posed differently: while ruling parties still have to manage national populations with the territorialized political machinery available to them, they no longer conceive of themselves as operating upon a naturally functioning and systemically integrated national population whose 'social' coherence is a condition for its economic security (cf. Hindess 1994b).[4]

The logics of social government were also problematized in other ways. As Hirschman (1991) has pointed out, there was a proliferation of 'rhetorics of reaction' about the paradoxical dis-welfares of the welfare state – its costs, its burdens, its injustices – which came from different parts of the political spectrum. There were also diverse criticisms of the expert powers installed by welfare states, and the discretionary scope that welfare systems accorded to professionals and bureaucrats (I have discussed these in detail elsewhere: Rose 1993b, 1993c). While these politico-ethical criticisms of social government were heterogeneous, they none the less have a certain 'family resemblance'. In particular, arguments made by libertarians of left and right, progressives, humanists, proponents of civil rights and advocates of empowerment shared a changed specification of the *subjects* of government. The human beings who were to be governed – men and women, rich and poor – were now conceived as individuals who are to be *active* in their own government. And their responsibility was no longer to be understood as a relation of obligation between citizen and society enacted and regulated through the mediating party of the State: rather, it was to be a relation of allegiance and responsibility to those one cared about the most and to whom one's destiny was linked. Each subject was now located in a variety of heterogeneous and overlapping networks of personal concern and investment – for oneself, one's family, one's neighbourhood, one's community, one's workplace. Central to the ethos of the novel mentalities and strategies of government that I have termed 'advanced liberal' is a new relationship between strategies for the government of others and techniques for the government of the self, situated within new relations of mutual obligation: the community.

The birth of the community

Until recently, the apparently 'a-moral' language of the market captured most attention in debates over changes in welfare – privatization, competition, financial calculation and so forth. But contemporary political rationalities also think in terms of another language which is just as important, which is highly morally invested and which intersects with markets, contracts and consumption in complex and surprising ways: 'community'. Consider the contemporary salience of the vocabulary of community care, community homes, community workers, community safety, for example. Consider the emergence of the idea of risk communities – drug abusers, gay men, carriers of particular genes, youth at risk. Consider the prominence of the language of community in debates over multi-culturalism and the problems posed for politicians, psychiatrists, police and others working in conditions of cultural, ethical and religious pluralism. All these seem to signal that 'the social' may be giving way to 'the community' as a new territory for the administration of individual and collective existence, a new plane or surface upon which micro-moral relations among persons are conceptualized and administered. I do not think this is merely a matter of changing professional jargon: it is indicative of a mutation, rather profound, if still uncertain, in the ways of thinking and acting that used to be conducted in a 'social' language. It is this mutation that also seems to lie at the heart of the recent prominence accorded to the language of community in political discourse from all sides of the political spectrum, and in the programmatic statements of political philosophers and advocates of the different versions of communitarianism. These new political languages are embodied in the ways in which a whole series of issues are problematized – made amenable to authoritative action *in terms of* features of communities and their strengths, cultures, pathologies. They shape the strategies and programmes that address such problems by seeking to *act upon* the dynamics of communities. They configure the *imagined territory* upon which these strategies should act – such as community mental health. And they extend to the *specification of the subjects* of government as individuals who are also, actually or potentially, the subjects of allegiance to a particular set of community values, beliefs and commitments.

We should not seek any single origin or cause of this complex reconfiguration of the territory of government. The social formed as a complex plane of interconnection among diverse minor lines of force, shifts in knowledge, in devices for charting populations and their vicissitudes, in practices of regulation and the pathways of action and calculation they traced out, contingent problematizations and ethical and political reformulations. Contemporary deployments of community are similarly heterogeneous, complex and mobile resultants of revised ways of representing, problematizing and intervening in a whole number of different arenas.[5] The term community, of course, has long been salient in political thought; it becomes governmental, however, when it is made technical. By the 1960s, community was already being invoked by sociologists as a possible antidote to the loneliness and isolation of the individual generated by 'mass society'. This idea of community as lost authenticity and common belonging was initially deployed in the social field as part of the language of critique and opposition directed against remote bureaucracy. Community activists were to identify, not with a welfare system that they saw as degrading, policing and controlling, but with those who were the subjects of that system – the inhabitants of the housing estates, projects and ghettos. More or less simultaneously, the language of community was utilized by authorities such as police to comprehend the problems they encountered in dealing with difficult zones – 'the West Indian community', the criminal community. Community here is a point of penetration of a kind of ethnographic sociology into the vocabularies and classifications of authorities; reciprocally, sociology itself intensified its investigations of collective life in terms of community and its anatomizing of the bonds of culture and the ties of locality that were thought to be essential conditions for its moral order. Within a rather short period, what began as a language of resistance and critique was transformed, no doubt for the best of motives, into an expert discourse and a professional vocation – community is now something to be programmed by Community Development Programmes, developed by Community Development Officers, policed by Community Police, guarded by Community Safety Programmes and rendered knowable by sociologists pursuing 'community studies'. Communities became zones to be investigated, mapped, classified, documented, interpreted, their vectors explained to enlightened professionals-to-be in countless college courses and to be taken into account in numberless encounters between professionals and their clients, whose individual conduct is now to be made intelligible in terms of the beliefs and values of 'their community'.

No doubt a whole range of other local shifts in vocabulary in diverse sites contributed to the emergence of community as a valorized alternative, antidote or even cure to the ills that the social had not been able to address – or even to the ills of the social itself. But what began to take shape here was a new way of demarcating a sector for government, a sector whose vectors and forces could be mobilized, enrolled, deployed in novel programmes and techniques which operated through the instrumentalization of personal allegiances and active responsibilities: *government through community*. It is this sense of community that has come to the fore in recent political arguments (e.g. Etzioni 1993; Grey 1996). Society is to be regenerated, and social justice to be maximized, through the building of responsible communities, prepared to invest in themselves (Commission on Social Justice 1994). As the current leader of the Labour Party put it, 'the search is on to reinvent community for a modern age, true to core values of fairness, co-operation and responsibility'.[6]

The re-figuring of the territory of government in terms of community has a number of significant features. The first is spatial: a kind of 'de-totalization'. The social, overarching all its stratifications and variations, was imagined as a single space, territorialized across a nation. Correlatively, government 'from the social point of view' posited a single matrix of solidarity, a relation between an organically interconnected society and all the individuals contained therein, given a politico-ethical form in the notion of social citizenship. Today, in contrast, a diversity of 'communities' is thought to, actually or potentially, command our allegiance: moral communities (religious, ecological, feminist . . .), lifestyle communities (defined in terms of tastes, styles of dress and modes of life), communities of commitment (to disability, problems of health, local activism) and so forth. Such communities are construed as localized, heterogeneous, overlapping and multiple. Sometimes they are defined in terms of the geographical co-ordinates of a micro-locale. Sometimes they are 'virtual communities' associated in neither 'real' space nor 'real' time but through a network of relays of communication, symbols, images, styles of dress and other devices of identification: the gay community, the disabled community, the Asian community (cf. Barry 1996). Such virtual communities are 'diasporic': they exist only to the extent that their constituents are linked together through identifications constructed in the non-geographic spaces of activist discourses, cultural products and media images.[7] And, while the language of community often locates discrete communities within a larger collectivity – a nation, a society, the planet itself, the nature of this superordinate allegiance is now most frequently posed as a problem. Hence arguments over 'multi-culturalism', the rise of political controversies over the implications of 'pluralism' – of ethnicity, religion, of sexuality, of ability and disability – together with conflicts over the competing and mutually exclusive 'rights' and 'values' of different communities.

A second significant feature of the birth of community is its changed ethical character. The social was an order of collective being and collective responsibilities and obligations. While the policies and programmes of the social accorded individuals personal responsibility for their conduct, this individual responsibility was always traversed by external determinations: the advantages or disadvantages conferred by family background, social class, life history, located within a wider array of social and economic forces such as changes in the labour market, booms, slumps, industrial cycles, the exigencies of urban environments, problems of housing supply. Of course, the extent to which such external determinants could or should mitigate personal responsibility was subject to continual dispute, as was the extent to which they could or should be compensated for in education, in the decisions of the criminal court and so forth. Nevertheless, this configuration of ethical vectors is re-organized under the sign of community. The subject is addressed as a moral individual with bonds of obligation and responsibilities for conduct that are assembled in a new way – the individual in his or her community is both self-responsible and subject to certain emotional bonds of affinity to a circumscribed 'network' of other individuals – unified by family ties, by locality, by moral commitment to environmental protection or animal welfare. Conduct is retrieved from a social order of determination into a new ethical perception of the individualized and autonomized actor, each of whom has unique, localized and specific ties to their particular family and to a particular moral community. Here we can locate the proliferation of debates on moral pluralism, and its diverse interpretations – as a relativistic threat to a necessary social agreement on moral absolutes or as the birth of a new era of enhanced ethical seriousness based upon individually sought and chosen allegiances in a cosmopolitan moral universe.

A third key aspect of the birth of community concerns the role of identification. The practices that assembled the social certainly entailed 'identification projects': programmes of mass schooling, of public housing, of public broadcasting, of social insurance and so forth had at their heart an image and a goal of the socially identified citizen, the person who, above all, understood themselves to be a member of a single integrated national society. The vocabulary of community also implicates a psychology of identification; indeed the very condition of possibility for a community to be imagined is its actual or potential existence as a fulcrum of personal identity. Yet these lines of identification are configured differently. Community proposes a relation that appears less 'remote', more 'direct', one which occurs not in the 'artificial' political space of society, but in matrices of affinity that appear more natural. One's communities are nothing more – or less – than those networks of allegiance with which one identifies existentially, traditionally, emotionally or spontaneously, seemingly beyond and above any calculated assessment of self-interest. Hence, like so many other similar loci of allegiance – class, civil society, ethnicity – arguments about community employ a Janus-faced logic (cf. Hindess 1993). Each assertion of community refers itself to something that already exists and has a claim on us: our common fate as gay men, as women of colour, as people with AIDS, as members of an ethnic group, as residents in a village or a suburb, as people with a disability. Yet our allegiance to each of these particular communities is something that we have to be made aware of, requiring the work of educators, campaigns, activists, manipulators of symbols, narratives and identifications. Within such a style of thought, community exists and is to be achieved, yet the achievement is nothing more than the birth-to-presence of a form of being which pre-exists.

'Government through community' involves a variety of strategies for inventing and instrumentalizing these dimensions of allegiance between individuals and communities in the service of projects of regulation, reform or mobilization. We can consider two examples which illustrate the complexity of these new governmental technologies.

My first example is security. Within social rationalities of government, a domain of collective security was envisaged to be maintained by the State on behalf of all citizens, through universal measures ranging from social insurance to the enforcement of the criminal law by a unified and socially funded police force. Today, this social image – and the practices to which it was linked – is displaced by a variety of different ways of imagining security, each of which mobilizes a particular sense of community. One image is of the 'gated city' preserving the security of its own residents, of the shopping mall policed by private security guards: that is to say, of a diversity of zones each circumscribing what Clifford Shearing has termed a 'contractual' community assuming – or being forced to assume – responsibility for 'its own' health, happiness, wealth and security (O'Malley 1992; Shearing 1995). Such patterns of re-configuring urban space can be observed in cities as distant as Sydney and Istanbul. The collective logics of community are here brought into alliance with the individualized ethos of neo-liberal politics: choice, personal responsibility, control over one's own fate, self-promotion and self-government. In a second image, community is promoted as an antidote to the combined depredations of market forces, remote central government, insensitive local authorities in new programmes for the regeneration of delimited locales – paradigmatically areas of disadvantaged inner cities (Etzioni 1993; Atkinson 1994). Here, new modes of neighbourhood participation, local empowerment and engagement of residents in decisions over their own lives will, it is thought, reactivate self-motivation, self-responsibility and self-reliance in the form of active citizenship within a self-governing community.[8] Government through the activation of individual commitments, energies and choices, through personal morality within a community setting, is counterposed to centralizing, patronizing and disabling social government. Paradoxically, given their apparent ideological differences, these opposed versions of security utilize similar images of the subject as an *active and responsible agent* in the securing of security for themselves and those to whom they are or should be affiliated. Equally, they envision the space of government in similar ways, no longer territorialized across a national space, but organized in terms of the relations of identification between the person and 'their community' – the particular collectivity to which each person is bound by kinship, religion, residence, shared plight or moral affinity. In each case, community is not simply the territory of government, but a *means* of government: its ties, bonds, forces and affiliations are to be celebrated, encouraged, nurtured, shaped and instrumentalized in the hope of producing consequences that are desirable for all and for each.

My second example concerns the health promotion programmes that have taken shape around HIV and AIDS. Gay communities of allegiance and identification pre-existed the HIV epidemic in the West, constructed most recently through the campaigning activities and lifestyle politics of gay activists. In the UK, Europe and the United States, it was largely in response to the political activism of these communities that national governments prioritized research and policies for HIV and AIDS (Ballard 1992). As politically funded agencies developed strategies for the government of sexual conduct in the name of health, gay organizations, first on their own, then in alliance with government health promotion campaigns, played a key role in the dissemination of new norms of sexual ethics and codes of sexual conduct to those who were 'at risk'. Not only in the publicity and health promotion materials, but also in the mass of social research into sexual attitudes and practices, identity and identification came to play a key role in the way in which sexual activity was rendered intelligible and in the development of strategies for its regulation – not only those targeted upon 'the gay community', but also those targeted upon other 'at risk groups'. Health promotion strategies were linked into the work of activist and self-help organizations, each strongly committed to the formation and valorization of the identity of its users and their communities. This established new forms of exclusion – for example, of haemophiliacs (cf. Watts 1994). New ways of problematizing the subjects to be governed emerged – for example, the way in which 'men who have sex with men' but who do not identify themselves as gay or bisexual have come to be seen as a major obstacle to current strategies for addressing the spread of HIV and AIDS (Bartos 1994). Government through community, even when it works upon pre-existing bonds of allegiance, transforms them, invests them with new values, affiliates them to expertise and re-configures relations of exclusion. This does not make 'communities' in some sense false. But it should alert us to the work entailed in the construction of community, and the implications of the logics of inclusion and exclusion, of responsibilization and autonomization, that they inescapably entail.

We can thus be governed *through* our allegiance to particular communities of morality and identity. Many programmes of government now operate upon the presupposition of such communities, even where the allegiances presupposed do not immediately appear to exist. Programmes of urban renewal, for example, imagine the plight of the inner city in terms of the loss of a 'spirit of community' with all the capacities of self-reliance, entrepreneurship and communal pride which such a spirit evokes. They attempt to 'empower' the inhabitants of particular inner-city locales by constituting those who reside in a certain locality *as* 'a' community, by seeking out 'community groups' who can claim to speak 'in the name of community' and by linking them in new ways into the political apparatus in order to enact programmes which seek to regenerate the economic and human fabric of an area by re-activating in 'the community' these 'natural' virtues which it has temporarily lost. Complementarily, imagined communities, created by the activity of local activists or emerging as the reciprocal, as it were, of such governmental projects, can form the locus of the articulation of demands upon political authorities and resistance to such authorities: the language of community and the identity which is its referent becomes the site of new contestations. Hence community mobilization can be for causes as diverse as the demand for funding for HIV research and services, the blocking of a new road driven through a residential area, the protesting of racial harassment and opposition to policies for housing within 'our' community those who do not belong – black, mad, disabled or whatever. These contradictions of community establish a new and agonistic territory for the organization of political and ethical conflicts.

This mutation, in which collective relations have been re-figured in such a way as to reduce the salience of 'the social' in favour of 'the community', has been accompanied by mutations along a number of other dimensions. In the remainder of this paper, I want to discuss three of these, which are linked in different ways to the birth of the community. Along the first, one sees a reshaping of strategies for governing economic life, decoupling the relations that previously existed between social welfare and economic strength. Along a second, one sees the subjects of government specified in new ways, in terms of an ethic of activity which establishes new divisions between those who are considered to be competent citizens and those whose are not. Along a third, one sees a reshaping of the relations between expertise and politics, and the emergence of a range of new expert technologies for governing expertise.

A de-socialization of economic government

A new configuration is taking shape for the government of economic life, in which techniques for the maximization of social welfare no longer appear necessary to secure economic well-being in a market constituted largely by private enterprises. As I have already noted, the formation of the notion of a national economy was a key condition for the separation out of a distinct social domain. Classical political economy effected a separation of a domain of 'economic' events with their own laws and processes from a 'moral' domain. Economic events were territorialized within a national space, seen as governed by laws and relations whose scope and limits seemed to map onto the territory of political rule. As they crystallized within nineteenth-century thought, 'economies' were organized within nations, limited by borders, customs and other restrictions on imports and exports, unified through a single supply of money, characterized by a set of functional relations between their components, and these unities were located in a wider space within which they could engage in 'foreign trade' with other national economies. The responsibility of the political authorities for the security of a nation, a state and a people, came to be understood in terms of their capacity to nurture natural economic processes to ensure national economic well-being (see the discussion in Tribe 1978). Further, over the course of the nineteenth century and into the twentieth, the solidity of these national economies was increased by the regular publication of various national indicators of economic performance, and by the gradual tracing out of a plane of 'economic policy', which concerned itself with the proper ways in which the strengths of such an economic system could be enhanced: action on the money supply, on the labour market, together with tariffs and restrictions on imports and so forth, especially as national wealth came to be understood in terms of competition between discrete economies and their struggle to gain access to sources of cheap raw materials, cheap labour or lucrative markets outside their own territorial bounds.

In the strategies of government that developed over the course of the twentieth century, the domains of the economic and the social were distinguished, but governed according to a principle of joint optimization. Economic activity, in the form of wage labour was given a new set of *social* responsibilities, seen as a mechanism which would link males into the social order, and which would establish a proper relationship between the familial, the social and the economic orders (Meuret 1981; Miller and Rose 1990; Rose 1990: II; Rose and Miller 1995; Walters 1994). Simultaneously, the privacy of the wage contract was weakened, as politicians came to accept that conditions of labour and pay should be regulated in the name of social peace. The production of a labour market itself became part of the responsibilities of economic government, and a range of interventions into the social would maximize the economic efficacy of the population as a work-force, from vocational guidance and labour exchanges to various methods of maintaining the social habits of labour among the unemployed. Gradually, over the next six decades, new indexes of economic activity were invented that would render the economy amenable to management, and new technologies of macro-economic regulations were brought into being. Through mechanisms of social insurance – unemployment benefit, accident insurance, health and safety legislation and so forth – and through an array of forms of economic government – tax regimes, interest rates and other techniques of 'demand management' – the state assumed responsibility for the management of a whole variety of risks – to individuals, to employers, to the state itself – in the name of society.

But the perception of 'the economy' which underpinned such endeavours is now undergoing a mutation (Hindess 1994b). 'An economy' is no longer so easily imagined as naturally co-extensive with the realm of a nation state, with different 'national economies' inhabiting a wider common field in which they traded, competed, exploited one another. Theorists and practitioners alike now construe economic relations as 'globalized', and this new spatialization of the economy is coupled with arguments to the effect that flexible economic relations need to be established in particular localities (Reich 1992; Hirst and Thompson 1992; both cited and discussed in Hindess 1994b). Overlaying this 'dialectic of the global and the local' are other trans-national spatializations of economic relations, such as the argument that there is a 'global economy' of 'world cities', in which Birmingham, Sydney, Baltimore, Budapest compete among one another for the economic benefit of company location, conferences, sporting events, tourism (Zukin 1991; Lash and Urry 1994).

Irrespective of the accuracy with which these trends are identified and portrayed, the economic problems of government are being re-thought in terms of a revised image of economic space and the means by which it can be acted upon. It appears that, while national governments still have to manage a national population, the economic well-being of the nation and of its population can no longer be so easily mapped upon one another and governed according to principles of mutual maximization. Government of the social in the name of the national economy gives way to government of particular zones – regions, towns, sectors, communities – in the interests of economic circuits which flow between regions and across national boundaries. The economic fates of citizens within a national territory are uncoupled from one another, and are now understood and governed as a function of their own particular levels of enterprise, skill, inventiveness and flexibility.

This is coupled with a shift in rationalities and techniques for the government of employment and unemployment. Unemployment is now understood as a phenomenon to be governed – both at the macro-economic level and at the level of the conduct of the unemployed person him or herself – through enhancing the activity of the individual in search of work, and obliging the individual to engage in a constant and active search for employment and for the skills that will provide employment. On the one hand, the general problem of unemployment is re-conceived in terms of the respective competitiveness of different labour forces, understood at least in part in terms of the psychological, dispositional and aspirational capacities of those that make them up. On the other, each individual is solicited as an ally of economic success through ensuring that they invest in the management, presentation, promotion and enhancement of their own economic capital as a capacity of their selves and as a lifelong project (Walters 1994; Dean 1995).

This emphasis upon the individual as an active agent in their own economic governance through the capitalization of their own existence is paralleled in a whole new set of vocabularies and devices for managing individuals within the workplace in terms of the enhancement of their own skills, capacities and entrepreneurship. These attempt an alliance between the desires of the worker or manager for self-enhancement and actualization through work and the perceived need of the enterprise to become flexible, competitive, agile, creative, etc. In labour, too, work is no longer to be construed as a social obligation, or its efficiency to be enhanced through maximizing the social benefits that the labourer finds in the workplace, or its primary role to be one of binding the individual into the collective through the socializing effects of the habit of work. Rather, the workplace itself – for labourers and for managers – is to be an area of self-promotion and the government of work is to be undertaken in terms of the enhancement of the active capacities of the entrepreneurial individual. No doubt, too, one could identify similar logics at work in the attempts to regenerate local economies, especially in urban areas: economic decline is to be halted through a range of devices that will enhance the activity of entrepreneurial individuals with skills and flexibility, and aspirations of self-promotion – exemplified, again, in the UK government's current strategies for urban renewal.

In short, one could suggest that, within those strategies of government that I have termed 'advanced liberal', one finds the emergence of a new way of conceptualizing and acting upon the relations between the government of economic life and the self-government of the individual: the economy is no longer to be governed in the name of the social, nor is the economy to be the justification for the government of a whole range of other sectors in a social form. The social and the economic are now seen as antagonistic, and the former is to be fragmented in order to transform the moral and psychological obligations of economic citizenship in the direction of active self-advancement. Simultaneously, government of a whole range of previously social apparatuses is to be restructured according to a particular image of the economic – the market. Economic government is to be de-socialized in the name of maximizing the entrepreneurial comportment of the individual.

The subjects of government

This transformation in the government of economic life links to a more general mutation in arrangements for the government of conduct. New ways are taking shape for understanding, classifying and acting upon the subjects of government, entailing new relations between the ways in which people are governed by others and the ways in which they are advised to govern themselves. Fundamental to this general field is a re-coding of dividing practices, revising the distinctions between the *affiliated* and the *marginalized*. By the affiliated I mean those who are considered 'included': the individuals and families who have the financial, educational and moral means to 'pass' in their role as active citizens in responsible communities. To remain affiliated one must 'enterprise' one's life through active choice, within authoritative terms and limits that have become integrated within all the practices of everyday life, sustained by a heterogeneous array of 'civilized' images and devices for lifestyle promotion. In rearing children, in schooling, in training and employment, in ceaseless consumption, the included must calculate their actions in terms of a kind of 'investment' in themselves, in their families, and maximize this investment with reference to the codes of their own particular communities. But the marginal are those who cannot be considered affiliated to such sanctioned and civilized cultural communities. Either they are not considered as affiliated to *any* collectivity by virtue of their incapacity to manage themselves as subjects or they are considered affiliated to some kind of 'anti-community' whose morality, lifestyle or comportment is considered a threat or a reproach to public contentment and political order. On this division between the affiliated and the marginalized are articulated two rather different sets of debates, and two rather different governmental strategies, neither of which seem to be undertaken from 'the social point of view'.

The problem of risk provides us with a point of entry for an investigation of these novel 'post-social' strategies for governing conduct. Many have pointed to the contemporary prominence of the notion of 'risk' as a way of understanding the troubles encountered by individuals and collectivities. Historical sociologies have suggested that the prevalence of the language of risk is a consequence of changes in the contemporary existential condition of humans and their world (Beck 1992). In contrast, genealogical studies have analysed risk as part of a *particular style of thinking* born during the nineteenth century (Ewald 1991). This entailed new ways of understanding and acting upon misfortune *in terms of risk*: risk thinking brought the future into the present and made it calculable, using the statistical intelligibility that the collective laws of large numbers seemed to provide (Hacking 1991). Most significant for present purposes have been genealogies of social insurance, that have traced the ways in which, over the course of the twentieth century, *security* against risk was socialized.

In the late nineteenth century, the respectable working man was urged to be *prudent*, an obligation which required him to take a range of active steps to secure himself, his family and his dependants against future misfortune: joining insurance schemes provided by trade associations or Friendly Societies, personal involvement in the selection of benefits and the making of regular payments and so forth (Defert 1991). These trade- or association-based schemes established rather direct connections between the individual responsibility of each member and the mutuality of the responsibility that was shared among the members as a whole. These mutualized relations of prudence were relatively short lived. By the end of the nineteenth century in Britain, Australia and the United States they were already being displaced by commercialized operations in which security was secured through individuals contracting into private insurance schemes run for profit (O'Malley 1995). At the turn of the century, in most European countries, these voluntary relations of prudence – mutual or commercial – were further transformed with the implementation of national schemes of compulsory social insurance. There were many different forces at work here, including political worries about the viability and integrity of the schemes, and concerns about the consequences to, and of, those who were left uninsured through failure of companies or through unwillingness or inability to be thrifty. But, as Ewald puts it, 'Insurance becomes *social* . . . because European societies come to analyse themselves and their problems in terms of the generalised technology of risk' (Ewald 1991): risk, responsibility and thrift became vectors of social government.

Social insurance was acquired as a benefit of citizenship. As is well known, schemes were structured with the aim that they would not 'demoralize' those who were their members through the inculcation of dependency, but, on the contrary, produce moral effects of responsibility, regularity of habits of labour and social obligation in those who were their beneficiaries (Gilbert 1966). Of course, the injunction to personal prudence on one's own behalf and that of one's dependants did not disappear over the twentieth century. But none the less, today, a strategic shift is occurring in the politics of security. Individuals are, once again, being urged by politicians and others to *take upon themselves* the responsibility for their own security and that of their families: to insure against the costs of ill health through private medical insurance, to make provisions for their future through private pensions, to take an active role in securing themselves against all that could possibly threaten the security of their chosen style of life. This 'new prudentialism' (O'Malley 1992) uses the technologies of consumption – advertising, market research, niche marketing and so forth – to exacerbate anxieties about one's own future and that of one's loved ones, to encourage us to subdue these risks and to tame our fate by purchasing insurance designed especially for us and our individual situation. There is obviously an industry of risk here, seeking out and creating markets for products in the interests of its own profit. But there is also a politics of risk, as politicians warn about the future of social pension and insurance schemes, and exhort responsible individuals to take primary responsibility for the management of risks to their own security and that of their families by disposing of their current income in the interests of their own future comfort. Thus, as in other technologies of consumption, a hybrid arrangement of forces and devices has been assembled together which acts to govern choice in the supposedly mutually reinforcing interests of personal security, private profit and public good.

This contemporary prudentialism differs from its nineteenth-century forebear in a number of ways. The person who is to be made prudent is no longer mutualized but autonomized. Thrift is recast as investment in a future lifestyle of freedom. Insurantial expertise is no longer a matter of actuarial wisdom, the assurance of stability and probity, and the personal relation with the contributions collector, but works through amplifying the very anxieties against which security is to protect and promoting the dreams of tranquillity and a golden future which insurance can provide, through the use of all the techniques of advertising and marketing. Further, insurance agents now offer themselves as versatile advisers in the techniques of risk reduction and risk management. As risk is simultaneously proliferated and rendered potentially manageable, the private market for 'security' extends: not merely personal pension schemes and private health insurance, but burglar alarms, devices that monitor sleeping children, home testing kits for cholesterol levels and much more. Protection against risk through an investment in security becomes part of the responsibilities of each active individual, if they are not to feel guilt at failing to protect themselves and their loved ones against future misfortunes. The ethics of lifestyle maximization, coupled with a logic in which someone must be held to blame for any event that threatens an individual's 'quality of life', generates a relentless imperative of risk management not simply in relation to contracting for insurance, but also through daily lifestyle management, choices of where to live and shop, what to eat and drink, stress management, exercise and so forth. Of course, this inaugurates a virtually endless spiral of amplification of risk – as risk is managed in certain zones and forms of conduct (e.g. shopping in malls scanned by security cameras; foetal monitoring; low fat diets and heart disease), the perceived riskiness of other unprotected zones is exacerbated (high streets; unsupervised pregnancies; the uneducated dietary habits of children and the poor). These arrangements within which the individual is re-responsibilized for the management of his or her own risk produces a field characterized by uncertainty, plurality and anxiety, thus continually open to the construction of new problems and the marketing of new solutions.

These assemblages of risk are related in complex ways to the valorization of community which I discussed earlier. The exhortation to risk management can itself be organized on the territory of community, where it can have a range of diverse effects, from consumer campaigns against the use of pesticides in fruit production to ecological mobilizations against the dumping of nuclear waste: 'not in our back yard' becomes a cliché to describe these responses to threatened introduction of new risks. But this is only one version of the more valued endeavours in which individuals seek, in the name of their own community, to reduce their risk, for example, as I have mentioned, by contracting into a 'gated' community which secures itself physically and spatially against risk. These new logics of risk management are thus capable of being deployed within a wide range of strategies. They not only multiply the points at which normative calculation and intervention are required but fragment the social space of welfare into a multitude of diverse pockets, zones, folds of riskiness each comprised of a linking of specific current activities and conducts and general probabilities of their consequences. In this new configuration, 'social insurance' is no longer a key technical component for a general rationality of social solidarity: taxation for the purposes of welfare becomes, instead, the minimum price that respectable individuals and communities are prepared to pay for insuring themselves against the riskiness now seen to be concentrated within certain problematic sectors.

This discussion of risk highlights certain more general features of the new 'post-social' technologies of governing conduct which are taking shape. Under the rationalities of welfare, social technologies were to civilize individuals, render them as citizens with obligations to conduct themselves with prudence in exchange for certain guarantees against uncertainty. In the new prudential regimes, individuals, educated through the mechanisms of marketing and the pedagogies of consumption and lifestyle, are to gain access to previously 'social' benefits such as educational advantage, health status and contentment in old age through purchase in a competitive market. Promotion of private insurance by market mechanisms thus exemplifies the widespread mechanisms through which consumption and markets have become powerful new mechanisms for the shaping of conduct. These are not guided by a political logic, but they none the less make it possible to transform political technologies for the government of subjectivity. Affiliation to communities of lifestyle through the practices of consumption displaces older devices of habit formation that enjoined obligations upon citizens as part of their social responsibilities. Consider, for example, the way in which advertising and marketing have transformed the role of the technologies invented in the early years of this century that targeted mothers – mothers-to-be in the schools, new mothers by health visitors, mothers as the guardians of hygienic and healthy homes by doctors and other experts in domesticity. Consumption regimes now operate as highly managed and carefully calibrated domains for the calculated regulation of the minutiae of private conduct through personal acts of choice. The politics of conduct at the end of the twentieth century is conducted, at least in part, through the selective amplification of passions, anxieties, allegiances and identities intrinsic to the commercial struggle to sell goods and maximize profits.

The commodification of identities and the instrumentalization of passions to which it is linked opens a heterogeneous and risky field – identities may be transgressive, identifications may lead to rave parties as much as to more salubrious lifestyles, the commodities promoted, such as alcohol or videos, may become identified with forms of conduct that themselves call forth demands for new areas of regulation. The injunction to healthy eating by politically funded programmes of health promotion is only one theme in a field that itself utilizes the opposition of wickedness to health to promote the consumption of all sorts of dangerous pleasure foods. Techniques of commodification of identities can be utilized by political authorities in calculated strategies such as those to reduce the spread of HIV, the use of drugs or the prevalence of drunken driving, but they can also be used in the spread of evangelical religions or pornography. The alliances forged here are always risky, provisional and revisable; none the less, from this point onwards, projects for the government of conduct will operate on a territory marked out by the vectors of identity, choice, consumption and lifestyle.

Governing the margins

It is, I think, only in relation to these logics of inclusion through choice, autonomy and consumption that one can understand the new ways that are taking shape for conceptualizing and acting upon those subjects who inhabit those zones that Beveridge termed the 'five giants on the road of reconstruction': Want, Disease, Ignorance, Squalor and Idleness – the five enemies that were to be attacked by 'a comprehensive policy of social progress' based on co-operation between the State and the individual (Beveridge 1942: 6). It would certainly be misleading to interpret the contemporary redrawing of the boundaries of the political as merely a 'reduction of the role of the State in society'. On the one hand, we have seen the spread of the mechanisms which Deleuze characterized under the rubric of 'societies of control', where conduct is continually monitored and reshaped by logics immanent within all networks of practice. In such practices we are continually subject to processes of functional integration: 'life long learning', 'continual retraining', 'constant job readiness', ceaseless consumption (Deleuze 1995). But these processes of continuous modulation of conduct have been accompanied by the intensification of direct, disciplinary, often coercive and carceral, political interventions in relation to particular zones and persons – the prison population is rising throughout Europe, for example. As civility is understood as affiliation by consumption, dividing practices are re-configured to problematize certain 'abjected' persons, sectors and locales for specific reformatory attention: the underclass, the excluded, the marginal.

It would be unwise to overstate the novelty of these divisions. One could write the history of the government of conduct in terms of its successive taxonomies and forms of division: the eighteenth-century division of poverty and pauperism; the Victorian proliferation of institutions for specific groups: fallen women, sailors out of work, blind children. At the end of the nineteenth century, there is a tension between those who would *unify* the social problem in terms of a degenerate constitution and those, in England most notably the Webbs, who would see the major requirement of a system of administration as a practice of *distinction*: the classification of socially problematic individuals into precise categories, each requiring its own distinct form of intervention. It would be foolish to deny the continued presence of these diagnostic and classificatory imperatives within the social machinery of the welfare state as it assembled over the middle decades of the twentieth century. Unlike France, where the language of social right provided a unifying milieu within which conflicting political positions could engage with one another, in England, social legislation, industrial tribunals, social security tribunals and many other apparatuses operated in terms of precise yet diverse criteria of eligibility and allowances. Nevertheless, at the programmatic level, codifiers such as Beveridge and Marshall constructed a vision in which security against hardship, like hardship itself, was social and to be provided by measures of benefit and insurance that, in name at least, were to be termed 'universal', including all within a unified 'social citizenship'.

Of course, even within this unified vision there were concerns with those who eluded the bonds of citizenship – one only has to consider the debate in the 1960s over the 'cycle of deprivation'. But the emergence of the notion of an 'underclass' in the United States at the end of the 1970s does seem to mark a moment in which the social vision of a continuous *quantitative* variability in levels of civility becomes re-coded as a *qualitative* distinction. 'Behind the [ghetto's] crumbling walls lives a large group of people who are more intractable, more socially alien and more hostile than almost anyone had imagined. . . . Their bleak environment nurtures values that are often at odds with those of the majority – even the majority of the poor. Thus the underclass produces a highly disproportionate number of the nation's juvenile delinquents, school dropouts, drug addicts and welfare mothers, and much of the adult crime, family disruption, urban decay and demand for social expenditures' (*Time*, 29 August 1977, quoted in Katz 1993: 4). The underclass was a heady mixture of long-term welfare recipients, hostile street criminals, hustlers in an alternative underground economy, traumatized alcoholics, vagrants and de-institutionalized psychiatric patients dominating the wastelands in the decaying industrial heartland of the cities of North America. In the UK, a less lurid picture was painted, but one in which the recipients of welfare were still portrayed in terms of a moral problematization: those lured into welfare dependency by the regimes of social security themselves, those unable to accept their moral responsibilities as citizens for reasons of psychological or other personal incapacity, those who might be enterprising, but wilfully refused to operate within the values of civility and responsible self-management, such as New Age travellers or drug abusers.

Of course these essentially moral characterizations, in terms of dependency, danger or depravity, were contested by social liberals and those on the left. Initially these contestations were posed in the familiar logics of social causation and social welfare. Yet, over the last decade, within British and European rationalities of social democracy, a new style of thought has taken shape, in which the old problems of inequality and social justice are analysed in a distinctive and recurring fashion. It is suggested that secular economic changes, exacerbated by policies which have sought to reduce welfare expenditure in the name of competitive tax regimes and the like, have led to the rise of a 'two-thirds, one-third' society, producing a widening gap between the 'included' majority who are seeing their standard of living rising and impoverished minorities who are 'excluded' (Levitas 1996). Thus, the European Commission, in a chapter entitled 'Social policy and protection – an active society for all', under the heading 'Promoting the social integration of all', a European Commission White Paper, argues that 'with more than 52 million people in the Union living below the poverty line, social exclusion is an endemic phenomenon . . . which threatens the social cohesion of each Member State and of the Union as a whole. . . . The marginalization of major social groups is a challenge to the social cohesion of the Union' (European Commission 1994: 49; cf. Hutton 1995; Commission for Social Justice 1994; Joseph Rowntree Foundation 1995).

Despite their great differences in notions of economic causation and personal responsibility, these different rationalities operate with a surprisingly consonant picture of the abjected persons and groups that are their object. On the one hand, they are dispersed. They are no longer seen as part of a single group with common social characteristics, to be managed by a unified 'social service' and 'generic social workers' who can recognize the common roots of all social problems. The marginalized, the excluded, the underclass are fragmented and divided; their particular difficulties thus need to be addressed through the activities of a variety of specialists each of whom is an expert in a particular problem – training schemes for those excluded through unemployment, specialist agencies working with those with disabilities, rehabilitation of addicts undertaken by specialist drug workers, education in social skills by workers with the single homeless, specialized hostels for battered women, for alcoholics, etc. Yet, on the other hand, these abjected subjects are re-unified ethically and spatially. Ethically, in that they are accorded a new active relation to their status in terms of their strategies and capacities for the management of themselves: they have either refused the bonds of civility and self-responsibility or they aspire to them but have not been given the skills, capacities and means. And spatially, in that the unified space of the social is re-configured, and the abjected are re-located, in both imagination and strategy, in 'marginalized' spaces: in the decaying council estate, in the chaotic lone-parent family, in the shop doorways of inner-city streets. It appears as if, outside the communities of inclusion, outside the control society, exists an array of micro-sectors, comprised of those who are unable or unwilling to enterprise their lives or manage their own risk, incapable of exercising responsible self-government, attached either to no moral community or to a community of anti-morality.

It is in this sense that it is possible to argue that new territory is emerging, after the welfare state, for the management of these micro-sectors, traced out by a plethora of quasi-autonomous agencies working within the 'savage spaces', in the 'anti-communities' on the margins, or with those abjected by virtue of their lack of competence or capacity for responsible ethical self-management: 'voluntary' endeavours (often run by users, survivors or philanthropists but funded by various grant regimes) – drug projects, disability organizations, self-help groups, concept houses and so forth (oppositional forces transformed into service providers). Private and for-profit organizations – old people's homes, hostels and so forth – make their money from private insurance or from the collection of the state benefits to their individual inmates. In the huge and murky industry of 'training' unemployment is re-problematized as a matter of the lack of individual and marketable skills among the unemployed themselves, to be countered by a multitude of training organizations that are private and compete in a market for public contracts and public funds. Within this new territory of exclusion, the social logics of welfare bureaucracies are replaced by new logics of competition, market segmentation and service management: the management of misery and misfortune can become, once more, a potentially profitable activity.

Experts of activity

I have suggested that the contemporary politics of competence construes subjects as, actually or potentially, active elements in their own self-government. This perception extends to those whom I have termed the abjected. Whether they be construed as excluded by socio-economic forces, marginalized by virtue of personal incapacity or pathology or morally alien on account of their dependency, depravity or delinquency, their alienation is to be reversed by equipping them with certain active subjective capacities: they must take responsibility, they must show themselves capable of calculated action and choice, they must shape their lives according to a moral code of individual responsibility and community obligation. I have argued elsewhere that in 'control societies', market mechanisms are increasingly utilized to link the active individual and family to expertise, and I have suggested that this opens new possibilities for questioning expertise as shown in the rise of consumers' and users' organizations of various sorts (Rose 1994). For those who are to be the subjects of expert attention, similar 'active' policies are being set in place, but this injunction to activity allows far fewer opportunities for contesting expert authority. Take the example of unemployment, which I have already discussed. In the UK, in the policies of the Organization for Economic Co-operation and Development and in Australia, the unemployed person is now portrayed as a 'jobseeker', whose 'job readiness' is the key point at issue, where a lapse into long-term unemployment is to be avoided by emphasizing the requirement for an 'active' programme of income support, and who is to be trained in the active skills of 'job search' (cf. Dean 1995; Walters 1994). The injunction to activity here limits the possibilities of resistance. Jobseeking conduct is to be continually subject to individualized evaluation and judgement and failure to manifest appropriately energetic conduct as specified in the manuals and criteria results in peremptory loss of benefit.

This injunction to activity extends to practices that might be thought more caring and progressive. Consider, for example, the widespread utilization of notions such as empowerment in the formulation of practices for a diversity of problematic categories (Cruikshank 1994; Baistow 1995). Experts still relate to their clients in a pedagogic and responsibilizing form. However, the emphasis has shifted. While clients were typically regarded as damaged individuals, with a personal pathology that may well have been triggered or sustained by social factors, hence requiring diagnosis and insight, the professional gaze has become more 'superficial': it now focuses upon conduct itself and the cognitive and moral organization of perception, intention, action and evaluation. In these new forms of practice, which are of course by no means universal but are spreading fast, the subject of expertise is now understood, at least for the purposes at hand, as an individual who lacks the cognitive, emotional, practical and ethical skills to take the personal responsibility for rational self-management. Of course, this empowerment, and the activity it is to generate, is not located within a closed disciplinary space, but upon the governable territory of cultural community. Empowerment, then, is a matter of experts teaching, coaxing, requiring their clients to conduct themselves within particular cultural communities of ethics and lifestyle, according to certain specified arts of active personal responsibility. Empowerment, with all its emphasis on strengthening the capacity of the individual to play the role of actor in his or her own life, has come to encompass a range of interventions to transmit, under tutelage, certain professionally ratified mental, ethical and practical techniques for active self-management. Under the sign of empowerment, one thus can observe the re-deployment of the whole panoply of psychological technologies for reforming conduct in relation to particular norms, from individual psychotherapy in various rational and cognitive forms, through the use of programmed behavioural techniques to group work. In line with the 'superficial' gaze of the new experts of conduct, however, these techniques are re-conceptualized so that they can be seen as having visible, identifiable and specifiable behavioural or mental outputs, leading to target behaviours that seem to be amenable to measurement and calculation. And, as we shall see, this emphasis on goals, targets and measurements is part of a new way not only of managing profession–client relations, but of managing professionals themselves.

Risk, community and expertise

The notion of risk once more provides a useful point of entry into the revised relations of expertise taking shape on the territory of community. In part this is because the capacity for personal 'power', or the lack of it, which is the object of empowerment technologies is itself re-thought in terms of the relations of risk and community which I discussed earlier: the risks posed to the individual themselves if they cannot adequately manage their life within the community, the risks the individual may pose to the community on account of their failure to govern themselves. It is also because the responsibilities of experts are themselves being re-formulated in terms of risk and community. In a range of domains, social workers, psychiatrists, doctors and others have been allocated accountability not so much for the cure or reform of clients, patients and other problematic individuals, but for their administration according to a logic of risk minimization (cf. Castel 1991; Rose 1996a). The novel intellectual techniques of risk identification, risk assessment and risk management bring into existence a whole new set of professional obligations – the obligation that each individual professional should calculate and reduce the risk of their professional conduct, instruct the subjects of their authority in the riskiness of the practices and procedures in which they are engaged and manage their clients in the light of the imperative to reduce the risk they may pose to others – their children, members of 'the general public'. Experts are thus increasingly required to undertake not so much an identification of a condition but a calculation of the riskiness of an individual or an event, with the obligation to take (legal, moral, professional, financial) responsibility for the calculations that they make, the advice that they give and the success of the strategies that they put into place to monitor and manage that risk. This is only one of the ways in which the re-configuring of the territory of government has been linked to new roles for experts in the government of the conduct of active individuals within their communities.

Social government was expert government. The devices of 'the welfare state' opened a multitude of new locales for the operation of expert judgements, based on knowledge, training, professional and bureaucratic ethics and specialist skills: bureaux of various types, benefit, social security and unemployment offices, dossiers, case records, case conferences and tribunals. In each of these locales, experts and their judgements were not only vital relays in the links between political objectives and personal conduct, they also had considerable capacities to 'enclose' themselves and their judgements, to make demands in terms of their own perceptions of their interests and the requirements of the apparatuses they operated – in short to deploy a range of tactics to render themselves difficult for politicians to govern, if not actually 'ungovernable'. While the problems posed by experts were bemoaned over many years and from many different perspectives, a number of new technologies are currently being deployed through which experts can be linked into the devices for the conduct of conduct. Locales and activities that were previously part of the assemblages of the 'social' are being autonomized from the machinery of politics and novel devices are being used to govern the activities of those who work within them. In a plethora of quasi-autonomous units, associations and 'intermediate organizations', experts are allocated new responsibilities and new mechanisms are developed for the management of professional expertise 'at a distance' – that is, outside the machinery of bureaucracy that previously bound experts into devices for the government of 'the social'. Previously 'social' experts such as social workers, benefit officers, doctors, social service bureaucrats and others now operate within a whole variety of quasi-private regulatory organizations: in the UK situation one could point to the Next Steps Initiative in the fragmentation and contractualization of the Civil Service; the establishment of 'agencies' to run even apparatuses previously considered to be essential to 'the State' such as the prison service; the proliferation of such hybrid public/private entities as Training and Enterprise Boards; the purchaser–provider split and case management techniques in social services, the fragmentation of health services into autonomous trusts and a range of other shifts popularly termed 'the quango-ization of the State'.[9] Three aspects are worth highlighting.

First, in the UK situation at least, there is a renewed emphasis upon the potential of a variety of legal and quasi-legal mechanisms to meet political obligations to address 'problems' – from discharged psychiatric patients to insider dealing – while refusing an extension of the politico-administrative machinery of the State. I am thinking here of the use of such statutorily specified and legally enforceable criteria as those governing minimum service standards and contracts specifying performance targets and outputs – numbers of patients to be treated, length of time a case must wait until dealt with, obligations for the relations between case managers, their clients and the providing organization and so forth. This should not be seen as the expansion of 'law' as a 'system' and its capture by a political apparatus. The mechanisms of legal regulation are complex and fragmented. Politicians, professionals and consumer groups organize around the production of codes of professional conduct which specify various rights for users and clients. A new 'litigious mentality' ensures that 'the shadow of the law' becomes a means of managing professional activity through the self-regulation of decisions and actions in relation to such formally promulgated codes and standards. Struggles over the regulation of expertise occur not only in the courts, but in campus sexual harassment offices, human rights committees and commissions, review bodies for appealing welfare decisions and in many new and diverse forums. These legal procedures are not in themselves new. None the less, the widespread utilization of these forms of regulation renders the actions and judgements of professionals governable in new ways – and, in the process, changes the very terms in which these judgements themselves are construed, prioritized, justified and enacted.

Perhaps even more significant has been the spreading of modes of financial calculation and budgetary obligations to areas which were previously governed according to bureaucratic, professional or other norms. The allocation of budgetary responsibilities to professionals – doctors, educationalists, civil servants, those working with excluded groups – requires them to calculate their actions not in the esoteric languages of their own expertise but by translating them into costs and benefits that can be given an accounting value. Coupled with the raft of other elements sometimes referred to as 'the new public management', this has transformed the governability of professional activity while, at the same time, apparently devolving more decisional power to those actually involved in devising and delivering services in local sites (cf. Hood 1991). Again, on the one hand, this has punctured the enclosures within which many forms of expertise were able to insulate themselves from 'political interference'. On the other, it has done so at the price of shifting powers to other forms of expertise – those of accountants and managers – and of changing the very terms in which experts calculate and enact their expertise.

Finally, it is worth remarking upon the ways in which the mechanisms of audit have become versatile ways of purporting to render accountable and judgeable the activity of professionals, managers, businessmen, politicians and many others (Power 1994). Audits of various sorts come to replace the trust that social government invested in professional wisdom and the decisions and actions of specialists. In a whole variety of practices – educational, medical, economic, organizational – audits hold out the promise – however specious – of new distantiated forms of control between political centres of decision and the autonomized loci – schools, hospitals, firms – who now have the responsibility for the government of health, wealth and happiness. Like the utilization of legal codes, and the allocation of budgetary responsibilities, government by audit transforms that which is to be governed: rendering something auditable shapes the processes that are to be audited, and the logics and technical requirements of audit displace the internal logics of expertise. Thus the emphasis on defined and measurable goals and targets in the work that professionals do with their abjected clients is an element within a much wider re-configuration of methods for the government of specialist activities. These arrangements retain the formal independence of the professional while utilizing new techniques of accountability to render their decisions visible, calculable and amenable to evaluation. No doubt many different factors converged to accord political priority to attempts to open up expertise to visibility and judgement according to criteria that purport to be publicly intelligible, rather than logics that are the esoteric preserve of the specialists themselves. And no doubt the consequences have frequently been costly and bureaucratic. But a politics of expertise also needs to recognize that such mechanisms may perhaps contain some innovative possibilities for contesting and reshaping the relations of power between experts and their subjects.

Conclusions

Many of the transformations to which I have drawn attention are themselves linked to a shift within the field of politics itself, in the ways in which political discourse itself configures the limits of the political and its relations with other domains. Confronted by supra-national associations and trans-national ecological movements, rival nationalisms fighting across a single geographical terrain, federalism, the politics of ethnic, cultural and linguistic minorities, and multi-culturalism, it is no longer easy for political thought to territorialize itself in an apparently 'natural' geo-political space in which the nation is coextensive with and delimited by a unified polity of social citizens (cf. Tully 1995). In the face of such 'strange multiplicities', to adopt Tully's term, in a variety of national contexts and from a variety of political positions, 'anti-political motifs' are on the rise within political discourse (Hindess 1994a). These motifs not only stress the corruption and ineffectiveness of the political classes but, more fundamentally, are based upon a sense of the limits of any politics that sees itself as omni-competent and articulates itself in terms of overarching political programmes. These 'anti-political' motifs have recently alighted upon 'community' – which in recent years had been a part of the mundane vocabulary of social policy and sociological investigation, valorized only by a small band of communitarian political philosophers and romantic or eccentric activists – as the space in which powers and responsibilities previously allocated to politicians might be relocated. Each of these emergent political rationalities – civic republicanism, associationalism, communitarian liberalism – in its different way, seeks a way of governing, not through the politically directed, nationally territorialized, bureaucratically staffed and programmatically rationalized projects of a centrally concentrated State, but through instrumentalizing the self-governing properties of the subjects of government themselves in a whole variety of locales and localities – enterprises, associations, neighbourhoods, interest groups and, of course, communities. Of course, it would be absurd to suggest that a politics of community is itself novel: as Tully points out, communitarianism may be regarded as one of the traditional themes of modern constitutional thought (along with nationalism and liberalism). But in these contemporary political rationalities, community is made calculable by a whole variety of reports, investigations and statistical enquiries, is the premise and objective of a range of governmental technologies and is to be acted upon in a multitude of authoritative practices and professional encounters. Community, that is to say, is to be governmentalized: it cannot be understood outside the other shifts to which I have tried to draw attention in this paper. What are of interest, therefore, are the problematizations through which collective existence has come to offer itself to thought in the form of community, and the new representations, techniques, powers and ethical relations that have been invented in the process.

It is too early to gauge the durability of these new ways of thinking about politics and government. For present purposes, their significance lies less in their success than in the evidence that they provide of an imperative felt at the heart of politics to fashion a revised way of governing, one which can, not only make itself consistent with the heterogeneity of the forms in which struggles are now carried out – nationalist, ethnic, religious, moral, environmental – but also connect up with the new conceptions of subjectivity through which the subjects of government increasingly have come to understand and relate to themselves. It is, of course, not a question of the replacement of 'the social' by 'the community': the spatialization and territorialization of political thought does not proceed in such linear sequences. None the less, the hold of 'the social' over our political imagination is weakening. While the social has no doubt been seen as a zone of failure since its birth, the solution to these failures is no longer automatically seen to be reinvention of the social. While our political, professional, moral and cultural authorities still speak happily of 'society', the very meaning and ethical salience of this term is under question as 'society' is perceived as dissociated into a variety of ethical and cultural communities with incompatible allegiances and incommensurable obligations.

We have still to begin the task of anatomizing the new relations of power brought into play on this new multiple and fragmented territory of government. In doing so, we should not assume that all is for the worst in this 'post-social' age. We need not simply to condemn the injustices and disadvantages entailed in the de-socialization of government, but also to engage inventively with the possibilities opened up by the imperatives of activity and the images of plural affinities. The role of such analyses should not be to praise or to blame, but to diagnose, to identify the points of weakness that might be exploited if we are to maximize the capacity of individuals and collectivities to shape the knowledges, contest the authorities and configure the practices that will govern them in the name of their freedoms and commitments.

Goldsmiths' College

Notes

1 This paper originated in comments prepared for a workshop on Radically Rethinking Regulation at Centre of Criminology, University of Toronto, 16–17 April 1994. A version was also given at a conference to mark the tenth anniversary of the

death of Michel Foucault held in London on 25 June 1994. My argument was intended to be open and speculative, and I have chosen to retain this in the written version. Barry Hindess helped me understand contemporary transformations in the government of 'the economy', but he is not responsible for my interpretation of his work. Thanks also to Mariana Valverde for perceptive criticisms of an earlier draft, to Clifford Shearing for insightful reader's comments, to Pat O'Malley for stimulating conversations on these topics and to Stephen Mugford for productive disagreements. The final version of the paper was prepared while I was a Visiting Research Fellow in the Political Science Program of the Research School of Social Sciences, Australian National University, and I would like to thank that institution for its support and hospitality. Comments from members of the *History of the Present* Research Network, especially Larry Barth, David Owen, Michael Power, Anne-Marie Singh and Grahame Thompson, helped me make some last minute revisions.

2 I take this phrase from Procacci (1989) but use it slightly differently.

3 On lines, see especially the discussion in Deleuze and Parnet (1987: 124–47).

4 Paul Hirst and Grahame Thompson have recently argued forcefully that the analysts and commentators have got it wrong, that economic relations were, in many ways, more 'globalized' in previous times than they are today, and that it is misleading and pernicious to argue that national governments are powerless (Hirst and Thompson 1996). For the purposes of my argument however, the truth effects of discourses of economic globalization are somewhat independent of the veracity of the analysis.

5 Obviously there are similarities between this argument and that concerning the construction of nations and identities in the form of 'imagined communities', which cannot be discussed here (cf. Anderson 1991).

6 In an article in the *Guardian* newspaper of 29 January 1996, timed to coincide with a speech to mark the tenth anniversary of the report of the Archbishop of Canterbury's Special Commission on Urban Priority areas, *Faith in the City*.

7 The term 'diaspora' which is sometimes employed here is interesting, implying that what is currently dispersed was once together – an essential unity scattered by the hand of fate or politics.

8 There are, of course, many other versions of this, most notably in the revival of civic republicanism. The 'advanced liberal' ethos of much contemporary civic republicanism is pointed out in Burchell (1995).

9 Quango is an acronym for Quasi-Autonomous Non-Governmental Organization.

References

Anderson, B. (1991) *Imagined Communities*, London: Verso.

Atkinson, D. (1994) *The Common Sense of Community*, London: Demos.

Baistow, K. (1995) 'Liberation and regulation? Some paradoxes of empowerment', *Critical Social Policy* 42: 34–46.

Ballard, J. (1992) 'Sexuality and the State in time of epidemic', in R. W. Connell and G. W. Dowsett (eds) *Rethinking Sex: Social Power and Sexuality*, Melbourne: Melbourne University Press.

Barry, A. (1996) 'Lines of communication and spaces of rule', in A. Barry, T. Osborne and N. Rose (eds) *Foucault and Political Reason: Liberalism, Neo-Liberalism and Governmentality*, London: UCL Press.

Bartos, M. (1994) 'Community vs. population: the case of men who have sex with men', in P. Aggleton, P. Davies and G. Hart (eds) *AIDS: Foundations for the Future*, London: Taylor & Francis.

Baudrillard, J. (1983) *In the Shadow of the Silent Majorities or 'The Death of the Social'*, New York: Semiotext(e).

Beck, U. (1992) *Risk Society: Towards a New Modernity*, London: Sage.

Beveridge, W. (1942) *Social Insurance and Allied Services* (Cmd. 6404), London: HMSO.
Burchell, D. (1995) 'Genealogies of the citizen: virtue, manners and the modern activity of citizenship', *Economy and Society* 24(4): 540–58.
Castel, R. (1991) 'From dangerousness to risk', in G. Burchell, C. Gordon and P. Miller (eds) *The Foucault Effect: Studies in Governmentality*, Hemel Hempstead: Harvester Wheatsheaf.
Clarke, P. (1979) *Liberals and Social Democrats*, Cambridge: Cambridge University Press.
Collini, S. (1979) *Liberalism and Sociology*, Cambridge: Cambridge University Press.
Commission on Social Justice (1994) *Social Justice: Strategies for National Renewal*, London: Vintage.
Cruikshank, B. (1994) 'The will to empower: technologies of citizenship and the war on poverty', *Socialist Review* 23(4): 29–55.
Dean, M. (1991) *The Constitution of Poverty*, London: Routledge.
—— (1995) 'Governing the unemployed self in an active society', *Economy and Society* 24(4): 559–83.
Defert, D. (1991) '"Popular life" and insurance technology', in G. Burchell, C. Gordon and P. Miller (eds) *The Foucault Effect: Studies in Governmentality*, Hemel Hempstead: Harvester Wheatsheaf.
Deleuze, G. (1979) 'Introduction', to Jacques Donzelot *The Policing of Families: Welfare versus the State*, London: Hutchinson.
—— (1995) 'Postscript on control societies', in *Negotiations*, New York: Columbia University Press.
Deleuze, G. and **Parnet, C.** (1987) *Dialogues*, London: Athlone.
Donzelot, J. (1979) *The Policing of Families: Welfare versus the State*, London, Hutchinson.
—— (1984) *L'Invention du Social*, Paris: Vrin.
Etzioni, A. (1993) *The Spirit of Community*, New York: Crown.
European Commission (1994) *European Social Policy: a Way Forward for the Union: a White Paper*, Luxembourg: Office for Official Publications of the European Communities.
Ewald, F. (1991) 'Insurance and risk', in G. Burchell, C. Gordon and P. Miller (eds) *The Foucault Effect: Studies in Governmentality*, Hemel Hempstead: Harvester Wheatsheaf.
Gilbert, B. (1966) *The Evolution of National Insurance in Great Britain*, London: Michael Joseph.
Gordon, L. (1989) *Heroes of their Own Lives: The Politics and History of Family Violence*, London: Virago.
Grey, J. (1996) *After Social Democracy*, London: Demos.
Hacking, I. (1991) *The Taming of Chance*, Cambridge: Cambridge University Press.
Hindess, B. (1993) 'Liberalism, socialism and democracy', *Economy and Society* 22(3): 300–13.
—— (1994a) 'Politics without politics: anti-political motifs in Western political discourse', paper delivered to Vienna Dialogue on Democracy, July.
—— (1994b) 'Governing what economy?', paper delivered to Governing Australia conference, Sydney, November.
Hirschman, A. (1991) *The Rhetoric of Reaction*, Cambridge, Mass.: Belknap Harvard.
Hirst, P. and **Thompson, G.** (1992) 'The problem of "globalization": international economic relations, national economic management and the formation of trading blocs', *Economy and Society* 21(4): 357–96.
—— and —— (1996) *Globalization in Question*, Cambridge: Polity.
Hood, C. (1991) 'A public management for all seasons', *Public Administration* 69(1): 3–19.
Hutton, Will (1995) *The State We're In*, London: Cape.
Joseph Rowntree Foundation (1995) *Enquiry into Income and Wealth*, 2 Vols, York: Joseph Rowntree Foundation.
Katz, M. B. (1993) *The 'Underclass' Debate: Views From History*, Princeton, NJ: Princeton University Press.
Kent, R. (1981) *A History of British Empirical Sociology*, Aldershot: Gower.

Lash, S. and **Urry, J.** (1994) *Economies of Signs and Spaces*, London: Routledge.
Levitas, R. (1996) 'The concept of social exclusion and the new Durkheimian hegemony', *Critical Social Policy* 16(1): 5–20.
Marshall, T. H. ([1949] 1963) 'Citizenship and social class', lecture given in 1949, in *Sociology at the Crossroads*, London: Heinemann.
Meuret, D. (1981) 'Political economy and the legitimation of the state', *I&C* 9: 29–38.
Miller, P. and **Rose, N.** (1990) 'Governing economic life', *Economy and Society*, 19(1): 1–31.
— and — (1991) 'Programming the poor: poverty, calculation and expertise', in J. Lehto (ed.) *Deprivation, Social Welfare and Expertise*, Helsinki: National Agency for Welfare and Health.
—— and —— (1995) 'Production, identity and democracy', *Theory and Society* 24: 427–67.
OECD (1990) *Labour Market Policies for the 1990s*, Paris: OECD.
O'Malley, P. (1992) 'Risk, power and crime prevention', *Economy and Society* 21(3): 252–75.
—— (1995) 'The prudential man cometh: life insurance, liberalism and the government of thrift', paper presented to the Annual Meeting of the Law and Society Association, Toronto, June.
Power, M. (1994) *The Audit Explosion*, London: Demos.
Procacci, G. (1989) 'Sociology and its poor', *Politics and Society* 17: 163–87.
Reich, R. (1992) *The Work of Nations: Preparing Ourselves for 21st Century Capitalism*, New York: Vintage.
Rose, N. (1990) *Governing the Soul: The Shaping of the Private Self*, London: Routledge.
—— (1992) 'Governing the enterprising self', in P. Heelas and P. Morris (eds) *The Values of the Enterprise Culture: The Moral Debate*, London: Routledge.
—— (1993a) 'Eriarvoisuus ja valta hyvinvointivaltion jalkeen' (Finnish translation of 'Disadvantage and power "after the Welfare State"'), *Janus* (Journal of the Finnish Society for Social Policy) 1: 44–68.
—— (1993b) *Towards a Critical Sociology of Freedom*, London: Goldsmiths' College.
—— (1993c) 'Government, authority and expertise in advanced liberalism', *Economy and Society* 22(3): 283–99.
—— (1994) 'Expertise and the government of conduct', *Studies in Law, Politics and Society* 14: 359–67.
—— (1996a) 'Psychology as a political science: advanced liberalism and the administration of risk', *History of the Human Sciences* 9(2): 000-000.
—— (1996b) *Inventing Our Selves: Psychology, Power and Personhood*, New York: Cambridge University Press.
Rose, N. and **Miller, P.** (1992) 'Political power beyond the state: problematics of government', *British Journal of Sociology* 43(2): 172–205.
Sabel, C. (1989) 'Flexible specialisation and the re-emergence of regional economies', in P. Hirst and J. Zeitlin (eds) *Reversing Industrial Decline*, London: Routledge.
Shearing, C. (1995) 'Reinventing policing: police as governance', in O. Marenin (ed.) *Policing Change: Changing Police*, New York: Garland Press.
Tribe, K. (1978) *Land, Labour and Economic Discourse*, London: Routledge.
Tully, J. (1995) *Strange Multiplicities: Constitutionalism in an Age of Diversity*, Cambridge: Cambridge University Press.
Walters, W. (1994) 'Social technologies after the welfare state', paper delivered to London History of the Present Conference, Goldsmiths College, April.
Watts, P. (1994) 'Absolutely positive: AIDS, the self and the performance of community in the user discourses of the Body Positive organisation', paper given to London History of the Present Research Network, June.
Zukin, S. (1991) *Landscapes of Power*, Berkeley, CA: University of California Press.

Part VI
Sovereignty, Globalization and the Rule of Law

[20]

STEALING THE NATURAL LANGUAGE: THE FICTION OF THE SOCIAL CONTRACT AND LEGALITY IN THE LIGHT OF NIETZSCHE'S PHILOSOPHY

*Jiří Přibáň**

. . . . Der du den Menschen schautest
so *Gott* als *Schaf* –,
den Gott *zerreissen* im Menchen
wie das Schaf im Menschen
und zerreissend *lachen* –

—Friedrich Nietzsche, 'Nur Narr! Nur Dichter!', from *Dionysos-dithyramben*, 1888

I. "Between Good and Evil": Nietzsche's Reflections on Hobbes and the Concept of Human Authenticity

In the first of his *Untimely Meditations*, Friedrich Nietzsche described Thomas Hobbes as "a bold spirit" and used the example of Hobbes's philosophy to criticize David Strauss's historicist moralism.[1] According to Nietzsche, Hobbes was a great and innovative thinker because he identified "*bellum omnium contra omnes*" as the first condition of moral principles. Hobbes's philosophy is, therefore, in sharp contradiction to much modern political and legal theory which is overloaded with moral normativity and false prescriptions for "the good life." War and force are an intrinsic part of our morals and shape the structure of the world. No absolutely "good" foundations of human life and

---

* J.P. lectures at the Cardiff Law School, University of Wales and is Professor of Jurisprudence and Sociology of Law at the Charles University in Prague. The author wishes to thank David Campbell for his extremely helpful comments and criticism.

[1] *See* 4 Friedrich Nietzsche, *David Strauss, The Confessor and the Writer* para. 7, *in* The Complete Works of Friedrich Nietzsche 1, 51 (Oscar Levy ed., Anthony M. Ludovici trans., 1964).

correlative calls for "unconditional duties"[2] may be justified. Morality as the essence of the real world is a gross falsification provided by modern thinking.[3] Good and evil, in fact, supplement each other. Evil is inseparable from good and human nature must recognize its evil as well as its good aspects. "[B]etween good and evil actions there is no difference of species, but at most of degree. Good actions are sublimated evil ones; evil actions are vulgarised and stupefied good ones."[4] In Nietzsche's philosophy, the duality of good and evil that gives a superior station to good is dismantled and the world becomes a flexible territory for the interplay of various meanings. In a legalistic manner, one might say with Nietzsche that good and evil have equal rights to be revealed and reflected in human culture, symbols and practices, while neither good nor evil can claim superiority or even sovereignty.[5]

The modern fiction of the social contract so influentially developed by Hobbes reflects a "marriage between heaven and hell," the outcome of which is the birth of civil political society and the principle of the rule of law. Through the social contract, the "evil" *bellum omnium contra omnes* is transformed into the "good" rule of law and an ordered political society. Nevertheless, this subjection of the chaotic world of war to the predictable, accountable and persistent world of legal rules may be done only by transferring the force and violence possessed by everyone in the natural state to the political sovereign. According to the fiction of the social contract, this is the beginning of politics and law. Apart from the formation of collective political will on the basis of expressed individual wills, the social contract also sets up a contract between good and evil that recognizes that it is impossible to provide ultimately "good" (or "evil") foundations to politics and opens up the possibility of exempting legality from the domain of moral normativism.

However, the modern fiction of the social contract also seeks to secure the stability of the political world. Many political and legal theories therefore make the social contract subject to natural

---

[2] 10 FRIEDRICH NIETZSCHE, *The Joyful Wisdom* Book I paras. 4-5, *in* THE COMPLETE WORKS OF FRIEDRICH NIETZSCHE 29, 40 (Oscar Levy ed., Thomas Common trans., 1964) [hereinafter NIETZSCHE, *The Joyful Wisdom*].

[3] *See* FRIEDRICH NIETZSCHE, *The Anti-Christ* para. 10, *in* TWILIGHT OF THE IDOLS AND THE ANTI-CHRIST 123, 133 (R. J. Hollingdale trans., 1990).

[4] 6 FRIEDRICH NIETZSCHE, *Human, All-Too-Human: A Book For Free Spirits* para. 107, *in* THE COMPLETE WORKS OF FRIEDRICH NIETZSCHE 1, 108 (Oscar Levy ed., Helen Zimmern trans., 1964).

[5] *See* 12 FRIEDRICH NIETZSCHE, *Nachlass 1885-1886*, *in* SÄMTLICHE WERKE 33 (1980) [hereinafter NIETZSCHE, *Nachlass 1885-1886*]. This reference is taken from PAVEL KOUBA, NIETZSCHE: FILOSOFICKÁ INTERPRETACE [NIETZSCHE: A PHILOSOPHICAL INTERPRETATION] 95 (1995).

laws and to the natural rights of man. The state of nature is then often interpreted not only as a state of permanent war, violence and fear, but also as a condition in which individuals can express themselves freely and authentically. The individual will in the state of nature is authentic because it is free of any subjection. This ideal of *human authenticity* is the background to a number of modern theories of legitimacy. Authentic life consists of a harmonized relationship between man's thinking and acting, and his own nature. The question of morality then becomes a question of listening to the voice of nature, which speaks through individual human existence. Politics and law, if they are to embody the virtue of justice, also must be an expression of the voice of nature and morality founded on that voice. The sovereignty of the "good" entrenched in nature returns into politics and denies the "evil" its political existence.

Rousseau's fiction of the social contract, which turns on the notion of a noble savage more ethical than a civilized man, is the typical example of such a theory of legitimation by authenticity. Here, the authentic behavior of man in the natural state stands in opposition to the artificial order and symbols of political culture. Ethics stands in opposition to law and state and, because it is founded on authentic human nature, has precedence over any legislative power. If civilization is to recapture the dimension of ethical community, it must subject itself to this original nature and its imperatives. Human nature and authenticity stand in contradiction to the "inhuman" structures of politics, economy, legality and science. This anarchistic and libertarian protest against law and state eventually leads to the metaphysical principle of authenticity, which found a new ethics and consequently posits new just and legitimate political order and laws to those ethics. In this reading, the social contract fiction becomes a servant to the sovereign principle of authenticity in politics. The renewal of human civilization will be the product of the power of an authentic natural law that acts directly and reveals a true face of humanity.

The belief that the development of social forms and structures leads to the progress of civilization but also to the decline of morals and humanity, is transformed into the call for a brotherly community in which no forms of social organization would lead to the exploitation (as in the modern capitalist economy), or the denigration (as witnessed in modern states and their legislation) of humanity. This belief in authenticity is present, for instance, in the work of Claude Lévi-Strauss, when he describes in *Tristes*

Tropiques[6] the implications of the lecture of writing in a village of Nambikwars. Lévi-Strauss displays a nostalgia for an authentic human nature which has not been corrupted, and describes how civilization, with its "writing," laws, power, economic exploitation and ideological indoctrination, comes to dominate the system of education.[7] Civilization and its laws are inauthentic and corrupt, while the small community of a "primitive" Indian tribe, in which everybody knows everybody, is closer to the ideal of humanity and authenticity.[8]

The legitimating force of authenticity shows its extraordinary strength just in the fiction of the social contract and the difference it posits between the natural and political state. The natural is authentic, while the political (is always) already an artificial construct, the legitimacy of which is founded on the act of contract. Contract is possible only as a departure from the natural state, which means that it is the result of an authentic acceptance of the conditions of political society. The authentic natural world determines the conditions of the legitimacy of political order and its law because natural laws and rights create the foundations of legitimate positive law. In this interplay of authenticity and the impersonal order of laws and politics, there lies the threat that politics and law may be legitimate only when they introduce violence into a "pure" life-world in which human existence achieves original—and therefore ethical—forms.

The fiction of the social contract and the natural state of mankind involve the danger that political institutions and laws function only as a form of the imposition of the fundamental ethics of authenticity and human nature. Politics then becomes a mere mediation of the authentic happiness of wo/man, his/her self-creation and individuation. This intellectual construction lies behind many modern political catastrophes, and, among other consequences, defines totalitarian politics and laws. If a legislator is both a guardian of human happiness and a sovereign body that defines this happiness, then the conditions of totalitarian domination are established. Paradoxically, the totalitarian domination of happiness also typically claims to represent human authenticity—which it transforms into structures of the state control of citizens. The communist concept of the historical law of the working class and the Nazi concept of the supremacy of race

[6] *See* CLAUDE LÉVI-STRAUSS, TRISTES TROPIQUES (John Weightman & Doreen Weightman trans., 1997).

[7] *See id.*

[8] *See* JACQUES DERRIDA, OF GRAMMATOLOGY 135 (Gayatri Chakravorty Spivak trans., 1976).

and nation also claim pre-political foundations. Therefore, they too enjoy the status of the authenticity of the "true" natural state of mankind that was to be respected by politics. Historical reason and racial order define the foundations of positive law, and expressions of will enacting such beliefs finally achieve the status of law. The Leader or the Party in these totalitarian regimes express historical reason and use political violence for the imposition of the natural order of history and political reality. True nature and the authentic existence of a nation or class are to speak through these structures guided by the will of a totalitarian political leadership. These structures finally impose authenticity upon an individual. Rousseau's notion of authentic freedom returns in the form of a map of the Gulag Archipelago and Auschwitz. In these structures of political violence, the original call for human authenticity and the modern revolutionary ideal of brotherhood was changed into an impersonal technique of human extermination. To Orwell's doublethink and newspeak slogans "Ignorance is force," "Freedom is slavery," "Peace is war" and "Love is hate" may be added the slogan "Authenticity is impersonality." Authenticity was eventually eliminated by those very political institutions which, according to the original plan, were to produce it.

II. STEALING THE NATURAL LANGUAGE OF AUTHENTICITY: THE RULE OF A FICTION AND NIETZSCHE'S EXPERIMENTAL THINKING

Despite all its attendant political risks and its possible disastrous consequences, authenticity has become an important virtue in modern society, reflecting its character and institutions through the fiction of social contract. The political demand of authenticity is often seen as a continuation and perfection of the modern ideal of individual autonomy entrenched in the Enlightenment.[9] Authenticity is to operate as a source of political and moral normativity and the integrity of democratic societies is to be founded on the principle of authenticity. The modern political project of democratic universalism abandons the normative character of individual autonomy and seeks to replace it with the ideals of both individual and collective self-creation.[10]

[9] For this interpretation of authenticity and its normative implications for democratic politics and philosophical universalism, see generally Alessandro Ferrara, *Authenticity and the Project of Modernity*, 2 EUR. J. PHIL. 241 (1984).

[10] For a critique of the liberal concept of justice and individual autonomy, see MICHAEL J. SANDEL, LIBERALISM AND THE LIMITS OF JUSTICE (1982).

"The ethics of authenticity" seeks to harmonize the authentic life of individuals and social groups with the "impersonal machinery" of the modern political system and representative democracy ruled by instrumental reason.[11] The concept of instrumental reason is criticized for being only a tool of man's domination over the world. There must be a deeper ethical background to modern rationality which, in our attempt to reformulate democratic politics, would guide us to make them more than the working of a decision-making machine ruled by the political majority, and instead, respecting all social differences so that individuals and groups can freely express themselves and realize the authentic life of self-fulfilment. The relation between the technology of power and the ideal of a free community in which all have the possibility of authentic self-generation is an unending struggle of contradictions.[12] Differences and uniqueness are recognized and respected in this community, but political decision-making and changes are impossible outside the framework of the state machine and the political majority principle. The problem, however, is how this machine, which is an expression of instrumental rationality, may be adjusted to the plurality and differences existing in modern societies.

Despite the deep reflection on the implications of plurality in political theories such as Taylor's ethics of authenticity, the argument usually is no more than a version of the common scheme in which political recognition means adaptation to general norms defining the space of modern politics. Despite his proclaimed advocacy of "good" politics, Taylor eventually must formulate his own version of a marital act or social contract between the "good" authentic motives of citizens and "bad" political power. A fragmented society must unite and different groups must act as one force in order to secure political recognition, equal treatment, independence and political freedom. It is, then, not surprising that the politics of resistance and struggle for authenticity as a foundation of the political system ends up in the rather conventional phrase of the "politics of democratic will-formation."[13] The formation of a common political space is done through democratic decision-making procedures and all humans subject themselves to these knowing that they will have to abandon part of their authenticity in order to form a common democratic political will. The force of the political system

[11] *See generally* CHARLES TAYLOR, THE ETHICS OF AUTHENTICITY (1991).

[12] *See id.* at 107. For the elaboration of the concept of authentic self, see CHARLES TAYLOR, SOURCES OF SELF: THE MAKING OF THE MODERN IDENTITY (1989).

[13] *See* TAYLOR, *supra* note 11, at 18.

determines the conditions that turn the call for authenticity into a political problem. Even Taylor must accept the language of the technology of power when he looks for political protection of the ethics of authenticity in democratic political society. Rousseau's problem of the subjection of political society to the laws of nature remains unresolved. It only finds another form in the ethics of authenticity.

In this context, it is noteworthy that another grand project of current practical philosophy and political theory—Jürgen Habermas's discourse ethics and theory of communicative reason—is rather hostile to the ambitious claims of the ethics of authenticity. Although Habermas understandably distinguishes between individual autonomy, drawing on *Selbstbestimmung*, and authenticity, drawing on *Selbstwirklichung*, he does not accept the concept of authenticity as a higher stage of the development of individual autonomy corresponding to the political conditions of our late modernity. Habermas perceives authenticity rather as a variant of autonomy.[14]

Habermas's reluctance to exploit all the possible political meanings of the concept of authenticity is entrenched in his critique of those streams of modern German philosophy—Heidegger's fundamental ontology, for example—which were critical of the "inauthentic" public sphere, democratic discourse and decisionmaking.[15] When analyzing the political limits of authenticity, an important case study turns out to be the dissident struggles in communist countries.[16] For instance, the Czech dissident movement was substantially inspired by Heidegger's critique of the inauthentic public sphere. It was used by dissidents in the form of a specific critique of communist totalitarianism. It helped dissidents to develop alternative politics that facilitated

[14] *See* JURGEN HABERMAS, THE PHILOSOPHICAL DISCOURSE OF MODERNITY: TWELVE LECTURES (Frederick Lawrence trans., 1987). For further insight into Habermas' philosophy, see JÜRGEN HABERMAS, BETWEEN FACTS AND NORMS: CONTRIBUTIONS TO A DISCOURSE THEORY OF LAW AND DEMOCRACY (William Rehg trans., 1996) [hereinafter HABERMAS, BETWEEN FACTS AND NORMS]; 2 JÜRGEN HABERMAS, THE THEORY OF COMMUNICATIVE ACTION: LIFEWORLD AND SYSTEM: A CRITIQUE OF FUNCTIONALIST REASON (Thomas McCarthy trans., 1987) [hereinafter HABERMAS, LIFEWORLD AND SYSTEM]; 1 JÜRGEN HABERMAS, THE THEORY OF COMMUNICATIVE ACTION: REASON AND THE RATIONALIZATION OF SOCIETY (Thomas McCarthy trans., 1984) [hereinafter HABERMAS, REASON AND RATIONALIZATION].

[15] *See* MARTIN HEIDEGGER, BEING AND TIME (John Macquarrie & Edward Robinson trans., 1962) (providing Heidegger's analysis and elaboration of the concept "das Mann").

[16] For further details and analysis of the dissident strategy, see JIŘÍ PŘIBÁŇ, DISSIDENTS OF LAW: ON THE 1989 VELVET REVOLUTIONS, LEGITIMATIONS, FICTIONS OF LEGALITY AND CONTEMPORARY VERSION OF THE SOCIAL CONTRACT (2002) [hereinafter PŘIBÁŇ, DISSIDENTS OF LAW].

parallel forms of social life independent of the dehumanizing techniques of the repressive political power and the facade of communist public life.[17] People like Václav Havel or Jan Patočka formulated the problem of authenticity with the help of Heidegger's vocabulary of "being" and "existence" because it corresponded well with the tension between individual life and the highly organized structure of political automatism which sought to control and pervade even the most intimate spheres of human life. The dissent against the communist system was clearly able to draw on the political ambivalence of Heidegger's philosophy.

The Czech dissent also manifests the political ambivalence of ethics of authenticity in general. In their struggle, the dissidents pursued the goal of authenticity and established alternatives to the existing political totality. Yet, this struggle also deprived them of authenticity because they had to enter the territory of highly structured political and legal arguments in order to point to totalitarian or authoritarian injustices. The dissident call for authenticity had to be eventually formulated in the language of "legality" and "human rights."[18] In order to prove the falsity of socialist legality and its repressive nature, dissidents had to adopt its language and arguments. The argument for authenticity, and against political terror, had to be formulated in a sophisticated artificial language, one of the main purposes of which was to facilitate such terror.

All advocates of legitimation by authenticity are forced to formulate their demand for authenticity in the language of legality and politics. However, law is a second-order semiological system *stealing the natural language*, similar to myths as Roland Barthes describes them.[19] The advocates of authenticity, be they political dissidents or philosophers, must consequently adapt to this theft and fight for natural language of authenticity by the use of formalized legal and political meta-concepts. The adoption of legal arguments is pragmatic and may not be perceived as a final defeat of the politics of authenticity. Yet nobody seeking to establish legitimation by authenticity is able to provide a foundationalist argument for politics and law in which all actions would be subject to the criterion of authenticity. An ultimate legitimation of politics and laws by authenticity is impossible because authenticity never enters the field of law and politics uncorrupted. Authenticity does not have an ultimate legitimation

[17] BARBARA DAY, SAMETOVI FILOSOFOVE [THE VELVET PHILOSOPHERS] 11 (1999).

[18] *See* Jiří Přibáň, *Legitimacy and Legality after the Velvet Revolution*, *in* THE RULE OF LAW IN CENTRAL EUROPE 29-55 (Jiří Přibáň & James Young eds., 1999).

[19] *See* ROLAND BARTHES, MYTHOLOGIES 129, 131 (Annette Lavers trans., 1993).

power. Yet it is present in modern legitimation strategies including the strategy of dissent and it plays an important role in the legitimation processes of modern law and political domination.

Soren Kierkegaard was also aware of the fact that authenticity cannot be reached directly. According to Kierkegaard, it is necessary to take the disguise of a seducer and use aesthetic, indirect descriptions to express what is authentic in human life. It is necessary to retreat to narratives and fictions. It is only in this indirect way, using inauthentic tools, that we can point to the ethically more valuable, higher and truer world that hides the authentic life in itself. A seducer's disguise is a necessary condition of authenticity, yet Kierkegaard does not understand not only the relationship between facts and fictions dialectically, but also as a hierarchical relation in which the function of a fiction is only secondary and subject to the order of authentic existence in the real world.[20] Disguises and fictions should support the ultimate modern search for human authenticity and individual self-creation.

Unlike the philosophy of the Christian existentialist Kierkegaard, Nietzsche's philosophy dismantles this hierarchical relation between facts and fictions and turns it into a play of various meanings, confrontations and riddles that finally makes the difference between fiction and reality unimportant. The authentic order of ethics, truth and reality is pulled down. Moral and philosophical concepts, including the concept of will, are a grammatical fiction.[21] The unique and authentic are thinkable when they are a part of the classification system of language.[22] Nietzsche's demand that thoughts should come to us in their "actual way" cannot be interpreted as a call for authentic being. Rather, it indicates the author's fear of manipulative power of philosophical concepts and categorical thinking. The actual is used as an opposite of metaphysics and philosophical systems.[23] When Nietzsche condemned his early metaphysics (late 1870s) of culture and the ideal of a genius speaking the words of nature, he described this period as one of *fanaticism*[24] requiring lengthy treatment. He condemned the idea that there is ultimate meaning to the world and replaced the totality of culture that provides freedom by positive meaning with the negative concept of freedom. It is freedom of:

---

[20] *See* CHRISTOPHER NORRIS, THE DECONSTRUCTIVE TURN 88 (1983).

[21] ROBIN HOLT, WITTGENSTEIN, POLITICS AND HUMAN RIGHTS 60 (1997).

[22] *See* DERRIDA, *supra* note 8, at 109-13.

[23] *See* MILAN KUNDERA, TESTAMENTS BETRAYED 150 (Linda Asher trans., 1995).

[24] 9 FRIEDRICH NIETZSCHE, *Nachlass 1880*, *in* SÄMTLICHE WERKE 47 (1980). This reference is taken from KOUBA, *supra* note 5, at 45.

> a man from whom the ordinary fetters of life have so far fallen that he continues to live only for the sake of ever better knowledge[. He] must be able to renounce without envy and regret much, indeed almost everything, that is precious to other men. He must regard as the *all-sufficing* and the most desirable condition; the free, fearless soaring over men, customs, laws, and the traditional valuations of things.[25]

Fanaticism entrenched in the prescriptive nature of metaphysics and human authenticity was challenged by Nietzsche in his elaboration of the notion of "eternal recurrence." This notion opens up the possibility of thinking of the world as chaos without any reason or higher purpose and ultimate ending.[26] However, this position is not cynical and does not mean that human life is meaningless and absurd, as is suggested by some streams of existentialism. It rather means that human life must be justified at every moment of its being because there is no hierarchy among human actions and thoughts. After it lost its metaphysical and systemic nature, the world became enigmatic and therefore a much bigger contest for human thinking and acting.[27] We cannot rely on the laws of nature facilitating the ordered world of rules, predictability, and stability for human conduct and social fabric. A reduction of reality to a system is impossible. Any reduction indicates the emergence of dogmatism in thinking. However, our thinking should retain its experimental nature.[28] The experiment involves the power and ability to live through and celebrate fictions, dreams and imaginations the status of which are not different from the "real" world.[29]

III. Performativity of Dissent, a Negative Will to Power, and Structural Changes in the Social Contract Fiction

The experimental nature of thinking and its positing of the world as a fiction and enigma should not be mistaken for intellectual arbitrariness and imagination without any limits. The fact that the world is chaotic and has lost its transcendental

[25] 6 FRIEDRICH NIETZSCHE, *Human, All-Too-Human: A Book For Free Spirits* para. 34, *in* THE COMPLETE WORKS OF FRIEDRICH NIETZSCHE 1, 51 (Oscar Levy ed., Helen Zimmern trans., 1964).

[26] *See* NIETZSCHE, *The Joyful Wisdom*, *supra* note 2, Book III para. 109, at 152-53.

[27] *See* NIETZSCHE, *Nachlass 1885-1886*, *supra* note 5, at 120.

[28] For the interpretation of Nietzsche's thinking as experimental and for his attack on philosophical systems, see KUNDERA, *supra* note 23, at 150, 174.

[29] *See* NIETZSCHE, *The Joyful Wisdom*, *supra* note 2, Book I para. 54, at 89.

meaning may not be interpreted, as Dostoyevsky did, as implying "anything is possible after the death of God." The process of thinking in a world that has lost its essence should not be mistaken for an arbitrary linking of different phenomena and attempt to attribute meaning to any intellectual construct. While we may not live under the laws of nature anymore, we are challenged by our obligation to engage in the "actual way" of thinking. Without a referential point of *essentia*, the human mind relies entirely upon its power to construct, use and subsequently dismantle fictions which set up a meta-referential framework about our otherwise inaccessible reality. Reality is made accessible by fictions, but we cannot abandon the concept of reality as our point of reference. Thinking and language are even turned into banality and *kitsch* if they are employed as tools of arbitrary imagination. Kitsch is interpretation blurring reality,[30] which violates the referential framework and ignores the semantic limits and potential of language and metaphors. It ignores the rules of the genre, breaks the possibility of critical thinking and, instead of facilitating it, puts an end to communication.

Metaphors and fictions require exactness whenever we deal with them and interpret them.[31] Fictions have an important role in setting up modes of communication about themes that would otherwise be impossible to communicate. They are able to dismantle the founding paradoxes of different themes that would be otherwise incommensurable. The founding paradoxes must enter the process of deparadoxification[32] and this process is possible because of fictions unifying the communication space about specific themes. This is exactly why Nietzsche treats Hobbes as a "brave mind."[33] Hobbes was the first one who, by using the fiction of social contract, "married" the "evil" state of natural war with the "good" political society governed by law and thus opened new and mutually independent modes of political, legal and moral communication. The contractual fiction facilitated the differentiation of each of these communication domains. It is almost paradoxical that the majority of modern political theories later adopted the opposite moral perspective, founded on the opposition between "good," which is natural and authentic, and "evil," which is political and systemic. Hobbes originally used the social contract fiction in order to point to authenticity as an urgent

30 KUNDERA, *supra* note 23, at 145-6.
31 *Id.* at 104.
32 *See* Gunther Teubner, *Economics of Gift–Positivity of Justice: The Mutual Paranoia of Jacques Derrida and Niklas Luhmann*, 18 THEORY, CULTURE & SOC'Y 29, 32 (2001).
33 *See* NIETZSCHE, *supra* note 1.

problem of emerging political societies, but he also contained its potentially destructive power within the system of positive law and political power. Moreover, he was very well aware of the fact that he could communicate about authenticity only within the artificial structures of the system of political and legal theory and avoided attempts to provide concrete historical evidence for the social contract fiction.

A call for the ultimate use of natural language of authenticity in politics and law is in vain. The social contract fiction may be an indirect expression of something signified as authentic, yet it cannot reconstruct authenticity. Authenticity may not be conceived as a pre-social/pre-systemic reality in the life of human beings that would respectively legitimate the public life of politics and law.[34] However, as the social contract fiction persuasively shows, authenticity is always a part of a symbolic order that shapes subjective opinions and beliefs by the force of constructed social reality. Legitimation takes place through the impact of the symbolic universe on individual beliefs, not as the establishment of social symbols from authentic human life.[35]

It is useful to return to the intellectual tensions entrenched in the social contract fiction. When Hobbes used it, he defined the framework of modern politics, law and their theory. It was purely a fictitious construct that was to facilitate the legitimation of law and political domination in the coming modern era. Yet, the logic of authenticity always represented an important component of modern political and legal theories because of the persuasive force it has always had in the process of legitimation. The contractual fiction facilitated the ethics of authenticity, but it also opened the space for political tyranny. It can never completely get rid of the dangers posed by the concept of authentic ethics and the understanding of law and politics as instruments for the pursuit of human happiness because those dangers are inherent in the contractual construction of the difference between the natural and political. Authenticity inscribed in the fiction of the social contract can always be easily used for the purpose of turning the world into a grand prescription with an ultimate set of rules of "good" behavior that nevertheless has to accommodate all of the world's "evil." In the fiction of the social contract and in political practices such as the strategy of dissent, the defense of authenticity requires the use of *indirect* arguments that respect the order of political

---

[34] For the pre-systemic and pre-social legitimating concept of authenticity, see AGNES HELLER & FERENC FEHER, THE POSTMODERN POLITICAL CONDITION (1989).

[35] *See* PETER L. BERGER & THOMAS LUCKMANN, THE SOCIAL CONSTRUCTION OF REALITY: A TREATISE IN THE SOCIOLOGY OF KNOWLEDGE 115 (1967).

power and the normative system of law. The demand for authenticity may be formulated only in its dependence on "impure" structures of our social life and thinking.

In the dissident struggle, authenticity is most commonly translated into the demand for protection of human rights. However, analyzing different functions of the political strategy of dissent, this struggle also turns out to be a specific example of current structural changes in the social contract. The original purpose of the social contract fiction was to disclose a mechanism that would have the power to establish a united community and legitimate political order. In the social contract, political unity was originally founded on the ideas of consensus and the moral integrity of a political community. On the other hand, every dissensual strategy shows the disunited nature of every modern political society. Even seemingly legitimate orders, defined by the language of legality, are finally exposed to many argumentative challenges from the outside. In the past, the social contract was a fiction of unity. Nowadays, it turned into a fiction securing the pluralistic character of political communities.

The social contract originally had distinctive *constative* features. The act of contract establishes a solid structure of political laws held to be legitimate because of the general consensus expressed by all parties to the contract. By their expressed will, those parties become citizens who must subject themselves to the general force of legitimate laws. The final purpose of the contract was to produce law and order. The social contract transforms the violence of the state of nature into a legitimate and stable power structure. On the other hand, dissent emphasises *performativity* in every political community, treating individuals as beings with the power to manifest and enforce their own political will. Dissent is derived from the unique character of every human being and his/her power to influence political life.

Every dissent includes a negatively formulated *will to power*, which is established by resistance to political power and an attempt to confront it with a different power protecting the political system from any totalitarian or authoritarian rule. Dissent cannot be formulated other than in a relationship with existing power structures. A performative dissident action must be formulated against a constative "state of affairs."[36] There is a permanent communication and mutual irritation between the constative and performative which characterize modern political

[36] For the constative/performative duality, see Jacques Derrida, *Mochlos; or, The Conflict of the Faculties*, *in* LOGOMACHIA 1, 21 (Richard Rand ed., Richard Rand & Amy Wygant trans., 1992).

societies and their legitimation fictions.[37] Dissent is imaginable only in the political condition, not as an anarchistic and spontaneous action that would be a pure expression of human nature.

IV. Human Rights, "Natural War" and the Rule of Law

One of the most interesting legacies of political dissent in communist countries is the differing use of the concept of human rights; particularly those uses that exceeded both the ethical and legal context. The adoption and elaboration of the human rights discourse by dissidents made any arguments about political justice inseparable from the concept of human rights. It established a perspective according to which historical and international political developments were determined by the struggle for human rights and humanity. This perspective constantly refers to what is neutralized in the context of legality, namely the concrete and authentic existence of human beings, their unique nature and their irreducibility to any category or general concept.

The logic of legal rules and concepts cannot govern ethics, which is established by responsibility for the other as a unique being. On the other hand, ethics is behind the concept of human rights.[38] Obligation to the other is irreducible to the obligations of man as a rational subject, the will of which is commensurable with the will of other citizens and creates the foundations of their political community and legal system. The liberal democratic-rule-of-law system is legitimate if it protects human rights by its power and technique. Yet, the legitimate structure of legality is defined by the crucial fact that the content and meaning of human rights escapes state institutions and the logic of social morality.

The world dominated by face-to-face social relations and experiences of authenticity is not; nevertheless, automatically a free world in which an individual has a bigger freedom of choice and individual self-creation.[39] This world is certainly more comprehensible, closer and intimate in comparison to the world of "big" social systems of law, politics and economy. On the other

[37] For political meaning of relations between the constative and performative, see Jacques Derrida, *Declarations of Independence*, 15 NEW POL. SCI. 7 (1986).

[38] This perspective is surprisingly close to the one provided by Emmanuel Lévinas. *See* EMMANUEL LÉVINAS, *The Rights of Man and the Rights of the Other*, *in* OUTSIDE THE SUBJECT 116-25 (Michael B. Smith trans., 1993).

[39] *See* NIKLAS LUHMANN, LOVE AS PASSION: THE CODIFICATION OF INTIMACY 16 (Jeremy Gaines & Doris L. Jones trans., 1986).

hand, the impersonal rules of big systems such as law make possible a higher flexibility of human action. The control and surveillance of the intimate and authentic experiences of a modern man may be extraordinarily strong, and the threat of "authentic" violence may be transformed into social relations of intimate surveillance of individual action. The ethics of authenticity and otherness has very ambivalent implications for freedom. Logos and laws must, therefore, supplement these ethics with foreseeability and the power of rules. The uniqueness and authenticity dominating the face-to-face relations with the other is inseparable from the impersonal social techniques of law and political power that divide social reality into private and public spheres and thus secure individual autonomy.

Unlike authenticity, autonomy is always a function of structures of law and politics. Man as an autonomous being is a result of the juridification of reality and the necessity of establishing the government of rules. "Citizens" and "the rule of law" are mutually dependent concepts. The social sphere providing the possibility of authenticity must be protected by the impersonal order of legality. "The iron cage of modernity,"[40] a part of which is legality, and human authenticity may be conceived only in their mutual interdependence. If authenticity were to be the foundation of legality, it would lead to the terror of human "nature" against "inauthentic" social conventions.

In liberal democracies there is nobody possessing absolute political sovereignty. The "people as a sovereign" is not one body claiming absolute political sovereignty in the name of its authentic self-creation and self-realisation. It consequently cannot be the only author of the supreme law from which normative discourse and the regime of legal rules might be derived.[41] The people must be represented in the process of drafting the constitution, and this "basic law" must respect some pre-existent rights independently of the people's will. The contemporary social and political situation is one of *the absence of a sovereign.* Inside contemporary liberal democratic political culture, the neutralizing force of legality exists together with "*natural war.*" Political conventions have a legal form, but this form is itself in a state of "war" with its environment. The relation between the *agora* of the liberal democratic rule of law and its social environment is a relation in which "tolerance of the rhetors (of liberal democracy) feeds on

---

[40] See, for instance, MAX WEBER, THE PROTESTANT ETHIC AND THE SPIRIT OF CAPITALISM 181 (Talcott Parsons trans., 1958).

[41] *See* JEAN-FRANCOIS LYOTARD, THE DIFFEREND: PHRASES IN DISPUTE 144 (Georges Van Den Abbeele trans., 1988).

intolerance of the tribes (fighting against liberal democracy)" and "intolerance of the tribes draws confidence from the tolerance of the rhetors."[42] Political leaders, rhetors, are cautious and aware of the modern crimes against humanity committed in the name of reason, better political order, or the greater happiness of humankind. They hesitate to legitimate the existing political order by reference to the rule of reason and its universal validity. The growing tolerance of leaders leads to bigger social insecurity and provokes tribalism, mutual clashes and intolerance. The modern democratic state and its laws continue to speak in the name of universality, but at the same time social space is privatized and isolated social fragments are filled with an intolerance produced by social uncertainty.[43]

The current liberal democratic rule of law is a political form in which the political and natural coexist and permanently interfere with each other. Law and legality are always a part of a pluralistic political situation, although their purpose is to overcome it by establishing a formal, politically neutral context and transforming it into the impersonal language of general laws. But inside legality, there are always different interpretations and strategies. Legality is contradictory, conflictual, and comprises different ideologies, worldviews and political interests and beliefs.[44] All legal interpretations and legality itself are just momentary outcomes of the struggle between different social forces and strategies using the law as their framework of reference. This conflictual character of legality, nevertheless, does not mean that legality is unstable. Legality can only exist because these forces and conflicts operate within its structures.[45] Force lies behind every act of law's application and creation, and represents an irrational element inherent of law. This force is, however, not a principle founding the legal system. It is a movement full of concrete social networks and practices. Legality is, then, not defined by a pre-existent framework of decision-making according general rules and universal political principles. It is politics in the sense of never-ending disputes between different particular beliefs, goals and interests that determines law and legality and comes very close to the original state of "natural war." However, there is no need to be worried about the Hobbesian war of all against all and

---

[42] ZYGMUNT BAUMAN, POSTMODERN ETHICS 238 (1993).

[43] *See id.* at 239.

[44] *See* STANLEY FISH, THERE'S NO SUCH THING AS FREE SPEECH: AND IT'S A GOOD THING, TOO 154 (1994).

[45] *See* STANLEY FISH, DOING WHAT COMES NATURALLY: CHANGE, RHETORIC, AND THE PRACTICE OF THEORY IN LITERARY AND LEGAL STUDIES 139 (Stanley Fish & Fredric Jameson eds., 1989).

complete anarchy, because persuasive force itself constitutes the main regulatory mechanism of law's pragmatic operations and defines its limits. This force is a repository of norms, standards or rules, not, as suggested for instance by adherents of analytical jurisprudence and theories of natural law and rights, a mortal threat to them. As Michel Serres writes, "war is a legal state."[46]

V. CONVERSATION, COMMON SENSE AND THE LEGACY OF THE CONTRACTUAL MODEL

In contemporary liberal democracies, there is no single mechanism with the power to unite the political community as an autonomous body and thus secure its complete legitimacy. Political consensus, which originally was the main purpose and practical political goal of the fiction of the social contract, has become a contingent structure determining human behavior only in certain parts of the political system of the liberal democratic rule of law. The sovereign people as a founding element of law and politics do not exist. The principle of autonomy is being dismantled and replaced with heteronomy as the first condition of the reproduction of liberal political communities.[47]

The role of compromise as a mechanism for the maintenance of political unity grows in any politically heterogeneous community. Consensus is being replaced by a broader phenomenon—*conversation*. The purpose of conversation is not only the achievement of various political goals. It also functions as an instrument to express differences and contradictions. Unlike democratic discourse ethics relying on the ideal starting point of political discussion under equal discursive conditions for all participants,[48] conversation respects plurality within the political community and does not seek to identify the winners and losers of political discussions. Instead, it aims to strengthen and increase the plurality of speaking voices.[49]

The political life of contemporary liberal democracies is not

---

[46] MICHEL SERRES, THE NATURAL CONTRACT 8 (Elizabeth MacArthur & William Paulson trans., 1995).

[47] *See* JEAN-FRANCOIS LYOTARD, POLITICAL WRITINGS 161 (Bill Readings & Kevin Paul trans., 1993).

[48] The concept of the discourse ethics has been elaborated by Jürgen Habermas in his critical theory of communicative reason. *See* HABERMAS, BETWEEN FACTS AND NORMS, *supra* note 14; HABERMAS, REASON AND RATIONALIZATION, *supra* note 14; HABERMAS, LIFEWORLD AND SYSTEM, *supra* note 14.

[49] *See, e.g.*, HILARY PUTNAM, REALISM WITH A HUMAN FACE (James Conant ed., 1990).

founded on political consensus. It derives from the amount of freedom of conversation. Instead of the culture of consensus with its sovereign auditorium, the importance of ever-growing and permanent dialogue grows. This permanent character of dialogue and conversation—between individuals, groups and even whole cultures and populations—stands behind the cultural movement[50] and supports the reflexivity of the structures of the democratic political power and the rule of law.

Unlike the culture of consensus, the political culture of conversation also involves a pre-political, existential dialogue as a search for identity and authenticity.[51] The culture of conversation, however, does not take this search and dialogue to be the foundational, sovereign discourse of modern politics. Conversation corresponds more closely to the absurdity of this search because, unlike Habermas's ideal speech situation, it does not rule out the possibility that participants will not understand each other at all. Conversation does not presuppose a minimum agreement or consensus, yet it still can be a very important political structure. This structure has a strong critical force and represents a necessary part of civic culture, which must not be the culture of assimilation founded on a politically enforceable *a priori* normative framework. It must be the culture of permanent communication, which is always "yet to set up and define" this framework. In conversation, citizens can mutually acknowledge their existence and political position without the necessity of accepting a pre-existing framework specifying permitted and prohibited communication. Wo/man becomes a free citizen only through his/her language and conversation.

However, conversation is never completely spontaneous. It is regulated by a *common sense*.[52] No message emerges without assuming that it will be understood and shared. It must have communicative power, otherwise it becomes a form of hermetism.[53] Common sense cannot be identified with the notion

[50] *See* CLAUDE LÉVI-STRAUSS, THE WAY OF THE MASKS (Sylvia Modelski trans., 1988).

[51] *See, e.g.*, GIANNI VATTIMO, THE END OF MODERNITY: NIHILISM AND HERMENEUTICS IN POST-MODERN CULTURE 150 (Jon R. Snyder trans., 1988).

[52] Common sense is politically ambivalent and its meaning may be both critical and conservative. From the position of common sense, it is possible to criticize the technologies of political power, economic exploitation and the expansion of instrumental reason and capital into the public sphere. At the same time, it is also possible to refer to common sense as a traditional and persisting structure of society, which resists the consequences of modernization. For historical, philosophical and humanist context of this rich concept, see, e.g., HANS-GEORG GADAMER, TRUTH AND METHOD 19-29 (Garret Barden & John Cumming eds., 1975).

[53] For this conclusion, see UMBERTO ECO, THE LIMITS OF INTERPRETATION *passim*

of norms of correct thinking or the metaphysical concept of human nature as the foundation of any legitimate community. Rather, common sense is an open framework of conversation proceeding in the pluralistic space of *forum*.[54] This space may not, therefore, be identified with truth, but rather with tolerance of the otherness of those entering into conversation with us. This ethos of tolerance belongs to the legacy of the fiction of the social contract and manifests the vital importance of the contractual model for the persistence of current liberal and democratic societies and the rule of law. The social contract is a fiction that still keeps a special appeal for liberal democratic communities and can facilitate their *modus* of political existence. It supplies them both with political limits in the form of law and, at the same time, makes it possible to question those limits set up by *civitas* in a particular place at a particular time. In short, the persuasive and legitimating force of the fiction of the social contract lies in its capacity to initiate a never-ending game between the constative and performative features of modern liberal democratic societies and their legal systems.

CONCLUSION

The social contract cannot survive as the grand project of modern politics and a sovereign fiction of the system of law providing a community with ultimate political integrity and consensual moral unity. Nevertheless, the contractual model manifests certain structural features which still make it an attractive model for contemporary political communities, their systems of political domination and legal legitimacy. Conversation as a process setting up the internal limits of the legitimation space is hardly conceivable without the contractual model. The analysis of the fiction of the social contract and its Nietzschean incorporation of the "evil" into the "good" brings us to the final remark that: political domination and laws in current liberal democratic societies must be the subject of permanent negotiation with its limits having the possibility of being permanently redefined. This is the legacy of the contractual model of a modern political society for our late, post-modern times.

(1990).

54 For the analysis and concept of forum, see PŘIBÁŇ, DISSIDENTS OF LAW, *supra* note 16, at 13-56.

[21]

"NOW THE MACHINE RUNS ITSELF": CARL SCHMITT ON HOBBES AND KELSEN

*David Dyzenhaus**

INTRODUCTION

Carl Schmitt claimed that the fundamental distinction of politics is the distinction between friend and enemy.[1] That distinction, he said, has to be put on a substantive basis, which, in the era of the nation state, he supposed must amount to an idea of the homogeneity of the people. Since liberal democracy is opposed to this kind of substance, Schmitt argued that liberalism cannot make the distinction between friend and enemy. It thus cannot defend itself against its enemies. It is no wonder that he remains the leading theorist of fascism.

Schmitt's work has recently attracted a great deal of attention and is likely to attract more. At a time when authoritarian nationalism is resurgent this is not surprising. What is surprising is that some of Schmitt's current followers advocate his view on the basis that Schmitt's concept of the state and politics will help us to resist the dangers which plague liberals and democrats. Their claim is that Schmitt, by alerting us to the problems of liberal democracy, teaches us how to save it from its enemies.

---

* Associate Professor of Law and Philosophy, University of Toronto. This article is part of a larger work in progress: *Truth's Revenge—Carl Schmitt, Hans Kelsen and Hermann Heller in Weimar*. For comments and discussion, I thank Heiner Bielefeldt, Cheryl Misak, the members of my philosophy graduate seminar on Schmitt and Hobbes, and faculty who attended my papers on these topics at the Benjamin N. Cardozo School of Law, the Philosophy Department of Wilfred Laurier University, and the Political Science Department of Yale University.

1 My account of Schmitt relies principally on the following works: CARL SCHMITT, THE CONCEPT OF THE POLITICAL (George Schwab trans., Rutgers Univ. Press 1976) (1932); CARL SCHMITT, THE CRISIS OF PARLIAMENTARY DEMOCRACY (Ellen Kennedy trans., MIT Press 1988) (1923); CARL SCHMITT, DER LEVIATHAN IN DER STAATSLEHRE DES THOMAS HOBBES: SINN UND FEHLSCHLAG EINES POLITISCHEN SYMBOLS (Hohenheim Verlag 1982) (1938) [hereinafter DER LEVIATHAN]; CARL SCHMITT, POLITICAL THEOLOGY: FOUR CHAPTERS ON THE CONCEPT OF SOVEREIGNTY (George Schwab trans., MIT Press 1985) (1922) [hereinafter POLITICAL THEOLOGY]; CARL SCHMITT, ÜBER DIE DREI ARTEN DES RECHTSWISSENSCHAFTLICHEN DENKENS (1934) [hereinafter DREI ARTEN]; CARL SCHMITT, VERFASSUNGSLEHRE (7th ed. 1989). References will in general be given only for direct quotes. In Schmitt's case, they will be given to the English editions cited here, although the translations are mine.

I fully agree with those recent responses to Schmitt observing that a project so driven by the urge to destroy liberal democracy is hardly likely to be harnessed in its defense. Nevertheless, I think that much can be learned from Schmitt once we understand why he would not have thought it possible that liberalism could adjust itself in light of his critique. This paper addresses these issues by exploring a paradox latent in Schmitt's work.

Schmitt thought of himself as *the* twentieth century Hobbesian. He ended his commentary on Hobbes's *Leviathan*[2] with a message across the centuries: "You shall no longer teach in vain, Thomas Hobbes!"[3] Schmitt also devoted himself to exposing what he considered to be the inherent contradictions of liberal legalism, in particular the contradiction he thought he had uncovered between liberal legalism and democracy. Schmitt found Hans Kelsen to be the theorist *par excellence* of the bourgeois *Rechtsstaat*.[4] To Schmitt, Kelsen's legal positivism and accompanying democratic theory were the exemplar of contradictory liberal legalism.

But in Schmitt's commentary on *Leviathan*, he seemed to claim that the *Rechtsstaat* is the logical terminus for Hobbes:

> It is the mark of . . . a rational state power that above all it accepts every political danger and in this sense accepts the responsibility for the protection and security of all subjects of the state. If the protection ceases, so the state itself ceases to be and with it any duty of obedience. Then the individual wins back his "natural" freedom. The "relation of protection and obedience" is the touchstone of Hobbes's conception of the state. It fits well with the concepts and ideals of the bourgeois *Rechtsstaat*.[5]

Thus, the paradox is as follows: Schmitt believes that by exposing contradictions in Kelsen's doctrine of legal positivism, he simultaneously exposes the contradictory nature of liberalism. Throughout this process he appeals, perhaps above all, to the authority of Thomas Hobbes; yet it appears that he regards the train of thought set in motion by Hobbes's publication of *Leviathan* as not only

---

2 THOMAS HOBBES, LEVIATHAN (C.B. MacPherson ed., Penguin Books 1986) (1651).

3 DER LEVIATHAN, *supra* note 1, at 132 (my translation).

4 For Kelsen I rely here principally on HANS KELSEN, DER SOZIOLOGISCHE UND DER JURISTISCHE STAATSBEGRIFF: KRITISCHE UNTERSUCHUNG DES VERHÄLTNISSES VON STAAT UND RECHT (Scientia Verlag 1981) (1928) (with emphasis on ch. 12); HANS KELSEN, REINE RECHTSLEHRE (1934), *reprinted in* HANS KELSEN, INTRODUCTION TO THE PROBLEMS OF LEGAL THEORY (Bonnie L. Paulson & Stanley L. Paulson trans., 1992) [hereinafter INTRODUCTION]; HANS KELSEN, VOM WESEN UND WERT DER DEMOKRATIE (Scientia Verlag 1981) (1929).

5 DER LEVIATHAN, *supra* note 1, at 113-14 (my translation).

having actually ended in the establishment of the *Rechtsstaat*, but as having *had* to end there.

I will argue here that, once the elements of this puzzle are unravelled, we will have a much better understanding not only of Schmitt's thought, but of his critique of liberalism as well. We will then be in a position to assess whether Schmitt speaks to contemporary debates in political and legal theory.

Schmitt's Understanding of Liberalism

Schmitt considers all political ideologies and doctrines to be metaphysical in the sense that they must ultimately appeal to something beyond actually existing practices. It is in this sense that he sees the conflict between ideologies as one between political theologies. Ideologies, even atheistic ones, assume the truth of their own vision of politics, and that is not a matter that can be adjudicated on the terrain of politics.

Liberalism, in his view, is a metaphysical system that, because of its allegiance to rationalism, not only denies its metaphysical foundation, but institutionalizes that denial. This denial, he argues, will prove to be liberalism's inevitable downfall.

Schmitt understands liberalism as the ideological manifestation of the bourgeois allegiance to the individualistic values of liberty and private property. In order to realize those values, liberalism had to make a pact with public power against the absolutist monarch who always threatens those values. Hence liberalism made a pact with democracy and sought successfully to channel democracy into parliamentarianism.

Parliamentarianism is a system which suits liberalism's purposes for several reasons. First, it leads to the eventual subordination of the monarch. Second, it establishes the normative order that provides the framework in which the requirements of a market society, such as security and predictability, are met. Third, through parliamentarianism liberalism can claim, by an appeal to representation, democratic legitimacy. Finally, parliamentarianism is itself balanced by the division of powers; for liberals the division is identical to constitutionality and ostensibly an effective constraint on public power.

However, by using parliament as the public means of establishing itself, liberalism, instead of achieving its individualistic aims, subjects the individual to the forces of civil society that can potentially exploit the liberties which liberalism originally guaranteed in its bid for power. Liberalism must make a transition from private to public in order to privilege the private, but it cannot do so without subverting itself; it cannot publicly manifest itself without privatizing the public sphere and thus rendering the public sphere prey to legions of private interest groups.[6]

For the most part, Schmitt describes this process of privatization as a logically necessary one following from the most basic liberal assumption of universal individual equality. Nevertheless, it is also important to bear in mind that he also sometimes describes this process as a deliberate deception:

> Still, one should not fail to recognize that there is a kind of democracy, namely parliamentary democracy, which has a plain interest in having certain antitheses remain latent so that they do not come to decision. Here the process of majority determination can be a suitable and desirable method to avoid and suspend political decisions. It can even be politically more shrewd not to decide oneself and to use the so-called majority decision in this way. Then the proposition "the majority decides" would belong to the arcane reaches of a particular political system, whose treatment goes beyond the framework of a "Constitutional Theory."[7]

---

6 Here are two representative quotes, both from the *Verfassungslehre*.

> For a consistent following through of election and vote by secret ballot leads to the metamorphosis of the citizen as the specific democratic, that is, political, figure, into a private individual, who renounces his voice and expresses a private opinion from within the sphere of the private. . . . Secret ballots mean that the voting citizen is isolated in the decisive moment. The assembly of the people as a presence and any acclamation is in this way made impossible, and the bond between the assembled people and the vote is torn asunder. The people no longer votes and elects as a people. In contemporary democracy, the methods of elections and plebiscites in no way contain the process of a genuine people's election or plebiscite, but organizes a process of individual voting by means of the addition of individual voices.

VERFASSUNGSLEHRE, *supra* note 1, at 244-45 (my translation).

> As soon as freedom of assembly leads to coalitions, that is, to associations, which fight each other and which oppose each other with specific social instruments of power like the strike or lockout, so the point of the political is reached and consequently an individual fundamental or liberty right is no longer in existence. The right of association, the right to strike, and the right to shutdown, are not liberty rights in accordance with the meaning of the liberal *Rechtsstaat*. When a social group achieves such potential for struggle, whether through express constitutional dispensation or by means of a practice of tacit tolerance, so the fundamental presupposition of the liberal *Rechtsstaat* has lapsed. And "liberty" no longer means the in-principle unlimited scope of activity of the individual, but the unlimited exploitation of social power by social organizations.

Id. at 165-66 (my translation).

7 *Id.* at 282 (my translation).

Schmitt talks often of liberalism's attempt to avoid the people and the sovereign, and thus the fundamental political decisions which he considers the very substance of politics. He also claims that every legal order is in some sense a concrete order in which some individuals rule over and subordinate others. As Schmitt never fails to point out, by definition it follows that liberalism too is a concrete order where one group, the bourgeoisie, attempts to rule over all others. The peculiarity of liberalism as a political doctrine resides, then, in its concealment, conscious or not, of its politics—a concealment which must, in Schmitt's opinion, empty politics of content and thus undermine liberalism.

Can Schmitt say both things of liberalism? On the one hand, he claims that liberalism provides a cloak for a power grab by private interest groups, and thus that their politics are the real politics of liberalism. On the other hand, he asserts that liberalism has no politics at all. It is important to see here that in Schmitt's view this is not a contradiction in his critique, but the contradiction which his critique exposes. It is a contradiction which pervades the doctrine to reside at its deepest level because liberalism's rationalist metaphysics is antimetaphysical. The contradiction is manifested on the surface in the apolitical or even antipolitical nature of liberal politics, exemplified in its legal order. Liberalism creates a society which desperately requires a sovereign decision but seeks at every point to postpone or prevent such a decision from being made.

Schmitt found the passage from rationality to contradiction most starkly illustrated in the transition from Hobbes's authoritarian positivism to Kelsen's liberal legal positivism.

Schmitt on Hobbes

As do Hobbes and Kelsen, Schmitt believes that traditional modes of justifying political authority are no longer available.[8] All three think that the disappearance of these modes means that we must accept the truth of relativism. Thus Schmitt, regardless of his own personal religious views, asserts that God is dead in the sense that different gods (including atheistic ideologies such as liberalism, fascism, and Marxism) now compete for our attention.

[8] It might be more accurate from Schmitt's perspective to say that there are no traditional modes of justifying political authority since the requirement of justification arises only when what had hitherto been taken for granted is thrown into question. In other words, strictly speaking, the problem has to do with the crumbling of tradition rather than the unavailability of traditional justifications.

Where he differs from Hobbes and Kelsen is in the conclusion that he believes follows from the fact that we live in a relativist age.

Hobbes and Kelsen try to provide a rational argument for their methods of justifying political authority in a relativist age. Liberalism offers an argument that is doubly rational in that it seeks to institutionalize its particular solution in the public order. Liberalism both appeals to individual rationality and structures its political institutions on the very model of individual rationality to which it appeals.

In contrast, Hobbes builds his theory of public order on an appeal to individual rationality, but then seeks to preclude individual rationality from any significant place in sustaining and recreating public order. To adopt a metaphor from Wittgenstein, Hobbes climbs a rational ladder to reach his solution, but, once he has reached the top, he kicks the ladder away. Schmitt believes that he can explain how Hobbes's logical terminus is Kelsen's liberal legal positivism in terms of Hobbes's inability to kick the ladder away.

Schmitt thinks that rationalism perforce undermines political authority. The idea of a rational public order is for him a contradiction in terms, evinced by the fact that liberalism inevitably subverts itself. He also thinks that Hobbes's absolutist or dictatorial solution is on the right track, but is necessarily undermined by its rational basis because that basis will eventually assert itself in the political superstructure. Thus, for Schmitt, the solution must be irrational in origin—a dictatorship which claims infallibility on the basis of a myth.

In *Leviathan*, Hobbes sets forth three main theses about law: (1) authority, and not truth, makes law; (2) legal subjects must take actually existing law as if it were a true interpretation of the laws of nature and, therefore, as morally binding; and (3) the supreme lawgiver is the sovereign—an entity or person that has ultimate legal authority yet stands outside of the law.[9]

These theses arise from Hobbes's fears about the state of nature. Since we cannot agree about truth in the state of nature, we need authority of a very particular kind—an authority whose desires are expressed in the form of commands rather than counsel, and whom we obey not because of our evaluation of the content of his commands, but because it is commanded. To use H.L.A. Hart's phrase, our reason for obedience is "content-independent."[10]

---

9 *See* HOBBES, *supra* note 2, at ch. 26.

10 H.L.A. HART, ESSAYS ON BENTHAM: STUDIES IN JURISPRUDENCE AND POLITICAL THEORY 254 (1982).

It is crucial to see that in order for the system of commands (the legal order) to be capable of supplying content-independent reasons for action to legal subjects, the actual content of the commands must be identifiable or determinable in a very particular way. Law must take the right form if it is to be effective.

Consider a standard example: the legislature decrees "no cruel and unusual punishment" and a court must determine whether the legislature intended to include execution in that category. If the interpretative tests mandated by the legal order in fact supply an answer to the question, then the law on this issue has the correct, or positive form. The law already supplies the answer and the judge's role is limited to simple application.

However, if there is no such answer, then, by definition, there is no law. The judges must decide whether execution should fall within the scope of cruel and unusual punishment. They will then engage in evaluative arguments as to what the law should be and can no longer be understood as taking the sovereign's command as a content-independent reason for action. Thus, in order for a command to function as its logical formal structure requires, it must have an identifiable content which does not require its subjects to engage in evaluative arguments to determine what the content should be.

According to Hobbes's model, when judges engage in evaluative arguments about what the law should be, although they are then acting as mini-sovereigns (or interpreters of the laws of nature), they are still subject to the sovereign's general command authorizing such activity.[11]

Furthermore, once these judges have made definitive pronouncements, legal subjects are under the same duty to obey the judge-made law as they would have been had the legislature made its intentions clear in the first place.

Hobbes was committed to believing that the fewer such cases the better. With regard to legal subjects, the more such cases exist, the greater the uncertainty in which the subjects live until judges or the sovereign clear up the uncertainty. Nonetheless, it is preferable that judges should, in so far as possible, merely execute the will of the sovereign rather than act as mini-sovereigns.

Hobbes therefore holds that law must have a particular form if it is to fulfill the function of providing the framework of a stable

[11] This command can be express or silent—it is silent when the sovereign simply refrains from overruling judicial decisions. *See* HOBBES, *supra* note 2, at ch. 26.

political order. There must be an intimate and highly political relationship between form and content. Law's content must be determinable and identifiable by factual tests which do not involve controversial moral-evaluative arguments.

Schmitt regards the argument which links form and substance favorably. He found it significant that Hobbes felt compelled to make it despite the fact that the most basic unit in Hobbes's theory is the atomistic individual. For Hobbes, the individual, whose instrumental reasoning power is the cause of the problems of the state of nature, is also someone to whom he appeals in order to initiate his rational argument, even though he ultimately reaches an authoritarian solution. In order to reach this solution, Hobbes appeals to the one end on which he believes all individuals can agree—that self-preservation is the ultimate good.

Schmitt thinks that the solution is compelling, but that it does not need the rational argument to be reached. In his view, authoritarianism is just the obvious solution once traditional modes of legitimizing political authority are no longer available. More accurately, Schmitt contends that Hobbes's argument robs the authoritarian solution of the kind of content or "substance" that can make it work. Further, Schmitt maintains that, without that substance, political order and law will become self-subverting. By relying on the rational argument, Hobbes sows the seeds of the Leviathan's destruction. Put differently, this rational argument leads naturally to Kelsen's liberal restatement of legal positivism.[12]

In Schmitt's opinion, Hobbes saw the need for a myth that would lend the positive legal order the right kind of substance. That was the reason Hobbes called his great work on political philosophy "Leviathan" and it was why he, in his second of the three references to the Leviathan, described the sea monster as a great man. But his third reference is to the Leviathan as a great machine. The product of his rationalist impulse was the destruction of the state's soul which rendered the state insubstantial and thus open to enemy capture.[13]

Despite Hobbes's outward denial of any room for individual rights against the state, Schmitt finds three related points in Hobbes's construction of the state where individualism manifests itself in a way that will eventually bring down the structure. Two will be addressed here and the third in the final section of this Article.

[12] *See supra* text accompanying note 5.

[13] For these references, see, respectively, HOBBES, *supra* note 2, at 81, 227, 362.

In Schmitt's view, the first manifestation is in Hobbes's emphasis on state structures that facilitate individual calculation of the consequences of action. This rational state apparatus is one which functions mechanically so as to ensure the rule of a framework of stable laws rather than the personalized and arbitrary rule of the sovereign. Schmitt found that this idea explained the image of Leviathan as a great machine that is also a man. This image is deeply metaphysical in that it challenges the power of other political symbols by seeking to erect the myth of the great machine in their place. It seeks to subvert all political myths, theologies, and religions by its claim to neutrality. But in a sense it is also antimetaphysical since the new god it creates is transcendent in only a juristic, not a metaphysical, sense. Thus, legitimacy is collapsed into legality, or formal legal validity.

But, according to Schmitt, in the very claim to do away with all other myths, it makes itself the most profound metaphysical claim of all. The idea of the ruler as a soul in a machine is nothing more than Descartes's idea of individuals as machines with souls. But the elevation of that idea to a political level makes a society organized on individualistic lines possible, and so throws into question all other forms of social organization. Eventually, as part of the logic of the process, all that will matter is that the machine functions, on the one condition that the subjects continue to enjoy protection so that they can go about their own lives. The actual ruler becomes wholly unimportant—as do the content of the laws. Hobbes can thus be justly seen as the founder of legal positivism. For him authority, and not truth, is the mark of a valid law.

But this is not to say that private judgment as to the truth has no place in Hobbes's system. Though he shares with Schmitt a deep distrust of allowing any matter of public importance to be determined by a conversation between individuals, Hobbes reserves to individuals the right to determine what is right or wrong for themselves. While Hobbes says in chapter thirty-seven of *Leviathan* that the sovereign can command conformity to any creed he chooses, and can determine what is a miracle and what is not, Hobbes also makes a distinction between faith and confession and states that all that the sovereign can ask of his subjects is that their actions conform to his commands, not that they believe his commands to be true.[14]

---

[14] *Id.* at 478 (ch. 37).

Here, according to Schmitt, is the second way in which Hobbes's reliance on individual rationality subverts his solution. It is here that one gets the decisive break in Hobbes's system which will eventually lead to the ideas of freedom of conscience and thought, and thus to the liberal constitutional system. With the distinction between faith and confession, the distinction between the inner and the outer spheres is born, and thus the seeds of the idea of civil society as one vast private sphere, the terrain of free individual action, are sown. And, given the disappearance of the soul from the great machine-state, the state becomes hollow, soulless, and vulnerable to capture by the indirect powers of civil society, each organized around its own myth. The seeds of the idea of civil society as the realm of the inner sphere are also the seeds of the Leviathan's death. The mythical forces which Hobbes's Leviathan were meant to combat are in fact unleashed by it to strike back.[15]

The actual change in the inner sphere's status, from something wholly marginal in Hobbes, to something central which should be given primacy over the outer, is, according to Schmitt, largely the work of Jewish philosophers such as Spinoza and Moses Mendelsohn, and which logically culminates in Kelsen.[16]

Schmitt on Kelsen

In Schmitt's view, Kelsen's restatement of legal positivism is the fulfillment of the Enlightenment project which attempts to subject human interaction to an impersonal order of rules: the rule of law and not men. The underlying concept is that no individual should be subject to the will of any other individual or group of individuals. If the sovereign is a highly personal entity existing outside the legal order, then the individual is subject to the sovereign's arbitrary will. The logical solution to this problem is to draw the sovereign into the legal order so that he is eventually dissolved into the rules of that order. The ultimate authorizing command of the order both requires obedience to the law and authorizes judges to interpret the law; it becomes a self-sustaining basis of the legal order. Hence Kelsen's "Grundnorm" or basic norm: "Now the machine runs itself."[17]

Both Schmitt and Kelsen try to emphasize the logical nature of this positivist conception of law. Kelsen emphasizes the appropriateness of the theory. In order to understand legal order scientifi-

[15] Der Leviathan, *supra* note 1, at 84-97 (my translation).

[16] *Id.* at 87-97, 108.

[17] Political Theology, *supra* note 1, at 62 (my translation).

cally, we must understand it as a logical structure. However, Kelsen believes that what makes such an order a logical structure is not that the content of any rule or norm can be derived from a higher norm, but that the structure is free from internal contradiction. Nor does Kelsen imagine such contradictions to be, in practice, impossible. The instance of illegal state action which he discusses at length in various places comes about simply because one agent of the state issues a norm whose content is in contradiction with the content of another norm. According to Kelsen, what preserves the noncontradiction is the premise that there will always be a higher norm to resolve the conflict.[18]

Schmitt thinks that Kelsen's line of argument illustrates that his solution is merely logical and thus of no practical effect. It dooms Kelsen's legal theory to recognizing as the law even acts which are illegal by the law's own standards, as long the acts are performed by an agent who has the "competence" to do so. Since it also follows from Kelsen's discussion of state illegality that such competence cannot be definitively constrained by law, Schmitt reckons that liberal legal positivism breaks down. In situations of conflict, most notably during a state of exception or emergency, not only is the conflict resolved by some personal act of will emanating from outside the law, the decision as to whether there even is a conflict is a personal one. The person who is the most important locus of power for such decisions is the sovereign.

In *Political Theology*, Schmitt argues that legal positivism exhibits the liberal trait of authority being undermined by rationalism. The necessity of decision in the "state of exception" is the flaw in the positivist legal order. Since the exception cannot be legally determined in advance, both the decisions as to when there is an exception and how it will be managed are not amenable to a prior, rational legal ordering. According to Schmitt, it follows that both the declaration that an exception exists and the means appropriate to deal with it are determined irrationally. Since the most fundamental challenges to a legal order are ones which throw its legitimacy into question and at the same time open up the possibility of a state of exception, it also follows that, if there is legitimacy, it derives from an irrational source.[19]

---

18 For example, the norm which embodies the doctrine of finality holds that an official mistake of law will, even if it contradicts the content of a higher norm, become the law at that time if it is allowed to stand. *See* Introduction, *supra* note 4, at 73-75.

19 Political Theology, *supra* note 1, at 5-15.

Schmitt writes, echoing the claim made by the main spokesmen for positivism in his day, that legitimacy in the age of rationality is nothing more than legality—the criteria which the law itself provides for valid law. His analysis of this claim is best summed up in the following quote:

> The positivist has no independent and therefore no eternal type of juristic thought. He subjects himself decisionistically to the decision of the legislature who is actually in possession of state power, because it alone has actual power to enforce its will; but he requires at the same time that this decision has a continuing, solid and unbreakable validity as a norm, which means that the legislature subjects itself to the norm. It is only this legal system that he calls the *Rechtsstaat*, although in the place of a *Rechtsstaat* he has a legislative state and in place of justice the security of the law. And then through the normativity of legality he raises himself again above the state's power to decide, which he had subjected himself to in the interests of security and certainty, and puts normative demands to the legislature. Thus he grounds his stance first on a will (the legislature or the statute) then against this will on an "objective" statute.[20]

Schmitt thinks that the decision to subject oneself (and all other legal subjects) to the decisions of the legislature is the decisionist component which makes positivism possible. But positivism refuses to inquire into the "metajuristic" moment of the decision. Thus it subjects itself to a sovereign power without conceiving of this power as an institution or as a concrete order, and without, above all, asking for what would be "by its own lights good law."[21] Moreover, the purer it becomes, and the more it is torn from the normal situation which it presupposes, the sharper the contrast it makes between the juristic and the worldly, between the economic, the social, and the political. The result is that positivism can no longer distinguish between law and not-law, objectivity and subjective arbitrariness.[22]

Although Schmitt does not make this explicit, it seems that for him the decisionist component of legal positivism has two main characteristics. First, there was the bourgeois's historical political decision to form an alliance with the democratic forces resulting in the concentration of legislative power in parliament. Second, there is the continuing and necessary moment of decision which should be both preserved and exhausted in the actual decisions made by

20 DREI ARTEN, *supra* note 1, at 35 (my translation).
21 *Id.* at 38.
22 *Id.* at 38-40.

the parliament. Thus, the legal positivist is in the impossible position of both subjecting himself unconditionally to parliament while requiring that parliament subject itself to law.

Schmitt asserts that this requirement is one that liberals sometimes try in vain to inject with content, namely the liberal value of protection of absolute liberty and private property. But its content can be nothing more than the result of the formalistic concept that laws will be recognized as such only when they are general norms properly enacted by parliament. Nor is this requirement merely formal; it acquired substance from parliament's subordination of the king in order to establish and preserve a concrete bourgeois political order. After that point, however, because it can take on any content, the legal order which legal positivism justifies is both empty and vulnerable to enemy capture.

Thus, it might seem that only the first aspect of legal positivism's decisionist component has any real content, and even then it is a content tied to its time. The decisionism preserved by reserving legislative power to parliament is in a sense not a genuine decisionism at all. Rather, it is a decision to avoid decisions, that is both characteristic of, and is what renders vulnerable, liberal politics.

Schmitt says that liberalism's "way of being is negotiation, procrastinating half-measures, in the hope that the final clash, the bloody battle of the decision, could be metamorphosed into a parliamentary debate and would allow itself to be suspended in an eternal discussion."[23] He regards the defects of this structure as a manifestation of liberalism's contradictory nature. Kelsen, despite his declarations of agnosticism, proclaims more than the disappearance of the state—he also proclaims the death of God. But Schmitt maintains that the death of God results not in the triumph of science but in a war between gods, just as he believes that the disappearance of the state results not in the disappearance of political power, but in the growth of private powers which captured the state.

Kelsen's myth, and the liberal myth in general—the political theology of liberalism—is antimythical, antitheological, and antipolitical. It is also antisociological in that it seeks to eliminate power both as a theoretical problem and as a fact of political life. The main feature of Kelsen's restatement is that the sovereign disappears. The idea of a sovereign entity as a personality which both

23 Political Theology, *supra* note 1, at 63 (my translation).

stands outside of the legal order and belongs to it is transformed into a mere personification of legal order. State and sovereign become merely different expressions for a valid legal order.

SCHMITT ON DEMOCRACY

Schmitt asserts that democracy and dictatorship are not contradictory, while liberal parliamentarianism and democracy are. This assertion is in part supported by showing how liberal democrats are, perhaps in spite of themselves, also driven to equate democracy with dictatorship. The identification of the minority will with the majority will after the majority has decided is one example of such an equation, as is the idea that the educated might know the will of the people better than the people know it themselves.

For Schmitt, these equations must have the same status as the liberal recognition that a state of exception is always possible. That is, liberalism cannot help but recognize, and seek to contain, some crucial factors in political life which potentially threaten its existence. However, liberalism is not only constitutionally incapable of containing such factors; it also provides them with a fertile breeding ground.

By inviting the collapse of the state into a society composed of a multitude of competing interest groups, liberalism creates the conditions for a general state of exception with which it cannot deal. And liberalism, in identifying the people's will with what the parliamentary majority decides, opens the door to a majority that can decide to destroy liberalism and requires the people to adopt that will as its own.

Thus, while liberalism must recognize the potentially dictatorial identity between ruler and ruled which Schmitt takes to be the essence of democracy, it cannot, in his view, become truly dictatorial. It is dictatorial only in that it provides a battleground for private interests and thus a means for groups organized around such interests to dictate to the rest.[24]

Given that Schmitt views democracy to be no more than an asserted identity between ruler and ruled, why does he find himself compelled to appeal to democracy? The answer to this question is that to Schmitt, an appeal to democracy is the only modern means to legitimize political authority. Claims based on tradition are no longer available. Claims based on rationality subvert authority and

24 Groups which are committed to liberalism cannot achieve a true dictatorship—all they will do is weaken the state and society. Groups which are committed to destroying liberalism by constitutional means can exploit that weakness to overthrow the constitution.

thus subvert democracy when one seeks to put democracy on a rational basis. But the appeal to democracy is necessary, since, in the absence of tradition, the people are the audience to which one must appeal and an appeal to the people is an appeal to democracy. Democracy is what is done in the name of the people—what one does when one can authentically assert that an action is identical to the people's will.

An appeal to democracy is then a necessity for any ideology that seeks to become dominant. In one sense, it is a purely formal requirement. But in another sense, it is not purely formal since only some appeals can give substance to the formal idea.

According to Schmitt, liberalism, like any ideology, had to make a pact with democracy. In order to make its pact, it had to relativize democracy through parliamentarianism, conceived (as Kelsen conceives it) as a model of competing private interests out of which the truth ostensibly should emerge. Liberalism thus aims at truth, but then undermines its aim by surrendering to the competition of atomistic interests, which it simultaneously attempts to render impotent by the division of powers.

Substance and Form in Political and Legal Theory

As we have seen, Schmitt holds that the structural weaknesses of liberalism are irreparable because they are inherent in liberalism's nature, which is to be neutral or substanceless. Of course, the very identification of these problems as structural depends upon Schmitt's claims about substance. One will not see the problems as structural and therefore irreparable, unless one also accepts the premise that liberalism needs a substance which it both does not and cannot have. If one provisionally rejects the structural claim, then Schmitt can be understood as pointing out problems in a useful way rather than seeking to subvert liberal democracy altogether.

The understanding of Schmitt as wanting to help liberalism is one which Schmitt encouraged after World War II and which his American disciples propagate today. But it makes nonsense of his work. One cannot understand that work without recognizing that it is driven by a particular purpose—to show the need for a myth based on an idea of substance.

There are two very abstract criteria for what can count as substance. The first is negative—and we will know it by its deep antithesis to liberalism. In particular, we will know it by its articulation of a vision that makes life worthwhile for individuals.

And, in Schmitt's view, this means a vision on whose behalf individuals can be asked to sacrifice their lives. One's life is worthless, he thinks, unless it has a purpose for which one is prepared to die. Liberalism cannot ask for the highest individual sacrifice since it makes the individual the ultimate judge of what is good for him or herself. It is in Hobbes's reservation to the individual subject of the right to resist the sovereign's attempt to kill him that Schmitt finds the third instance in which Hobbes's reliance on individual rationality subverts his authoritarian solution.[25]

The second criterion for substance is existential. It arises during a crisis situation in which one of the participants in the struggle is able to articulate a vision of who are the enemies of the people which meets with the people's acclaim. In an internal political struggle, the identification of the enemy will divide the participants into friends and enemies, but it will also bring the people into existence.

This abstract purpose is potentially very vulnerable. Since it invites any substantive ideology to replace liberalism, and does not discriminate further between the range of ideologies, it cannot, for example, close the door in late Weimar Germany on Nazism while trying to keep it open for some dictatorial union between Catholic aristocrats in the cabinet and the office of the President.[26]

Nevertheless, even if it does not provide us with a positive theory, Schmitt's analysis seems theoretically very powerful. Even if the problems he uncovers are not seen as structural unless one is driven by some abstract purpose, they are no less real or serious. The power arises because, even if one does not welcome the idea that some substantive ideology is the only alternative to substanceless liberalism, one might be driven to resign oneself to this idea if the problems are indeed structural. Schmitt's analysis of liberal ideology and of liberal institutions is constantly designed to ask whether this problem can be cured by a neutral, apolitical doctrine, when it is such a doctrine that appears to be the cause of the problem in the first place.

His strategy does not appear much different than the one adopted by Ronald Dworkin who argued for a conception of law built on the ideal of integrity. According to Dworkin, "[a]stronomers postulated Neptune before they discovered it.

---

25 It should be clear that I accept much of what Leo Strauss had to say in his review essay *Comments on Carl Schmitt's Der Begriff des Politischen*. *See* THE CONCEPT OF THE POLITICAL, *supra* note 1, at 81-105.

26 The latter was, of course, Schmitt's preferred solution to the problems of Weimar.

They knew that only another planet, whose orbit lay beyond those already recognized, could explain the behavior of the nearer planets. Our instincts . . . suggest another political ideal standing beside justice and fairness."[27] Generally, Dworkin's first crucial move is to suggest that something exists that naturally fills the gap repeatedly encountered during analysis of political morality's persistent problems. Indeed, the gap Schmitt and Dworkin claim to encounter seems to me to be the same—a lack of substance.

Interestingly, from the beginning, Dworkin believed that he had to remedy the problems of liberalism at two levels. First, he had to replace legal positivism with a theory of law that claimed a basis of moral substance immanent in the law. Second, he argued against utilitarian theories that adopted a view of politics similar to Kelsen's and for a substantive theory of individual rights based ultimately in a doctrine of equality.[28]

The difference between Schmitt and Dworkin is that Dworkin then positively argues for a particular way of filling in the ideal of integrity. Schmitt did not carry his theory so far because he, as a relativist, found it to be a liberal mistake to suppose that such positive justification is possible. If Schmitt is right, liberals who adopt something like Kelsen's relativist stance are in real trouble; for if he is right that the problems of such a stance are cured only by an absolutist leap which is not itself justified *but which provides its own justification* through success, then liberals have no better ground than he to discriminate between which destination the leap should bring.

One curious consequence should be noted. Schmitt does not argue that relativism is flawed because it cannot support the kind of moral absolutism he regards as the sole cure for its problems. If he were making that argument, he would refute himself since, as I have claimed, he is also a relativist. Rather, he seems to be arguing that there is a pragmatic necessity to move beyond relativism to absolutism or infallible dictatorship—but that liberalism's constitutional commitment to relativism renders it pragmatically incapable of making that move.[29]

Dworkin, of course, is an antirelativist. But Schmitt would probably want to try to show that antirelativism is inconsistent with

---

27 Ronald Dworkin, Law's Empire 183 (1986).

28 Ronald Dworkin, Taking Rights Seriously vii (1978).

29 One can, I think, plausibly understand the internal development of Schmitt's own thought as a gradual recognition of the nature of that necessity and of what was required to meet its demands.

liberalism. Following through with Schmitt's logic, it is significant that Dworkin finds it necessary to appeal to a substantive sounding idea like integrity, which, as Dworkin describes it, is meant to found a liberal community. But Dworkin's recognition of liberalism's need to acquire substance must, Schmitt would think, lead to the realization that liberalism cannot meet this need. Dworkin would either have to retreat from substance or recognize that there is no stopping point on the road to substance.

I offer the following example (with apologies to those feminists whose arguments I have cast in a Schmittian mold). According to Dworkin, the hope for a substantive basis to liberalism is equality. But in his critique of those feminists who argue for the censorship of pornography on the basis that it perpetuates inequality between the sexes, Dworkin is committed to absolute freedom of speech, even if its effect is to enable one group, in this case men, to use their superior resources to dominate another group.[30] His reason is that one must be agnostic or neutral on the subject of how individuals choose to live their lives, which means remaining neutral in regard to an individual's conception of what is in her or his own best interests. He therefore argues that, under a liberal democratic constitution, legislation accepting the arguments of feminists who would eradicate pornography would be unconstitutional. His neutrality thus favors one group over another and his concern is that if this stance of neutrality were to be modified, there would be no stopping point.

In Schmittian terms, one might say that the example shows that Dworkin is fundamentally committed to relativism since his stance is that each individual's preferences as to how to live must be considered by the state to be as good as those of any other individual. Thus, private choices trump a public choice and the political is reduced to private morality in which the state has no business to interfere. Dworkin's model allows a different covert politics to reign and demonstrates that the liberal ideal of universal equality is a cloak for power grabs by particular interest groups.

---

30 See his essays on this topic responding to Catherine MacKinnon in the *New York Review of Books*. Ronald Dworkin, *The Coming Battles over Free Speech*, N.Y. REV. OF BOOKS, June 11, 1992, at 55 (reviewing ANTHONY LEWIS, MAKE NO LAW: THE *Sullivan* CASE AND THE FIRST AMENDMENT (1993)); Ronald Dworkin, *Liberty and Pornography*, N.Y. REV. OF BOOKS, Aug. 15, 1991, at 12; Ronald Dworkin, *Women and Pornography*, N.Y. REV. OF BOOKS, Oct. 21, 1993, at 36 (reviewing CATHERINE A. MACKINNON, ONLY WORDS (1993)). I discuss Dworkin's responses to MacKinnon in my forthcoming article, *Pornography and Public Reason*. *See* David Dyzenhaus, *Pornography and Public Reason*, VII CAN. J. OF L. & JURISPRUDENCE (forthcoming 1994).

A Schmittian might also draw our attention to the fact that, from the liberal standpoint, Dworkin is correct to stick to his guns. For if he were to accept the equality-based feminist argument for censorship, there would in fact be no stopping point for the claims that competing interest groups would make of the state. Liberalism is damned if it does and damned if it doesn't.

My aim here is by no means to suggest that we should accept Schmitt's critique of liberalism. His own embrace of Nazism should warn us that his political existentialism is highly dangerous.[31] But there is, I think, something to his critique. Where it points productively is in the task liberalism must undertake and which he thought impossible. That is, liberalism must learn to manifest itself in the public realm in a way that does not privatize politics. Put differently, liberalism has yet to show that it can offer a convincing account of democratic citizenship.

[31] My view is that he was in principle committed to embracing Nazism, once it became the dominant ideology.

[22]

International Law as Political Theology: How to Read *Nomos der Erde*?

Martti Koskenniemi

I

Rarely in modern times have Europe and the United States drifted as far apart as they have today. It would be wrong to seek any single cause or a predominant theme for their separation. Much history and trauma, on both sides, is surely involved. A mutual *ressentiment* of the current intensity is not born overnight. But one of the more visible and perhaps sharper forms in which the divergence has appeared concerns thinking about international affairs. For the Americans, ever since September 11, the old truths of political realism seem to have overwhelmed any hopes for a more peaceful and united world that the end of the Cold War had brought about. The world is still as dangerous as ever, perhaps even more so, due to the extraordinary types of weapons and strategy possessed by America's enemies. A dangerous world requires a hardening of attitudes and more determinate, less conciliatory behavior. For decades, the United States has agreed to play the diplomatic game with the Europeans and an amorphous "international community," united often only by its implacable opposition to everything the United States stands for. Now this must stop.

The European view of the world could scarcely be more different. "Nowadays . . . the United Nations Charter has almost universally been recognized as the constitutional document of the international community of states."[1] Here is Antonio Cassese, former president of the International Criminal Tribunal for the Former Yugoslavia:

> at least at the normative level the international community is becoming more integrated and – what is even more important – . . . such values as human rights and the need to promote development are increasingly penetrating various sectors of international law that previously seemed impervious to them.[2]

Where Washington decision-makers and their academic epigones see the world as sharply divided between "us" and the "enemies of freedom," the Europeans have dusted off constitutional themes familiar from the interwar period, and apply them not only to the "paradise" of the European Union but, with an even greater sense of urgency, to the international scene. In policy and in doctrine, Europeans embrace the Kantian view that the international world will in due course organize itself analogously to the domestic one, as a vertically constraining system of law manifested in notions such as *jus cogens* or universal jurisdiction over crimes against humanity, and that it is the business of international institutions to bring this about.[3] For an old-European thinker such as Jürgen Habermas, the terms of the American-European controversy are clear: "The crucial issue of dissent is whether justification through international law can and should be replaced by the unilateral, world-ordering politics of a self-appointed hegemon."[4]

For reasons of polemic, but also in a genuine effort to understand, Europeans now often view American policies and attitudes through Carl Schmitt's writings during the interwar era and above all in his 1950 *Der Nomos der Erde im Völkerrecht des Jus Publicum Europaeum.* Whatever Schmitt's political choices, readers have been struck by the expressive force of his critiques when applied to contemporary events: the war on terrorism as a morally-inspired and unlimited "total war," in which the adversary is not treated as a "just enemy"; the obsoleteness of traditional rules of warfare and recourse to novel technologies – especially air power[5] – so as to conduct discriminatory wars against adversaries viewed as outlaws and enemies of humanity; Camp Delta in the Guantánamo naval base with its still over 500 prisoners from the Afghanistan war as a normless exception that reveals the nature of the new international political order of which the United States is the guardian – the source of the normative order, itself unbound by it.[6]

Such a view puts the "war on terrorism" squarely within the thematic of the last 100 pages of *Nomos der Erde*, which discuss "the question of the new nomos of the Earth." To be sure, Schmitt saw the new world order commence in the declarations of war on Germany by the allied and associated powers in the First World War and consolidated by the way the Versailles conference was conducted "against" (instead of "with") Germany, by the institution of the League of Nations as an instrument of British and American policy in Europe, and above all by the criminalization of the war of aggression in the 1928 Briand-Kellogg Pact and the 1945–46 Nuremberg War Crimes trial. To apply Schmitt's description of the new nomos to the behavior of the Western powers in Kosovo and Iraq, the 50-year interlude may be explained by the Cold War having prevented a full-scale moralization of international politics. Ironically, then, for half a century, the Soviet Union may have taken the role of the Schmittian *Katechon* – restrainer of the coming of the Antichrist.[7]

Nomos der Erde can be read from different perspectives. On its surface, far from appearing as Schmitt's "most idiosyncratic book,"[8] it appears to be a history of international law and international relations. Despite its sometimes esoteric mythological or etymological speculations, it recounts much that is commonplace for mainstream historiography in these fields: the importance of the turn from religious medieval "unity" to the secular system of territorially-limited sovereignty under the treaties of Münster and Osnabrück; the contrast between inter-European law and the state of nature projected onto the new world; and the turn to a pacifist universalism under the League Covenant. The direct influence of *Nomos der Erde* has been small: until very recently, it existed only in German, and even for German lawyers, referring to it may have been a *faux pas*.[9] Nevertheless, Schmitt's voice is clearly audible in German postwar histories of international law like those by Grewe and Ziegler.[10] Through the writings of Hans Morgenthau, Schmittian perspectives became absolutely central for international relations "realism" – a pedigree often left unrevealed.[11] *Nomos der Erde* is also often read biographically, as the most developed achievement in Schmitt's turn to international law after his fall from grace in the Nazi Party in 1936 and his consequent turn from *Staatsrechtslehre* to more innocent academic pursuits. From this perspective, *Nomos* (which was already finalized in 1945) appears to weave together Schmitt's interwar arguments on the League of Nations and the "discriminatory concept of war," aspects of his *Großraumlehre* (theory of greater spaces), and his war-time texts on the opposition of "Land and Sea," foreshadowing later commentary on international politics.

I will, however, read *Nomos* in the context of Schmitt's general *oeuvre* in order to make the point that the book's arguments should not be understood as mere historiography or contextualized against the background of Schmitt's turn to international politics. Instead, I see the mixture of *Ideengeschichte*, mythical speculation, and sharp insight into international politics as fragments from a political theology that is not explicitly articulated therein.[12] Reading it in this light might perhaps suggest a novel twist for the European-American controversy. The idea would be not (only) to employ Schmitt to understand the United States but to think *with* and *against* Schmitt in the interests of today's politics.

II

Like international law textbooks, Schmitt represents the history of international law in three stages: the medieval *respublica christiana* was a religiously-based, homogenous order that received its validity from God as mediated by the right ecclesiastic and secular authorities claiming universal jurisdiction. It was replaced by the territorial state as the principle of delimitation of spatial authority in Europe that realized a sharp distinction between secular and Church jurisdiction. The *jus publicum europaeum* that came to regulate the relationship between European states was consolidated through the great discoveries that opened up non-European territory as a field of unlimited European land-taking and made it thus possible for the European order itself to remain stable. The great merit of this system for Schmitt lay in the manner in which it was able to limit inter-European warfare by conceiving it as a public law status between formally equal sovereigns, by replacing the medieval notion of the *justa causa belli* by the formal concept of the *justus hostis*. This enabled enemies to be treated on an equal basis, through formal rules and without existential enmity.

War became a "duel," a regulated procedure for resolving inter-European rivalries.

Schmitt did not hide his admiration for the *jus publicum europaeum*, and though he recognized that there was no return to it, he still used it as the standard for his criticism of the liberal universalism that animated the post-Versailles system and buttressed the power of Western allies over their enemies, now targeted by a "discriminatory," in principle total war. By contrast, "[t]he interstate wars of 1815–1914 were in reality orderly procedures, encompassed neutral Great Powers and essentially juridical, in comparison to which modern police actions and pacification of the violators of peace appear as sinister attempts at annihilation."[13] In fact, *Nomos der Erde* is less a history of international law than political manifesto against the moralization of warfare that Schmitt saw as a cynical instrument to justify the enormous destruction Western technological superiority was inflicting on its adversaries. The moral arguments made by the British and the Americans in the twentieth century may have resembled the notions of just war but in fact had "nothing in common" with the moral basis of the medieval legal order, though Western jurists had started to celebrate sixteenth-century scholasticism (above all Francisco de Vitoria and Francisco Suárez) as their true predecessors. The replacement of true religion by a morality of secular "values" was in fact a nihilism. And "nihilism is worse than anarchy."[14]

Much in this critique seems correct. But what is problematic is its simple juxtaposition of a virtuous past in which legal rules channelled and limited intra-European warfare with a present period of hypocrisy and danger in which nothing stands in the way of the hegemonic pursuits of a single superpower. The problems are twofold. First, Schmitt's 1950 acceptance of the international law profession's own narrative about the *jus publicum europaeum* during the 400 years of European predominance is not based on a concrete analysis of European societies from 1500 to 1900, and even less on the reality of European warfare during that time. Instead, it is a projection of his 1922 dictum that "[a]ll significant concepts of the modern theory of the state are secularized theological concepts."[15] Through the use of the notion of "nomos," Schmitt gives the impression of describing a "concrete order" when he is simply describing the logical corollaries of a theory of domestic absolutism.

The second problem lies in Schmitt's apparently vehement rejection of the standpoint of the universal that seems to inform his critique of the nihilism of the secular "values" behind humanitarian internationalism. In fact, however, Schmitt's attack on the liberal humanists, the neutralizers and depoliticizers, is not based upon a rejection of universalism but on an unarticulated distinction between a "false" and a "genuine" universalism. This is, again, not apparent, since Schmitt refrains in 1950 from expressing the standpoint on which his own universalism is based and which he uses to make the distinction between the Catholic scholastics of the sixteenth century and the moralistic enthusiasm of the apologists for the new nomos.

III

Nomos der Erde grounds the European order on the emergence of the state as the political form that regulated the occupation and administration of land inside and outside Europe from the late fifteenth until the late nineteenth century. This history is constructed out of a definite relationship between three key Schmittian concepts: concrete order, the occupation of land, and statehood. That Schmitt did not tell European legal history in terms of the emergence and transformation of "great principles" – as had been done by the Alsatian Robert Redslob three decades before[16] – followed from his view of law as a "concrete order" (*konkretes Ordnungsdenken*), as opposed to what he characterized in 1934 as the alternative jurisprudential approaches of "normativism" and "decisionism."[17] That Schmitt always saw himself above all as a lawyer did not mean he thought he represented a marginal technical craft, and he positively abhorred the view of the legal scholar as a mere describer of the effects of legislation.[18] He understood law broadly as *Recht* (and *nomos*) in contrast to *Gesetz* or *loi*, as an expression of the fundamental – and irreducibly political – choice on which lay the unity of the human community – that is, during the European age, the state. It was both wider and narrower, and, above all, more fundamental, than the positive laws generated by what Schmitt ridiculed as the "motorized legislator" of the legislative state.[19] "The law is *always* wiser than the legislator."[20] For Schmitt, writing in 1943, historical jurisprudence remained the last carrier of this understanding – "the unity of the legal will as opposed to the multiplicity of egoistic parties and factions."[21] As "concrete-order thinking," jurisprudence would always need to go beyond mere positive laws or legislative "plans." It would need to grasp the substance of the choice on which a community's identity depends. This would not be a mere historiographical or legal-positivist task, but involved reaching towards a political standpoint: "The concept of the state presupposes the concept of the political."[22]

To elucidate the concrete order to which international law in the European period gave expression, Schmitt postulated a foundational relationship between order in the human community and the land it inhabited (*Ordnung-Ortung*).[23] If land-taking (*Landnahme*) was the primal act of community, then the method of effective land-distribution in a period provided its concrete order, its nomos. For four hundred years, since the Great Discoveries, the nomos of the earth had consisted of the division of European territory between European states and their expansion through acts of land-taking outside Europe. Since the end of the seventeenth century, this order had been supplemented by the alien aspect of the sea, dominated by the people of the sea – the British. But a reasonable equilibrium had been attained by the Peace of Utrecht (1713) between it and the states of the continent, especially through the safety-valve created by the unlimited possibility of occupation of land areas outside Europe.[24]

This new, state-centric system of public order, Schmitt argued, had had the extraordinary merit of limiting and channelling inter-European warfare.[25] This was an effect of the agnosticism of that law about matters of religion: *silete theologi in munere alieno*![26] From this followed the transformation of the religiously-inclined *just war* into a purely secular notion of the *formally legal* war between European states. In the European era – and this is central to Schmitt's normative argument – war became a regulated rivalry, a duel between formal states, conducted strictly following the procedures laid down by the *jus publicum europaeum*, while unlimited enmity was projected "beyond the line" – into the non-European world.[27]

This narrative is very dubious both in regard to the nature of the land-taking that it postulated and its categorical view of the principle of "no peace beyond the line."[28] But it is hardly insignificant that it was practically identical with the one told by representatives of the *jus publicum europaeum* themselves, in particular German public law experts such as Georg Friedrich von Martens (1756–1822) and Johann Ludwig Klüber (1762–1837), writing in the period of the post-Napoleonic restoration for diplomats and statesmen and restating the formal principles of *ancien régime* diplomacy. Their histories of *le droit public de l'Europe* restated the narrative of the fall of the medieval *respublica christiana* due to dissension, peaking in religious civil war and of the Peace of Westphalia, as a kind of social contract of mutual toleration – *cuius regio eius religio* – between European sovereigns.[29]

But in adopting the view of *le droit public de l'Europe*, Schmitt was in danger of characterizing it precisely in the formal and abstract terms he ridiculed in attempts to defend the Weimar constitution.[30] The treatises by von Martens and Klüber consisted of elaborate classifications and formal distinctions between different types of states, different classes of representatives, groups of treaties, and typologies of procedural relationships. Indeed, the thrust of *le droit public de l'Europe*, as understood by its dominant representatives themselves, lay precisely in its rigorous formalism, its absolute distance from the social lives of European nations.[31] That Schmitt could possibly identify this superficial network of diplomatic protocols as the nomos of the world and still believe that what he was describing was neither a naturalist abstraction nor an empty contractual positivism (*Vertragspositivismus*) was only possible by recourse to a background assumption about the intrinsic worth of European statehood conceived in the pre-revolutionary manner, that is, as *absolutist* statehood.

For Schmitt, as is well-known, the concept of the state presumes the concept of the political, and the political has to do with the opposition between friend and enemy. That Schmitt could see the European states-system of 1492–1890[32] as intrinsically beneficient followed from the way he saw it analogously to the Catholic Church as a political form that reduced the *complexio oppositorum* into a manageable set of territorial delimitations controlled by the balance of power between authoritarian units, each of which was able to maintain internal order and direct expansive energies to an unlimited rivalry outside Europe.[33] In other words – and though Schmitt avoids making this explicit in the *Nomos der Erde* – his endorsement of the old European order emerges from his prewar writings on the state, which supported precisely the kind of absolutist claims of sovereignty against which the Revolution had been initiated.[34]

Ostensibly, Schmitt based the concreteness of his analysis of 1950 on acts of land-taking (*Landnahme*) by European states. However, concentrating on claims of territorial jurisdiction by European states within a period of 400 years in fact obscures the wide divergence of forms and intensity of territorial rule in Europe between 1500 and 1900, ranging from the most fragile and tenuous, often *de facto* feudal or aristocratic regimes to centralized military dictatorships. That these various forms of domain came to be labelled "states" did not result from their attainment of some determinate form of social power or territorial control – indeed, territorial delimitation by means of maps and boundary stones or population censuses developed only in the eighteenth century[35] – but of the development of authoritarian political theory that secularized monotheism into the theory of the single sovereign. How this finally came about has been elegantly told by Ernst Kantorowicz through the idea that, annexed to his "natural body," the King also possessed a "body politic" that "contain[ed] his royal Estate and Dignity."[36] This ethereal body then joined all those to whom the King asserted his realm extended under his "rule," conceived in due course in the image of Roman ideas of jurisdiction – rulership through law, understood not as a general norm but a personal and concrete decision.[37]

Schmitt's *Landnahme* was less a sociological act of taking possession – after all, most non-European colonies were claimed by discovery, not by effective control until late nineteenth century, and even then only in part[38] – than a decision by the European monarch that could be interpreted as a "radical title," since it was now taken with the consciousness of taking place in a global system. Behind its complex formulations, Schmitt's nomos should be seen as the unity of certain events (namely of the voyages of discovery) with a certain consciousness about their meaning (that they take place in *global* history) that receive concreteness in the ordering act that the claim of public law jurisdiction is.[39]

Here, Roman law stood in a key position by making a difference between the claims by the feudal monarchs who tended to see their lands as private property and the claims of public law jurisdiction by modern European rulers.[40] The new nomos, as Schmitt explained, provided the very basis for that distinction.[41] Drawing attention to it, Schmitt was putting his finger on the fact that European statehood did not emerge alone but as the political form specific to capitalist social relations that presumed a constitutive distinction between public power, exercised through claims of sovereign jurisdiction (*imperium*), and private power, exercised by private law ownership (property, *dominium*), paradigmatically through the market.[42] The reception of Roman law gave expression to this transformation not only by differentiating between public law and civil law but, as Perry Anderson has pointed out, by conceiving sovereignty in equally absolute terms as private ownership under civil law.[43] Here – in the distinction between political and economic forms of power and in the absoluteness through which these powers were conceived – lay the social distinctiveness of early modernity as the concrete order Schmitt celebrated.

By conceiving the *jus publicum europaeum* in terms of the claims of public law jurisdiction (instead of ownership or control), Schmitt appears to be led into the trap of mainstream international thought, namely the awkward assumption of "an absolute form of rule which seems never to be absolute in practice even though, for some reason, the formal constitution of the international system rests on the assumption that it is so."[44] However, what indeed appears as an enigma of realist theories of sovereignty can be fitted within Schmitt's thinking once it is understood that his nomos is not at all derived from what takes place in the international social world but from a political theology conceived in support of domestic absolutism. As abstract sovereigns, units of the international system, European states of course varied in influence and were engaged in often fierce rivalries. But fluctuations between Spanish, Dutch, and French "epochs" failed to change the character of the *jus publicum europaeum*, which lay not in the identity of the leading power but in how the identity of the units – including the leading power – was conceived (including what was left outside as private economy). This was a system of states as seen by Schmitt's heroes Bodin and Hobbes – instruments for avoiding domestic chaos and civil war. "In the struggle of opposing interests and coalitions, absolute monarchy made the decision and thereby created the unity of the state."[45] At the same time, it emptied the international realm of any claim for obedience beyond *raison d'état* and the balance of power. Absolute internal sovereignty implied absolute external independence.[46] No relevant change in this regard took place as the locus of sovereignty shifted to the people. Indeed, for Schmitt democracy rested on a principle of homogeneity that presumed a no less determinate decision than absolute monarchy, while sometimes the difference between the two – as in Schmitt's theory of "commissarial dictatorship" – vanished completely.[47] Only when the liberal-constitutionalist ideas – originally stated in "the catastrophe of 1848" – began to prevail did the need for political decision come to be discarded: sovereignty was divided between state organs; its focus became legislation by general rules that aimed to regulate even their own suspension. Only then was the controlling capacity of sovereignty undermined and claims by an autonomous "universal" realm could be entertained.

The Schmittian view of European public law, whatever its virtues, is of an order between sovereigns that are absolute in the sense that their sovereignty involves the pre-legal decision that both grounds the domestic order and safeguards control of the international realm. The essence of sovereignty – against the liberal "neutralizers and depoliticizers" – is that it "is the highest, legally independent, underived power."[48] Such a view emerges from a political theology that is structurally homologous to Christian monotheism, historically continuous with religious teaching, and, above all, equipped by a supplement of faith that decides who is the enemy – "one's own question as the figure" – in a concrete situation.[49]

For Schmitt, here lies the wisdom of Bodin's theory of the state. *Auctoritas, non veritas facit legem.* The Prince is not bound by the law as he seeks to save the realm: even as the legal order is suspended, the state remains.[50] But the converse also is true: the "incapacity or the unwillingness to make [the distinction between friend and enemy] is a symptom of the political end."[51]

This danger arose only in the relatively calm times of the later eighteenth century. Enlightenment sought to banish the exception from politics as its theology did away with the miracle.[52] The last phase of the state's terminal decline began with the heyday of liberal constitutionalism and individualism in the late nineteenth century, when it was transformed into a "total state" out of weakness, kidnapped by special interests, equally unable to sustain the unity of the domestic realm and the *jus publicum europaeum* against the universalizing liberal moralists.

The *jus publicum europaeum* was not state-centric as such. It was *both* state-centric *and* absolutist, and it is the political theory of absolutism and not state-centrism that accounted for the virtues that Schmitt held dear. Humanitarian universalism is not antithetical to the state either. It reserves for the state a place in the administration of its hypothesized international society as the night-watchman guarding over the non-political politics of technological and economic progress. But what universalism cannot tolerate is sovereignty as the ultimate power to make the political decision from which each legal system would derive its force and its unity – unless, of course, it is itself precisely such a sovereignty.

IV

Schmitt's analysis and critique of modern international law in the last 100 pages of *Nomos* is both suggestive and incomplete. It is a strikingly sharp and original discussion that sheds light not only on the situation of international law in 1950, but also on what international lawyers today analyze in terms of the contradictory tendencies of the uniformization of the law under a single superpower and its functional and regional fragmentation into specialized technical regimes in fields such as trade, human rights, and the environment.[53] The replacement of a single, Eurocentric, public law-governed system of sovereignties by private law relations governing a global free market and the establishment of a morally-based imperial order that knows war only as a relation between the police and the criminal have rarely been analyzed with a sharper eye.

Yet these discussions are incomplete. Schmitt never really reveals the standpoint from which he writes, what it is that animates his attack on the new nomos. No doubt, Schmitt's writings emerge from an almost visceral anti-liberalism. But what gives force or provides direction to the attacks on technology, normativism, and "depolitizations and neutralizations" is no more evident in *Nomos* than in his other principal works. The 1950 book is difficult to classify. It is clearly not just a history of international law or a history of political thought or international relations. Schmitt's famous style, which prefers striking formulations and paradoxes – even his critics acknowledge their "rare poetic quality"[54] – over careful analysis, does nothing to make his narrative perspective any clearer. No conclusion emerges in *Nomos* to tie the critiques in a single thesis or position.

That *Nomos* is a critique of liberal "universalism" has understandably suggested to many readers that Schmitt is an anti-universalist, a committed supporter of a state-centered international order. Others focus on his "nihilistic" decisionism or his admiration of power. Still others assume that it emanates from his nationalism or the ideology of conservative revolution. Though there is something to such understandings, they remain incomplete. Schmitt is no *völkisch* nationalist, and he frequently indicates that "power" is insufficient for grounding an *acceptable* order. Though "statehood" is important to him, Schmitt understands it only as a contingent principle for ordering human communities. He expressly distinguishes his "concrete-order thinking" from positivistic – and as such "nihilistic" – decisionism.[55]

Schmitt is not an anti-universalist. He does not attack the Anglo-American, liberal world order because of its universalism, but because of its *false* and *nihilistic* universalism. The most plausible interpretation of *Nomos* is one that reads it in view of the opposition Schmitt made soon after its publication between a *philosophical* treatment of the historical problems it treated and a *theological* one, namely Schmitt's own.

In a 1951 talk in Madrid, Schmitt was uncommonly clear about this. A self-understanding of humanity that was based merely on a philosophy of history was poised between two alternatives. Either it condemned the human species to an "eternal return of the same" – this, in fact, is what political realism does[56] – or it recognized a fatal difference in humanity's technological and moral progress, and, having nothing to oppose their separation, marched humanity into Promethean suicide. In this regard, there was no difference between the ideologies of communism and capitalism, Schmitt wrote. Each was embedded in a fully secular understanding of itself, situating their struggle in alternative *philosophical* understandings of history. Schmitt's alternative was to move completely away from a philosophical-naturalist frame to a theological one, to interpret the present in light of a Christian conception of history.[57]

From this perspective, three insights would seem important for grasping the last 100 pages of *Nomos*. One is the interpretation of worldly conflict in terms of the struggle between the Christ and Antichrist which marks the persistence of historical time until, finally, "Babylonian" world unity will be attained with the victory on earth of the latter, and the end of historical time. The meaning of history from this perspective is not "progress" or unity, but *salvation*.[58] The irreducibility of the friend/enemy opposition that defined the political would then appear as a reflection of that fundamental opposition: pretending to "neutralize" or do away with it through secular norms or institutions would be to play the antagonist's game: "whoever wants to withstand Satan, must insist on enmity."[59] The second insight would be taking seriously the constant appearance of the figure of the *katechon* in *Nomos* and elsewhere as the secular "restrainer" of the coming of the Antichrist. This role would fall in different historical moments on different actors, and the important political decision would be to apprehend what or who at any moment plays it. The third insight would concern the uniqueness of each historical moment, the inability to make (political) decisions by reference to social laws or institutions, however conceived: "History is not the realization of rules or regularities or scientific, biological, or other types of norms. Its essential and specific content is *the event* that arrives only once and does not repeat itself."[60] These three insights – a Christian concept of time as the frame for salvation, the role of the *katechon* as the one that extends this time, and the single, undetermined event (the decision) as the carrier of all that is meaningful – ground a universalism which is from beginning to end based on an unquestioned faith, a faith that provides the only standpoint from which the critiques of the last 100 pages of *Nomos* receive their meaning and against which they can be united as a political rejection of everything represented by those that seek "world unity" under a secular philosophy of history and thus fall under what Apostle Paul wrote to the Thessalonians: "For when they shall say, peace and security, then sudden destruction cometh upon them."[61]

So what then is the force and direction of a political theologian's critique of international law? Again, *Nomos* remains unclear because its final sections focus on apparently random diplomatic events and doctrines: the change in the meaning of "war"; the nature of the Treaty of Versailles as continued discriminatory and limitless war against Germany; its generalization in the League of Nations; the asymmetrical and flexible use of the Monroe Doctrine; the changes in the law and practice of recognition; modern technologies as auguries for total war. Schmitt had already discussed such themes in his interwar writings. Because they are (intentionally) focused on concrete events and written so as to demonstrate the dominance of Anglo-American universalism, the temptation is to dismiss them as political polemics by a defeated enemy. This would be a mistake. They imply critiques of the main strands of international jurisprudence, which, though they are not made explicit in *Nomos*, appear in a small book from 1938.[62] This book is a critique of the views of Georges Scelle (1878–1961), Professor of International Law at Paris, a socialist and a "solidarist," and Hersch Lauterpacht (1894–1960), Professor of International Law at Cambridge University, who had emigrated from Galicia and Vienna to Britain in 1923. Scelle and Lauterpacht – and, as Schmitt saw it, the French and the British legal traditions – complemented each other so as to produce two different, partly conflicting, but parallel articulations of the *false* universalism of the new nomos.

The choice of Scelle and Lauterpacht was neither accidental nor misplaced. These were the two most influential international lawyers of the period. They also represented two major directions of international jurisprudence that had come to replace the "empty formalism" and the *Vertragspositivismus* of the immediate postwar years, which, in Schmitt's view, had only aimed to legitimize the

Versailles arrangement.[63] That their major works were published in 1933 and 1934 made them theorists of the "evening," bringing to fruition strands of thought and practice from the previous half century. Their projects – a sociologically-based institutionalism and a court-oriented, informal ("Victorian") naturalism – remain even today the basic alternatives for a liberal articulation of diplomatic practices in terms of international law. It is therefore useful to sketch them briefly before outlining the nature of Schmitt's critique.[64]

Scelle's left solidarism based international law on the social laws of modernity itself. Following Durkheim, Scelle explained social cohesion as an effect of organic solidarity, grounded in the biology of human needs and leading inexorably to federalism.[65] An implicit "social" constitution organized the government of common affairs through procedures for legislation, jurisdiction, and enforcement. None of this was a matter of choice. Legislation involved an essentially *scientific* task.[66]

Scelle's world consisted ("ultimately") of relationships between individuals, endowed by society with "essential competencies" and a sphere of discretion that grounded their freedom, conceptualized as the right to life, liberty, movement, trade, and economic establishment.[67] The state was a mere fiction: in "reality," only individuals existed, either as subjects of liberties, objects of behavioral regulation, or administrators (*gouvernants*), among whom the law distributed competencies to do what (objective) law required.[68] Hence his famous doctrine of the *dédoublement fonctionnel* – the situation where an individual has been put in a position to administer two or more societies – as where national parliaments or governments also administer international society.[69]

Lauterpacht's writings were altogether different in style and sensibility, constructing only an *implied* world federation from the "common law" created by international courts and tribunals. In his major works of 1927 and 1933, Lauterpacht gave articulation to the nature of international law as a "complete system" on a par with domestic law.[70] No realm of "politics" had autonomous power against the principles of international law, as employed in the work of international tribunals. An appeal to sovereignty, "vital interests," or "honor," for example, could always be transformed into the question of whether a rule of law provided that a state was free to act as it wished.

The great enemy of Lauterpacht and Scelle was political discretion, which they associated with "metaphysical" or atavistic doctrines of sovereignty, to be eliminated in due course by international federation. Lauterpacht's optimistic cosmopolitanism survived even the darkest times. Here he is speaking at the Royal Institute of International Affairs, Chatham House, London, in 1941, as bombs were falling over Coventry and the members of his family in Poland were being rounded up in a ghetto and soon killed:

> The disunity of the modern world is a fact; but so, in a truer sense, is its unity. Th[e] essential and manifold solidarity, coupled with the necessity of securing the rule of

> law and the elimination of war, constitutes a harmony of interests which has a basis more real and tangible than the illusions of the sentimentalist or the hypocrisy of those satisfied with the existing *status quo*. The ultimate harmony of interests which within the State finds expression in the elimination of private violence is not a misleading invention of nineteenth century liberalism.[71]

Scelle and Lauterpacht exemplified different but parallel articulations of a liberal-universalist jurisprudence which Schmitt totally rejected. Scelle's institutionalism extended at the international level the French theory of the "legislative state": law as an abstract project declaring objective social truths and legislation conceived as science and a social technique. What could be more in accord with the liberal tendency of neutralization and depoliticization? In Scelle's federalist utopia, politics would become extinct and the global institution would appear as the "total state" invaded by the economic and social interests between which the institution would preach total "neutrality." What could be less expressive of the seriousness of the struggles in the international world when interpreted from the perspective of political theology?

Today's international lawyers apply a sociology of globalization to articulate international law in terms of its fragmentation into technical "regimes" and invoke the need for its "constitutionalization" by hierarchical relations in view of universal values expressed in human rights or general notions such as *jus cogens*.[72] From Schmitt's perspective, such proposals only introduce a vocabulary that sustains the policies of those (liberal) actors well-placed in the diplomatic institutions that decide what they are to mean in concrete cases. As an Ersatz-theology, sociology only provides an apparently neutral scientific language for making political claims. As another Catholic-conservative jurist, Scelle's *nemesis* from the Paris law school, Louis Le Fur once remarked, "social solidarity" may mean anything one wants it to mean, not least the solidarity between the lion and the antelope, or the master and the slave.[73]

In order for "international society" or "globalization" (just like "the state" or "the individual") to receive meaning and applicability, an interpretative framework is needed. The framework of lawyers such as Scelle or Lauterpacht, as manifested in the quote above, is faith in the ultimate goodness of human beings and world harmony. By contrast, for Schmitt and Schmittian realists such as Hans Morgenthau, "all genuinely political theories presuppose man to be evil, i.e., by no means an unproblematic but a dangerous and dynamic being."[74] For the latter, even if successful, constitutionalization would have no intrinsic merit. It would merely consolidate an order based on somebody's effective decision and control – without guarantee that this decision would be *correct*.[75]

Lauterpacht's modest naturalism – his "Grotian tradition," the judge as the moral conscience of the international world[76] – avoids this trap but only at the cost of remaining unable to articulate itself in a philosophically plausible way. This view builds, as I have elsewhere argued, on late-nineteenth-century ideas about the civilizing power of pragmatic, liberal reasonableness, which, accompanied by an optimistic view of history, is still the mainstay of today's European international legal theory.[77] The problem is that by avoiding philosophical justification, such pragmatism rests on a faith that remains a mystery to itself as it conflicts with its avowed rationalism.[78] Closer to Schmitt than sociological ("scientific") theories of law, pragmatism emanates from an unself-conscious political theology, which, because it does not understand itself as such, could not be in sharper contrast with one that consciously interprets the world through the omnipresence of sin.

The critiques of the last 100 pages of *Nomos* are directed against diplomatic and political events and doctrines, not against legal theories. This may be because, from Schmitt's perspective, even if he could take them seriously in 1938, the Second World War had revealed their utter implausibility, perhaps their nihilism. But no novel approaches to international law have emerged since then. The international law Europeans invoke against the unilateralism of the US still emerges from two sources. One is a sociologically-informed federalism that views international institutions as necessary for the management of a globalized world and worries about their legitimacy in terms not unlike those current in the Weimar debates. The other is a pragmatic naturalism with a focus on courts and hierarchical notions such as universal human rights and *jus cogens* as manifestations of universal "values," grasped by private intuition rather than philosophical argument. The irony is that, taken as legal theories, they can be – and have been – invoked on both sides of the Atlantic, thus suggesting that they are, as Schmitt once suggested, best seen as surfaces over which political conflict is waged, vocabularies whose significance resides not in what they mean, but in who can authoritatively decide what action they suggest in concrete circumstances.

V

How should one then read *Nomos* in view of the present European-American controversy? One alternative is to suggest that its critical analysis is largely correct. The United States is embarked on a morally-inspired crusade opposed by a Europe that invokes the formal law of sovereign equality under the United Nations Charter. There is undoubtedly something right in such an analysis. It is especially hard to avoid thinking about the American rhetoric of freedom as an empty form through which the United States asserts its unconditional sovereignty over the world. This would be empire, and the only remaining question would be whether it is a "rational empire," inspired by genuine confidence in the universality of the moral truth for which Washington decision-makers see themselves as carriers (in Schmittian terms, the United States as a kind of "commissarial dictatorship" upholding the substantive constitution of the world by a suspension of its formal provisions); or whether the right characterization would be of a "cynical empire," lacking such faith though still using its language.[79] Both alternatives would be compatible with understanding American acts in terms of a political theology (of freedom) in the strict Vitorian sense: one's unconditional deference to right authority as the sole standard of evaluation, whereby one's acts would be automatically virtuous whether their consequences were good or evil.[80] This is the logic of (American) nationalism: the unquestioned authority of *my* (liberal-democratic) country as the sole normative standard.[81]

It is much harder to accept the (conservative) characterization of Europe as the representative of "international law" against American "hegemony." If the law is indeterminate in the way critics claim,[82] then there is no substantive legal system that could be distinguished from unilateral assertions of power. In such a case, the European appeal to "rules" – like Schmitt's invocation of the *jus publicum europaeum* – would appear as hegemonic techniques through which Europe would only seek to regain some control by inscribing its preferences on the surface of a legal vocabulary it claims as universal. "Moral empire" and "international law" would then both appear as languages that seek to encompass the universal, but do this from a particular point of view. Their clash would be a struggle over whose vocabulary – and thus whose institutions – would be entitled to claim to speak for everybody. This would be a true clash of incommensurate political theologies. But even if that (ultra-realist) conclusion were correct, it is hard to say what political consequences it would entail.[83]

Another direction is taken by those, like Habermas, who claim a special status for rule-systems and rule-applying institutions against unmediated moral truths. Habermas concedes the correctness of Schmitt's critique inasmuch as the "unmediated moralization of law and politics would in fact serve to break down those protected spheres that we as legal persons have good reason to want to secure."[84] Such moralization would result from the "false coding" of law in accordance with moral-political criteria of "good" and "evil," when in fact what is central to law is its claim of universality by presuming the judgment of external authority.[85] Claims of law are not (or not only) veiled moral claims; they are claims that decenter one's own position, that imply parity between the legal subjects and an unbiased "third party" that will decide. In fact, as Habermas notes, even the critique of indeterminacy is based on such an assumption: "any deconstructive unmasking of the ideologically concealing use of universalistic discourses actually presuppose the critical viewpoints advanced by these same discourses."[86]

The weakness of this is that there is no agreement on what the correct – "unbiased," "external" – procedure is: each contestant invokes institutions (the US Constitution and the UN Charter) the other regards as biased. Each views the very submission of itself to the procedure invoked by its adversary as *ab initio* prohibiting the articulation of its key claims. This type of "differend" would remain even if one were to concede, in principle, that the respective truth-claims do imply decentering and reference to a third party.[87] Even if Europe and the United States are committed by their own assumptions to turn their moral and political positions into generalizable claims about legal rights and duties, disagreement would remain about how this can be done in an unbiased way in view of the actually existing alternatives. The juxtaposition between the US claim that no legal order can be superior to its constitution and the European view that even such a position can only be invoked in terms of *legal* sovereignty (*Rechtssouveränität*) will lead to a dead end – unless it is viewed in pragmatic terms as a series of questions about the legitimacy and effectiveness of present domestic and international institutions. Granted, many Schmittian realists shun institutional reforms, perhaps regarding any engagement with existing institutions as giving in to the enemy. But if calling for such (continued) reform seems too mundane a conclusion in an age when even international lawyers are losing faith in the secular[88] – well, it can always be redescribed in the messianic language of present imperfection merely highlighting the brightness of law's promise:[89] international law as a self-correcting, secular project whose meaning would nonetheless be given by a horizon of transcendence.

NOTES

1. Bruno Simma and Andreas Paulus, "The 'International Community' Facing the Challenge of Globalization," *European Journal of International Law* 9 (1998): 274.
2. Antonio Cassese, *International Law* (Oxford: Oxford University Press, 2002), 45.
3. For a brief overview of the discussion, see Von Brun-Otto Bryde, "Konstitutionalisierung des Völkerrechts und internationalisierung des Verfassungsrechts," *Der Staat* 42 (2003): 61–76. For the tradition of reading of UN Charter as a constitutional document, see Andreas Paulus, *Die internationale Gemeinschaft im Völkerrecht. Eine Untersuchung zur Entwicklung des Völkerrechts im Zeitalter der Globalisierung* (Munich: Beck, 2001), 292–318.
4. Jürgen Habermas, "Interpreting the Fall of a Monument," *German Law Journal* 4 (2003): 706.
5. For Schmitt's reflections on the change wrought on the nature and regulation of warfare by air power, see Carl Schmitt, *Der Nomos der Erde im Völkerrecht der Jus Publicum Europaeum* (Berlin: Duncker & Humblot, 1988 [1950]), 293–8.
6. See, e.g., Giorgio Agamben, *État d'exception* (Paris: Seuil, 2003), 12–14, 41; Etienne Balibar, *L'Europe, l'Amerique, la guerre. Réflexions sur la médiation européenne* (Paris: Découvert, 2003), 141–57; Michael Hardt and Antonio Negri, *Empire* (Cambridge, MA: Harvard University Press, 2000), p. 16–17. See also the remarks by Jürgen Habermas and Jacques Derrida in Giovanna Borradori, ed., *Philosophy in a Time of Terror: Dialogues with Jürgen Habermas and Jacques Derrida* (Chicago: Chicago University Press, 2003), 38, 53–54, 100–102. Schmittian analysis also informs the useful Ulrich K. Preuss, *Krieg, Verbrechen, Blasphemie. Zum bewaffneten Gewalt* (Berlin: Wagenboch, 2002), esp. 43–48, as well as Günter Frankenberg, *Autorität und Integration. Zur Grammatik von Recht und Verfassung* (Frankfurt: Suhrkamp, 2003), 13–45. Among international lawyers, these themes are highlighted, e.g., in Frédéric Mégret, "War: Legal Semantics and the Turn to Violence," *European Journal of International Law* 12 (2002): 361–400; Gregor Noll, "Force, Partisanship, Dislocation: An Essay on International Law in the State of the Exceptional" and Jarna Petman, "The Problem of Evil in International Law" in Jarna Petman and Jan Klabbers, *Nordic Cosmopolitanism: Essays in International law for Martti Koskenniemi* (Leiden: Nijhoff, 2003), 207, 212–19; 126–28.
7. See section IV below.
8. Jan-Werner Müller, *A Dangerous Mind: Carl Schmitt in Post-war European Thought* (New Haven: Yale University Press, 2003), 88.

9. A French edition was published in 2001 as Carl Schmitt, *Le nomos de la terre*, tr. Liliyane Deroch-Gurcel, rev. and ed. Peter Haggenmacher (Paris: PUF, 2001).

10. See Wilhelm Grewe, *Epochen des Völkerrechts* (Berlin: de Gruyter, 1986), tr: *Epochs of International Law* (Berlin: de Gruyter, 2000). In 1948, Schmitt held Grewe to be the "foremost German international lawyer." Carl Schmitt, *Glossarium. Aufzeichnungen des Jahres 1947–1951* (Berlin: Duncker & Humblot, 1995), 203. For reviews highlighting the Schmittian perspective of Grewe's formidable history of international law, see Bardo Fassbender, "Stories of War and Peace: On Writing the History of International Law in the Third Reich and After," *European Journal of International Law* 13 (2002): 479–512 and Martti Koskenniemi, "Review of Grewe, Epochs of International Law," *Kritische Justiz* (2002): 277–81. The "hegemonic" perspective appears also in Karl-Heinz Ziegler, *Völkerrechtsgeschichte* (Munich: Beck, 1994).

11. See generally Martti Koskenniemi, *The Gentle Civilizer of Nations: The Rise and Fall of International Law 1879–1960* (Cambridge: Cambridge University Press, 2001), 413–509.

12. In this regard, my reading follows the "theological" interpretation of Schmitt's work, as influentially proposed in Heinrich Meier, *Carl Schmitt and Leo Strauss: The Hidden Dialogue*, tr. J. Harvey Lomax, foreward Joseph Cropsey (Chicago: University of Chicago Press, 1995) and *The Lesson of Carl Schmitt: Four Chapters on the Distinction between Political Theology and Political* Philosophy, tr. Marcus Brainard (Chicago: University of Chicago Press, 1998).

13. Schmitt, *Nomos*, 158. The dating here is odd. Modern histories of war do stress the limited and "institutional" nature of late-seventeenth- and early-eighteenth-century wars, while the post-Napoleonic era already captures mass armies motivated by nationalist ideas where "the purpose of the battle was to annihilate the enemy, not force him to surrender" – a "descent into total war." K.J. Holsti, *State, War, and the State of War* (Cambridge: Cambridge University Press, 1996), 33.

14. Schmitt, *Nomos*, 159.

15. Carl Schmitt, *Political Theology: Four Chapters on the Concept of Sovereignty*, tr. George Schwab (Cambridge, MA: MIT Press, 1985), 36.

16. Robert Redslob, *L'Histoire des grands principes de droit des gens* (Paris: Rousseau, 1923).

17. Schmitt's "concrete-order thinking" as a jurisprudential doctrine was expounded in his 1934 work *Über die drei Arten des rechtswissenschaftlichen Denkens*, 2e (Berlin: Duncker & Humblot, 1993).

18. See Carl Schmitt, "The Plight of European Jurisprudence" (from *Die Lage der europäischen Rechtswissenschaft*, 1943/44), *Telos* 83 (1990): 49. This aspect is usefully emphasised in Reinhard Mehling, *Carl Schmitt zur Einführung* (Hamburg: Junius, 2001) as well as William E. Scheuerman, *Carl Schmitt: The End of Law* (Boston: Rowman & Littlefield, 1999). Likewise Agostino Carrino, "Carl Schmitt and European Juridical Science," in Chantal Mouffe, ed., *The Challenge of Carl Schmitt* (London: Verso, 1999), 180–190.

19. See in particular Carl Schmitt, *Legalität und Legitimität* (Berlin: Duncker & Humblot, Berlin 1988 [1932]).

20. Schmitt, "The Plight of European Jurisprudence," 49.

21. Ibid. The article ends in an emphasis on Savigny's contemporary importance.

22. Carl Schmitt, *The Concept of the Political*, tr. and intr. George Schwab (Chicago: University of Chicago Press, 1996), 19.

23. Schmitt, *Nomos*, p. 13–20.

24. For Schmitt, the sea was always a principle specific for an umlimited, commercial and thus typically "British" and later "Anglo-American" order, in tension with the continent. See Schmitt, *Nomos*, 144–156 and "Das Meer gegen das Land" as well as "Staatlicher Souveränität und freies Meer. Über der Gegensatz von Land und See in Völkerrecht der Neuzeit"in *Staat, Grossraum, Nomos. Arbeiten aus den Jahren 1916–1969* (Berlin: Duncker & Humblot 1995), 395–400; 401–30.

25. Schmitt, *Nomos*, 112 and *passim*.

26. Ibid., 96.

27. Ibid., 142–52.

28. The unlimited nature of the warfare by the colonial powers outside Europe has been challenged in Jörg Fisch, *Die europäische Expansion und das Völkerrecht* (Stuttgart: Steiner, 1984).

29. G.F. de Martens, *Précis du droit des gens moderne de l'Europe, précedé d'une Introduction et completé par l'exposition des doctrines des publicistes contemporains et suivi d'une Bibliographie raisonnée du droit des gens par M. Ch. Vergé*, 2e[nd] (Paris: Guillaumin, 1864); J.L. Klüber, *Droit des gens moderne de l'Europe* (Stuttgart: J.G. Cotta, 1819).

30. Scheuerman, *Carl Schmitt*, 178–79.

31. See further Koskenniemi, *The Gentle Civilizer*, 19–28. See also Edward Keene, *Beyond the Anarchical Society: Grotius, Colonialism and Order in World Politics* (Cambridge University Press, 2002), 14–22.

32. Schmitt is not quite consistent in dating his system. These dates appear at *Nomos*, 150.

33. The interpretation of the Catholic Church is contained in Carl Schmitt, *Roman Catholicism and Political Form* (New York: Greenwood, 1996). The link between classical balance of power and domestic absolutism is often made. See, e.g., Paul W. Schroeder, *The Transformation of European Politics 1763–1848* (Oxford: Oxford University Press, 1994), 5–11.

34. Thus, for example, Schmitt's ironic remark that as the Jacobins attacked the *Kabinettkrieg* of the *ancien règime*, they paved the way for the *levée en masse* and total war, *Nomos*, 122–123.

35. Martin van Creveld, *The Rise and Decline of the State* (Cambridge: Cambridge University Press, 1999), 143–47.

36. Ernst H. Kantorowicz, *The King's Two Bodies: A Study of Mediaeval Political Theology*, with a new preface by William Chester Jordan (Princeton: Princeton University Press, 1997 [1958]), 9. Such a "taking over of theological notions for defining the state" – a "transference of definitions from one sphere to another, from theology to law [was] anything but surprising or even remarkable" (19).

37. This is the form Schmitt seeks to rehabilitate in *Political Theology*, 30–35 and 55–66.

38. See Koskenniemi, *The Gentle Civilizer*, 116 et seq, 143–66, and the still useful Julius Goebel, *The Struggle for the Falkland Islands* (New Haven: Yale University Press, 1927), esp. 47–173.

39. See the discussion of *Nomos* in Schmitt, *Über drei Arten*, 13. The way Nomos included both the original act of land-taking and its recognized continuation in time repeated, for Schmitt, the contrast between *pouvoir constituant* and *pouvoir constitué*, both of which he included here, as elsewhere, within his material notion of *Recht*, Schmitt, *Nomos*, 50–51.

40. Hagen Schulze, *States, Nations, Nationalism* (Oxford: Blackwell, 1996), 27.

41. Schmitt, *Nomos*, 16–17, 49.

42. See the very useful Justin Rosenberg, *The Empire of Civil Society* (London: Verso, 1994), 83–90, 126–29.

43. Perry Anderson, *Lineages of the Absolutist State* (London: Verso, 1976), 24–29.

44. Rosenberg, *Empire of Civil Society*, 127.

45. Schmitt, *Political Theology*, 48–9.

46. F.H. Hinsley, *Sovereignty*, 2e (Cambridge: Cambridge University Press, 1986), 158.

47. See Schmitt, *Die Diktatur*, 4e (Berlin: Duncker & Humblot, 1977 [1921]).

48. Schmitt, *Political Theology*, 17.

49. See especially Meier, *Lesson*, 1–25 and section IV below.

50. Schmitt, *Political Theology*, 8–10, 12.

51. Schmitt, *Concept of the Political*, 68.

52. Schmitt, *Political Theology*, 36–37.

53. For these tendencies, see, e.g., Mireille Delmas-Marty, *Trois défis pour un droit mondial* (Paris: Seuil 1998) or the various essays in Michael Byers, ed., *The Role of Law in International Politics* (Oxford: Oxford University Press, 2000). I discuss these at some length in Martti Koskenniemi, "International Law and Hegemony. A Reconfiguration," *Cambridge Review of International Affairs* 17 (2004): 197–218.

54. Mark Lilla, *The Reckless Mind. Intellectuals in Politics* (New York: New York Review of Books, 2001), 62.

55. Schmitt, *Über drei Arten*, 20–24.

56. See, e.g., Robert D. Kaplan, *Warrior Politics. Why Leadership Demands a Pagan Ethos* (New York: Vintage, 2003).

57. Schmitt, "L'Unité du monde" (1951), in *Du politique. Légitimité et légalité et autres essais* (Puiseux: Pardès, 1990), 244–49.

58. See on this esp. Meier, *The Lesson*, 158–173.

59. Ibid., 24.

60. Schmitt, "Unité du Monde," 248 (emphasis in the text).

61. 1 Thessalonians 5:3.

62. Carl Schmitt, *Die Wendung zum diskriminierenden Kriegsbegriff* (Berlin: Duncker & Humblot, 1988 [1938]).

63. Schmitt, *Wendung*, 2–5.

64. I have discussed the views of the two at length in Koskenniemi, *Gentle Civilizer*, 266 et seq., 327–38 (Scelle) and 353–412 (Lauterpacht).

65. Georges Scelle, *Précis du droit des gens*, 2 vols. (Paris: Sirey, 1932, 1934), I: 2–5.

66. This did not mean that anyone who disapproved of particular legislation could ignore it. Legislation enjoyed the presumption of being in accordance with the objective law (*hypothèse de bien légiféré*). Cf. Scelle, Précis, II: 297–99.

67. Scelle, "Théorie du gouvernment international," *Annuaire de l'Institut de droit public* (1935): 66.

68. Scelle, *Précis*, I: 9–14.

69. Cf. Scelle, "Théorie du gouvernment international," 54–57 and Antonio Cassese, "Remarks on Scelle's Theory of 'Role Splitting' (*dédoublement fonctionnel*) in International Law," *European Journal of International Law* 1 (1990) 210–34.

70. Hersch Lauterpacht, *Private Law Sources and Analogies of International Law* (London: Longmans, 1927) and *The Function of Law in the International Community* (Oxford: Clarendon, 1933).

71. Lauterpacht, "The Reality of the Law of Nations," in *International Law: Being the Collected Papers of Sir Hersch Lauterpacht*, 4 vols. (Cambridge: Cambridge University Press, 1970–1978), II: 26.

72. For a recent example, see Pierre-Marie Dupuy, *L'Unité de l'ordre juridique international. Cours général de droit international public*, 297 Recueil des Cours de l'Académie de droit international (Leiden: Nijhoff, 2003), esp. 207–399.

73. See my discussion in *Gentle Civilizer*, 316–27 and 338–42.

74. Schmitt, *Concept of the Political*, 61.

75. For Schmitt, after a period of hesitation, the political decision requires that one be "able to distinguish *correctly* the *real* friend and *real* enemy," *Concept of the Political*, 37 (emphases mine) and see comment in Meier, *Lesson*, 26–27.

76. See Hersch Lauterpacht, "The Grotian Tradition in International Law," *The British Year Book of International Law* XXIII. (1946): 1–53. See my analysis in *Gentle Civilizer*, 406–11.

77. Koskenniemi, "Lauterpacht: The Victorian Tradition in International Law," *European Journal of International law* 8 (1997): 215–63 and *Gentle Civilizer*, 353–412.

78. This is the great problem of the morality of "values" or of "human rights." On the one hand they are, as Michael J. Perry argues, "ineliminably religious." On the other hand, their raison d'être is precisely to replace the vacuum created by the absence of faith. See Perry, *The Idea of Human Rights. Four Inquiries* (Oxford: Oxford University Press, 1998), 11–41. For their inherent secularism, however, see Luc Ferry, *L'Homme-dieu ou le Sens de la vie* (Paris: Grasset, 1996).

79. For the opposition of "rational" and "cynical" empire, see my *Gentle Civilizer*, 489–94.

80. Francisco de Vitoria, *On the American Indians (De indis*, 1539*)*, in *Political Writings*, ed. Anthony Pagden and Jeremy Lawrance (Cambridge: Cambridge University Press, 1991), 235–37.

81. The is the explanation usually voiced to support American opposition to international organization: why would the US need to adhere to the wishes of often undemocratic regimes?

82. Something I have elaborated elsewhere. See Martti Koskenniemi, *From Apology to Utopia: The Structure of International Legal Argument* (Helsinki: Finnish Lawyers' Publishing, 1989).

83. See the discussion of the various left and right Schmittian reactions against the liberal universalism of "globalization" in Müller, *A Dangerous Mind*, 222–43.

84. Jürgen Habermas, "Kant's Idea of Perpetual Peace, with the Benefit of Two Hundred Years' Hindsight," in James Bohmann and Matthias Lutz-Bachmann, *Perpetual Peace: Essays on Kant's Cosmopolitan Ideal* (Cambridge, MA: MIT Press, 1996), 146.

85. Ibid., 147.

86. Habermas in Borradori, *Philosophy in a Time of Terror*, 42.

87. See famously, Jean-Francois Lyotard, *The Differend. Phrases in Dispute* (Minneapolis: University of Minnesota Press, 1988).

88. See David Kennedy, "Losing Faith in the Secular: Law, Religion and the Culture of International Governance," in Mark Janis and Carolyn Evans, eds., *Religion and International Law* (1999), 309–19.

89. See also Koskenniemi, "What is International Law For?" in Malcolm Evans, ed., *International Law* (Oxford: Oxford University Press, 2003), 105–11.

Martti Koskenniemi is Professor of International Law at the University of Helsinki, Global Professor of Law at New York University, and Member of the UN International Law Commission. He is the author of *From Apology to Utopia: The Structure of International Legal Argument* (1989) and *The Gentle Civilizer of Nations: The Rise and Fall of International Law, 1870–1960* (2001).

[23]

The Rule of Law in Transition: Revisiting Franz Neumann's Sociology of Legality

ROGER COTTERRELL

Queen Mary and Westfield College, University of London

THE RULE OF LAW is a concept with which so many writers have wrestled that it might be thought that little remains to be said. This article adopts a special focus to try to develop some manageable and relatively neglected themes in a vast, much discussed subject. It takes, as a basis, central ideas from the German jurist Franz Neumann's important but still insufficiently discussed work[1] on the Rule of Law and tries to pursue a tentative but specific inquiry in the spirit of Neumann.[2]

Neumann's historical study of the Rule of Law (1986; and see 1957), written in the 1930s, was strongly coloured by the experience of the constitutional turmoil of the Weimar Republic through which he had lived and worked as a practising lawyer and law teacher (see also Kirchheimer and Neumann, 1987). His work was concerned, in part, with exploring the changing social and political contexts in which the Rule of Law ideal, variously interpreted in different nations but with a certain common core of meaning, was invoked. For Neumann, it was important to emphasize in legal theory the emergence of a distinctively modern form of society – such as that of Germany of the 1920s but exemplified in important aspects by advanced western industrial nations in general – in which corporate organization of life had acquired important new forms. In this kind of society, which we might call 'corporate society', social and economic change, and especially the growth of monopolistic corporate economic power, had, in Neumann's view, undermined radically some of the most crucial social assumptions on which the ideal of the Rule of Law had been founded.

This article attempts three things: first, it tries to suggest in the idea of the Rule of Law a core of meaning reflecting the universal social as well as legal importance attached to this idea – whatever name is given to it in the various languages of western Europe. Second, it speculates as to how Neumann's thesis about the changing social conditions of existence of the Rule of Law in the modern (corporate) society of his time might be assessed and reinterpreted in the light of recent characterizations of contemporary (or, according to familiar current terminology, postmodern) western societies. Finally, it suggests how traditional thinking about the Rule of Law might be modified to take account of certain changed social and economic conditions of legal regulation in contemporary advanced western societies; conditions which can be directly related to those Neumann analysed. What follows is admittedly tentative: limited by space and time and the fact that any theoretical discussion, however confined, of the Rule of Law must cover much ground and refer to a very wide range of legal and social experience.

DIMENSIONS OF THE RULE OF LAW

The English idea of the Rule of Law seems to combine central elements of the German *Rechtssicherheit* (legal certainty or security) and *Rechtsstaat*[3] (legally regulated state) and related concepts in other legal systems (see Aubert, 1989: 66ff). For Neumann, the essence of the Rule of Law was the fusion or reconciliation of two vital elements of law which he termed *voluntas* and *ratio* (Neumann, 1986: 45–6; 1944: 440ff, 451–2; 1957: 26ff). *Voluntas* refers to the political authority which gives law its power of command, its non-optional, politically enforceable status. *Ratio* refers to the broad rationality of legal doctrine, the quality that makes it possible to reason with and analyse legal ideas in a principled and general way. Thus, the Rule of Law refers, for Neumann, to law that is not only reliably enforced but also general in application, applied uniformly to all cases within its terms. It is, therefore, predictable and calculable in its general consequences, permitting a sphere of freedom to the citizen. The Rule of Law is thus the enemy of particularistic regulation and administrative discretion.

Dicey's much earlier English statement of the Rule of Law (Dicey, 1959) has been strikingly called an 'unfortunate outburst of Anglo-Saxon parochialism' (Shklar, 1987: 5). Rather than prefiguring Neumann's abstract formulation of elements of a Rule of Law that might unite various meanings of the term in different western legal systems, Dicey had focused on specific features of the English common law as the essence of the Rule of Law. He gives the idea of generality of law a particular twist. Not only must law apply generally to citizens but they must be able to enforce all of their legal rights through a uniform system of ordinary common law courts (Dicey, 1959: 193–5). The stress on generality here becomes a prohibition on specialized expertise, for in Dicey's view continental administrative courts, with their special jurisdictions, are the enemy of the Rule of Law. General courts of common law can deal with the threat to liberties posed by administration.

In Dicey's vision, judges and the general common law principles they serve are ranged against executive discretion (see 1959: 188). Common-law judges as 'experts in non-expertise' (Kirchheimer, 1967: 435) are qualified as protectors of civil society – the common law community – from state infringement of the negative liberties of citizens. Courts express, as a by-product of their decisions on individual rights, the fundamental principles of the constitution. Common-law thought, developed in everyday judicial practice, sustains an environment of legal culture in which the problem of executive lawlessness has been largely dispelled. The 'rule, predominance, or supremacy of law' is 'the distinguishing characteristic of English institutions' (Dicey, 1959: 187). The implication seems to be that somehow *only* common-law courts can achieve such a happy state. And behind this implication seems to lie the familiar common-law mythology that puts the judge (merely by virtue of *being* a judge) in the centre of a notional moral and national community, as both its protector and spokesperson (see Postema, 1986: 32; Cotterrell, 1989: 33–5).

One great value of Franz Neumann's work for a British lawyer ought to lie in making it possible to hold Dicey at a distance and think of the Rule of Law in broader, less parochial terms. Neumann's writing portrays the long historical evolution of the *Rechtsstaat* and of the idea of government subject to law. In a similar context Judith Shklar (1987) has emphasized two contrasting themes running through the history of Rule of Law ideas.[4] One of these themes, which she traces to Montesquieu, is that of institutional restraints on government. The other, associated with Aristotle, is that of the Rule of Law as the 'rule of reason'.

The Aristotelian Rule of Law has vast ethical and intellectual scope ('an entire way of life') (Shklar, 1987: 1), but applies only to a limited range of persons who are (as office-holding citizens) full participants in the collective organization of the polity (see Barker, 1946: 93–5). It is concerned with the need to organize life collectively in a principled manner and seems indirectly reflected, for example, in Ronald Dworkin's contemporary conception of the Rule of Law as primarily embodied in the principled decision-making of courts (1978; 1986: 93–4). By contrast, Montesquieu's Rule of Law refers to 'a limited number of protective arrangements which are, however, meant to benefit every member of the society, though only in a few of their mutual relations' (Shklar, 1987: 2). These protective arrangements provide security against arbitrary exercises of discretionary power by government. But they are intended to protect also, indirectly, against other citizens and collectivities, insofar as the law that defines individual rights and duties is made secure from invasion by arbitrary discretions.

Montesquieu's version tends to dominate in lawyers' thought about the Rule of Law, since it emphasizes controlling rules and regulated institutions

– the kind of matters of planned social arrangements with which lawyers are typically most comfortable. But I argue that part of the problem of adjusting expectations of the Rule of Law to contemporary conditions lies in the need to recover the interrelation between the two directions of Rule of Law thought that Shklar usefully distinguishes.

The Rule of Law is the 'will-o'-the-wisp of political history' (Hutchinson and Monahan, 1987: ix). It is claimed as an 'unqualified human good' (Thompson, 1975: 266), yet is said to be almost impossible to explain without raising a doubt that it still exists as a practical virtue (Nonet, 1987: 127). No interest group is organized specifically to support it (Lowi, 1987: 56). If this is its situation, the reason may be that the Aristotelian version of the Rule of Law seems to entail such difficult challenges to deliver principle in an unprincipled world that only a few of the most ambitious philosophers now accept these challenges, and never with uncontroversial results. At the same time, Montesquieu's version of the Rule of Law demands protective arrangements that seem inadequate on at least two fronts.

On the one hand, they seem inadequate because their failure to safeguard citizens generally against arbitrary power appears increasingly transparent. The Rule of Law does not provide, at least for substantial sections of the population and in significant circumstances, the protection against governmental discretion, in the broadest sense, that is its apparent *raison d'être*. On the other hand, the emphasis on protection from public power through checks and balances in government and the limitation of governmental regulatory authority seems to ignore – or at least fail to address directly – problems of *private* power which are of no less significance for individual security, in particular the power of corporate capital to shape the lives of individuals, as consumers and employees as well as citizens.

In such circumstances a sense of insecurity may arise not from any disregard of the virtues of protective arrangements such as those associated with Montesquieu's version of the Rule of Law. It arises more typically from the apparent impossibility of applying the idea of the Rule of Law to important contexts in which relations of power require stabilization through regulation.

In contexts of social life where traditional regulation in the form of stable, relatively general rules operates, the Rule of Law often seems to represent an experienced reality. This will often be the case in the protection of traditional property entitlements and private transactions in a stable civil society not subject to restructuring on the basis of radical redistributive policies. So too, the reality of the Rule of Law is recognizable in the sense of general security felt at least in neighbourhoods where policing is considered to be 'by consent' and police discretions are exercised in 'reasonable' ways in the spirit of legal rules seen as maintaining a consensually supported status quo. The Rule of Law as limited but universal protective arrangements seems in general to remain a meaningful idea at least where the pace of regulatory change is slow, where populations are homogeneous and cases of conflict or dispute and claims of entitlement are relatively standardized, and where the values underlying regulation are generally understood and approved by the regulated population as a whole.

Over time, however, the images of law and society which could sustain a faith in the Rule of Law have been changing. Regulation now takes a wide variety of forms and is expected to do so. At one extreme it tends towards detailed technical prescriptions applicable to very specific cases; at the other it embraces the broadest, most open discretions. The lines between law and administration, and between legal and technical standards, seem to become increasingly hazy, and this development is no longer seen as a matter of aberrations which lawyers have long criticized but as a defining component of a changed general perception of legality (Cotterrell, 1995: ch. 13). Thus, in many fields of welfare or public-order regulation, it is assumed that governmental strategy can be expressed in almost any regulatory form, however technical and narrowly focused or however open and permissory it may be in controlling official actions. The Rule of Law remains theoretically intact as the presence of legal controls, 'protective arrangements' against unlawful applications of power. Yet much regulation slips through the guarantees of the Rule of Law, like sand through the fingers, because it seems impossible to say conclusively how general or how specific a lawfully established legal precept must be to be consistent with the Rule of Law's protective arrangements. The diversity and flexibility of contemporary regulatory forms make the practical meaning of the Rule of Law increasingly indeterminate.

Accompanying this general perception of change in the character of regulation is the sense of a significant pattern in the social contexts in which different kinds of regulation are used – a sense that the kinds of setting in which particular forms of regulation are often applied are not random but betray a sociological consistency. Typically, the more particularistic and discretionary forms of regulation are applied extensively, though certainly not exclusively, to areas beyond the assumed stable core of civil society. They are applied to what may be seen by government and lawmakers as 'problem populations', defined as appropriate objects of regulation. These regulatory forms tend to operate especially in areas where implementation of policy seems too urgent a matter to be trammelled routinely by clear rules, general in application; where direct and precise control of action may be more important than guiding citizens' autonomous decision-making; and where traditional ideas of legal protection may even seem a hindrance to effective resolution of pressing governmental tasks.

REINTERPRETING CORPORATE SOCIETY

One way to approach these issues is through Neumann's thesis on the Rule of Law. Neumann tried to relate the legal ideal of the Rule of Law to a specific historical context. Influenced by Max Weber, he linked the rise of the legal rational state, the *Rechtsstaat*, with the development of entrepreneurial capitalism. The competitive society of commodity traders and freely interacting property owners was favoured by the Rule of Law, which provided security of property holding and calculability and predictability in the legal consequences of transactions.[5] Neumann saw, controversially, the doctrine of precedent in the common law as providing the kind of legal security established in continental Europe by rational legal codes (1986: 241ff). It may be doubted whether he was any more successful than Weber in identifying a consistent link between the development of capitalistic economic activity and the establishment of a particular form of law. His interest, however, was not so much with the character of legal doctrine as with the more general values associated with it, which emphasized legal security and predictability, and non-intervention in private activity except insofar as necessary to secure a framework of known rules.

Accordingly, the Rule of Law supported the extension of markets, free access to them by entrepreneurs, the guarantee of general peace and security in which to trade and accumulate capital, and the security of capital acquisitions. Alongside its economic significance, the Rule of Law, in Neumann's view, enshrined virtues transcending the needs of the competitive society of entrepreneurial capitalism. It embodied an ideal of liberty that is of enduring value. Cherishing the legal conditions of individual freedom, the Rule of Law became, in the words of later writers, 'the central jewel in liberalism's crown' (Hutchinson and Monahan, 1987: ix).

The transition from the competitive society of entrepreneurial capitalism to a corporate society[6] of monopoly capitalism, dominated by cartels, giant business enterprises and other mass organizations, marked, in Neumann's analysis, conditions of crisis for the liberty-creating role of the Rule of Law. In a society no longer to be thought of as composed mainly of freely interrelating individuals, but rather as increasingly shaped by corporate interests and commitments powerfully influencing the conditions of life of citizens, the ideal of the generality of law favoured the corporate interest at the expense of the individual.

The Rule of Law emphasizes formal, not substantive, equality. Thus, in Neumann's view, it served the ends of equal liberty where the economic and social power of legal actors was not so unbalanced that formal legal equality and reliance on equal rights would merely entrench substantive inequality. In entrepreneurial capitalism the Rule of Law embraced the entire bourgeois class even if it failed to reach subordinate classes. But in modern society, the enfranchisement as citizens of those who had earlier been excluded from legal protection within the polity brought their demands for legal security and liberty into the political arena. At the same time, the concentration of capital in corporate structures removed the social conditions that had enabled the formal legal equality enshrined in the Rule of Law to parallel and promote a reasonable substantive equality in the life chances of citizens.

Corporations and cartels could benefit from the Rule of Law to protect their property and hence their economic power. They could use this power freely in bargaining and contracting with citizens and could counter government efforts to control it through special regulation, insofar as this regulation would fall foul of the corporation's right, as a legal person, to be treated legally in the same way as individual citizens. Thus, corporations could resist expropriation or other interference with their property using the same arguments that individual citizens might use – arguments grounded in the sanctity of individual liberty protected by the Rule of Law (see Kirchheimer, 1983).

The term *corporate society*, while useful to encompass what Neumann saw as defining conditions of modern society, seems inadequate today. 'Corporate' implies only certain aspects of the complexity of contemporary life and not necessarily the most significant. Indeed, the tendency today is to view corporate power more neutrally, not condemning or praising but treating it as socially inevitable. Power in general tends to be thought of in more positive terms than it was by Neumann during and immediately after the Weimar years. Again, aspects of corporate organization that were familiar to Neumann have become less so today. Trade unions, for example, play a less prominent role in social life in many contemporary western societies. And we tend to think in terms of disorganized capitalism (see Offe, 1985), recognizing a much less homogeneous economic organization than seemed apparent to radical social critics of Neumann's time. We speak less of corporate society than of consumer society, with its implications of individuals united only in their purchasing situation (Baumann, 1992: 49–53) and having a realm of individual choice that invalidates the idea of homogeneity produced by corporate constraints.

Nevertheless, the idea of corporate society remains important if supplemented appropriately. The consumer society is, after all, a society where what is chosen for consumption is, to a considerable extent, what is offered and promoted by corporate interests. Kinds of corporate economic structures that were familiar in Weimar times still exist, although their forms may have changed. But they must now be reconsidered in a much more international perspective. Their power is no longer shielded so much by Rule of Law principles of the nation state as by transnational economic imperatives that constrain state lawmakers.[7] Powerful nation states themselves can be regarded as pursuing their own corporate interests as political societies, sometimes through extraterritorial law enforcement, for example, in the imposition of terms in contracts of supply to contractors in other countries, whose freedom to resell products is thereby restricted as a condition of contracting. Again the political, and even military, power of nations is sometimes used to protect the nation's economic interests abroad, for example, as represented through multinational corporations, and to restrict the ability of less powerful states to control these corporations. In such ways the dominance of individual life by corporate interests may be made even harder to counter than the Rule of Law ideology seemed to Neumann to make it in Weimar times.

Correspondingly, however, corporate characteristics of other aspects of social organization have lost prominence since Neumann wrote. The privatization of life is reflected in the reduced influence of organized mutual welfare associations as foci of collective action. Postmodern society is held to be characterized in part by the decline of stable collective loyalties and the fragmentation of moral and political organization into loose, continually shifting interest group activity (Baumann, 1992: 181–3). The ideology of individual choice is seen to replace that of moral allegiance. The political party composed of committed activists dissolves into a myriad of single issue groups; national involvement transmutes into more local (or even merely individual) concern. The individual life is portrayed as increasingly atomistic. More may be known about the intimate personal circumstances of media stars and politicians (and, in Britain, at least, royalty) than about the lives of immediate neighbours. The moral bonds linking individuals into collectivities seem to weaken in the most rapidly developing patterns of contemporary social life, as sociological research has shown (Baumgartner, 1988).

Yet most of these developments can be seen as an extension rather than a reversal of the tendencies which Neumann and others associated with modern society. The political ideology of consumer choice offers a strictly limited perspective on social relations in a society dominated by corporate interests, which can express themselves far more effectively today than in Neumann's era. Corporate interests that dominate a market often seek to narrow the range of choice available to the consumer and standardize consumer demand so as to minimize corporate risk. The alliance between the public corporate interests of the state and the private corporate interests of capital, which Neumann emphasizes, is no less relevant than in his time. It is now cemented through the promotion of the ideology of the free market as both a political project (symbolizing political freedom) and an economic one (symbolizing future wealth). Half a century ago, Theodor Adorno and Max Horkheimer wrote of the 'world of the administered life' – a society structured by an alliance of bureaucracy and technology extending its normalizing controls into all aspects of social and cultural life (Adorno and Horkheimer, 1986). Today the notion of the administered life seems largely fused with a more general idea of 'mass society' – a society of homogeneous tastes and shared outlooks, promoted by global mass media controlled by a limited number of corporate organizations. The seemingly atomistic society of individual consumers thus exists alongside – indeed, as the other side of the coin from – the vast extension of Neumann's society of corporate interests.

LEGALITY IN CONTEMPORARY SOCIETY

Writers on postmodernity frequently portray contemporary western societies as marked by a profound loss of faith in the underpinnings of modernity. Five such underpinnings, in particular, might be identified: first, science as the intellectual basis of modernity; second, economic expansion as its material basis; third, the nation state as its affective, cultural basis; fourth, historical progress as its inspirational basis; and fifth, humanist and individualist morality as its moral basis. Modern law could be seen to a large extent as the instrument of all of these aspects of modernity; the expression, in part, of all of these foundations of modern life. In the perspective of *post*modernity, however, law tends to be seen as set free from the projects of modernity, which no longer appear as convincing underpinnings or justifications of legal regulation.

In this perspective, the situation of law seems profoundly ambiguous. Legal regulation is ubiquitous yet morally and culturally empty. For example, Jack Balkin, writing about United States constitutional law, remarks on the almost total divorce between, on the one hand, the prosaic, pragmatic practices of constitutional adjudication in the current United States Supreme Court and, on the other, the attempts of academic constitutional commentators to elaborate profound cultural meanings of the American constitution (Balkin, 1992: 1985–6). While philosophical efforts are made to infuse law with moral meaning, the reality of law as practised, produced and elaborated in the business of contemporary government is extremely mundane. In the most pessimistic postmodern views, law may be all there is to believe in. But that is not much, if something of greater cultural significance is sought than the endlessly pragmatic adjustment of regulation to increasing social complexity.

In particular, law is not much to believe in if what is held out as the object of belief is Montesquieu's version of the Rule of Law, as characterized by Shklar. We noted, earlier, the apparent inadequacy of this idea both in the light of perceived changes in the character of regulation – in the very image of legality that prevails (see Cotterrell, 1995: ch. 13) – and in the light of perceived social discrimination; that is, in the seemingly patterned application of different kinds of regulation to different kinds of social population.

If, however, we build on some of Neumann's themes, the vistas of so-called postmodern law and society can be approached with less hopelessness than many postmodernist analyses convey. The first matter of importance is to notice, as Neumann did, the Rule of Law's 'decisive ethical function' (1986: 256–7; 1957: 42). The Rule of Law implies not just specific political contexts or institutional structures but an appeal to transcendent *ideals*, which do not derive their validity from specific social conditions but are worth pursuing whatever the social context.

The moral essence of the Rule of Law in this sense lies in three values: equality, individual autonomy and security (Bobbio, 1987: 143–4). Equality refers mainly to procedural equality, or fair and equal governmental treatment of citizens; not to equal treatment of citizens in terms of substantive benefits. Individual autonomy refers to the treatment of the citizen as an independent, freely reasoning being, responsible personally for, but only for, his or her own rationally chosen actions and inactions. This value is typically expressed through the insistence that ignorance of the law is no excuse, through the requirement of intention (*mens rea*) generally in criminal law, and through the assumption that the discretion in action denied to government by the Rule of Law is available to citizens as the range of free decision left to them by clear general rules. Security, the third transcendent value of the Rule of Law, may be expressed in many other terms: as certainty, predictability, order or safety (see Aubert, 1989: 76). The guarantee to citizens of security, for example, of transactions, of property or of liberty, is one to which the state commits itself[8] by limiting its regulation to general, abstract rules.

The enduring project of the Rule of Law should be to promote these values even in the changed conditions of contemporary social life. Each of them, however, is challenged by contemporary conditions in a way that goes significantly beyond the challenges Neumann identified in corporate society.

Take first the value of *equality*. Formal equality before the law as an ideal has developed through several broad phases historically. Premodern notions of legal rights as dependent on personal status – itself determined by, for example, class, caste, religion, gender or age – were replaced by the modern idea of formal legal equality of all citizens. But lack of access to courts for subordinate sections of the population meant that the promise of the Rule of Law was mainly realizable only by the middle and upper classes. The class differentials in law application and enforcement in English history described by Weber (1968: 814) illustrate what can be termed the phenomenon of the 'dual state'. This involves the practical restriction of Rule of Law safeguards to certain population categories, and the regulation of other categories by means that do not incorporate such safeguards. But this familiar phenomenon has remained largely underemphasized in most celebrations of the Rule of Law, except when the duality has been instituted formally, even *de jure*, as in apartheid or other politically segregated societies (Shklar, 1987: 2).[9]

In contemporary western societies, particularly those where the institutions of the welfare state are weak or seriously challenged, the establishment of a *de facto* dual state is an ever-present threat. Judith Shklar (1987: 14) sees the reappearance of the dual state in the conditions of formal representative democracy as 'a constant possibility in our century'. It may exist insofar as sections of the population, often identified as a permanent 'underclass', become almost wholly separated, in terms of life-chances, economic resources, practical access to the legal system and political allegiances, from other citizens in civil society.[10] In such conditions their opportunities to benefit from the protections offered by the Rule of Law may be significantly less than those of other population groups.

Lack of resources (not merely economic but also resources of knowledge and of networks of support and aid) may make it very difficult to invoke the protections that the Rule of Law offers. Indeed, the Rule of Law is sometimes seen, from a governmental perspective, as threatened by the very existence of such an 'underclass'.[11] In fact, the term *underclass* seems to define a collective object of regulation rather than individual citizens as autonomous subjects of regulation. Control of the 'underclass' is often thought of from this perspective as an administrative matter no less than one of balancing rights and duties in terms of general legal rules. Consequently, control is achieved, to a significant extent, through a mixture of police and welfare discretions and highly particularized regulation. As noted earlier, these regulatory phenomena are not easily brought within the focus of Rule of Law protections.

Typically lacking any philosophy of action, any real possibility of engaging with the power and resources of law and the state except through isolated confrontations, many of those categorized as the 'underclass' may consider that they have little choice but to make a life substantially outside the scope of legal protections; a life either largely indifferent to the demands of law (living anarchistically) or sometimes calculatedly flouting those demands for purposes of survival (living through crime). What seems relatively new in this state of affairs in advanced western societies in recent times is that the underclass is both defined explicitly out of civil society in a host of ways and includes a great diversity of people who, deliberately, define themselves out. Hence, for this part of the population, the special characteristics of corporate society as well as its postmodern accretions may be largely irrelevant. The contemporary dual state adds to the inequalities of power existing in corporate society the inequalities that arise from the substantial exclusion of whole sections of the population from corporate society itself.

Consider next the Rule of Law's value of *individual autonomy*. The great achievement of liberal thought in what Neumann termed the competitive society of entrepreneurial capitalism was to remove special group statuses and elevate the individual human being as the explicit focus of almost all legal concern. But a recognition of the business corporation as a legal person, whose legal status was to be assimilated to the universal legal status of the individual citizen, made possible legally the inequalities of contractual and property-owning power that Neumann associates with modern (corporate) society (see Cotterrell, 1992: 123–30). Thus, the extension of legal individualism to accommodate the economic importance of the business corporation set in train a legal development, under the cloak of the Rule of Law, that has gradually undermined the legal significance of the autonomy of the individual citizen.[12] The internationalization of corporate power, previously noted, has subsequently further increased this power in ways that mainly escape Neumann's perspective, which is largely restricted to the context of the nation state.

At the same time, the idea that the individual person (whether citizen or business corporation) remains the necessary locus of rights and duties prevents constructive thought along lines that might strengthen the situation of citizens collectively, faced with overbearing concentrations of corporate power and the reinforcement through this power of the homogenizing features of 'mass society'. The value of individuality, as it has typically been interpreted in law, distracts attention from a full recognition of the importance of communities, however defined; groupings that might provide legally sanctioned forms of mutual support and collective action to protect and enhance the conditions of life of their individual members.

The development of corporate society has, as noted earlier, seen the individual's status enhanced as a consumer. But the value of individual autonomy has somehow been turned against itself, in the mass society of consumers, towards a celebration of privatized lifestyles. In contemporary society, economic developments have merely highlighted in new ways the elusiveness of individual autonomy as a legally promoted value.

Finally, consider the value of *security*. Security is provided legally through the consistent use of known rules, procedures and formalities.[13] In the competitive society of small entrepreneurs, legal security, according to Neumann, arises from the maintenance of a stable framework of general rules through which individuals can pursue their own lawful projects. With the emergence of large corporate economic interests, Neumann saw the need for government to act to control and organize these interests, not merely holding the ring but intervening with particularistic regulation to control specific concentrations of corporate power in the general interest of maintaining the security of the individual citizen. Indeed, government *has* increasingly intervened in economic planning and regulation, not necessarily to promote the security of the individual but to stabilize and control national economies, employment patterns, trade and commerce and industry in conditions determined increasingly by the internationalization of the corporate organization of economic life.[14]

This is merely a recent phase in the development of governmental management of society: 'the right disposition of things, arranged so as to lead to a convenient end'.[15] Michel Foucault (1991: 95) suggests that for such management purposes 'the instruments of government, instead of being laws, now come to be a range of multiform tactics'. Whether we call these instruments law or not, they are certainly in no way restricted to general legal rules. A traditional 'core' legal structure of civil society is provided by relatively general rules – clustered in fields of legal doctrine that often continue to be seen as the heart of law for the purposes of the academic education of lawyers. But around this traditional core – the heartland of the Rule of Law – a periphery of different forms of regulation extends. And the periphery seems in practice, if not in academic legal consciousness, to be turning into the core of regulation, while the traditional legal core is displaced to the periphery of regulatory experience for many citizens.

A general threat to the value of security in this state of affairs is the entrenchment of a wholly instrumental view of law and regulation (see Weinrib, 1987: 61). In such a view security is guaranteed not so much by maintenance of a stable framework of general rules as by appropriate ad-hoc regulatory responses to problems. When legality is viewed as an instrumental matter, there is a risk that the values of the Rule of Law themselves will be seen in purely instrumental terms. For example, court decisions identifying illegal acts of government officials and agencies may be treated as creating merely technical problems for government, rather than issues of principle.[16]

What has been previously stated is coloured by a certain interpretation of British experience, but the range of circumstances discussed can be put together to suggest an emerging general contemporary context of the Rule of Law which is not Neumann's corporate society, but recognizably derived from it. This context might be sketched, in necessarily highly schematic terms, as a kind of sociolegal hierarchy, to suggest how it provokes important further questions about the Rule of Law.

At the level of *the state*, contemporary conditions seem to encourage an instrumental view of legal regulation in general so that lines between law and policy, and between legal forms of regulation and other forms, are not only blurred but even increasingly regarded as unimportant. The consequence, when viewed in terms of the requirements of the Rule of Law, is that legality means something very different from what it meant to Neumann or, for that matter, Dicey. Legality as a virtue tends to lose its connection with moral demands rooted in cultural conditions. It becomes almost solely a matter of efficient government regulatory action.

At the level of *civil society*, dominated, on the one hand, by corporate entities and interests and, on the other, by a substantially privatized and atomistic life of individual citizens, law tends to be experienced increasingly as complex technicality. As such, it may be resented when it appears as the instrument of state agencies pursuing government policies that appear transient, remote from the moral conditions of everyday life, and at times ignorant, irrelevant or oppressive. The ordering in civil society is provided partly through instrumental lawmaking to ensure coordination and planning of complex social and economic conditions. However, insofar as government recognizes the limits of policy-driven law but appears largely unable to envisage any other form of legal innovation, it tends to rely also on promoting self-regulation, especially among the corporate entities that are seen as holding the keys to economic well-being in contemporary society.

Hence the Rule of Law is typically promoted as the rule of *minimum* law among those key sections of society that are considered able and motivated to regulate themselves largely without the state's intervention. But the combination of deregulation and the moral privatization of social life creates the possibility that individuals will be both morally isolated and legally unprotected; unable and unwilling to call either on legal agencies of the state or their fellow citizens for aid. Furthermore, while discriminatory law enforcement as between different sections of the populations participating in civil society is not a new phenomenon, the privatized character of social life may reduce sources of communal support and solidarity that otherwise provide some protection against or a means of compensating for the consequences of discriminatory legal ordering.

Finally, 'below' and outside civil society stand the various population sectors viewed from a certain governmental or law enforcement perspective as the *underclass*. As applied to this part of the population the Rule of Law may be taken to mean primarily the rule of strong discretionary controls or intricate particularized regulation. In contrast to the self-regulating subjects of civil society, the members of the 'underclass' are widely seen as appropriate *objects* of regulation. The Rule of Law appears in one aspect as a weapon to ensure adequate control of them. While in theory in contemporary democracies they can appeal to its protection no less than can other citizens, in practice their appeal will often be weakened not only by the inadequacy of Rule of Law protections in relation to the particular kinds of regulation often used against them but by the assumption that these populations threaten the conditions of general security, one of the central values associated with the Rule of Law.

THE RULE OF LAW AS A CONTEMPORARY PROJECT

The preceding discussion may seem wholly negative, since it sketches in general and schematic terms some largely unfavourable conditions in which the idea of the Rule of Law seems to exist today. Nevertheless, if emphasis is put on some long-standing traditions of Rule of Law thought and an effort made to relate them specifically to the kinds of social conditions that have been discussed a more productive view of possibilities is indicated.

Earlier a contrast was noted between traditions of Rule of Law thought linked, in Shklar's discussion, respectively with Aristotle and Montesquieu. The Aristotelian rule of reason indicates principled, fair and just government, though its benefits might not be extended to all within the regulated territory. The conception associated with Montesquieu emphasizes limited institutional protections for all citizens. What may need to be recaptured is the explicit combination of the universality of protection of the latter conception and the broad moral principle of the former. The jurist Lon Fuller, attempting to infuse a discussion of legality with explicit reference to moral principle, suggested that the lawmaker who governs through principles of the Rule of Law, as Fuller elaborated them (1969: ch. 2), thereby adheres to a relationship of reciprocity between rulers and ruled. The relationship is one of mutual trust, in which the authority of the lawmaker is founded on, or underpinned by, the confidence of citizens in the legislator's good faith. The idea that those who make law are no less subject to the laws, as made, than are other citizens is a powerful component of this confidence and trust.

The equal protection of the laws should not, therefore, be considered only as an affair of procedural technicalities but is, indeed, a matter of moral principle influencing not only the design of institutions to secure checks and balances but also the kinds of legal regulation created, the purposes for which it is created, and the manner in which its content is determined. The Montesquieu-derived conception of the Rule of Law properly insists on the protection of *all* by law, a situation rendered impossible by the existence of a formal or informal 'dual state' and of a population labelled as 'underclass' and substantially excluded from participation and protection as citizens.[17] At the same time, the value of individual autonomy as an object of the Rule of Law can, in contemporary conditions, be effectively promoted only by using law to aid citizens in confronting the corporate and bureaucratic power that shapes their lives by building *collective* strength through mutual support.

Hence the fulfilment of the promise of the Rule of Law requires not only the *universal* protection of the rights of all citizens to participate as members of the polity as a whole but also the *specific* protection of degrees of autonomy of groupings of citizens in partially self-regulating *communities* of many different kinds. The possibility for citizens to take more control of their lives can be enhanced through conditions of self-regulation, but only insofar as law ensures possibilities for all members to participate as full members of the communities to which they belong. Equally, government and law need to guarantee the minimum conditions of material life for individuals that make this participation worthwhile and that give them a serious stake in the various communities with which they may associate.

What of the problems for the Rule of Law posed by particularized and discretionary regulation? It might be suggested that a general problem here (leaving aside many specific justifications of these regulatory forms) is the frequent overextension of regulatory jurisdiction. Regulation by centralized government of frequently changing 'local' (for example, functionally or geographically specific) conditions may be possible only by creating extensive local official discretions. Conversely, attempts to legislate centrally to control 'local' complexity may sometimes lead to the temptation to cover every case or variation by a mass of particularistic regulation. The *general* issue in seeking to limit discretionary and particularistic regulation may be that of ensuring that the creation of regulation takes place in *reasonable proximity to the contexts to be regulated.* What is required is more extensive devolution of the creation of regulation from seemingly remote agencies of the centralized state to more local agencies representative of functional or geographical communities. Created, within certain limits of general principle, in these more localized settings, regulation might 'naturally' be particularized to local conditions. At the same time, necessary regulatory discretion might be better monitored democratically through greater proximity between regulator and regulated.

It seems ironic that ultimately the pursuit of these conditions requires, in pursuance of the Rule of Law, a further step that appears directly contrary to its doctrine. It has been argued earlier that the Rule of Law requires the equal treatment of individuals before the law of the state, but also the greater possibility of self-regulation within communities. In addition, however, and as a condition necessary to make these other requirements feasible and significant, the Rule of Law requires specific regulatory controls on corporate economic power. In recognizing the diversity of corporate structures and their effects, this regulation may need to dispense with the generality of legal rules addressed to individual citizens.[18] The equality, security and individual autonomy that exist as values served by the Rule of Law, may sometimes be promoted by the *unequal* or at least relatively particularistic treatment of large corporate entities. This is so where they dominate substantial sectors of economic life and their control in the general public interest needs to be specifically adapted to the perhaps unique patterns of their activities and social or economic effects.[19] Such an approach may undermine to some extent the security and autonomy of these entities. It does so, however, in the interests of the equality, autonomy and security of individual citizens at large, and of promoting the vitality of numerous forms of collective organization and cooperation not characterized by extensive capital accumulation and economic power. It recognizes, indeed, that large concentrations of capital and powerful corporate business enterprises should be treated – because of their special economic power – merely as instruments to serve the welfare of individual citizens generally.[20]

Thus, the Rule of Law is not only something to be preserved by negative controls imposed by legal doctrine on governmental processes. These aspects remain of great importance. Beyond them, however, are other matters that in contemporary conditions are even more fundamental. The Rule of Law needs to be *created* and *shaped* by positive acts of government and lawmaking. To speak of a society governed by the Rule of Law is hollow talk unless law's protection in practice reaches all sections of a population, giving enforceable rights and powers as well as imposing duties and constraints. The Rule of Law as a moral principle of government necessarily rejects any 'dual state'. At the same time, the Rule of Law as an embodiment of mutual trust between those who make laws and regulations and those who are subject to them requires for its fulfilment positive action to create and extend the conditions of this mutual trust – to enhance the conditions of reciprocity between rulers and ruled. The effort to promote democratic participation within communities that are able, as far as possible, to shape their own regulation and, thus, to take moral responsibility for it seems important here.

The Rule of Law is not an idea too vacuous to be taken seriously. Its seemingly unsatisfactory character derives partly from being considered merely as a set of institutional or procedural requirements divorced from a broader moral context. When the values of equality, individual autonomy and security implicit in it are given appropriate prominence, it ceases to appear as a limited requirement of procedural propriety and appears instead as an ambitious programme for responsible and responsive government.

Dissatisfaction with traditional modes of thought is deepened by attempts to work with familiar ideas of the Rule of Law in radically changed social and political circumstances. The society of freely interacting individuals, presupposed in much traditional thinking about the Rule of Law, has been replaced by the complex fusion of large-scale corporate organization and moral privatization that characterizes contemporary advanced western societies. Given these conditions, the Rule of Law should be seen as a dynamic project and not a static doctrine. Treated in this way much of its promise remains to be fulfilled. The corporate society of Neumann's time did not herald the end of the Rule of Law. It marked an historical moment in a process of sociolegal change which has made the reconstruction of the Rule of Law a contemporary necessity.

NOTES

This article is an adapted and extended version of the text of a lecture delivered at the Netherlands Instituut voor Sociaal en Economisch Recht (NISER), University of

Utrecht, on 27 October 1994. I am grateful to Roel de Lange, Anne-Marie Bos, Brian Tamanaha, Linda Cotterrell and Alan Norrie, in particular, for helpful comments and criticisms.

1. On Neumann's life and career see Jay, 1986; Wiggershaus, 1994: 223–9; Neumann, 1953a.
2. The following discussion builds on ideas in Cotterrell, 1995: ch. 8.
3. In the sense of the liberal (formal), rather than social, *Rechtsstaat*. See Böckenförde, 1991: ch. 3.
4. It is not necessary here to assess whether Shklar correctly identifies the sources of these contrasting themes in the history of ideas. The claim being made is only that the enduring tension between them is fundamentally important.
5. Neumann, 1986: 255–6; 1957: 40. See also Aubert, 1989: 81–3.
6. Neumann usually wrote in terms of 'monopoly capitalism' or, simply, 'modern society'; see 1986: ch. 15; 1957.
7. For a classic case study, see Carson, 1981.
8. 'Every legal rule also constitutes a guarantee to the legal subjects that the state is itself under an obligation for as long as the rule remains in force. . . . Before its subjects the state commits itself through the creative legal act – irrespective of how the law originates – to apply and enforce the law' (G. Jellinek, quoted in Aubert, 1989: 66).
9. Fraenkel, 1941, analysing the nature of the Nazi state, uses the term 'dual state' in a different sense to indicate parallel regimes of legality and political or administrative expediency, the last being cloaked by the former.
10. Among the now substantial literature focused – from a variety of political perspectives – on the concept of an 'underclass' in relation to US and UK society, see e.g. Auletta, 1982; Dahrendorf, 1985: ch. 3; MacNicol, 1987; Field, 1989; Mann, 1992; Morris, 1994, especially ch. 4.
11. In the remainder of this article, I use this controversial term (*underclass*) to indicate not a sociologically distinct group or social class but diverse categories of people often treated by governments and agencies of social control and public order as constituting a 'problem population' because of their perceived lack of a significant stake in the dominant economic order of society.
12. For important discussions of the empirical conditions in which corporate power may significantly limit the practical possibilities for individuals to enforce rights, secure redress or assert demands effectively through legal processes, see e.g. Galanter, 1974; Wanner, 1975; Hagan, 1982; Atkins, 1987; Wheeler et al., 1987.
13. On the contribution of legal formality to security see Fuller, 1941.
14. See e.g. Thompson, 1984a; 1984b; and, for a longer comparative perspective, Hall, 1986.
15. Guillaume de la Perriere, *Miroir Politique*, quoted in Foucault, 1991: 93.
16. See Zellick, 1985: 288–93, discussing examples of governmental practices in dealing with 'technical' illegalities.
17. At its broadest this problem is central to debates about the extension of social rights and benefits that have long surrounded the concept of the social *Rechtsstaat*. At its narrowest it refers to specific issues of access to justice, i.e. access to the machinery of justice through courts and other tribunals and to reliable legal advice and assistance.
18. For a discussion of related themes, see Lustgarten, 1988.
19. See Neumann, 1957: 52: 'The postulate that the state should rule only by general laws becomes absurd in the economic sphere if the legislator is dealing not with equally strong competitors but with monopolies which reverse the principle of

the free market.'

20. See Neumann, 1953b: 183, discussing limits on the 'civil right' of 'corporate property'.

REFERENCES

Adorno, T. and M. Horkheimer (1986) *Dialectic of Enlightenment, 2nd edition*. (tr. J. Cumming). London: Verso.

Atkins, B. (1987) 'A Cross-National Perspective on the Structuring of Trial Court Outputs: The Case of the English High Court', pp. 143–61 in J. R. Schmidhauser (ed.), *Comparative Judicial Systems: Challenging Frontiers in Conceptual and Empirical Analysis*. London: Butterworths.

Aubert, V. (1989) *Continuity and Development in Law and Society*. Oslo: Norwegian University Press.

Auletta, K. (1982) *The Underclass*. New York: Random House.

Balkin, J. M. (1992) 'What Is a Postmodern Constitutionalism?', *Michigan Law Review* 90: 1966–90.

Barker, E. (ed.) (1946) *The Politics of Aristotle*. Oxford: Clarendon.

Baumann, Z. (1992) *Intimations of Postmodernity*. London: Routledge.

Baumgartner, M. P. (1988) *The Moral Order of a Suburb*. New York: Oxford University Press.

Bobbio, N. (1987) *The Future of Democracy: A Defence of the Rules of the Game* (tr. R. Griffin). Cambridge: Polity.

Böckenförde, E.-W. (1991) *State, Society and Liberty: Studies in Political Theory and Constitutional Law* (tr. J. A. Underwood). Oxford: Berg.

Carson, W. G. (1981) *The Other Price of Britain's Oil: Safety and Control in the North Sea*. Oxford: Martin Robertson.

Cotterrell, R. B. M. (1989) *The Politics of Jurisprudence: A Critical Introduction to Legal Philosophy*. London: Butterworths.

Cotterrell, R. B. M. (1992) *The Sociology of Law: An Introduction, 2nd edition*. London: Butterworths.

Cotterrell, R. B. M. (1995) *Law's Community: Legal Theory in Sociological Perspective*. Oxford: Clarendon.

Dahrendorf, R. (1985) *Law and Order*. London: Sweet & Maxwell.

Dicey, A. V. (1959) *An Introduction to the Study of the Law of the Constitution, 10th edition*, by E. C. S. Wade. London: Macmillan.

Dworkin, R. (1978) 'Political Judges and the Rule of Law', pp. 9–32 reprinted in R. Dworkin (1985) *A Matter of Principle*. Cambridge, MA: Harvard University Press.

Dworkin, R. (1986) *Law's Empire*. London: Fontana.

Field, F. (1989) *Losing Out: The Emergence of Britain's Underclass*. Oxford: Blackwell.

Foucault, M. (1991) 'Governmentality' (tr. R. Braidotti), pp. 87–104 in G. Burchell, C. Gordon and P. Miller (eds), *The Foucault Effect: Studies in Governmentality*. London: Harvester Wheatsheaf.

Fraenkel, E. (1941) *The Dual State: A Contribution to the Theory of Dictatorship* (tr. E. A. Shils, E. Lowenstein and K. Knorr). New York: Oxford University Press.

Fuller, L. L. (1941) 'Consideration and Form', *Columbia Law Review*, 41: 799–824.

Fuller, L. L. (1969) *The Morality of Law, revised edition*. New Haven, CT: Yale University Press.

Galanter, M. (1974) 'Why the "Haves" Come Out Ahead: Speculations on the Limits of Legal Change', *Law and Society Review* 9: 95–160.

Hagan, J. (1982) 'The Corporate Advantage: A Study of the Involvement of Corporate and Individual Victims in a Criminal Justice System', *Social Forces* 60: 993–1022.

Hall, J. A. (1986) 'States and Economic Development: Reflections on Adam Smith', pp. 154–76 in J. A. Hall (ed.), *States in History*. Oxford: Blackwell.

Hutchinson, A. C. and P. Monahan (eds) (1987) *The Rule of Law: Ideal or Ideology*. Toronto: Carswell.

Jay, M. (1986) 'Foreword: Neumann and the Frankfurt School', pp. ix–xiv in F. L. Neumann, *The Rule of Law*. Leamington Spa: Berg.

Kirchheimer, O. (1967) 'The *Rechtsstaat* as Magic Wall, pp. 428–52 reprinted in F. S. Burin and K. L. Shell (eds) (1969) *Politics, Law and Social Change: Selected Essays of Otto Kirchheimer*. New York: Columbia University Press.

Kirchheimer, O. (1983) 'The Limits of Expropriation', pp. 85–129 reprinted in O. Kirchheimer and F. L. Neumann (1987), *Social Democracy and the Rule of Law* (tr. L. Tanner and K. Tribe). London: Allen & Unwin.

Kirchheimer, O. and Neumann, F. L. (1987) *Social Democracy and the Rule of Law* (tr. L. Tanner and K. Tribe). London: Allen & Unwin.

Lowi, T. J. (1987) 'The Welfare State, the New Regulation, and the Rule of Law', pp. 17–58 in A. C. Hutchinson and P. Monahan (eds), *The Rule of Law*. Toronto: Carswell.

Lustgarten, L. (1988) 'Socialism and the Rule of Law', *Journal of Law and Society* 15: 25–41.

McLennan, G., D. Held and S. Hall (eds) (1984) *State and Society in Contemporary Britain: A Critical Introduction*. Cambridge: Polity.

MacNicol, J. (1987) 'In Pursuit of the Underclass', *Journal of Social Policy* 16: 293–318.

Mann, K. (1992) *The Making of an English 'Underclass'?: The Social Divisions of Welfare and Labour*. Milton Keynes: Open University Press.

Marcuse, H. (ed.) (1957) *The Democratic and the Authoritarian State: Essays in Political and Legal Theory by Franz L. Neumann*. Glencoe, IL: Free Press.

Morris, L. (1994) *Dangerous Classes: The Underclass and Social Citizenship*. London: Routledge.

Neumann, F. L. (1944) *Behemoth: The Structure and Practice of National Socialism 1933–1944*. New York: Octagon reprint, 1983.

Neumann, F. L. (1953a) 'The Social Sciences', pp. 4–26 in F. L. Neumann et al., *The Cultural Migration: The European Scholar in America*. Philadelphia: University of Pennsylvania Press.

Neumann, F. L. (1953b) 'The Concept of Political Freedom', pp. 160–200 reprinted in H. Marcuse (ed.) (1957), *The Democratic and the Authoritarian State*. Glencoe, IL: Free Press.

Neumann, F. L. (1957) 'The Change in the Function of Law in Modern Society', pp. 22–68 in H. Marcuse (ed.), *The Democratic and the Authoritarian State*. Glencoe, IL: Free Press.

Neumann, F. L. (1986) *The Rule of Law: Political Theory and the Legal System in Modern Society*. Leamington Spa: Berg.

Nonet, P. (1987) 'The Rule of Law: Is That the Rule That Was?' pp. 125–40 in A. C. Hutchinson and P. Monahan (eds), *The Rule of Law*. Toronto: Carswell.

Offe, C. (1985) *Disorganised Capitalism: Contemporary Transformations of Work and Politics*. Cambridge: Polity.

Postema, G. J. (1986) *Bentham and the Common Law Tradition*. Oxford: Clarendon.

Shklar, J. N. (1987) 'Political Theory and the Rule of Law', pp. 1–16 in A. C. Hutchinson and P. Monahan (eds), *The Rule of Law*. Toronto: Carswell.
Thompson, E. P. (1975) *Whigs and Hunters: The Origin of the Black Act*. London: Allen Lane.
Thompson, G. (1984a) 'Economic Intervention in the Post-War Economy', pp. 77–118 in G. McLennan, D. Held and S. Hall (eds), *State and Society in Contemporary Britain*. Cambridge: Polity.
Thompson, G. (1984b) '"Rolling Back" The State?: Economic Intervention 1975–82', pp. 274–98 in G. McLennan, D. Held and S. Hall (eds), *State and Society in Contemporary Britain*. Cambridge: Polity.
Wanner, C. (1975) 'The Public Ordering of Private Relations: Part 2 – Winning Civil Court Cases', *Law and Society Review* 9: 293–306.
Weber, M. (1968) *Economy and Society: An Outline of Interpretive Sociology* (tr. E. Fischoff et al.) Berkeley: University of California Press edn, 1978.
Weinrib, E. J. (1987) 'The Intelligibility of the Rule of Law', pp. 59–85 in A. C. Hutchinson and P. Monahan (eds), *The Rule of Law*. Toronto: Carswell.
Wheeler, S., B. Cartwright, R. A. Kagan and L. M. Friedman (1987) 'Do the "Haves" Come Out Ahead? Winning and Losing in State Supreme Courts, 1870–1970', *Law and Society Review* 21: 403–45.
Wiggershaus, R. (1994) *The Frankfurt School: Its History, Theories and Political Significance* (tr. M. Robertson). Cambridge: Polity.
Zellick, G. (1985) 'Government beyond Law', *Public Law*?: 283–308.

[24]

Franz Neumann: Legal Theorist of Globalization?

William E. Scheuerman

Few facets of Franz Neumann's legal theory are as unfashionable today as his Marxist account of the decline of classical formal law. Even sympathetic commentators concede that Neumann relied on an idealized and probably unrealistic portrayal of classical liberal jurisprudence, as well as an excessively functionalist interpretation of legal development.[1] Far too often, Neumann offered an economistic *Verfallsgeschichte* that obscures key features of modern legal development at least as much as it helps make sense of them. Although Neumann sought to overcome the normative deficits of traditional Marxist legal theory by famously ascribing an "ethical function" to the rule of law, even this facet of his theory always remained underdeveloped. Neumann never fully liberated himself from a Weberian-Marxist intellectual background that ultimately minimizes law's immanent normative – and, more specifically, democratic – qualities.

Nonetheless, I would like to suggest that precisely those features of Neumann's thinking most criticized by contemporary commentators represent a surprisingly rich starting point for understanding key contemporary legal trends. My aim here is *not* to resurrect Neumann's Marxism. It is striking, however, that Neumann's famous account of the *economic* origins of anti-formal trends in contemporary law anticipates core legal attributes of the ongoing process of globalization. Furthermore, Neumann's explanation for those trends seems prescient as well. Globalization provides substantial empirical support for Neumann's thesis that the altered context of contemporary economic activity tends to reduce capital's traditional reliance on relatively formalistic modes of law and legal reasoning. Neumann's emphasis on the manner in which the traditional "elective affinity" between capitalism and formal law no longer obtains within contemporary capitalism offers a useful corrective to contemporary neoliberal conceptions of globalization, according to which market-oriented economic reforms and liberal legal reform necessarily represent two sides of the same coin.[2] In contrast to the dominant neoliberal view, globalization suggests that Neumann was justified in holding that the relationship between capitalism and law was likely to be complicated by a limited interest among privileged business interests in achieving strict, clear, public, and prospective forms of general law.

I begin with an explanation for why I do not consider it implausible to interpret Neumann as having tackled issues presently grouped under the rubric of globalization (I). I then revisit his Marxist account of the "functional transformation of law," before suggesting its virtues as a basis for interpreting ongoing trends in contemporary international economic law (II). Finally, I suggest ways in which the legal structure of economic globalization shows how Neumann's analysis of legal development might be revised.

I

The present tendency to ignore the ways in which globalization represents a long-term historical process[3] may lead us to miss the fact that features of the ongoing debate about globalization were anticipated by a series of heated disputes about international law in the 1930s and 40s. Neumann's main intellectual nemesis, Carl Schmitt, played a key role in those debates. Neumann's response to Schmitt represents a cautious attempt to grapple with what we nowadays describe as globalization.

Schmitt's infamous theory of the *Großraum* (greater region) has rightly been criticized, not the least because of its unabashedly Nazi and antisemitic connotations.[4] However despicable his political aims, Schmitt's account of the *Großraum* nonetheless succeeded in anticipating conspicuous features of the present-day debate about globalization. According to Schmitt's analysis, modern technology and contemporary forms of economic organization outstrip the legal and regulatory capacities of the nation-state; the increasingly supranational composition of such activity cries out for no less supranational forms of "regionalized" political and legal authority. Modern mass media allow political propaganda to reach the homes of foreigners living thousands of miles away at the blink of an eye; contemporary air warfare renders traditional national borders porous to an extent unfathomable to our nineteenth-century predecessors; markets and economic activity increasingly rest on complex cross-border networks. Existing nation-state borders thus tend ever more to possess limited relevance given the economic and technological possibilities of a globe that seems to shrink in size daily, and the modern nation-state is destined to be jettisoned for a set of "greater regions" better attuned to the functional imperatives of the "space revolution" (*Raumrevolution*) presently revolutionizing the time and space horizons of crucial forms of human activity.[5] In this conceptual context, Schmitt not only viewed Nazi imperialism as a fitting answer to the political challenges of his time, but he came to argue that a unified European continent (under German control, of course) might better answer the resultant problems at hand than America or Britain could. Eerily echoing some contemporary critics of neoliberalism, Schmitt insisted on the need for extensive state intervention within contemporary capitalism, while simultaneously insisting that indispensable forms of state coordination of the economy were destined to prove ineffective when undertaken on the global scale. In other words, a Nazi-dominated regionalized European *Großraum* might succeed in negotiating the regulatory challenges of contemporary social and economic life, whereas the US and British preference for a global "free market" – for Schmitt, nothing more than a specific form of imperialism derived from certain special traits of US and British experience – risked coming apart on the instabilities of laissez-faire capitalism.[6]

If we bracket the unsightly facets of this account for just a moment, we can see that Schmitt managed to foretell at least three features of the contemporary debate on globalization. First, he rightly identified the nation-state's declining capacity for providing effective regulatory answers to a host of core – especially economic – problems. Second, he no less accurately began to grapple seriously with dramatic ongoing changes in the space and time horizons of human activity, and he anticipated many facets of the present exchange among social theorists about the centrality of the process of "time and space compression" for understanding globalization. Well before Zygmunt Bauman, Anthony Giddens, and David Harvey, Schmitt rightly presaged that we could only make sense of the decline of the nation-state by focusing on the manner in which the heightened pace of human activity tends to minimize the significance of distance.[7] Third, he anticipated the increasingly widespread view that the best way to deal with the exigencies of globalization is by building regionally-based political and economic blocs able to protect their members from the vicissitudes of an unstable global neoliberalism under US auspices. Of course, Schmitt would hardly have defended a *social democratic* European Union as a bulwark against the neoliberal "race to the bottom." Yet he might have recognized in the EU an attempt to come to grips with some of his own worries about what he described as the irresponsible *Planfeindlichkeit* (hostility to planning) of Anglo-American models of market capitalism.

From his exile in New York City, Franz Neumann carefully followed the development of a distinct Nazi discourse on international law, and a substantial portion of his encyclopedic discussion of National Socialism, *Behemoth: The Structure and Practice of National Socialism*, is devoted to providing a detailed survey of it. Unlike contemporary Schmitt apologists, Neumann had no illusions either about Schmitt's moderately significant role in that debate, or the disturbing political implications of his reflections on the *Großraum*. Although legitimately disgusted by Schmitt's manifest enthusiasm for the Nazis, Neumann conceded that the technical and economic facets of Schmitt's defense of the *Großraum* raised difficult questions even for those hostile to Schmitt's normative and political preferences: "The decline of the state in domestic and international law is not mere ideology; it expresses a major practical trend."[8] In a wide-ranging discussion of Nazi imperialism, Neumann underscored the peculiarities of German development – in particular, Germany's status as a "late-comer" to industrialization – in order to explain the "efficiency and brutality" of Nazi imperialism.[9] In the context of a world divided among "powerful states, each of them committed to protect its own economy," free trade policies increasingly were an impossibility in interwar Europe.[10] Germany's far-reaching dependence on foreign trade thus meant that for Germany to integrate its neighbors' economies advantageously into its own, it could no longer rely on "mere economic exchange. . . . [O]nly with the help of political domination that incorporates the states into Germany's currency system" could Germany hope "to trade successfully with them, that is, to transfer from them more labor for less labor. . . ."[11] Notwithstanding its distinct developmental traits, however, for Neumann there was no question that Nazi imperialism was integrally linked to structural components of organized (or "monopoly") capitalism. According to the traditional Marxist argumentation at the core of *Behemoth*, Nazi expansionism represented the most barbaric manifestation of trends latent within contemporary capitalist development. To the extent that those trends were universal, the decline in the significance of national borders evinced by the case of Nazi imperialism suggested that the decay of the core institutions of the nation-state potentially constituted a universal phenomenon as well.

For Neumann, Schmitt's theory of the *Großraum* offered a particularly extreme answer to the challenges of contemporary capitalist economic development, just as the emergence of Nazism represented a paradigmatic attempt to achieve political and legal forms suitable to the profound pathologies of monopoly capitalism. Neumann offered two responses to the Nazi theoreticians of the *Großraum* of special interest for the present-day debate on globalization. First, he considered the claim that the achievement of a European *Großraum* would allow for the unshackling of Germany from the pressures of the world economy – wishful but misleading ideological talk; in contrast to a picture of the *Großraum* as a protective shield against global capitalism, Neumann pointed out that a German-dominated Europe would probably remain dependent on foreign trade (in particular, for raw materials), and that Germany's real aim was to manipulate its hegemonic position within a regionalized European economic and political bloc in order to gain protection from some imports while using its enhanced powers to gain greater access to foreign markets.[12] Neumann thereby rightly intimated that the relationship between regional blocs and the global economy might take a variety of distinct forms: in the Nazi case (and in Schmitt's corresponding theory of the *Großraum*), regionalization represented an assault on the indispensable achievements of universalistic liberal international law. Its claim to immunize Germany from the global economy in reality constituted a mask for improving the competitive position of Germany's leading capitalist interests within the global economy at large. Neumann's warnings on this point remain relevant today.[13] Second, Neumann seemed to interpret Schmitt's account of the decline of the nation-state as containing a kernel of truth, but as nonetheless overstated. Perhaps he would have accused Schmitt of succumbing to what David Held more recently has critically described as the "hyper-globalization thesis," according to which the traditional nation-state has now been stripped of *any* meaningful instruments for stemming the tide of globalization.[14] In any event, Neumann ultimately embraced a defensive position, according to which the gradual decline of the nation-state "expresses a major practical trend," while nonetheless continuing to insist on the lasting achievements of the Westphalian system of states in the face of the Nazi threat. For Neumann, the modern notion of the legal equality of states guarantees a modicum of predictability in international politics, and Schmitt's quest to replace the traditional state system with a narrow set of *Großräume* – each committed to developing a legal system appropriate to its "distinct" and particularistic ethnic and racial attributes – should remind us of the "progressive" functions of traditional notions of state sovereignty. The nation-state may be experiencing decay, but allowing it to be replaced by an international system that sheds the universalistic impulses of the modern state system would inevitably leave us with a system vastly more brutal than the existing one.[15]

Of course, whether Neumann would continue to insist on the progressive implications of state sovereignty in the context of contemporary attempts to develop *liberal-democratic* and – at least potentially – social-democratic forms of regional authority (for example, the EU) must remain an open question. At the very least, his skepticism forces those of us committed to developing new forms of transnational political and economic authority to make sure that they offer real gains in terms of self-government and the rule of law.[16]

II

These introductory comments place Neumann's account of the deformalization of classical formal law in a fresh light. Neumann, of course, believed that the decline of classical law was ultimately generated by the economic structure of contemporary monopoly capitalism, and thus represented a more or less universal trend. To the extent that "the antagonisms of capitalism are operating in Germany on a higher and, therefore, a more dangerous level," however, Nazi-dominated Europe provided a more unadulterated example of legal decay than the capitalist liberal democracies.[17] To the degree that non-formal law chiefly serves privileged private interests, for Neumann it was no accident that the legal order most immediately subject to the interests of the oligarchic sectors of capitalism, Nazi Germany, would ultimately abandon classical formal law in a more radical manner than its rivals. The destruction of the rule of law was most complete under Nazism chiefly because of the virtually unchallenged hegemony there of the most privileged capitalist classes, in contrast to the situation in liberal democracy where political and legal devices function to limit the influence of monopoly capital.

I am not interested in defending Neumann's Marxist interpretation of Nazism here; its weaknesses have been widely documented. Nevertheless, it is telling that Neumann's interpretation of Nazi imperialism at least indirectly suggests a provocative view of the nexus between law and economic globalization. As we saw above, Neumann was well aware of the manner in which Nazi-dominated Europe constituted a developmental response to the nation-state's declining ability to grapple with the technical and economic imperatives of contemporary society; Nazi *Großraum* plans provided an ominous answer to the growing mismatch between the traditional nation-state and the transnational scope of key technical and economic activities. So Neumann's account of the relationship between the

Nazi political economy and the decline of classical formal law, at least implicitly, amounts to suggesting that some features of what we presently describe as "globalization" are likely to exacerbate anti-formal trends in the law.

We need not engage in tortured textual exegesis, however, in order to construct an account of the relationship between globalization and legal development on the basis of Neumann's ideas. His best known claim is that the transition from competitive to contemporary monopoly capitalism undermines the economic basis for a legal order resting on clear, prospective, and public general norms. In an economy characterized by a rough equality among competitors, generality within the law was likely to be supported by a broad range of economic actors. General law was then not only legally advantageous but also economically sensible because individual legal interventions violate the principle of the equality of competition basic to a classical market economy.[18] In a mode of capitalism dominated by huge corporations possessing quasi-monopolistic status and numerous advantages vis-à-vis small entrepreneurs, general law becomes economically anachronistic:

> In a monopolistically organized system the general law cannot be supreme. If the state is confronted only by a monopoly, it is pointless to regulate this monopoly by general law. In such a case the individual measure is the only appropriate expression of the sovereign power.[19]

The key political question then becomes who possesses the authority to issue such individual measures, and whose interests are served by them. Neumann believed that the democratic welfare state provided a forum in which the interests of subordinate social groups could at least gain recognition by non-traditional forms of lawmaking; his own commitment to Weimar labor law represented a fervent attempt to establish new modes of post-classical law sensitive to the needs of the German working classes. But the collapse of Weimar indicated to him that such experiments were likely to prove fragile given the special position of monopoly capital within contemporary society. Privileged private interests would try to reduce the regulatory burdens placed on them in the democratic welfare state by pursuing a legal order better suited to their interests. They would tend to prefer legal forms in which their economic advantages might gain unmediated expression. For Neumann, the proliferation of vague, open-ended standards within contemporary law helped pave the way for the democratic welfare state. Non-formal legal forms might easily portend direct domination by large capitalist interests as well, however:

> Legal standards of conduct (blanket clauses) serve the monopolist. . . . Not only is rational law unnecessary for him, it is often a fetter upon the full development of his productive forces . . . rational law, after all, serves also to protect the weak. The monopolist can dispense with the help of the courts since his power to command is a satisfactory substitute.[20]

Unless effectively hemmed in by liberal-democratic political institutions along with welfare-state devices geared towards providing the working classes with some say in economic affairs, privileged economic interests are likely to make the most use of their *de facto* power advantages by minimizing meaningful legal constraints on their actions. Easily manipulable legal norms serve this purpose well, as do a host of related legal trends allowing large capitalist interests to avoid scrutiny by ordinary courts of law. According to Neumann, precisely this had occurred within Nazi Germany, and thus Nazism represented a forceful warning to defenders of the rule of law everywhere about the dangers posed to it by contemporary capitalism.

In a similar vein, Neumann believed that contract law was inevitably hollowed out by the transition from classical to contemporary capitalism. In early capitalism, the notion of a free contract rested on social as well as juridical postulates, since it presupposed a rough equality between economic competitors, and thus a real possibility that contractual relations might rest on a meaningful degree of reciprocity.[21] Contractual freedom, however, was soon reduced to its narrowly juridical features; even those contracts agreed to by manifestly unequal partners (between large and small businesses, for example) were deemed legitimate as long as a minimal set of formal-legal conditions were met. In this transformed view, contractual freedom was preserved even if the contract at hand managed to strengthen the position of a privileged monopolist. "Even when utilizing the form of the contract, his [that is, the monopolist's] economic power enables him to impose upon consumers and workers all those rules that he deems indispensable and that the other parties are forced to accept if they want to continue to exist."[22] Neumann worried that contemporary trends pointed to the demise of even those minimal protective functions performed by a narrowly juridical conception of contractual liberty, which at the very least guaranteed predictability in legal affairs by striving to provide a clear statement of the rights and obligations of parties to a transaction. For example, labor contracts obscure structural inequalities between capital and labor, yet fidelity to classical rule of law virtues (clarity, prospectiveness, and cogency) in labor agreements helps circumscribe capital's potentially awesome prerogatives. In Nazi Germany, Neumann hinted, monopoly capital found itself in the envious position of freeing itself from even such relatively minimal legal restraints: contracts were increasingly jettisoned in favor of untrammeled forms of discretionary command suited to the preservation of the hegemonic position of key capitalist interests. But even where contracts manage to survive in contemporary society, they often rely on vague, open-ended, and moralistic phrases lacking a precisely definable, justiciable meaning, thereby opening the door to their manipulation by economic interests in possession of the greatest *de facto* power.[23]

Now one surely could squabble with many features of this story. Nonetheless, for those familiar with the ongoing debate about globalization and the law, Neumann's diagnosis should seem remarkably prophetic. The most impressive study of global business regulation presently available notes that "the rule of law is not as influential in global regulatory regimes as it is in liberal nations. . . . International regulation is not characterized by a rule of law which constrains . . . .[24] The authors of the same study simultaneously point out that "the recurrently most effective actors" in global regulation are presently large corporations.[25] Those legal arenas pivotal to economic globalization are plagued by anti-formal trends arguably as far-reaching as those that grabbed Neumann's attention over fifty years ago. Core features of international economic law remain, to a substantial degree, *soft* law lacking in key classical rule of law virtues. Moreover, substantial evidence suggests that the most privileged sectors of the global economy tend to benefit disproportionately from this scenario. In accordance with the spirit of Neumann's own reflections, let me briefly underscore some crucial anti-formal trends within the normative structure of international economic law (A), before turning to the role of contracts in global business transactions (B):[26]

A. International business arbitration today is flourishing as a device for resolving disputes in the sphere of transnational transactions. Yet the legal structure of international business arbitration remains flexible and discretionary, characterized by a relative absence of the formal legal virtues of generality, publicity, clarity, and constancy. A vast legal literature now documents the manner in which arbitrators make use of the *Lex Mercatoria* and its indisputably vague clauses: made up substantially of "general principles" ("usages of faith," "good faith"), the *Lex Mercatoria* provides surprising support for Neumann's prediction that in *contemporary* capitalism large business firms are likely to dispense with formal law.[27] Although international business arbitration appears to be undergoing a process in which its limited legalistic features have recently been fortified, it remains a system in which confidentiality is far-reaching, and recourse to clearly focused legal rules (or precedents) circumscribed. Moreover, international business seems to be responding to evidence of a creeping legalization within international business arbitration by seeking alternative dispute resolution devices even more profoundly anti-formal in character. Traditional forms of commercial arbitration now face a whole range of competitors (including variants of mediation and conciliation geared towards the business community) promising the speedy resolution of conflicts; a key selling point to global business for these modes of dispute resolution is their limited reliance on traditional formalistic legal devices. Many practitioners of international business arbitration worry that it has become too akin to traditional judicial settings, aggressively demanding a rollback of even the rather limited formalistic attributes of present-day international commercial arbitration.[28]

Similarly, existing forms of transnational regulation for multinational corporations and international finance are weak on traditional rule of law virtues.[29] Thus far, attempts at the transnational level to develop a clear set of strict guidelines for multinational corporations have generally been successfully subverted by large firms promising to develop their own voluntary "codes of conduct." But voluntary corporate codes of conduct are typically vague and open-ended, enforcement procedures are feeble or even non-existent, and they rarely provide meaningful protection to those (especially employees) affected by them.[30] The dominant trend within transnational banking regulation is to move away from the model of imposing "strict, uniform, quantitative limits on the activities of the banks" in favor of outsourcing important elements of regulatory activity to the banks themselves.[31] Although much can be said in favor of this approach as a way of grappling with the dynamism of the financial sector, it not only raises difficult questions for defenders of traditional formal law, but even those sympathetic to it worry about its high price in terms of democratic legitimacy.[32] Neumann's anxieties about the specter of non-traditional modes of law that ultimately represent an abandonment of liberal law's normative bases of legitimacy remain apposite to contemporary debates about self-regulation within global business.

What then of more ambitious intergovernmental attempts – most notably, the WTO – to develop an effective transnational legal basis for the global economy? To be sure, the WTO clearly represents an attempt to develop a "hard" legal shell for the global economy, and there is no question that its enforcement procedures have been substantially strengthened in recent years. The WTO's dispute resolution devices hardly conform to traditional models of formal legality, despite the WTO's self-advertised loyalty to the "rule of law." The WTO Agreement is "riddled with exceptions – grandfather clauses, waivers, balance-of-payment exceptions," along with vague and open-ended clauses, loopholes, and sectoral exemptions.[33] It provides substantial leeway for a highly discretionary process of adjudication, and many of its decisions are likely to strike even those familiar with the complex norms making up the WTO legal system as controversial. WTO tribunals are confidential as well, and opinions expressed in the tribunal reports remain anonymous. This failing not only represents a violation of the modern ideal of the *publicity* of law, but it works in conjunction with the WTO's discretionary system of norms to raise the specter of a deeply irregular system of adjudication whose only real commitment is to the core neoliberal beliefs presently driving WTO policy.[34]

The question of which social groups are best served by anti-formal trends in present-day global economic law obviously is a complicated matter. But many commentators believe that so far they have proven especially opportune for privileged "global players" best able to exploit a "soft" legal structure porous to the influence of powerful economic groups.[35] International business arbitration is favored by transnational business in part precisely because it allows them to minimize the impact of other social constituencies on their activities; it represents an updated form of what Judith Shklar described as "arbitration under chamber of commerce auspices," whose very structure is geared towards maximizing the autonomy of businesses party to a dispute.[36] Multinational corporate codes of conduct too often provide a pseudo-legalistic window-dressing for the mistreatment of labor in poor countries; new modes of regulation within international finance arguably have helped rid the international financial system of its most blatant pathologies, yet consumers and others influenced by international finance have exercised little say over the emerging regulatory system. In any event, no one is plausibly arguing that existing global economic law is working to alleviate the injustices of contemporary capitalism or reduce the vast gap separating the rich from the poor on our ever more polarized planet.

B. The transnationalization of capitalism has spawned a number of ambitious recent attempts to harmonize contract law in order to facilitate cross-border transactions. In this vein, the UN Commission on International Trade Law (*UNICTRAL*), International Institute for the Unification of Private Law (*Unidroit*), and the Commission on European Contract Law are busily proposing reforms of contract law so as to make it better suited to the dictates of a global economy. Transnational economic activity continues to require a network of enforceable contracts; Neumann's Nazi-era expectation that contracts might disintegrate altogether remains unfulfilled. Nonetheless, substantial evidence confirms his prediction that fundamental changes in the nature of contemporary capitalism – in this case, the transition to an increasingly transnational economy – would likely contribute to anti-formal trends in contract law.

In the legal literature on globalization and contract law, a large number of voices now argue that transnational exchanges must be free of the excessively "static" as well as "inflexible and irrevocable legal remedies" presumably characteristic of earlier forms of contract law.[37] In this view, heightened possibilities for discretionary judicial activity are called for, and reliance on just those "general principles" whose implications Neumann considered so ambivalent is now identified as a central device for making discretion possible. Indeed, one object of Neumann's own anxieties, section 242 ("in good faith") of the German Civil Code, features strongly in the Unidroit *Principles of International Commercial Contracts* and the *Principles of European Contract Law* prepared by the European Commission on Contract Law.[38] A pervasive theme in the burgeoning legal literature on transnational contracts is the need for "dynamism" within contracts, along with growing skepticism concerning the virtues of traditional forms of codification: "many of us are becoming increasingly sensitive to the extent that codification of commercial law has not proven to be the most desirable goal."[39] Legal practitioners are no less unambiguous when describing the motivating force behind the general movement towards increased dependence on open-ended principles within transnational contracts. The changing contours of contract law are "primarily driven by business practice, not the grand theoretical structures of legal scholars" too often influenced by (allegedly) anachronistic and formalistic legal notions.[40] Commercial practice should directly shape contracts, and business practice in the global economy increasingly requires elasticity in the law:

> If a contract appears insufficiently explicit to furnish a direct statement of the parties' rights, duties, powers, and liberties, then the arbitrators will construct it and fill the gaps in it by recourse to their own knowledge of how commerce works in practice, and how commercial men [sic] in the relevant field express themselves. . .. What is important is the arbitrator should keep constantly in mind that he is concerned with international commerce, with all the breadth of horizon, flexibility, and practicality of approach which that demands.[41]

Of course, this trend hardly confirms Neumann's claim that anti-formal trends in contract law are of greatest benefit to the most privileged segments of the capitalist economy. In fact, Neumann's own account of the transformation of competitive into monopoly capitalism fails to offer a sufficient conceptual framework for making sense of the process of economic globalization; the economic developments at hand are far more multifaceted and complex, and many of Neumann's economic claims (for example, concerning the internal structure of the firm) are now badly in need in revision. The concept of monopoly capitalism is far too closely related to Fordist forms of capitalist production and accumulation that are increasingly of limited significance in some core areas of economic activity. If we keep in mind, however, that firms operating on the global level (and thus most likely to make use of the emerging contractual forms described here) likelier than not belong to the most privileged sector of the capitalist economy, Neumann's claim that the largest and most powerful capitalist interests tend to seek non-formal modes of law seems anything but outdated.

III

Neumann believed that powerful capitalist interests tried to escape the confines of Weimar's cautious quest to develop the outlines of the modern regulatory and welfare state by irresponsibly opting to support fascist dictatorship. As noted earlier, he considered the decline of classical formal law for the most part irreversible; which social interests could successfully harness anti-formal legal trends hence became the key political question. In the Weimar Republic, socially subordinate groups possessed a real chance to influence legislation. The Nazis promised to eliminate that influence, and key business interests thus were willing to take their chances with them.[42] Although it would be manifestly absurd to equate fascist dictatorship with globalization, it might be useful to apply elements of Neumann's analysis to contemporary legal development. Economic globalization rests on a panoply of distinct (technological, political, as well as immanently economic) sources. Nonetheless, it is striking that one of its more noteworthy facets consists of the attempt to release key forms of legal decision-making authority (international arbitration, for example, or the WTO) from the direct oversight of the regulatory and welfare states that came to determine the contours of nationally-based polities in significant segments of the developed world in the postwar era. Whatever its flaws, nation-state-based liberal democracy provided relatively substantial possibilities for social groups historically excluded from the political process to shape both legislation and the administration of justice in accordance with their needs. From the perspective of Neumann's analysis, it should come as no surprise that privileged business interests ultimately sought to throw off the burdens of the postwar regulatory and welfare state; globalization, in part, represents one result of that backlash. David Harvey's fascinating analysis of the manner in which the economic crisis of the 1970s played a powerful role in initiating the economic changes that we now associate with globalization accords disturbingly well with elements of Neumann's own analysis of how the Great Depression generated new economic and political strategies within German industry: in both cases, a crisis not only forced key business groups into an increasingly hostile political stance vis-à-vis the achievements of the regulatory and welfare state, but also unleashed a series of economic innovations (Harvey talks of "post-fordism") ultimately subversive of those achievements as well.[43]

The precise nature of the relationship between traditional forms of national authority and the emerging modes of transnational business regulation described above is a complicated matter that would take us beyond the scope of this essay. Yet the ascent of international business arbitration, proliferation of soft law and self-regulation, and establishment of the WTO arguably constitute ambitious attempts to minimize the potential impact of the democratic nation-state over the supervision of transnationally operating businesses. Non-formal modes of law were obviously commonplace in the postwar welfare and regulatory states, but they were undertaken by political bodies resting on liberal democratic procedures and committed to the ideals of the regulatory and welfare state. Whatever the legal ills of the regulatory and welfare state from the standpoint of traditional liberal jurisprudence, they often represented a worthwhile trade-off in the quest to assure democratic legitimacy and social stability. The same cannot be said about most present-day forms of transnational business regulation. In order to free itself from what Carl Schmitt angrily described as the regulatory burdens of the "weak quantitative total state," business groups in the 1930s pursued a risky – and occasionally self-destructive – alliance with right-wing dictatorship. At the beginning of the twenty-first century, powerful economic interests may no longer need the help of right-wing dictatorship in order to ward off challenges from below. Instead, they can preach the virtues of the "rule of law," while in fact establishing dispute resolution devices for the global economy that perpetrate their privileged position and make a mockery of traditional rule of law virtues. Where economic and technological innovations permit large-scale business to reduce the *de facto* and *de jure* significance of national regulation while simultaneously opting for an alternative supranational regulatory system lacking the minimal preconditions of formal legality (generality, clarity, prospectiveness, and publicity), we risk abandoning precisely those features of liberal democracy that allowed it to rein in privileged economic interests.

Many criticisms have rightly been directed at Neumann. My argument suggests two additional ones. First, like his colleagues in the Frankfurt School, Neumann was too quick to see the transition from liberal democracy to fascism as portending western civilization's general course of development. According to the argument developed here, he was right to worry about the "elective affinity" between contemporary capitalism and anti-formal legal trends, even if many details of his account today must be considered misleading and even incorrect. But he was clearly wrong to imply that the elective affinity between contemporary capitalism and anti-formal legal trends might only realize itself fully within fascist dictatorship; the present-day course of globalization suggests that alternative developmental paths cohere with the basic outlines of this trend as well. At the same time, even here Neumann still provides useful guidance. An immediate implication of his analysis is that one of the great political questions of our times is likely to concern the possibility of subjecting anti-formal trends in international economic law to democratic and social purposes. If I am not mistaken, this is precisely one of the key questions confronting participants in the ongoing debate about the prospects of transnational democracy and, on an even more immediate political level, the possibility of a democratic and socially sensitive European Union.

Second, Neumann's tendency to underscore the manner in which vague and open-ended legal clauses *directly* serve privileged economic interests means that his understanding of the nexus between capitalism and anti-formal trends in the law too often took an overly mechanistic form. The legal literature on globalization hints at a more complex picture. To be sure, substantial evidence confirms Neumann's expectation that large firms often prefer anti-formal law for reasons familiar to anyone who has spent time at the children's playground: when the rules of the game are vague or unclear, it is often the biggest boys (and sometimes girls) who succeed in enforcing their interpretation on the other players. This is only the tip of the iceberg, however. Transnational economic processes are characterized by high levels of simultaneity and instantaneousness, chiefly because new technologies (rapid-fire computerized economic transactions, for example) are playing a pivotal role in the global economy. The globalization of financial markets would be unimaginable without dramatic recent developments in information technology, as would numerous parallel developments among major "global players." Subcontracting, outsourcing, "small batch" and short production runs, and "just in time" inventory flows and delivery systems – each of these innovations can be interpreted as manifestations of a larger trend towards accelerating production and consumption, and each has been facilitated by technological changes allowing transnational enterprises to minimize the significance of distance and duration while maximizing the economic opportunities provided by new possibilities for instantaneousness and simultaneity. To be sure, modern capitalism has always operated to revolutionize the time and space horizons of economic activity. As Harvey reminds us, capitalism is a

> revolutionary mode of production, always searching out new organizational forms,

> new technologies, new lifestyles, new modalities of production and exploitation and, therefore, new objective social definitions of . . . time. The capacity to measure and divide time has been [constantly] revolutionized, first through production and the diffusion of increasingly accurate time pieces and subsequently through close attention to the speed and coordinating mechanisms of production (automation, robotization) and the speed and movement of goods, people, information, messages, and the like.[44]

Nevertheless, when high speed forms of informational technology make it possible for firms to produce distinct components of a single commodity in dozens of different countries, or when internet stock brokers in Hong Kong can communicate instantaneously with their peers in Toronto, it becomes difficult to deny that the time and space horizons of contemporary economic activity are experiencing especially far-reaching changes in our day and age. Although always essential to capitalism, the "compression of time and space" is now taking particularly dramatic forms, as evinced by a variety of economic innovations deriving from new technologically based possibilities for instantaneousness and simultaneity.

Neumann's legal theory never adequately thematizes this feature of capitalist development, notwithstanding its obvious centrality to Marx's own account.[45] Yet its implications are profound for legal development. The literature on globalization includes numerous suggestions that traditional formalistic legal procedures too often are rapidly rendered anachronistic given the dynamic character of contemporary economic change and high speed pace of innovation: the "half-life" of many forms of traditional legal regulation indeed appears to be undergoing a dramatic decline. The legal sociologist Boaventura de Sousa Santos adeptly captures the enigma at hand when he points out that the "speed and social acceleration" of contemporary social and economic processes means that "law will be easily trapped in the dilemma: either to remain static and be ignored, or to keep up with social dynamics and be devalued as a normative reference."[46] *Unidroit* justifies its own reliance on "soft" law by underscoring the necessity of contractual law able "to take account of the constantly changing circumstances brought about by the technological and economic developments affecting cross-border trade practice."[47] In a discussion of corporate codes of conduct, political scientist Kathryn Sikkink has suggested that large transnational corporations (TNCs) are often hostile even to relatively modest forms of strict, codified regulations because "[f]lexibility in export and marketing strategies is one of the essential requirements of a corporation, and . . . detailed, specific marketing regulations . . . could seriously hamper the TNC's ability to organize its activities globally."[48] In the same vein, a prominent international business lawyer observes that large transnational firms are now often hostile to "hard" transnational regulation because "[a]dvanced technology and organizational techniques permit MNCs to transmit information, shift production, alter marketing strategy, and otherwise adapt to changing business conditions on a scale and a pace unthinkable only a decade or two earlier."[49] The altered time and space horizons of crucial forms of transnational economic activity means that strict uniform norms are likely to constrain large firms so as to reduce unduly their capacity for dealing with the breathtaking pace of change in the global economy.

On one level, this diagnosis merely confirms Neumann's prescient observations from the 1930s and 40s: contemporary capitalism offers a surprising challenge to traditional conceptions of the rule of law as resting on strict, clear, prospective, general norms. But it also raises the ante for those of us sympathetic to a relatively traditional concept of the rule of law. To the extent that anti-formal trends in the law seem integrally related to the *dynamism* of contemporary economic development, how can we preserve that dynamism while simultaneously guaranteeing a reasonable measure of rule of law virtues? Must we choose between the rule of law and a system of production driven incessantly to accelerate the pace of economic life? Or might it be possible to preserve what is worthwhile about the dynamism of contemporary economic life – *and* achieve both greater social justice *and* the rule of law?

The intellectual legacy of Franz Neumann offers no easy answers to these questions. But Neumann's much-maligned legal theory provides an excellent starting point for helping us formulate them.

NOTES

An earlier version of this paper was presented at the conference on "Franz Neumann's Legacy: The Defense of the Democratic *Rechtsstaat* in Times of Changing Capitalism," Berlin (December 1–2, 2000). Special thanks to the conference organizers, Matthias Iser and David Strecker, for their efforts and helpful advice.

1. See, for example, many of the essays collected in Joachim Perels, ed., *Recht, Demokratie und Kapitalismus. Aktualität und Probleme der Theorie Franz L. Neumanns* (Baden-Baden: Nomos, 1984); also, William E. Scheuerman, *Between the Norm and the Exception: The Frankfurt School and the Rule of Law* (Cambridge, MA: MIT Press, 1994).

2. For an excellent critique of this view in reference to East Asia and inspired to some extent by Neumann, see Kanishka Jayasuriya, ed., *Law, Capitalism and Power in Asia: The Rule of Law and Legal Institutions* (London & New York: Routledge, 1999).

3. See David Held, Anthony McGrew, David Goldblatt, and Jonathan Perraton, *Global Transformations: Politics, Economics and Culture* (Stanford: Stanford University Press, 1999).

4. William E. Scheuerman, *Carl Schmitt: The End of Law* (Lanham, MD: Rowman & Littlefield, 1999), 141–74. But many German-language commentators long ago underscored the ominous political purposes of Schmitt's theory of international law; the English-language debate (and the works of Schmittians like Joseph Bendersky, Ellen Kennedy, Paul Piccone, and George Schwab) has badly lagged in this respect. Schmitt's antisemitism is now fully documented in Raphael Gross, *Carl Schmitt und die Juden. Eine deutsche Rechtslehre* (Frankfurt: Suhrkamp, 2000).

5. Carl Schmitt, *Völkerrechtliche Großraumordnung mit Interventionsverbot für raumfremde Mächte* (Berlin: Deutscher Rechtsverlag, 1939). The economic and technological elements of the *Großraum* theory are developed at many junctures: Schmitt, "Die Raumrevolution," *Das Reich*, 29 September 1940, 3; Schmitt, "Reich und Raum. Elemente eines neuen Völkerrechts," *Zeitschrift der Akademie für Deutsches Recht* 7, no. 13 (1940): 201–2; Schmitt, "Das Meer gegen das Land," *Das Reich* 9 (March 1941): 17–18; Schmitt, "Raum and Grossraum im Völkerrecht," *Zeitschrift für*

Völkerrecht 24 (1941): 145–49. More generally on the demise of traditional state structures: Schmitt, "Staat als konkreter, an eine geschichtlicht Epoche gebundenen Begriff" (1941), in Schmitt, *Verfassungsrechtliche Aufsätze aus den Jahren 1924–1954* (Berlin: Duncker & Humblot, 1973), 375–85. Schmitt's ideas about the impact of high-speed forms of weapons technology (in particular, air warfare) on the nation-state arguably influenced the fascinating study by John Herz, *The Nation-State and the Crisis of World Politics* (New York: McKay, 1976), which salvages the more plausible facets of Schmitt's empirical observations while cleansing them of the fascistic purposes for which Schmitt employed them.

6. See his references to the *Planfeindlichkeit* of Anglo-American liberalism (Schmitt, "Die Raumrevolution," 3), as well as his comment about the "chaos" of British liberal universalism (in Schmitt, "Raum und Großraum im Völkerrecht," 169). On the social and economic context and implications of Schmitt's theory, see the brilliant study by Ingeborg Maus, *Bürgerliche Rechtstheorie und Faschismus. Zur sozialen Funktion and aktuellen Wirkung der Theorie Carl Schmitts* (Munich: Wilhelm Fink, 1976).

7. Bauman describes the significance of the "new speed" in his *Globalization: The Human Consequences* (Cambridge: Polity, 1998); Giddens talks of the "distanciation" of time and space, for example, in *The Consequences of Modernity* (Stanford: Stanford University Press, 1990); Harvey analyzes "time and space compression" in *The Condition of Postmodernity* (Oxford: Blackwell, 1990).

8. Franz L. Neumann, *Behemoth: The Structure and Practice of National Socialism, 1933–1944* (New York: Harper & Row, 1944), 160.

9. Ibid., 199–200.

10. Ibid., 300.

11. Ibid., 331.

12. Ibid.

13. Not the least because of a flurry of populist attacks on "western" human rights unleashed by political elites in the developing world (in particular, in East Asia) eager to pursue an authoritarian developmental model without undue outside interference.

14. David Held, "The Transformation of Political Community: Rethinking Democracy in the Context of Globalization," in Ian Shapiro and Casiano Hacker-Cordon, eds., *Democracy's Edges* (Cambridge: Cambridge University Press, 2000), 97–8.

15. Neumann, *Behemoth*, 166–71.

16. The record of regional political blocs at the present time remains mixed, as evident by the contrast between the modest but worthy liberal-democratic achievements of the EU vis-à-vis the vastly more problematic case of NAFTA.

17. Neumann, *Behemoth*, 130.

18. For example, a legal standard determining the working day for one firm to be ten hours, whereas other firms are expected to respect the eight-hour day. In Neumann's account, the classical entrepreneur tends to be replaced by cartels and syndicates; capital and management functions separate; the "self-regulating" market tends to decline and state intervention becomes widespread; the elimination of many economic risks for the largest units results. Notwithstanding its flaws, important elements of this picture of capitalist development were widely shared in Neumann's time. See, for example, Joseph Schumpeter, *Capitalism, Socialism and Democracy* (New York: Harper & Row, 1950).

19. Neumann, "The Change in the Function of Law," in *The Rule of Law Under Siege: Selected Essays of Franz L. Neumann and Otto Kirchheimer* (Berkeley: University of California, 1996), 126.

20. Neumann, *Behemoth*, 446–47.

21. Unfortunately, his discussion of contracts in competitive capitalism tends to focus on the *history of political and legal ideas* rather than legal history itself. Thus, Neumann tends to rely on an exegesis of Adam Smith's jurisprudence in order to discuss early contracts. See Franz L. Neumann, *The Rule of Law: Political Theory and the Legal System in Modern Society* (Leamington Spa: Berg, 1986), 189–98.

22. Neumann, "The Change in the Function of Law," 132.

23. Neumann, "Labor Law in Modern Society" (1951), in *The Rule of Law Under Siege*, 233–34.

24. John Braithwaite and Peter Drahos, *Global Business Regulation* (Cambridge: Cambridge University Press, 2000), 30.

25. Ibid., 27.

26. The following section draws heavily on a series of papers that make up part of an ongoing research project. For support for some of the (broad) claims made below, for now I can only refer readers to the following: Scheuerman, "Economic Globalization and the Rule of Law," *Constellations* 6, no. 1 (1999): 3–25; "Globalization and the Fate of Law," in David Dyzenhaus, ed., *Recrafting the Rule of Law: The Limits of Legal Order* (Oxford: Hart, 1999), 243–66; "Reflexive Law and the Challenges of Globalization," *Journal of Political Philosophy* 9, no. 1 (2001): 1–22; "Global Law in our High Speed Economy," in *The Legal Culture of Global Business Transactions*, eds., Wm. Felstiner and Volkmar Gessner (Oxford: Hart, forthcoming); "False Humanitarianism? U.S. Advocacy of Transnational Labor Protections," *Review of International Political Economy* 8, no. 3 (2001).

27. Jarrod Wiener, *Globalization and the Harmonization of Law* (London: Pinter, 1999), 151-83.

28. For samples of this debate, see Albert Jan van den Berg, *International Dispute Resolution: Towards an International Arbitration Culture* (Hague: Kluwer, 1998); also R. Lillich and C. Brower, eds., *International Arbitration in the 21st Century: Towards Judicialization and Uniformity?* (Irvington: Transnational Publishers, 1994).

29. On taxation, see Sol Picciotto, *International Business Taxation: A Study in the Internationalization of Business Regulation* (London: Weidenfeld and Nicolson, 1992).

30. Harry Arthurs, "Private Ordering and Workers' Rights in the Global Economy: Corporate Codes of Conduct as a Regime of Labour Market Regulation," unpublished manuscript, York University (1999); L. Compa and T. Hinchliffe-Darricarrere, "Enforcing Labor Rights Through Corporate Codes of Conduct," *Columbia Journal of Transnational Law* 33 (1995): 663–89.

31. Wolfgang Reinicke, *Global Public Policy: Governing Without Government?* (Washington, DC: Brookings Institute, 1998), 120.

32. Ibid., 99–100.

33. David Kennedy, "The International Style in Postwar Law and Policy: John Jackson and the Field of International Economic Law," *American University Journal of International Law and Policy*10 (1995): 685. More generally on the legal structure of the WTO, John H. Jackson, *The World Trading System: Law and Policy of International Economic Relations* (Cambridge, MA: MIT Press, 1999).

34. L. Wallach and L. Sforza, *Whose Trade Organization? Corporate Globalization and the Erosion of Democracy* (Washington, DC: Public Citizen, 1999), 198.

35. Although rightly critical of orthodox Marxist accounts of globalization, Braithwaite and Drahos tend to confirm this view in their massive *Global Businesss Regulation*. Reminiscent of Neumann, they see strict antitrust laws as essential to reforming both the global economy and global economic regulation (602–29). In this vein, see Claire Cutler, "Global Capitalism and Liberal Myths: Dispute Settlement in Private International Trade Relations," *Millennium: Journal of International Studies* 24 (1995): 377–97; Cutler, "Public Meets Private: The International Unification and Harmonization of Private International Trade Law," *Global Society* 13 (1999): 25–48. I have tried to sketch out this argument as well in "Economic Globalization and the Rule of Law."

36. Judith N. Shklar, *Legalism: Law, Morals, and Political Trials* (Cambridge, MA: Harvard University Press, 1986), 16–17.

37. Peter Schlechtriem, *Uniform Sales Law: The UN Convention on Contracts for the International Sale of Goods* (Vienna: Manzsche Verlags- und Universitätsbibliothek, 1986), 1. More generally, see the symposium on commercial law in the *American Journal of Comparative Law* XL, no. 3 (1992).

38. Roy Goode, *Commercial Law in the Next Millennium* (London: Sweet & Maxwell, 1998), 19–20.

39. Arthur Rosett, "Unification, Restatement, Codification and Reform in International Commercial Law," *American Journal of Comparative Law* XL, no. 3 (1992): 687.

40. Ibid., 695.

41. Lord Justice Mustill, "The New *Lex Mercatoria*: The First Twenty-Five Years," *Arbitration International* 4 (1988): 118–19.

42. Far more clearly than Neumann, the late Tim Mason demonstrated that this political option ultimately proved dangerous for some key business groups. Tim Mason, *Nazism, Fascism and the Working Classes* (Cambridge: Cambridge University Press, 1990), 53–76.

43. Harvey, *The Condition of Postmodernity*, 121–200.

44. Harvey, *Justice, Nature & the Geography of Difference* (Oxford: Blackwell, 1996), 240–41.

45. On the account of globalization implicit in the *Communist Manifesto*, see Harvey, *Spaces of Hope* (Berkeley: University of California, 2000), 21–52.

46. Boaventura de Sousa Santos, "The Postmodern Transition: Law and Politics" in *The Fate of Law*, eds. Austin Sarat and Thomas Kearns (Ann Arbor: University of Michigan, 1993), 115.

47. International Institute for the Unification of Private Law (Unidroit), *Principles of International Commercial Contracts* (Rome: Unidroit, 1994), viii.

48. Kathyrn Sikkink, "Codes of Conduct for Transnational Corporations: The Case of the WHO/UNICEF Code," *International Organization* 40, no. 4 (1986): 836.

49. John Kline, "Advantages of International Regulation: The Case for a Flexible Pluralistic Framework," in *International Regulation: New Rules for a Changing World Order*, ed. Carol Adelman (San Francisco: Institute for Contemporary Studies, 1988), 36.

Name Index